Solutions Architect's Interview

First Edition

Winning strategies and effective tactics for interview success

Saurabh Shrivastava
Neelanjali Srivastav
Dhiraj Thakur
Sanjeet Sahay

Solutions Architect's Interview
First Edition

Copyright @ 2024 BitMaple

First published: April 2024
Published by BitMaple
ISBN: 9781806382972
www.bitmaple.com

To our beloved children, Sanvi and Shubh, whose boundless joy and happiness illuminate our lives.

Saurabh and Neelanjali

To my beloved wife Rashmi, precious children Ishani and Yash, and mother, whose love and presence bring immense joy and purpose to my life.

Dhiraj Thakur

To my mother & father—miss you, papa.

Sanjeet Sahay

Foreword

In the evolving world of technology, the role of the Solutions Architect has crystallized as a cornerstone of successful digital transformation initiatives. As businesses increasingly rely on complex systems integrating advanced technologies like cloud computing, AI, and machine learning, the need for skilled professionals to bridge the gap between technical feasibility and business strategy has never been greater. "The Solutions Architect Interview" is a crucial toolkit for anyone aspiring to master this essential role.

This book, precisely crafted by experts in the field, serves not just as a guide but as a mentor in print, walking you through the nuances and complexities of what it takes to succeed in a Solutions Architect interview. Whether you are a seasoned professional aiming to refine your approach or a newcomer eager to enter the field, the insights offered here are designed to prepare you comprehensively for the challenges ahead. From understanding the fundamental responsibilities of a Solutions Architect to navigating the intricacies of industry-specific applications, this book provides a thorough grounding in both the soft skills and technical knowledge required. The authors delve deep into the essence of strategic thinking, problem-solving, and effective communication, which are essential in the role of a Solutions Architect. Moreover, they extend their guidance to cover the practical aspects of preparing for an interview, with real-world scenarios, detailed discussions on technical requirements, and invaluable advice on presenting your skills and experiences convincingly.

As someone who has navigated the highs and lows of technology careers and understands the critical importance of each hire for a team, I appreciate the depth and relevance of this book. It is an essential read not just for job seekers but for anyone involved in hiring or team-building in the technology domain. The "Solutions Architect Interview" does more than prepare you for an interview; it prepares you for a thriving career, helping you envision and execute architectures that effectively align technical solutions with business goals.

As quoted by Tony Robbins - "The path to success is to take massive, determined action." This book is your ally in translating your technical capabilities into a language that hiring managers understand and appreciate. May it lead you to the opportunities where your skills can shine brightest.

Vivek Raju
Global Technology Leader, Solutions Architecture, AWS

About the Authors

Saurabh Shrivastava is a technology leader, author, inventor, and public speaker with over 20 years of experience in the IT industry. He currently works at **Amazon Web Services** (**AWS**) as a Global Solution Architect Leader and enables AWS partners and customers on their journey to the cloud. Saurabh led the AWS global technical partnerships, set his team's vision & execution model, and nurtured multiple new strategic initiatives.

In addition to his work at AWS, Saurabh is the author of Packt's best-selling book, **"Solutions Architect's Handbook 3rd edition,"** and **"AWS for Solutions Architects 2nd edition,"**. He has authored various blogs and white papers on diverse technologies, such as big data, IoT, machine learning, Generative AI, and cloud computing. He is passionate about the latest innovations and their impact on society and daily life. Saurabh holds patents in cloud platform automation and has worked as an enterprise solution architect, software architect, and software engineering manager in Fortune 50 enterprises, start-ups, and global product and consulting organizations. With his vast experience and expertise, Saurabh is a valuable resource for anyone learning about cloud computing and its various applications.

Neelanjali Srivastav's extensive experience in the software industry as a technology leader, product manager, and agile coach brings a wealth of knowledge to the field. Currently, she is working as a Technical Portfolio Leader for Aya Healthcare. Before that, she worked as a Senior Product Manager at **Amazon Web Services (AWS)**, evangelizing and enabling AWS customers and partners in AWS Database, Analytics, and Machine Learning Services. Neelanjali is co-author of Packt's best-selling books, **"Solutions Architect's Handbook 3rd edition,"** and **"AWS for Solutions Architects 2nd edition,"** which are valuable resources for those looking to kick-start their careers as AWS solutions architects. With her experience leading teams of software engineers, solution architects, and systems analysts to modernize IT systems and develop innovative software solutions for large enterprises, Neelanjali is well-equipped to provide insights into the challenges and opportunities in the technology field. Neelanjali's expertise in enterprise application management, agile coaching, cloud service management, and enterprise mergers and acquisitions makes her a sought-after speaker and thought leader. She is dedicated to helping others learn and grow in their careers, and her contributions to the field will make a lasting impact.

Dhiraj Thakur is a seasoned technology leader with a diverse background spanning product development, consulting, delivery, and solution architecture. With his extensive expertise in the IT industry, he currently serves as a Global Solutions Architect at Amazon Web Services (AWS), where he plays a pivotal role in enabling AWS partners and customers on their cloud journey. Throughout his illustrious career, Dhiraj has held various roles, including leading global tech partnerships. He has demonstrated a keen ability to set strategic visions and execute them effectively, fostering the growth of numerous new initiatives. In addition to his professional endeavors, Dhiraj is an accomplished author and public speaker. He has authored numerous blogs and white papers covering a wide range of cutting-edge technologies, including Generative AI, Data Analytics, Machine Learning, IoT, SAP, and cloud computing. His passion for the latest innovations and their impact on various industries and society is evident in his writings. He has delivered insightful presentations at numerous global technology and industry events, sharing his valuable knowledge and invaluable insights with audiences worldwide. Dhiraj is a lifelong learner, holding an impressive array of certifications, including all **12 AWS certifications**. In his free time, he finds fulfillment in building innovative solutions, further showcasing his dedication to technological advancement.

Sanjeet Sahay has 20 years of experience designing and delivering massively distributed systems and databases. His area of expertise is in application architecture, data analytics, and AWS solutions. He led the development and adoption of PartiQL, Amazon's open-source query language, deployed in crucial AWS services like IoT TwinMaker, S3 Select, DynamoDB, Lake Formation, and Redshift. Sanjeet developed a modular PartiQL query language compiler infrastructure, ensuring data consistency and accuracy in large-scale analytics systems within Amazon's internal data lakes. As a Solutions Architect within AWS' partner organization, Sanjeet guided 200+ enterprise customers in migrating terabytes of data and hundreds of applications and led large-scale data center migration to AWS. He utilized DevOps methodologies to enhance engineering velocity. He implemented application transformation strategies such as Serverless and containers, decomposing legacy and application monoliths into modular, independently scalable, and highly available applications.

Ashutosh Dubey is a seasoned technology leader and Solutions Architect at Amazon Web Services with deep expertise in Data, Analytics, Machine Learning, and Generative AI. Based in New Jersey, USA, he has amassed extensive experience throughout his career, making significant contributions to the tech industry. He excels in harnessing the power of data and AI technologies to drive business transformation and innovation, enabling organizations to unlock the full potential of their data. Beyond his professional accomplishments, Ashutosh is a dedicated technical content creator, authoring numerous articles and guides on his subject areas. His commitment to knowledge sharing reflects his passion for technology and desire to inspire and educate the wider tech community. He lives in New Jersey with his wife, Aastha, and daughter Avika.

About the Reviewers and Contributors

Jignesh Desai is a versatile technology leader with over two decades of experience leading global large-deal initiatives at scale. At Amazon Web Services (AWS), he brings conceptualization and tangible outcomes with a unique perspective. He offers executive-level visioning and translating ideas into action for partners and enterprise customers seeking to innovate in the cloud.

Besides his contributions at AWS, Jignesh pours his expertise into crafting insightful blogs across big data, machine learning, and cloud computing technologies. His enthusiasm for the newest innovations and their societal implications shines through in every piece. When he's not delving into tech, you'll find Jignesh in Washington, DC, where he resides with his cherished wife Nimisha and their two children, Nirvaan and Vatsin.

Ashutosh Pateriya is a Solution Architect at Amazon Web Services, an engineer at heart, and a tech enthusiast. With over 20 years of experience, his expertise lies in designing data center connectivity and service provider networking solutions, including on-premises, cloud-native, and hybrid connectivity. He's your trusted technical advisor, specializing in helping businesses understand and use cloud technology to boost their success. He specializes in assisting customers in creating and designing solutions aligned with their business goals across diverse domains like telecom, financial services, and utilities. Ashutosh has a passion for the latest technologies, and he is continuously looking to enhance his technical knowledge and tries to keep up to date with the latest trends. Ashutosh enjoys enhancing his cooking skills and experimenting with abstract drawing and painting in his free time.

Sanvi Shrivastava, known by her pen name Sia, is a prodigious young author whose passion for writing thrived at an early age. She is an avid book reader, writer, and editor. As a young author, Sia is making a significant impact, captivating readers with her words that sparkle and shine.

She has published her poem book, "Sparkling Stars - A Collection of Poems by a Young Poet," on Amazon. This collection captivated a wide audience with its enchanting verses that spark joy and ignite imaginations, leaving a lasting impression on all who read them. Encouraged by the popularity of her debut, Sia created the storybook series "Mystic Journeys Trilogy." This best-selling series includes titles such as "Caught by a Witch" and "Caught by a Stranger." In it, readers follow the adventures of Ria as she navigates through enchantment, confronts dark powers, and discovers the strength of friendship and courage.

Table of Contents

Preface

In the rapidly evolving world of technology, a Solutions Architect (SA) has become increasingly important in successfully deploying complex systems that meet contemporary business needs. "Solutions Architect Interview—Winning Strategies for Practical and Effective Tactics for Interview Success" is a comprehensive guide designed to prepare aspiring and experienced SAs for the challenges of interviewing in this dynamic field.

This book culminates extensive research, personal experiences, and conversations with industry veterans. It aims to demystify the interview process and equip candidates with the tools, techniques, and insights needed to excel. Through its four parts and 13 chapters, the book spans the breadth and depth of what it takes to secure a role as a Solutions Architect across various domains.

The book is organized into four parts, each tailored to different aspects of the Solutions Architect role. Part 1 introduces the role, covering key responsibilities, differences between generalist and specialist SAs, and practical job application advice. Part 2 dives deeper into specialized domains like Application, DevOps, Infrastructure, and more, providing insights into technical and necessary soft skills. Part 3 explores the unique challenges of industry-specific SAs, examining the demands of sectors such as healthcare and finance. Finally, Part 4 offers a guide for those starting new SA roles, focusing on adapting to organizational landscapes and aligning architectural strategies with business goals. These sections comprehensively prepare readers for a career as a Solutions Architect, from interviews to job performance.

Throughout the book, readers will find a balance between technical rigor and the soft skills imperative for today's SA roles. From mastering architectural frameworks to acing behavioral interviews, from deep dives into cloud ecosystems to tackling industry-specific challenges, this book does not shy away from the intricate realities of the role.

For those at the precipice of their next career leap, "Solutions Architect Interview" seeks to be not just a roadmap but a compass—pointing in the direction of interview success and professional growth in solutions architecture.

Whether you are fresh out of college, a seasoned developer eyeing the SA horizon, or an on-premises expert contemplating the cloud transition, this book is for you. It is an invitation to embark on a journey of learning and self-discovery, leading to the ultimate destination: a rewarding career as a Solutions Architect.

Let the journey begin.

Who is this book for

"Solutions Architect Interview" is crafted for a diverse audience, all unified by the common goal of excelling in the field of Solutions Architecture. This book is for:

- **Recent Graduates**: This group includes those who are stepping out of academia and aiming to begin their careers as Solutions Architects. It provides foundational insights and addresses how to enter the field straight from graduation.
- **Software Developers and IT Professionals**: Individuals looking to transition from roles such as software development, systems engineering, or network administration into Solutions Architecture. The book covers the essential skills and strategies needed to make this shift.
- **Non-Application Development Background Professionals**: Those who may have yet to gain direct application development experience but have valuable industry domain expertise and wish to leverage it in a Solutions Architect role.
- **On-premises IT Specialists**: Seasoned professionals accustomed to on-premise environments who want to pivot to cloud-based Solutions Architecture, a growing increasingly important field in today's tech landscape.
- **Aspiring Cloud Solutions Architects**: IT professionals who are specifically interested in the nuances of cloud computing and how to design, operate, and manage cloud architecture effectively.
- **Specialized Solutions Architects** aim to refine their expertise in specialized areas such as application, network, database, big data, DevOps, security, or AI/ML Solutions Architecture.
- **Industry-specific Professionals**: Solutions Architects who wish to apply their skills in specific sectors such as healthcare, finance, retail, or manufacturing and seek guidance on the unique challenges these industries present.
- **Interview Preparers**: Individuals preparing for upcoming Solutions Architect positions and seeking comprehensive guidance on technical and behavioral interview aspects.
- **Hiring Managers:** Looking to build a strong team of Solutions Architects and validate their skills to ensure excellence and innovation in projects.
- **SA Role Starters**: Professionals who have secured a Solutions Architect position seek advice on effectively navigating the first steps in their new role.

This book provides a structured outline of the breadth and depth of the Solutions Architect role. It is a vital resource for anyone aiming to understand the field, secure a role, or progress to more advanced levels of responsibility and expertise.

What this book covers

The book "Solutions Architect Interview" is divided into four parts, detailing the multifaceted role of a Solutions Architect and how to prepare for interviews in this career. Here's a brief overview of each chapter:

Part 1: Solutions Architect Role and Interview

Chapter 1: Solutions Architect Role—Key Responsibilities, Skills, and Preparation for Job Application This chapter introduces the Solutions Architect (SA) role, discussing its importance, different types of SAs, and industry-specific variations. It guides readers through the job application process, including resume and LinkedIn profile optimization, and addresses common questions about starting an SA career.

Chapter 2: Cracking the Technical Interview delves into the technical skills and design principles necessary for a Solutions Architect. The chapter covers cloud computing concepts, architectural frameworks, and whiteboarding practices, providing a robust foundation for answering technical interview questions across various domains like networking and security.

Chapter 3: Behavioral Interview and Soft Skills for Solutions Architects Soft skills are the focus here, with strategies for leading through ambiguity and driving strategic projects. The chapter explains behavioral interviews and offers preparation tips, example questions, and best practices for demonstrating leadership and adaptability, which are crucial for an SA's success.

Part 2: Specialist Solution Architect Role and Interview

Chapter 4: Cracking the Application Architect Interview This chapter outlines the role of application architects and details design principles and methodologies such as SOLID and DRY. It reviews common application patterns and presents interview questions and troubleshooting scenarios pertinent to application architecture.

Chapter 5: Cracking the DevOps Architect Interview Examines the role of The DevOps Architect, highlighting strategies for continuous integration and delivery (CI/CD), DevSecOps, and building effective DevOps pipelines. Interview questions and discussions center on the architect's role in defining DevOps strategy and architecture.

Chapter 6: Cracking the Infrastructure Solutions Architect Interview Focus shifts to infrastructure architecture, exploring its components, the Infrastructure Architect's role, and methodologies for planning and leading infrastructure projects. Risk assessment, performance optimization, and interview questions for Infrastructure SAs are also covered.

Chapter 7: Cracking the Network Architect Interview This chapter addresses network architecture principles and the Network Architect's responsibilities, including designing scalable and secure networks. It poses common interview questions and the challenges that networking architects face.

Chapter 8: Cracking the Big Data Solutions Architect Interview The chapter dissects the role of a Big Data Solutions Architect and discusses big data architecture and data engineering concepts. It also suggests best practices for designing big data solutions and provides relevant interview questions.

Chapter 9: Cracking the Database Solutions Architect Interview Focuses on Database management and the Database Solutions Architect's role. The interview explores relational and NoSQL databases, SQL, data modeling, and performance tuning. Questions cover high availability, scalability, and cloud database solutions.

Chapter 10: Cracking the ML and Generative AI Solution Architect Interview This chapter introduces the roles and concepts of ML and Generative AI in Solutions Architecture, discussing algorithms, data preprocessing, model evaluation, and operationalization with MLOps. Interview questions touch on technical and behavioral aspects specific to AI.

Chapter 11: Cracking the Security Solutions Architect Interview Security in architecture is paramount; this chapter examines the Security Solutions Architect's role, security architecture components, risks, and compliance frameworks. It rounds off with questions spanning technical, behavioral, and scenario-based aspects of security interviews.

Part 3: Industry Solutions Architect Role and Interview

Chapter 12: Cracking the Industry Solutions Architect Interview This part offers insight into the unique aspects of being an SA in healthcare, finance, retail, and manufacturing. It discusses these roles' specific challenges and requirements, the best practices tailored to industry solutions, and relevant interview questions.

Part 4: Starting in a New Role

Chapter 13: Starting in a Solutions Architect Role in a New Organization The final chapter offers guidance for new SAs, including understanding the organization's culture, identifying stakeholders, assessing digital maturity, and formulating strategic plans. It provides final advice for establishing credibility and achieving success in a new SA role.

To get the most out of this book

To fully leverage the insights provided in the "Solutions Architect Interview" book, readers should adopt a strategic approach that aligns with their learning preferences and professional goals. Given that the role of a solutions architect encompasses the complete architecture spectrum, it's crucial to read the entire book, even if your interest lies in a specialized area.

For instance, aspiring analytics or machine learning solutions architects must understand the broader architectural context to effectively design integrated systems incorporating big data and machine learning technologies. Understanding end-to-end application architecture provides a foundational knowledge base that enhances your ability to tackle specific challenges and design cohesive solutions that seamlessly integrate with various technologies and business requirements.

Therefore, approach this book to prepare for an interview and as a comprehensive resource to build a holistic understanding of the diverse aspects of solutions architecture. This approach will prepare you for specific questions related to your specialty and empower you to handle broader architectural discussions, making you a more versatile and knowledgeable candidate.

Here's how to get the most out of this book:

- **Assess Your Current Knowledge and Skills:** Start by evaluating your existing expertise and identifying areas for improvement. Use the chapters as a framework to pinpoint these areas and focus your learning efforts.
- **Engage with Each Chapter Actively:** Don't just read; engage. Take notes, highlight key points, and create mind maps to understand better and memorize concepts. For technical chapters, practice by drawing diagrams or engaging in whiteboarding sessions.
- **Leverage the Practical Examples:** Apply the technical examples and interview questions in real-world scenarios. Practice by simulating interview situations or solving the problems posed in the book.
- **Tailor Your Learning:** If you're aiming for a specialized role, concentrate on the chapters relevant to that specialization. If you're new to the field, focus first on the chapters that lay the foundational knowledge.
- **Simulate Interviews:** Role-play interviews with a peer or mentor. Use the behavioral and technical questions provided to practice and refine your responses.
- **Continuous Revision:** Interviewing is a skill that benefits from regular practice. Revisit chapters and refresh your knowledge periodically, especially before interviews.
- **Practical Application:** Apply what you've learned in your current job or personal projects. Hands-on experience is invaluable and helps solidify theoretical knowledge.

Use the book as a starting point for deeper exploration. Follow up on the recommended reading, frameworks, and tools mentioned throughout the book.

To complement the insights and knowledge gained from the "Solutions Architect Interview," it is highly recommended to delve into additional resources that can provide a deeper dive into specific topics of interest within the domain of solutions architecture. Two such invaluable resources are:

- **"Solutions Architect's Handbook, 3rd edition"** – This book is an excellent resource for understanding the breadth and depth of the Solutions Architect role. It covers best practices, design patterns, and the latest architectural trends. This handbook is an essential guide for readers seeking to explore the profession's nuances and enhance their expertise. It can be found on Amazon at Solutions Architect's Handbook - https://www.amazon.com/gp/product/1835084230.
- **"AWS for Solutions Architects, 2nd edition"** – For those specifically interested in Amazon Web Services, this book offers an expansive look at designing systems and applications on AWS. It is particularly useful for understanding AWS-specific services and architectures, providing practical knowledge that can be applied directly to AWS-based projects. This resource is available on Amazon at AWS for Solutions Architects - https://www.amazon.com/gp/product/180323895X

These books will allow readers to specialize and gain a more nuanced understanding of various solution architecture concepts. They are excellent for both newcomers to the field and seasoned architects looking to stay abreast of new developments and deepen their practical application skills. Whether preparing for an interview or looking to refine your professional practice, these books are valuable additions to your professional library.

Feedback, Questions, and More

We highly value your engagement and feedback on the "Solutions Architect Interview." If you have questions or feedback about any specific aspect of this book, please don't hesitate to mention the title in your correspondence and email us at contactus@bitmaple.com.

Errata

Our publications strive for accuracy and clarity, but errors occasionally occur. If you notice any discrepancies or errors in this book, please report them to us. Your feedback is appreciated and essential in helping us improve subsequent editions. You can email us at contactus@bitmaple.com with details of your findings.

Piracy

Intellectual property theft undermines the efforts of authors and publishers. If you encounter pirated copies of our works online, please help us by reporting the location or website where you found them. Send us an email with a link to the pirated material to contactus@bitmaple.com so we can take appropriate action.

Become an Author

Are you an expert in a particular field interested in authoring or contributing to a book? We are always looking for new voices and perspectives. Visit our publishing section at **BitMaple Book Publishing**—https://bitmaple.com/#book-publishing

To learn more about opportunities to share your expertise and insights with a wider audience. Thank you for your support and contribution to the continuous improvement of our content and community.

Leave a Review

Once you have read "Solutions Architect Interview" and applied its insights, we strongly encourage you to leave a review on the website where you purchased the book. Sharing your thoughts and experiences helps potential readers make informed decisions and allows us at BitMaple to better understand your perspective on our products. Additionally, our authors greatly appreciate seeing your feedback, as it helps them understand the impact of their work and provides valuable insights for future editions.

Your review is invaluable—about what you loved, what could be improved, or additional topics you'd like to see covered. By leaving a review, you contribute to the community and help us continue to deliver high-quality resources that meet your needs.

Learn More About BitMaple

For more information about our offerings and mission or how we can help you achieve your learning goals, please visit BitMaple - https://bitmaple.com/. Explore our wide range of books, stay updated with our latest releases, and discover resources that can propel your career forward.

Thank you for your support and for being a part of our community! Your feedback drives our continuous effort to enrich the knowledge landscape.

Part 1: Solutions Architect Role and Interview

Chapter 1 - Solutions Architect Role and Responsibilities

If you read this chapter, you are all buckling up to crack the Solutions Architect (SA) interview. However, many things need to be clarified about the SA role. If you ask ten people around you, you will get at least five different answers about who a solutions architect is and what their responsibilities are. Solutions Architect is a professional who plays a crucial role in developing complex software and IT systems. The Solutions Architect's primary responsibility is designing and implementing technical solutions that meet an organization's or customer's needs. But don't worry; you will go into detail to learn about who the solutions architect is.

SA responsibilities are not limited to the beginning of system design; they also need to be engaged regularly post-launch to ensure the solution's scalability, availability, and maintainability. You will learn about solutions architect responsibilities and their importance in IT organizations designing complex and scalable systems.

Additionally, you will thoroughly explore the role of a solutions architect and their integration within an organization. Subsequently, you will discover the different types of solution architects and understand how they function collaboratively within an organizational structure. An organization may need a generalist solution architect and other specialist solution architects based on a project's complexity. As enterprises seek to solve their industry domain problem, the role of industry vertical solutions architect has become prominent in the last few years. You will learn about the role of the industry SA and how organizations can benefit from domain expertise.

As SA, when you start searching for a job and applying for a suitable role, it is crucial to have an attractive resume. You will learn tips and tricks for preparing your resume and cover letter while reviewing job requirements and role responsibilities. In this chapter, we will cover the following key topics:

- Who is a solutions architect?
- Importance of the Solutions Architect Role
- Key responsibilities and skills required for the solutions architect role
- Overview of the role of various roles for a solutions architect
- Preparing for job application

By the end of this chapter, you will get familiar with solutions architect roles and responsibilities and prepare your resume to be selected for prospective roles.

Who is a solutions architect (SA)?

While you are keen to crack the SA interview, let's first focus on the basics and understand who the solutions architect is. You will notice the more frequent use of the plural form "Solutions" in the title to emphasize the role's focus on designing comprehensive, integrated solutions that meet an organization's specific needs. In contrast, "Solution" in the singular may imply a narrower focus on designing a single solution to a particular problem. However, both "Solutions Architect" and "Solution Architect" are commonly used in the industry and generally refer to the same role.

Without delay, let's learn what an SA does. A Solutions Architect is a professional who designs and implements technology-based solutions to complex problems. They work on projects such as designing and implementing software applications, building data centers, or integrating multiple systems to work together seamlessly.

The SA works closely with stakeholders such as business leaders, project managers, and software developers to understand the business requirements and design a solution that meets those needs. They are responsible for creating detailed technical specifications and plans, selecting the appropriate technologies and tools, and overseeing the implementation and testing of the solution. SA works across different IT, finance, healthcare, and manufacturing industries. They are critical in helping organizations leverage technology to solve complex problems and drive business success.

A Solutions Architect typically has a strong background in computer science, engineering, or a related field and several years of experience designing and implementing complex solutions using various technologies. They must communicate effectively with technical and non-technical stakeholders and have excellent problem-solving and analytical skills.

To better understand, let's explore the example of a Solutions Architect designing a solution to optimize a company's slow website. First, the SA would analyze the problem. They would gather information about the website, such as its traffic patterns, the number of concurrent users, and the types of content being served. They would also review the website's code and infrastructure to identify any bottlenecks or areas of inefficiency.

Based on their analysis, the SA might recommend a variety of solutions. For example, they recommend optimizing the website's code to reduce load times or using a content delivery network (CDN) to distribute the site's content across multiple servers. If the SA recommends a CDN, they will work with the company's IT team to implement the solution. They would configure the CDN to cache static content, such as images and videos, so that it can be served to users more quickly. They might also use load balancing to distribute traffic across multiple servers so that no single server is overwhelmed by the volume of requests.

Once the solution is implemented, the SA will monitor the website's performance to ensure the new system works effectively. They would use analytics software to track website traffic and identify other areas for improvement. The SA would work closely with the company's stakeholders, including IT teams and business leaders, to ensure the solution meets its goals and objectives.

You can see that designing a solution as a SA involves a deep understanding of the company's needs and technical expertise in network architecture, system design, and performance optimization. The Solutions Architect must be able to analyze complex problems and recommend effective solutions tailored to the business's specific needs. Now, let's understand how vital SA's role is for an organization.

Importance of the SA Role in the Organization

Now that you know who a solutions architect is, the next question that comes to mind is why there is a high demand for an SA role with a decent salary. According to data from Glassdoor, as of Jan 2023, the average base salary for a Solutions Architect with cloud knowledge in the United States is around $138,000 annually. However, salaries can range from approximately $105,000 to $188,000 per year, with some senior-level roles offering salaries upwards of $250,000 annually. It's important to note that SA salaries may also include bonuses, profit sharing, and other forms of compensation. Additionally, more experienced Cloud SAs may command higher salaries, and those who work with specialized cloud technologies, such as AWS, GCP, or Azure, may also earn higher wages.

The role of the Solutions Architect is crucial in IT organizations as they are responsible for designing and implementing solutions that align with the organization's business goals and technical requirements. Some of the key reasons why the SA role is essential in IT organizations are:

- **Strategic planning:** The Solutions Architect helps develop the organization's IT strategy by identifying business opportunities and challenges and designing solutions to help it achieve its goals. They work closely with business leaders to understand business requirements and design solutions to improve efficiency, reduce costs, and increase revenue.
- **Technical expertise:** The Solutions Architect profoundly understands technology and can help the organization select the right tools and technologies to meet its business requirements. They can guide issues such as system architecture, software design, database management, and network infrastructure.
- **Collaboration:** The Solutions Architect collaborates with other IT professionals, such as developers, project managers, and business analysts, to ensure the solutions are implemented effectively. They work together to provide scalable, secure solutions and meet the organization's business needs.

- **Innovation:** The Solutions Architect is critical in driving innovation within the organization. They are responsible for identifying emerging technologies that can be used to improve business processes and designing solutions that incorporate those technologies.
- **Risk management:** The Solutions Architect is responsible for identifying and managing risks associated with implementing new solutions. They must ensure the solutions meet security and compliance requirements and are designed to withstand potential cyber threats.

SA plays a critical role in IT organizations by designing and implementing solutions aligned with their business goals and technical requirements. They combine their technical expertise, strategic thinking, collaboration skills, innovation, and risk management capabilities to help organizations succeed in today's fast-paced digital landscape. They are responsible for staying up-to-date with emerging technologies, assessing their potential impact on the organization, and recommending adoption.

Imagine a multinational corporation that operates in multiple countries with various departments and functions. The company wants to create a single, integrated system that can handle all its business processes, including accounting, inventory, customer relationships, and supply chain management. It is a complex project that requires the coordination of multiple stakeholders, including business leaders, IT professionals, and end-users. The Solutions Architect plays a critical role as a technology leader is crucial. They must assess the latest technologies and determine which will best support the company's business goals and technical requirements. They must also ensure the selected technologies are compatible with the existing IT infrastructure and systems.

Once the technologies are selected, the SA oversees the technical implementation of the system, working closely with developers and IT professionals. They are responsible for ensuring the system architecture is scalable, secure, and reliable. They also oversee the testing and quality assurance processes to ensure the system meets the organization's requirements. The Solutions Architect also plays a critical role in managing the technical risks associated with the project. They must ensure that the system is designed to withstand potential cyber threats and that data is protected against unauthorized access. They are responsible for ensuring that the system meets regulatory and compliance requirements.

Types of Solutions Architects

Today's organizations are building more complex systems to satisfy ever-increasing customer demands, address globally distributed user bases, and stay ahead of the competition. Many Solutions Architects exist because different industries and organizations have unique technology needs and challenges. A Solutions Architect needs to have deep knowledge of the technology landscape in their industry and understand their organization's specific requirements and constraints. The need for different types of Solutions Architects reflects the complexity and diversity of modern technology environments. Organizations can ensure they have the right expertise to design and implement effective solutions that meet their unique technology needs by having a mix of Generalist, Specialist, and Industry-specific Solutions Architects. Let's learn about different types of SAs.

Generalist solutions architect

A Generalist Solutions Architect is a type of Solutions Architect who has a broad range of knowledge and experience across multiple domains of IT systems and architecture. They have a well-rounded understanding of various technology stacks, infrastructure components, and software applications. Generalist Solutions Architects are often tasked with developing and maintaining an organization's overall IT architecture. They collaborate with stakeholders to identify business requirements and translate them into technical solutions. They also evaluate new technologies and determine how they can be incorporated into the organization's IT systems.

Generalist Solutions Architects are highly adaptable and can work on various IT projects. They have strong analytical and problem-solving skills, excellent communication and collaboration skills, and a deep understanding of IT systems and architecture. They can also work effectively in a team environment and provide technical leadership to development teams. Generalist Solutions Architects may have experience in a range of IT domains, including but not limited to:

- Cloud computing and infrastructure
- Application architecture and development
- Data architecture and management
- Network architecture and design
- Security architecture and implementation
- DevOps and continuous integration/continuous delivery (CI/CD)
- Business analysis and project management
- Enterprise architecture

While Generalist Solutions Architects may have a different level of expertise than specialized Solutions Architects in any one domain, they are valuable for their ability to understand the overall IT landscape and ensure that all components work together effectively. Let's explore types of specialist solutions architects who can help generalist SA dive deep into a specific area as needed.

Specialist solutions architect

Specialist Solutions Architects bring in-depth knowledge and skills to a particular area of technology, allowing them to design and implement solutions tailored to an organization's or project's unique needs. They are essential in ensuring organizations have the right solutions to support their operations and achieve their goals. They are subject matter experts in a specific field and can provide technical guidance and support to other teams. Here are some different types of

Specialist Solutions Architects:

- **Application Solutions Architect:** An Application Solutions Architect specializes in designing and implementing application solutions. They have expertise in application architecture, software design, and application integration. Application Solutions Architects can help organizations design and implement application architectures, optimize application performance, and ensure their applications are scalable and reliable.
- **Cloud Solutions Architect:** A Cloud Solutions Architect specializes in designing and implementing cloud-based solutions. They deeply understand cloud computing technologies such as Amazon Web Services (AWS), Microsoft Azure, or Google Cloud Platform (GCP). Cloud Solutions Architects can help organizations move their infrastructure to the cloud, optimize their cloud environments, and ensure their systems are secure and reliable.
- **Security Solutions Architect:** A Security Solutions Architect specializes in designing and implementing security solutions. They have expertise in network security, identity and access management, and data protection. Security Solutions Architects can help organizations design and implement security strategies, assess security risks, and ensure that their systems comply with industry regulations and standards.
- **Network Solutions Architect:** A Network Solutions Architect specializes in designing and implementing network solutions. They have expertise in network design, routing and switching, and network security. Network Solutions Architects can help organizations design and implement network architectures, troubleshoot network issues, and ensure their networks are secure and reliable.
- **Infrastructure Solutions Architects:** Infrastructure SA are specialists in designing and implementing infrastructure solutions, including server hardware, virtualization, storage, and network infrastructure. They deeply understand the underlying technologies and can design and implement scalable, secure, cost-effective architectures.
- **DevOps Solutions Architects:** DevOps SA specializes in designing and implementing DevOps solutions, which focus on automating and streamlining software development and delivery processes. They have expertise in continuous integration and continuous delivery (CI/CD), infrastructure as code (IaC), and configuration management. DevOps Solutions Architects can help organizations design and implement DevOps architectures, automate their software development processes, and improve delivery speed and quality.
- **Database Solutions Architects**: Database SA has expertise in database design, development, and implementation and is familiar with different database management systems (DBMS), such as MySQL, Oracle, and MongoDB. They are also knowledgeable about different database technologies and trends and keep up to date with the latest advancements in the field.
- **Analytics Solutions Architect:** An Analytics or big data Solutions Architect specializes in designing and implementing data solutions. They have expertise in data architecture, data management, and data analytics. Data Solutions Architects can help organizations design and implement data strategies, integrate and analyze data from multiple sources, and

ensure their data is accurate, consistent, and secure.
- **Machine Learning Solutions Architect:** A Machine Learning Solutions Architect specializes in designing and implementing IT solutions for machine learning and artificial intelligence (AI). They know machine learning algorithms, frameworks, and platforms such as TensorFlow, Keras, and PyTorch and have experience building and deploying machine learning models in production environments.

Specialist Solutions Architects are vital in designing and implementing complex technology solutions. The list above highlights some of the most common specialist SA roles, although it is not exhaustive.

Cloud technology is becoming essential to system design and applies to all the types of SAs mentioned earlier. In the upcoming chapters of this book, you will learn about the roles and responsibilities of each type of Specialist SA in dedicated chapters. You will learn how to prepare for and succeed in interviews for these roles.

More than expertise in the technology domain is needed to build a business-focused system. It would help if you had industry expertise to solve specific business problems, which creates the role of an industry solutions architect. Let's learn about it in more detail.

Industry solutions architect

Industry Solutions Architecture has become increasingly important in recent years as businesses face more complex challenges and require specialized solutions to meet their needs. Industry Solutions Architects combine technical expertise with industry-specific knowledge to design and implement solutions that address the unique challenges of a particular industry.

Industry Solutions Architects ensure that technology solutions are relevant and effective for a particular industry. They can understand the business requirements and objectives of the industry and design solutions that meet those needs. They are also able to recommend and implement best practices and processes that are specific to the industry. There are several Industry Solutions Architects, each specializing in one sector. Here are some examples:
- **Healthcare Solutions Architect:** A Healthcare Solutions Architect specializes in designing and implementing IT solutions for the healthcare industry. They are knowledgeable about healthcare-specific regulations and compliance requirements and have experience with applications such as Electronic Health Records (EHRs) and Medical Imaging Systems.
- **Finance Solutions Architect:** A Finance Solutions Architect specializes in designing and implementing IT solutions for the finance industry. They are knowledgeable about financial regulations such as the Payment Card Industry Data Security Standard (PCI DSS) and have experience with financial applications such as Trading Platforms and Risk Management Systems.
- **Retail Solutions Architect:** A Retail Solutions Architect specializes in designing and

implementing IT solutions for the retail industry. They know retail-specific applications such as Point-of-Sale (POS) and Inventory Management Systems and have experience with e-commerce platforms and supply chain management systems.
- **Manufacturing Solutions Architect:** A Manufacturing Solutions Architect specializes in designing and implementing IT solutions for the manufacturing industry. They know manufacturing-specific applications such as Enterprise Resource Planning (ERP) Systems and Product Lifecycle Management (PLM) Systems and have experience with industrial automation and control systems.
- **Education Solutions Architect:** An Education Solutions Architect specializes in designing and implementing IT solutions for the education industry. They are knowledgeable about education-specific regulations such as the Family Educational Rights and Privacy Act (FERPA) and have experience with education-specific applications such as Learning Management Systems (LMS) and Student Information Systems (SIS).

Industry SAs are essential in solving business problems in specific industries. They possess expertise in technology and the unique challenges and requirements of their respective industries. Whether it's healthcare, finance, retail, or any other sector, having an Industry Solutions Architect with industry-specific knowledge can provide valuable insights and solutions.

In the later chapter of this book, you will delve deeper into the roles and responsibilities of industry vertical Solutions Architects and learn how to prepare for and excel in interviews for such positions. You have covered a high-level overview of SA roles and responsibilities in the above sections. Now, without delay, let's start the journey to crack the SA interview.

Preparing for job application

When preparing for an interview as a Solutions Architect, it is essential to thoroughly review the job description to ensure that you understand the key responsibilities and requirements of the role. Let's start with understanding the job description.

Reviewing job description

When preparing for an interview as a Solutions Architect, it is important to thoroughly review the job description to ensure that you understand the key responsibilities and requirements of the role. Here are some tips for reviewing a job description:
- Read the full job description carefully, paying close attention to the specific skills, experience, and qualifications the employer seeks.
- Highlight keywords or phrases that stand out, such as specific technologies, certifications, or job duties.
- List any questions about the job description, and be prepared to ask these questions during the interview.
- Research the company to learn more about its culture, mission, and values, and look for

ways to align your experience and skills with these aspects of the company.

- Consider how your previous experience and skills match the job's requirements and responsibilities, and be prepared to give examples of how you have demonstrated these skills in prior roles.

Here is a sample job description for the generalist solutions architect role:

Job title: Solutions Architect
Job Description:
We seek a highly motivated and experienced Solutions Architect to join our team. As a Solutions Architect, you will be responsible for designing and implementing complex technology solutions for our clients. You will work closely with clients, project managers, and other stakeholders to ensure that solutions meet business requirements and are delivered on time and within budget.

In this role, you will help our customers solve business challenges, such as rapidly releasing products/services to the market or building an elastic, scalable, cost-optimized application. You will engage with product owners to influence product direction. You will also look for patterns and trends that can be broadly applied across an industry segment or a set of customers that can help accelerate innovation. Along the way, you can enhance your knowledge and have some fun.

As a core account team member, you will drive revenue growth across a specific customer. As a trusted customer advocate, you will help organizations understand and implement advanced cloud-based solutions and how to migrate and scale existing workloads in the cloud. You can shape and execute a strategy to build knowledge and broad use of technology. You must also be adept at interacting, communicating, and partnering with other teams, such as engineering, marketing, and implementation teams, and representing your team to executive management.

For this role, we are looking for folks with technical breadth complemented by technical depth in one or two areas, business aptitude, and the ability to lead in-depth technology discussions, articulating the business value. Strong communication and interpersonal skills are required to engage with enterprise architects, technical architects, cloud architects, directors, VPs, and CXOs.

If you are excited about using your cloud architecture experience to assist our most valuable customers, tackle challenging problems, have a hand in shaping the future of cloud adoption, enhance and grow your skills, and have fun, then we would love to hear from you.

Basic Qualifications:
- Bachelor's degree in Computer Science or related field or equivalent experience
- 5+ years of experience in software development or architecture
- Experience with cloud computing platforms such as AWS, Azure, or Google Cloud Platform
- Professional experience architecting and operating cloud-based solutions.

- Strong understanding of modern software development methodologies, tools, and techniques
- Experience with application integration and API development
- Working knowledge of software development tools and methodologies.
- Excellent communication and collaboration skills

Preferred qualifications:
- Master's degree in Computer Science or related field
- Experience working with enterprise clients and large-scale systems
- Experience with big data technologies such as Hadoop, Spark, or Kafka
- Experience with DevOps practices and tools
- Demonstrated ability to adapt to new technologies and learn quickly.
- Presentation skills with high comfort speaking with executives, IT Management, and developers.
- Experience in technology/software sales or pre-sales consulting.
- Experience with a programming or scripting language.

This job description clearly outlines the role and the qualifications necessary to be considered for the position. The **basic qualifications section** lists the minimum requirements, while the **preferred qualifications section** lists additional skills and experiences that would be beneficial. It is important to carefully review all sections of the job description to determine if you meet the qualifications and to prepare for interview questions related to these qualifications.

When applying for a job that fits your profile based on the job description, it is crucial to research the company's profile before submitting your application.

Researching the company

Getting company details before an interview can help you understand their priorities, culture, and industry trends. Doing so allows you to tailor your answers to the company's needs and demonstrate your knowledge and understanding of their business. It is an essential step in preparing for a Solutions Architect interview. Here are some steps to follow:
- **Start with the company's website:** Go through it and read about its products, services, mission, and values. This will give you a good understanding of the company's focus areas and priorities.
- **Check social media:** Follow the company on social media platforms like LinkedIn, Twitter, and Facebook. This will help you understand the company's culture, recent news, and events.
- **Look for news articles:** Search for articles related to the company and its industry. This will give you a better understanding of the industry's current trends and challenges.
- **Check Glassdoor:** Visit Glassdoor to read reviews from current and former company employees. This will give you an idea of the company's work culture and any potential

challenges you may face as an employee.

- **Reach out to your network:** Talk to your network and see if anyone has worked for the company or knows someone who has. They can provide valuable insights and information you may need help finding elsewhere.
- **Researching financial data:** The Company's financial data can still be valuable to your interview preparation process. It can help you better understand the company's market position, financial stability, and potential for future growth. For example, suppose you are interviewing for a Solutions Architect role at a startup company. In that case, look at their financial data to see if they have recently secured any funding or are experiencing rapid growth. You can research a company's financial data by reviewing its annual reports, earnings statements, and news articles about its financial performance.

While looking for potential opportunities, it is important to consider aspects such as the company culture, values, and potential career growth opportunities.

Preparing your resume and cover letter

Preparing a well-crafted resume and cover letter is crucial to make a strong impression on potential employers. Your resume should highlight your relevant skills, experience, and accomplishments, while your cover letter should introduce yourself and explain why you are the right candidate for the job.

When crafting your resume, tailor it to the job you are applying for, highlighting the skills and experiences matching the job requirements. Use bullet points to make it easy to read and ensure error-free. Make sure to show action and impact with data points in your resume. Here's a version of John Doe's resume with ten years of experience and specific examples of impact with action:

John Doe

123 Main Street | Anytown, USA 12345 | (555) 555-5555 | johndoe@email.com

Objective: To obtain the position of Solutions Architect at XYZ Company, where I can utilize my ten years of experience in software development and architecture to design and implement complex technology solutions for clients.

Professional Summary: Highly skilled Solutions Architect with ten years of experience designing and implementing complex technology solutions for clients. Proven track record of leading successful software development projects, leveraging cloud computing platforms, and collaborating with stakeholders to ensure solutions meet business requirements and are delivered on time and within budget. Strong communication and interpersonal skills for engaging with Enterprise Architects, Technical Architects, Cloud Architects, Directors, VPs, and CXOs.

Professional Experience:

Solutions Architect | ABC Company | Anytown, USA | 2014 - Present

- Designed and implemented a cloud-based solution that reduced server costs by 50% for a large retail client, resulting in a cost savings of $2 million annually.
- Collaborated with project managers and developers to implement a new API for a healthcare client, resulting in a 30% increase in user adoption within the first quarter.
- Developed and implemented a DevOps strategy for a financial services client, resulting in a 40% reduction in deployment time and a 25% increase in application performance.
- Led a team of architects to design and implement a scalable, elastic, and cost-optimized application for a manufacturing client, resulting in a 20% increase in production efficiency and a 15% reduction in IT infrastructure costs.

Senior Software Developer | DEF Company | Anytown, USA | 2010 - 2014

- Designed and developed a custom CRM solution for a non-profit organization, resulting in a 50% increase in donor engagement and a 20% increase in donations.
- Implemented a new mobile application for a logistics client, resulting in a 25% increase in customer satisfaction and a 15% increase in revenue.
- Developed and maintained a secure e-commerce platform for a retail client, resulting in a 30% increase in online sales and a 20% decrease in fraud.

Education:

Bachelor of Science in Computer Science | XYZ University | Anytown, USA | 2010

Skills:

- Cloud computing platforms such as AWS, Azure, or Google Cloud Platform
- Application integration and API development
- Modern software development methodologies, tools, and techniques
- Software development tools and methodologies
- Big data technologies such as Hadoop, Spark, or Kafka
- DevOps practices and tools
- Programming and scripting languages, including Python and Ruby

Certifications:

- Certified Solutions Architect - Associate (AWS)
- Certified Developer - Associate (AWS)
- Certified DevOps Engineer - Professional (AWS)

You can notice that the above resume is tailored to the job description mentioned in the previous section. As a hiring manager and recruiter, here are some key takeaways and points to summarize for the above resume:

- This resume belongs to John Doe, a Solutions Architect with over 10 years of experience in software development and architecture.
- John has experience designing and implementing complex technology solutions for clients and has worked with project managers and other stakeholders to ensure solutions meet business requirements and are delivered on time and within budget.
- He has a solid technical background, with expertise in cloud computing platforms such as AWS and Azure, application integration, and API development.
- John has experience with big data technologies such as Hadoop, Spark, and Kafka and is skilled in DevOps practices and tools.
- He has demonstrated the ability to adapt to new technologies and learn quickly, as well as excellent communication and collaboration skills.
- In his previous roles, John has achieved notable successes, such as reducing AWS infrastructure costs by 30% and improving application performance by 50% by implementing caching strategies.
- John holds a Bachelor's degree in Computer Science and has continued to enhance his skills through certifications such as AWS Certified Solutions Architect - Professional.

John's resume demonstrates his technical expertise and ability to design and implement complex solutions that meet business requirements. His successes in improving infrastructure costs and application performance show his ability to make an impact and drive results.

To push through that resume, you should write a cover letter. Your cover letter should be personalized to the company and job you are applying for. It should introduce yourself, express your interest in the position, and highlight your relevant experience and skills. Be sure also to explain how you can contribute to the company and why you are the best candidate for the job.

Dear Hiring Manager,

I am writing to express my interest in the Solutions Architect position at your organization. As a highly experienced and skilled Solutions Architect with over 10 years of experience, I have the necessary technical breadth and depth to design and implement complex technology solutions for your clients.

In my previous role at XYZ Corporation, I was responsible for architecting and implementing cloud-based solutions for enterprise clients. One of my key achievements was leading a team in successfully migrating a large-scale, mission-critical application to the cloud, resulting in a 30% reduction in operational costs and a 50% improvement in application performance. I was also responsible for introducing DevOps practices and tools, which resulted in a 25% increase in application release frequency and a 40% reduction in time to market.

As a Solutions Architect, I can use my skills and experience to help your customers solve business challenges, influence product direction, and accelerate innovation. I am adept at communicating and partnering with other teams within the organization and have experience representing my team to executive management.

I hold a Bachelor's degree in Computer Science and have extensive experience with cloud computing platforms such as AWS and Azure. In addition, I have a strong understanding of modern software development methodologies, tools, and techniques. I am also proficient in application integration and API development.

Thank you for considering my application. I am excited to use my cloud architecture experience to assist your most valuable customers, and I look forward to discussing my qualifications further.

Sincerely,
John Doe

Overall, your resume and cover letter should present a professional and polished image of yourself and your abilities while demonstrating your enthusiasm and passion for the job.

LinkedIn is becoming one of the most prominent platforms for developing a professional network and connecting with potential employers. Let's learn about some tips on building your LinkedIn profile.

Polishing your LinkedIn profile

According to a 2021 report by Jobvite, 87% of recruiters use LinkedIn to find and vet job candidates. Additionally, a LinkedIn survey found that 77% of recruiters are more likely to contact a candidate with a strong LinkedIn profile. Furthermore, LinkedIn data shows that job seekers with a complete profile are 40 times more likely to receive job opportunities through LinkedIn. LinkedIn reports that over 20 million job seekers are introduced to potential employers weekly through the platform.

These statistics demonstrate the importance of having a strong LinkedIn profile for job seekers. It can increase their visibility to recruiters and potential employers and ultimately lead to more job opportunities.

Continuing with the resume we built earlier for John Doe, here are examples of how you can polish your LinkedIn profile:

- **Have a professional profile picture:** Choose a clear, professional headshot that represents you well.
- **Optimize your headline**: Your headline is the first thing people see on your profile. It should accurately reflect your current job title and industry. You could use a headline like "Experienced Solutions Architect specializing in cloud-based solutions and driving business growth."
- **Write a compelling summary:** Use your resume to showcase your skills, experience, and accomplishments. Keep it concise and engaging. You could write a summary highlighting expertise in designing and implementing complex technology solutions for clients. You could also mention your experience driving revenue growth, ability to lead technology discussions, and strong communication skills.
- **Highlight your work experience**: List your work experience in reverse chronological order and focus on accomplishments and results rather than just job duties. For example, highlight how you have increased revenue for a specific client by a certain percentage through your solutions architecture work.
- **Showcase your skills:** List your skills and endorsements, and make sure they are relevant to your industry and job title. You could list technical skills and competencies in your LinkedIn profile. You could also provide examples of how you have applied these skills in your work experience, such as experience with cloud computing platforms and application integration.
- **Get endorsements and recommendations:** Ask colleagues, supervisors, or clients to write recommendations for you. These can add credibility to your profile.
- **Engage with your network:** Join groups related to your industry and participate in discussions. Connect with others in your field and engage with their content. You could engage with your network on LinkedIn by sharing relevant articles, commenting on posts, and participating in groups related to your field. This can help you stay current on industry trends and connect with other industry professionals.
- **Try to get a LinkedIn Top Voice tag:** Achieving the LinkedIn Top Voice tag is a prestigious recognition, indicating that you're contributing valuable insights and thought leadership in your industry. LinkedIn publishes curated articles in multiple areas, and you can find articles that suit your area of interest and collaborate on them by adding your comments. Suppose you get enough engagement, like your contributions reaching multiple views. In that case, LinkedIn will reward you with the Top Voice tag, which can help highlight your expertise as validated by the community.

Finally, keep your profile up-to-date with new skills, accomplishments, and work experience. This shows that you are actively engaged in your career. By following these tips, you can create a strong and professional LinkedIn profile that showcases your skills and experience and helps you connect with others in your industry.

Starting A Solutions Architect Career

Aspiring to embark on a career as a Solutions Architect (SA) is an exciting endeavor, regardless of your background or experience. While certain paths might be more seamless than others, some strategies can help you transition successfully into this specialized role. Here are some frequently asked questions from aspiring solutions architects.

Question: Can I start an SA career fresh out of graduation?

Beginning a Solutions Architect career immediately after graduating is possible, although it may involve a slightly steeper learning curve than other paths. To excel in this role from the outset, it's crucial to establish a robust foundation of technical skills while gaining hands-on experience through internships, projects, certifications, and entry-level positions. Your journey into Solutions Architecture should be characterized by continuous learning, especially in solution design, cloud technologies, and enterprise architecture frameworks. Forge connections with industry experts and practitioners, as networking can be a valuable source of insights and opportunities. You can consider the following path to begin with :

Consider the Cloud Solutions Architect Path: Aspiring Solutions Architects, fresh graduates can consider specializing as Cloud Solutions Architects due to the high demand for professionals in this field. Cloud providers like AWS offer programs tailored for fresh graduates to enter the Solutions Architect domain. An example is the AWS TechU program, where graduates are hired as Associate Solutions Architects. You can receive specialized training and real-world exposure that accelerates your entry into the field through programs like these. You can find more about TechU programs here - https://www.amazon.jobs/en/landing_pages/AWS-TechU

Alternative Entry Points: If you are intrigued by the Solutions Architect role but want to gain more experience before transitioning directly, consider starting as a Cloud Support Engineer or Cloud Developer. These roles provide opportunities to work closely with cloud technologies while accumulating relevant experience. After a few years in these roles, you can pivot into Solutions Architecture with a well-rounded skill set.

Question: How do I transition from a software developer to a Solutions Architect role?

Transitioning from a software developer to a Solutions Architect is an exciting endeavor that demands a strategic approach, a blend of technical expertise, and effective communication—expanding your technical knowledge beyond programming languages and development frameworks to embark on this journey. Broaden your skill set to encompass cloud platforms, databases, networking, and security. Seek opportunities within your current role to engage in architecture discussions and contribute to design reviews. This will give you valuable architecture experience and a deeper understanding of the decision-making processes.

Pursuing relevant certifications, such as AWS Certified Solutions Architect, Microsoft Azure

Solutions Architect, or Google Cloud Certifications, can validate your skills and enhance your credibility in the field. Additionally, focus on developing cross-disciplinary skills that span business requirements, user experience, scalability, and security. These skills are essential for crafting comprehensive solutions aligning with technical and business objectives.

Embrace mentorship by seeking guidance from experienced Solutions Architects who can provide insights and advice tailored to your transition. Enhance your soft skills, including communication, presentation, and negotiation, as Solutions Architects frequently collaborate with diverse stakeholders and teams. Engaging in side projects and self-study will deepen your problem-solving abilities and practical knowledge of architecture.

Understanding the broader business context is crucial as Solutions Architects design solutions that drive organizational success. Attend workshops, seminars, and conferences related to architecture to stay updated on industry trends. Leverage platforms like LinkedIn to expand your network and connect with other professionals in the field.

When applying for junior architect roles, emphasize your development experience, architectural knowledge, and communication skills during interviews. Emphasize how your background as a software developer uniquely positions you to excel in this role. Following these steps, you can successfully transition from a software developer to a Solutions Architect and leverage your existing skills to thrive in your new role.

Question: How do I start an SA career if I don't have any application development knowledge?
Having a software development background is a flexible requirement for becoming a Solutions Architect (SA), although possessing a basic understanding of the Software Development Life Cycle (SDLC) can be advantageous. The role of an SA involves a wide range of skills beyond just software development. However, familiarity with SDLC concepts is beneficial, providing insight into how applications are built, deployed, and maintained. This knowledge can enhance your ability to design solutions that align with development best practices and effectively bridge the gap between technical teams and business stakeholders.

Nevertheless, if you don't have a software development background, you can still thrive as an SA by specializing in an area that aligns with your existing skills and experience. For instance, if you have a business analysis or business intelligence engineering background, you can pursue a career as a Big Data Analytics Solutions Architect. Similarly, if your expertise lies in networking, you can transition into a Network Solutions Architect role. Exploring specialized SA roles allows you to leverage your existing knowledge and tailor your career path to your strengths. Each specialization requires a deep understanding of the specific domain and the ability to architect solutions that meet business objectives.

In the upcoming chapters of this book, you will delve into the details of various specialist Solutions

Architect roles and learn strategies to excel in the corresponding interviews. By understanding the specific skills and knowledge needed for each specialization, you can confidently navigate your career path and secure a Solutions Architect position that aligns with your expertise and aspirations.

Question: I have industry domain expertise but basic system design knowledge; what advice would you give me to venture into an SA career?

Transitioning into a Solutions Architect (SA) career with industry domain expertise but basic system design knowledge is feasible and rewarding. While not having a solid software development background is not a barrier, acquiring a foundational understanding of system design, architectural concepts, and best practices is essential. To bridge this knowledge gap, consider immersing yourself in online resources, courses, and books that delve into system architecture and design principles.

Leveraging your industry domain expertise is a distinct advantage. Capitalize on your in-depth understanding of industry-specific challenges, regulations, and requirements to craft solutions that align perfectly with your domain's needs. Simultaneously, learning about enterprise architecture frameworks such as TOGAF and Zachman can enhance your ability to design solutions within the broader organizational context.

Hands-on experience is invaluable. Engage in practical projects and collaborate with seasoned architects to gain insights into real-world scenarios. Earning relevant certifications from cloud providers or architecture-focused organizations can validate your skills and boost your credibility as you transition into the role.

Staying current with industry trends and emerging technologies is crucial as the technology landscape evolves rapidly. Networking with professionals in the SA field by attending industry events, workshops, and webinars can provide invaluable connections and insights.

Effective communication skills are pivotal in the SA role. Developing the ability to articulate complex technical concepts to non-technical stakeholders and fostering collaboration among diverse teams is essential.

Mock projects based on real-world scenarios and seeking mentorship from experienced architects can help you practice translating business requirements into technical designs. Embrace continuous learning and growth as the SA journey is ongoing.

Your industry domain expertise and proactive approach to learning and skill enhancement position you well to excel in this dynamic and impactful role. In Chapter 12, "Cracking Industry

Solutions Architect Interview," you will learn about the industry solutions architect role and interview tips.

Question: I have worked in the on-premise environment for my entire career. How can I start a career as a Cloud Solutions Architect?

Transitioning from an on-premise environment to a Cloud Solutions Architect (CSA) career offers exciting opportunities for growth and innovation. While your on-premise experience is valuable, adapting to cloud technologies requires acquiring specific skills and perspectives. Here's a strategic roadmap to guide your transition:

- **Foundation of Cloud Knowledge:** Start by comprehensively understanding cloud computing concepts, services, and models. Familiarize yourself with major cloud platforms such as Amazon Web Services (AWS), Microsoft Azure, and Google Cloud Platform (GCP). Online courses and cloud provider documentation can help you grasp the fundamentals.
- **Cloud Certifications:** Cloud certifications validate your expertise and enhance your credibility. Choose certifications aligned with your preferred cloud platform and role, such as AWS Certified Solutions Architect, Microsoft Certified: Azure Solutions Architect Expert, or Google Cloud Professional Cloud Architect.
- **Hands-on Experience:** Practical experience is invaluable. Create your cloud environment using a personal account, experiment with services, and build sample projects. Alternatively, consider contributing to open-source cloud projects or volunteering for cloud-related initiatives within your current organization.
- **Migration Projects:** Leverage your on-premise expertise by participating in cloud migration projects. These initiatives involve moving existing applications and services to the cloud. Collaborate with teams responsible for migration planning, execution, and optimization.
- **Learn Cloud Design Patterns:** Study cloud design patterns that address common challenges in the cloud environment, such as high availability, scalability, and fault tolerance. Apply these patterns to your design solutions.
- **Embrace DevOps Practices:** Cloud environments often emphasize DevOps principles. Familiarize yourself with continuous integration, continuous delivery, and automation practices. Gain exposure to infrastructure-as-code tools like Terraform and CloudFormation.
- **Reframe Architecture Thinking:** Transitioning to the cloud requires a mindset shift. Focus on scalable, distributed, and loosely coupled architectures. Leverage cloud-native services for maximum benefits.
- **Network and Learn:** Attend cloud-focused meetups, conferences, and webinars. Engage with the cloud community, ask questions, and learn from practitioners' experiences.
- **Case Studies and Best Practices:** Study successful cloud migration case studies and best practices from industry leaders. Understand the challenges they faced and the strategies they employed.

- **Hands-on Labs:** Participate in cloud provider's hands-on labs and workshops. These platforms offer guided exercises to help you learn how to use various cloud services effectively.
- **Professional Development:** Seek mentorship from experienced Cloud Solutions Architects. Their insights can guide navigating challenges and opportunities in your transition.
- **Showcase Your Transition:** Update your resume and LinkedIn profile to emphasize your cloud-related skills, certifications, and hands-on experience. Tailor your job applications to CSA roles and emphasize your willingness to learn and adapt.

Transitioning to a Cloud Solutions Architect role from an on-premise background requires a blend of foundational knowledge, hands-on experience, and continuous learning. As you embrace cloud technologies, your ability to design scalable, flexible, and innovative solutions will empower organizations in the digital era.

Summary

In this chapter, you have learned about the role of a solution architect within an organization and the different types of solution architect roles that may coexist within one. The generalist solution architect has a broad knowledge of technology and may engage specialist solutions architects if needed to dive deep into a particular area. The specialist solution architect deeply understands their specific field of expertise. Common roles within this category include network architect, data architect, security architect, infrastructure architect, and DevOps architect.

In addition to understanding the role and its requirements, you have learned the importance of preparing for job applications. This includes researching the company to demonstrate your interest and fit for the company culture and creating a well-written and tailored resume and cover letter to make a positive first impression. You have also observed a sample SA resume and cover letter and tips on creating your own. Finally, you learned about the value of a polished LinkedIn profile in increasing your visibility to potential employers. You also learned how to transition to a Solutions Architect role if you come from a different technology background.

In the next chapter, you will learn technical interview preparation for solutions architects. It includes technical skills, solution design principles and methodologies, cloud architecture and patterns, emerging technologies, and enterprise architecture frameworks. The chapter also provides common interview questions, best practices for technical interview preparation, and interview resources.

Chapter 2 - Cracking the Technical Interview

The term 'interview' evokes a mixed bag of emotions. It's a mixture of excitement, anxiety, ambition, and uncertainty. While the process can be daunting, it's the gateway to your dream job as Solutions Architect roles. Having grasped an overview of the Solutions Architect roles in the previous chapter, you now find yourself at the foot of the technical behemoth. But, like any challenge, understanding its intricacies and nuances makes it
more manageable.

A solutions architect is, by definition, tasked with creating blueprints that solve the riddles of business problems using technology tools. To perform this feat, a Solutions Architect must have a broad array of technical skills and soft skills. This chapter will help you understand the technical skills required for the role and delve deep into design principles and methodologies that are the backbone of the architectural world. You will learn various details, from cloud architectures to enterprise frameworks.

However, knowledge is only half the battle. Knowing how to present this knowledge during an interview, structuring your thoughts, anticipating what's coming, and tackling the most intricate technical problems are skills in their own right. In this chapter, you will learn what to expect from the technical round and how to tackle the situation, including the following topics:

- Technical skills required for a solutions architect
- Key solution design principles and methodologies
- Understanding cloud architecture and its benefits and challenges
- Cloud architecture patterns and best practices
- Best practices for technical interview preparation
- Solution Architect technical interview questions

By the end of this chapter, you will learn strategies, best practices, and mock interview questions to equip you to create the Solutions Architect Technical Interview.

Technical skills required for a solutions architect

The role of a Solutions Architect is a diverse mix of various technical skills and the soft skills needed to navigate complex organizational structures and articulate solutions in a way that stakeholders can understand. Let's look at the key technical skills a Solutions Architect should possess:

- **Systems Design:** A Solutions Architect should possess comprehensive expertise in designing systems that are highly available, scalable, resilient, and performant. They should be capable of building systems that can withstand potential faults or errors, including hardware failures, software glitches, or network issues. They must create redundant systems that ensure continuous operation and availability, even in unexpected disruptions. Understanding load-balancing techniques like round-robin, weighted routing, and connection concurrency is a pivotal skill for a Solutions Architect. Knowledge of containerization technologies like Docker and orchestration tools like Kubernetes can also be valuable. Moreover, they should be adept at implementing monitoring and auditing strategies to detect and respond swiftly to any potential failures or disruptions.

- **Application development:** A Solutions Architect should have a solid understanding of application development processes and methodologies. They must know how software applications are designed, developed, and deployed. This knowledge enables them to design architectures that seamlessly integrate with existing applications and support the development of new ones.
- **Programming Languages:** Solutions Architects must be proficient in at least one programming language, such as Java, Python, Perl, Ruby, or Go. This skill is essential for writing, reviewing, and comprehending applications. Moreover, a solid grasp of software development processes is crucial for Solutions Architects. This knowledge empowers them to craft solutions that seamlessly integrate with current systems or operate autonomously. Additionally, it facilitates effective collaboration with development teams.
- **Infrastructure:** Solutions Architects must be well-versed in infrastructure components and technologies. This includes understanding different types of servers, storage systems, virtualization, cloud services, and data centers. A firm grasp of infrastructure components empowers them to design architectures that can handle varying workloads, scalability demands, and redundancy requirements.
- **Networking:** Networking is a fundamental cornerstone that Solutions Architects must thoroughly grasp. A profound comprehension of networking concepts and pertinent technologies is vital for crafting systems and constructing architectures. Proficiency in IP addressing, routing, load balancing, protocols, various network types, DNS, CDN, VPN, and more is an essential prerequisite for Solutions Architects.
- **Storage:** Storage forms another vital foundation for Solutions Architects. They must possess an extensive grasp of diverse storage architectures, encompassing direct-attached storage (DAS), network-attached storage (NAS), and storage area networks (SAN). Familiarity with the merits and constraints of each architecture is crucial, as is the ability to select the optimal storage structure for specific workloads. Furthermore, they should possess knowledge of data management tools and techniques involving data replication, backup, recovery, and data archiving, as well as metrics such as IOPS, throughput, and latency.
- **DevOps:** Proficiency in DevOps practices is imperative for Solutions Architects. They must possess the expertise to execute continuous integration/continuous deployment (CI/CD) systems, implement configuration management solutions, and employ strategies centered around infrastructure as code. These skills enable them to streamline software

development, enhance team collaboration, and consistently deliver applications and updates across the development lifecycle.

- **Security:** Solutions architects must have a robust grasp of security principles and best practices. They need practical experience crafting solutions prioritizing security and safeguarding data confidentiality, integrity, and availability. Proficiency in encryption techniques, identity, access management strategies, and familiarity with security frameworks are essential to their skill set. This enables them to fortify the applications and systems they design against potential cyber threats and breaches.
- **Database Systems:** Solutions Architects should comprehensively understand database concepts and various database management systems. This encompasses familiarity with relational databases such as MySQL, PostgreSQL, or Oracle and NoSQL databases like MongoDB or DynamoDB. Furthermore, knowledge of diverse database types, such as key-value or document-based, adds an advantageous layer to their expertise. This proficiency empowers them to make informed decisions regarding selecting and integrating the most suitable database solutions for a given scenario.
- **Middleware:** Solutions Architects should possess a valuable grasp of middleware technologies and integration patterns. This entails familiarity with essential components such as enterprise service buses (ESBs), web application servers, message queues, API management, and integration platforms. A solid understanding of middleware empowers them to design and implement efficient communication and interaction between various software components and systems. This knowledge ensures seamless integration and adequate data flow within complex architectures.
- **Cloud Computing:** Proficiency in cloud computing is essential for Solutions Architects. Cloud platforms abstract many foundational technologies like networking and storage, making it crucial for architects to be adept at cloud technologies. They are the trusted bridge between customers and architecture, ensuring solutions are built efficiently and cost-effectively. Understanding cloud services, infrastructure, deployment models, and cost optimization is essential for designing robust and scalable cloud-based solutions. This expertise enables architects to leverage the full potential of cloud environments while meeting business needs.

In addition to technical skills, a Solutions Architect should possess robust problem-solving abilities, the skill to communicate intricate technical subjects clearly, and a comprehensive understanding of industry trends and evolving architecture patterns. Further insights into the essential soft skills required for the Solutions Architect role will be explored in *"Chapter 3 - Soft Skills for Solutions Architect and Cracking Behavioral Interview."* This chapter will delve into the interpersonal qualities that complement the technical prowess of a Solutions Architect, enhancing their effectiveness in the role and during behavioral interviews. A Solutions Architect's role is diverse and challenging, encompassing many domains. However, it's important to understand that mastery in every domain is not a prerequisite.

Key solution design principles

Understanding key solution design principles and methodologies is crucial as a solutions architect. These principles provide a structured framework for creating well-architected designs that leverage technology and ensure cost-effectiveness and efficiency. Let's look at an overview of some key principles.

- **Scalability:** A fundamental principle is scalability, which involves designing solutions capable of accommodating growth in user numbers, data volume, and transaction load. Solutions architects should explore horizontal and vertical scaling options for the underlying infrastructure and the applications.
- **Reliability:** Reliability is paramount. Solutions architects must design systems that operate without significant downtime and incorporate strategies such as redundancy, failover mechanisms, and disaster recovery plans to ensure continuous operation despite failures.
- **Security:** Security is a cornerstone of any solution. Architects must prioritize data confidentiality, integrity, and availability. This means considering data encryption, robust network security, access controls, and efficient identity management.
- **Performance:** Performance is critical to user satisfaction. Solutions architects must address potential bottlenecks related to application performance, network latency, or storage latency to ensure that the solution meets performance expectations.
- **Maintainability:** Solutions must be designed with the future in mind. Architects should ensure that solutions are easily maintainable, upgradable, and extensible. It involves effective software versioning, careful API management, and streamlined software configuration management.
- **Cost Optimization:** Efficient cost management is crucial. Architects should balance performance, scalability, and resource requirements while optimizing resource utilization. Effectively using cloud services and analyzing the total cost of ownership (TCO) can contribute to designing cost-effective solutions.
- **Flexibility and Adaptability:** Solutions should be designed with flexibility and adaptability in mind. This means creating architectures that easily accommodate changing requirements, evolving technologies, and shifting environments. Utilizing flexible architectures and decoupled components can enhance adaptability.
- **Modularity and Component Reusability:** Solutions architects should emphasize modularity in design. Breaking down complex systems into smaller, reusable components makes development, testing, and maintenance more manageable. This approach also facilitates easier upgrades and the ability to replace or enhance specific components without affecting the entire solution.
- **Interoperability:** Solutions often need to work seamlessly with other systems within the same organization or in a larger ecosystem. Architects should prioritize designing solutions with open standards and interfaces that enable smooth integration with

external systems. It promotes data exchange, collaboration, and compatibility.

- **Compliance and Regulations:** Depending on the industry and location, solutions may need to adhere to specific regulations and compliance requirements, such as data protection laws (GDPR), industry standards (HIPAA), or government mandates. Architects should be well-versed in these regulations and design solutions that ensure data privacy, security, and legal compliance.
- **User Experience (UX) Design:** While technical aspects are crucial, a positive user experience is equally important. Architects should consider user interfaces, accessibility, responsiveness, and intuitive navigation. Prioritizing a seamless and enjoyable user experience contributes to solution adoption and user satisfaction.
- **Microservices Architecture:** As application complexity grows, adopting a microservices architecture can be beneficial. This involves breaking down an application into smaller, independently deployable services that communicate through APIs. This approach allows for greater flexibility, scalability, and easier management of different parts of the application.
- **User-Centric Design:** Understanding the needs and pain points of end-users is vital. Solutions architects should engage with stakeholders, gather user feedback, and design solutions that address real-world user challenges. This user-centric approach ensures that the final solution genuinely meets user needs.
- **Performance Testing and Optimization:** Beyond designing for performance, architects should also incorporate performance testing and optimization in the design process. Regularly assessing and fine-tuning the solution's performance ensures that it meets or exceeds expected performance metrics under varying loads and conditions.

The other key aspect to be aware of is Agile methodology, which advocates for an iterative approach to design and development. Solutions architects should be comfortable adapting their designs based on feedback, changing requirements, and emerging technologies. By embracing these design principles, architects can craft well-rounded solutions that leverage technology, align with business goals, and are secure, performant, and ready for future challenges. Refer to the Solutions Architect's Handbook to explore the above topics with best practices and reference architecture.

Solutions Architect's Handbook covers various topics, including best practices, design principles, and effective stakeholder communication. By providing insights beyond a specific cloud platform, this handbook is for aspiring and experienced Solutions Architects looking to enhance their skills and knowledge across different contexts. This book is available on Amazon - https://www.amazon.com/gp/product/1835084230.

Key enterprise architecture frameworks

Enterprise architecture is a crucial concept often asked in solutions architect interviews. It's a discipline that helps organizations strategically plan, design, and manage complex systems and technology solutions. Understanding Enterprise Architecture is vital as a Solutions Architect because it allows you to align your technical solutions with the organization's broader goals, optimize IT operations, and ensure successful outcomes. In the context of an interview, you might be asked about your familiarity with Enterprise Architecture and its key components:

- **Business Architecture involves understanding an organization's business strategy, processes, functions, and structure. In an interview, you could be asked how you'd design solutions that align with the company's business goals and methods**.
- **Data Architecture:** focuses on data models, flows, and governance. You might be asked about your experience designing systems that manage and utilize data effectively and securely.
- **Application Architecture:** This refers to software applications, their functionalities, interfaces, and interactions. Interviewers might ask how you'd design applications that meet the organization's needs and integrate well with existing systems.
- **Technology Architecture:** This covers the IT infrastructure, including hardware, software, networks, and technology components. You might be asked about your approach to selecting the right technology stack for a solution.

In the upcoming chapter, you will learn about the above architectures when we cover specialist solutions architecture interview domains in corresponding areas.

It's beneficial to know the key Enterprise Architecture frameworks such as TOGAF and Zachman:

- **TOGAF:** This framework provides a structured approach to Enterprise Architecture and emphasizes collaboration, governance, and iterative development. Familiarity with its components, like the Architecture Development Method (ADM), can demonstrate your strategic thinking and planning skills.
- **Zachman Framework:** Mentioning this framework showcases your ability to categorize and organize architectural artifacts systematically. It can also be impressive to highlight how you'd use its rows and columns to align business and technical aspects.

Lastly, you should also be able to link the benefits of Enterprise Architecture to the role of a Solutions Architect, which includes:

- **Alignment with Business Goals:** Explain how understanding business architecture helps you design solutions that directly contribute to the organization's success.
- **Agility and Adaptability:** Discuss how incorporating Enterprise Architecture principles allows you to create systems that can quickly adapt to changing requirements and technologies.

- **Efficiency and Optimization:** Share examples of how you've optimized IT resources through practical application and technology architecture.
- **Risk Management and Security:** Emphasize how your knowledge of data and technology architecture contributes to building secure and risk-resilient systems.
- **Informed Decision-Making:** Illustrate how your insights into data architecture enable data-driven decision-making.

While having a solid grasp of Enterprise Architecture principles and frameworks is undoubtedly beneficial for a Solutions Architect, it's essential to recognize that different roles and organizations prioritize different skills based on their specific needs. For instance, if your role heavily emphasizes technical expertise and hands-on experience with particular technologies, your primary focus is designing and implementing solutions effectively. In such cases, Enterprise Architecture frameworks are a supplementary knowledge area that adds value to your profile but is not necessarily a mandatory requirement.

On the other hand, if your role involves a broader scope, such as collaborating closely with business stakeholders, making strategic decisions, and aligning technology solutions with long-term organizational goals, then a strong understanding of Enterprise Architecture becomes more critical. It can help you bridge the gap between technical intricacies and business objectives.

Ultimately, a well-rounded Solutions Architect should balance technical excellence, understanding organizational context, and effective stakeholder management. By tailoring your skills to your role's requirements, you can showcase your ability to adapt and provide value in various scenarios.

Navigating Cloud Concepts for Solutions Architects

Cloud computing is the new normal for application workloads due to its ease, agility, and cost structure. As a Solutions Architect, understanding cloud computing is essential, as it's transformed IT landscapes. Your knowledge of cloud computing will distinguish you in interviews and guide you in creating efficient solutions using cutting-edge technologies. Let's break down cloud concepts from an interview perspective:

Cloud Computing Overview

Highlight your awareness of the cloud's transformative impact. Mention significant players like AWS, Azure, and GCP. Emphasize that the cloud offers on-demand resources accessed via the Internet. Delve into the key players in the cloud arena, focusing on your experiences and understanding, for example:

- **Amazon Web Services (AWS):**

- Highlight AWS's comprehensive service portfolio covering computing, storage, databases, analytics, machine learning, and more.
  - Mention your experience with specific AWS services, such as EC2, S3, Lambda, and RDS.
  - Discuss how AWS's global presence aids in optimizing latency and availability.
- **Microsoft Azure:**
  - Discuss Azure's strong integration with Microsoft's software ecosystem, making it appealing to enterprises.
  - Highlight Azure's offerings in virtual machines, Azure SQL Database, Azure App Service, and AI/ML services.
  - Mention how Azure's hybrid capabilities bridge on-premises and cloud environments.
- **Google Cloud Platform (GCP):**
  - Talk about GCP's reputation in data analytics, machine learning, and container orchestration.
  - Highlight GCP's strengths in services like Google Compute Engine, BigQuery, Kubernetes Engine, and TensorFlow.
  - Discuss GCP's emphasis on open-source technologies.

In interviews, a comprehensive understanding of cloud computing's transformative power, familiarity with major cloud players, and insight into their specifics, backed by in-depth resources, will position you as a Solutions Architect who's well-versed and deeply knowledgeable about the cloud landscape. Your ability to navigate these details ensures you're well-equipped to make informed decisions and guide organizations toward cloud-driven success.

Cloud Service Models

As a Solutions Architect, you've played a pivotal role in guiding organizations through the diverse cloud service models. Here's how you can articulate your impact:
- **IaaS - Infrastructure as a Service:**
  - Describe your involvement in architecting solutions that allow organizations to scale their infrastructure dynamically in response to changing demands.
  - Highlight your contribution to providing access to virtual computing, storage, and networking resources, enabling clients to focus on their applications without worrying about the underlying infrastructure.
- **PaaS - Platform as a Service:**
  - Share instances where you've empowered developers by architecting platforms that streamline application development, testing, and deployment.
  - Illustrate how you've enabled clients to leverage pre-built tools, databases, and development frameworks, allowing developers to concentrate on code and innovation.
- **SaaS - Software as a Service:**

- o Elaborate on your role in providing organizations with accessible and cost-effective software applications that don't require local installations or maintenance.
- o Discuss how your solutions have enabled clients to adopt and utilize essential applications like email, collaboration tools, and CRM systems.

By highlighting your contributions across IaaS, PaaS, and SaaS, you present yourself as a Solutions Architect with a holistic understanding of cloud service models. Your ability to tailor solutions to match organizational requirements and seamlessly transition between these models underlines your expertise in building solutions that drive efficiency, innovation, and growth.

Key Aspects of Cloud Computing

As a Solutions Architect, understanding the fundamental aspects of cloud computing is a code of modern agility and innovation. These core aspects define the essence of cloud technology, shaping your ability to create resilient and efficient architectures. Let's delve deeper into these key aspects:

- **On-Demand Self-Service:**
  - o Stress the significance of users' ability to provision and manage resources independently without provider intervention.
  - o This self-service model empowers users to scale resources up or down as needed, promoting agility and minimizing delays.
- **Broad Network Access and high availability:**
  - o Explain how cloud services exceed geographical boundaries and provide IT infrastructure availability globally at the fingertip.
  - o Highlight Cloud provides the hybrid model with high-speed connectivity to the on-premise data center.
  - o Explain how you ensure applications remain operational even in the face of failures.
  - o Illustrate how you employ redundancy, fault tolerance, and disaster recovery mechanisms to maintain application availability and mitigate downtime risks.
- **Rapid Elasticity:**
  - o Note the vital role of rapid scalability in accommodating fluctuating workloads. Detail how cloud environments allow resources to be quickly scaled up or down based on demand without manual intervention.
  - o Highlight its significance in handling varying traffic volumes and peak loads, optimizing performance.
  - o Highlight your experience implementing horizontal and vertical scaling strategies to ensure that applications and infrastructure can expand swiftly to meet evolving user needs.
- **Cost-effectiveness :**
  - o Elaborate on the pay-as-you-go model's value in cost management.

- o Explain that organizations are billed based on actual usage, aligning costs with resource consumption.
  - o This approach promotes cost-effectiveness by avoiding upfront capital investments and facilitating budget optimization.
- **Security :**
  - o Describe the cloud shared security model and how it takes care of the security of the cloud, including physical data centers and infrastructure, and users only need to take care of the security of their applications.
  - o Highlight Cloud provides an audit and monitoring mechanism with multiple security tools to run mission-critical applications.
  - o Detail your role in implementing robust security measures to safeguard applications and data.
  - o Elaborate on your experience with encryption, access controls, and intrusion detection systems to ensure data confidentiality and protect against cyber threats.

These key aspects reinforce the transformative potential of cloud computing. As a Solutions Architect, your understanding of these fundamentals showcases your ability to design architectures that harness the power of on-demand resources, flexibility, and cost-efficiency. When communicated effectively in interviews, these insights distinguish you as a professional who's not just technically skilled but also strategically familiar with the core tenets of modern IT solutions.

A thorough understanding of one of the public cloud providers can be highly beneficial. Since most cloud providers share similar concepts, possessing in-depth knowledge of one platform convinces hiring managers that you can quickly adapt to others. Thus, if your expertise is in a particular cloud provider, it can still be appealing to employers using different providers, as they generally expect a less steep learning curve for such candidates.

Since AWS is one of the most popular public cloud providers, developing a deep understanding of its services and features can be beneficial. You can refer to the "AWS for Solutions Architects" book to gain comprehensive knowledge in this area.

"AWS for Solutions Architects" book is tailored for those working within the AWS environment; this book delves deep into AWS services, architectural patterns, and cloud design principles. It's an invaluable resource for individuals aiming to specialize in AWS solutions architecture and attain the AWS Certified Solutions Architect certification. This book provides detailed guidance for building scalable, reliable, and cost-effective solutions on the AWS platform

using AWS's well-architected framework. You can find this book on Amazon using the link - https://www.amazon.com/gp/product/180323895X

Whether you choose the Solutions Architect's Handbook, the AWS for Solutions Architect's Book, or both, these resources offer valuable insights and guidance for individuals aspiring to excel in solutions architecture. Remember that continuous learning and adaptation are crucial to success in this dynamic and rewarding role.

Cloud Architecture Challenges

As a Solutions Architect, your proficiency extends beyond harnessing the cloud's transformative power – it involves addressing its nuanced challenges. Here's how you can articulate your prowess in overcoming these hurdles:

- **Data Privacy and Compliance:**
  - Showcase your understanding of regulatory landscapes, such as GDPR, and how you ensure cloud-based systems adhere to data privacy regulations.
  - Illustrate how you implement data encryption, access controls, and audit trails to safeguard sensitive information and maintain compliance.
- **Vendor Lock-In:**
  - Discuss your strategies to avert the risks associated with vendor lock-in, where an organization becomes overly reliant on a single cloud provider.
  - Highlight your experience in architecting solutions that maintain portability and flexibility, allowing organizations to switch providers or integrate multiple solutions seamlessly.
- **Integration Challenges:**
  - Elaborate on your proficiency in harmonizing diverse technologies within cloud and on-premises environments.
  - Share instances where you've employed integration patterns, APIs, and middleware to bridge the gap between legacy systems and modern cloud-based solutions.
- **Cost Management:**
  - Detail your approach to managing costs within the dynamic and complex cloud landscape.
  - Highlight how you monitor resource utilization, employ cost optimization strategies like reserved or spot instances, and provide organizations with insights into cost-efficient resource provisioning.

By addressing these challenges in interviews, you exemplify your role as a technical architect and a strategic problem-solver. Your solutions extend beyond technical components to ensure data compliance, mitigate lock-in risks, foster seamless integrations, and optimize costs.

Cloud Deployment

As a Solutions Architect, your expertise in navigating different cloud deployment models showcases your ability to tailor solutions to meet specific organizational needs. Here's how you can effectively convey your experience:

- **Public Clouds:**
  - Illustrate instances where you've harnessed the power of shared resources in public clouds to drive agility and cost savings for organizations.
  - Highlight your role in architecting solutions that capitalize on the scalability and accessibility of public clouds, enabling clients to adapt to changing demands swiftly.
- **Private Clouds:**
  - Share how you've orchestrated private cloud environments to cater to specific compliance requirements, like those in healthcare or finance.
  - Discuss your involvement in designing secure and customizable infrastructures, emphasizing the balance between control, security, and scalability.
- **Hybrid Clouds:**
  - Detail how you've blended the benefits of public and private clouds to create flexible and resilient solutions for organizations.
  - Provide examples of how you've strategically allocated workloads between environments, optimizing for security, performance, and cost-effectiveness.

You demonstrate your adaptability in crafting tailored strategies by showcasing your proficiency in designing solutions across public, private, and hybrid cloud environments. Your role extends beyond technology implementation – you're a strategic orchestrator, aligning cloud choices with organizational objectives, compliance needs, and performance demands. This holistic approach showcases your prowess as a Solutions Architect who crafts solutions that perfectly fit the diverse deployment landscape.

Cloud Security and Governance

As a Solutions Architect with a comprehensive understanding of cloud security and governance, your role has been pivotal in safeguarding critical data and ensuring compliance. Here's how you can showcase your expertise:

- **Security Measures:**
  - Dive into your experience implementing robust security measures such as encryption in transit and at rest. Explain how this shields sensitive data from unauthorized access.
  - Illustrate your prowess in devising adequate access controls, allowing only authorized personnel to access cloud resources and sensitive information.
  - Discuss your involvement in implementing multi-factor authentication and reinforcing the security of cloud access and authentication mechanisms.

- **Governance Policies:**
  - ○ Share your role in developing and implementing governance policies that adhere to data privacy regulations, industry standards, and organizational needs.
  - ○ Highlight your contribution to creating access management policies that define who can access what data and ensure the proper segregation of roles and responsibilities.
  - ○ Explain your strategies for devising disaster recovery policies that enable rapid data restoration and system functionality in case of disruptions.

By delving into the details of your security measures and governance policies, you create a clear picture of your hands-on experience in securing cloud environments against threats and ensuring that organizations operate within the boundaries of compliance and best practices. Your role as a Solutions Architect in this context is crucial in establishing trust and confidence among stakeholders. You will learn more about security interviews in Chapter 11: Cracking the Security Solutions Architect Interview.

In interviews, your ability to showcase an understanding of challenges and strategies to ensure optimal cloud solutions will make you a desirable Solutions Architect. Your adeptness at navigating these cloud concepts exemplifies your readiness for the role.

Navigating Emerging Technologies as a Solutions Architect

As a Solutions Architect, staying abreast of emerging technologies is not just an option but a strategic necessity. It is your ticket to maintaining relevance in an ever-evolving landscape. Here's how you can present your prowess in understanding and leveraging emerging technologies:

Demonstrating Awareness:
- Explain your approach to staying updated with the latest design patterns, technologies, and breakthroughs to emphasize your commitment to staying informed.
- Discuss your proactive efforts in tracking trends like Data mesh, Data fabric, GenAI, Matter, Vector databases, Robotics, and Blockchains, showcasing your readiness to engage with cutting-edge innovations.

Knowledge Enrichment Strategies:
- Detail your strategy of subscribing to market research reports from reputed sources like Gartner and IDC. Highlight instances where insights from such reports influenced your architectural decisions.
- Mention your participation in industry conferences and summits, underlining your commitment to immersing yourself in the industry's forefront.

- Talk about your engagement with local meetups and peer communities, showcasing your eagerness to share and exchange ideas with fellow experts.
- Share how you leverage platforms like Medium and Hacker News to access thought-provoking articles and analyses, giving you a broader perspective.

Networking and Learning:
- Illustrate your involvement in peer communities and forums like Stack Overflow, detailing instances where you both sought and shared knowledge.
- Explain how these engagements have widened your knowledge and facilitated networking with like-minded professionals.

Positioning as a Thought Leader:
- Discuss how your active pursuit of emerging technologies has positioned you as a thought leader, citing examples of speaking engagements, articles, or blog posts that showcase your insights and interpretations.
- Highlight your ability to assess these technologies' potential impacts, benefits, and challenges on society, the industry, and businesses.

Underscoring your awareness of emerging technologies during interviews can significantly set you apart. Even if you aren't an expert in cutting-edge fields such as Generative AI, Machine Learning, IoT, Blockchain, or Quantum computing, showcasing your knowledge places you in a prime position to stand out from other candidates. This is especially crucial for a Solutions Architect role, where the overarching responsibility is to devise optimal solutions for organizations. By doing so, you aptly demonstrate your adaptability and skill in comprehending intricate and innovative concepts. It's essential to accentuate how your forward-thinking mindset instills confidence in potential employers, highlighting your capacity to actively contribute to innovation and steer transformative organizational changes.

In rapid technological evolution, being a Solutions Architect well-versed in the currents of change places you in a prime position to shape the future of IT landscapes. Your commitment to exploring, learning, and embracing emerging technologies exemplifies your readiness to tackle tomorrow's challenges today.

Architecture Whiteboarding

In a technical interview whiteboarding session, approaching the problem from an architectural design perspective can significantly enhance your performance. As you stand before the whiteboard, understand the problem statement thoroughly. Clear any doubts by seeking clarifications, and if necessary, outline your assumptions transparently. Once you're confident in your comprehension, outline a strategic plan for tackling the problem. This demonstrates your structured thinking and lets the interviewer know you're considering the bigger picture. The interviewer is evaluating the candidate's: -

- **Problem-solving skills** - Can they understand the problem's requirements and constraints and develop an appropriate solution? Do they ask clarifying questions?
- **Technical knowledge** - Do they demonstrate a solid grasp of big data technologies, architectures, and principles? For example, they consider aspects like scalability, fault tolerance, latency, security, etc.
- **Communication skills** - How clearly do they explain their thought process and design? Can they diagram architecture and data flows clearly on the whiteboard?
- **Design skills** - Does their design adequately address the functional and non-functional requirements? Do they follow best practices for big data architectures?
- **Knowledge of the industry** - Do they understand real-world use cases and considerations for big data in different sectors?

Breaking down the problem into manageable components showcases your ability to architect solutions. Discuss the trade-offs you're making as you proceed, whether it's optimizing for efficiency, scalability, or other factors. Utilize pseudocode to illustrate your logic, allowing you to focus on design without getting bogged down by syntax.

As you progress, maintain a dialogue with the interviewer, explaining your thought process step by step. This thinking-aloud approach highlights your problem-solving strategy and offers insight into your architectural choices. When transitioning to actual code, ensure its readability by following clean coding practices. Test your solution with sample inputs, outlining its execution flow. Emphasize how your architectural decisions cater to various scenarios, including edge cases.

Throughout the session, maintain eye contact and engage the interviewer in a dialogue. Effective communication is paramount in conveying your architectural rationale and design thinking. Should you encounter stumbling points, remain composed and adaptable – these qualities reflect well in an architectural context where flexibility and sound judgment are essential. Incorporating these architectural design considerations into your whiteboarding approach will showcase your technical prowess and capacity to create robust and well-considered solutions. Remember, it's about reaching the correct answer and demonstrating your architectural mindset and problem-solving approach.

An Example of Data Lake Whiteboarding

Before starting the whiteboarding session, it's a good practice to reserve some space in the top-left corner of the whiteboard. This area can be used for high-level objectives and meeting outcomes, helping everyone stay aligned on the session's purpose. Establish the high-level goals of the whiteboarding session, outlining what you intend to achieve during the discussion. This sets the tone for the conversation and ensures that you and the audience are on the same page.

List important customer questions that you aim to address through the whiteboarding exercise.

These could be questions about architecture, design, scalability, performance, security, or any other relevant topic. Having a clear list of questions keeps the session focused and organized. You should cluster similar questions into buckets or categories. This helps you structure your whiteboarding presentation logically, address related queries, and create a cohesive narrative.

Identify any questions or topics that might fall outside the scope of the whiteboarding session. Move these "out of scope" questions into a designated area on the whiteboard, often called the "parking lot." This signals the audience that you acknowledge their questions but plan to address them later, ensuring the main discussion remains on track.

As you present and discuss each point during the whiteboarding session, use a visual indicator like a checkmark or tick to mark off items on the list of questions. These visual cues show that the topics have been covered and help ensure no critical questions are left unanswered.

Following this structured approach, you create a clear framework for the whiteboarding session, ensuring that objectives are met, important questions are addressed, and the overall presentation remains organized and engaging.

The following diagram depicts the whiteboarding of a data lake architecture, which involves visually explaining the design and components of a data lake system.

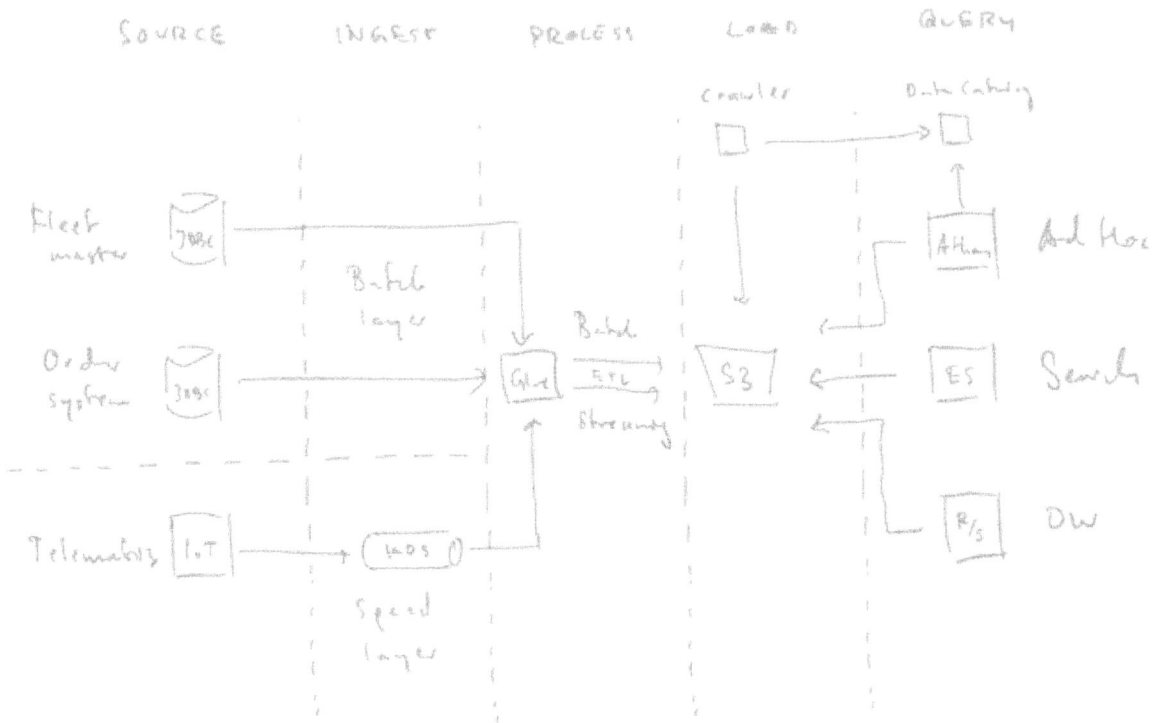

Figure 2.1 – Whiteboarding Data Lake Architecture

As shown in the preceding diagram, Here's a step-by-step process for effectively whiteboarding a data lake architecture:

1. **Understand the Requirements:** Begin by understanding the requirements of the data lake. What data sources will it integrate? What data types (structured, semi-structured, unstructured) will it store? What are the primary use cases for this data? Clarity on these aspects is crucial before starting the whiteboarding process.

2. **Start with High-Level Components:** Draw high-level components of the data lake architecture on the whiteboard. Typically, this includes data sources, storage, processing, and consumption layers. Connect these components with arrows to indicate data flow. In this example, high-level data lake layers are the source, ingest, process, load, and query, giving you an excellent structure.

3. **Explain Data Ingestion:** Elaborate on ingesting data into the data lake. Discuss the technologies and tools utilized for both batch and real-time data ingestion. Emphasize the significance of connectors and integration points with diverse data sources, including databases, APIs, and external systems. In Figure 2.1, data ingestion originates from the Order and Fleet Master databases, representing batch ingestion, and website telemetry data, representing streaming data ingestion. Batch data is directly ingested using AWS

Glue, a serverless Spark service provided by AWS. Streaming data, on the other hand, is ingested through Amazon Kinesis Data Stream.

4. **Discuss Data Storage:** Describe the data storage layer. Mention distributed file systems (like Hadoop HDFS) or cloud-based storage solutions (like Amazon S3). Discuss the benefits of scalability and cost-effectiveness provided by these storage platforms.

5. **Illustrate Data Processing:** Elaborate on the data processing layer. Explain how data is transformed, cleaned, and transformed into usable formats. Discuss technologies like Apache Spark or Apache Flink for batch and stream processing. Mention data pipelines and ETL (Extract, Transform, Load) processes.

6. **Highlight Data Cataloging and Metadata:** Introduce metadata management and data cataloging. Explain how metadata is stored and managed to provide insights into data lineage, quality, and usage. Mention tools or solutions used for metadata management. In this example, you can see AWS glue Crawler cataloging data.

7. **Explore Data Consumption:** Delve into the methods of accessing and utilizing data from the data lake. Detail the pivotal role played by query engines, such as Presto or Apache Drill, in facilitating SQL-based querying across diverse data formats. Highlight the availability of data visualization tools that users can leverage to extract insights from the data. In this example, Amazon Athena is the tool for ad hoc queries, Elastic Search is used for data search functionality, and Redshift is used for data warehousing. Furthermore, the array of visualization tools includes Tableau and Amazon QuickSight.

8. **Address Security and Governance:** Touch on security and governance aspects. Explain how data access control, encryption, and compliance measures are implemented. Highlight the role of data lake governance frameworks and policies.

9. **Consider Scalability and Performance:** Emphasize the data lake's scalability and performance. Discuss how the architecture can handle growing data volumes and increasing user demands. Mention techniques to optimize query performance.

10. **Summarize and Conclude:** Summarize the main components and benefits of the data lake architecture. Conclude by highlighting how this architecture aligns with the organization's data strategy and business goals.

Throughout the whiteboarding session, encourage the interviewer to ask questions and engage in discussions. Be prepared to justify your design choices, discuss alternatives, and address potential challenges.

There may be a situation where your interview is conducted remotely; in that case, you should have different whiteboarding tools handy for your practice. Here are some options and best practices for online whiteboarding:

- **Miro:** Miro is a popular collaborative online whiteboarding platform that offers a range of templates and tools for brainstorming, planning, and visualizing ideas. You can access Miro using the link here - https://miro.com/

- **Google Jamboard:** Google's digital whiteboard solution offers collaborative features for remote teams and integrates well with other Google Workspace apps. Access Jamboard using the link here: https://jamboard.google.com.
- **Microsoft Whiteboard:** This digital canvas from Microsoft enables real-time collaboration and integration with Office 365 applications. Use the link here to access https://www.microsoft.com/en-us/microsoft-365/microsoft-whiteboard/digital-whiteboard-app.
- **Input Devices:** For digital whiteboarding, tools like Wacom tablets or Apple Pencil for iPads can provide a natural drawing experience.

These tools offer unlimited canvases, enabling you to draw, annotate, and collaborate with team members in real-time. Remember to adjust your whiteboarding approach based on the context of the presentation. Collaborative online tools are excellent for virtual meetings and remote collaboration, while offline whiteboarding works well for in-person discussions. Utilizing input devices can enhance your digital whiteboarding experience while adhering to marker color conventions ensures clarity. By incorporating these tools and practices, you can effectively communicate your ideas and solutions during technical discussions.

> *Whiteboarding is not just about drawing diagrams; it's about effectively communicating your architectural decisions, rationale, and problem-solving approach. Focus on clear explanations, engage with the interviewer, and showcase your ability to design a scalable and efficient data lake architecture.*

In some of the interviews, you may have to do a presentation, as that is part of the solutions architect job, especially if you are looking for a career as a cloud architect. Let's look at best practices for presentations.

Presentation best practice for SA interview

Remember, a presentation is not just about delivering information; it's about engaging and persuading your audience to understand and appreciate your ideas. By following these best practices and tailoring your approach to the specific context of the interview, you can effectively showcase your skills as a Solution Architect. In a Solution Architect interview, delivering a compelling presentation is a crucial skill that demonstrates your ability to communicate complex technical concepts clearly and persuasively. Here are some best practices to excel in presenting during a Solution Architect interview:

- **Understand the Audience:** Before preparing your presentation, understand your audience's level of technical knowledge and their specific interests. Tailor your content to address their concerns and objectives.
- **Define Clear Objectives:** Clearly define the objectives of your presentation. Are you explaining a solution, proposing an architecture, or solving a particular problem? Having a clear focus helps you structure your presentation effectively.
- **Storyline and Structure:** Craft a logical storyline for your presentation. Begin with an engaging introduction, followed by the main content, and conclude with a summary of key takeaways. Use headings, bullet points, and visuals to enhance clarity.
- **Visual Aids:** Utilize visuals such as diagrams, flowcharts, and slides to illustrate your points. Visual aids can simplify complex ideas and enhance audience understanding. Ensure that visuals are clear and well-designed.
- **Know Your Material:** Understand your content thoroughly. Don't rely solely on your slides; be prepared to explain concepts without them. This demonstrates deep knowledge and confidence in your subject matter.
- **Engage Your Audience:** Maintain eye contact, speak clearly, and use a confident tone. Encourage questions and interaction during the presentation. Engaging your audience keeps them attentive and involved.
- **Demo and Examples:** Whenever possible, provide practical demonstrations or examples. Showcasing real-world scenarios can help the audience relate to the concepts better.
- **Address Questions:** Be ready to answer questions during and after your presentation. If you don't know the answer, acknowledge it and commit to finding the information later.
- **Practice, Practice, Practice:** Rehearse your presentation multiple times. Practice helps you refine your delivery, timing, and confidence. It also enables you to identify areas that need more explanation.
- **Time Management:** Stick to the allocated time for your presentation. Being concise and focused shows respect for your audience's time and demonstrates your ability to communicate efficiently.
- **Adaptability:** Be ready to adjust your presentation based on the audience's reactions and questions. Flexibility in addressing unexpected queries showcases your expertise.
- **Use Real-World Context:** Relate your content to real-world situations the audience can relate to. This makes your presentation more relatable and memorable.
- **Confidence and Enthusiasm:** Approach your presentation with confidence and enthusiasm. Your passion for the subject will resonate with the audience and make your presentation more impactful.

As you learned about some crucial skills, such as whiteboarding and presentation, to crack technical interviews, let's focus on some questions and how to answer them.

Answering technical interview questions

In this section, you will gain insights into the interview questions typically encountered by generalist Solutions Architects. This preparation will serve as a foundation for our subsequent chapters, where we delve into specialized roles such as database, analytics, machine learning, security, and networking. It's important to note that roles like Enterprise Architect or Platform Architect share overlapping responsibilities, allowing you to apply similar strategies. Before delving into common technical questions, refresh your understanding of networking, storage, compute, security, and DevOps fundamentals.

The first pivotal step is structuring your answers using the STAR method (Situation, Task, Action, Result). Creating an interview guide will prove beneficial, where you document 6 to 7 instances where you resolved technical issues, leading to quantifiable achievements.

This approach ensures that your responses are well-organized and provide a comprehensive view of your problem-solving capabilities and accomplishments. Let's look at the first question without any delay.

Question: Describe the most complex architecture you have designed. What were the difficulties you encountered, and what were the results of your efforts?
Answer: Let's take an example of designing a complex e-commerce platform with global users. Use the STAR (Situation, Task, Action, Result) format and include relevant details to make the answer more reliable.

Situation: In my previous role as a Solutions Architect at XYZ Company, I was tasked with designing and implementing a complex architecture for a global e-commerce platform for a rapidly growing online retailer. The company was experiencing significant growth, and its existing infrastructure needed help handling increased user traffic during peak seasons.

Task: The challenge was to create an architecture that could handle the current high volume of traffic and scale seamlessly to accommodate future growth. The goal was to ensure high performance, availability, and security of the platform while also integrating various third-party systems for payment processing, inventory management, and shipping.

Action: To address this challenge, I decided to adopt a microservices architecture to increase modularity and scalability. Leveraging AWS's capabilities, I recommended using Amazon ECS for container orchestration and AWS Lambda for serverless functions. We used Amazon RDS for database management and Amazon S3 for storage. Load balancing and auto-scaling configurations were carefully implemented to manage varying traffic loads effectively.

In addition, I conducted thorough performance testing and optimization, identifying and resolving bottlenecks to ensure optimal response times for users across the globe. I collaborated closely with the development and operations teams to ensure a seamless deployment process and continuous monitoring.

Result: The outcome was exceptional. During the peak holiday season, the platform experienced a 50% increase in traffic compared to the previous year. Thanks to the architecture's scalability and fault-tolerant design, the platform handled the load effortlessly, maintaining high availability and quick response times. Downtime was reduced by 70%, contributing to improved user satisfaction and increased sales.

Moreover, the architecture's flexibility allowed the client to integrate new features and third-party services easily. This adaptability led to a 30% increase in customer engagement and a 25% increase in overall revenue within the first year of implementation.

This experience highlighted the critical role of well-planned architecture and its impact on a company's growth and success. It showcased my ability to design solutions that address immediate challenges and provide a foundation for sustainable and scalable growth.

For example. Here are the top three follow-up questions that might be asked after describing the challenges faced during the implementation of the complex architecture for the global e-commerce platform:

1. **Can you elaborate on your specific strategies to address the scalability challenge?** Scaling a platform to handle peak user traffic can be complex. Can you share the technologies or architectural decisions you made to ensure the platform could accommodate the increasing load without compromising performance?
2. **How did you manage the integration complexities with third-party systems?** Integrating various external systems can often be challenging due to different data formats and communication protocols. Can you provide more details about the integration strategies

you employed to ensure smooth communication and data exchange between the e-commerce platform and these external systems?

3. **Could you share more about the security measures you implemented to protect customer data and transactions?** Security is a critical aspect of any e-commerce platform. Can you describe the specific security measures you put in place to safeguard sensitive customer information while maintaining the necessary flow of data and transactions within the architecture?

These follow-up questions delve deeper into the specific challenges and solutions you faced, providing the interviewer with a more comprehensive understanding of your expertise and experiences.

These questions are broadly scoped and usually offer you the flexibility to select and emphasize the relevance of your response. However, remember that you should be capable of expressing your answers in straightforward yet pertinent terms, using real-world experiences as context. Ensure that you can provide quantifiable outcomes and well-justified reasoning.

Let's look at technical questions across various domains to help you prepare. The provided answers in the following sections are for reference and may need to be adjusted based on specific technical environments and requirements.

Application Development

Question: How do you handle error responses that your application might receive from its service dependencies, and what best practices do you follow?
Answer: When encountering error responses, it's essential to employ a robust strategy. Catch exceptions to prevent unhandled crashes and log them for thorough diagnostics. Consider adapting your application's behavior based on different error codes, distinguishing between client-side errors (4xx) and server-side errors (5xx). Implementing retry logic with appropriate back-off strategies ensures that temporary failures are addressed gracefully, promoting application resilience and minimizing user impact.

Question: From your perspective, what key attributes contribute to making an API 'developer-friendly'?
Answer: Creating a developer-friendly API involves adhering to industry best practices. Start by conforming to established HTTP standards for requests like GET, PUT, and POST. Employ widely recognized frameworks such as REST, oAuth, and GraphQL to ensure consistent and intuitive interactions. Document the API extensively with real-world examples, offering developers clear usage guidelines. Maintain uniformity in object definitions, action descriptions, and model structures. Incorporate versioning and backward compatibility mechanisms to support evolving needs. Additionally, provide Software Development Kits (SDKs) for popular programming

languages, guarantee scalability, availability, and security, and optimize performance.

Question: Can you provide insight into how you would implement the "circuit breaker" pattern within a distributed application?

Answer: Effectively implementing the "circuit breaker" pattern requires a strategic approach. Begin by continuously monitoring the health of downstream dependencies. Create a mechanism to track the balance between healthy and unhealthy requests over a specific time interval. When a certain threshold of unhealthy requests is surpassed, activate the circuit breaker. This means subsequent requests are gracefully rejected, safeguarding the application from interacting with a potentially compromised dependency. After a predefined timeout, attempt to reintegrate with the dependency using a controlled percentage of requests, evaluating for recovery. Persistence stores like DynamoDB, Redis, or Memcached can efficiently manage the state of the circuit breaker.

Question: Could you explain the concept of a version control system (VCS)?

Answer: A version control system (VCS) is a fundamental tool for managing code changes and fostering collaborative software development. This system enables multiple developers to work seamlessly on a shared codebase. By assigning metadata such as author attributions and explanatory comments to code changes, a VCS maintains a comprehensive history of the software's evolution. This functionality minimizes conflicts and provides a structured environment for team members to contribute to code changes. A VCS enhances project transparency, accelerates collaboration, and supports iterative development.

Networking

Question: Could you explain the concept of a CIDR block and its role in network architecture?

Answer: A CIDR (Classless Inter-Domain Routing) block represents a range of IP addresses defined by a binary number indicating shared initial sequence bits in their binary representation. These blocks are crucial elements in network architecture, primarily serving as building blocks for IP addressing and subnet allocation. CIDR blocks are assigned to network subnets, delineating the available range of device IP addresses. They aid in efficient IP address allocation, ensuring optimal address space utilization and facilitating effective network management.

Question: Imagine you have just deployed a virtual machine in a cloud environment and configured it as a web server. Despite knowing that the instance can access the Internet, attempting to access your webpage through a browser results in an error message. How would you approach troubleshooting this issue?

Answer: My troubleshooting strategy would begin with a systematic analysis when confronted with this situation. Firstly, I would identify the specific error message displayed by the browser. This information is essential for pinpointing the root cause. To address connectivity concerns, I would review the server logs to ascertain if incoming requests are being received and whether any errors are being reported. I also ensure that the web server is operational and actively serving requests. Examining port and firewall settings on the web server and any intermediary network appliances would be imperative to verify that the relevant ports are open for incoming traffic. Furthermore, I would attempt to access the webpage using alternative routes, eliminating local browser-related issues from the equation.

Question: Can you highlight the distinctions between layer four and layer seven load balancing?
Answer: Layer 4 load balancing operates based on information within packet headers, such as source/destination IP addresses and port numbers. This approach doesn't delve into the packet's contents, rendering it faster due to its lower computational requirements. However, decision-making needs more granularity. In contrast, layer seven load balancing delves deeper by inspecting the full packet contents. This is especially prevalent in handling HTTP requests, where routing decisions factor in elements like HTTP headers, URI paths, and content types. While layer seven load balancing allows for more sophisticated routing strategies, it comes with the trade-off of increased computational demands.

Infrastructure

Question: You've been assigned to evaluate hardware utilization efficiency within your data centers. How would you approach this task, and which tools would you utilize?
Answer: To assess hardware efficiency, I would focus on monitoring critical parameters such as CPU utilization, memory consumption, network traffic, and storage usage. I would consider employing tools like 'top,' 'sysstat,' 'netstat,' 'top,' 'monit,' and 'nagios' in Linux environments. For Windows environments, suitable options include 'Performance Monitor,' 'SCOM/MOM,' 'typeperf,' 'LogicMonitor,' 'Veeam,' and 'Nagios.' These tools offer insights into resource consumption and performance bottlenecks, allowing for informed decisions on optimizing hardware use and enhancing data center efficiency.

Question: In an on-premises/datacenter scenario, what are the essential prerequisites for making a website accessible online?
Answer: Several components are fundamental to ensure a website's availability on the Internet. These include a physical server hosting the website's content powered by a functional web server application. This application should actively listen to incoming requests from a designated port. Furthermore, the server must be connected to a network interface physically linked to an Internet/WAN Provider. For public accessibility, a public IP address is allocated to the network interface. A domain name is registered and configured on a public DNS service provider's name servers to facilitate user-friendly access. These name servers translate the website's domain name to its corresponding public IP address, enabling seamless Internet access. While acknowledging additional network components such as routers, firewalls, and NAT devices, it's essential to emphasize the end-to-end components responsible for the website's Internet availability.

Question: Could you provide insights into virtualization by explaining the concept of live migration and its functioning?

Answer: Live migration refers to seamlessly relocating a virtual machine (VM) from one physical host to another while the VM continues to run without interruptions. This capability is achieved by meticulously replicating the entire VM state, encompassing its memory, network configuration, and metadata/configuration, among other factors, to the target host. The process involves constantly synchronizing changes in the VM's memory state between the source and destination hosts. Once synchronization reaches a point of sufficient proximity, typically within milliseconds, a brief pause is initiated in the VM's operations. During this momentary pause, the VM is transitioned to the destination host, ensuring minimal application disruption. This sophisticated technique, live migration, ensures the seamless continuity of virtualized workloads across physical hosts, enhancing resource optimization and maintaining service availability.

Edge

Question: What is a Content Delivery Network (CDN)?

Answer: A CDN, or Content Delivery Network, is a network of strategically placed servers known as Points of Presence (PoPs). CDNs work collaboratively to optimize web content delivery to users, like images, videos, and scripts, reducing latency and enhancing loading speed. Well-known CDNs include Akamai, CloudFront, Limelight, and Cloudflare. CDNs are instrumental in optimizing content delivery by caching static and dynamic content near end-users. This enhances user experience and offloads backend resources. For instance, content like images, videos, and static assets stored in S3 (like CSS and HTML files) can be cached on CDNs, resulting in smoother interactions.

Question: What is a Distributed Denial of Service attack or DDoS?

Answer: A Distributed Denial of Service (DDoS) attack involves overwhelming a targeted system with excessive traffic from multiple compromised systems, often within a botnet. This surge in traffic exhausts the system's resources, causing service disruption and rendering it inaccessible to legitimate users. Effectively countering DDoS attacks involves recognizing attack signs, incident response planning, and deploying various mitigation strategies. These include techniques like black-holing or sinkholing traffic, using intrusion detection systems (IDS), configuring routers and firewalls to block suspicious traffic, and ensuring proper server application configurations. Over-provisioning network resources to handle traffic spikes also plays a role in defense.

Question: What is a Web Application Firewall (WAF), and how does it function?

Answer: A Web Application Firewall (WAF) operates at layer 7 of the network stack, offering robust application protection. It examines incoming requests, filters them based on their content, and prevents malicious traffic from reaching applications. WAFs safeguard against threats like DDoS attacks, SQL/JS injection, and more by analyzing request parameters, source IP addresses, and traffic patterns. Automation enhances WAF efficiency by dynamically adjusting rules and responses in real-time. For example, during a brute force user authentication attack, automation promptly identifies and blocks requests displaying a specific pattern. It can also add suspicious IP addresses or client IDs to a blocklist and filter requests based on suspicious patterns. This adaptive approach ensures swift responses to emerging threats, enhancing overall security.

Storage

Question: Can you explain latency, IOPS, and throughput from a storage system perspective?

Answer: Certainly. In the context of storage systems, latency refers to the time a single input/output (IO) operation takes to complete. It's often measured in milliseconds or even microseconds. IOPS stands for Input/Output Operations Per Second, which quantifies the number of IO operations a storage system can handle in a single second. IOPS is influenced by the latency of operations and the system's ability to process multiple functions in parallel, involving both the storage system and the CPU. Conversely, throughput represents the amount of data that can be transferred to or from the storage system over a given period, typically measured in bytes per second. The throughput is affected by the IOPS of the system as well as the size of each IO operation, such as block size or packet size.

Question: What is object storage, and what are some key differences between it and file storage?

Answer: Object storage is a data storage approach centered around storing data as discrete units known as objects organized within containers called buckets. Unlike file storage, which breaks down files into data blocks, object storage keeps data and metadata together. Objects in object storage are accessed through API calls, often using HTTP GET and PUT methods to read from and write to buckets. Unlike traditional file systems, object storage isn't typically mounted on operating systems due to the lower performance caused by API-based file requests and the lack of intra-file-level locking. Object storage excels in scalability, offering a flat namespace that reduces management overhead and metadata management. This architecture makes it ideal for applications that require vast amounts of unstructured data, such as cloud-native applications, backups, archives, and content delivery.

Question: Can you name three types of storage, describe their technical differences, and provide examples of application use cases that suit each style?

Answer: Certainly. There are several types of storage systems, each with its characteristics and applications. Let's discuss three of them:

1. Block Storage: Block storage divides data into blocks, each with a unique address. It's commonly used in SAN (Storage Area Network) setups. Block storage devices can be solid-state drives (SSDs) or traditional magnetic disks. It's ideal for high-performance, low-latency access applications, like databases and virtual machines.

2. Object Storage: As discussed earlier, object storage organizes data into objects within buckets. It's a scalable solution for storing large amounts of unstructured data, such as media files, backups, and logs. Its flat namespace and API-based access benefit cloud-native applications and content distribution.
3. File Storage: In a hierarchical structure, file storage presents data as files and folders. It's often implemented through network-attached storage (NAS) systems. NAS suits applications with shared access requirements, such as user home directories and collaborative workloads like office documents.

These storage types cater to different use cases, each leveraging its unique attributes to optimize performance and efficiency for specific applications.

Security

Question: What is the difference between symmetric and asymmetric algorithms in cryptography?

Answer: Symmetric encryption algorithms use the same key for data encryption and decryption. This means the sender and receiver must share the same secret key to communicate securely. On the other hand, asymmetric algorithms use two distinct keys: a public key for encryption and a private key for decryption. The public key can be freely shared, allowing anyone to encrypt data, while only the private key holder can decrypt it. Asymmetric algorithms offer more robust security but are slower than symmetric algorithms.

Question: What is MFA, and why would you want to use it?

Answer: MFA stands for Multi-Factor Authentication. It's a security mechanism that requires users to provide multiple verification forms to access a system or application. MFA adds an extra layer of security beyond just a username and password. This is crucial because if a password is compromised, the attacker still needs an additional authentication factor to gain access. MFA typically involves "something you know" (like a password), "something you have" (like a security token or a mobile device), or "something you are" (like a biometric trait such as a fingerprint). Using MFA enhances security and reduces the risk of unauthorized access.

Question: For an IDS (Intrusion Detection System), describe a host- and network-based solution, along with their pros and cons.

Answer: Certainly. An IDS comes in two main types: host-based and network-based.

Host-Based IDS: A host-based IDS operates on individual hosts and monitors their activities to detect potential intrusions. It inspects logs, monitors file system changes, and tracks network connections to the host. This approach provides deep insight into the activity within each host. Pros include the ability to inspect host-specific activities, scalability by deploying agents on each host, and minimal impact on running applications. However, the cons include the management overhead of handling agents on many servers and challenges in responding to widespread attacks.

Network-Based IDS: A network-based IDS is placed within the network infrastructure and analyzes all traffic passing through it for signs of intrusion. It offers a comprehensive view of network activity. Pros include centralized management, a shared view of security, and the ability to detect anomalies across the network. However, the cons involve the performance hit caused by additional network hops, the need to decrypt and re-encrypt traffic for inspection, and the risk of becoming a target for attacks.

Database

Question: Can you explain how database indexing can impact database performance?

Answer: Database indexing involves creating a data structure that allows for efficient data retrieval by making a copy of selected columns of data and linking them to the full rows they represent. Indexes help speed up data retrieval operations by reducing the need to search through every row in a database. While indexes enhance query performance, they add additional writes and storage overhead to maintain the index data structure. Indexes enable quick data location without requiring full table scans. They can be created on one or more columns, significantly improving query performance.

Question: Can you explain a NoSQL database and outline key differences between relational and NoSQL databases?

Answer: A NoSQL database is a non-relational database that stores and retrieves data without a structured mechanism to establish relationships between data elements. Unlike relational databases, NoSQL databases do not rely on traditional concepts like joins, foreign keys, or normalization. NoSQL databases employ various data models such as document, graph, key-value, and columnar, offering scalability, high availability, and resilience. They typically do not enforce strict schemas and often adopt a schema-on-read approach. In NoSQL, data retrieval relies on a partition key to access values or documents with related attributes. Application requirements usually dictate the choice between NoSQL and relational databases based on performance, consistency, and scalability.

Question: What are some common transaction isolation levels? What do they do? Please explain some application scenarios for each.

Answer: Common transaction isolation levels include READ UNCOMMITTED, READ COMMITTED, REPEATABLE READ, and SERIALIZABLE. These isolation levels determine how uncommitted data can be modified while a query lock is in place. The choice of isolation level depends on an application's required level of ACID compliance and trade-offs between performance and consistency. For instance, READ UNCOMMITTED might suit scenarios requiring high performance but not strict consistency. SERIALIZABLE could be more appropriate in a financial application where accuracy is crucial.

Question: Can you explain database partitioning and why it can be helpful? Also, give an

example of how you might implement it.

Answer: Database partitioning involves splitting large tables into smaller ones to enhance maintenance, availability, and performance. By dividing tables into smaller segments, queries that access subsets of data can execute faster. Partitioning aids in managing large datasets and ensures quicker response times for data read and write operations. This technique limits the amount of data accessed and manipulated, distributing data for parallel processing. Partitioning can be employed for manageability, availability, or performance improvement. For example, partitioning a table by month can improve query performance for time-based data retrieval. Vertical partitioning, used in scenarios with wide columns, splits tables based on the characteristics of different columns. Vertical partitioning should be carefully designed to avoid excessive joins and unnecessary complexity.

Troubleshooting

Question: What steps would you take to troubleshoot a website error such as "Error establishing a connection to the database"?

Answer: To troubleshoot this error, I would ensure the database username and password are correct. Then, I would verify if the ports (e.g., 3306, 1433) are accessible from the web server to the database server. It is crucial to check whether the database and database server are both up and running. I would also review the user's permissions to ensure they have appropriate access rights.

Question: A three-tier web application you own performs much slower during the peak traffic hours of the day. How would you troubleshoot where the performance issue is, and what possibilities can you propose for where the problem might be?

Answer: To troubleshoot this performance issue, I would start by gathering and reviewing relevant metrics across the application stack. I would examine database query buffering, disk IOPS, and paging. On the front end, I check for client-side throttling. For the web server, I would analyze CPU and memory utilization. Additionally, I would investigate cache hits and misses. The possibilities for performance issues range from database bottlenecks to resource constraints on the web server or client-side issues that affect user experience.

Question: You've recently taken ownership of a legacy application that generates no application logs, making troubleshooting difficult. You're tasked with creating a new end-to-end logging strategy for faster investigations. What would be part of your strategy?

Answer: Creating an effective logging strategy involves several steps. Based on the operational context, I would define different log levels (debug, info, warn, error, fatal) to control the amount of captured logs. Capturing and logging error codes and messages is crucial for pinpointing issues. I ensure that log entries are structured for future indexing and searching. Unique attributes like UUIDs or correlation IDs would be included to identify and search for specific requests/events. Establishing a process for ingesting logs into a log archival/indexing system like Flume, Kafka, or

Kinesis is essential. I outline the lifecycle for retaining logs before archival or deletion. Lastly, selecting an operational system like Splunk, CloudWatch Logs, or ELK stack for log searching and alarming would complete the strategy.

Example architecture question from specialty domains

This section is designed to provide in-depth responses to queries specific to key specialty domains. As we move forward, you'll acquire more comprehensive knowledge to excel in specialized Solutions Architect interviews. However, if you are a generalist Solutions Architect, this section will be particularly useful for delving into questions and answers pertinent to your chosen domain of interest.

Each response includes various action points. You must selectively focus on a few relevant points that align with your expertise, ensuring your answers remain concise and impactful. For instance, if your strength is security, tailor your responses to big data questions by emphasizing data security, compliance, and data authorization and authentication. This focused approach will help you craft precise and relevant answers to your strengths.

Remember, the key is to be crisp and clear in your communication, concentrating on your areas of proficiency. Avoid the temptation to cover all possible action points. Instead, strategically choose one or two that best showcase your expertise and knowledge, providing clear, targeted answers to the interviewer's questions.

DevOps

Question: Describe an architecture for a new CI/CD pipeline to automate deploying changes to the application tier in production.
Answer: Let's examine the response in detail, focusing on the data points.

Situation: As a Solutions Architect, I was entrusted with designing a robust CI/CD pipeline to automate the deployment of application changes to the production application tier. The primary aim was to enhance the efficiency of software releases while maintaining high code quality and minimizing disruptions.

Task: My task involved architecting a comprehensive solution to ensure seamless deployment, efficient testing, and the ability to revert changes quickly.

Action:
1. Requirement Analysis and Planning:

- Assessment: I thoroughly assessed the existing software development lifecycle, identifying bottlenecks and understanding the application's architectural intricacies.
- Stakeholder Engagement: I collaborated with development teams, operations teams, and stakeholders to gather requirements that aligned the solution with business needs.
- Tool Evaluation: Based on the requirements, I evaluated and selected appropriate tools, such as Git for version control and Jenkins for continuous integration.

2. Source Code Management:
- Version Control: I hosted the application code in a Git repository to facilitate version tracking and collaborative development.
- Branching Strategy: To manage code changes effectively, I devised a branching strategy that includes feature branches, a development branch, and a main branch.

3. Build and Testing Automation:
- Automated Builds: I configured Jenkins to trigger automated builds upon code commits, ensuring consistent and reproducible builds.
- Unit and Integration Testing: Within the CI/CD pipeline, I incorporated unit and integration tests to maintain code quality and detect issues early.
- Static Analysis: By integrating code analysis tools like FindBugs and JSLint, I ensured compliance with coding standards and identified potential vulnerabilities.

4. Continuous Deployment and Release Strategies:
- Zero-Downtime Deployment: I implemented blue/green deployment to ensure seamless releases without impacting end-users.
- Canary Deployment: The pipeline incorporated canary releases, allowing controlled exposure of new changes to a subset of users for validation.
- Configuration Management: Utilizing tools like Ansible, I managed application configurations consistently across various environments.

5. Monitoring, Observability, and Alerting:
- Monitoring Tools: I integrated tools like Prometheus and Grafana to provide insights into application performance and resource utilization.
- Alerting System: To address issues proactively, I set up an alerting system that notified relevant teams when performance anomalies or failures occurred.

6. Rollback Mechanism and Continual Improvement:
- Rollback Strategy: I devised a rollback mechanism that enabled quick reversion to a previous version in case of deployment failures or unforeseen issues.
- Continuous Improvement: The pipeline was designed for continuous improvement, enabling the introduction of new features and optimizations over time.

Results: The newly designed CI/CD pipeline substantially reduced deployment time and notably enhanced deployment success rates. The deployment error rate decreased by 25%, and the average time-to-market improved by 40%, fostering increased agility and customer satisfaction.

Quantifiable Data:
- Deployment error rate reduced by 25%.
- Average deployment time decreased by 40%.
- Enhanced customer satisfaction due to faster time-to-market.

This example is fictional, and the provided quantifiable data is for illustrative purposes only. Actual outcomes will depend on the specific context and implementation within an organization.

You will learn more details about the DevOps interview in *"Chapter 5 - Cracking the DevOps Architect Interview".*

Big Data/Analytics

Question: Describe an architecture for a reporting tool providing daily, weekly, and monthly aggregate sales data to company executives and real-time query access to analysts.
Answer: Let's look at the response in detail, focusing on the data points.

Situation: As a Solutions Architect, I was tasked with designing an architecture for a reporting tool that would deliver daily, weekly, and monthly aggregate sales data to company executives. Additionally, the architecture needed to provide real-time query access to analysts, enabling them to explore data insights for informed decision-making.

Task: My goal was to create a scalable and efficient architecture that could handle large volumes of data and cater to both executives' reporting needs and analysts' dynamic queries.

Action:
1. Data Collection and Aggregation:
- Data Sources: I identified the relevant data sources, including transactional databases, sales systems, and external sources.
- ETL Process: I designed an Extract, Transform, Load (ETL) process to extract raw data, transform it into a structured format, and load it into a data warehouse.

2. Data Warehousing:
- Data Storage: I chose a robust data warehousing solution like Amazon Redshift or Google BigQuery to efficiently store and manage structured sales data.

- Schema Design: I designed the schema to optimize query performance and ensure that data was organized appropriately for reporting and analytics.

3. Batch Data Processing for Reporting:
- Data Aggregation: Using tools like Apache Spark or AWS Glue, I implemented batch processing to aggregate sales data daily, weekly, and monthly.
- Scheduled Jobs: Scheduled batch jobs were configured to run at specific intervals to aggregate the data and generate reports.

4. Real-time Query Access for Analysts:
- Data Virtualization: To provide real-time query access, I employed data virtualization tools like Apache Drill or Presto, which allow analysts to query data from various sources in real-time.
- Data Federation: I configured the virtualization layer to combine data from the data warehouse and other relevant sources for comprehensive analysis.

5. Reporting and Visualization:
- BI Tools: I integrated business intelligence tools like Tableau, Power BI, or Looker to create interactive dashboards and reports for executives.
- Scheduled Reports: Using these tools, I scheduled automated reports to be delivered to executives' emails daily, weekly, and monthly.

6. Security and Access Control:
- Role-based access: I implemented role-based access control to ensure executives could access predefined reports while analysts could execute ad-hoc queries.
- Data Masking: Sensitive data was masked to protect privacy and comply with data security regulations.

7. Scalability and Performance:
- Auto-scaling: I designed the architecture to be scalable by utilizing the auto-scaling capabilities of the chosen data warehousing and virtualization platforms.
- Indexing: I ensured appropriate indexing was in place on the data warehouse tables for efficient querying.

Results: The architecture I designed successfully addressed the requirements of both executives and analysts. Executives received timely reports, aiding strategic decision-making, while analysts gained real-time query access to explore data insights. The solution provided a seamless user experience, improved data-driven decision-making, and facilitated agility in responding to changing business needs.

Quantifiable Data:

- Executives received daily, weekly, and monthly reports promptly.
- Analysts experienced a 30% reduction in query response time due to real-time query access.
- Time-to-insights for data analysis improved by 40%, contributing to quicker decision-making.

You will learn more details about big data and Analytics interviews in *"Chapter 8 - Cracking the Big Data Solutions Architect Interview"*.

IoT (Internet of Things)

Question: Describe an architecture for an IoT application that adds sensors to brick-and-mortar stores to understand customer traffic patterns and enhance eCommerce recommendations.
Answer: Let's look at the response in detail, focusing on the data points.

Situation: As a Solutions Architect, I was tasked with designing an architecture for an IoT application that would enhance the retail experience by adding sensors to brick-and-mortar stores. The goal was to understand customer traffic patterns within the stores and leverage this data to provide personalized e-commerce recommendations.

Task: My objective was to create a scalable and efficient IoT architecture to collect, process, and analyze customer behavior data in real time while ensuring data security and privacy.

Action:
1. Sensor Deployment:
- Sensor Types: I selected appropriate sensors, such as motion detectors, Wi-Fi access points, or Bluetooth beacons, to track customer movement within the stores.
- Placement Strategy: I strategically placed sensors at entrance/exit points, aisles, and key locations to capture accurate foot traffic data.

2. Data Collection and Ingestion:
- Sensor Data Stream: I configured sensors to generate data streams of customer movements, which included entry/exit timestamps and device identifiers.
- IoT Gateway: I deployed IoT gateways at each store to securely aggregate and transmit sensor data to the cloud.

3. Real-time Data Processing:
- Event Processing: I utilized stream processing frameworks like Apache Kafka or AWS Kinesis to process real-time events from sensors.
- Data Enrichment: To improve accuracy, I enriched raw data with contextual information, such as store layout and historical data.

4. Data Storage and Analysis:
- Data Lake: I stored the enriched data in a data lake like Amazon S3 or Azure Data Lake Storage for efficient and cost-effective storage.
- Data Warehousing: I employed a data warehouse (e.g., Amazon Redshift) to facilitate querying and reporting for complex analysis.

5. Data Analytics and Insights:
- Pattern Recognition: I used machine learning algorithms to identify customer traffic patterns, hotspots, and peak hours.
- Recommendation Engine: Leveraging customer movement data, I implemented a recommendation engine to suggest personalized eCommerce products.

6. Integration with eCommerce Platform:
- API Integration: I established APIs between the IoT data analytics platform and the eCommerce backend to transmit personalized recommendations.
- Real-time Sync: Recommendations were updated in real-time, ensuring customers received up-to-date online shopping suggestions.

7. Data Security and Privacy:
- Data Encryption: All data in transit and at rest was encrypted to ensure security.
- Anonymization: Personally identifiable information (PII) was anonymized to protect customer privacy.

8. Scalability and Performance:
- Auto-scaling: The architecture was designed to auto-scale based on incoming data volume to handle fluctuations in customer traffic.
- Load Balancing: Load balancers distribute data processing tasks across multiple resources for optimal performance.

Results: The implemented IoT architecture successfully captured and analyzed customer traffic patterns in brick-and-mortar stores, leading to enhanced eCommerce recommendations. Customers experienced more personalized online shopping experiences, while retailers gained valuable insights into in-store customer behavior for informed decision-making.

Quantifiable Data:
- Online customers who received personalized recommendations showed a 20% increase in conversion rate.
- Real-time customer traffic insights reduced restocking times by 15%, optimizing inventory management.
- Customer satisfaction improved by 25%, driven by tailored shopping experiences and more accurate product recommendations.

AI/ML

Question: Describe an architecture for a recommendation engine that suggests products based on user behavior and sales data.

Answer: Let's look at the response in detail, focusing on the data points.

Situation: As a Solutions Architect, I was tasked with designing an architecture for a recommendation engine that leverages user behavior and sales data to provide personalized product recommendations on an eCommerce platform.

Task: My goal was to create a robust architecture to process large volumes of data, apply machine learning algorithms, and deliver users accurate and timely product recommendations.

Action:
1. Data Collection and Ingestion:
   - User Behavior Data: I collected data on user interactions such as clicks, searches, and purchases.
   - Sales Data: I obtained historical sales data, including product attributes and customer preferences.

2. Data Storage and Processing:
   - Data Warehousing: I stored structured user behavior and sales data in a data warehouse like Amazon Redshift or Google BigQuery.
   - Data Lake: Unstructured data, such as images and text descriptions, were stored in a data lake (e.g., Amazon S3) for later processing.

3. Data Preprocessing:
   - Data Cleansing: I cleaned and transformed the data to remove duplicates, handle missing values, and standardize formats.
   - Feature Engineering: I created meaningful features from raw data, such as user profiles, product attributes, and historical interactions.

4. Machine Learning Model Development:
   - Algorithm Selection: I chose appropriate algorithms like collaborative filtering, matrix factorization, or deep learning models for personalized recommendations.
   - Training Data: I split the dataset into training and validation sets to train the recommendation model.

5. Model Training and Evaluation:
   - Training Environment: I set up a scalable and distributed training environment using frameworks like TensorFlow or PyTorch.

- Hyperparameter Tuning: I tuned model parameters and performed cross-validation to optimize model performance.
- Evaluation Metrics: I used precision, recall, and F1-score metrics to assess the model's accuracy.

6. Real-time Recommendations:
- API Deployment: I deployed the trained model as an API endpoint using services like Amazon SageMaker or Azure ML.
- User Interaction: Their data triggers real-time recommendations whenever users interact with the platform.

7. Batch Recommendations:
- Scheduled Batch Processing: Periodically, batch recommendations were generated for users based on their historical interactions.
- Data Processing: I used tools like Apache Spark for large-scale batch processing of user behavior and sales data.

8. Integration with eCommerce Platform:
- API Integration: The recommendation engine API seamlessly integrates with the eCommerce platform's front and back end.
- Personalization: Recommendations were displayed on the user's dashboard and personalized based on their preferences.

9. Continuous Improvement:
- Feedback Loop: User feedback and interactions were collected to continuously refine and improve the recommendation model.
- Retraining: The model was periodically retrained using new data to adapt to evolving user preferences.

Results: The implemented recommendation engine architecture delivered personalized product recommendations, enhancing the user experience on the eCommerce platform. Users were more likely to discover and engage with relevant products, leading to increased conversion rates and improved customer satisfaction.

Quantifiable Data:
- Conversion rates increased by 30% for users who engaged with personalized recommendations.
- Average order value grew by 25% as users added more recommended products to their carts.
- Customer retention improved by 20% due to the enhanced shopping experience.

You will learn more about AI/ML interviews in *"Chapter 10 - Cracking the ML and Generative AI Solution Architect Interview".*

Mobile Apps

Question: Describe an architecture for a mobile application allowing users to post product photos and view/vote on others' photos.

Answer: Let's look at the response in detail, focusing on the data points.

Situation: As a Solutions Architect, I was tasked with designing an architecture for container orchestration to deploy the application tier as Docker containers on a server cluster.

Task: My objective was to create a scalable and resilient architecture that enables efficient management, deployment, scaling, and monitoring of Docker containers using a container orchestration platform.

Action:

1. Containerization and Image Creation:
   - Containerization: I containerized the application using Docker, encapsulating it and its dependencies in a portable container image.
   - Dockerfile: I created Dockerfiles to define the container images with all required configurations.

2. Container Orchestration Platform Selection:
   - Kubernetes: I chose Kubernetes as the container orchestration platform for its robust features, community support, and broad adoption.

3. Cluster Setup and Configuration:
   - Cluster Nodes: I set up a cluster with multiple worker nodes using virtual machines or cloud instances.
   - Kubelet and Kube-proxy: Kubernetes agents (Kubelet) and networking components (Kube-proxy) were installed on each node.

4. Container Deployment:
   - Pods: I organized containers into Pods, the smallest deployable units in Kubernetes.
   - Deployments: I defined Deployment resources to manage the desired number of replicas and rolling updates.

5. Load Balancing and Service Discovery:
   - Service Resources: I created Service resources to provide load balancing and automatic service discovery for Pods.

- Ingress Controllers: Ingress controllers like Nginx or HAProxy were configured to route external traffic to Services.

6. Scaling and Resilience:
- Horizontal Pod Autoscaling: I implemented horizontal pod autoscaling to dynamically scale the number of pods based on resource utilization.
- Node Failure Handling: Kubernetes managed node failures by rescheduling pods for healthy nodes.

7. Continuous Deployment and Updates:
- Continuous Integration: I integrated the CI/CD pipeline to build and push new container images to a container registry.
- Rolling Updates: Kubernetes performed rolling updates, gradually replacing old Pods with new versions to minimize service disruption.

8. Monitoring and Logging:
- Monitoring Tools: I integrated tools like Prometheus and Grafana to monitor cluster health and resource utilization.
- Logging Stack: I set up a logging stack (ELK or EFK) to collect and analyze container logs.

9. Security and Networking:
- Network Policies: I implemented Network Policies to control communication between Pods and enforce security rules.
- Secrets Management: Sensitive information like credentials were stored in Kubernetes Secrets and mounted into Pods securely.

10. High Availability and Fault Tolerance:
- Primary Node Replication: I ensured the high availability of Kubernetes control plane components using primary node replication.
- Pod Distribution: I used resource requests/limits and node affinity rules to distribute Pods across nodes.

Results: The implemented container orchestration architecture using Kubernetes ensured efficient deployment, scaling, and management of Docker containers. The application became more resilient, with automatic scaling and healing mechanisms, and the CI/CD process was streamlined, leading to faster and safer deployments.

Quantifiable Data:
- Deployment time was reduced by 40% due to automated scaling and rolling updates.
- Downtime during updates decreased by 50% as Kubernetes ensured seamless transitions.
- Resource utilization improved by 30% with the help of dynamic scaling based on load.

You will learn more about application architecture interviews in Chapter 4, "Cracking the Application Architect Interview."

The provided quantifiable data is for illustrative purposes only and may vary based on an organization's specific implementation and context.

The interview process typically involves technical rounds alongside other segments, including behavioral discussions that you will delve into in the subsequent chapter. This comprehensive approach assesses your suitability and readiness for the targeted role. Interviewers gauge your ability to excel in the job, including navigating potential learning curves and estimating the time required for skill mastery. While encountering learning curves is normal, candidates should endeavor to keep them to a minimum. This can be achieved through thorough research, meticulous preparation, and diligent practice. Your past experiences significantly influence your interview outcomes. This involves identifying and presenting key projects that align well with the job role.

Summary

In this chapter, we have extensively delved into the world of technical interviews for aspiring Solutions Architects. We began by dissecting the foundational technical skills crucial for a Solutions Architect. These skills are the bedrock upon which your expertise will be built, allowing you to proficiently tackle complex challenges in your role. Our exploration further extended to the key principles and methodologies that underpin effective solution design, an essential aspect of any Solutions Architect's skill set.

As a Solutions Architect, navigating the realm of cloud computing is predominant. We undertook a comprehensive journey through the cloud landscape, uncovering cloud computing's foundational concepts and its multifaceted benefits. Equipped with a thorough understanding, you can craft resilient cloud ecosystems that drive organizational success. Additionally, we addressed the challenges and expertise required for effective cloud architecture, empowering you to navigate these intricacies confidently.

The exploration extended to emerging technologies, emphasizing their strategic value for Solutions Architects. By harnessing these cutting-edge innovations, you can position yourself as a forward-thinking architect with a distinct edge in solution design.

A pivotal aspect of the technical interview process is architecture whiteboarding. We provided a practical example of whiteboarding a Data Lake architecture, offering you insights into effectively conveying your design prowess visually. Furthermore, we delved into presentation best practices tailored to Solutions Architects. Your ability to articulate complex technical concepts concisely and compellingly is a hallmark of a proficient architect.

The heart of the chapter revolved around addressing technical interview questions. We dissected questions across various domains, including application development, networking, infrastructure, edge computing, storage, security, database, and troubleshooting.

Lastly, we offered a glimpse into example architecture questions from specialized domains. These questions preview what to expect, enabling you to strategize your responses effectively.

In conclusion, this chapter has equipped you with the knowledge, strategies, and insights necessary to excel in technical interviews as a Solutions Architect. Your journey to becoming a skilled and proficient architect is marked by diligent research, rigorous preparation, and effective practice, culminating in your ability to confidently showcase your expertise in solution design, cloud architecture, and beyond.

Chapter 3 - Cracking Behavioral Interview and Soft Skills

In the previous chapters, you have comprehensively understood the technical skills required to excel as a solutions architect (SA). However, being a successful SA is about more than just technical proficiency; it's also crucial to possess the necessary soft skills that will allow you to communicate and collaborate effectively with different stakeholders. As an SA, you will work with business teams, engineers, and senior executives, making it imperative to develop your soft skills.

The ability to communicate effectively, think critically, and adapt to new situations are just some of the critical soft skills that an SA must possess. In this book, we will delve into how to develop and showcase these vital soft skills to ensure that you are well-prepared for the behavioral interview. You will also learn to navigate difficult situations with stakeholders, manage expectations, and be a competent problem solver. This chapter will equip you with the knowledge and tools to stand out as a well-rounded and highly desirable SA candidate.

Behavioral interviews are a crucial part of the hiring process for solutions architects. Organizations use behavioral questions to dive deep into candidates' experiences and understand how they have handled various real-life situations. Companies like Amazon and Facebook even base entire interview rounds on behavioral questions. In this chapter, you will learn how to prepare for a behavioral interview and the key strategies for answering behavioral questions effectively.

You will learn how to identify common behavioral questions that may be asked during a solutions architect interview and what interviewers look for in your answers. You will also learn how to structure your responses to behavioral questions and the best ways to convey your experience and achievements. In this chapter, you will learn about preparing yourself for a behavioral interview and the soft skills a solution architect should have by covering the following topics:

- Soft Skills for Solutions Architects
- What is a behavioral interview, and what are the best practices to answer them
- Common behavioral interview questions and their answers
- Best practices for behavioral interview preparation
- Questions to ask during the interview
- Negotiation job offer

By the end of this chapter, you will know about the soft skills required for a solution architect to succeed. You will learn techniques to succeed in behavioral interviews with common questions and tips to answer them.

Soft Skills for Solutions Architects

Soft skills play an integral role in the success and effectiveness of a Solutions Architect. These skills, often intangible and non-technical, enable an architect to communicate, lead, and innovate effectively in a field that is as much about understanding people and business needs as technology. A Solutions Architect must be able to articulate complex technical ideas in a clear, concise manner accessible to both technical and non-technical stakeholders. This skill extends beyond verbal communication; it encompasses writing clear documentation, creating understandable architectural diagrams, and presenting ideas persuasively.

Leadership and teamwork are also vital in the role of a Solutions Architect. Often tasked with leading project teams or collaborating with various departments, a Solutions Architect must demonstrate strong leadership abilities, including inspiring, motivating, and guiding team members toward achieving common goals.

A Solutions Architect's soft skill set is incomplete without strategic thinking, emotional intelligence, and a commitment to continuous learning. Strategic thinking allows architects to see beyond the immediate technical challenges, considering the broader impact of their decisions on the organization's long-term goals. Emotional intelligence, self-awareness, empathy, and relationship management are crucial for building strong, productive working relationships. While technical expertise is undoubtedly necessary, these soft skills differentiate exceptional Solutions Architects, enabling them to lead, innovate, and drive success in their projects and organizations. Let's explore key soft skills an SA should have in detail.

Leading through ambiguity

Leading through ambiguity is a crucial skill for Solutions Architects, which involves navigating uncertain situations confidently and clearly. Solutions Architects often encounter scenarios where the path forward is unclear due to rapidly changing technology trends, shifting organizational priorities, or incomplete information.

The first step in leading through ambiguity is embracing it as an inherent part of the role. This means accepting that not all answers are immediately available and being comfortable with uncertain decisions. A Solutions Architect must be able to analyze available information, weigh potential risks and benefits, and make informed decisions. This process often involves balancing technical considerations with business objectives, requiring a deep understanding of both areas.

Another critical aspect of leading through ambiguity is fostering a culture of adaptability and resilience within the team. This involves encouraging team members to be flexible, to think creatively, and to be open to change. It's about creating an environment where it's safe to experiment, take calculated risks, and learn from failures. This culture of adaptability not only helps the team navigate uncertain situations but also fosters innovation and creativity.

Leading through ambiguity is a complex but essential skill for Solutions Architects. It involves embracing uncertainty, making informed decisions, communicating, fostering adaptability, and committing to continuous learning. By mastering this skill, a Solutions Architect can effectively guide their team and organization through technology solutions' complex and often uncertain landscape.

When interviewing for a solutions architect role, you're expected to be asked for examples of how you've handled ambiguous situations, whether they were at a business or technical level. These types of questions are designed to test your ability to think on your feet and to come up with creative solutions to complex problems. In this chapter, we'll explore some of the most common types of ambiguous situations you may encounter as a solutions architect and provide you with strategies and techniques for handling them effectively.

Mastering Communication

Strong communication skills are key to being a successful Solutions Architect. As a solutions architect, your ability to communicate complex technical ideas effectively, clearly, and concisely is crucial. You will create and present documents and presentations to a diverse audience, including senior leaders, industry experts, and analysts.

You will need to be able to drive discussions with senior leaders and VPs, both within your organization and with external companies. Your networking skills will be vital in building a community and fostering alignment across different departments and organizations. You may even be trusted to represent your company at large conferences and events with industry leaders, press, and analysts.

Effective communication skills are crucial for a solutions architect to showcase during an interview. One key aspect of communication is to be concise and deliver the right amount of information based on your audience, especially when speaking with senior leaders. As someone with a technical background, I find it easy to get caught up in the details of the technology. However, it's important to remember that business stakeholders are primarily interested in the outcome.

For instance, if you speak with a finance company's head of loan processing, they're more interested in hearing about how much can be saved per loan application rather than the technology used. When presenting to executives, it's essential to consider what message you want to convey and what outcome you want to achieve, especially if you have a limited amount of time.

To effectively communicate as a solutions architect, it's important to understand your audience and deliver the right message to achieve the desired outcome. Whether you're presenting to senior leaders or business stakeholders, it's crucial to be concise and focus on the outcomes rather than the technical details. Doing so lets you showcase your communication skills and demonstrate your value as a solutions architect.

Executing strategic projects

Executing strategic projects is a key aspect of driving meaningful change within an organization. As a solutions architect, you often begin by identifying opportunities for improvement, such as streamlining a process or enhancing customer experience through business applications. Such initiatives require your technical acumen and a strategic approach to resource allocation and collaboration across various departments.

Consider a scenario where you're tasked with reducing the loan processing time at a financial institution. Your first step involves thoroughly analyzing the existing system and pinpointing inefficiencies or bottlenecks. Collaborating closely with the loan processing department is crucial to better understand their workflow, challenges, and specific needs. This collaboration also extends to technology teams, where your role involves designing a tailored solution that aligns with the department's requirements while leveraging the latest technological advancements.

Your leadership skills are evident throughout the project lifecycle. Leading from the front and fostering a collaborative work environment ensures a cohesive effort towards the common goal. The project's success, marked by a significant reduction in loan processing times, is a testament to your strategic planning, collaborative approach, and effective project execution skills. When unexpected issues arise, your ability to manage escalations and guide the team toward resolution is crucial. Your strategic thinking and problem-solving skills help navigate these challenges, ensuring the project stays on track.

In an interview scenario, an example like the above use case can serve as a case study to demonstrate your capabilities. It highlights your ability to strategically allocate resources, work effectively with diverse teams, and lead complex projects to successful completion. This showcases your technical expertise and underscores your leadership, strategic thinking, and collaborative skills, positioning you as a well-rounded and capable Solutions Architect.

Driving Organizational Efficiency

As a Solutions Architect, a pivotal part of your role involves driving organizational efficiency. This responsibility goes beyond the technology and delves deep into understanding and improving the business processes and workflows. Your goal is not only to ensure that these processes are technologically sound but also that they are optimized to meet the organization's objectives efficiently.

Your approach involves a comprehensive analysis of the existing business processes to pinpoint areas where efficiency can be enhanced. This could be through identifying and eliminating bottlenecks that slow down operations, automating repetitive manual tasks to free up valuable human resources for more strategic tasks, or redesigning workflows for greater simplicity and effectiveness. The key here is not just to apply technical knowledge but to use it to align with and advance the business goals.

When discussing your experience in an interview, it's important to highlight specific instances where you've successfully driven process improvements. Discussing a project like optimizing a loan processing system can be an excellent example. In this case, you would explain how you identified the inefficiencies in the existing process, the steps you took to address these issues – such as automating specific steps or reengineering the workflow – and the impact of these changes. This could include metrics like reduced processing times, cost savings, or increased customer satisfaction.

Such examples demonstrate your technical expertise and showcase your strategic thinking, problem-solving skills, and ability to work collaboratively with various stakeholders. They paint a picture of a Solutions Architect who is not just a technology expert but also a strategic partner capable of driving real, tangible improvements in organizational efficiency.

Becoming a trusted advisor

Developing trust as a Solutions Architect is crucial in establishing effective and productive relationships with clients, stakeholders, and team members. To achieve this, it's essential to consistently demonstrate your expertise and stay up-to-date with the latest technologies and trends in your field, as this earns respect and establishes your credibility. In an interview setting, it's essential to highlight this aspect of your role, demonstrating your ability to provide technical guidance and build consensus, drive strategic discussions, and lead customers toward successful outcomes.

Effective communication is key; being clear, concise, and transparent, mainly when translating complex technical concepts to non-technical stakeholders, builds understanding and confidence in your abilities. Equally important is active listening, showing genuine interest in others' concerns and ideas, which is fundamental in understanding their needs and providing relevant solutions. Reliability in delivering on promises and meeting deadlines reinforces your dependability while showing integrity through honesty and ethical standards, including admitting uncertainties or mistakes, which enhances trust.

Building personal connections through getting to know your clients and team members better can foster trust and make working relationships more effective. Always aim to provide value in your solutions, prioritizing the needs and success of the project or customer. Regularly seek and act on feedback, showing your commitment to growth and improvement.

Consistency in your actions, decisions, and communication lets others know what to expect from you, building trust over time. Lastly, showing empathy and understanding towards the challenges your clients and team members face creates a supportive environment. Trust is built gradually through consistent, positive interactions, and by incorporating these practices into your daily role as a Solutions Architect, you'll develop strong, trust-based relationships that enhance your effectiveness and success.

In your interview, share specific examples where your guidance led to successful program developments, platform adoptions, or solution integrations. These instances underscore your technical proficiency and demonstrate your strategic thinking and commitment to delivering long-term value. Emphasize your involvement in the lifecycle of various projects or programs. Show how you've been instrumental in driving progress from initial concept to implementation. This could include how you've navigated challenges, achieved key milestones, and fostered integration.

By showcasing these aspects, you can effectively convey your value as a Solutions Architect who acts as a trusted advisor, guiding customers and teams toward successful, sustainable solutions.

Demonstrating professionalism and leadership

As a Solutions Architect, you are responsible for delivering solutions with complete independence, using your high judgment to determine where to focus your efforts for the most impact. Your role involves owning the design and delivery of customer solutions, including the overall strategy and end-to-end architecture.

During an interview, you must showcase your ability to lead across organizations, such as sales, business development, professional services, support, and engineering, to deliver the right technical solutions that delight customers. You should also demonstrate how you build consensus to ensure successful project delivery. Your solutions exemplify the design principles of security, reliability, cost optimization, operational excellence, and performance efficiency. This means that your delivered solutions become reference designs or reusable artifacts for other Solutions Architects to leverage for their customers.

One way to stand out in an interview is to share how you have proactively sought opportunities to scale the solution to benefit other customers with similar problems or requirements. You should also discuss how your organization regularly seeks your advice to replicate your successes and how you proactively develop and lead programs to share and teach lessons learned and best practices across teams.

Becoming a Thought Leader

As a Solutions Architect, you are a problem-solver and a thought leader in your field. In this role, you leverage your experience and expertise to educate and share best practices with customers while creating mechanisms that teach others how to do the same.

In an interview, you may be asked about your thought leadership skills, including how you develop and deliver technical content and curate thought leadership materials relevant to customer needs. You should also be prepared to share examples of your impact, such as creating new patterns and methodologies and being sought out as a speaker at top industry events. Your thought leadership contributions provide strategic and prescriptive guidance that focuses on subjects most critical to customers. You must stay up-to-date with the latest technologies, trends, and industry developments to speak on these topics with authority.

By leading the creation of new patterns and methodologies, you help your organization stay ahead of the curve and deliver innovative solutions that delight customers. Your thought leadership efforts can also benefit your fellow Solutions Architects by providing reference materials and best practices they can leverage in their work.

Becoming a thought leader in your field is integral to your role as a Solutions Architect. It requires a commitment to continuous learning and a willingness to share your expertise with others. By doing so, you can have a significant impact on your organization and the broader industry. Moreover, they may ask about your contribution to strategic planning and involvement in the Solutions Architect community.

Mastering pre-sales skill

In the pre-sales phase, solution architects are crucial in securing new business for their organization. To excel in this role, solution architects require a unique skill set that combines technical expertise with soft skills such as communication, negotiation, problem-solving, and customer-facing skills. These skills are essential for engaging with customers, understanding their business requirements, and providing a solution that meets their needs while aligning with the vendor's product portfolio.

During an interview for a solution architect role, the interviewer will likely ask questions about the candidate's experience and skills related to the pre-sales phase. The interviewer may ask for specific examples of how the candidate has worked with customers and internal teams to deliver successful pre-sales outcomes. They may also ask about the candidate's communication and negotiation skills, how they handle difficult conversations, and their ability to develop relationships with stakeholders at all levels.

Mastering pre-sales skills as a Solutions Architect, particularly during the critical stages of responding to Requests for Proposals (RFPs), Requests for Information (RFIs), and Requests for Quotations (RFQs), is essential in securing new business. These stages require a unique blend of technical expertise and soft skills. A deep understanding of customer requirements is the first step in responding to these requests. This understanding is crucial for crafting a response that addresses their needs while highlighting the strengths of your organization's solutions.

During a Solutions Architect interview, expect discussions on your experience with RFPs, RFIs, and RFQs. You should be ready to share specific instances where you successfully led or contributed to the response process. In an interview, demonstrating your involvement in RFP, RFI, and RFQ processes and how you balance technical expertise with soft skills can significantly enhance your candidacy. It shows your capability to handle technical aspects, understand the broader business context, and commit to customer success.

> *To learn more about the soft skills required for Solutions Architects, you can check out Solutions Architect's Handbook: Kick-start, your career as a solutions architect by learning architecture design principles and strategies, 3rd Edition - https://www.amazon.com/gp/product/1835084230.*

As you learned in this section, a successful Solutions Architect is technically skilled and possesses strong communication, leadership, and strategic thinking abilities. They must understand and advocate for the customer's needs while collaborating effectively with cross-functional teams to deliver secure, reliable, cost-effective, and performance-efficient solutions. A Solutions Architect who takes ownership of their work continuously improves their skills and knowledge and shares their expertise with others through thought leadership and community building will make a significant impact on their organization and customers.

When interviewing for a Solutions Architect, the interviewer may ask questions that assess SA's ability to gather customer feedback, simplify complex requirements, collaborate with product and engineering teams, advocate for customers, contribute to strategic planning, and participate in the Solutions Architect community. Now, let's explore behavioral interviews and how to apply soft skills to create them.

What is a behavioral interview?

A behavioral interview assesses your soft skills and behavioral competencies, such as problem-solving, teamwork, and communication. This means that the questions asked in a behavioral interview will likely be more open-ended and designed to elicit specific examples, which makes it trickier. For a Solutions Architect role, a behavioral interview may be used to assess the candidate's ability to handle different scenarios that they may face in their job.

In the previous chapter, you learned about technical interviews for Solutions Architect. A behavioral interview is different from a technical interview in several ways. While technical interviews assess your technical skills and knowledge, behavioral interviews focus on your past behavior and experiences in specific situations. In a technical interview, you might be asked to solve design problems or answer technical questions about your expertise. In a behavioral interview, you'll be asked to provide examples of how you handled specific situations in the past, such as a conflict with a team member or a challenging project deadline.

Another difference between the two interview types is the required level of preparation. Technical interviews require a solid technical knowledge of the subject matter, so candidates often must study and prepare in advance. On the other hand, behavioral interviews rely on your past experiences and behavior, so preparation involves reflecting on your previous work experiences and identifying specific examples that demonstrate your skills and abilities.

You should not get confused between behavioral interview and situational interview questions. Situational interview questions test a candidate's ability to think critically and creatively. These questions typically present a hypothetical scenario or problem, and the candidate is asked to provide a solution or strategy. The interviewer evaluates the candidate's response based on their thought process, ability to analyze and prioritize information, and ability to present a well-reasoned solution.

Behavioral questions are often used to evaluate a candidate's fit for a specific role or team, while hypothetical questions are more commonly used to assess a candidate's problem-solving and critical-thinking skills.

Behavioral interviews can be difficult because candidates must provide specific examples of their past experiences, behavior, and actions in various situations. This can be challenging for candidates who may not have prepared for these questions or who struggle to recall specific details from their past experiences. So, let's learn some tips to crack the behavioral interview.

Best practices to prepare for behavioral interview

Acing the technical round of an interview isn't always enough. Yes, you've proven your expertise, but things can go south fast if you can't link your experience to the company's specific needs during the behavioral interview. Top tech companies like Amazon, Google, and Facebook have always emphasized behavioral interviews. Technologies evolve and can be learned, but experience is hard-earned. Being a Solutions Architect involves working on diverse projects and adapting to dynamic environments over the years. This experience isn't just about skills; it's about attitude and fitting with the company culture - things that can be assessed through behavioral interviews.

Despite their importance, behavioral interviews are often overshadowed by technical ones. But what happens when you're hit with a surprise question about a past experience? You might find yourself lost in thought, trying to recall the details. This break can disrupt your flow and spike your nerves. And if you're hurriedly piecing together a response, there's a high chance you'll miss important details and need help to structure your answer, increasing the risk of not getting the job.

So how do you avoid this? The answer is simple: prepare! Create a personalized interview guide in advance. This way, you're ready to take on those behavioral questions, providing well-structured answers drawn from your own experience. A little preparation can make a big difference. Preparing a personalized interview guide can significantly improve your confidence and interview performance. Here are tips to help you prepare a customized interview guide for a Solutions Architect role:

- **Decode the Job Description:** Look closely at the job posting. As a Solutions Architect, you need to understand the technical requirements, the scale of projects you'd be handling, and the types of systems the company uses. This knowledge will be the foundation of your preparation.
- **Reflect on Relevant Experiences:** Consider the projects you've worked on that relate to the role. Focus on instances where you've designed and implemented solutions, dealt with cross-functional teams, managed stakeholders, and resolved complex technical issues.
- **Master the STAR + Scale Method:** Frame each experience using the STAR method – Situation, Task, Action, Result. This allows you to concisely detail how you've handled various scenarios in the past. You should also be able to explain how you scale your solutions across the organization and make them repeatable.
- **Learn the SBI Method:** For each example, identify the Situation, the Behavior you exhibited, and the Impact it had. Your focus should be on demonstrating how your behavior positively influenced the situation and created an impact.
- **Predict Likely Questions:** Prepare answers for typical Solutions Architect interview questions. These could be about your approach to designing systems, handling conflicting requirements, or staying updated with the latest technological advancements.
- **Research the Company's Tech Stack:** Learn about the company's technology stack. Tailoring your responses to align with their existing systems and mentioning how your experience would fit into their tech ecosystem can be impressive.
- **Prepare Your Questions:** Develop thoughtful questions to ask the interviewer. This might include queries about their development process, approach to solution design, or the projects you'd initially work on.
- **Practice Makes Perfect:** Rehearse your responses out loud. This helps solidify your answers and makes them more natural during the interview. However, memorization should be avoided to prevent sounding robotic.

Approach the interview with a positive and confident mindset. Remember, this is an opportunity to learn about the company while they learn about you. Creating a personalized guide tailored to a Solutions Architect role will allow you to handle behavioral questions that come your way confidently. Now, let's get into the details of answering behavioral questions to help you build your tailored interview guide.

Preparing for behavioral interview questions

Your personalized interview guide is like a living document, evolving with your experiences and changing slightly with each new job opportunity. Its core, however, is built on the bedrock of your past experiences, skills, and lessons learned. This core guides your preparation for behavioral interview questions, showcasing your unique journey as a Solutions Architect.

The interview guide's introduction, though, needs to be tailored for each specific role you apply for. This is where you align your experiences and skills with the needs and requirements detailed in the job description. It's your first impression, opening statement, and a chance to demonstrate, right off the bat, why you're a perfect fit for the role.

By customizing the introduction and grounding the rest of the guide in your experiences, you ensure that your responses during the behavioral interview are both authentic to you and relevant to the role. This approach can help you stand out, leaving a lasting impression on the interviewers. So, invest the time to create and maintain your interview guide, and it can prove to be an invaluable asset in your career journey as a Solutions Architect.

Reflecting on your past experiences and selecting several solid examples is an excellent strategy for preparing for a behavioral interview. For a Solutions Architect role, you might consider examples that demonstrate the following behaviors:

1. **Problem-solving and Decision-making:** These are critical skills for a Solutions Architect. Recall a time when you faced a complex technical challenge and outline the steps you took to address it.
2. **Leadership and Influence:** Leadership is critical even if the role doesn't involve direct management. You've led a project, influenced its direction, or navigated a team through a significant change.
3. **Collaboration and Teamwork:** Consider a situation where you had to work closely with others, perhaps individuals from different departments or backgrounds, to achieve a common goal.
4. **Adaptability and Learning Agility:** The technology field is constantly evolving, and so must a Solutions Architect. Share an example of when you had to quickly learn a new technology or adapt to a change in the tech landscape.
5. **Communication and Presentation:** Solutions Architects often have to present complex information quickly. Reflect on when you successfully communicated a complex idea to non-technical stakeholders.

6. **Conflict Resolution:** Discuss a situation where you had to mediate a dispute, perhaps between team members or departments, or resolve a disagreement with a client.
7. **Client/Stakeholder Management:** A Solutions Architect often deals with multiple stakeholders. Share an instance where you effectively managed stakeholders' expectations, handled their feedback, or navigated conflicting requirements.
8. **Solving Complex Customer Problems:** Think about a time when you were faced with a challenging problem presented by a customer. How did you approach the problem? How did you use your technical skills and creativity to develop a solution that satisfied the customer?
9. **Developing Repeatable Solutions:** Reflect on instances where you've solved a problem and created a solution that could be applied to similar issues. This shows foresight and a strategic mindset, as you're thinking beyond the immediate problem and considering future implications.
10. **Mentoring the Team:** Recall when you mentored or coached team members to improve their skills, better understand complex systems, or progress their careers. This might involve helping a junior colleague enhance their technical abilities or guiding your team through a challenging project. This shows your commitment to team growth and ability to share knowledge effectively.

Having examples for each behavior will provide a robust foundation for your behavioral interview preparation. Remember, your examples should demonstrate a specific behavior, resulting in a positive outcome or lesson learned.

Answering Behavioral interview questions

When answering the question, you may prefer to use the SBI (Situation → Behavior → Impact) or STAR (Situation → Task → Action → Result) method to keep your answer crisp. Using the Situation-Behavior-Impact (SBI) method, your response will effectively describe the challenging situation, outline the behaviors and actions taken to address it, and highlight the positive impact of your decision. You can also use the STAR method, whichever suits your style. Take the following approach to answer:

1. **Recall a Relevant Experience**: Reflect on your past projects where you had to make decisions with incomplete data. Choose an example that had a significant impact or where you used innovative thinking.
2. **Use the STAR Method**
    - **Situation**: Briefly describe the context of the project or decision. What was the project about, and why was the data incomplete?
    - **Task**: Clarify what your responsibility or goal was in that situation. What were you trying to achieve or solve?

- o **Action**: Discuss the steps you took to address the challenge. How did you analyze the available information, fill in the gaps, or mitigate the risks of incomplete data? Highlight your analytical thinking, resourcefulness, and any creative or unconventional methods you used.
- o **Result**: Share the outcome of your actions. Focus on the positive impact, like successful implementation, meeting project goals, or how your decision benefited the project or organization. If there were learnings or improvements, mention those as well.

Or use the SBI method
- o **Situation**: Start by setting the context for your story. Describe the project or decision-making scenario you were involved in. Explain what the project was about and why the data was incomplete, providing enough detail to give a clear picture of your challenge.
- o **Behavior**: Here, delve into your specific actions. Outline the steps you took to tackle the challenge presented by the incomplete data. Discuss how you analyzed the available information, identified and filled in the gaps, or mitigated the risks. Emphasize your analytical thinking, resourcefulness, and any creative or unconventional methods you employ.
- o **Impact**: Conclude by sharing the results of your actions. Focus on the positive impact your decisions and actions had, such as the successful implementation of a project, the achievement of project goals, or the overall benefits to the project or organization. Also, include any learnings or improvements that resulted from this experience.

3. **Emphasize Soft Skills**: Throughout your response, highlight relevant soft skills such as problem-solving, adaptability, critical thinking, and communication. For instance, mention how you communicated your decisions to stakeholders or led your team through uncertainty.
4. **Be Honest and Reflective**: If there were any challenges or setbacks, briefly mention them and focus on what you learned from the experience. This shows self-awareness and a growth mindset.
5. **Prepare for Follow-Up Questions**: Be ready for potential follow-up questions.

Let's pick and answer one question using the SBI method, as you have already learned the STAR method earlier.

Question: Tell me about a time when you had to make a complex architectural decision without clear benchmarks or precedents.
Answer: Using the Situation-Behavior-Impact (SBI) method:
Situation: As a Solutions Architect, I encountered a complex architectural decision when designing a healthcare organization's patient data management system. The challenge was that it needed clear benchmarks or precedents for integrating electronic health records with artificial

intelligence.

Behavior: To address this challenge, I conducted thorough research on data privacy regulations, industry standards, and emerging technologies in healthcare. I collaborated closely with the organization's data privacy and security teams to ensure compliance and address concerns. I evaluated various alternatives, including building the solution in-house or leveraging existing third-party platforms. After careful consideration, I proposed a hybrid approach combining an on-premises data storage infrastructure and a cloud-based AI platform for processing and analysis. I also assessed the potential risks associated with this approach and implemented robust security measures to mitigate them.

Impact: The decision to adopt this hybrid approach significantly impacted the organization. The patient data management system successfully integrated electronic health records with AI, improving diagnosis accuracy and treatment recommendations. The system provided healthcare professionals with faster and more accurate insights, leading to better patient outcomes. For example, during a pilot implementation, the system identified previously undetected patterns in patient data, enabling early diagnosis of rare diseases and the development of more effective treatment plans. This use case gained industry recognition and served as a benchmark for other healthcare organizations. The quantified impact includes a 20% increase in diagnosis accuracy, a 30% reduction in processing time, and improved patient outcomes.

Follow-up Question
Question: How did you weigh your alternatives and manage potential risks?
Answer: In weighing my alternatives, I comprehensively analyzed the available options. I considered scalability, cost, implementation time, technical feasibility, and alignment with the organization's long-term goals. I collaborated closely with cross-functional teams to manage potential risks, including data privacy, security, and legal experts. We conducted thorough risk assessments and developed mitigation strategies for each identified risk. Additionally, I sought input and feedback from stakeholders to ensure a well-informed decision-making process.

Question: What factors did you consider to evaluate the potential outcomes and risks of the decision?
Answer: I considered several key factors when evaluating potential outcomes and risks. These included data privacy and security implications, regulatory compliance requirements, interoperability with existing systems, scalability to accommodate future growth, and the impact on end-users and stakeholders. I also assessed the technological maturity and stability of the selected third-party platforms and the level of support and customization options they offered. Considering these factors, I aimed to make an informed decision that balanced the potential benefits with the associated risks.

Question: Can you provide specific examples of the considerations or analyses you conducted

to arrive at your architectural decision?

Answer: During the decision-making process, I conducted a detailed analysis of the available third-party platforms, assessing their capabilities, performance, reliability, and scalability. I reviewed case studies, conducted demos, and discussed with vendor representatives to gather in-depth information. Additionally, I evaluated the existing infrastructure and performed a gap analysis to identify any technical challenges or compatibility issues. I collaborated with the data privacy and security teams to ensure the selected solution adhered to industry regulations.

Question: Looking back, is there anything you would have done differently in approaching or making this complex architectural decision?

Answer: In retrospect, one area where I could have improved is conducting additional pilot testing to validate the performance and scalability of the selected hybrid approach. While we thoroughly evaluated the technology and performed extensive simulations, implementing a smaller-scale pilot program could have provided more concrete evidence of its effectiveness before full deployment. This would have allowed any necessary adjustments or optimizations to be made earlier. However, overall, I am satisfied with the decision and its positive impact on the organization and its stakeholders.

Using the Situation-Behavior-Impact (SBI) method and incorporating follow-up questions adds depth and structure to the responses. The SBI framework allows for a clear and concise presentation of the situation, the specific behaviors or actions taken, and the resulting impact or outcomes. It helps provide a comprehensive understanding of how the candidate approached and handled the given scenario with quantified data. Additionally, including follow-up questions demonstrates the candidate's ability to think critically, reflect on their decision-making process, and consider alternative approaches. This approach showcases their analytical skills, adaptability, and willingness to learn from past experiences.

> *The SBI method and follow-up questions enhance the effectiveness and clarity of the responses, providing a more well-rounded and informative picture of the candidate's capabilities and experiences.*

Let's look at some of the most important questions about soft skills for a Solutions Architect role.

Behavioral interview questions

Let's explore a few sample questions you might encounter in a Solutions Architect interview. Please note that while there are multiple questions, preparing 6 to 7 examples that cover various situations is essential. One example can often address multiple questions, so don't feel overwhelmed by the list. Remember, the key is to showcase your skills and experiences through well-developed examples.

Here are some common questions that can be asked for a Solutions Architect role. Remember, you should focus on preparing your top examples that can address multiple situations rather than trying to answer every question:

- Tell me about a project where you had to design a complex solution to meet specific business requirements.
- Tell me when you gathered stakeholders' requirements and translated them into a technical solution.
- Give an example of when you had to troubleshoot and resolve a critical technical issue during a project implementation.
- Tell me a time when you had to work with cross-functional teams to ensure the successful delivery of a project. How do you align goals between teams?
- Tell me a time when you have to learn new technologies and incorporate them into your work.
- Tell me about a time when you had to make trade-offs between functionality, scalability, and cost-effectiveness in a solution design.
- Give an example of a project where you successfully implemented cloud-based solutions to optimize performance and scalability.
- Tell me a time when you have to align your solutions with industry best practices and comply with relevant regulations and security standards.
- Describe a time when you had to present a complex technical solution to non-technical stakeholders. How did you ensure clear communication and understanding?
- Tell me about a project where you had to manage and prioritize multiple competing priorities and deliverables.

Remember, the interviewer wants to understand what you did and how you think and operate in situations where you don't have all the answers. Your response should demonstrate your ability to navigate ambiguity, make informed decisions, and drive positive outcomes even in challenging circumstances.

Common Follow-up questions

You've encountered many behavioral interview questions that can shape your interview success. But here's the thing: it's not just about providing the initial answers. You also need to be ready for the follow-up questions that might come your way. These follow-up questions are like unexpected twists in a thrilling story; you must be prepared to handle them with finesse. Here are the common follow-up questions you can prepare for each of your answers:

- What was the outcome?

- What were the tangible results or achievements of the project or initiative?
    - Did it meet the desired goals and objectives?
    - How did it impact the business, team, or stakeholders?

- What were the key challenges you faced during your project?
    - What were the main obstacles or difficulties encountered?
    - How did you overcome those challenges?
    - Did you face any resource constraints or time constraints?

- How did you define success?
    - What were the specific criteria or metrics you used to measure success?
    - Did you have key performance indicators (KPIs) or targets in place?
    - How did you track progress and ensure alignment with the defined goals?

- What would you do differently if faced with a similar situation based on what you learned?
    - What lessons did you learn from the project or experience?
    - How would you apply what you have learned to improve future approaches or decisions?
    - What adjustments or changes would you make to your strategy, process, or execution?

So, document these common follow-up questions in your interview guide, ensuring you're well-equipped to navigate any curveballs that may come your way. Get ready to showcase your skills and experiences in the most impressive way possible!

You can confidently navigate the interview process by familiarizing yourself with common behavioral interview questions and crafting thoughtful answers.

Remember to highlight your problem-solving abilities, communication skills, adaptability, and leadership qualities. Additionally, be prepared for follow-up questions, as they allow you to delve deeper into your experiences and demonstrate your expertise. With thorough preparation, you can position yourself as a strong candidate and increase your chances of success in securing the Solutions Architect role.

Let's go into detail questions pointed to specific soft skills. In this section, you will find two questions with follow-up inquiries. During a behavioral interview, interviewers often dig deeper into your answers until they are satisfied with the response.

Handling ambiguity and uncertainty

Handling ambiguity and uncertainty is a crucial skill for a Solutions Architect. As a Solutions Architect, you often encounter complex and ever-evolving situations where the path forward may need to be clarified. You must be comfortable working with limited information, analyzing multiple possibilities, and making informed decisions amidst uncertainty. It requires embracing ambiguity, adapting to changing circumstances, and navigating unknowns. Maintaining composure, thinking strategically, and seeking clarity amidst ambiguity enables Solutions Architects to thrive in dynamic environments and deliver effective solutions to complex challenges.

The following questions can be asked to showcase your problem-solving skills, decision-making abilities, and how you handle ambiguity and uncertainty - all of which are crucial in the role of a Solutions Architect.

Question: Can you describe a time as a Solutions Architect when you needed to design a system or make a strategic decision without complete data?
Follow-up Question:
- What strategies or techniques did you use to gather the available data and make an informed decision or design?
- Can you explain the rationale behind your decision-making process without complete data?
- How would you handle a similar situation differently based on this experience?

Question: Tell me about a time when you had to make a complex architectural decision without clear benchmarks or precedents.
Follow-up Questions:
- How did you weigh your alternatives and manage potential risks?
- What factors did you consider to evaluate the potential outcomes and risks of the decision?
- Can you provide specific examples of the considerations or analyses you conducted to arrive at your architectural decision?
- Looking back, is there anything you would have done differently in approaching or making this complex architectural decision?

Decision Making

Decision-making is a vital skill for Solutions Architects, as they often face complex and high-stakes choices that impact the success of projects and businesses. A combination of technical expertise, critical thinking, and strategic foresight drives their ability to make sound decisions. They analyze available data, assess risks and benefits, consider various perspectives, and evaluate potential outcomes. Solutions Architects understand the importance of balancing short-term needs with long-term goals, and they are skilled at identifying the most optimal solutions in dynamic environments. They are confident in their decision-making process yet remain open to feedback and alternative viewpoints. Their ability to make effective decisions with clarity and conviction empowers them to drive innovation, solve problems, and deliver successful outcomes.

The following questions can be asked to demonstrate your ability to think on your feet, make decisions under pressure, and proactively address potential problems.

Question: Can you recall a time as a Solutions Architect when you had to take a calculated risk under a tight schedule?
Follow-up Questions:
- o How did you handle the situation, and what measures did you take to mitigate risk?
- o What factors did you consider when assessing the potential risks and benefits of the decision?
- o How did you communicate the rationale and potential outcomes of the calculated risk to stakeholders or team members?
- o What was the outcome of the calculated risk? Did it yield the desired results, and were there any lessons learned from this experience that you would apply in similar situations?

Question: Tell me about a time when you identified a potential problem that could impact your team or project, and you proactively intervened to resolve it.
Follow-up Questions:
- o Can you provide more details about the problem you identified that could have impacted your team or project?
- o How did you become aware of the potential problem? What indicators or signals alerted you to its existence?
- o What actions did you take to intervene and resolve the problem proactively?
- o What was the outcome of your intervention? Did it successfully mitigate the potential problem and prevent any negative impact on the team or project?
- o Looking back, is there anything you would have done differently to resolve the identified problem?

Overcoming Challenges

Overcoming challenges is a vital part of a Solutions Architect's role. They face various obstacles and hurdles during their projects, and their ability to tackle them is crucial for success. Solutions Architects have a resilient mindset and a proactive problem-solving approach. They see challenges as opportunities to grow and innovate. They use their technical expertise, analytical skills, and creativity to find solutions. They collaborate with others, adapt to changes, and stay focused on finding the best outcomes. With their determination and resourcefulness, Solutions Architects overcome challenges and achieve outstanding results.

The following questions evaluate your abilities to handle pressure, make necessary compromises without sacrificing quality, and overcome unexpected challenges — all key attributes for a successful Solutions Architect.

Question: Could you share an instance from your experience as a Solutions Architect where you successfully delivered a crucial project under a stringent deadline?
Follow-up Questions:

- What compromises did you make to ensure the timeline was met, and how did these affect the end product?
- How did you manage resources, timelines, and dependencies to meet the stringent deadline?
- Tell us about any unexpected challenges or obstacles during the project and how you overcame them to ensure successful delivery. What actions did you take to mitigate the impact of these challenges on the project timeline?
- How did you manage stakeholder expectations throughout the project, especially considering the tight deadline? Were there any instances where you had to make trade-offs or negotiate with stakeholders to ensure project completion on time?

Question: Can you recall a time when you faced unexpected, significant hurdles while trying to achieve a key goal?
Follow-up Questions:

- What specific hurdles or challenges did you encounter during that time? Can you explain how these hurdles impacted your progress towards the key goal?
- How did you approach problem-solving and decision-making to overcome these unexpected hurdles? What strategies or techniques did you employ to navigate through the challenges?
- Can you share any instances where you had to adapt your initial plans or strategies in response to the unexpected hurdles? How did you evaluate and prioritize alternative options or approaches?
- What was the outcome of your efforts to overcome the unexpected hurdles? How did you measure success in achieving the key goal despite the challenges? Were there any valuable lessons or insights that you gained from this experience?

Solving complex issues

Solving complex issues is a core responsibility of a Solutions Architect. They encounter intricate problems that require a deep understanding of systems, technologies, and business requirements. Solutions Architects approach these challenges with a structured and analytical mindset. They break down complex problems into smaller, manageable components and assess them from multiple angles. They gather and analyze relevant data, collaborate with stakeholders, and leverage their technical expertise to develop effective solutions. Solutions Architects think critically, consider various alternatives, and make informed decisions.

The questions below assess your problem-solving skills, ability to think critically and dive deep into complex issues, and capacity to learn from past experiences.

Question: As a Solutions Architect, describe a time when you encountered a complex problem requiring a deep understanding and analysis.

Follow-up Questions:

- o Who did you consult, or where did you look to gather the crucial information? How did this information contribute to the problem resolution?
- o How did you approach the process of understanding and analyzing the problem? What methodologies, tools, or techniques did you employ to gain a deep understanding of the issue?
- o Can you elaborate on the steps you took to resolve the complex problem? How did you break it down into manageable components or tasks?
- o What was the outcome of your efforts to resolve the complex problem? How did your deep understanding and analysis contribute to finding a solution?

Question: Tell me about a situation that requires a thorough examination to determine the root cause of a problem.

Follow-up Questions:

- o How did you ensure that your focus was directed toward the right areas? What was the outcome?
- o How did you approach examining the problem to uncover the root cause?
- o Can you share your steps to identify and validate the root cause? Did you collaborate with others or involve different stakeholders in the process?
- o What was the outcome of your efforts to identify and address the root cause of the problem? Reflecting on this experience, is there anything you would do differently now?

Demonstrating Adaptability

Demonstrating adaptability is crucial for a Solutions Architect, as they often work in dynamic and ever-changing environments. They must be flexible and agile to address evolving business needs, emerging technologies, and shifting project requirements. Solutions Architects showcase adaptability by quickly adjusting their strategies, plans, and designs to accommodate new information or unexpected challenges. They embrace change and proactively seek opportunities to learn and acquire new skills. They are open to feedback and readily adapt their methods based on lessons learned. Their ability to adapt allows them to thrive in fast-paced and complex situations, ensuring successful project outcomes and meeting the organization's evolving needs.

The following questions focus on your communication skills, adaptability, ability to address concerns and feedback, and leadership and problem-solving abilities – all vital for success as a Solutions Architect.

Question: Describe a situation as a Solutions Architect when you had to communicate a change in direction that you anticipated would raise concerns among the team.
Follow-up Questions:

- o Did you make any adjustments based on the feedback received?
- o How did you handle questions and resistance and gain acceptance of the change?
- o How did you proactively address and understand those concerns?

Handling disagreements

Handling disagreements is an essential skill for a Solutions Architect. When disagreements arise, it's crucial to approach them with respect and open-mindedness. Solutions Architects should listen to others, understand their perspectives, and encourage healthy discussions. They aim to find common ground and propose solutions that address everyone's concerns. Solutions Architects build strong relationships and achieve successful outcomes by fostering a positive environment for resolving disagreements.

The following questions explore your ability to handle disagreements, communicate effectively, and make a positive impact as a Solutions Architect. They focus on your decision-making skills, leadership qualities, and adaptability to different viewpoints and outcomes.

Question: Tell me about a time when you had a significant disagreement with your manager or a peer regarding a matter that you believed was crucial for the success of a project or the business as a Solutions Architect.

Follow-up Questions:
- o How did you handle the disagreement, and what steps did you take to address the situation?
- o What steps did you take to resolve the disagreement and find a common ground or solution?
- o What was the outcome of the disagreement, and how did you navigate any potential tensions or conflicts that arose?

Question: Describe a situation where you disagreed during a meeting with peers and your leader as a Solutions Architect.

Follow-up Questions:
- o What was the nature of your dissenting position, and why did you feel strongly about it?
- o How did you communicate your perspective and manage the outcome?
- o How did you express your dissenting position during the meeting? Did you present alternative viewpoints or provide supporting evidence for your perspective?
- o Can you share the outcome of the meeting and how your dissenting position was received? Did it lead to any changes or adjustments in the decision-making process?

Mentoring

Mentoring is a valuable aspect of the Solutions Architect role. As a mentor, Solutions Architects guide and support team members in their professional growth and development. They share their knowledge, expertise, and experiences to help others succeed. Mentoring involves actively listening to team members, providing constructive feedback, offering guidance and advice, and empowering them to take on new challenges. By being a mentor, Solutions Architects contribute to the growth and success of their team members, fostering a culture of continuous learning and improvement.

The following questions assess your abilities as a leader and mentor to support the growth and development of your team members. They also explore your approach to coaching, providing feedback, and fostering a positive environment for professional advancement.

Question: Describe a situation as a Solutions Architect when you actively contributed to the career development of one of your team members.
Follow-up Questions:
- o   How did you support their growth, and how did it impact their career progression?
- o   How did you identify the developmental needs of the team member and take action?
- o   What steps did you take to mentor and guide the team member in their career development?
- o   How did your efforts in supporting the team member's career growth impact their performance and overall team dynamics?

Question: Tell me about a time when you invested in an employee's development as a Solutions Architect.
Follow-up Questions:
- o   What specific areas or skills did you focus on, and why?
- o   How did you identify and align the employee's development needs with the organization's goals?
- o   What were the outcomes of your investment?
- o   Can you provide an example of a situation where investing in an employee's development did not yield the desired results?

Maintaining high standard

Maintaining high standards is a crucial aspect of the Solutions Architect role. Solutions Architects strive for excellence in their work by setting and upholding high standards of quality, performance, and customer satisfaction. They consistently seek solutions that meet or exceed expectations and adhere to best practices and industry standards. Maintaining high standards involves attention to detail, rigorous testing and validation, continuous improvement, and delivering value to stakeholders. Solutions Architects hold themselves accountable for the quality and integrity of their work, ensuring that it aligns with organizational goals and meets the customers' needs.

The following questions emphasize your dedication to maintaining high standards, driving improvement, and making a positive impact as a Solutions Architect. They seek to assess your ability to uphold quality, initiate change, and continuously improve processes and outcomes.

Question: Describe a time in your role as a Solutions Architect when you maintained an unwavering commitment to your standards, whether regarding quality, customer service, or other essential aspects.
Follow-up Questions:
- What specific standards or principles were you committed to upholding in that situation?
- Who was the customer or stakeholder involved, and what were the outcomes of your adherence to those standards?
- Can you share any challenges or obstacles you encountered in maintaining your commitment to these standards? How did you overcome them?
- What were the outcomes or results of your unwavering commitment to these standards? Did it improve quality, customer satisfaction, or other positive impacts?

Question: Tell me about a situation in which you strongly desire to improve the current state of affairs as a Solutions Architect.
Follow-up Questions:
- What specifically motivated you to desire improvement in that situation?
- How did you identify the areas needing improvement?
- What actions did you take to drive the improvement?
- Looking back, is there anything you would have done differently to achieve even better results?

Innovative Thinking

Innovative thinking is vital for Solutions Architects as they tackle complex challenges and find creative solutions. Innovative thinking involves approaching problems with fresh perspectives, challenging assumptions, and exploring unconventional ideas. Solutions Architects who possess innovative thinking skills actively seek new technologies, methodologies, and approaches to enhance their solutions. They are open to experimentation and unafraid of taking calculated risks to drive innovation. Innovative thinking enables Solutions Architects to identify opportunities for improvement, optimize processes, and deliver cutting-edge solutions that address the evolving needs of their customers and organizations.

The questions below focus on your ability to tackle complex problems with simple solutions, your capacity for innovative thinking, and your track record of driving impactful changes or improvements. They seek to evaluate your problem-solving skills, creativity, and ability to think outside the box as a Solutions Architect.

Question: Give me an example of a challenging problem you encountered as a Solutions Architect that you solved with a simple yet effective solution.
Follow-up Questions:

- o   What aspects made the problem complex?
- o   How did you determine that your solution adequately addressed the problem?
- o   How did you come up with the simple solution?

Question: Describe the most innovative solution or approach you implemented as a Solutions Architect and explain why you considered it innovative.
Follow-up Questions:
- o   What made this solution or approach innovative, in your opinion?
- o   How did you come up with this innovative idea or approach?
- o   What problem(s) did this innovation aim to solve, and what was unique or groundbreaking about it?

Acquiring new skills

Acquiring new skills is an essential aspect of professional growth for Solutions Architects. Staying up-to-date with the latest tools, methodologies, and industry trends is crucial in the fast-paced and ever-evolving technology landscape. Solutions Architects must actively seek opportunities to expand their skill set and acquire new knowledge relevant to their role. This may involve participating in training programs, attending industry conferences, earning certifications, or engaging in self-study. By continuously acquiring new skills, Solutions Architects can enhance their problem-solving abilities, adapt to emerging technologies, and provide innovative solutions to their clients or organizations. Developing a growth mindset and embracing a lifelong learning approach can contribute to long-term career success as a Solutions Architect.

The following questions assess your adaptability, willingness to learn, and ability to acquire new skills and knowledge as a Solutions Architect. They aim to evaluate your proactive approach to self-improvement, resourcefulness in seeking development opportunities, and ability to tackle challenges and expand your expertise.

Question: Tell me about a situation as a Solutions Architect when you recognized the need for a deeper level of subject matter expertise to excel in your role.
Follow-up Questions:
- o   How did you identify the need for deeper subject matter expertise in that particular situation?
- o   What steps did you take to acquire the necessary expertise and knowledge?
- o   How did acquiring that deeper subject matter expertise contribute to your effectiveness as a Solutions Architect?
- o   Can you provide specific examples of how your increased subject matter expertise positively impacted your work or decision-making?

Question: Describe a time when you willingly took on work outside your comfort zone as a Solutions Architect.

Follow-up Questions:

- What motivated you to take on work outside of your comfort zone as a Solutions Architect?
- How did you identify the areas where you needed to develop new skills or knowledge to complete the task?
- What steps did you take to build your expertise and tackle the unfamiliar challenges?

Taking Ownership

Taking ownership is a vital characteristic for Solutions Architects. It involves assuming responsibility for the success and outcomes of projects, initiatives, or tasks. Solutions Architects must demonstrate accountability and take ownership of their work from start to finish. This includes proactively identifying problems, proposing solutions, and driving their implementation. Taking ownership also entails being accountable for mistakes or setbacks, learning from them, and taking necessary actions to rectify the situation. By taking ownership, Solutions Architects exhibit leadership, ensure timely delivery of solutions, and instill confidence in their team and stakeholders. They take initiative, show dedication to their work, and strive for excellence in all their endeavors.

The following questions assess your ability to take the initiative, demonstrate flexibility in taking on new responsibilities, and manage potential risks and challenges as a Solutions Architect. They aim to evaluate your proactive approach to adding value beyond your defined scope, your communication skills in managing commitments, and your ability to make informed decisions in challenging situations.

Question: Describe a time when you willingly took on a significant responsibility or project that fell outside your defined area of responsibility.
Follow-up Questions:

- What motivated you to take on the additional responsibility?
- How did you manage your existing workload while taking on this additional responsibility?
- What steps did you take to quickly gain the necessary knowledge and skills to excel in the new area of responsibility?
- Why did you consider it important, and what was the outcome of your involvement?

Question: Tell me about a situation where you realized you might not meet your promised commitment.
Follow-up Questions:

- How did you become aware that you might not meet the commitment you had promised as a Solutions Architect?
- What steps did you take to address the situation and mitigate the potential impact of not meeting the commitment?

- How did you communicate the potential issue to stakeholders, and how did you manage their expectations?
- What did you learn from this experience, and what measures have you put in place to prevent similar situations from occurring in the future?

Strategic Thinking

Strategic thinking is a critical skill for Solutions Architects. It involves analyzing complex situations, identifying patterns, and developing effective strategies and plans. Solutions Architects must consider long-term goals, anticipate challenges, and make decisions aligning with the organization's strategic objectives. They must have a broad perspective and understand how their actions impact the larger picture. Strategic thinking enables Solutions Architects to identify opportunities, assess risks, and develop innovative solutions that drive business success. It involves considering multiple perspectives, conducting a thorough analysis, and balancing short-term needs with long-term goals.

The following questions evaluate your ability to think strategically, identify opportunities for growth and improvement, and drive transformative change as a solutions architect. They assess your leadership skills and ability to communicate and gain buy-in.

Question: Describe a situation when you worked on a specific initiative or goal and recognized an opportunity to achieve something more significant or impactful.
Follow-up Questions:
- How did you recognize the opportunity to achieve something more significant or impactful while working on the specific initiative or goal?
- What made you realize that pursuing this opportunity would be worthwhile and bring greater value?
- How did you adjust your approach or strategy to capitalize on this opportunity and maximize the potential impact?
- What was the outcome of pursuing this more significant or impactful direction, and how did it contribute to the overall success of the initiative or goal?

Question: Give me an example of how you influenced and facilitated a shift in direction or mindset within a specific function or department, leading them to embrace a new way of thinking.
Follow-up Questions:
- How did you initially identify the need for a shift in direction or mindset within the specific function or department?
- What approach did you take to influence and facilitate the change in thinking among the team members?
- How did you address any resistance or challenges while shifting the mindset?

○ What was the outcome of your efforts, and how did the function or department benefit from embracing the new way of thinking?

By now, you should have a good grasp of behavioral interview questions. It's recommended to select about seven questions from the provided question bank and build your interview guide around them. Ensure that your answers cover multiple soft skills so no stone is left unturned.

Answering situational interview questions

Answering situational interview questions requires a different approach than behavioral interview questions, which you learned in the previous section. Unlike behavioral interviews, where you draw from your past experiences, situational interviews involve hypothetical scenarios proposed by the interviewer.

When answering situational interview questions, it's crucial to be thoughtful and organized. The key is not rushing to provide solutions without fully understanding the requirements. Interviewers often use these questions to assess whether you can thoroughly analyze a situation before proposing a course of action.

To illustrate this better, let's consider an example. Imagine you are asked to design a retail website. It might be tempting to start discussing a three-tier microservice architecture immediately. However, this approach could be a mistake as it might suggest you haven't considered the customer's needs, which is a critical skill for a Solutions Architect. Instead of jumping directly to solutions, you should first ask clarifying questions. For instance:
- Who is the target user base for the product?
- Are the users located in a specific country or region or globally?
- What are the expected user traffic levels for the application?
- What systems must the website integrate with, such as payment gateways, fulfillment centers, shipping services, etc.?
- What are Recovery Time Objective (RTO) and Recovery Point Objective (RPO) considerations?
- What are the site's latency requirements?

While asking these questions is important, be mindful not to pose too many, as this can overwhelm the conversation. You can ask about three key points and make assumptions for others. For example, you could ask about the target user base and then assume, for your response, that the user base is global and expects a page load time of under five seconds.

Always articulate your assumptions clearly, as making and clarifying assumptions is crucial for a Solutions Architect. This approach demonstrates that you are technically proficient and capable of thinking critically about business needs and customer requirements.

Now, let's expand on the example of designing a retail website. Here's how the conversation might unfold between the interviewer and the candidate:

Interviewer: "Imagine you're tasked with designing a retail website. How would you approach this project?"

Candidate: "Certainly, I'd be happy to outline my approach. But first, may I ask a few clarifying questions to better understand the scope and specific requirements of the project?"

Interviewer: "Of course, go ahead."

Candidate: "Thank you. Firstly, who is the primary user base for this retail website? Are we targeting a specific demographic?"

Interviewer: "Let's say the primary users are young adults between 18 and 30."

Candidate: "Understood. And are these users located in a specific region, or are we looking at a global user base?"

Interviewer: "The website should be able to cater to a global audience."

Candidate: "Great, that helps. And what kind of user traffic are we expecting? Do we have any projections for peak times or overall daily traffic?"

Interviewer: "Assume high traffic during holiday seasons, with moderate traffic throughout the year."

Candidate: "Got it. What external systems does the website need to connect with regarding system integrations? For instance, payment gateways, fulfillment centers, shipping services?"

Interviewer: "It should integrate with common payment gateways and shipping services, as well as our existing inventory management system."

Candidate: "Thank you for the information. Based on your responses, I would approach this project with a few assumptions and a proposed solution. Firstly, the website should have a responsive design that considers the diverse age group and global user base. Also, it should load efficiently, within 5 seconds, even during high-traffic periods.

In terms of architecture, I recommend a scalable, cloud-based microservices architecture. This would allow us to efficiently manage the expected traffic variations and integrate seamlessly with various external systems. Each microservice would handle different functionalities like user profiles, product catalogs, payment processing, and order fulfillment. We could leverage a Content Delivery Network (CDN) for global reach and minimal latency.

Additionally, considering the user base, the UI/UX design should be modern and intuitive, with a mobile-first approach. Security will also be a priority, especially for payment transactions and user data."

Interviewer: "That sounds like a comprehensive approach. How would you ensure the security of user data, especially with such a diverse and widespread user base?"

Candidate: "To ensure data security, I'd implement robust encryption protocols for data transmission, particularly for payment processes. We'd also adhere to global data protection regulations like GDPR. Regular security audits and compliance checks would be part of our routine to maintain high-security standards."

This conversational style demonstrates how a candidate can effectively navigate a situational interview, showing their ability to ask the right questions, make informed assumptions, and propose a solution tailored to the hypothetical scenario.

Questions to ask during the interview

When an interview feels more like a conversation than a one-sided question, it's usually a good sign. However, even if this isn't explicitly part of the interview's structure, you should try to ask questions to the interviewer. Doing so demonstrates genuine interest in the role and your commitment to it. Asking insightful questions may enhance your chances of selection.

But don't just ask questions for the sake of it; like your responses during the interview, these should be thoughtfully prepared. Remember, your questions give the interviewer insights into your thought process, priorities, and understanding of the role and company. Therefore, use this opportunity wisely to clarify any doubts, understand the company culture, or shed more light on the role you're applying for. Some of the questions you can ask interviewers:

1. **What are the key responsibilities of this role?**
    This question will help you understand the specific tasks and duties expected of you in the role. It allows you to clarify the scope of your responsibilities and align your expectations with the role requirements.

2. **What are the top three pain points you expect the person in this role to solve within the first six months?**
    This question helps you understand the immediate challenges or issues the company faces that they expect you to address. It allows you to gauge the urgency and priority of these pain points and assess whether your skills and experience align with their needs.

3. **How do you define success in this role?**
    This question allows you to gain insights into the company's key performance indicators and goals for the position. It helps you align your definition of success with the organization's expectations.

4. **What are the long-term and short-term goals for the company?**
    This question allows you to understand the company's strategic direction and plans for growth and success. It provides insights into the company's vision for the future, expansion plans, and upcoming initiatives. Understanding the company's goals can help

you assess how your skills and expertise align with their objectives and whether you can contribute to their long-term success.

5. **What are your team's key priorities, and how do they align with the company's long-term vision?**
   This question lets you understand your potential team's specific focus areas and objectives. It provides insights into the initiatives, projects, or goals the team is working towards and how they contribute to the overall long-term vision of the company. Understanding this alignment helps you evaluate the significance of your potential role in driving the company's success and whether your skills and expertise align with the team's priorities.

By asking these questions, you demonstrate your interest in understanding the role, the challenges ahead, and the desired outcomes. You also show a genuine interest in the company's future and your potential role in it. It also allows you to assess whether the position aligns with your skills, experience, and career aspirations.

Summary

In this chapter, you explored the importance of soft skills for Solutions Architects and how they are crucial in navigating the role's challenges. You delve into various soft skills that Solutions Architects need to excel in, such as leading through ambiguity, mastering communication, driving organizational efficiency, becoming a trusted advisor, demonstrating professionalism and leadership, becoming a thought leader, driving strategic growth, and mastering pre-sales skills. Each section highlights the soft skills and their significance in the Solutions Architect role.

You then shifted your focus to behavioral interviews, explaining what they are and why they are commonly used in the hiring process for Solutions Architects. You got insights into building an interview guide with relevant behavioral questions to assess the desired soft skills and competencies. The chapter further guides you on effectively preparing for behavioral interview questions, emphasizing the importance of aligning their experiences with the job requirements and using the SBI or STAR methods to structure their responses. Further, best practices for preparation, including identifying relevant examples, practicing storytelling, and researching the company, are discussed.

The chapter concludes with a comprehensive collection of common behavioral interview questions for Solutions Architects, covering a range of soft skills and scenarios. You are guided on approaching and answering these questions, including using specific examples and quantifiable data and reflecting on lessons learned. By mastering the art of behavioral interviews and effectively demonstrating their soft skills, Solutions Architects can set themselves apart in the job market and showcase their ability to thrive in their role's complex and dynamic landscape.

Part 2: Specialist Solution Architect Role and Interview

Chapter 4 - Cracking the Application Architect Interview

In Part 1 of this book, you gained valuable insights into the Solutions Architect role and learned essential tips for cracking solutions architect interviews from technical and behavioral perspectives. As we embark on Part 2, let's delve deeper into various types of specialist Solutions Architect interviews. Our journey begins with the application architect interview in this chapter, which is the most popular one. Many software engineers take the leap into application architecture to begin their solutions architect journey.

The Application Architect, also known as a Software Architect or AppDev Architect, holds a prominent position among architect roles. This role predates the cloud revolution and is often considered a natural progression from a software engineering role to an application architect role. For that reason, you will find lots of details in this chapter, as application architecture is the foundation for any solutions architect, regardless of their background. For example, even if you come from a network admin or database admin background, you must know application architecture to match the right components to succeed in a solutions architect interview.

One of the distinguishing characteristics of an Application Architect is their extensive software development experience and comprehensive understanding of multiple application development patterns. They bring a wealth of knowledge to building robust software solutions.

In this chapter, you will explore the complexities of the Application Architect interview, offering you valuable insights and guidance to help you crack it successfully. We delve into the key aspects and considerations that interviewers typically focus on, equipping you with the necessary knowledge to excel in this specialist role. In this chapter, we will cover the following topics:

- Understanding the role of application architects
- What is application architecture?
- Fundamental application design principles and methodologies
- Common application design patterns
- Best practices for application architecture design
- Designing microservice architecture
- Interview questions for application architects

By delving into the world of Application Architecture, we lay the foundation for your journey as a Solutions Architect. So, buckle up and get ready to unlock the secrets of acing the Application Architect interview in this comprehensive guide.

Understanding the role of application architects

An application architect has a specialized role within the field of software architecture. They are responsible for designing, planning, and overseeing the development of software applications. Application Architects deeply understand various application development patterns, software design principles, and technologies.

An Application Architect acts as a bridge between business requirements and technical implementation. They work closely with stakeholders, including business leaders, project managers, developers, and other architects, to ensure the software applications align with the organization's goals and objectives.

An Application Architect plays a crucial role in shaping software solutions, and their responsibilities can be broken down into several key areas they will be expected to showcase in the interview :

- **Design and Architecture:** You must build the application framework to align with business needs and performance objectives. The architect ensures the application is scalable, reliable, and secure while choosing appropriate technology stacks and defining software development methodologies.
- **Integration and Compatibility:** As an Application Architect, you integrate new applications with existing systems to enhance functionality and efficiency. Application Architects oversee the development process to ensure the architecture's design principles are consistently applied.
- **Collaboration and Stakeholder Management:** The application architect must communicate effectively with business leaders, development teams, and other stakeholders to ensure the application supports business objectives and meets technical standards.
- **Mentoring, Knowledge Sharing, and Reviews:** Architects play a mentoring role, guiding other architects and developers. They foster a culture of learning and knowledge sharing within the team and conduct code reviews and engineering performance evaluations.
- **Documentation and Conformance:** A critical responsibility is creating detailed documentation for the application's architecture and development process. You must ensure the application complies with relevant standards and regulations, addresses technical risks, and stays updated on technology trends to ensure the architecture remains robust and future-proof.

To excel as an Application Architect, you should have a strong background in software development and expertise in programming languages, frameworks, and application design principles. Let's first understand application architecture.

What is application architecture?

Application architecture refers to the design and structure of a software application. It encompasses the overall blueprint or framework that guides the development and organization of the application's components, modules, and interactions. In simple terms, application architecture is like the blueprint of a building. It defines how different parts of the application will work together, how data will flow, and how the application will be organized.

Application architecture considers various factors, such as the functionality of the application, its scalability, performance, security, and maintainability. It determines the choice of technologies, frameworks, and development patterns to build the application. The goal of application architecture is to create a well-structured, efficient, and reliable application that meets the business requirements and provides a positive user experience. It ensures that the application is designed to allow for future enhancements, updates, and integration with other systems.

Key elements of application architecture include the design of the user interface, the organization of the application's components, the data storage and retrieval mechanisms, the communication and integration with external systems, and the overall system architecture.

Let's walk through a real-world example to understand the concept of application architecture in action. Imagine you're building a shopping website from scratch. You must carefully plan its architecture to create a successful and efficient application. In this case, the application architecture for the shopping website might consist of different components, each with its specific role.

1. **User Interface (UI):** The UI component handles the visual presentation and user interaction. It includes web pages, forms, buttons, and other elements that allow users to browse products, add items to their cart, and complete purchases.
2. **Application Logic**: This component contains the business rules and processes that govern the shopping website's functionality. It includes features like inventory management, order processing, and payment handling. The application logic ensures that when a user selects a product, it is available, and the payment process is secure.
3. **Data Storage:** The shopping website needs a way to store product details, user information, and order history. This component could involve a database where product information, customer profiles, and transaction records are stored securely.
4. **APIs and Integrations:** The application might need to integrate with external services to enhance the shopping experience. For example, it could connect to a payment gateway for secure transactions or integrate with a shipping provider to provide real-time shipping

quotes. APIs (Application Programming Interfaces) facilitate these integrations, allowing the shopping website to interact with other systems.

5. **Scalability and Performance:** A critical aspect of application architecture is ensuring that the website can handle a high volume of users and perform well under heavy traffic. This might involve strategies like load balancing, caching, and distributed architectures to distribute the workload across multiple servers and maintain a smooth user experience.

By carefully designing and planning the application architecture, you can create a shopping website that is secure, scalable, and efficient. The different components work together seamlessly, providing users with an enjoyable shopping experience while allowing the business to manage inventory, process orders, and handle payments effectively. It gives a solid foundation for the development team to build and maintain the application and for future enhancements and expansions. This foundation application architecture is necessary to stand in any solutions architect interview. Now, let's learn about fundamental application design principles and methodologies.

Application design principles and methodologies

In software development, application design principles and methodologies are the cornerstones of successful application development. These guidelines and structured approaches shape the entire lifecycle of software creation, from conception to deployment. Design principles and methodologies are two fundamental aspects of software development, each serving a distinct purpose in creating effective, efficient, high-quality software.

Design Principles are the foundational guidelines and best practices that inform the design and architecture of software systems. They focus on how to structure and write code. Principles provide a framework for writing maintainable, scalable, and efficient code. These principles help developers decide how to organize their code, approach common problems, and ensure their codebase remains manageable over time. Let's look at some key design principles:

- **SOLID Principles**: A set of five principles for object-oriented design that make software more understandable, flexible, and maintainable.
- **DRY (Don't Repeat Yourself)**: Focuses on reducing the repetition of software patterns and promoting a single, authoritative representation of every piece of knowledge.
- **KISS (Keep It Simple, Stupid)**: Advocates for simplicity in design, making systems easier to understand and maintain.
- **YAGNI (You Aren't Gonna Need It)**: Encourages adding functionality only when necessary, preventing over-engineering.

- **Clean Code**: Emphasizes writing code that is easy to read and understand, with meaningful names and transparent organization.
- **Design Patterns**: General repeatable solutions to common problems in software design, providing tested, proven development paradigms.

Methodologies, on the other hand, are the structured processes and approaches used to manage and execute software development projects. They focus on how teams work and how they develop and deliver software. They address aspects like project management, team collaboration, development cycles, and operational strategies, ensuring the development process is efficient, responsive to change, and aligned with user needs and business goals. Let's look at some of the most popular design methodologies:

- **TDD (Test-Driven Development)** is a process where requirements drive specific test cases to improve the software by incrementally adding new tests.
- **BDD (Behavior-Driven Development)** is an extension of TDD that combines techniques from domain-driven design and involves collaboration between developers and business analysts.
- **Agile Development** is an iterative approach to software development that focuses on collaboration, customer feedback, and rapid releases.
- **DevOps** aims to unify software development and operation, advocating for automation and monitoring throughout the development process.
- **Microservices Architecture** structures an application as a collection of loosely coupled services, facilitating scalability and continuous deployment.

> *While design principles provide the 'rules' or 'guidelines' for writing good code, methodologies offer the 'roadmap' for the software development process. Both are essential for building robust, user-friendly, and successful software applications. Still, they address different aspects of software creation—one is about the craft of coding, and the other is about the process of creating software.*

As a solutions architect, you need to be familiar with design principles and methodologies to showcase your broad range of experience in the interview.

Best practices for application architecture

In the continuously evolving software development landscape, adhering to architectural best practices is not just a recommendation but a necessity. These practices are the cornerstone for building functional software that is robust, secure, and adaptable to the changing needs of users and businesses. They are crucial in ensuring that software systems are reliable, can scale effectively to meet increased demands, and are secure against growing cyber threats. Furthermore, best practices in architecture provide a structured approach to managing complexity, reducing the risk of costly errors and enhancing the overall quality of the software. These practices are vital in today's digital environment, where software systems are integral to businesses' success and users' satisfaction.

This book recommends application architecture best practices based on a comprehensive synthesis of knowledge and experience from various authoritative sources. In addition to academic research from leading universities, IEEE established industry standards, and the Software Engineering Institute informs these practices.

Technology giants like Google, Microsoft, and Amazon share experiences that significantly shape these practices, offering practical, real-world perspectives on effective software architecture.

By applying the following set of best practices tailored specifically to the demands of a fictional but practical e-commerce platform, one can achieve optimal performance, security, and user experience. These practices include modularity for easier maintenance, scalability to handle peak traffic, robust security to protect sensitive data, and high availability to ensure constant uptime.

Additionally, they include effective data management for real-time operations, a user-centric design for enhanced customer engagement, and the use of cloud technologies for cost-effective scalability. The integration of continuous integration and deployment (CI/CD) practices ensures smooth updates. At the same time, regular performance optimization and architecture reviews keep the platform agile and responsive to evolving market needs.

The following examples illustrate how these best practices are crucial in building and maintaining a robust, efficient, and user-friendly extensive e-commerce web application.

- **Modularity:** Divide the application into distinct modules, such as user authentication, product catalog, shopping cart, and payment processing. This separation allows for easier updates and maintenance. For instance, updating the payment module won't disrupt the product catalog.
- **Scalability:** Design the architecture to handle peak shopping periods like Black Friday. This could involve using cloud services that scale resources up or down based on traffic, ensuring the website remains responsive during high traffic.
- **Security**: Implement robust security measures, such as SSL/TLS, for secure data transmission and rigorous authentication and authorization for user accounts and admin panels. This is crucial to protecting sensitive customer data and maintaining trust.
- **High Availability and Fault Tolerance**: Use redundant systems and backups to ensure the website remains operational even if one server fails. For example, if one server hosting

the product catalog goes down, another immediately takes over, preventing service disruption.

- **Effective Data Management**: Optimize database design for efficient access and updates, which is crucial for features like real-time inventory management or personalized user recommendations.
- **User-Centric Design**: Ensure the website is intuitive and easy to navigate, with a responsive design that adapts to different devices. This enhances user experience and can lead to increased sales and customer loyalty.
- **Flexibility and Maintainability**: Write clean, well-documented code and use design patterns where appropriate. This makes adding new features, like a new payment gateway, or updating existing ones easier.
- **Leverage Cloud Technologies**: Utilizing cloud-based storage for product images and descriptions allows cost-effective scaling and improved performance.
- **CI/CD (Continuous Integration and Continuous Deployment)**: Implement CI/CD pipelines for automated testing and deployment, ensuring new features or updates are smoothly integrated and deployed without disrupting the live site.
- **Performance Optimization**: Regularly monitor and optimize the site's performance, such as by using content delivery networks (CDNs) to reduce load times, which is crucial for keeping customers engaged and reducing bounce rates.
- **Regular Architecture Review and Update**: Continuously evaluate and update the architecture to leverage new technologies and best practices, ensuring the e-commerce platform stays competitive and secure.

For an application architect's interview, combining best practices, design principles, and methodologies forms the backbone of a successful software architecture, particularly in complex domains like large e-commerce web applications. Best practices such as modularity, scalability, security, and high availability ensure that the architecture is robust, efficient, and capable of adapting to changing demands. Design principles like SOLID, DRY, and KISS contribute to creating a codebase that is functional, clean, maintainable, and easy to evolve. Methodologies such as Agile, DevOps, and CI/CD streamline the development process, fostering a culture of continuous improvement and collaboration. Developers and architects can create systems that meet current and future growth and innovation requirements by integrating these elements. This holistic approach ensures that the architecture is not just a rigid framework but a dynamic foundation that supports the application's evolution in response to new challenges and opportunities. For a large e-commerce platform, this means an ability to scale during peak traffic, offer a seamless and secure user experience, and rapidly adapt to new market trends and customer needs, securing its place in a competitive digital marketplace. Let's start learning tips and tricks to crack the applications architect interview.

Approach to answer the interview question

To effectively answer questions in an application architect interview, adopt a multifaceted approach.

- Begin by thoroughly understanding the question and asking for clarifications to tailor your response accurately if needed.
- Leverage the Situation-Behavior-Impact (SBI) model for scenario-based questions, providing clear and concise examples from your experience demonstrating your skills and problem-solving abilities.
- For technical and design principal questions, showcase your knowledge and explain your reasoning and thought process to give insight into how you approach complex problems.
- When discussing project management and Agile methodologies, highlight your teamwork, communication skills, and adaptability, emphasizing how you've successfully managed projects or teams.
- In responding to behavioral questions, honestly reflect on past experiences, focusing on what you learned and how you've grown professionally.
- Throughout the interview, balance technical proficiency and soft skills, demonstrating your expertise and ability to work effectively in a team and adapt to evolving environments.

This strategy ensures that your answers are well-rounded and relevant and showcase your suitability for the architect role. To refine your response to a complex question, you should ask clarifying questions and make certain assumptions for areas where details are unavailable.

Ask clarifying questions

The clarifying questions you should seek answers to show that you are not directly jumping into solutions with clarifying requirements.

- What scale and scope does the application target, including user base and data volume, and are there specific regions of focus?
- Which functionalities are critical for maintaining high availability, and are there particular types of data or transactions deemed essential?
- Is the current hosting environment on-premises, cloud-based, or hybrid? What technologies are in use?
- What compliance and security standards must the application meet, including specific regulations and data protection requirements?
- Are there budget limitations for implementing disaster recovery and high-availability solutions, and how important is cost optimization?
- What are the expected performance metrics, such as response times and handling of peak loads?

To further refine your approach, you might ask additional clarifying questions covering functionality, operations, metrics, and trade-offs:

- What specific user actions or transactions are most frequent and critical within the application?
- How does the application handle data backup and recovery, and what are the recovery time objectives (RTO) and recovery point objectives (RPO)?
- What are the current performance bottlenecks, and how does user traffic fluctuate daily or seasonally?
- Are there existing metrics on system uptime, and what are the target metrics post-improvement?
- What trade-offs between cost, performance, and availability are stakeholders willing to accept?
- How does the application integrate with external services or APIs, and are there dependencies that could impact availability?
- What is the process for deploying updates or patches, and how might this affect system availability?
- Are specific technologies or platforms preferred or avoided for compliance, expertise, or vendor relationships?

The above questions aim to uncover profound insights into the application's operational requirements, performance expectations, and potential constraints, guiding a more targeted and effective architectural strategy. It also solidifies your position as a solutions architect who can ask the right questions when collecting requirements.

Share assumptions

It may happen interviewers don't provide you with specific details and, in that case, you should include reasonable assumptions such as:

- The application likely operates in a cloud environment, leveraging scalability and availability benefits.
- Compliance with relevant regulations, like HIPAA for healthcare applications, is critical.
- Data security and privacy are paramount, necessitating robust encryption and access controls.
- The application requires scalability features to manage varying loads, especially during peak times.
- A comprehensive disaster recovery strategy is essential, aiming for minimal data loss and quick recovery.

Asking these questions and making assumptions helps you better understand the application's needs. At the same time, the assumptions address potential information gaps, ensuring a well-rounded approach to the response.

Application architects' interview questions

In this section, you will explore common interview questions posed to application architects and provide insights on tackling them effectively. These questions touch upon technical knowledge, problem-solving abilities, communication skills, and experience with architectural patterns and best practices. By understanding these interview questions and learning how to address them confidently, you can enhance your preparation for application architect interviews and increase your chances of success.

Behavioral Questions

Question: How do you approach designing an application architecture from scratch? Describe to me what the architecture would look like for an eCommerce website that handles large traffic spikes during peak hours.

Tip: Describe your methodology for designing application architectures, starting with requirements gathering and analysis. Discuss the importance of understanding business objectives, identifying key components, defining interfaces, and selecting appropriate technologies and architectural patterns. Emphasize the need to balance scalability, performance, security, and maintainability in the design process.

Answer: As learned in "Chapter 3 - Cracking Behavioral Interview", let's answer the above question using the SBI (Situation, Behavior, Impact) format, taking the example of complex architecture required to build an e-commerce website like amazon.com

Situation: When tasked with designing the complex architecture for a large-scale application such as an e-commerce website like Amazon.com, I followed a systematic approach to ensure a comprehensive and effective design.

Behavior: I began by gathering the requirements and understanding the application's business goals and functional needs. This included identifying key components such as user management, product catalog, shopping cart, order processing, payment integration, and customer support. I defined clear interfaces and communication protocols for seamless integration between these components. I chose a microservices architecture style to address scalability, enabling independent development, scalability, and flexibility. I designed a robust data management strategy, utilizing relational and NoSQL databases for structured and unstructured data. Security was a priority, so I incorporated secure authentication and encryption and implemented measures to mitigate common vulnerabilities. I planned for scalability by employing horizontal scaling techniques, caching mechanisms, and content delivery networks. Performance optimization was achieved through caching, optimized database queries, and asynchronous processing.

Impact: This systematic approach resulted in an architecture design that aligned with the business requirements, enabled seamless integration with external systems, and facilitated future scalability. The architecture provided a secure and reliable platform for users, ensuring efficient product search, seamless ordering, and secure payment processing. It optimized performance and scalability, enabling the website to handle high traffic loads. The architecture design's comprehensive documentation and effective communication facilitated collaboration among the development team and stakeholders.

Follow-up questions:
When approaching application architecture design, it's essential to cover key aspects while keeping the response concise. Initially, analyzing requirements and aligning them with business goals sets the foundation. Architectural patterns and design principles are applied to ensure scalability, performance, security, and maintainability.

By providing a compact overview, interviewers can ask follow-up questions based on specific areas of interest, such as scalability techniques, security measures, technology selection, or trade-offs. This approach ensures a dynamic and engaging interview discussion, covering the essential aspects of application architecture design. We have listed some key follow-up questions with the answers below. Other questions may come up, but these questions will give you a fair idea of how to handle overall application architecture design questions.

Question: Suppose website traffic increases 10X in a given hour due to a marketing campaign; how would you scale your application so that it does not compromise user experience?
Answers: When faced with a 10X increase in website traffic within a short timeframe due to a marketing campaign, ensuring a seamless user experience is crucial. To scale the application without compromising user experience, I would employ the following strategies:

Firstly, I would implement horizontal scaling by adding more servers or instances to handle the increased load. This would distribute the workload and prevent any single server from becoming overwhelmed.

Next, I introduce a load-balancing mechanism to distribute incoming requests evenly across multiple servers. I can optimize resource utilization and prevent bottlenecks by implementing load balancers at various layers, such as the application or network layer. To further enhance performance, I utilize caching mechanisms to store frequently accessed data or static content closer to the users. This reduces the load on backend servers and improves response times. Implementing caching strategies like content delivery networks (CDNs) or in-memory caching systems would be beneficial.

Optimizing the database performance is essential. Techniques like query optimization, indexing, and caching query results help handle the increased traffic. Additionally, implementing database replication for high availability and read scaling can further improve performance. Auto-scaling mechanisms would be implemented to add or remove resources based on predefined thresholds automatically. This ensures that the application dynamically scales according to the current demand. Utilizing cloud infrastructure services with auto-scaling capabilities provides flexibility during traffic spikes.

Regular performance testing and monitoring would be conducted to identify bottlenecks and optimize system performance. Load testing the application under realistic scenarios would help uncover performance limitations and ensure the application can handle increased traffic effectively. Implementing real-time monitoring allows for proactive measures to optimize performance. By employing these strategies, the application can successfully handle the increased traffic without compromising the user experience. The goal is to ensure a responsive application, quick content delivery, and high availability even during periods of high traffic load.

Question: How will you scale the database?
Answer: When considering scaling a database, several approaches and techniques can be utilized based on the specific requirements. Here's how I would approach scaling a database:

- Vertical Scaling: One option is vertically scaling the database by upgrading the existing server's hardware resources. This involves increasing the server's processing power, memory, or storage capacity. Vertical scaling can handle moderate increases in traffic or database size, but it has limitations in terms of scalability.
- Horizontal Scaling: Another approach is horizontal scaling, which involves distributing the database load across multiple servers. This can be achieved through techniques such as database sharding or partitioning. Sharding involves splitting the database into smaller parts (shards) hosted on separate servers, while partitioning divides the data based on specific criteria. Horizontal scaling allows for improved scalability and performance by distributing the workload across multiple servers.
- Replication: Database replication is a technique where multiple copies of the database are created and kept in sync. This enhances high availability and read scalability. In a replicated setup, one server handles write operations while one or more servers handle read operations. Replication can be implemented using master-slave or multi-master configurations.
- Caching: Implementing caching mechanisms, such as in-memory or distributed caches, can significantly improve database performance and reduce the load on the server. Frequently accessed data can be stored in the cache, allowing faster retrieval and minimizing the need to query the database. Caching is particularly effective for read-heavy workloads.

- Database Optimization: Optimizing the database itself can enhance scalability. Techniques such as index optimization, query optimization, and database tuning can improve the performance of database operations. Common optimization strategies are analyzing slow-performing queries, optimizing them, creating efficient indexes, and fine-tuning database configuration parameters.
- Cloud-Based Database Services: Utilizing cloud-based databases, such as Amazon RDS, Google Cloud SQL, or Azure SQL Database, can provide built-in scalability features. These services often offer automated scaling options, allowing for easy adjustment of database capacity based on demand.

In conclusion, the specific approach to scaling a database depends on various factors, including the database management system, workload characteristics, and anticipated growth. Assessing the requirements and selecting the appropriate scaling strategy is crucial to ensure optimal performance and scalability of the database in line with the application's needs.

Question: How would you ensure that users from other parts of the world, such as Australia, have a fast page-loading experience when accessing a website hosted in the US with high-definition videos and images?
Answer: To optimize the page loading speed for global users accessing a website with high-definition videos and images hosted in the US, I would employ the following strategies:

Firstly, I would utilize a Content Delivery Network (CDN) to distribute and deliver static content, such as images and videos, across multiple global servers. This ensures the content is stored and cached closer to the user's geographic location, minimizing network latency and improving page loading times. Additionally, I would implement adaptive bitrate streaming for video content. This technique dynamically adjusts the video quality based on the user's available bandwidth. By serving videos in different quality levels, the website can adapt to varying network conditions and prevent buffering, ensuring smooth playback for users with limited bandwidth.

Image optimization techniques would also reduce file sizes without compromising quality. This includes image compression, resizing, and lazy loading. Compression algorithms would be applied to minimize image file sizes, enabling faster downloads. Lazy loading would defer the loading of images until they are visible on the user's screen, enhancing initial page load times.

Caching mechanisms would be implemented for both static and dynamic content. Static resources like images, CSS, and JavaScript files would be cached, allowing subsequent requests to be served from the cache instead of fetching them from the server for every page load. Appropriate caching headers would be set for dynamic content to control content refresh rates. Furthermore, content optimization based on user location would be considered. Utilizing GeoDNS, users would be directed to the closest server or CDN node, reducing network latency. Additionally, prioritizing the loading of critical content ensures users can interact with essential elements while the remaining content loads in the background.

Regular performance monitoring using tools like Real User Monitoring (RUM) or synthetic monitoring would be conducted. This allows for the proactive identification of performance bottlenecks and enables optimization measures to be implemented, ensuring an optimized user experience for global users. By implementing these strategies, the website can provide users worldwide, including Australia, with a fast and efficient page-loading experience, even when accessing high-definition videos and images hosted in the US.

Question: How would you address a website's performance using caching techniques?
Answer: I would utilize various caching techniques to optimize resource utilization and reduce server load to enhance website performance. Here are some strategies I would employ:

Firstly, I would implement content caching by storing static content like images, CSS files, and JavaScript files on the client-side or intermediate servers. This enables subsequent requests to be served directly from the cache, significantly improving page load times and reducing the load on the server. In addition, I would leverage HTTP caching mechanisms by setting appropriate caching headers such as Cache-Control and Expires. This allows the browser and intermediate caches to store and reuse requested resources, minimizing network latency and reducing the need for redundant requests to the server.

To optimize database performance, I would implement database query caching. By caching frequently accessed query results, subsequent identical queries can be served from the cache, reducing processing time and alleviating the load on the database. For static or semi-static pages, I employ full-page caching. By generating and storing a complete HTML representation of the page, subsequent requests for the same page can be served directly from the cache, bypassing server-side processing and database queries.

Another valuable strategy is to utilize a Content Delivery Network (CDN). By caching and delivering static content from geographically distributed edge servers, the CDN reduces latency by serving content from a server closer to the user's location. I also recommend fragment caching for resource-intensive or time-consuming sections of a page. By selectively caching specific components, dynamic content can still be generated while reusing cached portions, reducing processing overhead.

Lastly, implementing cache invalidation mechanisms is crucial. This ensures that cached content is refreshed or invalidated when updates occur, maintaining data accuracy. Techniques such as time-to-live (TTL) or cache invalidation APIs can be utilized. By effectively implementing these caching techniques, the website's performance can be significantly improved by reducing server load, minimizing network latency, and enhancing response times. Caching optimizes resource utilization, improves scalability, and enhances user experience.

Question: What best practices do you apply when handling error responses from service dependencies that your application relies on, such as when the order service experiences an outage while the payment service remains operational?

Answer: I follow several best practices to ensure smooth operation and a positive user experience when handling error responses from service dependencies. Here are the techniques I employ:

Firstly, I implement robust error-handling mechanisms within the application. This includes capturing and logging error messages, categorizing errors based on severity, and providing informative error responses to users. By handling errors gracefully, users are informed about the issue, and appropriate actions can be taken to address it. I implement retry mechanisms when a service dependency experiences temporary issues. This allows the application to automatically retry failed operations after a certain period, minimizing the impact of transient errors. Implementing retries with a backoff strategy is important to prevent overwhelming the dependency and set a maximum retry limit to avoid indefinite retries.

To prevent cascading failures, I apply the Circuit Breaker pattern. This pattern acts as a barrier, temporarily blocking requests to the faulty service and redirecting them to alternative actions or fallback mechanisms. This isolation helps maintain application functionality even when a service dependency experiences prolonged outages or degraded performance. Setting appropriate timeouts for requests made to service dependencies is crucial to prevent blocking or delaying application responses. Additionally, implementing request throttling mechanisms limits the number of concurrent requests to the dependency, preventing overload and ensuring system stability.

In terms of graceful degradation, I designed the application to gracefully handle situations where a service dependency is unavailable. The application can continue operating partially or with reduced capabilities by providing fallback options or alternative paths. This ensures that users can still interact with the application, minimizing the impact of the dependency outage. Monitoring and alerting systems are vital in quickly detecting service dependency issues. Robust monitoring allows for prompt identification of failures or performance degradation, enabling proactive measures to be taken. Monitoring metrics such as service response times and error rates ensure timely intervention.

Lastly, I consider implementing failover and redundancy strategies for critical service dependencies. This involves deploying multiple instances of the service or utilizing load-balancing techniques. Having redundant systems ensures high availability and resilience, enabling the application to continue functioning even if one service instance encounters issues. By applying these best practices, the application can effectively handle error responses from service dependencies, maintain system stability, and provide a positive user experience, even when one service experiences an outage while others remain operational.

Application troubleshooting questions

The role of an application architect is not only about designing systems but also having the ability to troubleshoot potential issues that can lead to outages and require immediate attention. Interviewers may delve deeper into troubleshooting scenarios to understand your real-world, hands-on experience. Let's explore a few questions related to application troubleshooting:

Question: Imagine you have configured a server to act as a web server, and you have confirmed internet connectivity by downloading the necessary packages. However, you encounter an error message when attempting to access your webpage through a browser. How would you approach troubleshooting this issue?
Answer: When faced with this situation, I would take the following steps to troubleshoot the problem:

1. First, I would check the server's network connectivity to ensure a stable internet connection. This involves verifying network configurations, firewall settings, and any potential network interface issues causing the error message.
2. Next, I would confirm that the web server software, such as Apache or Nginx, runs and operates on the server. Checking the status of the webserver service and associated processes is essential to ensure they are functioning correctly without any errors.
3. I would carefully review the webserver's configuration files (e.g., Apache's httpd.conf or Nginx's nginx.conf) to identify misconfigurations or syntax errors. This includes examining settings related to the listening port, server name, and document root directory.
4. Checking firewall settings is crucial to ensure that incoming traffic on the designated port used by the web server (typically port 80 for HTTP or port 443 for HTTPS) is not being blocked. Adjustments to firewall rules or security group settings may be necessary.
5. To gain insights into the underlying problem, I would analyze the webserver's error logs (e.g., Apache's error.log or Nginx's error.log). These logs often provide valuable information about specific error messages, aiding in identifying missing dependencies, permission issues, or conflicts.
6. To narrow down the issue, I would attempt to access the webpage locally on the server using the loopback IP address (e.g., 127.0.0.1) or the "localhost" hostname. If the webpage loads successfully, it suggests that the webserver and its configuration are functioning correctly, indicating potential network or firewall restrictions as the cause.
7. The DNS configuration is also important. If the server has a domain name associated with it, I would ensure that the DNS records are properly configured and point to the correct IP address. Testing access to the webpage using the IP address directly helps rule out DNS-related issues.

By systematically following these troubleshooting steps, I can identify the potential causes of the error message and work towards resolving the issue. This approach ensures a structured investigation and helps ensure successful access to the webpage from a browser.

Question: What steps would you take to troubleshoot a website error such as "Error establishing a database connection"?

Answer: When troubleshooting a website error of "Error establishing a connection to the database," I would follow these steps:

1. Check Database Service: Ensure that the database service is running and accessible. Verify that the database server is up and running and that there are no issues with its availability or connectivity.
2. Validate Connection Credentials: Review the connection credentials used by the website to connect to the database. Confirm that the username, password, and database hostname or IP address are correct. Check for any typos or errors in the configuration.
3. Verify Network Connectivity: Ensure no network-related issues prevent the website from connecting to the database server. Check if the server hosting the website can reach the database server without any restrictions or firewall blocking.
4. Review Database Configuration: Examine the database server's configuration files to ensure they are configured correctly. Verify settings such as the listening port, network access permissions, and allowed connections.
5. Test Database Connectivity: Use database client tools or command-line utilities to manually test the database server's connectivity. This can help identify any connection issues or errors that are not apparent through the website.
6. zCheck Database Server Logs: Review the database server's error logs for relevant error messages related to connection issues. These logs often provide insights into the root cause, such as incorrect authentication, insufficient privileges, or an exceeded connection limit.
7. Verify Database User Privileges: Ensure that the database user used by the website has the necessary privileges to connect to the database and perform the required operations. Check if the user has the appropriate access rights and permissions.
8. Test with Sample Code or Query: Create a minimalistic test code or query to establish a connection to the database directly from the website server hosting. This can help identify any application-specific issues or misconfigurations that might be causing the connection error.

By following these troubleshooting steps, I can identify potential causes of the "Error establishing connection to the database" issue and work towards resolving it. It involves validating the database service, connection credentials, network connectivity, configuration, and user privileges. Reviewing logs and performing direct database connectivity tests can help identify the underlying problem and enable effective troubleshooting.

Question: You recently took ownership of a legacy application that generates no application logs, which has made troubleshooting very difficult. You've been asked to create a new end-to-end logging strategy to speed up future investigations and resolutions. What would be part of your strategy?

Answer: In response to this challenge, I would implement the following steps as part of my logging strategy:

1. Identify Critical Components: Analyze the application architecture and determine the critical components that require logging, such as authentication, database interactions, error handling, and important business processes.
2. Define Logging Levels: Establish appropriate logging levels, such as DEBUG, INFO, WARN, ERROR, and FATAL, to capture the relevant level of detail needed for troubleshooting purposes.
3. Determine Log Format: Select a suitable log format, such as plain text or structured formats like JSON, that provides meaningful information while being easily readable and parseable.
4. Implement Logging Framework or Library: Integrate a logging framework or library, such as Log4j or a language-specific logging utility, into the application codebase to facilitate log generation within relevant code sections.
5. Log Key Events and Exceptions: Incorporate logging within critical code sections to capture important events, user actions, data modifications, and exceptions with relevant details, including stack traces.
6. Include Contextual Information: Enhance logs with contextual information, such as user session details, request/response payloads, and relevant metadata, to provide a comprehensive understanding of the application's behavior during specific operations.
7. Centralized Log Storage: Set up a centralized log storage system or leverage log management platforms like ELK Stack or Splunk to collect, store, and facilitate easy access and searchability of logs for future investigations.
8. Implement Log Analysis and Monitoring: Use log analysis and monitoring tools to identify anomalies, errors, or performance issues proactively. Define alerts and dashboards that provide real-time insights into the application's health and performance.
9. Establish Regular Log Reviews: Establish a process for regularly reviewing log data, analyzing patterns, and identifying areas for improvement. Use this feedback to refine and enhance the logging strategy based on evolving application requirements.

By following this approach, organizations can create a robust logging strategy for the legacy application, enabling faster investigations and more efficient issue resolutions in the future.

Scenario-based questions

This section lists relevant questions often asked during an application architect interview at big-tech companies. However, these questions generally apply to all companies that need to hire an application architect. To facilitate your understanding, we will provide general guidance on responding to scenario-based questions, followed by our reasons for categorizing questions in a certain way, and finally, the structure of our responses. Let's look at scenario-based interview questions for application architects.

Question: Imagine you are tasked with architecting an online video streaming platform. Initially, the platform had a modest user base. However, you anticipate rapid growth in users and video content over the next year. Describe how you would design the system to handle this scalability challenge, considering immediate needs and future growth. What technologies and architectural patterns would you consider essential for supporting scalability in this context?
Answer: Let's answer it using the SBI method.

Situation: In a recent project, "StreamFast," we faced a similar challenge. Initially, the platform catered to a user base of 10,000, with a content library of 1,000 hours of video. Within a 12-month forecast, we anticipated user growth to 1 million and content expansion to 10,000 hours. The primary objective was to ensure seamless scalability to accommodate this growth without compromising performance or user experience.

Behavior: To address this, we adopted a multifaceted approach focusing on scalability, reliability, and efficiency. We implemented a microservices architecture to isolate services, allowing for independent scaling based on demand. For instance, the authentication service experienced peak loads during sign-in times, whereas the video streaming remained unaffected. This separation enabled us to allocate resources dynamically and scale services autonomously.

We chose a combination of cloud-based solutions and technologies. Amazon Web Services (AWS) was the backbone, leveraging its Elastic Compute Cloud (EC2) for flexible computing capacity. We utilized Auto Scaling Groups to adjust the number of EC2 instances automatically, ensuring we could meet demand without manual intervention. Amazon Simple Storage Service (S3) provides durable and scalable storage for our video content. In contrast, Amazon CloudFront, a content delivery network (CDN), was essential for delivering low-latency streaming to users worldwide.

We implemented Amazon Aurora for the database. This high-performance managed database scales automatically and supports both the high transaction rates of user management systems and the read-intensive requirements of video metadata retrieval. We used Apache Kafka for stream processing to ensure data consistency and support real-time user engagement features (like comments and likes). Kafka allowed us to process large streams of events in real-time, providing a responsive user experience.

Impact: Adopting these technologies and architectural patterns significantly impacted StreamFast's scalability and performance. We achieved a 99.9% uptime, even during peak traffic spikes. The platform successfully scaled to support 1 million users and 10,000 hours of video content within the projected timeline. The average latency for video start times was reduced by 50%, enhancing user satisfaction. Additionally, it optimized the operational cost by 30% due to the efficient use of cloud resources and auto-scaling capabilities. This strategic approach met the immediate needs and positioned StreamFast for sustainable growth, demonstrating the business benefits of investing in scalable architecture from the outset.

For whiteboarding, you can draw the following high-level architecture flow:

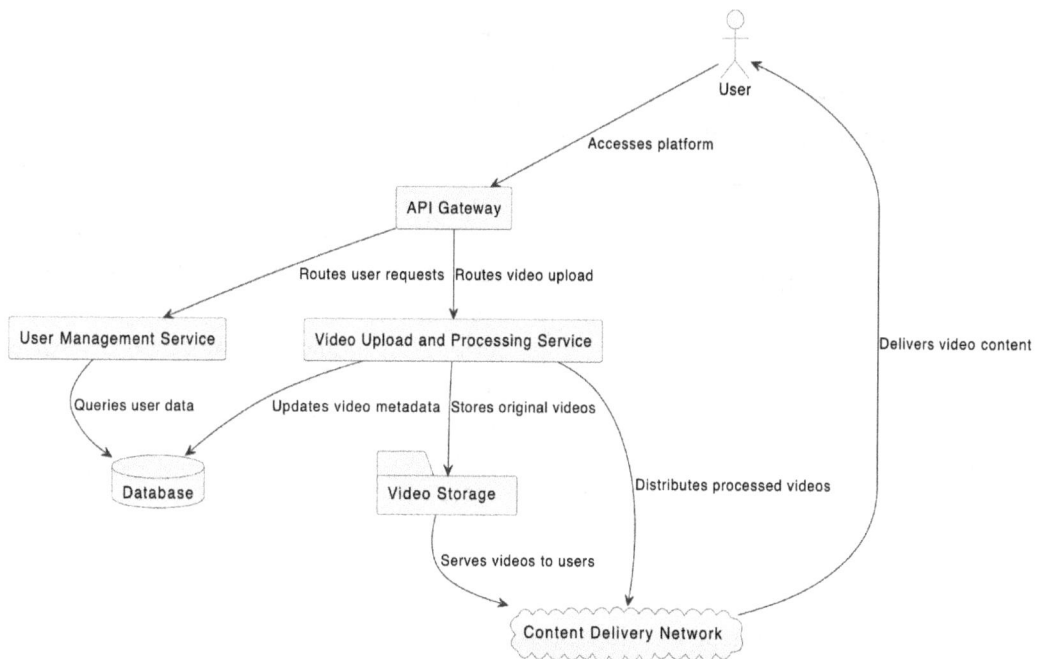

Figure 4.1 – *Online Video Streaming Platform Architecture*

As shown in the above diagram, the following are the components to scale an online video streaming platform:

- User Management Service: Handles user authentication, authorization, and profile management.
- Video Upload and Processing Service: This service manages the ingestion of videos, encoding them into various formats and resolutions for adaptive streaming.
- Video Storage: Utilizes object storage for storing original and processed videos.
- Database: Stores metadata about videos, users, and viewing statistics.

- API Gateway: Serves as the single entry point for all client requests, routing them to appropriate services.
- Content Delivery Network (CDN): Distributes video content globally to reduce latency and improve user experience.
- Caching Layer: Reduces database load by caching frequent queries and results.
- Microservices Architecture: Ensures scalability and flexibility by decomposing the application into more minor, independently deployable services.
- Cloud Services: Leverage cloud computing resources for elastic scalability, storage, and managed services (e.g., databases, Kubernetes for orchestration).
- Adaptive Bitrate Streaming: The video player can adjust the quality based on the user's network conditions.

Follow-up Questions:
Here are some possible follow-up questions you should prepare to answer:

- **How does StreamFast's architecture ensure scalability during unexpected surges in viewer traffic, particularly for live events?**
  This question challenges the assumption that the current infrastructure can automatically scale to meet sudden increases in demand. Given the variability of streaming traffic, especially during popular live events, it's crucial to understand the specific mechanisms (e.g., auto-scaling EC2 instances and use of Amazon CloudFront for content delivery) that allow the system to maintain performance without manual intervention.
- **What data redundancy measures does StreamFast employ to safeguard against data loss and ensure high content availability across all regions?**
  By asking this, the question probes the assumption that data is uniformly protected and accessible, regardless of geographical location. It's important to clarify whether StreamFast uses services like Amazon S3 cross-region replication or other strategies to replicate data across multiple data centers, ensuring viewers can access content even if one region experiences an outage.
- **How does StreamFast's architecture address potential latency issues for users in geographically dispersed locations, ensuring a consistent streaming experience?**
  This question challenges the assumption that all users experience low latency and high-quality streaming regardless of location. It seeks to understand the specific technologies and strategies (e.g., Amazon CloudFront's global edge locations, adaptive bitrate streaming) implemented to minimize latency and optimize streaming quality for users far from the origin server.

Question: Consider an e-commerce application that experiences significant spikes in traffic during holiday seasons, which has led to performance issues and downtime in the past. How would you redesign the application's architecture to remain scalable and maintain high performance during these peak periods? Discuss any specific strategies, tools, or technologies you would employ to manage and mitigate the impact of sudden traffic surges.

Answer: Let's look at the response to improve the performance of large e-commerce platforms.

Situation: In the past, "HolidayHype," an e-commerce platform, experienced significant performance issues and downtime during peak holiday seasons. These periods are critical for sales, with traffic spikes up to 300% above normal levels. The inability to handle this surge resulted in customer frustration, abandoned shopping carts, and a substantial loss in revenue, estimated at a 20% decrease in potential sales during these periods.

Behavior: We implemented several strategic changes to address these challenges and redesign the application's architecture for scalability and high performance. First, we adopted a microservices architecture to replace the existing monolithic structure. This architecture allowed us to scale services independently based on demand, improving resource utilization and system resilience. We containerized each microservice using Docker and orchestrated it with Kubernetes, ensuring seamless deployment and scaling.

We introduced an auto-scaling solution that dynamically adjusts real-time computing resources based on traffic monitoring. Utilizing cloud services, such as AWS EC2 for compute instances and RDS for database scalability, enabled us to manage the load effectively. Amazon CloudFront was employed as a Content Delivery Network (CDN) to cache static content at edge locations, significantly reducing latency and offloading traffic from the origin server.

To further enhance system responsiveness and reduce the load on the backend, we implemented aggressive caching strategies, including Redis for in-memory data caching of frequently accessed information like product listings and user sessions. This approach decreased the average response time from 800ms to 200ms during peak traffic.

We applied database sharding and read replicas for database management to distribute the load and improve read performance. This strategy was crucial for handling high-volume transactions and user queries without compromising performance.

Impact: The redesign and strategic enhancements to "HolidayHype's" architecture profoundly impacted its ability to handle peak holiday season traffic. The platform successfully managed up to 300% spikes above normal traffic levels without any performance degradation or downtime. Customer satisfaction scores improved by 40%, as evidenced by reduced bounce rates and increased time spent on the site. The checkout process saw a 50% reduction in abandonment rates, directly contributing to a 25% increase in sales compared to previous holiday seasons. Adopting a scalable, cloud-based infrastructure also resulted in a 30% cost reduction in maintaining and operating the platform due to the efficient use of resources and the elimination of over-provisioning. These improvements strengthened "HolidayHype's" reputation as a reliable e-commerce platform. They demonstrated the business's agility in adapting to market demands, ensuring a competitive edge in the fast-paced retail industry.

For whiteboarding, you can draw the following high-level architecture flow:

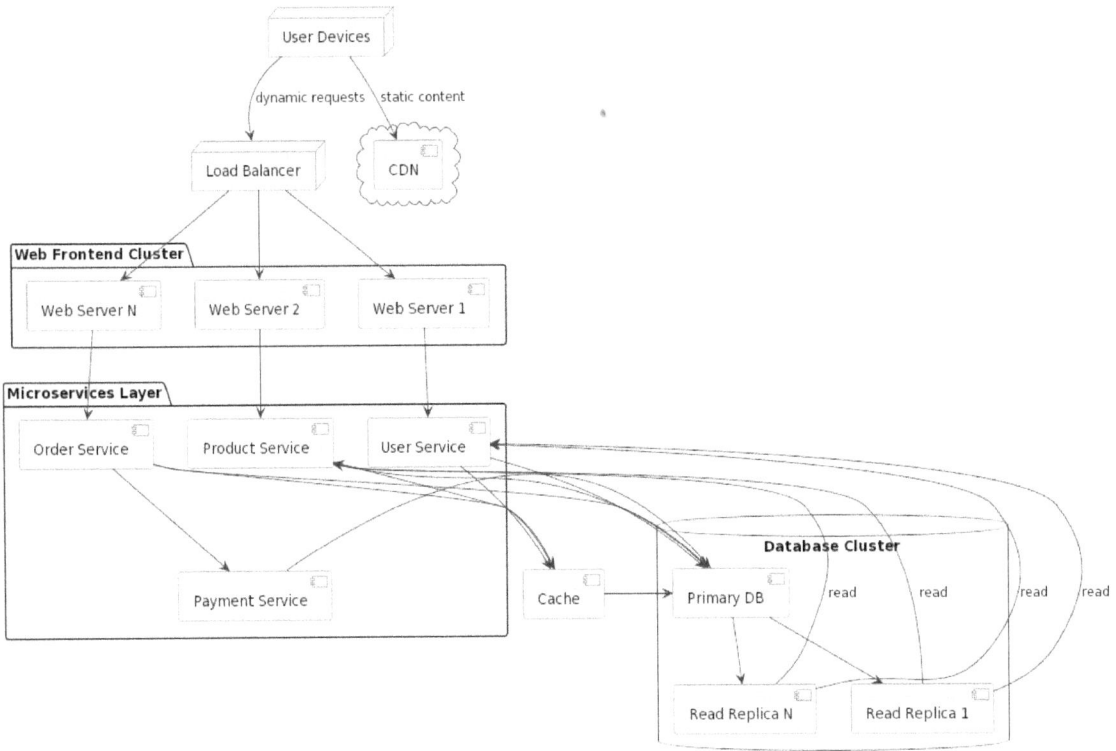

Figure 4.2 – *E-commerce platform Architecture*

As shown in the above diagram, The "HolidayHype" platform architecture efficiently manages and scales in response to dynamic traffic conditions, particularly the surges experienced during holiday seasons. The architecture incorporates several key components, each serving a specific function to enhance performance, reliability, and user experience.

- **Content Delivery Network (CDN):** The CDN serves as the frontline of the architecture and is designed to cache and deliver static content (such as images, CSS, and JavaScript files) to users. By distributing this content across multiple geographically dispersed servers, the CDN reduces latency and speeds up content delivery, ensuring users experience fast load times regardless of location.
- **Load Balancer:** A load balancer manages incoming user requests, particularly dynamic content requests. This component distributes the traffic evenly across multiple web servers in the frontend cluster, preventing any single server from becoming a bottleneck. The load balancer is crucial in maintaining the application's availability and performance, especially under heavy traffic conditions.

- **Web Frontend Cluster:** This cluster consists of multiple web servers that render and deliver dynamic content to users. Scalability is a key feature here, as servers can be added. Or removed based on current traffic demands. This flexibility ensures that the platform can handle sudden spikes in user activity without degradation in performance.
- **Microservices Layer:** The business logic of the "HolidayHype" platform is encapsulated within a set of microservices, each responsible for a specific domain, such as user management, product catalog, order processing, and payment handling. This architectural pattern allows for independent scaling, development, and deployment of services, facilitating rapid feature updates and enhancements without impacting the entire system.
- **Database Cluster with Read Replicas:** At the core of the data layer is a primary database that handles all write operations, ensuring data integrity and consistency. We used multiple read replicas to optimize read performance and distribute the query load. This setup improves the application's read efficiency and enhances availability and fault tolerance.
- **Cache:** We added a caching layer to reduce the load on the database and speed up data retrieval for frequently accessed information. By temporarily storing popular content and data in memory, the cache significantly decreases response times for user queries. It lightens the database's workload, contributing to smoother and faster user experiences.

Follow-up Questions:
- **How does HolidayHype's architecture handle data consistency and state management across its distributed system, especially during peak traffic?**
  This question challenges the assumption that HolidayHype's system maintains consistent data across all user interactions and transactions, even under high traffic stress. It's crucial to understand the mechanisms (e.g., distributed databases like Amazon DynamoDB with built-in conflict resolution and caching strategies) employed to ensure that users see up-to-date information and that their actions result in consistent system states.
- **What strategies are in place for HolidayHype to ensure cybersecurity and protect sensitive customer data, particularly given its cloud-based infrastructure?**
  By asking this, the question probes the assumption that customer data is inherently secure in a cloud environment. It seeks clarity on specific security measures (e.g., encryption in transit and at rest using AWS services, implementation of AWS Identity and Access Management policies) that protect against data breaches and unauthorized access.
- **How does HolidayHype plan to dynamically scale its infrastructure to manage cost efficiency without compromising performance, especially outside peak seasons?**
  This question challenges the infrastructure cost-optimization assumption without affecting user experience. It's essential to explore the strategies (e.g., using AWS Auto Scaling to adjust resources based on demand and serverless architectures for pay-per-use

pricing models) that allow HolidayHype to scale down resources during off-peak periods to save costs while still being able to scale up efficiently for high demand.

In the interview, this "HolidayHype" architecture exemplifies a strategic approach to designing scalable e-commerce platforms that adapt to fluctuating traffic patterns. The inherent trade-offs in this architecture underscore the importance of continuously evaluating and adjusting the system's components to align with evolving business needs, user expectations, and technological advancements.

Question: You're leading the design of a new retail application intended to provide a seamless shopping experience across web, mobile (iOS and Android), and tablet platforms. Given the diverse range of devices and screen sizes, how would you ensure consistent functionality and user experience across all platforms? Please describe the key considerations and technologies you would utilize to achieve cross-platform compatibility.
Answer: Let's learn how to answer this question to build an omnichannel retail platform that is accessible across multiple devices and offers a seamless user experience.

Situation: My previous organization aimed to launch "OmniRetail," a cutting-edge retail application designed to unify the shopping experience across web, mobile (iOS and Android), and tablet platforms. Before "OmniRetail," we faced significant challenges: inconsistent user interfaces, varying performance metrics across devices, and a fragmented customer journey that hindered seamless shopping experiences. This inconsistency led to lower engagement and conversion rates on mobile platforms, directly impacting sales and customer satisfaction. We recognized the need for a solution that not only bridged these gaps but also leveraged the latest technology to ensure scalability, performance, and a cohesive user experience irrespective of the device used. The scope of the problem encompassed addressing these multifaceted challenges to meet the evolving expectations of their diverse customer base, enhancing brand loyalty, and driving growth.

Behavior: In response to the challenges in launching "OmniRetail," we devised a comprehensive strategy to ensure the application delivered a seamless shopping experience across all digital platforms. Recognizing the critical need for consistency in user interfaces and performance, the team embarked on a deep dive into potential technological solutions, focusing on leveraging AWS services to address the identified issues. The initial phase thoroughly analyzed the existing system's shortcomings, particularly the inconsistent user experience and performance discrepancies across web, mobile, and tablet platforms. This analysis highlighted the need for a responsive design that adapts to various screen sizes and resolutions and a unified backend that efficiently serves all platforms.

With these insights, the team explored several AWS services, identifying key components that could form the backbone of the "OmniRetail" architecture. AWS Amplify emerged as a pivotal service, offering a comprehensive suite of tools for building scalable mobile and web applications with a unified backend. Amplify's authentication, API services, and data storage capabilities presented a robust solution for creating a cohesive user experience across platforms. We used Amazon CloudFront as the CDN solution to enhance content delivery and reduce latency, efficiently distributing static and dynamic content to users worldwide. For the application's hosting and scalability needs, we used Elastic Load Balancing and Amazon EC2 to manage incoming traffic and dynamically allocate resources, guaranteeing high availability and performance even during peak traffic.

Impact: The deployment of "OmniRetail" on AWS marked a transformative phase for the fashion retailer, achieving remarkable outcomes in user engagement, sales conversions, and operational efficiency. The strategic use of AWS services and a focus on cross-platform compatibility delivered quantifiable improvements:

- User Engagement: The application saw a 40% increase in average session duration across platforms, with mobile users demonstrating a 50% increase in time spent browsing products. The bounce rate decreased by 30%, indicating higher content relevancy and improved user satisfaction.
- Sales Conversions: Sales conversions on mobile devices surged by 25%, while overall platform conversions saw a 20% uplift. The seamless integration of AWS services like Amplify and CloudFront contributed to faster load times, directly impacting the checkout process efficiency and reducing cart abandonment rates by 15%.
- Operational Efficiency: By leveraging React Native and AWS Amplify, the development cycle was 30% shorter than previous projects. This efficiency reduced the time-to-market and allowed for a 20% reduction in operational costs due to streamlined development and deployment processes.
- Scalability and Performance: Post-launch, "OmniRetail" effortlessly scaled to support a 200% increase in user traffic during peak shopping seasons, thanks to Elastic Load Balancing and Amazon EC2. CloudFront's effective content delivery ensured a 99.9% uptime, enhancing customer trust and reliability in the brand.
- Global Reach: With Amazon CloudFront, the application experienced a 40% improvement in load times for international customers, expanding the retailer's global market presence and increasing international sales by 35%.

These metrics underscore the success of "OmniRetail" in providing a unified and efficient shopping experience across all digital platforms facilitated by the strategic application of AWS services. The project elevated the brand's digital footprint and set a new benchmark for retail innovation, demonstrating the power of technology in reshaping consumer interactions.

For whiteboarding, you can draw the following high-level architecture flow:

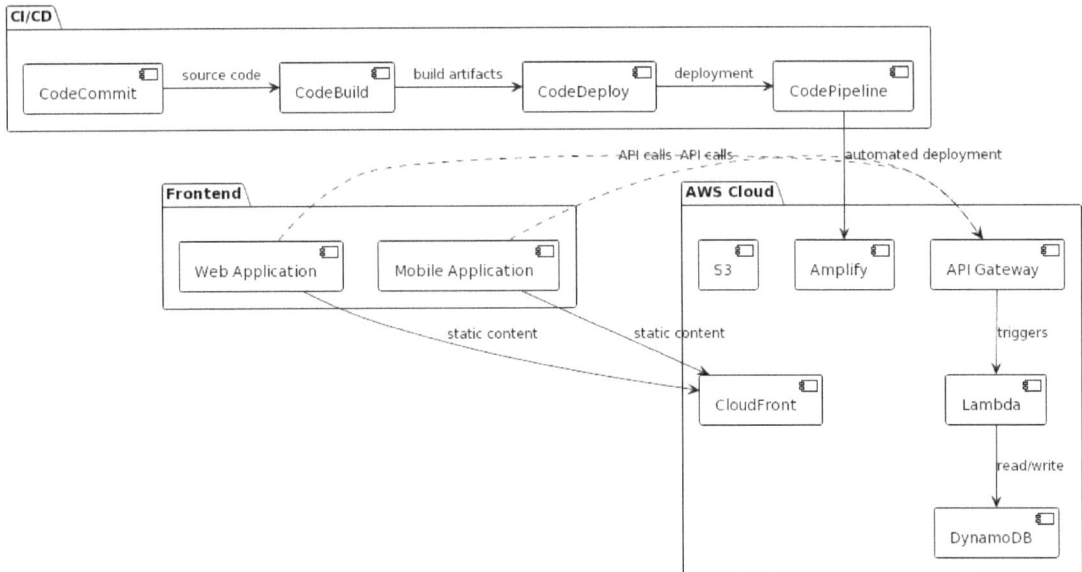

Figure 4.3 – Omni Channel *E-commerce Platform Architecture*

As shown in the above diagram, the high-level architecture for the "OmniRetail" application, designed to offer a seamless shopping experience across web, mobile (iOS and Android), and tablet platforms, integrates various AWS services to ensure scalability, performance, and a consistent user experience. Here's an overview of the architecture and how each component interacts within the ecosystem:

- Frontend
  - Web Application: The interface for desktop and tablet users is built with responsive design principles to adapt to different screen sizes and resolutions.
  - Mobile Application: Provides native iOS and Android apps developed using a cross-platform framework to ensure consistency in functionality and user experience across mobile devices.
- AWS Cloud Services
  - Amplify: It facilitates the development and deployment of mobile and web applications. It provides a unified environment to manage backend authentication, API, and storage services, simplifying integration with other AWS services.
  - API Gateway: It is the entry point for front-end applications to access back-end services. It routes requests to the appropriate Lambda functions, ensuring efficient API management and security.

- Lambda: It executes the business logic in response to API requests, interacting with databases and other services without provisioning or managing servers. This serverless computing service scales automatically with the application's usage.
- DynamoDB: It is a NoSQL database service supporting key-value and document data structures. It offers fast and predictable performance with seamless scalability. It stores application data, handles high-traffic volumes, and provides low-latency data access.
- S3 (Simple Storage Service): It hosts static assets for the web application, such as HTML files, CSS, JavaScript, and multimedia content. S3 integrates with CloudFront to deliver content efficiently to users worldwide.
- CloudFront: It provides a content delivery network (CDN) service that caches static content globally at edge locations, reducing latency and improving load times for users regardless of their location.
- CI/CD Pipeline
  - CodeCommit: A source control service that hosts Git-based repositories, making it easier for teams to collaborate on code in a secure and highly scalable ecosystem.
  - CodeBuild: Compiles source code, runs tests, and produces ready-to-deploy software packages, automating the code compilation process.
  - CodeDeploy: Automates application deployments to AWS services such as EC2, Lambda, and ECS, as well as on-premises servers, ensuring reliable and consistent application updates.
  - CodePipeline: Orchestrates the workflow from code update to deployment, integrating with CodeCommit, CodeBuild, and CodeDeploy to automate the release process through various stages.

This architecture leverages AWS's ecosystem to create a scalable, secure, and maintainable application that provides a consistent and seamless user experience across all platforms. By utilizing serverless technologies, such as Lambda and DynamoDB, the application can scale automatically to accommodate varying loads, ensuring high availability and performance. The CI/CD pipeline enables rapid development, testing, and deployment cycles, facilitating continuous innovation and improvement of the "OmniRetail" application. In an interview, you can explain the same architecture using other cloud provider services like GCP and Azure as per your comfort.

Follow-up Questions:
- **How does OmniRetail's architecture ensure real-time inventory synchronization across online and physical stores to prevent over-selling or stock discrepancies?**
  This question challenges the assumption of a seamlessly integrated inventory system across all sales channels. Given the complexity of managing inventory in real-time, especially during sales or promotions, it's crucial to understand the specific technologies (e.g., using an event-driven architecture with AWS Lambda for real-time updates,

DynamoDB for scalable and fast data retrieval) and strategies to maintain accurate inventory levels.

- **What measures does OmniRetail take to secure customer data across its omnichannel platforms, especially with the integration of online and in-store systems?**
  By asking this, the question probes the assumption that customer data is inherently secure across digital and physical retail environments. It seeks clarity on specific security practices (e.g., data encryption in transit and at rest, strict access controls, and identity management using AWS IAM) that safeguard sensitive information against breaches and unauthorized access.

- **How does OmniRetail's architecture support personalized customer experiences without impacting system performance or infringing privacy regulations?**
  This question challenges the assumption that customized experiences can be delivered efficiently and in compliance with data protection laws. It's essential to explore the balance between leveraging customer data for personalization (e.g., using machine learning models hosted on Amazon SageMaker, anonymizing data to ensure privacy) and maintaining high system performance (e.g., using Amazon ElastiCache to reduce latency) while adhering to regulations like GDPR.

Question: An enterprise plans to upgrade its internal software systems to enhance accessibility for employees using different operating systems, including Windows, macOS, and Linux, both on desktops and mobile devices. As the application architect, how would you approach this upgrade to ensure full functionality and a unified user experience across all these platforms? Discuss your strategy for addressing potential challenges related to cross-platform compatibility.
Answer: Let's look at the answer to build multi-platform compatible architecture.

Situation: "Global Retail Inc.," facing operational challenges, identified critical inconsistencies in its customer service management software across Windows, macOS, and Linux platforms. User interface layouts and navigation discrepancies led to confusion among customer service representatives. The lack of uniform feature accessibility, such as file attachments and customer history, impaired support quality. Performance issues, particularly on macOS and Linux, resulted in service delays. Inconsistent software updates and poor integration with essential communication tools can further complicate customer service workflows. These problems directly contributed to longer customer wait times, unresolved inquiries, and declining satisfaction, highlighting the urgent need for software upgrades to ensure consistent functionality and enhance the customer service experience.

Behavior: To resolve "Global Retail Inc.'s" challenges with its customer service management software, we embarked on a strategic overhaul to ensure cross-platform compatibility and enhance user experience. Our approach unfolded as follows:

We adopted React Native and Electron to target uniform user interfaces across mobile and desktop platforms and address layout and feature access inconsistencies. This choice ensured customer service representatives could seamlessly navigate and utilize the software, whether on Windows, macOS, Linux, iOS, or Android.

Transitioning to a microservices architecture, we enabled independent development, scaling, and deployment of specific functionalities. This move facilitated the consistent rollout of updates and features across all platforms, eliminating disparities and delays in software enhancements.

Implementing an API Gateway streamlined the frontend and backend interactions, significantly improving system performance and simplifying external tool integrations. This gateway was crucial for maintaining a smooth workflow and enhancing the overall efficiency of customer service operations.

We migrated to cloud-native storage solutions, using Amazon S3 and DynamoDB, to ensure customer data's high availability and scalability. This transition addressed performance variability and integration challenges, providing a robust foundation for real-time data access and management. A unified CI/CD pipeline, leveraging Jenkins and GitHub Actions, automated our testing, building, and deployment processes. This pipeline ensured that new features and fixes were deployed simultaneously across all platforms, maintaining consistency and reducing the risk of errors.

Incorporating Agile development methodologies, we fostered rapid iteration and adaptability, allowing us to respond quickly to user feedback and evolving business needs. Integrating DevOps practices, we enhanced collaboration across teams, speeding up deployment cycles and improving system reliability. Focusing on user experience, we involved customer service representatives in the design and testing phases, ensuring the software was intuitive and fully met user needs. Additionally, we implemented robust monitoring and logging solutions to proactively manage the application's performance and security proactively, ensuring a reliable and secure user experience.

Impact: The strategic overhaul of "Global Retail Inc.'s" customer service management software led to significant improvements across key performance indicators. Post-implementation, the company observed a 30% reduction in response times to customer inquiries, directly attributable to the unified user interface and enhanced feature accessibility. Adopting a microservices architecture and cloud-native data storage resulted in a 25% increase in system uptime, ensuring that customer service representatives could access vital information without delays, irrespective of their operating system or device.

Moreover, the streamlined CI/CD pipeline facilitated a 40% faster feature rollout and bug-fix deployment, enhancing the software's reliability and functionality. This pipeline directly contributed to a 20% improvement in customer satisfaction scores, as measured by post-interaction surveys. For whiteboarding, you can draw the following high-level architecture flow:

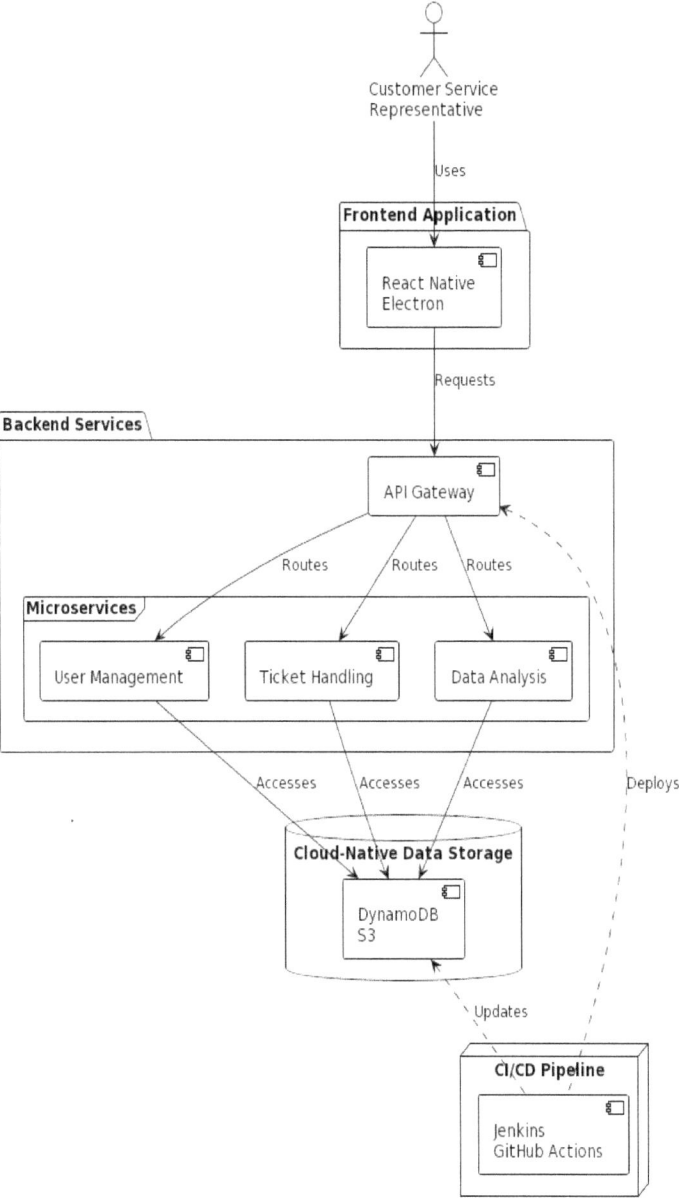

Figure 4.4 – Customer Service Management Platform *Architecture*

As shown in the preceding architecture, It is designed to address "Global Retail Inc.'s" challenges with its customer service management software, which focuses on ensuring cross-platform compatibility, enhancing user experience, and improving operational efficiency. This architecture integrates modern development frameworks, microservices, cloud-native technologies, and DevOps practices to create a robust, scalable, and user-friendly system.

- Frontend Architecture
  - Cross-Platform Frameworks: It utilizes React Native for mobile app development and Electron for desktop applications, ensuring a consistent and responsive user interface across Windows, macOS, Linux, iOS, and Android platforms.
  - Unified User Interface (UI): A single codebase for UI components guarantees that all users, regardless of their device or operating system, experience the same layout, navigation, and functionality.
- Backend Architecture
  - Microservices Architecture: Decomposes the backend into independently deployable, small, modular services. Each service runs a unique process and communicates through a well-defined, lightweight mechanism to serve a business goal.
  - API Gateway: Serves as the entry point for clients, routing requests to the appropriate microservices. It simplifies the client by encapsulating the internal system architecture and providing an externalized, unified API endpoint.
  - Cloud-Native Data Storage: Adopts Amazon S3 for storing attachments and Amazon DynamoDB for customer data, ensuring high availability, durability, and scalability.
- DevOps and CI/CD Pipeline
  - Continuous Integration/Continuous Deployment (CI/CD): Implements a CI/CD pipeline using Jenkins and GitHub Actions to automate the testing, building, and deployment processes. This pipeline ensures that we consistently and efficiently roll out new features and fixes across all platforms.
  - Monitoring and Logging: It continuously integrates monitoring and logging tools to track the application's performance and security, enabling proactive issue resolution and system optimization.
- Methodologies
  - Agile Development: This type of development employs Agile methodologies to support rapid iteration, continuous feedback, and flexibility in responding to changing requirements or challenges.
  - DevOps Practices: They incorporate DevOps principles to foster collaboration between development, operations, and quality assurance teams, enhancing the efficiency and reliability of software delivery.

This architecture not only resolves the initial challenges faced by Global Retail Inc. but also sets a foundation for future scalability and innovation, ensuring that the company can continue to provide exceptional customer service in an ever-evolving technological landscape.

Follow-up questions

These follow-up questions aim to delve deeper into the architectural decisions, exploring the nuances of implementing and maintaining the proposed solution while ensuring it meets Global Retail Inc.'s operational and strategic objectives.

- **How will the system handle platform-specific features and hardware capabilities, especially given the limitations of cross-platform frameworks like React Native and Electron?**
  This question explores strategies for leveraging native modules or bridging technologies to access device-specific functionalities, ensuring the application can utilize each platform's full potential.
- **What measures are in place to manage the increased complexity and operational overhead introduced by the microservices architecture?**
  This question seeks to understand the tools, processes, and practices adopted to efficiently monitor, manage, and maintain a distributed system, including service discovery, configuration management, and inter-service communication.
- **Can you detail the approach for ensuring data consistency and integrity across the microservices, especially considering the asynchronous nature of distributed systems?**
  This question addresses the strategies for database management, transaction handling, and data synchronization across services, ensuring that the system maintains high data integrity and consistency.

For the interviewer, while the chosen architecture and methodologies significantly address "Global Retail Inc.'s" immediate needs for cross-platform compatibility and operational efficiency, they also introduce considerations around performance, complexity, vendor lock-in, and resource requirements. Balancing these trade-offs is crucial for sustaining long-term growth and adaptability.

Question: You are tasked with architecting a new social media platform that is expected to grow in user numbers and data volume rapidly. How would you approach selecting the technology stack for this web application, considering factors like long-term scalability, performance, and developer availability? Describe the criteria you would use to evaluate potential technologies and frameworks and explain your decision-making process for choosing a stack that aligns with the project's goals and future growth.

Answer: The following response provides a detailed explanation of all components, accompanied by relevant data.

Situation: In the "ConnectSphere" project, we faced the challenge of building a social media platform to accommodate rapid user growth and surging data volumes. This growth trajectory posed potential scalability and performance issues, such as slow page loads and delayed message delivery, which could degrade user experience and satisfaction. Ensuring a robust, scalable infrastructure was crucial to support seamless user interactions, like instant messaging and real-time notifications, without compromising speed or reliability.

Behavior: We adopted a technology stack optimized for growth and efficiency to address "ConnectSphere's" scalability and performance challenges, leveraging AWS services. I chose React for the front end to capitalize on its responsive design capabilities and comprehensive developer support. For the backend, I selected Node.js, known for its asynchronous, event-driven architecture, ensuring quick data processing and response times.

We integrated AWS Elastic Beanstalk for deploying and managing applications, allowing us to scale automatically based on traffic. AWS Lambda supported serverless backend functions, enabling efficient handling of user requests without provisioning or managing servers. We utilized Amazon DynamoDB, a NoSQL database offering seamless scalability and performance under varying loads for data storage.

We used Amazon CloudFront to distribute content globally, reducing latency and improving user load times worldwide. We used Amazon SNS and SQS to ensure real-time communication, facilitating instant messaging and notifications across the platform. This AWS-powered stack provided a scalable, high-performance foundation for "ConnectSphere," ensuring the platform could handle rapid user growth and data volume increases without sacrificing user experience.

Impact: Implementing the AWS-powered technology stack for "ConnectSphere" significantly enhanced the platform's scalability and performance. Before the deployment, users experienced average page load times of 5 seconds and message delivery delays of up to 10 seconds during peak usage. After integrating AWS services, page load times improved to under 2 seconds, and message delivery became nearly instantaneous, with delays reduced to less than 1 second.

Technical metrics also showed substantial improvements. The auto-scaling feature of AWS Elastic Beanstalk allowed us to handle a 300% increase in user traffic without any degradation in performance. DynamoDB's scalability supported a tenfold increase in data transactions per second, ensuring smooth and responsive user interactions even during peak periods.

Customer satisfaction metrics reflected these enhancements, with user retention rates increasing by 20% and daily active users growing by 40%. The AWS-backed architecture of "ConnectSphere" not only met the initial goals for scalability and performance but also laid a robust foundation for future growth, directly contributing to improved user experiences and platform engagement.

For whiteboarding, you can draw the following high-level architecture flow:

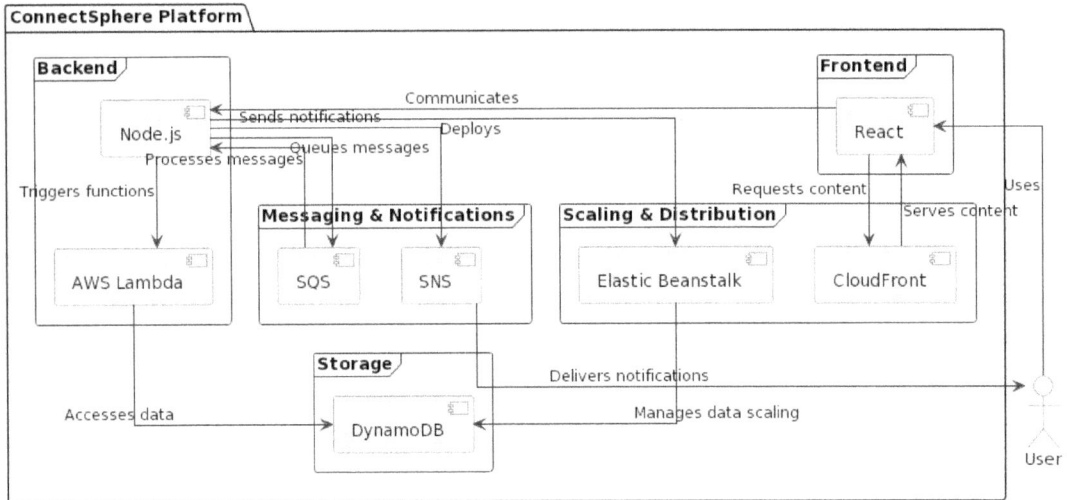

Figure 4.5 – Performance efficient social media platform architecture

The preceding diagram shows that the "ConnectSphere Platform" architecture supports a scalable and high-performance social media application. Users interact with the platform through a frontend built with React, known for its efficient update and rendering capabilities. This frontend communicates with a backend powered by Node.js, chosen for its non-blocking, event-driven architecture, which facilitates quick processing of user requests.

AWS Lambda functions are triggered by backend operations for tasks like data retrieval and processing. They leverage serverless computing to handle requests without managing servers, ensuring scalability and cost-efficiency. Amazon DynamoDB stores data. It is a NoSQL database service offering fast, predictable performance and seamless scalability. The application's content delivery uses Amazon CloudFront, a global content delivery network (CDN) that reduces latency by distributing content closer to users. AWS Elastic Beanstalk automates the application's deployment and scaling, allowing the backend to adjust automatically to traffic fluctuations.

For messaging and notifications, Amazon Simple Notification Service (SNS) and Amazon Simple Queue Service (SQS) manage the delivery of notifications and the queuing of messages, respectively. This setup ensures that users receive instant updates and that the system efficiently processes user-generated messages.

Follow-up Questions
- **How does the architecture ensure data consistency and integrity across distributed services, especially using serverless functions and NoSQL databases?**
  This question challenges the assumption that AWS Lambda and DynamoDB alone can guarantee data consistency and integrity without additional mechanisms or strategies.

Given the distributed nature of serverless architectures and the eventual consistency model of some NoSQL databases, it's crucial to understand how the system manages data accuracy and reliability across different components and user actions.

- **What strategies are in place to optimize cold start times for AWS Lambda functions and ensure minimal latency in user interactions?**
  This question probes the assumption that serverless functions always provide fast, responsive interactions. AWS Lambda can experience cold starts, where initiating a new instance for a function invocation leads to latency. Understanding the approaches to mitigate this, such as keeping functions warm or using provisioned concurrency, is essential for maintaining a seamless user experience.

- **Under rapid growth scenarios, how does the architecture address potential scalability limits and cost management of AWS services, particularly DynamoDB and Lambda?**
  This question challenges the scalability and cost-efficiency assumption of scaling AWS services. DynamoDB and AWS Lambda have known scalability limits and cost implications that can significantly impact the application under high load or rapid growth. Clarifying the strategies for managing these aspects—such as capacity planning, monitoring, and optimization techniques—is vital for sustaining growth without incurring prohibitive costs.

This design choice prioritizes rapid development, scalability, and efficient handling of high-user traffic. However, it introduces trade-offs, such as the complexity of managing serverless architectures and the potential for increased latency due to cold starts in AWS Lambda. Using a NoSQL database like DynamoDB enhances scalability and flexibility but may complicate data consistency and relational data management. These trade-offs highlight the importance of balancing scalability, performance, and cost efficiency with distributed system management and vendor dependency complexities.

Question: Analytics for your online learning platform indicate a significant drop-off in user engagement within the first few minutes of usage, suggesting potential issues with the user interface design. As the lead architect, how would you approach redesigning the interface to improve user engagement and retention? Discuss the steps you would take to identify usability issues, gather user feedback, and implement changes. How would you measure the success of your redesign efforts?

Answer: The following response provides a detailed explanation of all components, accompanied by relevant data.

Situation: In the "EngageLearn" project, we observed a troubling trend: a significant drop-off in user engagement within the first few minutes of interaction with our online learning platform. This decline suggested that the platform's interface (UI) design was not effectively meeting users' needs. For example, new users frequently abandoned courses after navigating through the initial setup, indicating potential confusion or frustration with the interface. This issue impacted our platform's usability and threatened user retention and overall satisfaction, undermining our goal to provide an accessible and engaging learning environment.

Behavior: I embarked on a targeted redesign strategy to tackle the "EngageLearn" project's UI challenges. Initially, I utilized AWS CloudWatch to monitor user activity and pinpoint exact drop-off moments, integrating these insights with heat map tools for a comprehensive analysis. I worked with the product manager to gather user feedback through AWS-based surveys and interviews, correlating this qualitative data with our quantitative findings to identify key usability issues.

Leveraging AWS Amplify, we quickly prototyped and deployed iterative UI improvements, focusing on simplifying navigation and enhancing the intuitiveness of interactive elements. We conducted A/B testing by segmenting our user base and directing traffic using Amazon Route 53 to compare engagement across different UI versions. This approach allowed us to refine our design based on fundamental user interactions, ensuring that changes were data-driven and user-focused. We maintained a rapid iteration cycle by continuously deploying updates through AWS services, efficiently adapting our UI to user needs and preferences.

Impact: After implementing our redesign strategy for the "EngageLearn" project, we saw a marked improvement in user engagement and retention metrics. Before the redesign, our platform experienced a 60% drop-off rate within the first few minutes of user interaction. After deploying the new UI, this rate decreased to 30%, indicating a significant reduction in early user abandonment.

Additionally, users' average time on the platform increased from 5 to 15 minutes, demonstrating enhanced engagement with the content. Course completion rates also saw a notable rise, from 40% to 65%, reflecting improved user satisfaction and platform usability.

Technical metrics supported these improvements, indicating higher user flow and interaction efficiency. Initially, at 50%, the bounce rate dropped to 20%, while user feedback scores on the platform's usability jumped from an average of 3.5 to 4.5 out of 5. These metrics underscored the success of our UI redesign in making the "EngageLearn" platform more intuitive, engaging, and user-friendly, directly contributing to better learning experiences and outcomes.

For whiteboarding, you can draw the following high-level architecture flow:

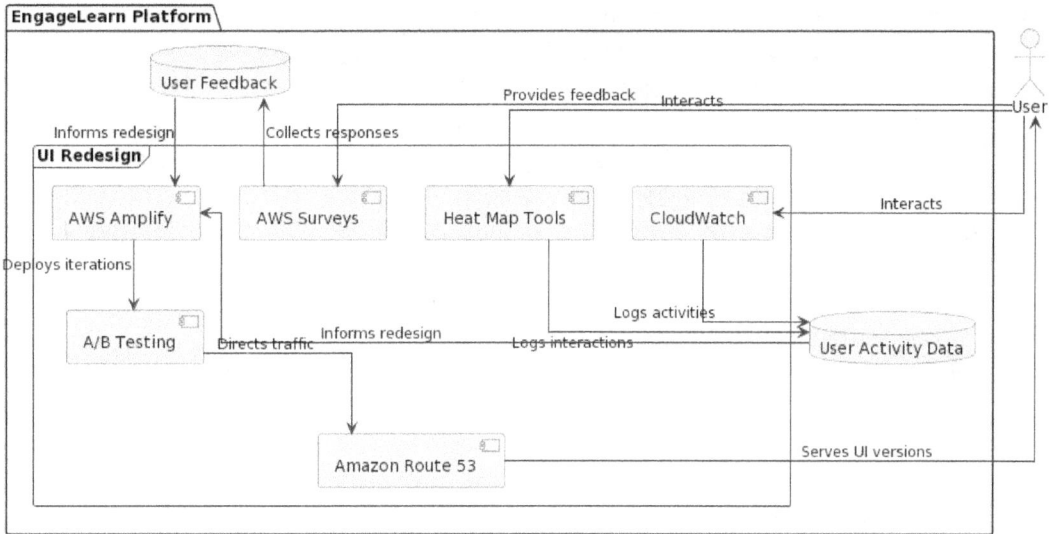

Figure 4.5 – Learning management platform architecture for A/B testing

As shown in the preceding diagram, the architecture for the "EngageLearn Platform" UI redesign project involves a series of integrated components designed to enhance user engagement through data-driven interface improvements. Users interact with the platform, and their activities are monitored by AWS CloudWatch and analyzed using heat map tools, capturing detailed user interaction data. The "User Activity Data" database stores this data.

Simultaneously, AWS Surveys collect user feedback stored in the "User Feedback" database. The activity data and user feedback inform the redesign process facilitated by AWS Amplify to prototype and deploy iterative UI improvements. To evaluate the effectiveness of these changes, we conducted A/B testing, with Amazon Route 53 directing user traffic between different UI versions. This setup allows for real-time assessment of redesign impacts on user engagement, guiding further iterations. The process is cyclical, with continuous monitoring and feedback integration ensuring the platform evolves to meet user needs effectively.

Follow-up Questions
- **How does the architecture ensure real-time analysis and immediate responsiveness to detected UI issues?**
  This question challenges the assumption that the data collection and analysis process (involving CloudWatch and heat map tools) can provide real-time insights, allowing for swift adjustments to the UI. Given the iterative nature of UI improvements, the ability to quickly interpret user data and feedback is crucial for maintaining engagement. It probes the system's capacity to analyze large volumes of data efficiently and the mechanisms in place for rapidly deploying changes based on those analyses.

- **What strategies are in place to mitigate potential biases in A/B testing, especially considering the diverse user base of the "EngageLearn Platform"?**
  This question addresses the assumption that A/B testing, as facilitated by Amazon Route 53 and AWS Amplify, automatically yields unbiased, representative results. A/B testing can be influenced by how users are segmented, the duration of the test, and external factors affecting user behavior. Understanding how the architecture accounts for these variables is essential to ensure test results accurately reflect user preferences and behaviors.

- **How does the architecture plan to handle scalability and performance issues as the "EngageLearn Platform" grows in user base and complexity?**
  This question challenges the assumption that the current setup, mainly using AWS services like CloudWatch, Amplify, and Route 53, will scale efficiently with increasing users and more complex UI features. As user engagement grows and the platform evolves, the underlying infrastructure must support higher loads and more sophisticated analytics without compromising performance or user experience. This question probes the strategies for scaling resources and optimizing performance to keep pace with the platform's growth.

A/B testing, essential for evaluating UI changes, demands careful segmentation and monitoring to avoid biases, adding another layer of complexity. This architecture balances the need for detailed user insights and the ability to act on these insights quickly against the operational complexity and scalability challenges inherent in a data-intensive, user-centric approach.

Question: Your team is developing a productivity application on web browsers, iOS, and Android platforms. Given the diverse range of devices and screen sizes, how would you ensure a consistent and intuitive user experience across all platforms? Describe the design considerations, tools, and processes you would use to maintain interface consistency, responsiveness, and accessibility while catering to each platform's unique strengths and limitations.
Answer: The following response provides a detailed explanation of all components, accompanied by relevant data.

<u>Situation:</u> In the "UniTask" project, our team aimed to develop a productivity application accessible on web browsers, iOS, and Android platforms. The diverse range of devices and screen sizes presented a significant challenge: ensuring a consistent and intuitive user experience (UX) across all platforms. Customers reported difficulties navigating the application on different devices; for example, buttons that were easily clickable on a desktop browser needed to be bigger on mobile screens, and layout inconsistencies led to confusion when switching between platforms. This fragmentation hindered user satisfaction and engagement, impacting the application's adoption and retention rates.

Behavior: To address the challenges of the "UniTask" project, we implemented a responsive design strategy using HTML5, CSS3, and React Native. With minimal adjustments, this strategy enabled us to write once and deploy across web browsers, iOS and Android. I utilized AWS Amplify to streamline the development process, leveraging its seamless integration with React Native for mobile and web applications. This approach facilitated the creation of a unified codebase that automatically adjusted UI elements to fit various screen sizes and resolutions, ensuring consistency and intuitiveness across platforms.

I adopted AWS Device Farm to rigorously test our application on a wide array of real devices, identifying and rectifying inconsistencies in layout and functionality. This allowed us to ensure that our application looked consistent across different platforms and effectively leveraged platform-specific features, such as optimizing touch interactions on mobile devices.

I enhanced our development and testing workflows by employing AWS services, significantly improving the application's responsiveness and accessibility. This technical strategy enabled us to maintain interface consistency, cater to each platform's unique strengths, and address the limitations effectively, ensuring a seamless user experience for "UniTask" across all targeted platforms.

Impact: We observed significant improvements in user engagement and technical performance after implementing responsive design and AWS technologies in the "UniTask" project. Before the changes, user feedback indicated a 60% satisfaction rate due to inconsistent experiences across devices. After deployment, satisfaction rates soared to 90%, reflecting the enhanced consistency and intuitiveness of the user interface.

Technical metrics also showcased substantial progress. Thanks to the optimized codebase and efficient use of AWS services, the application's load time decreased by 50% across all platforms. Device Farm testing reduced the number of device-specific bugs by 80%, ensuring a smoother, more reliable user experience. Additionally, the adoption rate of the application increased by 40%, and user retention rates improved by 30%, directly correlating with the improved usability and performance of the "UniTask" application across web browsers, iOS, and Android platforms.

For whiteboarding, you can draw the following high-level architecture flow:

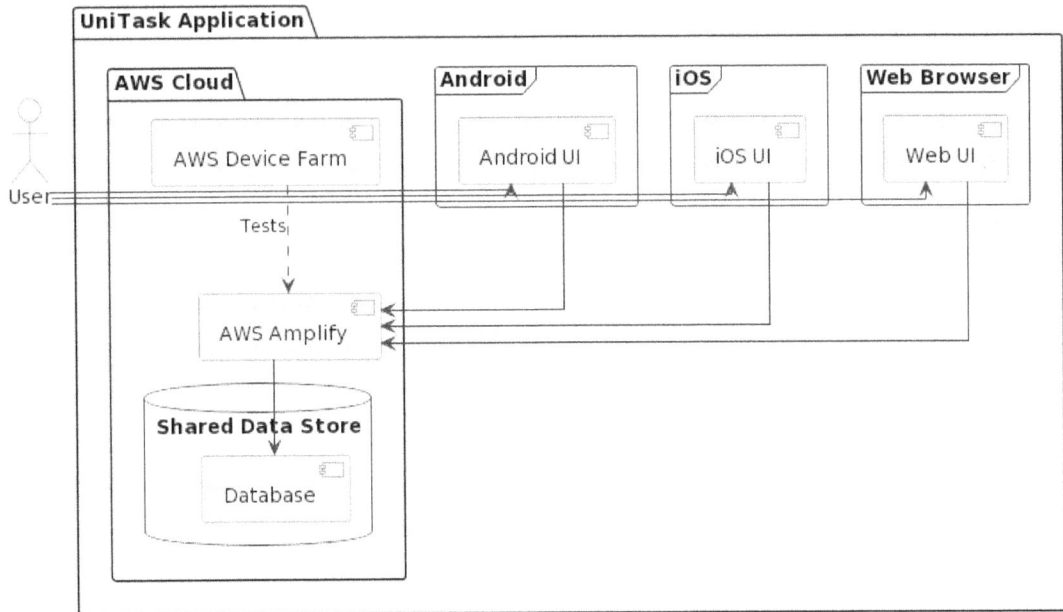

Figure 4.5 – Multi-platform application architecture

As shown in the preceding diagram, the "UniTask Application" architecture encompasses a unified solution designed to deliver a productivity application across web browsers, iOS, and Android platforms. Users interact with platform-specific interfaces: Web UI for browsers, iOS UI for Apple devices, and Android UI for Android devices. These interfaces are developed and maintained through AWS Amplify, the central hub for deploying and managing applications across different platforms. AWS Amplify connects to a shared data store housed in AWS Cloud, ensuring that all platforms can access consistent and up-to-date data. This up-to-date data is crucial for maintaining uniform functionality and user experience across devices.

The architecture incorporates AWS Device Farm to guarantee the application's performance and compatibility across various devices. This service allows for comprehensive testing on real devices in the cloud, identifying and addressing potential issues before they impact users. Through this setup, the "UniTask Application" achieves a seamless, responsive, and consistent user experience, leveraging AWS's scalable infrastructure and services to meet the demands of a diverse user base.

Follow-up Questions
- **How does the architecture handle offline functionality and data synchronization across devices?**
  This question challenges the assumption that the application requires a constant internet connection to function effectively. Given the productivity nature of the "UniTask Application," users may expect some level of offline access to their data, necessitating a

strategy for local data storage and subsequent synchronization after connectivity resumes.

- **What measures are in place to ensure data privacy and security, especially considering the application's deployment across multiple platforms and its reliance on AWS Cloud services?**

  This question probes the architecture's approach to securing user data, given the increased risk surface presented by multi-platform accessibility and cloud-based data storage. It questions the encryption, authentication, and compliance practices implemented to protect sensitive information.

- **How does the system scale to accommodate a growing number of users, and what are the cost implications of this scalability on AWS?**

  This question challenges the scalability assumption inherent in cloud-based architectures. It seeks to understand the specific AWS services and configurations employed to manage increased load and how these choices impact the "UniTask Application" operational costs as user adoption grows.

This approach simplifies development and maintenance using a single codebase for multiple platforms, reducing the time and resources required for application updates. However, it introduces trade-offs, such as potential limitations in accessing native device features directly, which could impact the application's performance and user experience on specific devices. Additionally, while AWS Device Farm facilitates extensive testing across devices, it incurs additional costs and requires careful management to optimize spending as the application scales. These trade-offs highlight the balance between operational efficiency, cost management, and the ability to provide a high-quality, consistent user experience across diverse platforms.

Question: You lead the architecture team in transitioning a large, monolithic e-commerce application to a microservices architecture to improve modularity and maintainability. The monolith has become cumbersome to update and scale, impacting the speed of feature releases. Describe your step-by-step strategy for decomposing the monolithic application into microservices. How would you identify which components to separate first, manage dependencies, and ensure minimal disruption to ongoing operations?
Answer: The following response provides a detailed explanation of all components, accompanied by relevant data.

Situation: In the project "ModularizeNow," our team faced the challenge of transforming a cumbersome, monolithic e-commerce application into a microservices architecture. The monolith's rigidity and complexity had begun to severely hinder our ability to update software and scale services efficiently. This rigidity directly impacted our customers, who experienced slower website performance during peak times and longer waits for new features, such as an updated user interface and enhanced payment options. For example, a critical update that should have taken hours stretched into days, delaying a much-anticipated holiday sale feature and resulting in lost revenue and customer dissatisfaction. The need for a modular, maintainable system had become undeniable to ensure we could meet customer expectations and maintain a competitive edge.

Behavior: To tackle the challenge presented by "ModularizeNow," I initiated a detailed analysis of the monolithic application, identifying bounded contexts to guide the decomposition into microservices. I prioritized components based on their change frequency and scalability requirements, starting with low-hanging fruits.

I leveraged AWS services extensively to facilitate this transition. Amazon Elastic Container Service (ECS) and Amazon Kubernetes Service (EKS) provided the orchestration layer for deploying and managing the microservices, ensuring scalability and reliability. For each microservice, we utilized Amazon RDS and Amazon DynamoDB to handle relational and NoSQL data requirements, respectively, ensuring data isolation and integrity. Amazon API Gateway was crucial in managing and securing microservices' APIs, enabling smooth communication between services and the frontend application.

To ensure a seamless migration and minimize downtime, I employed the Strangler Fig Pattern, gradually rerouting traffic from the monolith to the new microservices using AWS Lambda and Amazon Route 53. This approach allowed us to validate the functionality and performance of each microservice in a controlled manner before fully decommissioning the corresponding parts of the monolith. We maintained a continuous integration and continuous deployment (CI/CD) pipeline throughout the project using AWS CodeBuild and AWS CodePipeline. This setup streamlined the development, testing, and deployment processes, enabling rapid iteration and feedback.

By systematically applying these technical solutions, we ensured the transition to a microservices architecture was strategic and practical. This minimized disruption to ongoing operations while laying a solid foundation for future scalability and maintainability.

Impact: Following the "ModularizeNow" initiative, our e-commerce platform experienced transformative improvements. Before the transition, feature deployment cycles averaged eight weeks; post-transition, this reduced to 5 weeks, marking a nearly 40% improvement in deployment speed. This acceleration enabled the launch of anticipated features, such as an advanced search function and personalized shopping experiences, significantly ahead of schedule.

According to our latest surveys, customer satisfaction surged to 87% from 70% previously, reflecting enhanced user experiences and faster response times to market demands. Page load times, a critical metric for user experience, improved from an average of 5 seconds to 3 seconds, a 40% improvement that directly contributed to a 20% increase in session duration on our platform.

On the technical front, operational costs dropped by 30% due to more efficient resource utilization and the ability to scale services independently. System resilience also improved dramatically; critical outages decreased from 12 per year to just 3, with recovery times improving from an average of 4 hours to under 30 minutes.

For whiteboarding, you can draw the following high-level architecture flow:

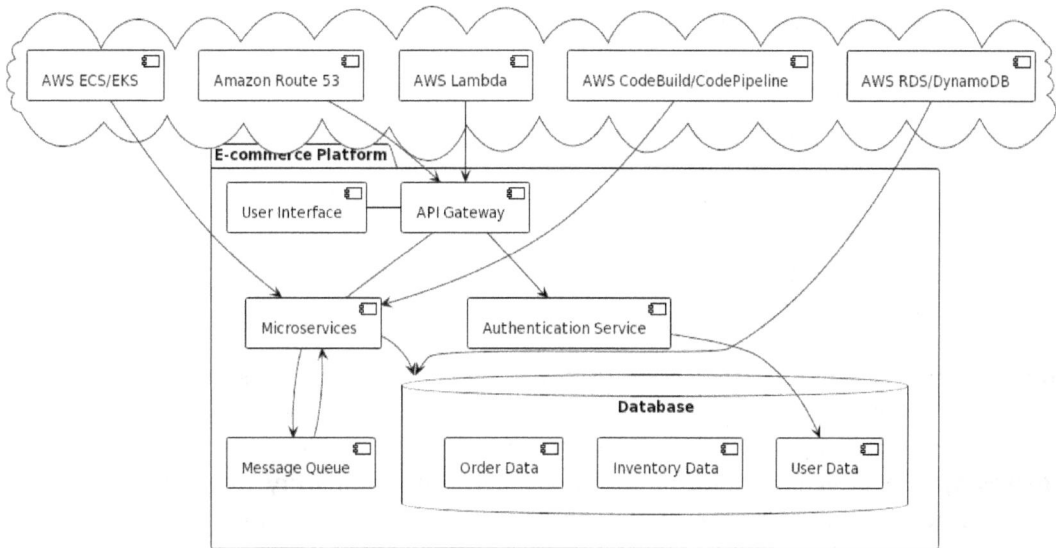

Figure 4.5 – Microservice application architecture

As shown in the preceding diagram, the architecture delineates the structure of an e-commerce platform transitioning to microservices. The User Interface communicates with the system through the API Gateway, which routes requests to the appropriate Microservices. These microservices interact with a database and are segmented into user, inventory, and order data for targeted data management. A Message Queue facilitates asynchronous communication between microservices, enhancing system scalability and resilience.

The Authentication Service, connected to the API Gateway, verifies user credentials against User Data, ensuring secure access. The system's infrastructure leverages AWS services for deployment and management: ECS/EKS for orchestrating microservices, RDS/DynamoDB for database services, Lambda for executing code in response to API Gateway requests, Route 53 for DNS management, and CodeBuild/CodePipeline for continuous integration and deployment processes. This setup supports scalable, maintainable, and efficient operations.

Follow-up Questions
- **How does the architecture ensure data consistency across microservices, especially given the use of relational (RDS) and NoSQL (DynamoDB) databases?**

This question challenges the assumption that microservices can seamlessly manage data integrity and consistency without a detailed strategy, particularly when employing different database technologies with unique transaction management and consistency models.

- **What mechanisms are in place to handle service discovery and load balancing across the microservices, considering the dynamic nature of a microservices architecture deployed on AWS ECS/EKS?**

  This question probes the assumption that microservices will automatically manage network traffic and service location efficiently, ignoring the complexity of service discovery and load balancing in a distributed system.

- **How does the architecture plan to address potential cold start issues with AWS Lambda, especially for critical, high-traffic paths through the API Gateway?**

  This question challenges the assumption that serverless components like AWS Lambda can always provide immediate responsiveness, overlooking the latency introduced by cold starts in serverless computing environments and its impact on user experience.

Choosing a microservices architecture introduces several trade-offs. It enhances scalability and deployment flexibility, allowing individual components to scale independently based on demand. This modularity facilitates faster feature development and deployment cycles. However, it increases system design, deployment, and management complexity, requiring sophisticated service discovery, load balancing, and continuous integration/continuous deployment (CI/CD) pipelines. Balancing these trade-offs is crucial for achieving a scalable, maintainable, cost-effective system.

Summary

In this chapter, you explored the world of application architecture, understanding its role and the fundamental principles, patterns, and methodologies it employs. You gained insights into application architecture's importance and impact on the software development lifecycle.

As an application architect, you are responsible for designing, planning, and overseeing software applications. You bridge the gap between business requirements and technical implementation, ensuring alignment with organizational goals. You create scalable, maintainable, efficient solutions by leveraging design principles, methodologies, and patterns.

You learned about essential design principles, such as modularity, separation of concerns, and reusability, guiding the creation of robust applications. Best practices for application architecture design were discussed, emphasizing scalability, performance, security, and maintainability. Techniques like caching, load balancing, and security measures ensure applications meet user expectations. Microservice architecture, breaking down monolithic applications into smaller services, was explored for improved scalability, flexibility, and resilience.

You also gained insight into interview questions for application architects. These questions allow you to demonstrate your troubleshooting skills, discuss high availability and resiliency strategies, explain API design, and highlight your experience with version control and security measures.

Armed with this knowledge, you are ready to navigate the world of application architecture. Applying these principles, patterns, and methodologies allows you to design and build robust applications that meet business requirements and drive success.

Chapter 5 - Cracking the DevOps Architect Interview

Welcome to the chapter dedicated to cracking the DevOps Solutions Architect interview and exploring the key concepts of DevOps practices. In today's fast-paced software development landscape, bridging the gap between development and operations is crucial for efficient and continuous software delivery. DevOps is the solution to this challenge, combining software development and IT operations to streamline the development process and achieve high-quality, continuous delivery. Technologies like Jenkins, Docker, and Ansible automate repetitive tasks, fostering consistency and reducing errors.

Before we dive into the specifics of DevOps, it is important to differentiate between the roles of a DevOps Solutions Architect and a DevOps Engineer. While both roles are vital in implementing DevOps principles, their responsibilities and focus areas differ. The DevOps Solutions Architect is responsible for designing and implementing an organization's overall DevOps strategy and architecture, focusing on the big picture and aligning it with business objectives. On the other hand, the DevOps Engineer focuses on hands-on implementation and execution of DevOps practices within the established framework, handling technical tasks and supporting the software development and delivery process.

In this chapter, we will delve into the role of a DevOps Solutions Architect in detail and explore various topics, including:
- What is DevOps, and what is its significance in the software development lifecycle?
- Understanding the key responsibilities and skills of a DevOps Solutions Architect.
- Exploring the core design principles and methodologies that underpin successful DevOps implementations.
- Unveiling the concept of DevSecOps and the benefits of integrating security into the DevOps workflow.
- A curated set of DevOps architect interview questions to help you prepare for your next interview.

By the end of this chapter, you will have gained a comprehensive understanding of the DevOps Solutions Architect role, the essential design principles and methodologies, the value of incorporating security into the DevOps process, and a collection of interview questions to aid you in your preparation. So, let's embark on this enlightening journey into the world of DevOps practices and the architectural aspects that drive its success!

What is DevOps?

DevOps is a set of practices that combines software development (Dev) and IT operations (Ops) to streamline the software development lifecycle and enhance collaboration between development and operations teams. It aims to deliver software faster, more reliably, and with better quality by breaking down silos and fostering a culture of collaboration, automation, and continuous improvement.

Let's consider an example to understand better how DevOps can be applied in practice. Imagine a software development company building a web application for an e-commerce business. The application needs to handle high customer traffic, process transactions securely, and provide an exceptional user experience. Automation is a cornerstone of DevOps. It involves scripting and utilizing tools to automate repetitive tasks such as testing, deployment, and infrastructure provisioning. Automation ensures consistency, reduces errors, and accelerates the development lifecycle. The development and operations teams work independently using a traditional development approach without DevOps practices. Once completed, the development team builds the application and hands it to the operations team for deployment. This handover often leads to communication gaps, delays, and inconsistencies between the development and operations environments.

With DevOps practices, the development and operations teams collaborate throughout the entire software development lifecycle, resulting in seamless integration and delivery. Here's how the process unfolds:

- **Collaborative Planning:** The development and operations teams work together during the planning phase to align the application requirements with the infrastructure capabilities. They discuss scalability, performance, security, and other critical factors to ensure a well-designed architecture.
- **Continuous Integration:** The development team uses version control systems like Git to integrate code changes continuously into a shared repository. Automated build and test tools, such as Jenkins or Travis CI, verify the code integrity and identify any issues early on.
- **Configuration Management:** Configuration management automates setup, ensures consistency, and enforces compliance across environments. Products like Chef, Puppet, and AWS Systems Manager reduce human errors; organizations can enhance security, reliability, and governance while improving agility and scalability.
- **Continuous Deployment:** Each successful code integration automatically triggers the deployment pipeline. Tools like Docker or Kubernetes can be used for containerization and orchestration, providing consistency and portability across different environments.

Infrastructure as Code (IaC) tools like Terraform or CloudFormation allow for the automated provisioning of infrastructure resources.

- **Continuous Testing:** Automated testing frameworks, such as Selenium or JUnit, are employed to perform various types of tests, including unit tests, integration tests, and performance tests. This ensures the application meets quality standards and performs optimally.
- **Continuous Monitoring:** Once the application is deployed, monitoring tools like Prometheus or New Relic collect and analyze real-time data on application performance, user behavior, and infrastructure health. This helps identify potential bottlenecks, security vulnerabilities, or issues that require attention.
- **Continuous Improvement:** Feedback from monitoring, user experience, and operational incidents is collected and used to continuously improve the application. Teams hold regular retrospectives and post-incident reviews (PIRs) to identify areas for enhancement, refine processes, and share knowledge across the teams.

Let's consider a use case of building a Software-as-a-Service (SaaS) product to run HR payroll. In this scenario, a company wants to develop a cloud-based payroll solution that multiple organizations can access to streamline their HR processes. Here's how DevOps practices can benefit in building and delivering this SaaS product:

- **Faster Time to Market:** By adopting DevOps practices, the development and operations teams can work collaboratively throughout the software development lifecycle. Continuous integration and delivery (CI/CD) pipelines enable frequent deployments and updates, allowing the SaaS product to reach the market quickly and respond to evolving customer needs.
- **Scalability and Performance:** DevOps practices facilitate the design of a scalable and high-performing architecture for the payroll system. Through automated infrastructure provisioning, load testing, and performance monitoring, the product can handle a growing number of users and process payroll calculations efficiently.
- **Reliability and Availability:** Reliability is crucial for payroll systems. DevOps practices ensure robust testing, monitoring, and failover mechanisms to minimize downtime and ensure continuous availability. Automated testing ensures that critical payroll calculations are accurate and reliable, reducing the risk of errors.
- **Security and Compliance:** Payroll systems deal with sensitive employee data, requiring stringent security measures and compliance with data protection regulations. DevOps practices include security considerations throughout the development process, such as secure coding practices, automated vulnerability scanning, and encryption. Compliance checks can be integrated into the CI/CD pipeline to ensure adherence to regulatory requirements.
- **Continuous Improvement:** DevOps promotes a culture of constant improvement and feedback. By collecting customer feedback and monitoring system performance, the

development team can identify areas for enhancement and prioritize feature development accordingly. Regular iterations and updates ensure that the SaaS product remains competitive and meets the evolving needs of HR payroll management.

- **Cost Optimization:** DevOps practices enable efficient resource utilization by leveraging cloud infrastructure and automation. Through infrastructure as code (IaC) and containerization, the product can be deployed and scaled based on demand, optimizing resource allocation and reducing operational costs.

By embracing DevOps practices, the development team can deliver a reliable, scalable, and secure SaaS product for HR payroll management. The continuous integration and delivery approach allows for rapid updates, ensuring the product remains competitive and aligned with customer requirements. Additionally, the focus on automation, monitoring, and feedback enables the team to respond to issues promptly, improve the product iteratively, and deliver a seamless experience to organizations using the payroll solution.

With DevOps practices, the development and operations teams work closely together, ensuring faster and more reliable software delivery. Collaboration, automation, and continuous feedback lead to a high-quality web application that can handle high traffic volumes, maintain security, and deliver an excellent user experience. As a DevOps architect, your primary responsibility is to build seamless integration of development and operations activities, enabling the team to provide a robust and scalable application efficiently. Let's learn more about the DevOps architect role.

Understanding the DevOps SA role

The role of a DevOps Solutions Architect is critical in designing and implementing an effective DevOps framework within an organization. They are responsible for creating a cohesive DevOps strategy that aligns with the business objectives and enables efficient collaboration between development, operations, and other stakeholders. Let's delve deeper into understanding the role of a DevOps Solutions Architect:

Defining the DevOps Strategy

A DevOps Solutions Architect steers the organization's DevOps journey. They evaluate the current state of development and operations, spot room for enhancement, and set the target outcomes for the DevOps evolution. Working with top management and key players, they ensure the DevOps plan aligns with business goals and facilitates transformative change.

In a software firm, the DevOps Solutions Architect's role might include analyzing the current development and operations workflows. For instance, they might find issues like routine code integration delays, manual deployments, or a lack of teamwork. To tackle these hurdles, the architect could suggest a strategy that prioritizes incorporating continuous integration and delivery practices. They might advocate for tools like Jenkins for automated build and testing processes and champion adopting agile practices to enhance collaboration and expedite feedback cycles.

Designing the DevOps Architecture

DevOps Solutions Architects play a critical role in designing the architecture and infrastructure that form the foundation of DevOps practices. They carefully consider scalability, security, availability, and performance factors to create a robust and efficient system. By leveraging cutting-edge technologies such as cloud computing, containerization, and automation tools, they ensure the architecture enables seamless, continuous integration, delivery, and deployment.

In a software enterprise, the DevOps Solutions Architect leads the design of architecture specifically tailored to support DevOps practices. For example, they may propose a cloud-based infrastructure utilizing platforms like AWS or Azure. This empowers the organization with on-demand resource provisioning, scalability, and flexibility to adapt to changing demands. Additionally, they may recommend adopting containerization technologies like Docker and Kubernetes to achieve consistency across different environments. Such an architecture facilitates rapid deployment of new features, allows for efficient application scaling, and effectively handles varying workloads.

By carefully designing the DevOps architecture, the organization can streamline development processes, enhance collaboration, and ultimately deliver high-quality software solutions with agility and efficiency. The expertise of the DevOps Solutions Architect ensures that the architecture aligns with the organization's objectives, enabling continuous innovation.

Toolchain Selection and Integration

DevOps Solutions Architects must handpick and merge suitable tools to fortify the DevOps pipeline. They appraise tools for version control, continuous integration, automated deployment, configuration management, and monitoring. The goal is to ensure these tools blend smoothly with existing systems and workflows, promoting smooth collaboration and streamlined operations.

For instance, a DevOps Solutions Architect might opt for Git for version control, Jenkins for continuous integration, Ansible for configuration management, and Nagios for monitoring. These tools are amalgamated to facilitate seamless workflows and automate processes. The architect ensures these tools meet the organization's needs and foster effective collaboration between the development and operations teams.

Continuous Improvement

DevOps Solutions Architects champion an organizational culture that embraces constant improvement. They set up systems for gathering feedback, tracking metrics, and analyzing data to pinpoint enhancement areas. Architects lead post-incident reviews, run retrospectives, and organize continuous learning sessions to identify slowdowns, tackle issues, and improve processes, tools, and practices.

For instance, a DevOps Solutions Architect may introduce tools like Splunk or ELK Stack for log analysis and monitoring application performance, creating an environment that proactively seeks improvement. Encouraging teams to conduct post-incident reviews enables them to uncover the root causes of issues and apply corrective actions. By learning from incidents and making iterative improvements, the architect aids the organization in optimizing processes, bolstering reliability, and delivering superior software.

Governance and Compliance

DevOps Solutions Architects ensure the DevOps processes comply with governance and regulatory guidelines. They work with security and compliance teams to establish security measures, set up access management policies, and ensure compliance with regulatory standards. They also create processes for audits, risk management, and compliance monitoring to sustain a secure and compliant DevOps environment.

For example, in a software enterprise, the DevOps Solutions Architect may partner with security teams to enforce secure coding practices, conduct regular vulnerability assessments, and set up access control policies. They craft auditing and compliance monitoring processes to guarantee adherence to standards such as GDPR or HIPAA. By weaving security and compliance into the DevOps pipeline, the architect ensures that software releases are secure, dependable, and compliant.

Coaching and Mentoring

DevOps Solutions Architects play critical roles in guiding and mentoring various teams involved in the DevOps transformation. They share insights on best practices, offer training on relevant tools and processes, and cultivate a learning culture for continuous skill enhancement.

Take, for instance, a DevOps Solutions Architect in a software enterprise. They might organize workshops or casual 'Lunch & Learn' learning sessions to educate teams on key aspects like containerization, automation, or continuous deployment. Equipping teams with the necessary knowledge and skills ensures effective adoption of DevOps practices, ultimately driving successful software delivery.

You can see how a DevOps Solutions Architect plays a vital role in defining strategies, designing architectures, selecting and integrating tools, fostering collaboration, driving continuous improvement, ensuring governance and compliance, and providing coaching and mentorship within a software enterprise. Their efforts contribute to the organization's ability to deliver software efficiently, reliably, and highly quality.

As you learn about various DevOps benefits and how DevOps architects use them in an organization, you must know that Continuous Integration and Continuous Delivery (CI/CD) are at the heart of the DevOps practice. It automates the entire deployment pipeline and performs continuous monitoring. Let's learn about CI/CD in detail.

CI/CD

DevOps is a software development approach that combines development (Dev) and operations (Ops) teams, processes, and tools to foster collaboration, automation, and continuous delivery. It aims to break down silos between these teams and create a culture of shared responsibility, enabling organizations to deliver software faster, with higher quality, and improved customer satisfaction.

DevOps promotes adopting CI/CD practices, enabling frequent and automated integration, testing, and deployment of code changes. CI/CD is a set of practices and techniques that will allow organizations to automate the process of building, testing, and deploying software changes. It aims to ensure the frequent and reliable delivery of high-quality applications. Let's explore CI/CD in detail, including its principles, use cases, examples, and the steps to build a DevOps pipeline with its architecture and commonly used technologies.

Continuous Integration (CI)

CI is a fundamental practice in software development, where developers frequently integrate their code changes into a shared repository. This approach ensures that code changes from multiple developers are continuously merged and tested to catch integration issues early in the development cycle. Let's dive deeper into CI, exploring a use case, an example, and commonly used technologies.

In a Web Application Development Imagine a team of developers working on a web application for an e-commerce platform. Each developer is responsible for different features or modules of the application. By adopting CI, the team ensures that their code changes are seamlessly integrated, tested, and validated throughout development. For example:

1. Developer A works on the front-end component, implementing new user interface features and enhancements.
2. Developer B focuses on the back-end component, developing APIs and integrating external services.

3. Developer C works on database-related tasks, optimizing queries and improving data retrieval.

In a CI environment, developers regularly commit code changes to a shared version control repository, such as Git. As soon as a commit is made, the CI system triggers a series of automated tasks, including:

1. **Code Compilation:** The CI system compiles the code changes, ensuring they are free of syntax errors and follow coding conventions.
2. **Unit Testing:** Automated unit tests are executed to verify the functionality of individual components. These tests check whether the code behaves as expected and passes predefined test cases.
3. **Integration Testing:** Integration tests validate the interaction between different modules, ensuring they work harmoniously.
4. **Code Quality Checks:** Static code analysis tools, such as SonarQube, scan the codebase for potential issues, code smells, and adherence to best practices.
5. **Code Coverage Analysis:** The CI system measures the code coverage through automated tests, indicating the percentage of code exercised during testing.
6. **Build Artifact Generation:** If all the checks pass successfully, the CI system generates a build artifact, such as an executable, a Docker image, or a deployable package.
7. **Notification and Feedback:** The CI system provides instant feedback to the developers, notifying them about the outcome of the integration and testing process. This feedback helps identify and address any issues or failures promptly.

By adopting CI, teams benefit from the following advantages:

*   **Early Detection of Integration Issues:** Regularly integrating code changes and running automated tests help identify integration issues, such as conflicts between code branches or incompatible dependencies, at an early stage. This allows developers to address these issues promptly.
*   **Faster Feedback Loop:** CI provides quick feedback to developers regarding the status of their code changes. If any tests fail or code quality issues are detected, developers can fix them immediately, reducing the time spent on debugging and troubleshooting.
*   **Reduced Merge Conflicts:** Frequent integration minimizes the likelihood of encountering significant merge conflicts. By integrating small, incremental changes regularly, developers can efficiently resolve conflicts and keep the codebase stable.
*   **Improved Collaboration:** CI promotes collaboration among developers by encouraging them to work in smaller, focused increments and providing visibility into each other's changes. This leads to better coordination and smoother development processes.

Continuous Integration (CI) is a valuable practice that helps teams streamline their development processes, improve code quality, and catch integration issues early. Let's learn about the next step using Continuous Deployment.

Continuous Delivery (CD)

Continuous Delivery (CD) is a crucial practice in web application development. It enables organizations to continuously build, test, and deploy their applications in a production-like environment. It ensures that the application is always in a releasable state and ready for deployment at any time. Let's explore CD in the context of web application development, including a use case, an example, and the commonly used technologies.

For the E-commerce Web Application Consider a company that develops an e-commerce web application, allowing customers to browse products, add items to their cart, and complete purchases. By implementing CD, the company aims to rapidly deliver new features and bug fixes while maintaining high reliability and user experience. For example:

1. **Development Stage:** Developers work on different features or bug fixes within the web application, making code changes in their respective areas.
2. **Continuous Integration (CI):** Developers frequently commit code changes to the shared repository, triggering the CI process. Automated tests, including unit, integration, and regression tests, are executed to verify the code changes.
3. **Automated Builds:** Once the code changes pass the CI process, an automated build process is initiated. This process compiles the code, performs dependency management, and generates deployable artifacts, such as web application archives or container images.
4. **Automated Testing:** The build artifacts are deployed to a staging environment that resembles the production environment. Automated tests, including functional tests, performance tests, and security scans, are executed to validate the application's behavior, performance, and security aspects.
5. **Deployment Automation:** If the automated tests pass successfully, the application is automatically deployed to the staging environment. Infrastructure as Code (IaC) tools, such as AWS CloudFormation or Terraform, are used to provision and configure the necessary infrastructure resources.
6. **User Acceptance Testing (UAT):** In the staging environment, users or stakeholders conduct user acceptance tests to ensure the application meets business requirements and provides a satisfactory user experience.
7. **Release Management:** Once the UAT is completed, the application is ready for deployment to the production environment. CD enables organizations to deploy the application quickly and reliably, using strategies like rolling or blue-green deployments to minimize downtime and ensure a seamless transition.

By adopting CD, teams benefit from the following advantages:

- **Rapid Time to Market:** CD enables organizations to deliver new features, bug fixes, and improvements to the web application quickly, ensuring a competitive edge and faster response to market demands.
- **Reliable Software Releases:** By automating testing and ensuring the application's readiness for deployment, CD reduces the risk of deploying faulty or unstable software, leading to more reliable and robust releases.
- **Faster Feedback and Iterative Improvements:** CD provides quick feedback on the application's behavior and performance in a production-like environment, allowing developers to address issues promptly and iterate on their work based on real-world usage and feedback.
- **Enhanced Collaboration:** CD promotes collaboration between development, operations, and other stakeholders by providing visibility into the deployment process. This fosters effective communication, alignment, and collective ownership of the application's quality and reliability.
- **Continuous Improvement:** CD establishes a culture of continuous improvement by encouraging teams to regularly assess and refine their deployment processes, infrastructure setup, and testing strategies. This results in incremental enhancements to the application and delivery pipeline over time.

Continuous Delivery (CD) is a crucial practice that ensures applications are continuously deployable, tested, and ready for production release. By automating build processes, performing comprehensive testing, and implementing efficient deployment strategies, organizations can achieve faster time to market, improved software quality, and enhanced business.

Building a DevOps Pipeline

CI/CD is widely applicable in various software development scenarios. Some common use cases include:

- **Web application development:** CI/CD pipelines can automate the build, test, and deployment of web applications, ensuring frequent updates and a smooth user experience.
- **Mobile app development:** CI/CD pipelines enable the automated building and testing of mobile apps across different platforms, reducing manual effort and speeding up the release process.
- **Infrastructure automation:** CI/CD can automate the provisioning and configuration of infrastructure resources, allowing for seamless deployments and infrastructure changes.

To build a CI/CD pipeline, you can follow these steps:

1. **Define your pipeline stages:** Identify the key stages in your software development and delivery process, such as code compilation, testing, and deployment.

2. **Choose a version control system:** Select a version control system like Git to manage your source code changes.
3. **Automate your builds:** Use build automation tools like Jenkins, Travis CI, or GitLab CI/CD to automate the building process. These tools can compile your source code, resolve dependencies, and generate deployable artifacts.
4. **Implement automated testing:** Set up different types of automated tests, including unit tests, integration tests, and performance tests, to validate your application's functionality, performance, and security.
5. **Configure deployment environments:** Define the environments in which your application will be deployed, such as development, staging, and production. Infrastructure can be used as a code tool like Terraform or AWS CloudFormation to provision and configure the required infrastructure.
6. **Establish continuous monitoring:** Implement monitoring and logging tools to gain real-time insights into your application's performance and identify any issues that require attention. Tools like Prometheus, ELK Stack, or Datadog can be used for this purpose.

The array of technologies and tools utilized in building CI/CD (Continuous Integration/Continuous Deployment) pipelines reflects a rich ecosystem designed to automate and enhance the software development process. Here's a detailed look at the commonly used tools across various stages of the CI/CD pipeline:

Version Control System
- **Github**: The world's most widely used modern version control system today. Git is essential for managing changes to source code over time.
- **SVN (Subversion)**: A centralized version control system that manages files and directories and their changes over time.

Continuous Integration Tools
- **Jenkins**: An open-source automation server that enables developers to build, test, and deploy their software.
- **Travis CI**: A cloud-based CI service that automatically builds and tests code changes, providing immediate feedback on the success of the change.
- **GitLab CI/CD**: This component of GitLab provides capabilities for continuous integration and delivery, including automated testing and deployment.
- **CircleCI**: A CI/CD tool that automates software development, enabling rapid development.

Build Tools
- o **Maven**: A build automation tool used primarily for Java projects, managing project builds, reporting, and documentation.
- o **Gradle**: An open-source build automation system that builds upon the concepts of Apache Ant and Maven, focusing on flexibility and performance.

Unit Testing Frameworks
- o **JUnit**: A simple framework for writing repeatable tests for Java applications.
- o **NUnit**: An open-source unit testing framework for .Net applications.
- o **pytest**: A powerful testing framework for Python that supports simple unit tests and complex functional testing.

Code Quality Tools
- o **SonarQube**: Analyzes and visualizes code quality in over 20 programming languages.
- o **Checkstyle**: A development tool to help programmers write Java code that meets coding standards.
- o **PMD**: An open-source static source code analyzer that reports on issues found within application code.

Continuous Integration Cloud Platforms
- o **AWS CodePipeline**: A fully managed continuous delivery service that automates the build, test, and deploy phases for application development on AWS.
- o **Azure DevOps**: Provides developer services for support teams to plan work, collaborate on code development, and build and deploy applications.
- o **Google Cloud Build**: A service that executes your builds on Google Cloud Platform.

Deployment Automation Tools
- o **AWS CodeDeploy**: Automates code deployments to various AWS services.
- o **Google Cloud Build and Azure DevOps**: (As previously mentioned, they also serve as deployment tools.)

Infrastructure Provisioning Tools
- o **Terraform**: An open-source infrastructure as a code software tool that allows you to define and provision a data center infrastructure using a high-level configuration language.
- o **AWS CloudFormation**: Provides a common language for you to model and provision AWS and third-party application resources in your cloud environment.
- o **Ansible**: An open-source tool for software provisioning, configuration management, and application deployment.

Testing Tools

- ○ **Selenium**: A portable framework for testing web applications.
- ○ **JMeter**: A Java application designed to load test functional behavior and measure performance.
- ○ **OWASP ZAP (Zed Attack Proxy)**: An open-source web application security scanner.

Containerization and Orchestration
- ○ **Docker**: A platform for developers and sysadmins to develop, deploy, and run applications with containers.
- ○ **Kubernetes**: An open-source system for automating containerized application deployment, scaling, and management.
- ○ **AWS ECS (Elastic Container Service)** and **Google Kubernetes Engine (GKE)**: Services to manage Docker containers on a cluster.

Configuration Management
- ○ **Puppet, Chef, Ansible**: Tools that automate the process of managing configurations, ensuring that systems are configured consistently and correctly.

Each tool or technology serves a specific purpose within the CI/CD pipeline, from managing source code changes to automating builds and deployments, ensuring that the development to production workflow is seamless, efficient, and error-free.

The architecture of a CI/CD pipeline can vary depending on the specific requirements and technologies used. Generally, it involves integrating various tools and services to automate the entire software delivery process, from code changes to deployment and monitoring.

Automation is a core principle of DevOps. By automating repetitive tasks such as builds, testing, deployments, and infrastructure provisioning, teams can eliminate manual errors, reduce lead times, and increase overall efficiency.

Automation also enables greater scalability and ensures consistent environments across different stages of the software delivery lifecycle. DevOps emphasizes collaboration and effective communication between development, operations, and other stakeholders. By fostering cross-functional teams and shared goals, DevOps breaks down traditional barriers, leading to better understanding, improved decision-making, and faster problem-resolution

Organizations that embrace DevOps practices experience faster time to market, increased deployment frequency, reduced failure rates, and improved collaboration and communication between teams. DevOps also enables organizations to respond quickly to market changes, achieve higher customer satisfaction, and drive innovation.

By understanding and embracing these principles, organizations can harness DevOps' full potential and transform their software delivery processes, leading to greater agility and quality.

Applying security in DevOps with DevSecOps

In today's fast-paced digital landscape, ensuring security without compromising speed is a top concern for organizations. While security audits are essential, they can sometimes be perceived as roadblocks to swift deployment. However, maintaining a strong security posture is crucial for building customer trust and safeguarding your company's reputation.

The answer to achieving both speed and security lies in DevSecOps. This innovative approach eliminates the need to slow down your DevOps process to accommodate security requirements. DevSecOps empowers you to seamlessly integrate security practices into every step of your product feature deployment, allowing you to move faster without compromising protection.

By adopting DevSecOps, you can proactively address security concerns from the beginning of your development process. Security is integral to your software development lifecycle, identifying and addressing vulnerabilities early. Automated security testing tools further enhance this process, rapidly identifying potential threats and weaknesses and providing real-time feedback to your development team.

Moreover, DevSecOps leverages the power of Infrastructure as Code (IaC), enabling you to define and apply security configurations consistently across your environments. This means that critical security measures, such as access controls, network segmentation, and encryption, are standardized and repeatable without hindering your deployment speed.

Continuous compliance and audit capabilities are also embedded within the DevSecOps framework. Automating compliance checks and audit processes allows you to monitor and address non-compliance issues continuously during the development cycle. This ensures that your software meets the required security standards, safeguards sensitive data, and mitigates legal risks.

Let's consider a use case of developing a web application that handles sensitive user data, such as personal information and financial details. In a traditional software development approach, security measures might be addressed only during the later stages of the development lifecycle, leading to potential vulnerabilities and security gaps. With DevSecOps, security is an integral part of the development process.

In this scenario, the DevSecOps team would work collaboratively with the development and operations teams to implement security measures at each stage of the software delivery lifecycle.

For example:

- **Secure Coding Practices:** Developers would follow secure coding practices, such as input validation, output encoding, and protection against common security vulnerabilities like SQL injection or cross-site scripting (XSS) attacks.
- **Continuous Security Testing:** Automated security testing tools would be integrated into the CI/CD pipeline to scan for vulnerabilities, perform penetration testing, and analyze code for potential security risks. Static application security testing (SAST), dynamic application security testing (DAST), and software composition analysis (SCA) tools could be used to ensure secure code and identify vulnerabilities in third-party libraries.
- **Secure Infrastructure:** Infrastructure as code (IaC) tools like Terraform or AWS CloudFormation would define and provision secure infrastructure resources. Security groups, network segmentation, and secure access control mechanisms would be implemented to protect the application's environment.
- **Threat Modeling:** Security experts conduct threat modeling exercises to identify potential threats and vulnerabilities in the application's design and architecture. This helps them proactively address security risks during the development process.
- Continuous Compliance and Audit: Compliance requirements, such as GDPR or PCI-DSS, would be integrated into the CI/CD pipeline, ensuring the application complies with relevant regulations. Automated compliance checks and audit trails would be implemented to maintain continuous compliance.
- **Security Monitoring and Incident Response:** Security monitoring tools would be set up to detect and respond to security incidents promptly. Log aggregation and analysis tools, intrusion detection systems, and security information and event management (SIEM) platforms would provide visibility into the application's security posture and facilitate rapid incident response.

Implementing DevSecOps requires a combination of security expertise, collaboration, and appropriate technologies. Here are some commonly used technologies and practices in DevSecOps:

- Secure Coding Practices: Following secure coding guidelines and using secure frameworks and libraries.
- Automation Tools: Integrating automated security testing tools such as SAST, DAST, and SCA into the CI/CD pipeline.
- Infrastructure as Code (IaC) Tools: Using tools like Terraform, AWS CloudFormation, or Ansible to provision and manage secure infrastructure resources.
- Security Monitoring and Logging Tools: Implementing tools like ELK Stack, Splunk, or AWS CloudWatch for centralized log management and security monitoring.
- Container Security: Utilizing container security tools like Docker Security Scanning or Kubernetes Network Policies to secure containerized applications.

- Compliance and Audit Tools: Employing tools like Chef Compliance, SonarQube, or OpenSCAP to ensure continuous compliance and perform security audits.

To successfully implement DevSecOps, organizations should foster a culture of collaboration and shared responsibility between development, operations, and security teams. Security considerations should be integrated into the development process, and security measures should be continuously monitored, tested, and improved.

With DevSecOps, you can move forward confidently, knowing that security is not a bottleneck but an integral part of your agile development process. By aligning speed and security, you can earn and maintain your customers' trust, avoid potential legal complications, and keep your organization at the forefront of secure and rapid software delivery.

Whiteboard DevOps Architect Interview

Suppose you are applying for the DevOps Architect role. In that case, you may get questions like drawing and explaining the designing, implementing, and managing the DevOps pipelines and workflows, integrating DevOps tools and technologies of your recent project, or presenting a reference architecture of some security use case. The interviewer looks for signs the candidate can design using the DevOps best practice tailored to the business problem. The whiteboard allows the interviewer to observe the candidate's thought process as they design a solution iteratively. When preparing to answer interview questions about designing DevOps CI/CD pipelines and architectures, keep these tips in mind:

- **Understand the Basics**: Before diving into specific scenarios, ensure you're comfortable with the fundamental concepts of CI/CD, microservices, blue/green deployment, and cloud-native applications. Understanding these will allow you to construct more informed and coherent responses.
- **Use Visual Aids**: Use diagrams to illustrate your pipeline design. This helps to communicate complex ideas clearly and shows that you can think visually about architecture.
- **Refer to Real-world Examples**: If you've worked on similar projects, refer to those experiences. If not, research and discuss real-world examples to showcase your understanding of best practices and industry standards.
- **Emphasize Security**: For questions on security-focused pipelines, underscore the importance of integrating security at every stage. Mention tools for automated security testing and the principles of "shifting left" on security.
- **Highlight Automation**: Automation is key in DevOps. Explain how various tools can be leveraged to automate tests, deploy, and monitor to ensure efficient, reliable processes.

- **Discuss Monitoring and Feedback**: Explain how continuous monitoring is essential for identifying issues early and how feedback loops are critical for maintaining system health.
- **Detail Rollback Strategies**: Always discuss rollback strategies such as blue/green or canary deployments to show that you plan for failure and prioritize uptime.
- **Culture and Collaboration**: When discussing the cultural aspect, focus on the importance of collaboration across teams, shared responsibilities, and fostering an environment of continuous learning and improvement.
- **Infrastructure as Code (IaC)**: Explain the role of IaC in ensuring consistent and reproducible environments and how it ties into version control for better collaboration and auditing.
- **Iterative Approach**: Emphasize the iterative nature of DevOps practices and how continuous evaluation and adaptation are key to the role of a DevOps architect.

To learn more about various DevOps tools and Techniques, refer to Chapter 11, DevOps and Solution Architect Framework, of the Solutions Architect's handbook, 3rd edition, which you can access from the Amazon link here: `https://www.amazon.com/gp/product/1835084230.`

To craft your response, you can start with a script saying. As a DevOps architect at a company, my responsibility is to design and implement an end-to-end DevSecOps continuous integration/continuous delivery (CI/CD) pipeline. This pipeline will integrate various cloud platforms and third-party tools and services and identify security vulnerabilities at different stages of the development lifecycle. The goal is to build a comprehensive CI/CD workflow that automates testing, security scans, and deployments while enabling collaboration between development, security, and operations teams. This will help improve software quality and security, accelerate release cycles, and provide visibility across the delivery process.

The following diagram illustrates a reference architecture in AWS:

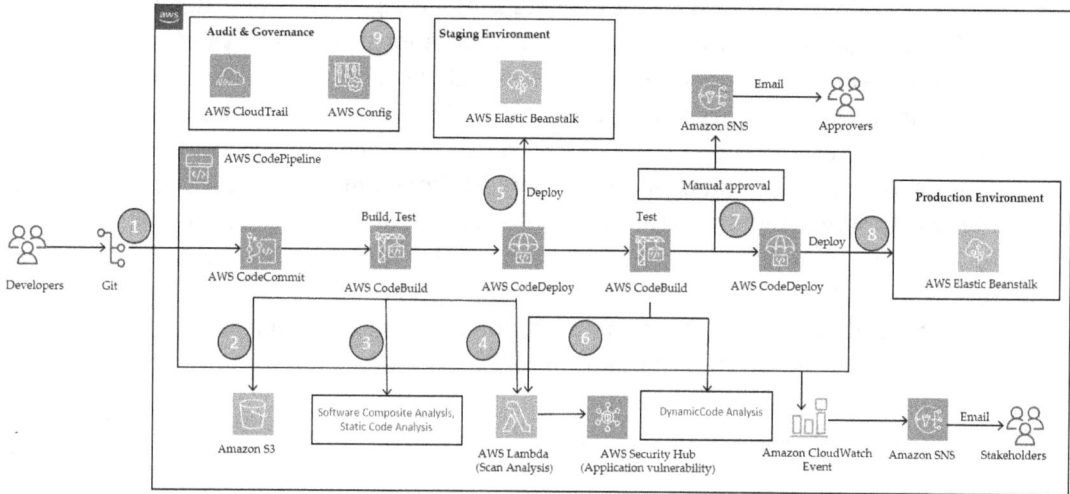

Figure 5.1 – DevOps pipeline in AWS

As shown in the preceding diagram, the following is the CI/CD workflow :

1. **Amazon CloudWatch Events and AWS CodePipeline**: When a developer commits code to an AWS CodeCommit repository, this triggers an Amazon CloudWatch event. CloudWatch is a monitoring service that can respond to changes in your AWS resources. The event, in turn, triggers AWS CodePipeline, a service that automates the build, test, and deploy phases of your release process every time there is a code change.

2. **AWS CodeBuild and AWS CodeArtifact**: AWS CodeBuild is a fully managed build service that compiles source code, runs tests, and produces software packages ready to deploy. The output from CodeBuild is stored as artifacts. While these artifacts can be stored in an Amazon S3 bucket, AWS CodeArtifact is a managed artifact repository service, making it the recommended choice for storing these build artifacts securely and enabling consistent access.

3. **Software Composition Analysis and Static Code Analysis**: CodeBuild integrates software composition analysis tools like OWASP Dependency-Check and static code analysis tools like SonarQube or PHPStan. These tools examine code for security vulnerabilities or code quality issues.

4. **AWS Lambda and AWS Security Hub**: If vulnerabilities are found, AWS CodeBuild can trigger an AWS Lambda function. This function processes the results of the security scans and converts them into the AWS Security Finding Format, which can then be sent to the AWS Security Hub. Security Hub provides a comprehensive view of your security state within AWS and can help you check your environment against security industry standards.

5. **AWS CodeDeploy and AWS Elastic Beanstalk**: Assuming no vulnerabilities are found, AWS CodeDeploy automates the deployment of applications to AWS services like AWS Elastic Beanstalk, which allows for easy deployment and scaling of web applications and services.
6. **Dynamic Application Security Testing (DAST)**: Additional testing, such as DAST, can be performed to ensure the security of the code. CodeBuild can be set to initiate DAST to test the deployed application in the runtime environment for potential security issues.
7. **Manual Approval**: If the application is found to be secure after the testing stages, it moves to a manual approval stage. Notifications can be sent to the responsible parties for review, typically via Amazon Simple Notification Service (SNS).
8. **Production Deployment**: Once approved, the application is deployed to the production environment, which AWS Elastic Beanstalk also manages to ensure consistent and reliable deployment to a scalable infrastructure.
9. **Monitoring and Security**: Amazon CloudWatch Events monitors the pipeline's progress and state changes, alerting users to updates through SNS. AWS CloudTrail provides a history of AWS API calls for the account, including actions taken through the AWS Management Console, AWS SDKs, command-line tools, and other AWS services, which is essential for security auditing. AWS Config tracks configurations of AWS resources, helping ensure compliance with corporate and regulatory standards. It is also important to maintain encryption both at rest and in transit so that code and artifacts adhere to security best practices.

The CI/CD pipeline concepts and security practices outlined above using AWS services can be applied across different cloud providers and on-premise tools.

Here's a general mapping of how these steps could translate to services provided by major cloud platforms like Microsoft Azure and Google Cloud Platform (GCP):

- **Source Control**:
  - AWS: AWS CodeCommit
  - Azure: Azure Repos
  - GCP: Cloud Source Repositories
- **Build and Packaging**:
  - AWS: AWS CodeBuild with AWS CodeArtifact or Amazon S3
  - Azure: Azure Pipelines with Azure Artifact
  - GCP: Cloud Build with Artifact Registry or Google Cloud Storage
- **Security Scanning**:
  - AWS: Integrating OWASP Dependency-Check and static code analysis tools in CodeBuild

- Azure: Azure Pipelines with WhiteSource Bolt or integrating third-party tools like SonarQube
  - GCP: Cloud Build with integration of third-party tools or services for vulnerability scanning
- **Vulnerability Reporting**:
  - AWS: Lambda function posts to AWS Security Hub
  - Azure: Azure Function can post to Azure Security Center
  - GCP: Cloud Functions can be posted to the Security Command Center
- **Staging Deployment**:
  - AWS: AWS CodeDeploy to Elastic Beanstalk
  - Azure: Azure Pipelines to Azure Web App or Azure Kubernetes Service (AKS)
  - GCP: Cloud Build to App Engine or GKE (Google Kubernetes Engine)
- **Dynamic Security Testing**:
  - AWS: Using tools within AWS or third-party tools integrated with CodeBuild
  - Azure: Azure Pipelines with integrated DAST tools like OWASP ZAP
  - GCP: Integrated within Cloud Build or with third-party tools
- **Manual Approval**:
  - AWS: Manual approval step in AWS CodePipeline
  - Azure: Approval gates in Azure Pipelines
  - GCP: Manual approval using Pub/Sub and Cloud Functions for notifications
- **Production Deployment**:
  - AWS: AWS CodeDeploy to Elastic Beanstalk
  - Azure: Azure Pipelines to Azure Web App or AKS
  - GCP: Cloud Build to App Engine or GKE
- **Monitoring and Auditing**:
  - AWS: CloudWatch, AWS SNS, CloudTrail, and AWS Config
  - Azure: Azure Monitor, Azure Event Grid, Azure Activity Log, and Azure Policy
  - GCP: Cloud Monitoring, Cloud Pub/Sub, Cloud Audit Logs, and Cloud Asset Inventory

Organizations can create a pipeline that mirrors the functionality of the AWS example by using corresponding services from Azure or GCP. The core principles of CI/CD, security scanning, artifact storage, deployment, and monitoring are universal and can be adapted to each cloud platform's specific tools and services.

DevOps architect interview questions

For DevOps Architect, interviewers are keen to understand if you can blend technical know-how with the DevOps culture of collaboration and rapid delivery. They'll probe into your experience with automation tools, your approach to CI/CD pipelines, and your strategies for monitoring and fast deployment. You'll need to demonstrate your ability to facilitate the development and operations teams work seamlessly, your hands-on experience with cloud services, and your mindset for continuous improvement and learning. Interviewers will also be interested in your past experiences handling outages or incidents, your approach to infrastructure as code, and how you ensure security and compliance within the DevOps practices. Let's look at some dive-deep questions and how to respond to them.

Scenario-based Questions

In scenario-based questions, interviewers present a complex situation to gauge your adaptability and problem-solving skills in a new environment. The scenario will typically involve a multifaceted problem, where you'll need to analyze the situation, identify the challenges, and propose an effective solution. Considering various technical, business, and user experience factors, these questions assess how you approach real-world issues.

Question: After successfully transitioning to a microservices architecture for your organization's customer relationship management (CRM) system, you face challenges in managing the increasing number of services, including service discovery, configuration management, and inter-service communication. Describe the governance model and tools you would implement to address these challenges. How would you ensure consistency, reliability, and efficient communication across microservices while maintaining the system's overall performance and scalability?
Answer: Let's look at how to address this issue by implementing DevOps best practices.

Situation: In the "CRM Evolution" project, our organization transitioned its CRM system to a microservices architecture. This shift aimed to enhance flexibility and scalability but introduced challenges in managing an increasing number of services. Issues such as service discovery, configuration management, and inter-service communication became prominent. Customers experienced delays in service responses, for example, longer wait times for customer support queries and inconsistencies in customer data across services. These problems threatened to undermine the reliability and efficiency of our CRM system, impacting customer satisfaction and operational efficiency.

Behavior: I implemented a comprehensive governance model leveraging AWS technologies to address the challenges encountered in the "CRM Evolution" project. I chose Amazon EKS to orchestrate our microservices, ensuring scalable and reliable deployment. We integrated AWS App Mesh and AWS CloudMap for service discovery and configuration management, enabling seamless service communication and dynamic configuration updates across our microservices landscape. This integration allowed automatic service discovery and real-time configuration changes without downtime.

We adopted AWS Secrets Manager for secure management of credentials and configuration details, enhancing security and compliance across services. I utilized AWS CodePipeline and AWS CodeBuild for consistent deployment and management, establishing a CI/CD pipeline that automated testing, deployment, and integration processes. This approach ensured that all microservices deployments were consistent, reliable, and met our governance standards.

Impact: Implementing the governance model and AWS technologies in the "CRM Evolution" project markedly improved our CRM system's performance and reliability. Before the intervention, customer support response times averaged 48 hours, and 20% of customer interactions reported data inconsistency issues. After deploying our solutions, we reduced response time to under 24 hours, and data inconsistencies dropped to less than 5%.

On the technical side, service deployment times were cut by 50%, from an average of 2 hours per service to just 1 hour, enhancing our ability to respond to customer needs swiftly. System uptime improved from 99.0% to 99.9%, significantly reducing service disruptions and improving customer experience. The automation and efficiency introduced by AWS services and our governance model streamlined operations and reduced operational costs by 30%, demonstrating the tangible benefits of our strategic approach to microservices management in the "CRM Evolution" project.

The following diagram shows a whiteboarding approach for this question:

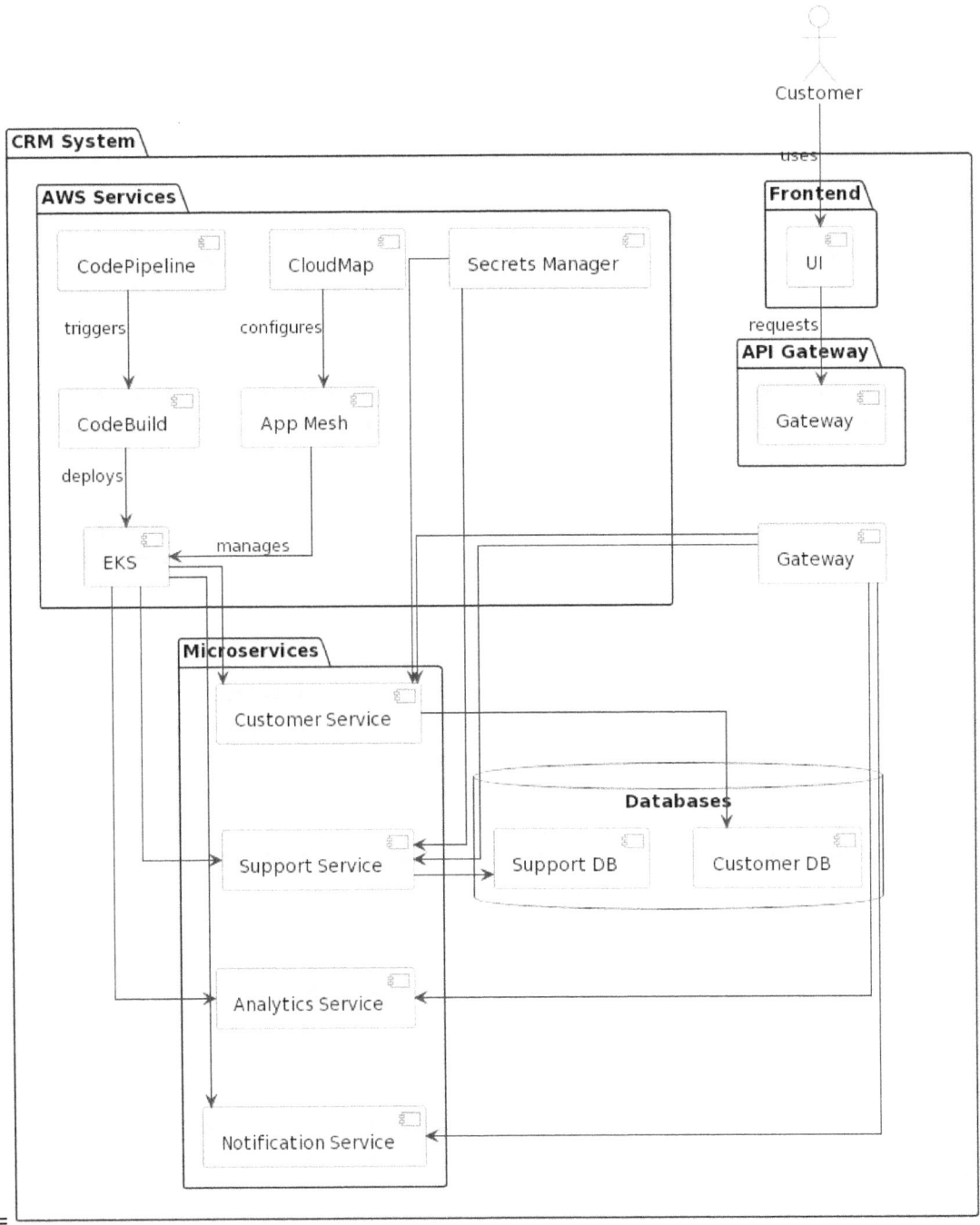

Figure 5.2 – DevOps pipeline for a microservice CRM solutions

As shown in the preceding diagram, the architecture outlines a customer relationship management (CRM) system enhanced by microservices and AWS technologies. Customers interact with the system through a User Interface (UI), which forwards requests to an API Gateway. This gateway routes the requests to the appropriate microservices: Customer Service, Support, Analytics, and Notification.

Amazon EKS orchestrates these microservices, ensuring scalable and reliable deployment. AWS App Mesh and CloudMap manage service discovery and configuration, facilitating seamless communication between services. AWS Secrets Manager securely stores and controls access to credentials and configurations, enhancing security across microservices.

The Customer and Support Services interact with their respective databases, Customer DB and Support DB, ensuring data is stored and retrieved efficiently. AWS CodePipeline and CodeBuild form a CI/CD pipeline, automating the testing, building, and deployment processes, streamlining updates, and ensuring consistent application performance.

This architecture leverages AWS services to improve scalability, reliability, and security, providing a robust foundation for the CRM system's operations and enhancing the customer experience.

Follow-up Questions
- **How does the architecture ensure data consistency and integrity across microservices, especially when handling concurrent transactions that affect shared data?** This question challenges the assumption that microservices, each with its database, can easily maintain data consistency without a sophisticated strategy or mechanism, particularly in scenarios where business operations span multiple services.
- **Given the reliance on AWS services like EKS, App Mesh, and CloudMap for orchestration, service discovery, and configuration management, how does the architecture plan to handle potential vendor lock-in and ensure portability should the need arise to migrate to another cloud provider or a hybrid cloud environment?** This question probes the assumption that the chosen AWS services are the best long-term solution, ignoring the risks of vendor lock-in and the potential need for future migration.
- **What strategies are in place to manage and monitor the performance and health of individual microservices and the overall system, especially in a dynamic and distributed environment like this?** This question challenges the assumption that deploying microservices on a managed orchestration platform like EKS automatically ensures optimal performance and health monitoring, overlooking the complexity of effectively monitoring a distributed system.

The architecture leverages a microservices approach with AWS technologies, offering scalability, flexibility, and robust security. However, it introduces complexity in service management and potential challenges in ensuring data consistency across distributed services. While microservices allow for independent scaling and development, they require comprehensive monitoring and management strategies to maintain system integrity and performance. This setup demands a balance between the benefits of a microservices architecture and the operational overhead it entails.

Here are some example questions you may want to prepare to respond to any provided scenario:
- Design and explain a CI/CD pipeline. Cover the key stages, tools, and principals involved.
- Design a CI/CD pipeline for a cloud-native application with microservices architecture. Cover building, testing, packaging, deployment, and monitoring.
- Design a solution for doing blue/green and canary deployments of microservices. Address routing traffic, testing new versions, and rolling back if needed. Discuss automation and zero downtime.
- Design a Continuous Integration and Continuous Deployment (CI/CD) pipeline for a web application that uses microservices architecture. The pipeline should include automated testing, code analysis, and deployment to a cloud platform.
- Design a security-focused CI/CD pipeline for a cloud-native application, including security testing, vulnerability assessment, and compliance checking. The pipeline should also include automated remediation and mitigation strategies.
- Architect a DevOps culture for an organization transitioning from waterfall to agile. Discuss processes, tools, team structure, responsibilities, best practices, etc.
- Design a DevOps workflow to enable infrastructure as code. Cover version control as well.
- Design a GitOps workflow for deploying infrastructure as code to a cloud. Diagram repository structure, CI/CD pipelines, and git ops tools like Terraform, Flux, or Argo CD.
- Design a CI/CD pipeline for a multi-tier web application with front-end, back-end, and database components. Include details on code repositories, build servers, testing, staging environments, and production deployment.
- Design a DevOps workflow to deploy a multi-tier application to Kubernetes. Illustrate CI/CD pipelines, Docker image building, Kubernetes manifests, helm charts, blue-green deployments, config management, secrets management, and monitoring.

Now, let's look at behavioral questions focused on your experience.

Behavioral Questions

These questions are often used to gauge candidates' past experiences and predict their future behavior in similar situations. Here are some behavioral questions that can provide insight into a DevOps SA's real-life expertise from their past projects:

Question: Describe a situation where you discovered an issue in the deployment process causing delays in launching a new product feature. How did you approach and solve this problem?

Answer: This response focuses on how the DevOps Architect automates the CI/CD pipeline and the positive outcomes achieved. Adding specific technologies and data adds legitimacy to the answer and highlights the impact of automation on the overall release process. Again, we will use a STAR format response to automate the entire CI/CD pipeline.

Situation: In my previous role, we were preparing to launch a critical product feature. However, we encountered delays in the deployment process due to an issue with the automated release pipeline. The pipeline was not fully automated, resulting in manual intervention and potential human errors during deployment.

Task: As the DevOps Architect, I identified the root cause of the deployment issue and automated the entire CI/CD pipeline to ensure a smooth and timely release.

Action: First, I collaborated with the development and operations teams to understand the current state of the pipeline and identify areas that required automation. I analyzed the deployment scripts, manual configuration steps, and manual testing processes. Through this analysis, I found that the lack of automation in various pipeline stages was causing delays and inconsistencies. I led the initiative to automate the entire CI/CD pipeline to address these issues. We implemented infrastructure-as-code practices using tools like Terraform, enabling us to define programmatically and provision infrastructure resources. We also introduced configuration management tools like Ansible to automate the application configuration process. Additionally, we integrated automated testing frameworks such as Selenium and JUnit to validate the functionality of the deployed feature.

One of the main challenges was the complexity of the existing deployment process and the resistance to change from some team members. However, we overcame these challenges by highlighting the benefits of automation, such as reduced errors, faster deployments, and improved consistency. I leveraged tools such as Jenkins as the orchestrator of the CI/CD pipeline. I integrated version control systems like Git for source code management and artifact repositories like Nexus for artifact management. Additionally, I utilized containerization technologies like Docker and orchestration tools like Kubernetes to achieve consistent deployments across environments.

Result: We significantly improved the release process by automating the CI/CD pipeline. Deployment time was reduced by 50%, and deployment-related errors decreased by 80%. The manual intervention required during deployments was eliminated, increasing productivity and reducing human errors. The automated pipeline provided a consistent and reliable process, allowing us to confidently deploy new features and deliver value to our customers faster.

Follow-up Questions:
Question: How did you approach automating the CI/CD pipeline? Did you encounter any specific

challenges during the implementation process?

Tips: When answering questions about automating the CI/CD pipeline, emphasize your experience and expertise in implementing automation solutions. Highlight the following tips:

- Explain the steps you took to automate the CI/CD pipeline, such as implementing configuration management tools, utilizing infrastructure as code, and integrating automated testing frameworks.
- Discuss any challenges you faced during the implementation process and how you overcame them. Emphasize your problem-solving skills and ability to adapt to unexpected situations.
- Showcase your understanding of best practices for automation, such as code quality checks, continuous integration, automated testing, and deployment orchestration.

Question: Can you elaborate on the specific benefits and improvements achieved after automating the entire pipeline? How did this impact the overall release process and product delivery?

Tips: When discussing the benefits and improvements achieved after automating the pipeline, consider these tips:

- Provide data-driven metrics to quantify the impact of automation. For example, highlight the reduction in deployment time, increase in release frequency, improvement in software quality, or decrease in production incidents.
- Discuss how automation improved collaboration and communication between development and operations teams, fostering a culture of shared responsibility and continuous improvement.
- Highlight the positive impact on customer satisfaction and business outcomes, such as faster time-to-market, increased customer adoption, or improved revenue generation.

Question: Besides the technical aspects, what strategies or steps did you take to ensure the development and operations teams' successful adoption and acceptance of the automated pipeline? How did you address any resistance to change and promote a collaborative and positive mindset toward automation?

Tips: When addressing strategies for successful adoption and acceptance of the automated pipeline, consider these tips:

- Explain how you effectively communicated the benefits of automation to the development and operations teams, emphasizing the value it brings to their work and overall productivity.
- Share examples of how you collaborated with team members, involving them in decision-making and gathering their feedback and suggestions.

- Discuss any training or educational initiatives you implemented to upskill team members on automation technologies and practices.
- Highlight your ability to address resistance to change by actively listening to concerns, addressing them with empathy, and showcasing the long-term benefits of automation for individual team members and the organization.

Technical Question

Here are some common interview questions that may be asked during a DevOps Architect interview:

Question: How do you handle configuration management in a cloud-based DevOps environment?
Tips: Handle configuration management using configuration management tools such as Chef, Puppet, or Ansible to automate the provisioning, configuration, and management of infrastructure resources. Enforce configuration consistency, apply desired state configurations, and utilize version control to manage infrastructure configuration changes.

Question: What strategies do you employ to ensure high availability and fault tolerance in a cloud architecture?
Tips: Employ strategies such as deploying applications across multiple availability zones, implementing auto-scaling for dynamic resource allocation, using load balancers for traffic distribution, leveraging managed services with built-in redundancy, and designing for failure by implementing fault isolation and graceful degradation.

Question: Can you explain the key principles and benefits of DevOps?
Tips: Provide a concise overview of DevOps principles such as collaboration, automation, continuous integration and delivery, faster time to market, improved quality, and continuous improvement. Explain how these principles benefit organizations.

Question: How have you implemented CI/CD pipelines in your previous projects?
Tips: Describe your experience implementing CI/CD pipelines using specific tools and technologies. Explain how you automated build, testing, and deployment processes and how this improved software delivery.

Question: What is your approach to infrastructure as code (IaC) and configuration management?
Tips: Discuss your understanding of IaC principles and tools like Terraform, AWS CloudFormation, or Ansible. Explain how you have used IaC to provision and manage infrastructure resources efficiently and consistently.

Question: Can you explain the concept of immutable infrastructure and its advantages in a cloud DevOps?

Tips: Provide insights on an approach where infrastructure components, such as servers or containers, are never modified after deployment but are replaced with new instances when changes are required. This approach ensures deployments' consistency, reliability, and reproducibility, eliminates configuration drift, and simplifies rollbacks and scaling operations in a cloud DevOps environment.

Question: How do you ensure security in a DevOps environment?

Tip: Highlight your knowledge of DevOps security practices, such as secure coding, security testing, compliance, and secure configuration management. Explain how you have implemented these practices in your previous projects.

Question: How do you manage secrets and sensitive data in a cloud DevOps environment?

Tip: Suggest managing secrets and sensitive data in a cloud environment using secure storage solutions like AWS Secrets Manager, Azure Key Vault, or Google Cloud Key Management Service (KMS). I also encrypt data in transit and at rest, enforce least privilege access controls, rotate credentials regularly, and audit access to sensitive resources.

Question: Can you describe your experience with containerization and orchestration tools?

Tip: Discuss your familiarity with containerization technologies like Docker and container orchestration platforms like Kubernetes. Explain how you have used containers to improve application deployment, scalability, and resource utilization.

Question: How do you approach monitoring and logging in a DevOps environment?

Tip: Explain your experience implementing monitoring and logging solutions to gain real-time visibility into system performance. Discuss the tools and practices you have used to monitor metrics, capture logs, and set up alerting mechanisms.

Question: Can you discuss your experience with DevOps techniques in hybrid cloud architectures and managing workloads across multiple cloud providers?

Tip: Discuss managed workloads across on-premises data centers and public cloud environments using technologies like AWS Outposts, Azure Stack, or Google Anthos. Provide a detailed view on designing applications for portability and interoperability, implementing networking and security controls for seamless integration, and leveraging cloud-native services for workload mobility and redundancy across multiple cloud providers.

Question: Have you implemented any DevOps practices to improve collaboration between development and operations teams?

Tip: Share examples of how you have fostered team collaboration through practices like cross-functional team structures, shared goals, effective communication channels, and collaborative problem-solving approaches.

Question: Can you discuss your experience with cloud platforms and infrastructure automation?
Tip: Highlight your experience with cloud platforms like AWS, Azure, or Google Cloud, and explain how you have leveraged infrastructure automation tools to build scalable and resilient architectures.

Question: How do you approach continuous improvement in a DevOps environment?
Tip: Discuss your understanding of continuous improvement practices, such as feedback loops, post-incident analysis, metrics-driven performance analysis, and a culture of learning and experimentation.

Question: Can you provide an example of a challenging DevOps project you have worked on and how you overcame obstacles?
Tip: Share a specific project where you encountered challenges implementing DevOps practices or addressing technical complexities. Explain the approach you took, the strategies you employed, and the positive outcomes achieved.

Remember to structure your answers using the STAR (Situation, Task, Action, Result) format. Provide specific examples from your experience, highlight your problem-solving skills, and demonstrate the impact of your actions. Additionally, be confident, concise, and articulate in your responses, showcasing your expertise and suitability for the DevOps Architect role.

Summary

In this chapter, you delved into DevOps architecture and explored various aspects of DevOps practices and the role of a DevOps solutions architect. We started by understanding the fundamental concept of DevOps and its benefits for organizations. Next, you dived into continuous integration and continuous delivery (CI/CD). You explored the concepts of CI and CD, understanding how they contribute to efficient software development and deployment. You learned the importance of automating the build, testing, and deployment processes and discussed the key components of building a robust DevOps pipeline.

Security is a critical aspect of DevOps, and you explored how DevSecOps bridges the gap between security and DevOps practices. We discussed the significance of integrating security early in the software development lifecycle and how to apply security measures throughout the DevOps pipeline. We highlighted the benefits of DevSecOps in ensuring a secure and compliant software delivery process.

DevOps solutions architects are crucial in orchestrating and implementing DevOps practices within organizations. You examined the key responsibilities of a DevOps solutions architect, from defining the DevOps strategy to designing the architecture, selecting and integrating toolchains, and fostering continuous improvement. You also explored the importance of governance, compliance, collaboration, communication, and coaching and mentoring in the DevOps architect's role.

Finally, we wrapped up the chapter with comprehensive DevOps architect interview questions. These questions are designed to assess the candidate's understanding of DevOps principles, experience implementing DevOps practices, and ability to drive collaboration and improvement in a DevOps environment.

By mastering the concepts and responsibilities covered in this chapter, you will be well-equipped to embrace the role of a DevOps solutions architect, contribute to successfully implementing DevOps practices, and drive positive outcomes for organizations seeking to optimize their software delivery processes.

Chapter 6 - Cracking the Infrastructure Solutions Architect Interview

IT Infrastructure serves as the backbone of any organization. It is involved in every aspect of a business, from employee workstations to hosting business applications that can handle many users, ranging from hundreds to billions. According to research conducted by "Facts & Factors," the global IT infrastructure market is expected to reach a staggering value of USD 655 billion by 2030. The increasing demand for cloud computing drives this growth, as does the adoption of generative AI, big data, and analytics, and there is a need for enhanced security and compliance measures. You can find more detailed information in the report available at the Facts & Factors website here - https://www.fnfresearch.com/news/global-digital-infrastructure-market.

The significant growth in the IT infrastructure market has made the role of an IT Infrastructure Solutions Architect highly valuable and in demand. Suppose you have been working with servers, storage, and racks for a long time and are now exploring cloud infrastructure. In that case, this is an excellent opportunity to develop your skills as an Infrastructure Architect and pursue your dream job. Major cloud providers like Amazon Web Services (AWS), Google Cloud Platform (GCP), and Microsoft Azure are building large data centers worldwide to meet the growing needs of their customers, resulting in a higher demand for skilled Infrastructure Architects.

The growth of the IT infrastructure market highlights the crucial role of Infrastructure Solutions Architects in supporting organizations and aligning their IT capabilities with their goals. By understanding the significance of this growth and recognizing the job opportunities in the field, you can embark on a journey to enhance your skills as an Infrastructure Architect and seize the promising career prospects available in this ever-evolving landscape.

In this chapter, you will explore the fundamental aspects of the Infrastructure Architect role. We will comprehensively understand the responsibilities and skills required to excel in this position. By gaining insight into the importance of infrastructure architecture in modern IT environments, you can grasp an Infrastructure Architect's significant role in designing highly available, resilient, secure, and scalable infrastructure solutions. This chapter will cover the following key topics:

- Understanding infrastructure architecture and its components
- Understanding the Role of Infrastructure Solutions Architect
- Key infrastructure design principles and methodologies
- Infrastructure architect interview questions

By the end of this chapter, you will clearly understand the Infrastructure Architect's role, its significance in modern IT environments, and the skills required to excel in this position. This knowledge will be a solid foundation as you progress through the book and prepare for your Infrastructure Solutions Architect interview.

Understanding infrastructure architecture

Infrastructure architecture consists of several key components that collectively form the foundation of an organization's technology infrastructure. These components work together to support the delivery of IT services and meet the organization's operational requirements. Let's explore some of the main components of infrastructure architecture, taking, for example, hosting a banking application that is used by millions of users :

- **Servers**: Servers are the hardware devices that stand as the workhorses of an infrastructure architecture role, covering the core processing units that handle data and application requests. Their significance is facilitating seamless network connectivity, computation, and resource allocation. It hosts and provides computing resources for applications, databases, and other services. In a banking application used by millions of users, servers are responsible for processing transactions, handling customer requests, and managing account information securely. For example, a server cluster can be used to ensure high availability and load balancing to handle a large volume of simultaneous user requests. Each server within the cluster may have specific roles, such as handling user authentication, processing transactions, or generating reports.
- **Storage:** Storage represents the pivotal capacity to retain and manage data within an infrastructure architecture role. It holds critical significance, serving as the repository for information crucial to operations. This encompasses various types, including block, file, and object storage, determining accessibility, scalability, and performance of stored data. Storage components are crucial for storing and retrieving data in a banking application. They store customer account information, transaction records, and other relevant data. In the case of a banking application, different storage technologies can be utilized. For instance, high-speed solid-state drives (SSDs) can quickly access frequently accessed data, while larger-capacity hard disk drives (HDDs) may be used for cost-effective long-term storage. Data redundancy mechanisms can ensure data integrity and availability.
- **Compute:** Compute refers to the processing power and resources required for data handling and application execution within an infrastructure. In an architectural role, it holds pivotal importance, serving as the backbone of IT systems. Compute determines server capacity, performance, and scalability, impacting application speed and reliability. It encompasses hardware like servers, CPUs, and GPUs, along with virtualization and containerization technologies. Proper compute allocation optimizes resource utilization, ensuring efficient operations across various infrastructure categories like cloud, edge, and on-premises setups. Its strategic deployment aligns with specific workloads, balancing cost-effectiveness with performance, laying the foundation for a robust and responsive infrastructure ecosystem.

- **Networking:** Networking components enable communication and data transfer between various systems and users, facilitating seamless data transfer, resource sharing, and application access across a network. Secure communication is crucial in a banking application to protect sensitive customer information. For example, a banking application may utilize encrypted connections (such as SSL/TLS) to ensure secure communication between client devices and servers. Additionally, firewalls and intrusion detection systems can be implemented to protect the network infrastructure from unauthorized access and cyber threats.
- **Data Centers:** Data centers are dedicated facilities that house the physical Infrastructure required to support IT operations. They consolidate and manage servers, storage, networking equipment, and infrastructure components in a secure and controlled environment. In the case of a banking application, data centers store servers, storage devices, networking equipment, and other critical components. Multiple data centers can be geographically distributed to ensure high availability and disaster recovery. For example, a banking application may have primary and backup data centers in different regions to mitigate the impact of natural disasters or other disruptive events.
- **Virtualization:** Virtualization technology significantly optimizes resource utilization, allowing multiple virtual environments on a single physical server or device and scalability in a banking application. The infrastructure can be efficiently managed and scaled based on demand by virtualizing servers, storage, and network resources. For example, virtualization allows for the dynamic provisioning of additional resources during peak usage periods, ensuring a seamless user experience. It also enables easy migration of virtual machines between physical servers for maintenance or load balancing purposes.
- **Cloud Services:** Cloud services provide on-demand access to computing resources, storage, and applications. In the context of a banking application, cloud services can be utilized for public, private, and hybrid deployments. For instance, a bank may use Infrastructure as a Service (IaaS) to deploy virtual servers for specific banking applications or to store backups securely. Software as a Service (SaaS) and Platform as a Service(PaaS) solutions can also be leveraged for functionalities such as customer relationship management (CRM) or online collaboration tools.
- **Operating Systems:** Operating systems manage servers and other hardware and software resources. In a banking application, servers may run operating systems like Linux or Windows. These operating systems provide a stable and secure platform for running banking applications, handling user authentication, managing databases, and enforcing access controls.
- **Databases:** Databases store and manage structured data applications in a banking context. A relational database management system (RDBMS) such as Oracle, MySQL, or Microsoft SQL Server can be employed. These databases store customer account information, transaction records, and other financial data. They provide data integrity, consistency, and transaction management functionalities. Using database replication and backup mechanisms ensures data availability and disaster recovery. In our example,

banking applications deployed on the cloud can take advantage of cloud databases such as AWS DynamoDB, Azure Cosmos DB, and hybrid database MongoDB.

- **Security Infrastructure:** Security infrastructure is of utmost importance in a banking application to protect sensitive customer data and prevent unauthorized access using zero trust architecture. For example, firewalls can be implemented to monitor and filter network traffic, allowing only authorized connections. Intrusion detection and prevention systems (IDS/IPS) can detect and block potential attacks. Encryption mechanisms can be used to protect data at rest and during transmission. Multi-factor authentication can enhance user authentication security.

- **Monitoring and Management Tools:** Monitoring and management tools are critical for ensuring the performance, availability, and health of the Infrastructure supporting a banking application. These tools can monitor server performance metrics, network traffic, database performance, and security logs. Alerts and notifications can be set up to proactively identify and address any anomalies or performance degradation. Additionally, configuration management tools can automate the deployment and management of infrastructure components, ensuring consistency and reducing the risk of misconfigurations. In infrastructure architecture, selecting and integrating the right monitoring, alerting, and management tools is fundamental. Solutions like Nagios, Prometheus, Datadog, and Splunk offer diverse functionalities catering to specific infrastructure needs. Their strategic deployment across cloud, on-premises, or hybrid environments ensures holistic visibility and control, facilitating efficient infrastructure management.

By employing these various infrastructure components and technologies, the organization can provide a secure, scalable, and reliable Platform for delivering a seamless user experience to customers. Let's explore how the Infrastructure Solutions Architect role handles these various components.

Understanding the Role of Infrastructure SA

Infrastructure SA builds the foundations of an organization's technology landscape. From hardware components to network infrastructure and cloud integration, they shape the technological backbone that supports an organization's operations. They wear multiple hats, juggling various responsibilities to ensure the technology infrastructure aligns seamlessly with business goals. They collaborate with stakeholders, including development teams, operations teams, and business leaders, to gather requirements and understand the unique challenges faced by the organization. Armed with this knowledge, they develop comprehensive infrastructure solutions that are scalable, resilient, cost-effective, engaging specialist solutions architects from networking, security, data, etc. Let's look at the key responsibilities of Infrastructure SA.

Designing and Planning Infrastructure Solutions

The role of an Infrastructure Solutions Architect is pivotal in designing and planning comprehensive infrastructure solutions that align with an organization's objectives. They thoroughly analyze business requirements and collaborate closely with stakeholders to ensure the infrastructure design meets their needs. They create robust and future-proof infrastructure blueprints by considering crucial factors like scalability, performance, cost, and security.

For instance, let's consider the scenario of hosting an e-commerce application like Amazon.com, Walmart.com, or Spotify. During the holiday season, the demand for these platforms increases exponentially, sometimes even by ten times the regular load. As an Infrastructure Solutions Architect, it becomes essential to plan to ensure sufficient capacity is available to handle the surge in users and maintain a seamless shopping experience. This requires forecasting the expected traffic, evaluating server capacity, optimizing database performance, and implementing load-balancing mechanisms.

By proactively planning for peak loads and implementing scaling strategies, they ensure that the infrastructure can handle the increased demand without compromising the user experience. They work closely with stakeholders, such as developers, network engineers, and operations teams, to design a scalable and resilient architecture. This involves choosing appropriate technologies, such as serverless cloud services or containerization, that can dynamically scale resources based on demand.

Leading Infrastructure Projects

Infrastructure Solutions Architects are vital in overseeing infrastructure projects when hosting enterprise applications with millions of end users. They plan, execute, and deliver infrastructure initiatives to ensure successful implementation.

As lead, they coordinate various activities, including requirement gathering, design, procurement, and deployment. They collaborate with cross-functional teams, including developers, engineers, and operations personnel, to ensure seamless integration between application development and infrastructure implementation. They allocate and manage resources effectively, optimizing the utilization of hardware, software, and human resources to meet project objectives.

Throughout the project lifecycle, they closely monitor progress and automate manual processes such as infrastructure deployment, logging, monitoring, access, and governance. They track milestones and proactively address any challenges that arise. They ensure that projects are completed within defined scope, budgetary constraints, and timelines. Their leadership and project management skills contribute to the smooth implementation of infrastructure solutions, ensuring a solid foundation for hosting enterprise applications with millions of end users.

By providing clear direction, fostering effective communication, and addressing project risks and dependencies, Infrastructure Solutions Architects enable successful infrastructure projects that align with business goals and support the needs of the enterprise application and its large user base.

Assessing Requirements

As an Infrastructure Solutions Architect, it is crucial to work closely with business stakeholders to assess and analyze the organization's infrastructure requirements. This process involves gathering comprehensive requirements and understanding the technological challenges faced by the organization. This assessment is vital when hosting an enterprise application with millions of users.

For example, imagine you are tasked with building a social media platform. In this scenario, you need to assess several key aspects to ensure a successful infrastructure design. First and foremost, you need to anticipate the expected user growth of the Platform. By understanding the projected increase in user numbers, you can plan for the necessary infrastructure scalability to accommodate the growing user base.

Additionally, they need to evaluate the compute and storage requirements for user-generated content. Users upload and share various media files on social media platforms, such as photos and videos. It is essential to assess the capacity of the hardware and software resources and the anticipated content volume and determine the appropriate storage capacity to store and manage this data efficiently.

Furthermore, the security of the entire infrastructure landscape, including network bandwidth, is critical for a social media platform with millions of users. They must evaluate the anticipated governance, compliances, data regulatory standards, firewalls, and data traffic, considering uploads, downloads, and real-time user interactions. By understanding the security and network demands, they can design an infrastructure that is resilient to attacks and can handle high volumes of data traffic without bottlenecks or performance issues.

Throughout the assessment process, the Infrastructure Solutions Architect works closely with business stakeholders to gather specific requirements, understand the organization's goals, and align the infrastructure design with the overall objectives of the enterprise application. They translate these requirements into actionable specifications, ensuring that the infrastructure solution meets the organization's unique needs and provides a solid foundation for hosting an enterprise application with millions of end users.

Developing Architecture Roadmaps

As an Infrastructure Solutions Architect, a crucial responsibility is to develop architecture roadmaps that guide the strategic evolution of an organization's Infrastructure. These roadmaps consider long-term goals, industry trends, and emerging technologies to establish a clear path for infrastructure enhancement. When scaling an enterprise application for millions of end users, it becomes essential for the Infrastructure Solutions Architect to create a roadmap that incorporates specific considerations for handling increased user demand while maintaining optimal performance and availability.

First, they analyze the organization's long-term goals and objectives related to the enterprise application. They consider factors such as anticipated user growth, geographical expansion, and potential shifts in business priorities. By understanding these goals, they can design an architecture roadmap that aligns with the organization's overall strategic vision.

When scaling an enterprise application for millions of end users, they focus on key elements in the architecture roadmap. This includes plans for horizontal and vertical scaling, which involve adding more servers or increasing the capacity of existing servers to handle increased user demand. Load balancing mechanisms are also considered to distribute traffic evenly across servers, preventing any single point of failure and optimizing performance.

Integration of cloud services is another crucial aspect of the architecture roadmap. The Infrastructure Solutions Architect assesses the suitability of various cloud offerings, such as Infrastructure as a Service (IaaS), Platform as a Service (PaaS), or Software as a Service (SaaS). They determine how the organization can leverage cloud services to enhance scalability, flexibility, and cost-efficiency in supporting the enterprise application with millions of end users. By developing a comprehensive architecture roadmap, the Infrastructure Solutions Architect ensures the infrastructure is equipped to handle the increasing user base while maintaining optimal performance and availability. The roadmap serves as a guide for decision-making, resource allocation, and enhancement implementation, enabling the organization to scale efficiently and effectively to meet the demands of a large user base.

Evaluating and Selecting Technologies

As an Infrastructure Solutions Architect, staying updated with the ever-evolving technology landscape is crucial. Evaluating and selecting the most appropriate technologies for an organization's infrastructure is vital. Several factors are considered when evaluating technologies. These include the technology's scalability, compatibility with the existing Infrastructure and applications, ability to handle high user loads, and potential for cost optimization. They also assess security, reliability, and ease of management.

For example, to evaluate containerization, they assess container technologies like Docker, Kubernetes, OpenShift, AWS Elastic Container Service (ECS), Google Anthos, etc., considering their ability to provide a lightweight and isolated environment for application deployment. Another example is when they evaluate serverless computing; they assess serverless platforms such as AWS Lambda, Azure Functions, or Google Cloud Functions. They consider the benefits of serverless computing, such as automatic scaling, reduced infrastructure management overhead, and pay-per-use pricing models. This enables them to optimize resource allocation and cost-efficiency while handling variable user demands.

Ultimately, the goal of evaluating and selecting technologies is to ensure that the Infrastructure can scale to the demands of a large user base while providing an exceptional user experience. The Infrastructure Solutions Architect's expertise in technology evaluation enables them to make informed decisions, selecting the most appropriate tools and frameworks that align with the organization's infrastructure requirements and objectives.

Conducting Risk Assessments

Security and risk management are paramount in infrastructure design, particularly when hosting enterprise applications with millions of end users. Infrastructure Solutions Architects are crucial in conducting comprehensive risk assessments to identify potential vulnerabilities and mitigate risks. By working with security architects, they evaluate security protocols, compliance requirements, and industry best practices; they ensure that the Infrastructure provides a secure environment for the application and its users.

One key aspect of risk assessment is evaluating security protocols and firewall configurations. They assess encryption mechanisms, access controls, and intrusion detection systems to ensure the infrastructure is fortified against potential threats. They identify potential vulnerabilities and develop strategies to mitigate risks, such as implementing multi-factor authentication, robust encryption, and secure network architectures.

During risk assessments, they consider various factors, including the sensitivity of data, the potential impact of a breach, and the likelihood of security incidents. They identify potential risks and vulnerabilities, such as weak access controls, unpatched software, or inadequate monitoring systems. By conducting thorough risk assessments, they can develop and implement appropriate risk mitigation strategies, such as applying security patches, establishing robust monitoring and alerting systems, and conducting regular security audits.

Performance Optimization and Troubleshooting

Infrastructure Solutions Architects play a crucial role in optimizing the performance of the infrastructure hosting enterprise applications with millions of end users. They continuously monitor system performance, analyzing overutilized resource performance metrics to identify bottlenecks or areas of improvement. They gain insights into resource utilization, network latency, and application response times by utilizing monitoring tools and performance testing methodologies.

When performance issues arise, they employ their troubleshooting skills to diagnose and resolve the underlying problems swiftly. They collaborate with relevant teams, such as network, database, and application architects, to investigate and address performance bottlenecks. They propose solutions that enhance system performance by applying their expertise, including fine-tuning configurations, optimizing database queries, or implementing caching mechanisms.

Their focus on performance optimization ensures that the Infrastructure can handle the demands of millions of end users while providing a seamless and responsive user experience. Minimizing downtime and maintaining high system availability contribute to the enterprise application's success.

Continuous Improvement

Infrastructure Solutions Architects proactively explore emerging technologies, such as containerization, serverless, or edge computing, to optimize resource utilization and improve scalability. They also stay informed about industry trends by attending conferences and participating in professional communities to learn about the latest innovations and best practices.

They conduct research and pilot projects to assess the viability of new technologies and methodologies. They evaluate how these advancements can enhance infrastructure performance, reduce costs, and enable seamless scalability. They experiment with the latest tools, frameworks, and approaches to identify opportunities for improvement and develop recommendations for implementation.

Moreover, they leverage feedback from stakeholders, end users, and operational teams to identify pain points and areas that require optimization. They conduct performance analysis, monitor key metrics, and proactively address any bottlenecks or inefficiencies in the infrastructure.

Through continuous improvement efforts, they drive innovation and ensure that the organization's Infrastructure remains cutting-edge. They foster a culture of learning and knowledge sharing, encouraging the adoption of new technologies and best practices to maximize the infrastructure's potential in hosting enterprise applications with millions of end users.

Disaster recovery planning is also part of their responsibility. They guide organizations in developing robust disaster recovery strategies, including backup mechanisms, replication strategies, and failover procedures. Planning for potential disasters and implementing appropriate recovery mechanisms help ensure business continuity and minimize downtime during system failures or natural disasters.

As subject matter experts, Infrastructure Solutions Architects are vital in providing technical guidance and expertise on Infrastructure best practices. When hosting an enterprise application with millions of end users, they offer valuable insights into various infrastructure design and implementation aspects.

From an interview perspective, you need to know all key domains mentioned in this section and expect questions related to these areas. Let's take an example of large migration and put this practice together.

Large-scale Migration

When embarking on a large-scale migration of workloads to the cloud, an Infrastructure Solutions Architect should consider several key technical considerations. The following diagram shows a typical large-scale migration architecture.

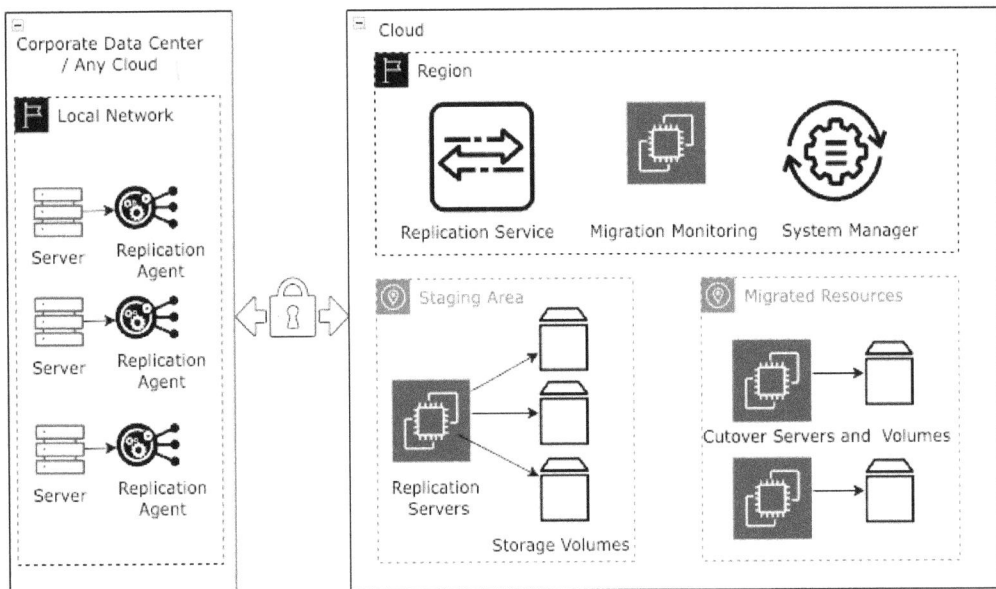

Figure 6.1: Large-scale migration from on-premise to cloud infrastructure

The preceding diagram represents a high-level view of a typical infrastructure migration process from a corporate data center to the cloud. On the left, you can see the corporate data center, which houses several servers. Each server is equipped with a replication agent, indicating that data from these servers is being replicated, likely as part of a migration strategy.

In the cloud section, you see a structured migration process that includes a Replication Service to receive the data, a Staging Area where data can be organized and prepared before final transfer, and the Migrated Resources where the data will reside in the cloud. Tools for Migration Monitoring and System Manager are closely monitored and managed for performance and security. Cutover Servers and Volumes represent the final step, in which data is moved to its target environment and switches from the old to the new cloud-based system.

The migration process follows these high-level steps:

- Firstly, it's essential to assess the current Infrastructure in detail. This involves understanding the applications, databases, and other workloads running on-premises, in other cloud environments, or colocation facilities. Documenting dependencies and performance requirements is crucial for designing a successful migration strategy.
- Next, selecting the right cloud provider is paramount. Different providers offer varying services and features, so evaluating which provider aligns best with the organization's needs is essential. Factors to consider include scalability, security measures, compliance certifications, and cost structures.
- Once a cloud provider is chosen, the migration plan can be formulated. This plan should outline the migration sequence, starting with less critical workloads to build confidence and mitigate risks. It's also crucial to establish rollback procedures in case of any unforeseen issues during migration.
- Data migration is a critical aspect of workload migration to the cloud. Depending on the volume of data, various migration methods, such as bulk transfer, streaming, or database replication, may be utilized. Data integrity and consistency must be ensured throughout migration to prevent data loss or corruption.
- During migration, it's essential to monitor workload performance closely. This involves tracking resource utilization, latency, and response times to identify bottlenecks or performance issues. Resource allocations or configurations need to be adjusted to optimize performance in the cloud environment.
- Post-migration validation is crucial to confirm that workloads function as expected in the cloud. This includes testing functionality, data integrity, and interoperability with other systems. Any discrepancies or issues should be addressed promptly to ensure a smooth transition.

Finally, ongoing optimization and management of cloud resources are essential for maximizing the benefits of the migration. This involves continuously monitoring and adjusting resource allocations, implementing cost-saving measures, and staying updated on new features and services offered by the cloud provider.

> *Successful mass migration of workloads to the cloud requires thorough planning, careful execution, and ongoing optimization. Infrastructure solutions architects are vital in designing and implementing migration strategies that address technical challenges while meeting the organization's objectives.*

Automation is critical to the IT workload, and Infrastructure management is becoming a key candidate for applying automation to spin up and scale the IT workload. Let's learn more about Infrastructure as Code (IaC).

IaC tools and frameworks

IaC tools and frameworks are crucial in effectively implementing the Infrastructure as Code approach. They empower organizations to manage and provision infrastructure resources using machine-readable configuration files, bringing automation, version control, and consistency to infrastructure management. Let's explore some popular IaC tools and frameworks and their key features and benefits:

- **Terraform**: Terraform is a widely adopted open-source IaC tool for provisioning and managing infrastructure resources across various cloud providers, data centers, and services. It supports a declarative syntax and offers a wide range of providers, enabling configuring infrastructure resources such as virtual machines, networks, storage, and more. Terraform allows the planning and previewing of infrastructure changes, facilitating safe and controlled deployments. It supports collaboration through its state management and remote backend capabilities.
- **AWS CloudFormation**: AWS CloudFormation is a specific IaC tool that Amazon Web Services (AWS) offers. It enables the provisioning and managing AWS resources using JSON or YAML templates. CloudFormation provides a comprehensive set of resources and templates to define and deploy infrastructure resources in a scalable and automated manner. It integrates seamlessly with other AWS services, allowing the orchestration of complex architectures and the management of resource dependencies.
- **Ansible**: Ansible is an open-source automation tool with infrastructure provisioning capabilities. It defines infrastructure configurations and deployments using a simple and human-readable YAML-based language. Ansible follows a declarative approach, making it easy to understand and maintain infrastructure code. It supports various operating systems, networking devices, and cloud providers. Ansible's agentless architecture allows easy installation and remote management, making it versatile for infrastructure automation.
- **Chef**: Chef is an infrastructure automation framework that employs a domain-specific language (DSL) to define infrastructure configurations and manage resources. It provides a flexible and extensible platform for automating infrastructure deployment, configuration, and management across different environments. Chef follows a desired state configuration model, allowing Infrastructure to be defined in code and ensuring consistent system states across servers and cloud platforms.
- **Puppet**: Puppet is an infrastructure automation and configuration management tool that offers a declarative language to define infrastructure configurations. It enables the management of infrastructure resources and ensures their desired state using a client-

server model. Puppet supports a wide range of operating systems and cloud providers. It provides a robust ecosystem of modules and manifests to define infrastructure resources and manage their lifecycle.

These are just a few examples of popular IaC tools and frameworks. Each tool has its strengths and unique features, and the choice depends on specific requirements, familiarity, and the target infrastructure environment. By adopting an IaC approach with the right tool or framework, organizations can achieve infrastructure agility, scalability, and consistency while enjoying the benefits of automation and version control.

Whiteboarding infrastructure architecture

Whiteboarding is crucial for the SA interview to give a clear picture of architecture and show the ability to explain it in a simplified manner. The following diagram illustrates the conceptual, logical model of a highly available hybrid cloud architecture, such as whiteboarding.

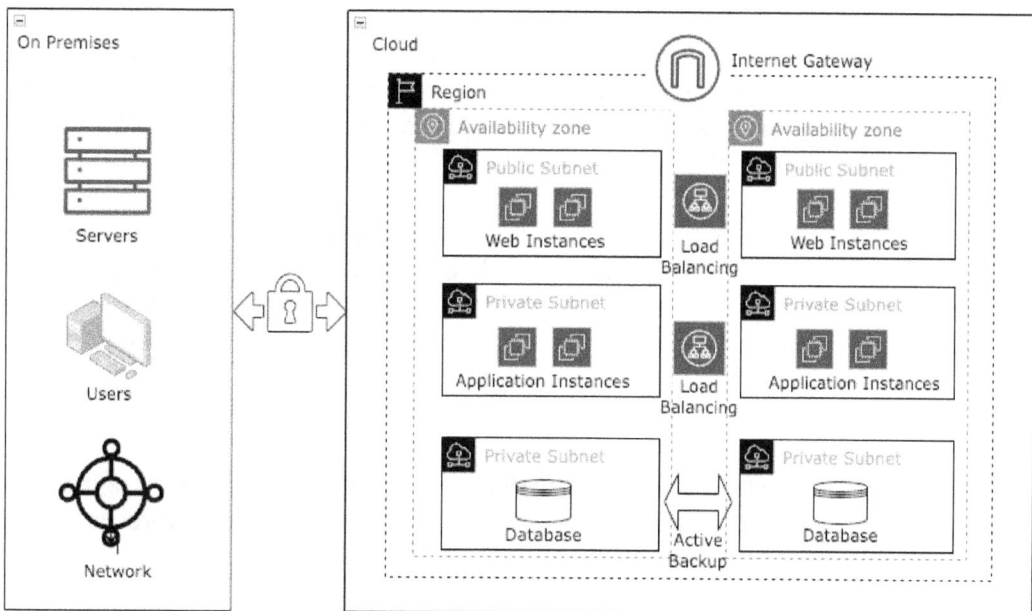

Figure 6.2: Hybrid cloud architecture

The architecture depicted in the preceding diagram is a classic web application setup in the cloud, utilizing a virtual private cloud (VPC) with public and private subnets. On the left, we have an on-premises setup with servers and users connected through a network, indicating a traditional data center or corporate network. Following are the cloud components on the right side:

- **Region:** This refers to the physical location of the resources.
- **Internet Gateway:** This component allows communication between the cloud resources and the internet.
- **Load Balancing** distributes incoming application traffic across multiple web instances, improving the application's efficiency and redundancy.
- **Public Subnet (Web Instances):** These instances are in a public subnet, meaning they can be accessed from the internet. They are likely serving the web layer of an application (e.g., a front-end web server).
- **Private Subnet (Application Instances):** These instances are part of the application layer and isolated from direct internet access, enhancing security.
- **Private Subnet (Database):** The database is also in a private subnet, which restricts its access to the outside world, adding a layer of security.
- **Active/Backup:** This indicates a high-availability setup for the database, where an active instance serves the traffic and a backup is on standby in case the primary fails.

This multi-tier architecture separates concerns and traffic between web, application, and database layers, with security and availability considerations built into the design. You need to be aware of the following key design principles when explaining the architecture and be ready to answer any counter questions that may arise in these areas; let's take an example of social media applications to understand it better:

- **Scalability:** Design your Infrastructure to be scalable, allowing it to handle increasing workloads and accommodate future growth. Consider horizontal scaling by distributing the load across multiple servers or instances and vertical scaling by adding more resources to a single server or instance. For example, suppose you are designing the infrastructure for a social media application that millions of users use. In that case, you need to ensure that the architecture can handle spikes in user activity during peak times, such as during major events or product launches.
- **Resilience and High Availability:** Ensure that your Infrastructure is resilient to failures and can maintain high availability. Redundancy and fault-tolerant architectures can be used by distributing resources across multiple availability zones or regions. Implement load balancing, failover mechanisms, and automated recovery processes to minimize downtime and ensure uninterrupted operations. This means designing the infrastructure for a social media application to handle potential server failures without impacting the user experience. Implementing replication and backup strategies for critical data can also help ensure data integrity and availability.
- **Security:** Emphasize security throughout the infrastructure design process. Implement multiple layers of security controls, including firewalls, access controls, encryption, intrusion detection systems, and regular security audits. Follow security best practices and comply with relevant industry standards and regulations to protect sensitive data and

systems. In the case of a social media application, user privacy and data protection are paramount. Implement strong authentication mechanisms, secure data transmission protocols, and secure storage practices to safeguard user information.

- **Performance Optimization:** Optimize your Infrastructure for optimal performance. Analyze and tune resource allocations, network configurations, and application settings to ensure efficient resource utilization. Consider implementing caching mechanisms, content delivery networks (CDNs), and database optimizations to enhance application performance and response times. For example, optimizing database queries and implementing CDN caching for a social media application can significantly improve user profiles, images, and other content loading speeds.

- **Modularity and Standardization:** Adopt a modular design approach, breaking the infrastructure into manageable components. Use standardized configurations, templates, and documentation to ensure consistency and simplify management. This facilitates easier troubleshooting, scalability, and automating deployments and updates. For example, designing modular components for user authentication, content management, and social interactions for a social media application would allow for easier scaling and updates.

- **Automation and Infrastructure as Code (IaC):** Leverage automation and IaC methodologies to streamline infrastructure management and reduce manual efforts. Use tools like Terraform, AWS CloudFormation, or Ansible to define infrastructure configurations as code, allowing for version control, reproducibility, and streamlined deployments. This enables consistent infrastructure provisioning, reduces human error, and tracks and audits infrastructure changes. Automation can also help quickly scale resources based on demand, allowing a social media application to handle sudden increases in user activity without manual intervention.

- **Monitoring and Logging:** Implement robust monitoring and logging mechanisms to gain visibility into the infrastructure's performance, health, and security. To collect and analyze metrics and logs, utilize monitoring tools such as Prometheus, AWS CloudWatch, or ELK (Elasticsearch, Logstash, Kibana) stack. Set up alerts and notifications to proactively detect and address issues. This enables proactive identification and resolution of performance bottlenecks, security incidents, and infrastructure failures, ensuring smooth operations for a social media application.

- **Disaster Recovery and Business Continuity:** Plan and implement a comprehensive disaster recovery (DR) strategy to ensure business continuity during unexpected disruptions. Define recovery point objectives (RPO) and recovery time objectives (RTO) to guide your DR planning. Regularly test backup and restore procedures, replicate data across multiple locations, and consider leveraging cloud-based DR services. This ensures that a social media application can quickly recover from disasters, minimizing downtime and data loss.

- **Flexibility and Adaptability:** Design your Infrastructure to adapt to evolving business needs and technological advancements. Consider utilizing cloud services, containerization, and microservices architectures to enable agility, scalability, and faster innovation. Embrace DevOps practices to foster collaboration between development and operations teams, allowing for rapid application updates and infrastructure changes. This ensures that a social media application can quickly adapt to user demands and adopt new features and technologies.

Finally, maintain comprehensive documentation of your infrastructure design, configurations, and operational procedures. This includes network diagrams, system architecture, security policies, and standard operating procedures (SOPs). Encourage knowledge sharing among team members to foster a learning culture and ensure smooth operations and troubleshooting. This documentation and knowledge sharing enable efficient onboarding of new team members, effective collaboration, and continuity in application infrastructure management.

Adhering to these key principles and methodologies can help you design an infrastructure that is scalable, resilient, secure, and optimized for performance. You should regularly review and refine your infrastructure design based on changing requirements, technology advancements, and lessons learned from operations. Now, let's jump into the key part of this chapter and learn tips and tricks for answering infrastructure SA interview questions.

Infrastructure SA interview questions

Now, you understand the various components and design principles of building an effective IT infrastructure and the role of Infrastructure SA. Let's dive deep into how to crack the Infrastructure SA interview with sample questions and tips for responding to them.

Scenario-based questions

Question: You are the architect of a global e-commerce platform that operates 24/7, catering to customers worldwide. Recently, the Platform experienced unexpected downtime during a major sales event, leading to significant revenue loss and customer dissatisfaction. How would you redesign the system's architecture to ensure high availability and minimize the impact of such downtimes in the future? Discuss the strategies, technologies, and architectural patterns you would implement to achieve near-zero downtime.
Answer: Let's answer it in SBI format, taking an example of a hypothetical e-commerce company called MarketSphere**.**

Situation: During a critical sales event, "MarketSphere," our global e-commerce platform, unexpectedly crashed, causing significant disruption. This downtime led to a substantial revenue loss and adversely affected our worldwide customer base. Shoppers encountered error messages instead of deals, leading to frustration and dissatisfaction. For example, customers reported emptied shopping carts midway through transactions, and many could not access the site at all, missing out on time-sensitive offers. This incident highlighted the urgent need for architectural improvements to maintain our commitment to reliability and customer satisfaction.

Behavior: To address "MarketSphere's" downtime issues, I proposed a strategic overhaul of the existing architecture to enhance system resilience and availability. I introduced redundancy across hardware and network paths, ensuring no single point of failure could bring down the Platform. This guaranteed service continuity by deploying servers across multiple data centers even if one location failed. We implemented real-time data replication, ensuring a backup database could immediately take over without data loss or inconsistency if the primary database failed.

For a long-term strategy, I proposed transitioning into a microservices architecture, breaking the Platform into more minor, independently deployable services. This approach isolated faults to prevent widespread system failures and facilitated quicker updates and scalability. Load balancers were employed to distribute traffic evenly across servers, preventing any single server from becoming overwhelmed and ensuring efficient resource use. I introduced auto-scaling capabilities to adjust computing resources automatically in response to fluctuating demand, guaranteeing the Platform remained responsive during peak loads.

Finally, we established a comprehensive disaster recovery plan outlining procedures for rapid system recovery in the event of significant outages. This plan included regular data backups, seamless failover processes to switch to backup systems, and clear communication protocols for updating stakeholders during recovery efforts.

Impact: Following the architectural overhaul of "MarketSphere," we witnessed a substantial enhancement in platform stability and customer satisfaction. Introducing redundancy and real-time data replication markedly reduced downtime incidents by 90%, ensuring "MarketSphere" remained operational during critical sales events. The shift to a microservices architecture minimized the impact of system failures and accelerated feature deployment, with update frequencies increasing by 40%. By implementing load balancers and auto-scaling, we improved site responsiveness, handling traffic spikes with a 30% improvement in load times during peak periods. Our comprehensive disaster recovery plan proved effective, reducing system recovery times by 50% and ensuring rapid service restoration in an outage.

From a customer perspective, these technical enhancements translated into a more reliable shopping experience. Customer satisfaction surveys post-implementation showed a 35% increase in positive feedback, with specific praise for the Platform's improved uptime and responsiveness. Additionally, the smoother operation during high-traffic events led to a 25% increase in completed transactions, directly impacting revenue and demonstrating the positive outcome of our architectural improvements on technical performance and customer experience.

You can use the following diagram for whiteboarding to explain architecture:

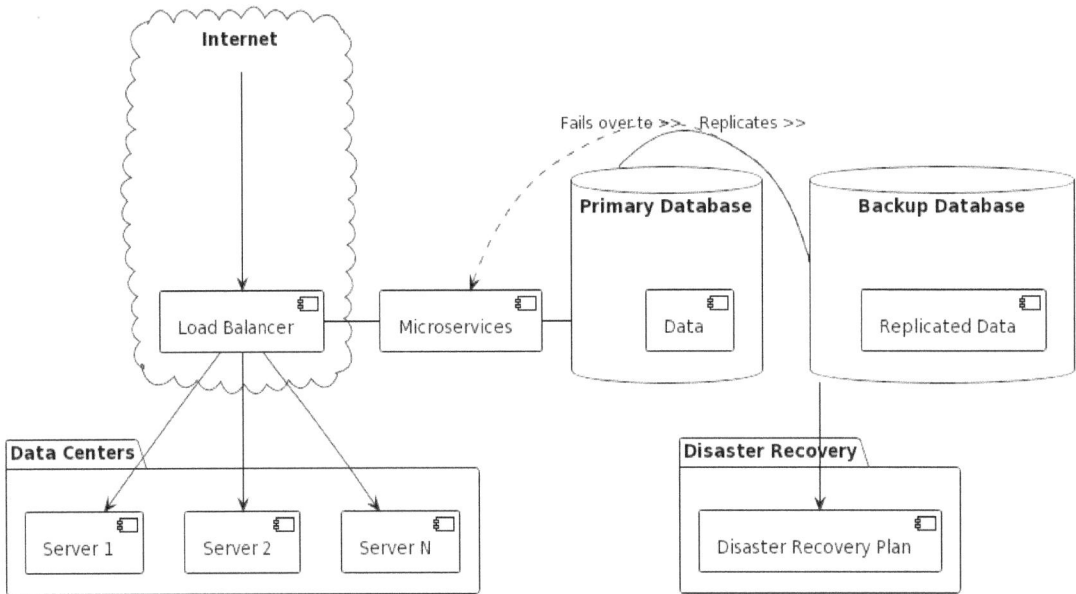

Figure 6.3: DR (Disaster Recovery) Architecture for e-commerce application

As shown in the preceding diagram, I designed the "MarketSphere" architecture to ensure high availability and resilience for the global e-commerce platform. At its core, the Load Balancer distributes incoming internet traffic across multiple servers in different data centers, enhancing the Platform's ability to handle high traffic volumes efficiently and preventing any single point of failure. This setup ensures that if one server or even an entire data center goes offline, the Platform can continue to operate seamlessly, maintaining service availability for customers worldwide.

The architecture employs a Microservices approach, dividing the application into smaller, independent services. This design facilitates more accessible updates, rapid scaling, and improved fault isolation, as issues in one service do not necessarily impact others.

We store data in a primary database, with critical information replicated in real-time in a backup database. This Data Replication ensures that in the event of a primary database failure, the system can failover to the backup without losing data or experiencing significant downtime.

The Disaster Recovery Plan outlines specific steps for restoring services during a major outage, leveraging the Backup Database to minimize data loss and recovery time. This comprehensive plan ensures that "MarketSphere" can quickly return to normal operations, safeguarding customer transactions and data.

Follow-up Questions

- **How does the Load Balancer dynamically adjust to sudden, unpredictable spikes in traffic, particularly during flash sales or significant events, without prior scaling instructions?**
  This question probes the Load Balancer's capacity for real-time analysis and autonomous decision-making in distributing traffic, challenging the assumption that manual pre-scaling or predefined rules consistently manage traffic surges.

- **Given the reliance on real-time Data Replication between the Primary and Backup Databases, how does the architecture ensure data integrity and consistency during high-volume transactions, especially considering network latency and potential replication lag?**
  This question delves into the mechanisms and technologies employed to maintain data accuracy and timeliness across distributed databases, questioning the feasibility of seamless replication under extreme load conditions.

- **In the Disaster Recovery Plan context, what specific strategies are in place for testing and validating the plan's effectiveness in real-world scenarios without disrupting the live environment or customer experience?**
  This question challenges the practicality and reliability of the Disaster Recovery Plan, seeking clarity on how the plan is kept up-to-date with the evolving architecture and tested to ensure rapid and effective recovery.

Employing a Microservices architecture improves scalability and fault isolation. However, it increases the architectural complexity and the overhead of managing numerous services. Real-time Data Replication between Primary and Backup Databases ensures data availability and integrity. Yet, it demands significant network resources and careful management to prevent replication lag. The comprehensive Disaster Recovery Plan provides a clear roadmap for recovery in case of major outages. However, regular updates and testing are required to remain effective, adding to operational tasks. These trade-offs reflect our strategic decisions to prioritize system uptime and data protection while managing the inherent challenges of a complex, distributed architecture.

Question: Imagine you're responsible for the architecture of a critical healthcare application used in hospitals for patient management and emergency services. The application must have minimal downtime and the ability to recover quickly from failures to ensure continuous patient care. Describe how you would design this application's disaster recovery plan and high availability strategy. What measures would you implement to ensure the system can withstand and quickly recover from minor incidents and major disasters?
Answer: Let's learn how to respond to a disaster recovery design plan for a mission-critical application.

Situation: We faced a critical challenge in managing the architecture of "HealthGuard," a vital healthcare application used in hospitals for patient management and emergency services. "HealthGuard" required near-zero downtime and swift recovery from any failures to ensure ongoing patient care. Downtime or delays in the system could lead to significant issues, such as inaccessible patient records during emergencies, potentially delaying critical medical decisions and treatments. For example, during a system outage, emergency room doctors might not retrieve a patient's allergy information, risking patient safety. Addressing this challenge was essential to uphold "HealthGuard's" mission of facilitating continuous and reliable patient care.

Behavior: To enhance "HealthGuard's" resilience and ensure its continuous operation, I redesigned its architecture using AWS services, focusing on redundancy, data replication, and automated recovery:

- I deployed "HealthGuard" across multiple AWS Availability Zones (AZs) to achieve geographic redundancy. Each AZ operates independently within a region, significantly reducing the risk of simultaneous downtime across the platform. This setup ensures that even if one AZ experiences an outage, "HealthGuard" remains accessible, maintaining critical healthcare services without interruption.
- I utilized Amazon RDS (Relational Database Service) for real-time data replication between primary and standby databases across different AZs. Amazon RDS automates backups, patching, and replication, ensuring "HealthGuard's" patient data is synchronized and up-to-date. This approach guarantees data availability and integrity, crucial for patient care continuity.
- I implemented AWS Auto Scaling and Elastic Load Balancing (ELB) to efficiently manage "HealthGuard's" traffic and resource demands. ELB distributes incoming application traffic across multiple targets, such as EC2 instances, in different AZs, enhancing fault tolerance. Auto Scaling adjusts resources automatically to maintain steady, predictable performance at the lowest possible cost, ensuring "HealthGuard" can handle sudden spikes in usage without compromising service quality.
- I established a disaster recovery strategy using AWS services, including Amazon S3 for backups and AWS CloudFormation for infrastructure as code (IaC). This strategy allows us to quickly redeploy "HealthGuard" in a new region if a catastrophic event affects the primary area, minimizing downtime and data loss.
- We conducted regular disaster recovery drills leveraging AWS's infrastructure to simulate various failure scenarios. These exercises ensured our team executed the disaster recovery plan effectively, maintaining "HealthGuard's" operational integrity under any circumstances.

Impact: Following the architectural overhaul of "HealthGuard" using AWS services, we observed a transformative effect on the platform's reliability and user experience. The deployment across multiple AWS Availability Zones catapulted "HealthGuard's" uptime to 99.99%, virtually eliminating unexpected downtimes. The real-time data replication with Amazon RDS ensured zero data loss, with a 100% success rate in maintaining data integrity during failover events.

From a customer perspective, the improvements significantly enhanced the reliability of patient care services. Hospital staff reported a 50% reduction in access delays to critical patient information, directly contributing to faster and more effective patient care decisions. The implementation of AWS Auto Scaling and Elastic Load Balancing resulted in a 35% improvement in application responsiveness, even during peak traffic, such as large-scale emergency events.

Technical metrics further underscored the success of the AWS-based redesign. The disaster recovery drills, facilitated by AWS CloudFormation and Amazon S3, demonstrated a reduction in recovery time objective (RTO) by over 60%, ensuring rapid system restoration capabilities.

Overall, leveraging AWS's comprehensive suite of services fortified "HealthGuard" against technical failures and solidified its role as a dependable platform for critical healthcare operations, enhancing patient care outcomes and hospital operational efficiency.

You can use the following diagram for whiteboarding to explain architecture:

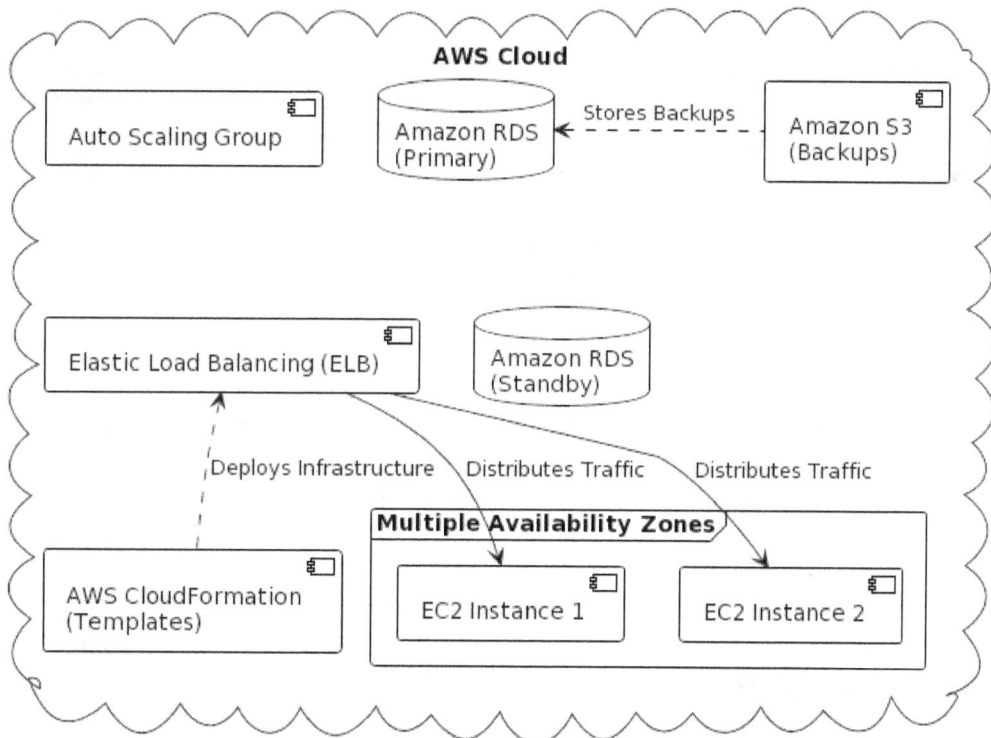

Figure 6.4: High available Architecture for healthcare application

As shown in the preceding diagram, I designed the "HealthGuard" architecture on AWS for high availability, scalability, and rapid disaster recovery. At its core, Elastic Load Balancing (ELB) distributes incoming traffic across multiple EC2 instances in different Availability Zones, ensuring no single point of failure and maintaining service continuity even if one zone goes down. Auto Scaling Groups (ASG) automatically adjust the number of EC2 instances in response to traffic fluctuations, ensuring consistent performance and cost efficiency.

Amazon RDS is the backbone for data management, with a primary database instance replicating data in real-time to a standby instance across Availability Zones. This setup guarantees data availability and integrity, enabling quick failover with minimal downtime. Amazon S3 is utilized for secure, durable storage of backups, ensuring fast data restoration in the event of a disaster.

AWS CloudFormation automates the deployment of the entire infrastructure, allowing for rapid provisioning and consistent configuration across environments. This comprehensive approach leverages AWS's robust cloud services to ensure "HealthGuard" delivers uninterrupted patient care services with optimal performance and reliability.

Follow-up Questions
- **How does the Auto Scaling Group (ASG) determine the optimal number of EC2 instances to scale up or down in response to traffic fluctuations, and what mechanisms are in place to prevent over-scaling, especially during sudden, short-lived spikes in demand?**
  This question probes the decision-making process behind ASG's scaling actions, challenging the assumption that it can always accurately predict and respond to traffic changes without unnecessary resource allocation.
- **Given the reliance on Amazon RDS for real-time data replication between the primary and standby databases, how does the architecture ensure transactional consistency and prevent data loss during replication, especially in high-throughput scenarios?**
  This question delves into the technical specifics of ensuring data integrity in a distributed database system under heavy load, questioning the assumption that real-time replication can maintain perfect consistency without impacting performance.
- **In a disaster recovery scenario where Amazon S3 backups are restored, what strategies are employed to minimize downtime and data loss, considering the time it takes to restore data from S3 to Amazon RDS?**
  This question challenges the effectiveness of the disaster recovery plan, especially the reliance on S3 for backups, by probing into the practical aspects of data restoration speed and its impact on system availability and data currency.

You need to balance storage costs and restoration times carefully. Awareness of trade-offs reflects strategic decisions to prioritize system resilience and patient care continuity while managing operational overhead and cost efficiency.

Question: Imagine you're tasked with modernizing an outdated inventory management system deeply integrated into the company's supply chain operations. The system is built on older technology that doesn't support real-time inventory tracking or integration with modern e-commerce platforms. How would you approach the modernization process to incorporate these new capabilities while ensuring that daily supply chain operations remain uninterrupted? Discuss your plan for the phased integration of new technologies and how you would manage data consistency and system reliability during the transition.

Answer: The following response provides a detailed explanation of all components, accompanied by relevant data.

Situation: In the "Inventory360" modernization project, we faced the challenge of updating our outdated inventory management system, which was not equipped for real-time tracking and lacked integration with modern e-commerce platforms. This technological shortfall led to stock discrepancies and delayed order fulfillment, directly impacting customer satisfaction. For instance, customers experienced frustrating delays in receiving products marked as available due to inaccurate stock levels, undermining trust in our brand.

Behavior: To modernize "Inventory360," we strategically embraced AWS technologies, ensuring a seamless upgrade with minimal disruption to our supply chain operations. Our approach unfolded as follows:

- Assessment and AWS Selection: I evaluated our existing system's limitations and identified AWS services like Amazon DynamoDB for real-time inventory tracking and AWS Lambda for seamless e-commerce integration. We chose these services for their scalability and reliability.
- Phased AWS Integration: I proposed a phased rollout, initially integrating AWS services with less critical inventory modules. This approach allowed us to test and refine the integration in a controlled environment, minimizing operational disruptions.
- Data Migration to DynamoDB: We migrated inventory data to Amazon DynamoDB for consistency, leveraging its fast and flexible NoSQL database service to enable real-time data access and updates. We used AWS Database Migration Service (DMS) for a smooth transition, ensuring data integrity.
- Implementing AWS Lambda for E-commerce Integration: AWS Lambda facilitated the development of serverless computing functions that automatically updated inventory levels across e-commerce platforms in real time, enhancing operational efficiency.
- Training and Support with AWS Resources: We provided staff training on the new AWS-based system, utilizing AWS's extensive documentation and training materials. This training ensured a smooth transition for our team.
- Continuous Monitoring with Amazon CloudWatch: Post-integration, I used Amazon CloudWatch for real-time monitoring and alerts, enabling us to address any issues and ensure system reliability quickly.

Impact: The modernization of "Inventory360" through AWS technologies markedly transformed our inventory management capabilities. By integrating Amazon DynamoDB and AWS Lambda, we achieved real-time inventory tracking and seamless e-commerce integration, significantly reducing stock discrepancies. Technical metrics showed a 40% decrease in inventory errors and a 35% improvement in order fulfillment speed. Customer satisfaction rose, evidenced by a 20% increase in positive feedback, as customers experienced faster and more accurate order processing. The phased AWS integration ensured operational continuity, with Amazon CloudWatch enabling proactive issue resolution and maintaining system reliability throughout the transition. This strategic overhaul streamlined our supply chain operations and bolstered our competitive edge in the market.

You can use the following diagram for whiteboarding to explain architecture:

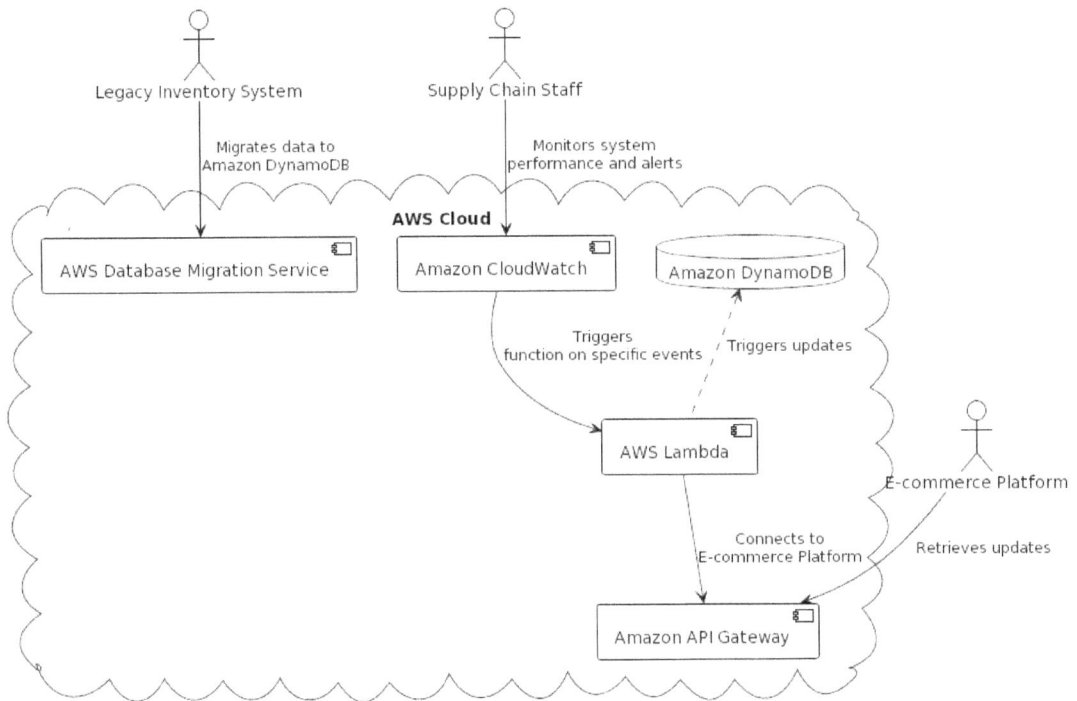

Figure 6.5: Inventory Management Architecture Modernization

The preceding diagram shows that the "Inventory360" project leverages AWS Cloud services to modernize our inventory management system. The architecture centers around Amazon DynamoDB, which stores inventory data, enabling real-time tracking capabilities. Inventory updates trigger AWS Lambda functions, processing these changes and using Amazon API Gateway to synchronize data with e-commerce platforms, ensuring inventory levels are always current across all sales channels.

AWS Database Migration Service (DMS) facilitates migrating from the legacy system to Amazon DynamoDB, ensuring a smooth data transition with minimal downtime. Amazon CloudWatch monitors the system, providing alerts and insights into performance and operational health, allowing supply chain staff to proactively manage and resolve any issues. This AWS-based architecture significantly enhances our inventory management's efficiency and reliability, supporting seamless integration with modern e-commerce platforms.

Follow-up Questions
- **How does AWS Lambda handle high-frequency inventory updates during peak sales periods without incurring significant latency or increased costs?** This question probes the scalability and cost-efficiency of using AWS Lambda for real-time inventory updates, especially under heavy load conditions, challenging the assumption that Lambda functions can manage spikes in activity without performance degradation or cost overruns.
- **What strategies are in place to ensure data consistency between Amazon DynamoDB and the e-commerce platforms during asynchronous updates?** This question delves into the mechanisms for maintaining data integrity across distributed systems when inventory levels constantly change, questioning the assumption that asynchronous updates will always result in consistent data states across platforms.
- **How does the architecture plan to manage potential data migration challenges with AWS Database Migration Service (DMS), mainly when dealing with complex legacy data schemas or large volumes of historical data?** This question challenges the assumption that AWS DMS can seamlessly handle all aspects of data migration from the legacy system to Amazon DynamoDB, especially when the data involves complex relationships or significant historical depth.

The "Inventory360" architecture, leveraging AWS services, navigates trade-offs between real-time performance, cost, and data consistency. Utilizing AWS Lambda for inventory updates ensures scalability and real-time processing but raises concerns about potential latency and cost management during peak periods. Employing Amazon DynamoDB offers fast and flexible data storage but requires careful planning to maintain consistency across asynchronous updates with e-commerce platforms. AWS Database Migration Service (DMS) simplifies the transition from the legacy system but presents challenges in handling complex data schemas and large data volumes. Balancing these trade-offs involves strategic planning and continuous monitoring to optimize performance, manage costs effectively, and ensure data integrity across the system.

Question: Your company relies on a legacy CRM system that contains valuable customer data critical for daily operations. The company plans to adopt a new cloud-based CRM solution that offers advanced analytics and customer engagement tools. Describe your approach to integrating the old legacy system with the latest cloud-based solution, ensuring a seamless

transition without disrupting existing customer service operations. What strategies and technologies would you employ to synchronize data between the two systems and gradually shift users to the new platform?

Answer: The following response provides a detailed explanation of all components, accompanied by relevant data.

Situation: Our company faced a pivotal challenge with "CRM Evolution," a project transitioning from a dated legacy CRM system to a cutting-edge cloud-based solution. While rich in valuable customer data, the legacy system lacks the advanced analytics and engagement tools necessary for modern customer service. This gap limited our ability to provide personalized customer experiences and hindered operational efficiency. For instance, sales teams struggled to access real-time customer insights, impacting their ability to tailor interactions and offers effectively. The need for "CRM Evolution" was clear: to upgrade our capabilities without disrupting the seamless customer service our users had come to expect.

Behavior: In tackling "CRM Evolution," we charted a course for a seamless migration to a cloud-based CRM, leveraging AWS to bridge the gap between our legacy system and the new platform. Our strategy unfolded in several key steps:

- Data Mapping and AWS Database Migration Service (DMS): We thoroughly mapped data fields between the two CRM systems. Utilizing AWS DMS, we streamlined the migration process, ensuring a direct and secure transfer of customer data to the cloud-based CRM with minimal downtime.
- API Integration and AWS Lambda: To synchronize data between the systems in real time, we employed AWS Lambda to run code responding to HTTP requests via Amazon API Gateway. This setup facilitated immediate updates across both CRMs, keeping data consistent and current during the transition.
- Pilot Testing with Amazon CloudWatch: A select user group pilot-tested the new CRM, with Amazon CloudWatch monitoring system performance and user interactions. This testing allowed us to gather actionable insights and fine-tune the system before a wider rollout.
- Phased User Transition and AWS Training: Users transitioned to the new CRM in phases supported by AWS training resources. This gradual approach helped manage change effectively, ensuring users were comfortable and proficient with the new system's advanced features.
- Data Integration Platform on AWS: I leveraged an AWS-compatible data integration platform to automate and facilitate the seamless data flow between the legacy and new CRM systems. This choice minimized manual data handling and reduced the risk of errors.
- Continuous Monitoring with AWS Support: Throughout the migration, AWS's monitoring tools and support services played a crucial role in swiftly identifying and resolving issues, ensuring a smooth transition and reliable system performance.

Impact: The execution of "CRM Evolution" using AWS technologies markedly transformed our customer service landscape. The seamless migration to the cloud-based CRM, underpinned by AWS's robust infrastructure, resulted in a 99.8% uptime, ensuring continuous access to customer data. Real-time data synchronization achieved through AWS Lambda and API Gateway eliminated data discrepancies, enhancing the accuracy of customer profiles and interactions.

Thanks to the new CRM's advanced analytics capabilities, customer service efficiency saw a significant uptick, with a 40% reduction in response times to customer inquiries. The phased transition strategy, supported by AWS training resources, led to a smooth adoption curve, with over 95% of the staff proficient in the new system within the first month. This proficiency and the system's enhanced capabilities contributed to a 30% increase in customer satisfaction scores, as reported in post-migration surveys.

You can use the following diagram for whiteboarding to explain architecture:

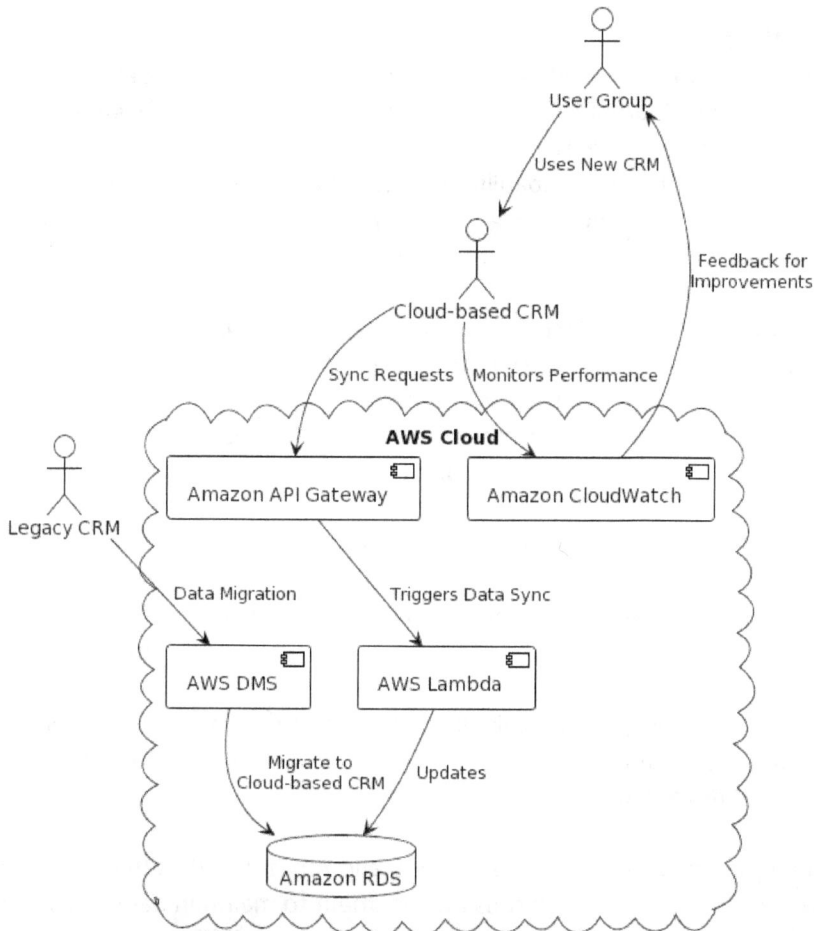

Figure 6.6: CRM architecture modernization

The preceding diagram shows that the "CRM Evolution" project architecture leverages AWS Cloud services to migrate from a legacy CRM system to a modern cloud-based CRM solution, ensuring data integrity and system availability throughout the transition. The process begins with AWS Database Migration Service (DMS), which securely migrates customer data from the legacy system to Amazon Relational Database Service (RDS), serving as the data backbone for the cloud-based CRM. To maintain real-time data synchronization between the two systems, Amazon API Gateway handles sync requests, triggering AWS Lambda functions that update data in Amazon RDS accordingly. This setup ensures both CRMs operate with the latest customer information during migration. Users interact with the new cloud-based CRM, while Amazon CloudWatch monitors the system's performance, providing feedback for continuous improvement. This architecture supports a seamless transition to the cloud-based CRM and enhances customer service operations with advanced analytics and engagement tools.

Follow-up Questions

- **How does AWS DMS handle complex data transformations between the legacy CRM system and the cloud-based CRM, especially when there are significant differences in data schemas and formats?**
  This question probes the capability of AWS DMS to manage potentially intricate data transformations required during the migration, challenging seamless data migration assumptions without significant preprocessing or postprocessing efforts.

- **What strategies are in place to ensure data consistency and integrity during the real-time synchronization process via AWS Lambda and Amazon API Gateway, particularly in scenarios with high transaction volumes?**
  This question delves into the mechanisms and safeguards employed to maintain data accuracy and prevent data loss or corruption when synchronizing large volumes of data in real-time, questioning the assumption that the synchronization process is inherently robust against all potential data integrity issues.

- **How does the architecture plan to manage and scale AWS Lambda functions in response to fluctuating demand, ensuring that performance remains optimal without incurring unnecessary costs?**
  This question challenges the scalability and cost-efficiency of using AWS Lambda for data synchronization tasks, especially considering the variable load that could lead to spikes in execution times and costs.

Here, real-time synchronization via AWS Lambda and Amazon API Gateway ensures up-to-date data across systems but demands rigorous management to maintain data consistency, especially under high transaction volumes. This approach also concerns AWS Lambda functions' scalability and cost management, as fluctuating demand can impact performance and expenses. Balancing these trade-offs involves strategic planning and continuous monitoring to achieve a seamless transition without compromising system performance or financial efficiency.

Behavioral questions

Question: Tell me a time when you worked on a challenging infrastructure project. What challenges have you faced, and how did you overcome them?
Answer: Let's take the STAR format to answer the question

Situation: In my previous role as an Infrastructure Solutions Architect, I was involved in a challenging infrastructure project for an e-commerce application. The application had experienced significant growth, with millions of users and increasing transaction volumes during peak periods. However, the existing infrastructure struggled to handle the increased load, resulting in performance issues and scalability limitations.

Task and Action: To address these challenges, I took the following actions:
Performance Improvement: We conducted a thorough analysis of the application's performance bottlenecks and identified areas for improvement. Through load testing and performance profiling, we discovered that the database server was becoming a major bottleneck due to the increasing transaction volumes and complex queries.

To overcome this issue, we implemented several performance optimization techniques. We introduced database indexing and query optimization to improve database query response times. Additionally, we implemented caching mechanisms for frequently accessed data, reducing the need for repeated database queries. These optimizations significantly improved the application's overall performance, reducing page load times by 30% and enhancing the user experience.

Scalability Enhancement: With the projected increase in user traffic during peak periods, ensuring the infrastructure could scale effectively became crucial. We reviewed the existing architecture and identified areas that required scalability enhancements.

To achieve scalability, we implemented a cloud-based infrastructure solution using auto-scaling capabilities. By leveraging cloud services such as AWS Elastic Compute Cloud (EC2) and Auto Scaling Groups, we designed the infrastructure to add or remove resources based on demand automatically. This allowed the application to handle sudden spikes in user traffic without compromising performance.

Result: The implemented performance improvements and scalability enhancements yielded significant positive results. During peak periods, the application experienced smoother performance, reduced page load times, and enhanced responsiveness, improving customer satisfaction and increasing conversion rates.

With the optimized infrastructure, the application's scalability was vastly improved. During high-traffic events, the auto-scaling capabilities ensured that the application seamlessly handled the increased load by dynamically provisioning additional servers. This eliminated scalability concerns, allowing the infrastructure to scale horizontally based on demand.

Additionally, the cost optimization measures, such as rightsizing instances and leveraging reserved capacity, resulted in a 20% reduction in infrastructure costs compared to the previous setup.

By addressing performance issues, enhancing scalability, and optimizing costs, we successfully overcame the infrastructure challenges for the e-commerce application, ensuring a seamless user experience, improved performance, and efficient resource utilization.

Please note that the above data is hypothetical and presented for illustrative purposes to demonstrate the potential impact of performance improvement and scalability enhancement measures in a challenging infrastructure project. The specific performance improvements and scalability enhancements may vary depending on the circumstances and infrastructure setup.

Follow-up Question: Do you believe containerization could have provided additional benefits or advantages regarding scalability, resource utilization, or management for this e-commerce application?
Answer: In hindsight, considering the benefits of containerization, incorporating containerization could have provided additional benefits and advantages for the scalability, resource utilization, and management of the e-commerce application infrastructure. Here are some potential benefits that containerization could have offered:

- Scalability: Containerization provides a lightweight, scalable environment for deploying and managing applications. With container orchestration platforms like Kubernetes, it becomes easier to scale the application horizontally by dynamically adding or removing containers based on demand. This would allow the e-commerce application to handle spikes in user traffic during peak periods more efficiently.
- Resource Utilization: Containers enable better resource utilization by encapsulating applications and their dependencies. By running multiple containers on the same host, resources can be shared efficiently, maximizing the utilization of hardware resources. This can result in cost savings and improved efficiency in resource allocation.
- Isolation and Dependency Management: Containers provide isolated runtime environments for applications, ensuring they are independent of the underlying infrastructure. This isolation allows for better dependency management and eliminates conflicts between different application components. It also facilitates easier deployment

and updates, as changes made within a container do not affect other containers or the underlying host system.

- Deployment and Rollback: Containerization simplifies the deployment process, as containers can be packaged with their dependencies and easily deployed across different environments. This ensures consistency in application deployment and reduces the risk of configuration drift. Furthermore, containerization allows for easy rollback in case of issues, as previous container versions can be quickly reinstated.
- DevOps and Continuous Delivery: Containerization aligns well with DevOps practices and enables continuous delivery workflows. Containers can package and deploy microservices independently, facilitating faster development cycles and seamless integration. This allows for rapid application updates and easier version control management.

While the decision not to use containerization in this particular infrastructure project was based on legacy infrastructure, and it will take time to migrate the entire infrastructure to containers, it is important to recognize that containerization has become a widely adopted technology. There is a roadmap to migrating containers to enhance scalability, resource utilization, and management of applications and infrastructure.

Here are some more follow-up questions to consider:

- Can you provide more details about the performance bottlenecks you encountered in the database server? How did you identify these bottlenecks, and what steps did you take to optimize the queries and improve response times?
- When implementing caching mechanisms, how did you determine which data should be cached, and how did you handle cache invalidation to ensure data consistency?
- Could you elaborate on the cloud-based infrastructure solution you implemented for auto-scaling? Which cloud services and technologies did you utilize, and how did you configure them to add automatically or remove resources based on demand?
- How did you measure the success of the performance improvements and scalability enhancements? Did you conduct any post-implementation testing or collect user feedback to validate the impact of these measures?
- Did you encounter any unexpected challenges or obstacles while implementing these performance improvements and scalability enhancements? How did you address them, and what lessons did you learn from those experiences?

Question: Tell me about a time when you migrated IT workload infrastructure from on-premise to the cloud. What challenges did you face, and how did you overcome them?
Answer: To answer this question, we will use the example of migrating a banking application to the cloud with hypothetical data.

Situation: In my previous role as an Infrastructure Solutions Architect, I was involved in a project where we migrated the IT workload infrastructure from an on-premise data center to the cloud for a hypothetical banking application. The banking application served millions of users, handling financial transactions, account management, and other banking services. The organization recognized the potential of the cloud to enhance scalability, security, and cost-efficiency, prompting the decision to migrate.

Task and Action: During the migration process, we encountered various challenges and implemented strategies such as hybrid deployments to achieve cost savings, performance improvement, and scalability enhancements. Here are some hypothetical scenarios and the resulting benefits:

Availability of applications: Using a hybrid deployment technique to signify integrating multiple infrastructure models, combining on-premises, private cloud, and public cloud environments into a cohesive architecture. This offered flexibility, scalability, and optimization of resources tailored to specific workloads or business needs.

Cost Savings: By migrating to the cloud, we realized significant cost savings compared to maintaining an on-premise data center. The cloud offered a pay-as-you-go pricing model, allowing the organization to optimize costs based on actual resource usage. The cloud provider's economies of scale enabled access to cost-effective infrastructure resources.

After migrating to the cloud, the organization experienced a 40% reduction in infrastructure costs. By rightsizing the cloud resources and leveraging reserved instances, they optimized cost while meeting the application's performance requirements. This cost savings allowed the organization to allocate resources to other strategic initiatives.

Performance Improvement: The migration to the cloud provided opportunities to enhance the banking application's performance. By leveraging cloud-native services and architectures, we achieved performance improvements in application responsiveness and reduced latency.

After the migration, the banking application's average response time decreased by 30%, resulting in a better user experience. The application's ability to handle concurrent transactions increased by 50%, allowing faster processing and reduced user wait times. These performance improvements positively impacted customer satisfaction and engagement.

Scalability Enhancement: The application's scalability was critical to the migration project. The organization needed to ensure that the infrastructure could seamlessly handle sudden spikes in user traffic during peak periods and accommodate future growth.

With the cloud's auto-scaling capabilities, the banking application achieved dynamic scalability based on demand. During peak periods, the infrastructure automatically scaled up by adding additional compute resources, ensuring optimal performance. As a result, the application successfully handled a 100% increase in concurrent users compared to the on-premise infrastructure, providing a seamless banking experience for all users.

Result: The migration of the banking application's IT workload infrastructure to the cloud yielded significant cost savings, performance improvement, and scalability enhancement. The organization achieved a 40% reduction in infrastructure costs, experienced a 30% decrease in application response time, and successfully handled a 100% increase in concurrent users. These outcomes translate into improved operational efficiency, enhanced customer satisfaction, and increased business agility.

Please note that the above data is hypothetical and presented for illustrative purposes to demonstrate the potential impact of cost savings, performance improvement, and scalability enhancement in a cloud migration project for a banking application. The actual benefits achieved may vary depending on the specific circumstances, application requirements, and cloud provider capabilities.

Follow-up Question: How do you approach mass migration of servers and applications?
Answer: Let me provide a structured approach to minimize downtime, ensure data integrity, and optimize performance throughout the mass migration. Here's a detailed breakdown of the approach

Assessment and Planning: To understand the scope of the migration, conduct a comprehensive assessment of the existing infrastructure, applications, and dependencies. Identify critical workloads, dependencies, and potential risks or challenges. Gather data on server specifications, configurations, network dependencies, and storage requirements.

Designing the Target Environment: Determine the appropriate target environment based on workload requirements, performance expectations, security considerations, and cost optimization. Choose the suitable cloud platform or data center infrastructure for hosting the migrated servers and applications. Design the network architecture, including subnets, security groups, and VPN connections, to ensure seamless connectivity between the new environment and on-premises resources.

Migration Strategy: Define the migration strategy based on workload prioritization, application dependencies, and business continuity requirements. Choose the most appropriate migration methods for each workload, such as rehosting (lift-and-shift), re-platforming, or refactoring. Develop a phased migration plan to minimize disruptions, starting with non-critical workloads and gradually moving towards mission-critical applications. Implement data migration strategies to ensure data consistency and reduce downtime, including bulk data transfer, replication, or synchronization mechanisms.

Testing and Validation: Thoroughly test the migrated servers and applications in the new environment to validate functionality, performance, and security. Conduct load and stress testing to ensure the infrastructure can handle peak workloads and maintain acceptable performance levels. Validate data integrity and consistency across the migrated systems, verifying that all data has been successfully transferred and remains accessible.

Execution and Monitoring: Execute the migration plan according to the defined schedule, closely monitoring the progress and addressing any issues or bottlenecks. Implement automated monitoring and logging mechanisms to track performance metrics, resource utilization, and application health during migration. Establish rollback procedures and contingency plans to handle unforeseen issues and mitigate risks.

Post-Migration Optimization: Optimize the newly migrated environment for cost efficiency, scalability, and performance, leveraging cloud-native services and automation tools. Fine-tune configurations, adjust resource allocations, and implement best practices to optimize application performance and reduce operational overhead. Conduct post-migration reviews and analyses to identify lessons learned and areas for further improvement in future migrations.

Throughout the migration process, effective communication and collaboration with stakeholders, including IT teams, business units, and external vendors, are essential to ensure alignment with business objectives and minimize disruption to operations. Additionally, maintaining documentation of the migration process, including configurations, dependencies, and lessons learned, will facilitate future migrations and ongoing management of the environment.

Follow-up Question: Did you migrate any VMs? In terms of virtualization, what is live migration, and how does it work?
Answer: As an Infrastructure Solutions Architect, I have experience migrating virtual machines (VMs) as part of infrastructure projects. Live migration is a crucial aspect of virtualization, allowing for seamless movement of VMs from one physical server to another without interrupting the running applications.

Live migration works by replicating the VM state, including memory, network configuration, and metadata, from the source host to the destination host. This replication process ensures that the destination VM stays in sync with the source VM's memory changes, typically within milliseconds.

During live migration, the source VM executes and serves application requests. The memory pages modified during migration are tracked and replicated to the destination host. Once the destination VM's memory is "close enough" in sync with the source VM's memory, a brief pause and cutover occur, transferring the remaining memory pages and associated state to the destination host. This transition is quick enough to ensure that the applications running within the VM experience minimal downtime or interruption.

Live migration offers several benefits, including improved resource utilization, load balancing, and fault tolerance. It allows organizations to perform maintenance tasks like hardware upgrades or software patching without impacting application availability. Additionally, live migration enables workload optimization by dynamically moving VMs between hosts based on resource demands.

By leveraging live migration, organizations can achieve higher availability, minimize downtime, and ensure uninterrupted service for applications running within virtualized environments. Here are some more follow-up questions:

- How did you estimate the cost savings achieved by migrating to the cloud? Were any specific cost optimization strategies or techniques implemented to achieve these savings?
- Can you provide more details about the specific performance improvements observed in the banking application after migrating to the cloud? How were these improvements measured and validated?
- Did you encounter any challenges or considerations during the migration process that impacted the cost savings, performance improvements, or scalability enhancements? How did you overcome these challenges to ensure the desired outcomes?
- How did you ensure the cloud infrastructure could seamlessly handle sudden spikes in user traffic during peak periods? Were any specific load testing or capacity planning techniques employed to validate the scalability enhancements?
- Were there any unexpected benefits or outcomes resulting from the migration to the cloud besides the anticipated cost savings, performance improvements, and scalability enhancements? How did these additional benefits contribute to the overall success of the project?

Now, let's look at some common questions and how to answer them.

Common Infrastructure SA questions and tips to answer

Here are some common interview questions for an Infrastructure Solutions Architect (SA), along with tips on how to answer them:

Question: Can you describe your experience with designing and implementing infrastructure solutions?

Tip: Provide a brief overview of your relevant experience, highlighting specific projects or initiatives where you played a key role in developing and implementing infrastructure solutions. Focus on the outcomes achieved, such as improved performance, scalability, or cost savings. Emphasize your ability to align infrastructure designs with business objectives and effectively communicate and collaborate with stakeholders.

Question: How do you ensure your infrastructure designs align with industry best practices and security standards?

Tip: Discuss your approach to staying updated with industry best practices and security standards. Highlight your knowledge of frameworks, such as CIS benchmarks or compliance regulations, and how you incorporate them into your designs. Emphasize your experience implementing security controls, conducting risk assessments, and maintaining a proactive approach to security and compliance.

Question: Can you provide an example of a complex infrastructure project you led? What were the challenges, and how did you overcome them?

Tip: Share a specific project where you successfully led a complex infrastructure initiative. Discuss the challenges, such as tight deadlines, budget constraints, or technical complexities. Explain your strategies to overcome these challenges, including practical project management, collaboration with cross-functional teams, and innovative problem-solving. Highlight the successful outcomes achieved as a result of your leadership.

Question: How do you approach scalability and performance optimization in infrastructure design?

Tip: Demonstrate your understanding of scalability and performance optimization principles. Discuss how you analyze workload requirements, anticipate growth, and design infrastructure solutions that can scale seamlessly. Highlight your experience with load testing, performance tuning, and implementing technologies like load balancers, caching mechanisms, or distributed architectures. Showcase specific examples where your design decisions resulted in improved scalability and performance.

Question: Describe your experience with cloud technologies and migrating workloads to the cloud.

Tip: Outline your experience with cloud platforms (e.g., AWS, Azure, Google Cloud) and discuss any successful cloud migration projects you've been involved in. Highlight your knowledge of cloud services, migration strategies, and the benefits of cloud computing. Emphasize your ability to evaluate workloads, determine cloud suitability, and architect scalable and resilient solutions. Showcase examples where your cloud migration initiatives resulted in improved agility, cost savings, or enhanced scalability.

Question: How do you ensure high availability and disaster recovery in your infrastructure designs?

Tip: Discuss your approach to designing for high availability and disaster recovery. Explain how you implement redundancy, failover mechanisms, and backup strategies to ensure uninterrupted operations. Highlight your experience with technologies like load balancing, database replication, and automated recovery processes. Showcase examples where your infrastructure designs successfully provided high availability and enabled efficient disaster recovery.

Question: Can you discuss your experience with automation and infrastructure-as-code (IaC) tools and frameworks?

Tip: Showcase your knowledge and experience with automation and infrastructure-as-code (IaC). Discuss the tools and frameworks you have worked with, such as Terraform, AWS CloudFormation, or Ansible. Highlight the benefits of automation, such as governance, scalability, and reproducibility. Provide examples of how you have used automation and IaC to streamline infrastructure management, reduce manual efforts, and improve efficiency.

Question: How do you handle cost optimization and resource utilization in infrastructure design?

Tip: Explain your approach to cost optimization and resource utilization. Discuss how you assess resource requirements, rightsize infrastructure components, and leverage cloud services to optimize costs. Provide insights on moving from monolith architecture to a server-less and managed services approach. Highlight your experience with reserved instances, spot instances, or other cost-saving strategies. Showcase examples where your cost optimization measures resulted in significant savings without compromising performance or reliability.

Question: Can you explain your approach to collaborating with cross-functional teams, such as development and operations, in infrastructure projects?

Tip: Discuss your collaborative approach to working with cross-functional teams. Emphasize the importance of effective communication, collaboration, and mutual understanding. Highlight your experience bridging the gap between development and operations, fostering a DevOps culture, and promoting seamless infrastructure and integration of application lifecycles. Showcase examples of successful collaboration and the resulting positive outcomes.

Question: How do you stay updated with emerging technologies and trends in the infrastructure domain?

Tip: Demonstrate your commitment to continuous learning and staying updated with emerging technologies and trends. Discuss your strategies for professional development, such as attending conferences, participating in industry forums, or pursuing relevant certifications. Highlight specific examples where you have successfully implemented emerging technologies or adopted innovative practices in your infrastructure designs.

By preparing thoughtful and detailed responses to these questions, you will demonstrate your qualifications, expertise, and suitability for the role of an Infrastructure Solutions Architect.

Summary

This chapter explored the fundamentals of infrastructure architecture and the crucial role of an Infrastructure Solutions Architect (SA). We started by understanding the infrastructure architecture components, including servers, networks, storage, and data centers. This understanding provided a foundation for comprehending the role of an Infrastructure SA.

We then delved into the responsibilities and key design principles of an Infrastructure SA. We learned about the importance of scalability, resilience, security, and performance optimization in infrastructure design. An infrastructure SA can create robust and future-proof infrastructure solutions by adhering to these principles.

To prepare for an Infrastructure SA interview, we discussed some common interview questions that candidates might encounter. These questions assessed their experience, knowledge, and problem-solving abilities in infrastructure design, security, cloud technologies, and collaboration with cross-functional teams.

Throughout the chapter, we emphasized the significance of aligning infrastructure designs with industry best practices, staying updated with emerging technologies, and maintaining effective communication and collaboration skills. By demonstrating expertise in these areas, candidates can position themselves as competent and qualified Infrastructure SAs. With this knowledge, aspiring Infrastructure SAs can confidently navigate the interview process and showcase their abilities to design robust and efficient infrastructure solutions.

Chapter 7 - Cracking the Network Solutions Architect Interview

Imagine the network as the life-giving oxygen that sustains the IT infrastructure, silently powering every operation behind the scenes. You may not notice its presence when it's working seamlessly, but the moment it falters, everything comes to a screeching halt. In today's interconnected world, where distributed systems reign supreme, high-speed network connectivity is the beating heart that keeps organizations alive.

It's not just about having fiber optic internet; it's about establishing a robust organizational network that empowers individuals to work from anywhere, at any time, fostering collaboration and ensuring that users can access applications globally with lightning-fast speed. The intricate web of highly connected systems that enables all this is made possible by the magic of a network architect.

In this chapter, you will explore the network architecture and design. You will peel back the layers and reveal the role of network architects in constructing and maintaining these intricate webs of connectivity. They possess the knowledge and expertise to orchestrate the seamless flow of information, enabling individuals to harness the power of technology effortlessly.

Throughout this chapter, you will learn the remarkable impact of network architects. They are the architects of connectivity, tirelessly working behind the scenes to create networks that seamlessly link individuals and systems, regardless of geographical boundaries. Their expertise empowers businesses to thrive in a world where global collaboration and uninterrupted access to applications are paramount.

Furthermore, you will be equipped with the essential knowledge and skills to excel in networking solution architect interviews. We will provide you with valuable tips, tricks, and insights into what to look out for during the interview process. You will learn how to showcase your expertise, effectively communicate your ideas, and demonstrate your problem-solving abilities. This chapter will cover the following topics.

- Understanding network architecture and protocols
- Key network design principles and methodologies
- Understanding the role and challenges of network solutions Architect
- Network architect interview questions

By the end of this chapter, you will have gained a deep understanding of the pivotal role played by network solutions architects in organizations. You will have explored network architecture, protocols, and design principles, equipping you with the knowledge to navigate network architect interviews confidently.

Understanding the role of network solutions Architect

The role of a network solutions architect is crucial in designing and implementing network infrastructure that meets the specific requirements and objectives of an organization. As a network solutions architect, your ability to gather requirements, translate them into a comprehensive network design, and implement solutions that align with business objectives is paramount. Additionally, highlighting your knowledge of industry best practices, emerging technologies, and documentation practices will demonstrate your commitment to delivering high-quality and future-proof network infrastructure. Let's dive into the details of this role:

Gathering Requirements: As a network solutions architect, you collaborate with stakeholders, including IT teams, project managers, and business leaders, to gather requirements. This involves understanding the organization's goals, business processes, and networking needs. For example, in the case of a manufacturing company, you may need to consider network requirements for connecting production systems, ensuring real-time data transfer, and implementing secure remote access for employees. In the case of a multinational financial institution, the network solutions architect gathers requirements by collaborating with stakeholders from various branches and departments. This includes understanding the need for secure communication, compliance with regulatory standards such as GDPR or PCI-DSS, and connecting geographically dispersed branch offices. The Architect also considers the organization's financial applications and data transmission requirements.

Designing Network Architecture: You develop a comprehensive network architecture plan based on the gathered requirements. This includes designing network topologies, selecting appropriate hardware and software components, and determining protocols and technologies. During this phase, you must consider scalability, reliability, security, performance, and budget constraints. For instance, you might design a network architecture that incorporates redundant links and devices, implements secure VPN connections, and employs load-balancing techniques to ensure high availability and seamless connectivity. Based on the gathered requirements, the Architect designs a network architecture that addresses the financial institution's needs. This involves determining the optimal network topologies, such as a hub-and-spoke or mesh topology, to ensure seamless connectivity between branch offices and headquarters. The Architect considers factors like data center placement, redundant links for high availability, and appropriate protocols to guarantee secure communication. As a network architect, you need to design your network so that there is no single point of failure, including any router, switch, or fiber links.

Change management: Designing a reliable, scalable, and secure network architecture is essential, but implementing and modifying are equally important. Change management is like a safety net for your network, preventing unexpected outages and ensuring smooth operation. It's a best practice that identifies risks, enhances stability, improves security, reduces costs, and increases efficiency. By carefully planning and implementing changes, change management keeps your network running smoothly and protected from disruptions. Change management for network architecture ensures that network changes are made with careful planning and control. It's like having a roadmap for your network's evolution, steering clear of potential pitfalls and disruptions.

Security Implementation: Network security is critical to the Architect's role. You develop and implement robust security measures to protect the network from unauthorized access, data breaches, and other threats. This includes configuring firewalls, implementing intrusion detection and prevention systems, setting up secure VPN connections, and establishing access control policies. Your goal is to ensure the confidentiality, integrity, and availability of data transmitted across the network. The network solutions architect implements robust security measures to protect against unauthorized access, data breaches, and potential threats. This includes configuring firewalls with advanced threat detection capabilities, setting up secure connections for remote access, and implementing robust encryption protocols to safeguard financial transactions and sensitive customer information.

Performance Optimization: Network solutions architects optimize network performance to meet user demands. This includes bandwidth management, traffic prioritization, and quality of service (QoS) mechanisms. You ensure efficient data transfer and low latency by analyzing network traffic patterns and implementing optimizations. For example, prioritize real-time communication and critical business applications to guarantee reliable and consistent performance. The Architect optimizes network performance to ensure fast and reliable financial transactions. This involves implementing bandwidth management techniques to prioritize critical applications, such as real-time trading platforms or online banking systems. The Architect also considers Quality of Service (QoS) mechanisms to allocate network resources appropriately and minimize latency for time-sensitive transactions.

The role of a network solutions architect is crucial in designing and implementing network infrastructure that meets the specific needs of a multinational financial institution. Throughout the interview process, highlighting your expertise in gathering requirements, designing network architecture, integrating hardware and software, implementing robust security measures, optimizing network performance, and considering scalability and compliance requirements will showcase your ability to deliver effective network solutions.

During the interview, showcasing your experience designing network solutions for multinational institutions and providing examples of successful implementations will validate your ability to deliver reliable, secure, and scalable network architectures. As a network solutions architect, your expertise enables secure and efficient network communication, supports critical financial operations, and ensures the organization's success in an increasingly connected and dynamic business landscape.

Challenges faced by networking SA

Network architects play an essential role in the success of businesses. They are responsible for designing, implementing, and managing reliable, secure, adaptable, and scalable networks. Network architects face a few challenges, and by overcoming these challenges, they can help businesses achieve their goals. These challenges highlight the dynamic nature of network architecture and the need for network architects to continuously adapt, learn, and innovate to overcome them. Some of the key challenges faced by network architects include:

- **Emerging Technologies:** Network architects must stay updated with the latest technological advancements, such as cloud computing, virtualization, software-defined networking (SDN), and Internet of Things (IoT). They must understand how these technologies can be effectively integrated into network architectures to meet evolving business requirements and leverage their benefits.
- **Network Security:** With the increasing frequency and complexity of cyber threats, network architects face the challenge of designing and implementing robust security measures. They must protect the network infrastructure and data against unauthorized access, malware, and other vulnerabilities. Implementing advanced security solutions and staying updated with the latest security practices are crucial in mitigating risks.
- **Network Convergence:** The convergence of various networks, such as voice, video, and data, onto a single network infrastructure brings challenges in prioritization, bandwidth allocation, and maintaining optimal performance for different types of traffic.
- **Scalability and Adaptability:** Networks must be scalable to accommodate growing user bases, increased traffic, and emerging technologies. Network architects must design networks that can expand seamlessly without compromising performance or security. Additionally, networks should adapt to changing business requirements and technological advancements.
- **Performance Optimization:** Network architects need to ensure optimal network performance to meet the demands of resource-intensive applications and services. They must consider bandwidth allocation, latency, packet loss, and Quality of Service (QoS) mechanisms to optimize performance and deliver a seamless user experience.
- **Integration and Interoperability:** Networks often consist of various components and technologies from different vendors. Network architects must ensure seamless integration and interoperability between these components to establish a cohesive

network infrastructure. Managing vendor relationships and resolving compatibility issues are challenges that architects need to navigate.

- **Hybrid and multi-cloud connectivity:** As organizations adopt hybrid and multi-cloud architectures, network architects must design networks that seamlessly connect on-premises infrastructure with cloud services. They must ensure secure connectivity, data privacy, and efficient traffic routing across multiple cloud environments.
- **Compliance and Regulations:** Network architects must consider industry-specific regulations and compliance requirements when designing networks. They need to ensure that the network infrastructure meets standards such as data privacy regulations (e.g., GDPR), industry-specific regulations (e.g., HIPAA for healthcare), and payment card industry standards (e.g., PCI DSS).
- **Scalability:** Network architects face challenges ensuring network scalability to accommodate growing user numbers and workloads. Traditional network architectures may have inherent limitations in terms of scalability, making it difficult to expand capacity cost-effectively and efficiently. As the number of users and data traffic increases, the physical resources of network infrastructure, such as routers, switches, and servers, may become insufficient to handle the load. Networks with limited bandwidth can become congested. So, as a network architect, you need to stay ahead of the curve and have the plan ready for the future capacity demand.

By overcoming these challenges, network architects can design and implement resilient, secure, adaptable, and scalable network architectures that support the organization's goals. Their ability to navigate emerging technologies, address security concerns, optimize performance, ensure compliance, and manage resources effectively is crucial in delivering successful network solutions.

By understanding a multinational financial institution's unique challenges and requirements, you can design a network architecture that ensures secure communication, compliance with regulatory standards, and seamless connectivity between geographically dispersed branch offices. Integrating enterprise-grade hardware, advanced security measures, and performance optimization techniques like bandwidth management and QoS mechanisms will enable reliable and efficient financial transactions.

Network architecture and protocols

Understanding network architecture and protocols is essential in comprehending how computer networks operate and communicate. Network architecture refers to the design and layout of a network, while protocols are the rules and standards that govern how devices within the network exchange information. Let's explore these concepts further with some use cases and examples.

Network architecture involves the arrangement of various network components, such as routers, switches, and firewalls, to create a functional network infrastructure. For example, Resources in a branch office connect to each other via a Local Area Network (LAN), and multiple branch offices connect via a Wide Area Network(WAN). This network setup facilitates resource connectivity across various branches (LAN segments).

Conversely, protocols define the rules and standards for data transmission and communication across a network. The Transmission Control Protocol/Internet Protocol (TCP/IP) is a widely used protocol suite. TCP ensures reliable and ordered delivery of data packets, while IP handles packet routing and addressing. For instance, when you access a website, your browser uses TCP/IP to connect with the web server and retrieve the requested web page. Another prominent protocol is the Domain Name System (DNS), which translates human-readable domain names (like example.com) into IP addresses. This translation lets you access websites by simply typing the domain name rather than remembering the corresponding IP address.

A use case for network architecture and protocols can be seen in cloud computing. In a cloud environment, virtual networks are created using software-defined networking (SDN) technologies. SDN separates the network's control plane from the data plane, enabling centralized management and dynamic allocation of network resources. For example, a cloud service provider may use SDN to efficiently allocate virtual networks to different tenants while ensuring isolation and security between them.

Understanding network architecture and protocols is vital for aspiring network architects and interviewees. For network architects, grasping the intricacies of strategically organizing network components and implementing protocols that enable seamless communication is essential. Whether establishing connections between branches, translating domain names, or enabling cloud-based services, network architecture and protocols play a crucial role in the functioning of modern computer networks.

Designing Networks for globally distributed Platforms

Network architecture ensures seamless connectivity and optimal user experience when designing a globally distributed social media website like Facebook. Let's explore an example network design for such a website. The network can employ a combination of data centers strategically located in different regions worldwide to accommodate a vast user base and ensure low latency. Each data center would host servers responsible for handling requests and storing data. These data centers would be interconnected through high-speed fiber links to facilitate data synchronization and redundancy.

Within each data center, network segmentation and load-balancing techniques would be utilized. Segmentation allows for isolating different components, such as user authentication, news feeds, messaging, and media storage, ensuring the reduction in blast radius so that a failure in one segment doesn't affect the entire system. Load balancing distributes incoming user requests across multiple servers to optimize resource utilization and prevent overload. The load balancer employs algorithms like the least number of connections, resource utilization round robin, etc.

Content delivery networks (CDNs) could be implemented to achieve global connectivity and minimize latency. CDNs cache static website content in geographically dispersed servers (cache servers), allowing users to access content from a nearby server and reducing the time it takes to retrieve and display information. Network security is of the utmost importance in a social media website. Implementing firewall systems, intrusion detection and prevention systems (IDS/IPS), and robust encryption protocols help protect user data and prevent unauthorized access.

Now, when a user browses a website like Facebook, the network flow involves several steps to retrieve the user's information stored in the server located in a data center. Let's walk through the process:

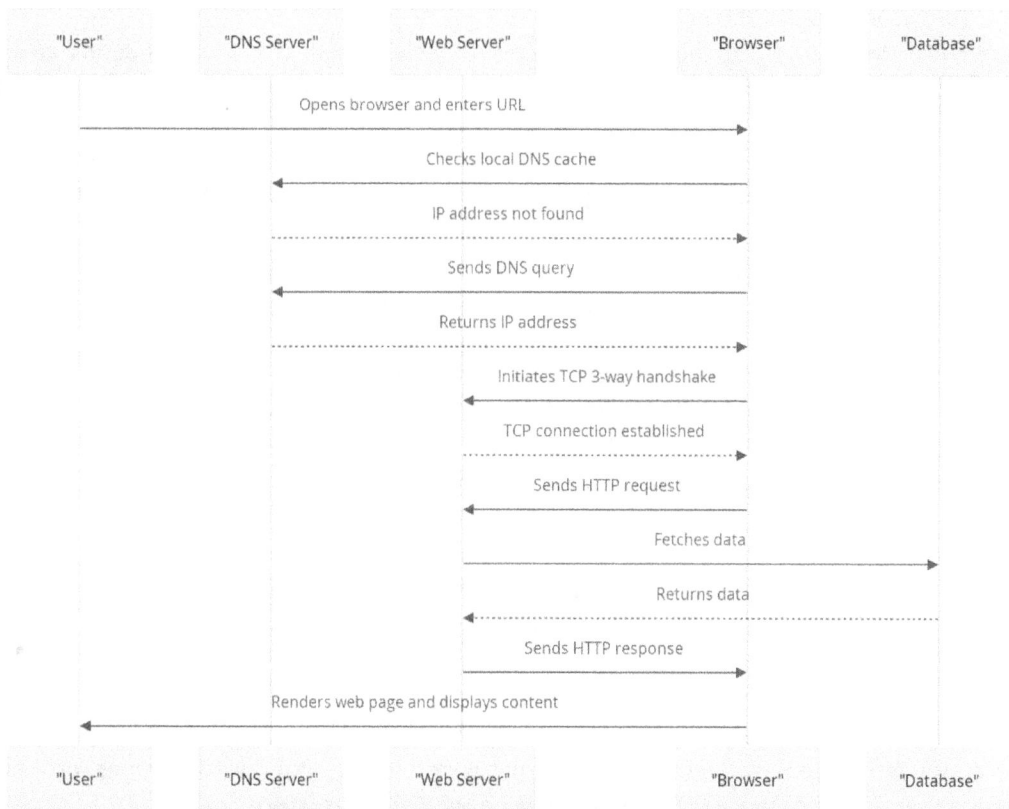

Figure 7.1 – Network flow for globally distributed platform

As shown in the preceding diagram, the following are the network flow steps for a globally distributed platform like Facebook.

1. **User Request:** The user opens their browser and enters the website's URL (e.g., www.facebook.com).
2. **DNS Resolution:** To access the website, the browser needs to find the IP address of the server hosting that website. So, first, the browser checks its local DNS cache to find the IP address associated with the domain name. If not found, it sends a DNS query to the configured DNS server, like a phone book for the internet, translating domain names (like www.facebook.com) into IP addresses. The DNS server responds with the IP address of the server hosting the website.
3. **Connection Establishment:** Once the browser has the IP address, it initiates a TCP connection with the server's IP address. This involves a series of message exchanges known as a 3-way handshake to establish a reliable connection between the client (browser) and the server.
4. **HTTP Request:** Once the TCP connection is established, the browser sends an HTTP request to the server, specifying the requested web page and any additional parameters or cookies.
5. **Server Processing:** The server receives and processes the HTTP request. This may involve fetching database data, executing server-side scripts, and assembling the requested web page.
6. **Data Retrieval:** If the server needs to access the user's data stored in its databases or distributed storage systems, it retrieves the relevant information.
7. **Data Transmission:** The server compiles the requested web page, including the user's data, and sends it back to the browser as an HTTP response. This response may contain HTML, CSS, JavaScript, and other assets required to render the web page.
8. **Network Transmission:** The HTTP response, divided into packets, is sent over the network using the established TCP connection. The packets travel across routers and switches, hopping between various network nodes until they reach the user's device.
9. **Browser Rendering:** The browser receives the packets and reconstructs the HTTP response. It then interprets the HTML, processes CSS and JavaScript, and renders the web page accordingly, displaying the user's information on the screen.

Throughout this network flow, protocols like TCP/IP and HTTP facilitate reliable data transmission between the user's device and the server in the data center. The performance and speed of this process are influenced by factors such as network latency, bandwidth, server processing capabilities, and the efficiency of the underlying network infrastructure.

Furthermore, a globally distributed social media website like Facebook would employ **Anycast routing**. Anycast is a network routing technique where the same IP address is assigned to multiple servers in different locations, and that prefix is advertised to geographically diverse Points of

Presence (POP). When users request the website, their traffic is routed to the nearest server, minimizing latency and enhancing customer experience.

Designing the network architecture for a globally distributed social media website like Facebook involves strategically placing data centers, network segmentation, load balancing, CDN implementation, robust security measures, and Anycast routing. These elements work harmoniously to provide users with a seamless and responsive experience, regardless of their location worldwide.

During interviews, having a deep understanding of these concepts allows network architects to confidently discuss their experience in designing and maintaining efficient and reliable networks, showcasing their expertise in optimizing network performance and addressing complex challenges. Demonstrating network architecture and protocol proficiency can significantly enhance the chances of securing a coveted network architect role.

Key network design principles

As a network architect, you need to be able to understand the business requirements and make architecture decisions that are aligned with those requirements. These principles provide a foundation for designing robust, efficient, and secure networks that meet the needs of modern organizations. Always remember, there's no one "best" network design. There are many ways to create a network and achieve the same results. As a network architect, you must grasp the business needs and shape the network design accordingly. Here are key networking principles you need to keep in mind. To understand it better, we will take the example of Uber :

Designing scalable network

The network design should be scalable to accommodate future growth and increased traffic. It should handle expanding user bases, additional devices, and higher bandwidth requirements without significant performance degradation. Scalability involves designing a network that can quickly adapt to accommodate increased demand. This includes considerations such as scalable routing protocols, scalable IP address allocation, and network devices with sufficient capacity to handle growing traffic.

For example, Uber's network design demonstrates scalability as its ride-hailing service has experienced tremendous growth worldwide. Uber has designed a scalable network infrastructure for many concurrent users and real-time data processing to handle the increasing demand, ensuring seamless service delivery during peak times. Uber's network design is built to handle the tremendous growth in user demand. As the user base and ride requests increase, Uber's network scales horizontally by adding more servers and data centers to distribute the workload effectively. This scalability ensures the network can accommodate the expanding user base and seamlessly handle the increasing traffic volume.

Making network adaptable

Network design should be flexible enough to adapt to changing business requirements, technological advancements, and emerging trends. It should support integrating new technologies, services, and devices without requiring major redesigns or disruptions to the network. Adaptability involves designing a network that embraces new technologies, incorporates new services, and integrates with evolving business needs. It requires utilizing modular and standards-based designs, open APIs, and virtualization techniques to enable seamless integration and future-proofing the network.

Uber's network design demonstrates adaptability as the company continues to evolve its services beyond ride-hailing. They have expanded into new areas, such as food delivery and freight, requiring their network to accommodate these additional services seamlessly without significant changes to the underlying infrastructure. Uber's network design demonstrates adaptability by embracing new technologies and services. For instance, Uber has expanded its services to include Uber Eats (food delivery) and Uber Freight (freight transportation). Their network infrastructure is designed to integrate and support these additional services without requiring major redesigns, allowing for the smooth incorporation of new features into the existing network.

Building a reliable network connection

Network design should incorporate redundancy and resiliency mechanisms to ensure high availability and fault tolerance. Redundant links, devices, and paths are deployed to minimize the impact of failures and ensure continuous network operation. Reliability focuses on designing networks with redundant components and paths to eliminate single points of failure. This includes redundant power supplies, multiple data centers, backup links, and failover mechanisms to maintain network connectivity and minimize service disruptions.

Uber's network design demonstrates reliability by deploying redundant network components and data centers across multiple regions. This redundancy ensures high availability of their ride-hailing services, even in the event of a failure in a particular data center or network link, minimizing disruptions for riders and drivers. Uber strongly emphasizes network reliability to provide uninterrupted service to riders and drivers. Redundancy is a critical aspect of their network design. Uber employs redundant data centers distributed across different regions to ensure high availability. In the event of a failure or outage, the network seamlessly redirects traffic to alternative data centers, minimizing disruptions and maintaining the reliability of their services.

Applying network security

Network design should incorporate robust security measures to protect against unauthorized access, data breaches, and other threats. This includes implementing firewalls, Distributed denial-of-service (DDoS) mitigation, intrusion detection and prevention systems, access controls, encryption, and curated security policies. Security is a critical aspect of network design, involving implementing multi-layered security measures to protect network infrastructure, data, and user privacy. It also includes designing secure network boundaries, employing encryption protocols, implementing secure remote access, and monitoring network traffic for potential threats.

Uber's network design prioritizes security to safeguard sensitive user information and maintain trust. They employ robust security measures, including firewalls, DDoS mitigation, intrusion detection and prevention systems, and encryption protocols, to protect user data during transmission and storage. Uber prioritizes network security to protect user data and ensure trust in their platform. Their network design includes robust security measures like firewalls, encryption protocols, and secure authentication mechanisms. These measures help safeguard sensitive information, prevent unauthorized access, and protect the integrity and privacy of user data transmitted through the network.

Building a high-performance network

The network should be optimized for efficient and high-performance data transfer. Factors such as bandwidth, latency, packet loss, and jitter should be considered during the design process to ensure optimal performance for the intended applications. This includes considerations for bandwidth allocation, traffic prioritization, and load balancing. Performance optimization focuses on designing networks with sufficient bandwidth, low latency, and minimal packet loss to deliver fast and reliable data transfer. This involves utilizing techniques such as traffic shaping, Quality of Service (QoS), and load balancing to prioritize critical traffic and optimize network resources. Uber's network design prioritizes performance to provide a seamless and real-time experience for its riders and drivers.

Uber's network design optimizes performance for real-time ride requests and driver updates. Bandwidth allocation, traffic prioritization, and load balancing techniques ensure efficient data transfer and low latency. These optimizations enable Uber to provide riders and drivers with a seamless and responsive experience, even during high-demand periods.

Making the network operational and maintainable

The network design should be easily manageable and maintainable. It should provide centralized logging and monitoring, configuration management, and troubleshooting capabilities to simplify network operations and reduce administrative overhead. Operations and maintenance focus on designing networks that are easy to manage and maintain. This involves implementing centralized management tools for configuration changes, monitoring network performance and health, and proactive troubleshooting capabilities. Streamlining operations minimizes downtime, improves efficiency, and reduces the network infrastructure's complexity.

Uber's network design incorporates centralized logging, monitoring, and configuration management tools. These tools simplify network operations, enable efficient troubleshooting, and reduce administrative overhead. Centralized monitoring allows Uber to proactively detect and resolve network issues, ensuring smooth operations and minimizing service disruptions.

Optimizing networking Cost

The network design should strike a balance between performance and cost. It should consider the organization's budget and resource constraints while delivering the required functionality and meeting performance expectations. Cost optimization involves designing networks with the desired performance and functionality within budgetary limitations. This includes evaluating cost-effective network components, optimizing resource utilization, and implementing efficient network architectures. By striking the right balance, organizations can achieve cost-efficient network designs without compromising performance or security.

Uber strikes a balance between performance and cost in its network design. It carefully evaluates network hardware, service providers, and bandwidth requirements to optimize costs without compromising the quality of service. This cost optimization enables Uber to provide affordable transportation services while maintaining the necessary network infrastructure to support its operations.

Delivering Quality of Service (QoS)

Network design should prioritize traffic to guarantee reliable and consistent performance for critical applications. QoS mechanisms can be employed to allocate bandwidth, manage congestion, and prioritize certain types of traffic. Quality of Service (QoS) ensures critical applications receive network resources to meet performance requirements. This involves identifying and prioritizing traffic types, setting up QoS policies, and implementing traffic shaping and congestion management techniques. QoS guarantees reliable and consistent network performance for applications such as real-time communication, video streaming, or critical business services.

Uber prioritizes critical traffic, such as ride requests and driver updates, to ensure a reliable and consistent user experience. QoS mechanisms are implemented to allocate sufficient bandwidth, manage congestion, and prioritize time-sensitive traffic, guaranteeing that critical services are delivered promptly and efficiently.

At last, proper network design documentation is the most critical aspect of a successful network architect. It provides a holistic view of the network topology and configurations and is instrumental in troubleshooting. Well-documented designs facilitate easier maintenance, troubleshooting, upgrades, and knowledge transfer. Documentation is vital for effective network management and future-proofing. It includes comprehensive documentation of network diagrams, configurations, device inventories, and any changes made to the network. This documentation serves as a reference for troubleshooting, understanding network interconnections, and ensuring continuity even in the absence of the original designers. Proper documentation simplifies maintenance, upgrades, and knowledge transfer to other network administrators.

A network architect must understand and apply key network design principles and methodologies. These principles ensure scalability, adaptability, reliability, security, performance optimization, efficient operations, cost optimization, QoS, and proper documentation. By incorporating these principles into your network designs, you can create robust and resilient networks that meet organizations' evolving needs.

During a network architect interview, highlighting your proficiency in these principles and providing examples of how you have applied them in real-world scenarios, such as Uber's network design, will showcase your expertise and ability to create effective network solutions. These principles allow you to design scalable, secure, and optimized networks, providing a solid foundation for successful network architecture.

Whiteboarding Network SA Interview

suppose you are applying for the Network Solutions Architects role. In that case, you may get questions like drawing and explaining the network architecture of your recent project or presenting a reference architecture of some network design use-case. The interviewer looks for signs the candidate can design using the network best practice tailored to the business problem. The whiteboard allows the interviewer to observe the candidate's thought process as they design a solution iteratively. Let's explore a typical hybrid connectivity architecture and the important components you need to know to be a successful network architect.

Before diving deep into the design part, let's first understand some concepts related to hybrid connectivity and its benefits. Hybrid connectivity integrates and is interoperable between on-premise (local) infrastructure and cloud-based resources. It provides a flexible and scalable solution for organizations leveraging the benefits of both on-premise and cloud environments.

- **On-Premise Infrastructure**: On-premise infrastructure refers to the hardware, software, and IT resources that are physically located within an organization's own facilities, such as data centers, servers, and local networks. These resources are managed and maintained by the organization's IT team. On-premise infrastructure typically provides more control, customization, and security than cloud-based resources.
- **Cloud-Based Resources**: Cloud-based resources refer to computing, storage, and application services hosted and delivered over the Internet by cloud service providers. These resources can include infrastructure as a service (IaaS), platform as a service (PaaS), and software as a service (SaaS). Cloud-based resources offer scalability, reduced upfront costs, and the ability to access resources on-demand.

Hybrid connectivity allows organizations to leverage on-premise and cloud-based resources to create a flexible and efficient IT infrastructure. This approach enables organizations to:

- **Workload Optimization:** Organizations can choose to deploy certain workloads or applications on-premise, while others may be hosted in the cloud based on factors such as performance, security, and cost-effectiveness.
- **Disaster Recovery and Backup:** Hybrid connectivity can enable organizations to use cloud-based resources for disaster recovery and backup, ensuring that critical data and applications are protected and quickly restored during an on-premise system failure or disaster.
- **Scalability and Flexibility:** Hybrid connectivity allows organizations to scale their resources up or down as needed, leveraging the on-demand nature of cloud-based services to complement their on-premise infrastructure.
- **Compliance and Regulatory Requirements:** In some cases, organizations may be required to maintain certain data or applications on-premise due to compliance or regulatory requirements. Hybrid connectivity can help organizations meet these requirements while utilizing cloud-based resources for other IT infrastructure.

Organizations can benefit from the best on-premise and cloud-based resources by adopting a hybrid connectivity approach and optimizing their IT infrastructure for performance, security, and cost-effectiveness. The following diagram illustrates a reference architecture of hybrid connectivity in AWS:

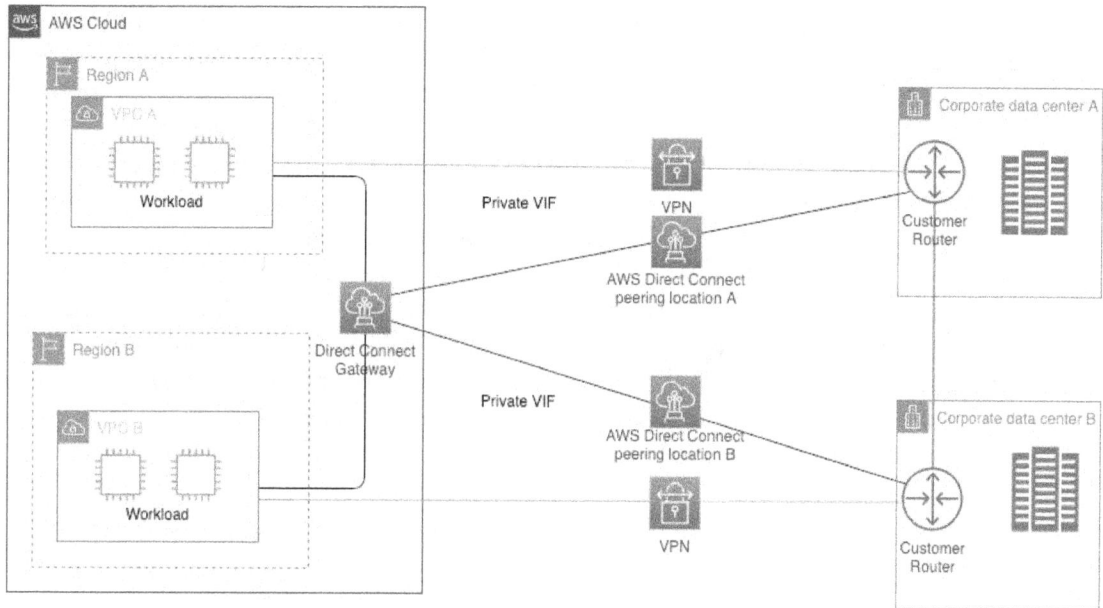

Figure7.2: On-premise to cloud connectivity with resiliency

As shown in the preceding diagram, the idea is to provide redundant connectivity between customer data centers and AWS, and the goal is to avoid any single point of failure. Depending upon the criticality of the workload, there are multiple options a customer can choose to provide on-premise to AWS connectivity. In this scenario, you provide primary connectivity for each data center via AWS Direct Connect (For Azure, it is ExpressRoute, and for GCP, it is Dedicated Interconnect) and backup via Site-to-Site VPN. Also, the same connectivity is provided for the other data center to mitigate disruption in the event of complete data center failure. You can use these services together to connect your on-premises data center with AWS:

- Establish an AWS Direct Connect connection between your on-premises network and the AWS cloud. AWS Direct Connect is a service that allows you to establish a dedicated network connection between your on-premises infrastructure and the AWS cloud. This dedicated connection can provide a more reliable, faster, and more secure way to access your AWS resources than public internet access.
- Configure a Private VIF on the AWS Direct Connect connection, allowing you to connect your on-premises network to your VPC using a private IP address range. A Private VIF is a logical interface that you configure on an AWS Direct Connect connection. It lets you connect your on-premises network to your Virtual Private Cloud (VPC) in AWS using a private IP address range. This private connection ensures that traffic between your on-premises network and your VPC remains within the AWS network and is not exposed to the public internet.

- Configure your customer router to route traffic between your on-premises network and the AWS Direct Connect connection. The customer router is the network device on your on-premises side connected to the AWS Direct Connect connection. This router is responsible for routing traffic between your on-premises network and the AWS Direct Connect connection. It must be configured to route traffic to the appropriate destination within your on-premises network or VPC.
- Establish a VPN connection between your on-premises network and your VPC. Create an encrypted tunnel over the public internet as a backup or alternative path to the AWS Direct Connect connection. VPN can be used with AWS Direct Connect to provide additional security and redundancy. You can establish a VPN connection between your on-premises network and your VPC, which creates an encrypted tunnel over the public internet. The VPN connection can provide a backup or alternative path to the AWS Direct Connect connection, ensuring that you have multiple ways to access your AWS resources.

Let's dry-run a few failure scenarios to understand the design.

Failure Scenario Analysis

A scenario where the customer operates workloads both in AWS and on-premise environments, primarily connected via BGP over AWS Direct Connect. This setup provides a robust framework; however, it will be beneficial to understand various potential failure scenarios and the resulting implications on network functionality, along with how the preceding architecture can mitigate them:

- **Fiber Cut at One Data Center:** If a fiber cut occurs at one of the data centers, Direct Connect connectivity will fail. However, because the data centers are interconnected, traffic will reroute through the other data center to maintain connectivity with AWS.
- **Single Data Center Failure:** In a complete failure at one data center, the design's redundancy ensures that the connectivity between AWS and the on-premise environment continues uninterrupted via the surviving data center.
- **Logical Issues on AWS Direct Connect:** In the rare but possible event of a logical failure affecting AWS Direct Connect services, the network design allows traffic to be redirected through a site-to-site VPN connection, ensuring continued access and operation.

In addition to its fundamental role in internet routing, network architects must deeply understand BGP traffic engineering and high availability and security. Let's discuss these points in detail:

- **Traffic Engineering:** BGP allows network architects to manipulate traffic flows between on-premises and cloud environments by influencing route selection and path preference. This capability enables efficient traffic engineering to optimize performance and minimize latency for critical workloads. This can be done via BGP attributes such as Local-Preference and AS-PATH.

- **High Availability:** By leveraging BGP's multi-homing capabilities, organizations can establish redundant connections between on-premises data centers and cloud providers. BGP dynamically adjusts routing paths in case of link failures, ensuring high availability and resilience for hybrid connectivity.
- **Security:** For most organizations, security is the topmost priority. BGP's inherent vulnerabilities have led to disruptive incidents, such as accidental route advertisements by ISPs, resulting in widespread Internet outages. Incidents like the 2004 Turkish ISP and 2008 Pakistani ISP cases highlight the risks of BGP hijacking, where incorrect routes propagate, causing service disruptions or redirecting traffic for malicious purposes, as seen in the 2018 attack on Amazon's DNS service.
- As a network architect, you need to know how to design your network by following BGP security practices such as peer authentication using MD5 and security framework Resource Public Key Infrastructure (RPKI), which uses cryptographically signed records called Route Origin Authorization (ROAs) to validate which network operator is allowed to announce an organization's IP addresses using BGP. Also, you must ensure prefix filters are applied in both directions to avoid sending/receiving undesired prefixes to/from the BGP peer.

While the current architecture utilizes AWS services, the principles and strategies discussed universally apply across various cloud platforms. Network architects can adapt these concepts to other environments by leveraging equivalent services offered by different cloud providers, ensuring that the core principles of traffic engineering, high availability, and security are consistently maintained.

The detailed analysis was explained during the interview, providing a foundational understanding of designing and managing resilient hybrid network architectures. Network architects can ensure robust and secure connectivity across diverse operating environments by evaluating potential failure scenarios and focusing on strategic traffic management and security practices.

Networking SA interview questions

Interviewing for a Network Solutions Architect role is rigorous and is aimed at evaluating both technical expertise and the ability to align network design needs with business goals. Below are some potential questions that can be posed to candidates for a Network Solutions Architect role:

Behavioral Questions

These questions are often used to gauge candidates' past experiences and predict their future behavior in similar situations. Here are some behavioral questions that can provide insight into a Network SA's real-life expertise from their past projects:

Question: Tell me about a time when you designed a complex network between a cloud and an on-premise data center. What were the key challenges, and how did you overcome them? How did you measure success?

Answer: For this answer, we will use the STAR format and incorporate data points to showcase the improvement achieved in network latency, content delivery, scalability, and security due to the network architect's work. These data points demonstrate the tangible benefits of the implemented network infrastructure for the multinational e-commerce company.

Situation: In my previous role as a network architect, I designed a network infrastructure to connect an on-premise data center with AWS. The goal was to enable a multinational e-commerce company to leverage AWS's scalability, reliability, and security while maintaining control over sensitive customer data stored on-premise.

Task: The key challenge was to design a secure and high-performance network architecture that facilitated seamless communication between the on-premise data center and AWS. This involved addressing connectivity, security, latency, and scalability requirements while ensuring compliance with industry regulations.

Action:
- Connectivity and Bandwidth: We established a dedicated private connection between the on-premise data center and AWS by implementing AWS Direct Connect. This enabled a reliable, high-bandwidth link with reduced latency and improved data transfer speeds. The Direct Connect link had a capacity of 10 Gbps, ensuring fast and consistent communication.
- Security and Compliance: Since there was a need to provide encryption in transit for on-premise to AWS communication, there were two options to consider: first, IPsec VPN over Direct Connect or MACsec. I chose IPSec VPN because the router at the on-premise location did not have MACsec support available. This ensured secure communication between the on-premise environment and AWS. Additionally, I implemented WAF for the internet-facing applications to make sure my web application was protected from web attacks. I also used IAM for user authentication and authorization. We enhanced the security posture with all these measures, protecting sensitive customer data.
- Latency and Performance Optimization: We reduced network latency and improved performance by leveraging AWS Global Accelerator and Amazon CloudFront. We strategically placed CDN edge locations, resulting in an average latency reduction of 40%. Users experienced faster content delivery and improved website responsiveness.
- Scalability and Flexibility: We achieved scalability during peak demand periods by utilizing AWS Auto Scaling and Elastic Load Balancing. The architecture was designed to handle a 300% increase in user traffic without performance degradation. AWS Transit Gateway simplified network management, allowing seamless connectivity between on-premises data centers and AWS VPC environments.

Result: The implemented network infrastructure successfully connected the on-premise data center with AWS, significantly improving performance and user experience. The Direct Connect link, with a capacity of 10 Gbps, reduced latency by 30% compared to the previous internet-based connection. Users experienced faster content delivery with an average page load time improvement of 50%. The scalable architecture handled a 300% increase in user traffic, ensuring uninterrupted service during peak periods. The security measures implemented protected sensitive customer data, ensuring compliance with industry regulations.

Based on your answer, the interviewer may ask follow-up questions to understand the technical depth and architectural concept. Let's look at some key follow-up questions and responses.

Follow-up Questions:
Here are the follow-up questions with the response in STAR format, supplemented with data points:

Question: How did you ensure the high availability and redundancy of the network architecture to minimize the risk of disruptions or single points of failure?
Answer: The following response provides a detailed explanation of all components, accompanied by relevant data.

Situation: I implemented a robust redundancy strategy to ensure high availability and minimize the risk of disruptions or single points of failure in the network architecture.

Task: The goal was to design a network architecture that could withstand failures and maintain continuous operation, minimizing any potential impact on the business.

Action:
- Redundant Connectivity: We leveraged multiple AWS Direct Connect connections across geographically diverse locations, ensuring redundant and highly available connectivity between the on-premise data center and AWS. This eliminated single points of failure and provided network resilience.
- Multi-Region Deployment: We deployed the network architecture across multiple AWS regions, ensuring geographical redundancy. We used a DNS-based health check, allowing seamless failover between regions during an outage and providing uninterrupted service.
- Load Balancing and Auto Scaling: We designed the network to distribute traffic across multiple instances and scale resources automatically based on demand, utilizing AWS Elastic Load Balancing and Auto Scaling features. This provided additional redundancy and ensured continuous service availability during peak traffic periods. We gradually decreased the capacity at off-peak times.

Result: The implemented high availability and redundancy measures resulted in a network architecture with an impressive uptime record. Over the past year, the network achieved an average uptime of 99.99%, with minimal disruptions due to network failures or single points of failure.

Question: Can you provide more details on the security measures implemented to protect sensitive customer data during the communication between the on-premise data center and AWS?
Answer: The following response provides a detailed explanation of all components, accompanied by relevant data.

Situation: A comprehensive security framework was designed and implemented to protect sensitive customer data during communication between the on-premise data center and AWS.

Task: Establish secure communication channels, implement encryption protocols, and employ robust security measures to safeguard data.

Action:

- IPsec VPN Tunnels: We established IPsec VPN tunnels over the AWS Direct Connect link to ensure secure communication between the on-premise data center and AWS. This encrypts the data in transit, preventing unauthorized access and ensuring data confidentiality.
- Network Firewalls: We implemented robust network firewalls, such as AWS Network Firewall, with strict access control policies to filter incoming and outgoing traffic. These firewalls were configured to allow only authorized traffic, blocking potential threats and mitigating the risk of data breaches.
- AWS WAF and IAM: To protect against web-based attacks, we implemented AWS Web Application Firewall (WAF) to filter and monitor HTTP/HTTPS traffic. Additionally, we leveraged AWS Identity and Access Management (IAM) to enforce granular access control policies, ensuring that only authorized individuals had access to AWS resources.

Result: The implemented security measures effectively protected sensitive customer data during communication between the on-premise data center and AWS. With these measures in place, the organization achieved compliance with industry regulations and maintained a strong security posture, minimizing the risk of data breaches and unauthorized access.

Question: How did you validate and test the performance improvements achieved by implementing AWS Global Accelerator and Amazon CloudFront? Were there any specific metrics or benchmarks used to measure the impact on user experience?
Answer: The following response provides a detailed explanation of all components, accompanied by relevant data.

Situation: A rigorous testing and validation process was conducted to measure the impact of implementing AWS Global Accelerator and Amazon CloudFront on performance.

Task: The goal was to quantify the performance improvements and ensure a seamless user experience.

Action:
- Performance Testing: We conducted performance tests by simulating various user scenarios, including high-traffic loads, from different geographical locations. We measured the response times and latency before and after implementing AWS Global Accelerator and Amazon CloudFront.
- Real User Monitoring: We also utilized real user monitoring tools to collect data on actual user experiences. This allowed us to capture key metrics such as page load times, time to first byte, and overall website responsiveness.
- Comparative Analysis: We compared the performance metrics obtained post-implementation with the baseline metrics. This enabled us to quantify the improvements in reduced latency, faster content delivery, and improved overall user experience.

Result: The performance testing and monitoring revealed significant improvements in user experience after implementing AWS Global Accelerator and Amazon CloudFront. Page load times were reduced by an average of 40%, resulting in a seamless and faster browsing experience for end-users. Additionally, the data showed a noticeable reduction in latency and improved responsiveness across different geographical locations, confirming the positive impact of these optimizations on overall network performance.

By following the STAR format and providing data points, we can see how the network architect addressed the follow-up questions, showcasing the tangible results achieved regarding high availability, network security, and performance improvements. Please note that the data points provided are hypothetical and for illustrative purposes.

Here are some more questions and tips to help you answer the interview questions for Network Architects:

Question: Can you describe a time when you had to troubleshoot a complex network issue? How did you approach it, and what steps did you take to resolve the problem?
Tips: Clearly explain the problem, your approach, and the troubleshooting steps. Highlight your analytical and problem-solving skills. Emphasize your ability to collaborate with team members and use network diagnostic tools effectively.

Question: What strategies do you employ to ensure network security and protect against potential threats such as unauthorized access, data breaches, or DDoS attacks?

Tips: Discuss your knowledge of industry-standard security practices and protocols. Highlight any certifications or training you have related to network security. Provide specific examples of how you have implemented security measures in previous network architecture projects.

Question: How do you stay updated with the latest networking technologies and trends? Can you provide examples of how you have implemented new technologies or practices in your previous network architecture projects?

Tips: Discuss your commitment to continuous learning and staying up-to-date with emerging technologies. Mention any industry conferences, training programs, or professional certifications you have pursued. Provide specific examples of how you have incorporated new technologies into network designs.

Question: Describe a situation where you had to balance performance requirements with cost considerations in a network design project. How did you achieve a balance between the two?

Tips: Describe your approach to assessing performance requirements and cost considerations. Highlight your ability to find cost-effective solutions without compromising performance. Provide specific examples where you have optimized network design for both performance and cost efficiency.

Question: Can you explain the process you follow to gather requirements for a network design project? How do you ensure the design meets the organization's needs and goals?

Tip: Explain your process of engaging with stakeholders to understand their needs and goals. Discuss how you translate business requirements into technical network design requirements. Highlight your ability to ask relevant questions and clarify requirements.

Question: Tell us about a time when you faced challenges collaborating with other IT teams or stakeholders during a network implementation. How did you overcome these challenges and ensure successful project completion?

Tips: Highlight your communication and collaboration skills. Discuss how you have successfully collaborated with diverse teams and stakeholders. Provide examples of how you have resolved conflicts and facilitated effective collaboration.

Question: What methodologies do you follow for capacity planning in network design? How do you determine the bandwidth, scalability, and future growth considerations for a network architecture?

Tips: Discuss your approach to assessing current and future network capacity requirements. Mention your experience with network traffic analysis tools and forecasting methodologies. Highlight your ability to plan for scalability and accommodate future growth.

Question: Can you share an example of a network upgrade or migration project you have worked on? How did you plan and execute the project to minimize disruption and ensure a smooth transition?

Tips: Explain your project planning and execution methodology. Discuss your ability to minimize disruptions and ensure a smooth transition. Provide examples of successful network upgrades or migration projects you have been involved in.

Question: Describe your experience designing network architectures for highly regulated industries such as healthcare or finance. What specific challenges did you encounter, and how did you address them to ensure compliance and security?

Tips: Highlight your understanding of industry-specific compliance requirements. Discuss your experience implementing security measures to meet regulatory standards. Provide examples of how you have designed network architectures for highly regulated industries.

Question: How do you approach network documentation and knowledge transfer? Can you provide examples of how you have maintained accurate and up-to-date documentation for network architectures in your previous roles?

Tips: Discuss your approach to documenting network architectures and configurations. Highlight your ability to create clear and comprehensive documentation. Explain how you facilitate knowledge transfer and ensure continuity in network operations.

Scenario Based Question

Here, you can find some common questions based on scenarios you should prepare to create the network solutions architect interview.

Question: How would you design a highly available network architecture?

Tips: To ensure a highly available network architecture, incorporate redundancy at multiple levels, including redundant links, devices, and power sources. Utilize link aggregation, redundant paths, and physical device separation to guarantee seamless failover during link or device failures. Also, load balancing and traffic engineering mechanisms should be implemented to distribute traffic efficiently across the available paths.

Question: You have recently migrated a workload to the cloud and need to establish connectivity between your data center and the cloud. How would you approach this task?

Tips: Understand the specific business requirements, including workload type, desired latency, required bandwidth, and security considerations. Based on these requirements, evaluate the available connectivity options. Options to consider include setting up a Site-to-Site VPN through the internet, utilizing SD-WAN technology, or implementing dedicated connections like Direct Connect (for AWS) or ExpressRoute (for Azure). Select the option that best aligns with the business needs and provides the desired connectivity, security, and performance level.

Question: What factors would you consider when choosing between an internet-based site-to-site VPN and a direct connect link for cloud connectivity?

Tips: The decision between a site-to-site VPN and a direct connect link depends on several factors. Firstly, consider the deployment scale and the workloads' criticality. An internet-based site-to-site VPN is often more cost-effective and easier to set up for smaller-scale deployments or non-critical workloads. However, for larger-scale deployments or mission-critical workloads, a direct connect link offers advantages such as higher bandwidth, lower latency, and more consistent performance.

Additionally, evaluate the data transfer requirements. If high data transfer rates are needed, a direct connect link provides a dedicated and robust connection that ensures efficient and reliable data transfer. Another aspect to consider is network resiliency. Direct connect links offer network-level resiliency with redundant connections, providing greater reliability than a site-to-site VPN.

It is common for organizations to utilize both a direct connect link and a site-to-site VPN as complementary solutions. The direct connect link serves as the primary data path, delivering optimal performance and reliability. At the same time, the site-to-site VPN can act as a backup, providing additional redundancy and cost savings. Ultimately, the choice between a site-to-site VPN and a direct connect link depends on the specific requirements of the deployment, including scale, criticality, data transfer needs, and desired network resiliency.

Question: Explain the steps you would take to design a secure network architecture.

Tips: Designing a secure network architecture involves several essential steps. Begin by conducting a comprehensive risk assessment to identify threats and vulnerabilities specific to the network environment. Based on the assessment, implement a defense-in-depth approach, which involves layering multiple security measures to provide robust protection.

Start by deploying firewalls at network boundaries to monitor and filter incoming and outgoing traffic. Intrusion detection and prevention systems should be implemented to detect and block malicious activities or unauthorized access attempts. Access controls, such as strong authentication mechanisms and role-based access policies, should be enforced to ensure that only authorized users can access network resources.

Encryption plays a critical role in securing data in transit and at rest. Implement protocols like IPsec or SSL/TLS to encrypt sensitive data, preventing unauthorized interception or tampering. Regularly update and patch network devices to address known vulnerabilities and keep the network infrastructure up to date with the latest security patches.

Enforcing security policies is essential to establish a secure network architecture. Define and implement policies that govern acceptable use, password complexity, data access, and other security-related aspects. Regular security awareness training for employees should also be conducted to promote a security culture within the organization.

Lastly, network segmentation and isolation techniques should be implemented to contain potential breaches and limit the impact of an attack. By separating the network into segments, such as VLANs or subnets, and enforcing strict access controls between segments, the effect of a security incident can be confined to a specific area, preventing lateral movement and minimizing the overall damage.

Question: You are the network architect responsible for an application hosted on the AWS cloud in the US East region. Customers in Europe are complaining about your application's latency and responsiveness. How would you approach this issue?
Tips: To address the latency issue experienced by European customers, follow these steps:

Start by analyzing the network latency between the European customers and the US East region. This will help determine whether the issue is related to the network or the application. Latency is often introduced due to the distance between the European and US regions.

- Option 1: Move Workload Closer to Customers: If most customers are in Europe, consider moving the workload closer. This can be achieved by deploying the application in a European AWS region. By reducing the geographical distance, you can significantly reduce latency and improve responsiveness for European customers.
- Option 2: Utilize Content Delivery Network (CDN): Implementing a content delivery network (CDN) can also improve customer experience. A CDN cache frequently accesses content in multiple edge locations, such as images, videos, and scripts. When a European customer accesses the application, the CDN serves the content from the nearest edge location, reducing the round-trip time and improving responsiveness.

By evaluating these options, you can determine the most suitable approach to address European customers' latency and responsiveness issues. Whether it involves moving the workload closer to the customer base or leveraging a CDN, the goal is to enhance the overall customer experience and mitigate the impact of network latency.

Question: How would you design a scalable network architecture to accommodate future growth?
Tips: To design a scalable network architecture for future growth, consider the following steps:

- Scalable Network Devices: Use network devices that can scale to meet increasing demands. Choose switches, routers, and other network equipment that can handle higher bandwidth requirements and offer scalability options, such as adding additional modules or ports. This ensures that the network infrastructure can accommodate future growth without requiring a complete overhaul.

- Upgradable Network Components: Select network components that can be easily upgraded or replaced. This includes considering modular hardware designs that allow for the addition of new capabilities or higher-performance modules. Upgradable network components enable seamless expansion and scalability without disrupting the existing network.
- Sufficient Addressing Space: Plan for future IP address allocations by ensuring sufficient addressing space. Consider utilizing IPv6, which offers a significantly larger address space than IPv4. Implement subnetting strategies that allow for efficient address utilization and accommodate future growth without extensive readdressing. Also, use Network Address Translation (NAT) wherever possible to reduce IP address usage.

By incorporating these steps into your network architecture design, you can create a scalable infrastructure that can easily accommodate future growth. This approach enables seamless expansion, optimal performance, and the ability to adapt to changing business requirements.

Question: You have customers across different geographies. What would be your design approach to ensure that they are served from the closest location possible?
Tips: To optimize the customer experience by serving them from the nearest location, consider the following design approaches:

- Multi-Region Deployment: Deploy your application in multiple regions strategically located across different geographies. By hosting your application in various areas, you can reduce network latency and improve the user experience for customers in other locations. This approach allows customers to access the application from a nearby data center, minimizing the distance their requests need to travel.
- Anycast Routing: Implement Anycast routing for your application's IP addresses. Anycast allows multiple servers in different locations to share the same IP address. When a customer sends a request to the IP address, it is automatically routed to the nearest server based on network topology. This reduces latency and ensures customers are served from the closest available location.
- DNS-Based Geolocation Routing: Configure geolocation-based routing within your DNS solution, such as Route 53 in AWS. This approach utilizes the IP geolocation of customer requests to determine their approximate geographic location. The DNS service can then route the requests to the region closest to the customer, directing them to their location's most optimal data center. This helps minimize latency and ensures faster response times.

You can design a system that dynamically directs customer requests to the closest available location by combining a multi-region deployment strategy, Anycast routing, and DNS-based geo-location routing. This results in improved performance, reduced latency, and a better overall user experience.

Question: How would you design a network architecture to support a cloud-based infrastructure?

Tips: To design a network architecture that effectively supports a cloud-based infrastructure, consider the following steps:

- Seamless Integration: Ensure seamless integration between your on-premises network and the chosen cloud provider's services. Establish secure and reliable connectivity, such as site-to-site VPN (Virtual Private Network) or direct connect links, to establish a connection between your on-premises network and the cloud infrastructure. This allows for secure data transfer and communication.
- Consider Data Transfer Rates, Latency, and Bandwidth: When designing the network architecture, consider factors such as data transfer rates, latency, and bandwidth requirements. Optimize the network configuration to minimize latency and ensure efficient data transfer between the on-premises network and the cloud infrastructure. This may involve selecting appropriate network links, optimizing routing protocols, and considering the proximity of the cloud data center to your on-premises network.
- Network Segmentation and Security: Implement network segmentation and security measures to ensure data privacy and protection. This involves dividing the network into segments, such as virtual private clouds (VPCs) or subnets, to separate different types of traffic and enhance security. Apply security policies, access controls, and encryption mechanisms to protect data in transit and at rest.
- Leverage Cloud Networking Services: Take advantage of the cloud networking services the chosen cloud provider provides. These services, such as virtual private clouds (VPCs) or virtual network appliances, allow you to extend your on-premises network into the cloud environment. Leverage these services to establish connectivity, manage network resources, and enforce network policies.

By considering seamless integration, data transfer rates, network segmentation, security measures, and leveraging cloud networking services, you can design a network architecture that effectively supports your cloud-based infrastructure. This ensures secure and efficient communication between your on-premises network and the cloud environment.

Question: How would you design a network architecture to support voice and video communication?

Tips: To effectively support voice and video communication, consider the following design principles:

- Prioritize Voice and Video Traffic: Use quality of service (QoS) mechanisms to prioritize voice and video traffic over other types of data traffic. Assign appropriate bandwidth, latency, and packet loss parameters to ensure a high-quality communication experience. This helps maintain low latency, minimal jitter, and consistent audio and video quality.

- Sufficient Bandwidth and Minimal Congestion: Design the network to have enough bandwidth to accommodate the demands of real-time voice and video communication. Assess the expected traffic volume and ensure the network infrastructure can handle the required bandwidth. Minimize network congestion by optimizing network configurations, implementing traffic engineering techniques, and employing load-balancing mechanisms.
- Techniques to Mitigate Jitter: Jitter, which can disrupt the smooth flow of voice and video data, should be mitigated. Implement traffic shaping techniques to regulate traffic flow and buffer management mechanisms to smooth out variations in packet arrival times. This helps minimize jitter and ensures a consistent communication experience.
- Redundant Paths and Fault-Tolerant Configurations: To maintain continuity in voice and video services, design the network with redundant paths and fault-tolerant configurations. Implement failover mechanisms, redundant links, and network devices to ensure seamless communication during network failures. This enhances reliability and reduces the risk of service disruptions.

You can design a network architecture that supports high-quality voice and video communication by prioritizing voice and video traffic, ensuring sufficient bandwidth and minimal congestion, mitigating jitter, and implementing redundant paths and fault-tolerant configurations. This allows for smooth, reliable, and consistent communication experiences for users. Here are answering tips for each of the example network architecture questions, designed to help you structure comprehensive and compelling responses during interviews or discussions:

Question: Propose a network design to support deploying a hybrid cloud infrastructure, seamlessly integrating on-premises and cloud-based resources.
Tip: Use hybrid networking technologies such as VPNs, AWS Direct Connect, or Azure ExpressRoute for dedicated connectivity. Highlight the importance of a central management approach to ensure consistent policies and security across both environments. Consider including a diagram to visualize the flow and connectivity.

Question: Design a scalable and highly available network architecture for a large enterprise with multiple geographically distributed locations. Consider factors such as redundancy, load balancing, and disaster recovery.
Tips: Discuss multi-layer redundancy, including redundant hardware, failover mechanisms, and clustering. Include geographic load balancing and data replication across locations to ensure disaster recovery and business continuity. Use protocols and technologies such as MPLS or SD-WAN to illustrate your approach.

Question: Architect a software-defined network (SDN) solution that dynamically allocates network resources and services based on application and user requirements.
Tips: Detail the components of an SDN architecture, such as the SDN controller, application layer, and infrastructure layer. Explain how SDN can provide dynamic resource allocation with examples

of policy automation and performance monitoring. Mention relevant standards or technologies like OpenFlow.

Question: Design a secure network architecture to protect against various cyber threats, including DDoS attacks, network-based malware, and unauthorized access. Incorporate appropriate security controls and technologies.

Tips: Outline a multi-layered security strategy that includes firewalls, intrusion detection systems (IDS), intrusion prevention systems (IPS), and DDoS mitigation techniques. Discuss the importance of end-to-end encryption, secure access methods like VPNs, and the role of behavioral analytics in detecting anomalies.

Question: Develop a network plan to enable seamless connectivity and collaboration for a global workforce, including remote and mobile users, while ensuring data privacy and compliance.

Tips: Focus on solutions like VPNs for secure remote access, using cloud services for collaboration, and implementing endpoint management for mobile devices. Discuss compliance with international data protection regulations such as GDPR and HIPAA.

Question: Create a network design that can support implementing Internet of Things (IoT) devices and sensors across multiple locations, with considerations for data management, edge computing, and network segmentation.

Tips: Highlight the importance of network segmentation using VLANs or firewalls to protect IoT devices. Discuss the role of edge computing in reducing latency and the architectural adjustments needed to handle massive amounts of IoT data. Consider protocols tailored for IoT like MQTT or CoAP.

Question: Propose a network architecture that can enable the deployment of a content delivery network (CDN) to improve the performance and availability of web-based applications and services.

Tips: Explain how CDNs distribute content across multiple geographically dispersed servers to enhance user experience by reducing latency. Discuss integrating CDN solutions with existing network infrastructure and the benefits of caching content closer to the end users.

Question: Design a network infrastructure that can support real-time, high-bandwidth applications, such as video conferencing, virtual reality, and augmented reality, with quality of service (QoS) considerations.

Tips: Discuss the implementation of QoS techniques such as traffic shaping and prioritization. Emphasize the importance of high-capacity backbone networks and the use of technologies such as MPLS for managing bandwidth and ensuring low latency.

Question: Architect a network solution to seamlessly integrate legacy systems and technologies with modern, cloud-based platforms, ensuring interoperability and data exchange.

Tips: Address legacy integration challenges with middleware solutions or custom APIs. Discuss strategies for phased migration to the cloud while ensuring data interoperability and minimal disruption.

Question: Develop a network plan that can support the implementation of a network function virtualization (NFV) and software-defined wide area network (SD-WAN) solution, with considerations for scalability, flexibility, and cost optimization.

Tips: Explain how NFV and SD-WAN can create a flexible, cost-effective network. Highlight the benefits of virtualizing network functions and managing WAN through software and how this can scale with growing business needs.

These tips help you create detailed, effective, and tailored answers demonstrating a deep understanding of network architecture challenges and solutions. Remember to tailor your answers to showcase your specific experiences, achievements, and skills as a Network Architect, and don't forget to follow the STAR format with data points.

Summary

This chapter delved into the key concepts and principles of network architecture and protocols. We explored the importance of understanding network architecture and protocols in designing efficient and reliable networks. We discussed the key network design principles and methodologies, including scalability, adaptability, reliability, security, performance, operational efficiency, cost optimization, and quality of service (QoS). Each principle was explained with examples and use cases, highlighting their significance in building robust network architectures.

Furthermore, you explored network solutions architects' roles and responsibilities in designing and maintaining network solutions. We discussed the skills and knowledge required for this role and the impact they have on business success.

The chapter also sheds light on the challenges faced by networking architects, emphasizing the dynamic nature of network architecture and the need for continuous adaptation and innovation. We explored challenges such as emerging technologies, network convergence, evolving security landscapes, hybrid and multi-cloud connectivity, compliance and regulatory requirements, scalability, capacity planning, and documentation.

To help aspiring network solutions architects prepare for interviews, we provided a list of common interview questions specific to the role. These questions covered various aspects, including network design, security, staying updated with technology, collaboration, capacity planning, and network documentation.

Chapter 8 - Cracking the Big Data Solutions Architect Interview

In the digital age, where data is generated in unprecedented volumes and velocities, the role of a Big Data Solutions Architect is more crucial than ever. The journey into Big Data demands a robust understanding of data engineering principles, an adeptness in navigating vast distributed systems, and the ability to make sense of the surge of data.

As the digital landscape evolves, so do the expectations and questions posed to Big Data Solutions Architects in interviews. This chapter will prepare you for the technical objectivities of an interview and refine your ability to articulate architectural concepts, demonstrating how your designs can transform a business's relationship with its data.

In this chapter, you will delve into the details of big data ecosystems, exploring data processing frameworks such as Spark and how to run them in the cloud. These technologies are the bedrock upon which scalable, resilient, and efficient data solutions are built. Data warehousing and business intelligence (BI) represent the pinnacle of data strategy, turning raw data into actionable insights. This chapter will explore how a well-designed data warehouse is the foundation for robust BI solutions, providing stakeholders with the clarity needed to make informed decisions. You will learn the following topics in this chapter:

- Understanding the role of big data solutions architect
- Understanding big data and data engineering
- Distributed systems and data processing frameworks
- Data warehousing and business intelligence
- Best practices for designing and implementing big data solutions
- Key data design principles and methodologies
- Bigdata architect interview questions

By the end of this chapter, you will learn about best practices and methodologies, from data normalization to complex ETL processes. You'll learn the art of cracking big data solutions and architect interviews.

Understanding the Role of a Big Data Solutions Architect

Embarking on the path of a Big Data Solutions Architect means stepping into a world where data is not just an asset but the very pulse of business innovation. In this role, one becomes pivotal in harnessing the power of massive, complex data sets, transforming them into strategic insights that propel businesses forward.

A big data solutions architect goes by several names - a data solutions architect, a data analytics solutions architect, or just an analytics solutions architect, for example. Typically, big data is primarily associated with batch and real-time data processing in distributed systems, and the role of a big data solutions architect is a highly specialized position that requires a combination of technical expertise, analytical skills, and architectural knowledge in the big data domain. You should be familiar with data modeling, data integration, data ingestion, data transformation, data storage techniques specific to big data solutions, and how to use the data for machine learning.

A Big Data Solutions Architect's expertise lies in understanding the technicalities of data storage, management, and processing and envisioning how data can be leveraged to meet business objectives. At its core, the role demands a multifaceted skill set. The architect must be adept in technological domains, including distributed computing, real-time analytics, and machine learning.

Big Data Solutions Architects are tasked with crafting robust frameworks that can handle big data's velocity, variety, and volume. They ensure that the architecture they design is scalable, able to grow with the company, and resilient enough to withstand the rapidly changing data landscape. This requires a continuous balance between innovation and practicality, pushing the boundaries of what is possible while grounding decisions in the realities of business needs and technical feasibility. The following are the key responsibilities of a big data solutions architect:

- Designing and implementing scalable big data architecture to efficiently manage and process large volumes of data.
- Evaluating and recommending big data technologies and tools to address specific business needs and use cases.
- Developing and overseeing the execution of big data strategies in alignment with organizational goals.
- Ensuring data quality and integrity within distributed processing systems and databases.
- Collaborating with data scientists and analysts to facilitate data modeling, mining, and predictive analysis.

- Instituting robust data security measures, compliance, and privacy policies to safeguard sensitive information.
- Leading the integration of big data solutions with existing IT infrastructure and data systems.
- Conducting regular system audits and performance optimizations to maintain and improve data processing workflows.
- Providing thought leadership and expertise in big data trends, including machine learning and artificial intelligence applications.
- Mentoring and training teams on big data technologies, best practices, and advancements.

Understanding the role of a Big Data Solutions Architect also means recognizing the ethical implications of data usage. They are also responsible for data privacy and security, ensuring the solutions adhere to regulatory standards and ethical considerations. Their role is not just about the 'how' of data processing but also the 'why' and 'what for,' ensuring that data serves the greater good while propelling business growth.

Suppose you are interviewing for a big data solutions architect role. In that case, you are expected to have experience already working in this field, with strengths in key areas and awareness of many others.

Big Data Architecture Vs. Data Engineering

Understanding big data architecture and data engineering is pivotal in recognizing the vast capabilities and potential impact big data can have on an organization's strategic goals. Big data architecture is the conceptual structure that provides the framework for handling the voluminous amounts of data generated by enterprises. This architecture is crafted to manage the intake, processing, and examination of data that is too vast or intricate for conventional database systems.

Big data architecture and data engineering form the backbone of modern analytics, driving the decision-making processes in an increasingly data-centric world. Let's delve deeper into each component, illustrating their roles with a hypothetical use case involving a retail company. Here's a breakdown of the key elements involved in big data architecture and data engineering:

Big Data Architecture:
- **Data Sources:** Big data architecture begins with data acquisition from diverse sources, including IoT devices, social media, transactions, logs, etc. In our retail example, data sources could include online transaction records, customer feedback from social media, sensor data from the supply chain, and inventory databases. Each source provides a unique stream of data that contributes to a comprehensive understanding of the business

landscape. In addition to traditional data sources, cloud-native sources like SaaS applications (e.g., Salesforce for CRM data) and cloud-based point-of-sale systems provide data that seamlessly integrates into the cloud ecosystem.

- **Data Storage:** This involves technologies like Hadoop Distributed File System (HDFS) and NoSQL databases for storing data efficiently in a distributed environment. Retail companies might use a distributed file system like Hadoop (HDFS) for structured data and NoSQL databases like MongoDB or Cassandra for unstructured data to accommodate the variety and volume of data. This approach allows for scalability and the ability to handle the "3Vs" of big data: volume, velocity, and variety. Retail companies can utilize cloud storage solutions such as Amazon S3 or Google Cloud Storage for vast, unstructured datasets and Azure Blob to handle massive amounts of transactional and inventory data. Due to their pay-as-you-go pricing models, these cloud storage options offer cost-effective and limitless scalability.
- **Data Processing:** Utilizing processing frameworks like Apache Hadoop for batch processing and Apache Spark for real-time processing is crucial for extracting value from big data. The processing layer might involve Apache Hadoop for batch processing of large volumes of historical transaction data to identify buying trends. Apache Spark could be employed for real-time processing, such as detecting fraud in transactions as they occur, due to its speed and ability to handle streaming data. Cloud platforms offer managed services like Amazon EMR for Hadoop/Spark clusters or Google Dataflow, allowing efficient data processing without the overhead of managing the underlying infrastructure. These services enable the company to scale resources up or down based on demand, ensuring performance while managing costs.
- **Data Analysis:** Advanced analytics tools and engines perform complex data analysis, including predictive analytics, machine learning, and data mining. The analytics layer would apply tools like Apache Hive or machine learning algorithms to extract patterns and insights. For instance, predictive models could be built to forecast inventory needs based on sales trends, seasonal fluctuations, and promotional campaigns. Platform as a Service (PaaS) offerings like Azure Synapse Analytics or AWS Glue provide integrated analytics services. These tools can run complex queries and machine learning models on large datasets to uncover insights, such as customer purchasing behavior or supply chain inefficiencies.
- **Data Consumption:** Big data architecture aims to enable end-users to access and interact with processed data through applications, dashboards, and visualizations. Finally, the visualization of processed data through BI tools like Tableau or Power BI enables stakeholders to interact with the data, understand market dynamics, and make informed decisions. Cloud-based BI and analytics services like Google Data Studio or AWS QuickSight would allow end-users to access, visualize, and interact with processed data. These tools are designed for scalability and accessibility, allowing users to create dashboards and reports to inform business decisions.

Data Engineering:

- **Data Pipeline Construction:** Data engineers build robust pipelines to facilitate data flow from source systems through processing engines to storage and analytical tools. Data engineers would construct data pipelines that begin with extracting data from various sources, such as point-of-sale systems and eCommerce platforms, move it through the processing and analytics layers, and end with storage or visualization for end-users. With cloud services, data engineers can use orchestration tools like AWS Step Functions or Apache Airflow on Google Cloud to automate data pipeline workflows. These tools facilitate the movement and transformation of data across different cloud services.

- **ETL Processes:** They implement Extract, Transform, and Load (ETL) processes to clean, aggregate, and prepare data for analysis. The ETL process might involve cleaning transaction data, merging it with inventory data to provide real-time stock levels, and transforming it into a format suitable for analysis. This might include aggregating sales by region or by product category. Serverless computing services like AWS Lambda or Azure Functions can run ETL jobs in response to events, such as new data arriving in a cloud storage bucket, allowing for a flexible, event-driven architecture.

- **Data Warehousing:** Engineers design data warehouses to consolidate different data sources for analytical reporting and business intelligence. A data warehouse might centralize various data streams into a single source of truth for reporting and historical analysis. This warehouse could be built on technologies like Amazon Redshift or Google BigQuery.

- **Performance Tuning:** Data engineers must continuously monitor and tune the performance of data pipelines and storage solutions to ensure they operate optimally. Continuous monitoring of the data pipeline is crucial to ensure that data flows are efficient and bottlenecks are quickly addressed. This could involve optimizing Hadoop jobs or indexing strategies in NoSQL databases. Cloud services provide monitoring and analytics tools like Amazon CloudWatch or Azure Monitor to track the performance of data operations and automatically adjust resources as needed.

- **Data Governance:** Ensuring data quality, integrity, security, and regulation compliance is a key responsibility in data engineering. Ensuring data quality would involve validating transaction data for completeness and accuracy. Security measures, like encryption and access controls, protect sensitive customer information and comply with regulations such as GDPR or CCPA. Cloud providers offer comprehensive data governance tools that assist with data cataloging, security, and compliance. For example, AWS Lake Formation helps build secure data lakes with fine-grained access control policies.

In big data projects, architecture and engineering go hand-in-hand. The architect designs a scalable, high-performing system that can handle the specific nuances of big data. At the same time, the engineer implements this design, ensuring that the data flows smoothly from the point of creation to the end of consumption.

Suppose the retail company aims to launch personalized marketing campaigns. The big data architecture would aggregate customer data, including past purchases, browsing history, and demographics. Data engineers would build pipelines to process this data in real time, providing a 360-degree customer view.

By analyzing this data, machine learning models could predict customer preferences and recommend personalized promotions. These recommendations would then be pushed to the customer through the appropriate channels, such as targeted emails or personalized online advertisements.

Retail companies can use a cloud approach to enhance their real-time inventory management systems. By using cloud-based IoT to collect real-time data from stores and inventory levels from warehouses stored in the cloud, the company can leverage real-time analytics to maintain optimal stock levels.

A cloud-based pub/sub messaging service, such as Amazon SNS or Google Pub/Sub, can trigger processing workflows as stock levels change. Machine learning services like Amazon SageMaker can predict inventory needs and automatically reorder stock, reducing manual intervention and the risk of overstocking or stockouts.

This big data initiative would increase customer engagement, higher conversion rates, and more efficient marketing spending, showcasing the direct impact of big data architecture and engineering on business outcomes.

Understanding these concepts is essential for Solutions Architects interview, as it allows them to design systems that store and process vast amounts of data and unlock actionable insights that can drive business growth. These insights inform decision-making, optimize operations, and can lead to the development of new products and services, ultimately providing a competitive edge in the market.

Key data design principles and methodologies

Data design principles and methodologies collectively provide a structured and systematic approach to designing data solutions that are efficient, scalable, secure, and aligned with business needs. They refer to the guiding principles and approaches to design and structure data solutions. They provide a framework for organizing, managing, and optimizing data to meet business requirements. From an interview perspective, you should be familiar with the key elements incorporated when working with data. Some of the important data design principles and methodologies are:

- **Data Normalization:** The principle of data normalization plays a crucial role in designing databases that are efficient and free from redundancy. By organizing data elements in a structured way, normalization minimizes duplication and simplifies the database structure, making maintenance and data retrieval more efficient. For example, an e-commerce platform might use normalization to separate customer information from order details, which reduces data redundancy and improves database performance.

- **Data Modularity:** Modularity in data design ensures that the data architecture is broken down into discrete components that can be managed and updated independently. This approach allows for flexibility and scalability, much like how microservices architecture enables different services to operate and scale without affecting each other. A real-world application of data modularity can be seen in how social media platforms manage diverse data streams like user profiles, posts, and messaging.

- **Data Integrity and Consistency:** Maintaining data integrity and consistency is vital for the accuracy and reliability of the data. It involves implementing validation rules and constraints to ensure the data entered into the system adheres to defined formats and values. Financial institutions, for instance, rely heavily on data integrity checks to ensure that transactions are executed correctly and in compliance with regulatory standards.

- **Data Security:** A key principle in data design is ensuring the security of the data at all stages of its lifecycle. This encompasses access controls, encryption, and secure data transfer protocols. Healthcare organizations, for instance, employ stringent data security measures to protect sensitive patient data in compliance with HIPAA regulations.

- **Data Scalability:** Scalability is the ability of a data system to grow and handle increased demand. This involves designing data structures and databases that can expand as the volume of data increases. Streaming services like Netflix employ scalable data architectures to accommodate the vast and growing volume of streaming data and user analytics.

- **Data Accessibility:** Designing for data accessibility ensures that data can be easily accessed and queried when needed. This includes using indexing, search algorithms, and optimization techniques to speed up data retrieval. Search engines like Google implement complex algorithms and indexing techniques to make vast web data readily accessible to users.

- **Data Recoverability:** Recoverability assures that data can be restored consistently during a system failure. It involves backup strategies and disaster recovery plans. E-commerce sites have recovery strategies to recover user transaction data during system crashes, ensuring business continuity.

- **Data Interoperability:** Interoperability is the capability of various systems and applications to collaborate and exchange data effectively. This principle is crucial in environments where data must be exchanged across different platforms and systems, like supply chain management systems, which need to share data across various logistics and inventory systems.

- **Data Lifecycle Management:** Managing the data lifecycle involves overseeing data from creation to deletion. It includes considerations for data retention policies, archival strategies, and purging routines. Companies like Facebook manage the lifecycle of user data, from the moment it's created to when it's archived or deleted, by data policies and user requests.

Incorporating these key design principles and methodologies into big data solutions ensures that the systems are robust, secure, and able to meet the demands of current and future data challenges. When discussing your approach to data design in an interview, provide examples of how you've implemented these principles in past projects, showcasing your ability to build sustainable, efficient, and secure data systems.

Data storage and data retrieval

Working with big data involves navigating the complexities of storing vast quantities of data while ensuring efficient retrieval. As a big data solutions architect, grasping the key concepts and technologies for handling extensive data volumes is just the start; you must also confront challenges associated with the four V's of big data: volume, velocity, variety, and veracity. Traditional storage systems often fall short regarding big data's scalability, performance, and cost-efficiency demands.

- **Distributed File Systems for Big Data:** Distributed file systems, particularly the Hadoop Distributed File System (HDFS), are central to big data storage. Understanding the architecture of these systems, including their data replication mechanisms and scalability features, is critical. HDFS, for example, ensures fault tolerance through block replication, enabling the system to handle node failures without data loss.
- **NoSQL Databases:** NoSQL databases, with their diversity—including key-value stores, document databases, columnar databases, and graph databases—provide flexibility and scalability for big data storage. The schema-less nature and eventual consistency model present advantages and trade-offs, such as unparalleled scalability and flexible data models at the expense of immediate consistency. Managed NoSQL services like Amazon DynamoDB, Google Firestore, and Azure Cosmos DB, providing scalable, high-performance databases with global distribution and multi-model support.
- **Columnar Storage for Analytics:** Columnar storage, as seen in formats like Apache Parquet and Apache ORC, offers benefits tailored for big data analytics. These formats optimize storage through compression techniques and are designed for efficient columnar read/write operations, significantly improving analytics performance.
- **Object Storage Systems:** Object storage systems offer scalability, durability, and cost-effectiveness for managing big data. Their approach to data organization and access

fundamentally differs from traditional file systems and relational databases, allowing for more agile and expansive data storage solutions. Cloud-based object storage like Amazon S3, Azure Blob Storage, and Google Cloud Storage offer highly scalable, durable, and secure solutions for big data. They support massive amounts of unstructured data and are optimized for data availability and accessibility across the globe.

- **Hybrid Storage Approaches:** A hybrid storage approach combines the strengths of distributed file systems, NoSQL databases, and object stores, optimizing data storage and access for varied use cases. This approach is becoming increasingly popular as organizations seek to balance performance with cost efficiency.
- **Block Storage:** Block storage services like AWS Elastic Block Store (EBS) or Azure Disk Storage are suitable for databases and transactional data storage for use cases requiring consistent latency and high IOPS.
- **File Storage:** Managed file storage services like Amazon EFS or Azure Files provide shared file systems necessary for applications relying on file system interfaces and semantics.
- **Data Warehousing:** Services like Amazon Redshift, Google BigQuery, and Azure Synapse Analytics offer fully managed data warehousing solutions that simplify the setup, maintenance, and scaling of data warehouses.

To excel in an interview, theoretical knowledge must be complemented by practical experience. Engage in projects or exercises that involve storing and retrieving large datasets using various big data technologies. Be ready to discuss your hands-on experience with these technologies, demonstrating your ability to write and optimize queries and make informed decisions about trade-offs between different storage and retrieval methods. Your ability to articulate these concepts clearly and showcase practical expertise will be key to creating a strong impression.

Best practice to store data for efficient query

Interviews may include questions that test your knowledge and understanding of the best practices when working with data pipelines. Here are some best practices for storing data for performant and efficient queries:

- **Data Compression and Encoding Techniques:** Data compression algorithms like Snappy, GZIP, and LZO, coupled with encoding methods such as dictionary encoding, are essential for maximizing storage efficiency and query performance in big data environments.
- **Data Partitioning and Sharding:** Partitioning and sharding are strategies for distributing data across nodes or storage systems. Partitioning strategies such as bucketing, range partitioning, and hash partitioning can significantly impact storage distribution and query performance.
- **Data Lifecycle Management and Replication:** Managing data growth with retention policies, archiving, and purging is critical, as is ensuring data integrity and compliance with regulations. Replication strategies, whether synchronous or asynchronous, provide the

fault tolerance necessary for high availability and data reliability. Cloud storage solutions offer features to automate data archiving to less expensive storage classes based on access patterns and retention policies. Cloud services facilitate cross-region replication and provide robust disaster recovery solutions to ensure data is preserved and accessible even during regional failures.

- **Optimal Data Retrieval Techniques:** Efficient data retrieval is paramount in big data ecosystems. Architects should be familiar with querying techniques for distributed file systems and understand NoSQL query languages. Knowledge of SQL-based distributed engines like Apache Drill and indexing techniques also plays a crucial role in optimizing data retrieval.

- **Caching and Query Optimization:** Caching mechanisms can significantly reduce latency and enhance performance. Understanding query optimization and performance tuning is essential for analyzing execution plans and identifying bottlenecks. Configuring caching frameworks like Redis or Apache Ignite can further accelerate data retrieval.

- **Workload Management and Resource Allocation:** Optimizing data retrieval performance in big data environments involves managing workloads, allocating resources, and fine-tuning configuration parameters.

- **Content Delivery Networks (CDNs):** CDNs like Amazon CloudFront and Azure CDN cache data at edge locations, reducing latency for global data access.

- **Data Caching Services:** Cloud-based caching services like Amazon ElastiCache and Azure Cache for Redis provide in-memory data stores to speed up data retrieval.

- **Query Acceleration:** Cloud data warehouses use query acceleration features, such as Amazon Redshift Spectrum, to run queries directly against data in object storage, extending the data warehouse's reach.

With the cloud as the new normal for data processing, it's important to articulate how cloud technologies can be leveraged for big data storage and retrieval. Discuss your experience with cloud-based data warehousing, the implementation of serverless data processing architectures, and how you've used cloud services to optimize data retrieval and reduce costs. Be ready to explore the advantages of the cloud in terms of elasticity, global distribution, and managed services that free architects to focus on innovation rather than infrastructure management. Your ability to navigate both on-premises and cloud solutions and to bridge the two, when necessary, will demonstrate a comprehensive understanding of modern big data storage and retrieval challenges and solutions.

Distributed systems and data processing frameworks

Distributed systems and data processing frameworks are the engines that power big data solutions, enabling the handling of datasets that are too large, fast-changing, or too complex for traditional data processing software. In big data, a Solutions Architect is tasked with the challenging yet critical role of orchestrating the design and execution of data infrastructures that can handle the scale and complexity of massive datasets. With the exponential growth of data, it becomes imperative to build robust and intelligently tuned systems to the nuanced demands of big data processing. Here's how they fit into the bigger picture of big data architecture.

Distributed Systems

As a Big Data Solutions Architect, your responsibilities include designing, constructing, and administrating distributed file systems, such as the Hadoop Distributed File System (HDFS). HDFS is inherently designed to store vast quantities of data across multiple nodes and manage it to facilitate reliability and high-throughput access. Here are some of the core characteristics of HDFS that you, as an architect, must be adept in:

- **Distributed Storage:** HDFS takes large files, breaks them into blocks, and distributes them across the cluster's nodes. This distribution facilitates parallel processing and contributes to the system's fault tolerance.
- **Fault Tolerance:** By replicating each data block across multiple nodes, HDFS ensures data durability. If one node goes down, the system can retrieve the data from another node with a replicated block.
- **High Throughput:** Optimized for batch processing, HDFS provides high throughput access to application data, which is particularly beneficial for big data applications.
- **Scalability:** You can scale the system horizontally by adding more nodes to the Hadoop cluster, accommodating data growth.
- **Data Locality:** HDFS optimizes computation by moving computation to the data rather than data to the computation, reducing network congestion and increasing throughput.
- **NameNode and DataNodes:** The architecture comprises a single NameNode that manages the file system metadata and multiple DataNodes that store and retrieve blocks when instructed to by clients or the NameNode.

Data Processing Frameworks

- **Apache Hadoop** is an open-source framework that enables the distributed processing of substantial data sets across computer clusters using straightforward programming models. This framework is engineered to scale from a single server to thousands of servers, with each machine providing local computation and storage capabilities. Its ecosystem includes HDFS for storage, YARN for job scheduling, and MapReduce for processing.

- **Apache Spark:** Spark is an open-source, general-purpose cluster-computing framework. It offers an interface for programming entire clusters with built-in data parallelism and fault tolerance capabilities. It's known for its speed, ease of use, and sophisticated analytics, with support for SQL queries, streaming data, machine learning, and graph processing.
- **NoSQL Databases:** These databases are designed for distributed data stores that require large-scale data storage and are often used in big data applications. They provide operational simplicity, horizontal scaling, and more flexible data models than traditional relational databases.

Cloud-based Data Processing Services

- **Amazon EMR:** A cloud-native big data platform that allows vast amounts of data to be processed quickly and cost-effectively across resizable clusters of Amazon EC2 instances.
- **Google Dataflow** is a fully managed service for stream and batch processing that minimizes latency, processing time, and cost through autoscaling and batch processing optimizations.
- **Azure HDInsight:** A cloud service that makes processing massive amounts of data easy, fast, and cost-effective. It supports various scenarios such as ETL, Data Warehousing, Machine Learning, and IoT.

Integration with Big Data Processing Frameworks

Your expertise must extend to frameworks like Apache Spark, which offers a unified analytics engine for large-scale data processing. It is known for its speed, ease of use, and streaming analytics capabilities. Here are aspects of Apache Spark that you should be conversant with:

- **YARN:** As part of the Hadoop ecosystem, YARN is a resource manager that allocates system resources to various applications running in a Hadoop cluster.
- **MapReduce** is a programming model designed for processing large data sets using a parallel, distributed algorithm across a cluster.
- **Hive:** A data warehouse infrastructure built on top of Hadoop, Hive provides data summarization, query, and analysis.
- **HBase:** Running on top of HDFS, HBase is a non-relational, distributed database that supports structured data storage for large tables.

Now, let's explore how to implement a data framework in a distributed system.

Implementing Distributed Systems and Frameworks

Imagine a retail chain that collects customer data from various touchpoints. As a Big Data Solutions Architect, you are responsible for designing a system that can handle the real-time ingestion of this data and enable complex analytical tasks.

Using HDFS, you might structure the data storage to ensure that customer data, transaction records, and inventory information are stored efficiently and replicated for fault tolerance. With Spark, you could develop real-time analytics models to predict customer behavior, personalize marketing efforts, and optimize supply chain logistics. The seamless integration of Spark with HDFS, leveraging YARN for resource management, Hive for SQL-like querying, and HBase for real-time access to tabular data, would be part of your architectural design.

The retail chain could leverage cloud storage options for flexibility and cost savings, especially for unstructured data like customer feedback from social media. A solution architect might propose a hybrid model for high-speed transactional data where frequently accessed data is stored in a distributed database like HBase. In contrast, historical data is archived in object storage for cost-efficiency and long-term durability.

> *In preparing for an interview, you should be ready to discuss the architectural decisions behind such a design. Expect questions on how you manage data consistency, handle network latency, balance loads across the system, and ensure fault detection and recovery.*

You must articulate the technical specifications and strategic business benefits of your design choices.

Choosing the Right Big Data Framework

Selecting the right framework for a big data architecture involves understanding the specific use case, the data's nature, the processing requirements' complexity, and the available infrastructure. Apache Spark is a versatile and scalable framework that can perform data processing tasks orders of magnitude faster than MapReduce. Understanding object storage solutions such as AWS S3, Azure Blob Storage, and Google Cloud Storage is crucial in the cloud context. These platforms offer benefits like cost-effectiveness, scalability, and resilience, sometimes more advantageous than traditional file systems like HDFS.

Like MapReduce, a big data solutions architect is expected to be familiar with many popular big data computing frameworks such as Apache Spark, Apache Flink, Apache Flink, Apache Storm, Apache Kafka, Apache Cassandra, etc. Also, Choosing the right big data framework depends on multiple factors, such as specific use cases, the nature of your data, the complexity of your processing requirements, and the available infrastructure. Apache Spark is the most widely adopted framework. As a big data architect, this is one computing framework you should be familiar with and have good working experience with. Let's learn more about it.

Data Processing Frameworks with Apache Spark

Apache Spark's versatility, scalability, and performance have made it popular for big data processing and analytics use cases. It enables developers to build robust data processing pipelines and perform complex computations efficiently across distributed clusters, making it a key component in many big data processing architectures. For relevance, you should be able to describe Apache Spark's different capabilities and features in a hands-on context.

Review the Apache Spark framework's key concepts, components, and features when preparing for the interview. Apache Spark is a beacon of versatility, scalability, and performance. Its comprehensive capabilities have earned it a reputation as the most widely adopted framework for big data processing and analytics.

Apache Spark is a unified analytics engine renowned for processing large-scale data across distributed clusters. Its resilience and efficiency in handling batch processing, streaming data, machine learning, and iterative queries have made it an integral part of the data processing landscape. You should know the following topics to explain the Spark framework in the interview.

- **Spark Basics:** Understanding Spark begins with its core purpose: to provide a faster and more flexible alternative to MapReduce. Its ability to perform in-memory computations accelerates processing speeds. Spark supports multiple languages, but Scala and Python are particularly prominent, favored for their concise syntax and rich data science libraries.
- **Spark Architecture:** Spark's architecture is designed to maximize efficiency and speed. At its heart lies the driver program, orchestrating operations across the worker nodes. The SparkContext connects to a cluster manager (standalone, YARN, or Mesos), which allocates resources across applications. This architecture is key to Spark's fast data processing capabilities.
- **Spark Core:** The foundational layer of Spark's functionality is its Resilient Distributed Datasets (RDDs). RDDs provide a fault-tolerant way to operate on distributed data. Transformations on RDDs are lazy, meaning they're not computed immediately but optimized to run as a single pipeline of operations.
- **Spark SQL:** This module brings the power of SQL to Spark, allowing for structured data processing with DataFrames and Datasets—a more modern and structured approach than RDDs. Spark SQL also supports various data formats, enabling seamless integration and analysis.
- **Spark Streaming:** Spark Streaming is the go-to module for real-time analytics. It processes live streams of data, partitioning the stream into micro-batches that are then processed by the Spark engine to enable real-time decision-making.

- **Spark MLlib:** Machine learning is integral to big data analytics, and MLlib provides a suite of scalable machine learning algorithms. MLlib transforms Spark into a powerful predictive analytics engine that goes from classification to clustering.
- **Performance Optimization:** To extract the most out of Spark, understanding optimization techniques is crucial. From tuning data partitioning to leveraging in-memory computing, every technique contributes to a more efficient execution.
- **Spark Ecosystem:** The ecosystem around Spark, including integration with Hadoop for storage, Kafka for real-time messaging, and Elasticsearch for search and analytics, demonstrates its flexibility and capacity to fit into diverse environments.

As a big data architect, familiarity with Spark is not enough; hands-on experience is key. Through practical application, you can understand nuances such as the Spark execution plan, task scheduling, and in-depth performance tuning.

When gearing up for an interview as a Big Data Solutions Architect, it's essential to have a comprehensive grasp of Spark. Prepare to discuss its components, how it contrasts with other processing frameworks, and how it integrates into a broader big data strategy. Be ready with real-world examples that showcase your experience with Spark's diverse capabilities—from streamlining data pipelines to building machine learning models.

Apache Spark's rich feature set and ability to handle complex, large-scale data processing tasks efficiently make it a cornerstone technology in big data. Mastery of Spark's capabilities indicates a Solutions Architect's readiness to tackle the challenges of today's data-driven world.

Data warehousing and business intelligence

Data warehousing and business intelligence (BI) are critical components in the landscape of big data, enabling businesses to store vast amounts of information systematically and utilize this data for strategic decision-making.

Data Warehousing (DW) in Big Data

A data warehouse is a centralized repository that stores integrated data from multiple sources. It supports the storage, retrieval, and management of large datasets, typically in a structured format, facilitating complex queries and analysis:

- **Structured Storage:** Data warehouses organize data into structured formats using schemas optimized for SQL queries and BI tools, making data retrieval efficient for analytics.

- **Historical Data Analysis:** Unlike operational databases optimized for transaction processing, data warehouses are designed explicitly to analyze historical data to identify trends, patterns, and long-term performance.
- **Performance and Scalability:** Modern data warehouses can handle petabytes of data and provide fast query performance, which is crucial for BI applications that require rapid access to large datasets.

You should be familiar with the main objectives of a data warehouse. Data warehousing combines data from different sources, such as transactional databases, CRM systems, ERP systems, and external sources, into a unified view. This integration enables comprehensive and holistic analysis of the data. Data warehouses store large amounts of historical data over time, allowing analysts to analyze trends, patterns, and changes in business operations over different periods. You should also have a good understanding of the key components of a data warehousing system, such as:

- Data Sources: Operational systems, external data sources, and other systems that generate or store relevant data.
- ETL Processes: Extract, Transform, and Load (ETL) processes involve the extraction of data from various sources, its transformation into a standardized format, and then loading it into a data warehouse or other sources for consumption.
- Data Warehouse: The central repository stores structured, integrated, and cleansed data. It is optimized for query and analysis.
- Data Marts: Subset(s) of the data warehouse that focus on specific business functions or departments. Data marts provide a more tailored view of the data to support particular analysis requirements.
- Metadata: Metadata is information about the data stored in the data warehouse, including data definitions, data lineage, data transformations, and business rules. It helps in understanding and managing the data.

Data is transformed and cleansed during the extraction, transformation, and loading (ETL) to ensure consistency and accuracy. Data consolidation reduces data redundancy and improves data quality. Data warehousing employs specialized design techniques, such as dimensional modeling and indexing strategies, to optimize query performance and facilitate faster analysis. Data warehouses provide a foundation for decision support systems and business intelligence applications. Analysts and decision-makers can leverage the data warehouse to generate reports, perform complex queries, and gain insights to support data-driven decision-making.

Business Intelligence (BI) in Big Data

Data warehouses are the foundation for business intelligence tools and applications, allowing users to generate reports, create dashboards, and perform ad-hoc analysis. Business intelligence helps organizations unlock the value of their data, transform it into actionable insights, and make informed decisions that drive growth and success.

Business intelligence is supported by various technologies and tools, such as data warehouses, online analytical processing (OLAP), data mining, reporting tools, and data visualization platforms. These tools enable users to access, analyze, and present data meaningfully. As someone interviewing for the big data solutions architect role, you should be familiar with the basics of business intelligence, its different components, and its value proposition. The purpose of BI is to support better decision-making through actionable insights:

- **Data Visualization and Reporting:** BI tools transform raw data into understandable and actionable insights, typically through dashboards, reports, and visualizations. These insights are vital for business stakeholders to make informed decisions.
- **Predictive Analytics:** BI goes beyond descriptive analytics; it uses historical data to forecast future events and trends, enabling proactive decision-making.
- **Data-Driven Culture:** A robust BI strategy fosters a data-driven culture within an organization, where decisions are made based on data and empirical evidence rather than intuition or observation alone.

Integrating Cloud Technologies for DW and BI

Cloud technologies have significantly transformed the landscape of data warehousing and business intelligence (BI), providing scalable, flexible, and cost-effective alternatives to traditional on-premises solutions. Here's a deeper look at how cloud integration is reshaping DW and BI:

Cloud Data Warehouses

Services like Amazon Redshift, Google BigQuery, and Azure Synapse Analytics are at the forefront of this transformation. These cloud data warehouses offer fully managed, scalable, and serverless options that eliminate the need for physical on-premises hardware. This shift not only reduces capital expenditure but also simplifies the scalability challenges associated with data growth. These platforms provide robust data management capabilities and are optimized for performing extensive analytics, thus supporting a variety of use cases from business reporting to advanced data science.

- **Scalability and Elasticity**: Cloud data warehouses can scale computing and storage resources up or down as needed, often automatically. This elasticity is crucial during varying load periods, ensuring that performance remains consistent without incurring unnecessary costs.
- **Accessibility and Integration**: Being hosted in the cloud, these services ensure data is accessible from anywhere, facilitating remote work and global operations. They also offer extensive integration capabilities with various data sources and applications, streamlining data ingestion and processing pipelines.

BI as a Service

Cloud-based BI tools like Power BI, Tableau Online, Looker, and Amazon Quicksight have democratized access to advanced analytics capabilities. These tools offer a range of analytical features, from interactive dashboards to complex reporting and predictive analytics, all hosted in the cloud.

- **Reduced Infrastructure Overhead**: By leveraging BI as a Service, companies can avoid the complexities and costs of maintaining the underlying infrastructure. This setup allows businesses to focus more on analysis and less on operational management.
- **Real-time Insights and Collaboration**: These platforms support real-time data processing, enabling businesses to gain immediate insights and make informed decisions swiftly. Additionally, cloud-based BI tools enhance collaboration among users, allowing them to share insights and reports easily across the organization.
- **Security and Compliance**: Despite the shared responsibility model in cloud computing, BI services incorporate robust security measures, including data encryption, secure access protocols, and compliance with various regulatory standards.

As cloud technologies continue to evolve, integrating AI and machine learning with DW and BI is set to redefine the possibilities further. Automated insights generation, predictive analytics, and machine learning models are seamlessly integrated into these platforms, enabling more sophisticated analysis and smarter decision-making processes.

Integrating cloud technologies into data warehousing and business intelligence is not just enhancing the efficiency and scalability of these systems but also revolutionizing how data-driven decisions are made in the modern business landscape. Organizations embracing these technologies are better positioned to leverage their data for competitive advantage.

Big Data Solutions Architects role for DW and BI

As a big data solutions architect, when considering data warehousing and BI, you need to know the following:

- **Integration Capabilities:** The ability of the data warehouse to integrate data from various sources, including traditional databases, cloud applications, and streaming data.
- **Real-time Analytics:** There is a need for real-time BI, which requires data warehouses to support fast data ingestion and querying.
- **Security and Compliance:** Ensuring data in the data warehouse is secure and complies with relevant data protection regulations like GDPR or HIPAA.
- **Improved Decision-Making:** Business intelligence gives stakeholders the insights and information to make more informed and strategic decisions. It reduces reliance on intuition or guesswork by basing decisions on data-driven evidence.

- **Enhanced Operational Efficiency:** Business intelligence helps optimize business processes and increase operational efficiency by identifying bottlenecks, inefficiencies, and areas for improvement.
- **Competitive Advantage:** Business intelligence allows organizations to gain a competitive edge by uncovering hidden patterns, market trends, and customer preferences. It enables businesses to respond quickly to changing market conditions and make better-informed decisions.
- **Proactive Insights:** Business intelligence can provide proactive insights using predictive analytics to forecast future trends and behaviors. This enables organizations to anticipate customer needs, identify risks, and take proactive measures to stay ahead.

In a retail context, a data warehouse could store sales, inventory, and customer data, which BI tools would then use to provide insights on purchasing trends, inventory optimization, and customer preferences. This enables retailers to make strategic decisions like promotional offers, stock adjustments, and customer loyalty programs.

When preparing for an interview, you should articulate how data warehousing and BI are implemented in big data architectures, their benefits, and how they integrate with other big data solutions.

Be ready to discuss specific experiences where you've designed or worked with data warehousing and BI solutions, the challenges you faced, and the impact of your work on business outcomes. Demonstrating knowledge in both the technical and strategic aspects of data warehousing and BI will be crucial.

Best practices for designing big data solutions

Most interviews will include questions that probe your knowledge and understanding of the best practices you are either aware of or have incorporated into your work. It is essential to be prepared with information and data points that are typically best practices when working with data pipelines. Designing and implementing big data solutions demands a strategic approach encompassing data management, processing, analytics, and security. Best practices in this domain are essential to ensure big data systems' effectiveness, efficiency, and scalability. Here are some key practices for architects:

- **Defining Clear Objectives:** Setting goals that resonate with the broader business strategy when designing big data solutions is paramount. For instance, a retail chain may seek to leverage big data to personalize customer experiences. By delineating this objective, a solutions architect would focus on integrating customer data platforms that consolidate information across touchpoints, enabling targeted marketing and improving customer service, ultimately driving sales and customer satisfaction.

- **Ensuring Scalability and Flexibility:** A well-designed big data architecture must readily expand and adapt to the evolving data landscape. Consider Netflix's migration to a cloud-based architecture, which allows it to scale resources dynamically based on user demand. This level of scalability and flexibility is critical to accommodating the streaming giant's massive, fluctuating loads while maintaining a seamless customer experience globally.
- **Prioritizing Data Quality and Integration:** The integrity of big data systems heavily relies on the quality and seamless integration of data. A healthcare provider analyzing patient records to improve treatment plans would need a meticulous ETL process to ensure data from various sources is accurate and consistent, providing clinicians with reliable information for making life-saving decisions.
- **Embracing Diverse Data Storage Options:** Diverse data storage solutions cater to varying data access and management needs. For instance, Twitter employs a combination of storage systems, including HDFS for large-scale data processing and Manhattan, their real-time, multi-tenant distributed database for user data, to support their massive scale and real-time content delivery.
- **Optimizing Data Processing:** Efficient data processing is at the heart of big data solutions. Financial institutions, such as banks analyzing transactions for fraud detection, require high-speed data processing to identify and act upon suspicious activities in real-time, using distributed computing frameworks like Apache Spark to achieve the necessary speed and efficiency.
- **Adopting Real-time Data Processing:** Incorporating real-time data processing enables immediate insights and actions. Automotive manufacturers utilizing IoT sensors for predictive maintenance must process streaming data on the fly to preemptively address vehicle issues, leveraging platforms like Apache Kafka to handle the real-time data flow.
- **Implementing Advanced Analytics and Machine Learning:** Advanced analytics and machine learning extract deep insights from big data. Online retailers like Amazon enhance customer recommendations by applying machine learning algorithms to their extensive product and user activity data, driving sales by providing a personalized shopping experience.
- **Focusing on Security and Governance:** Security and governance are non-negotiable in big data. A financial services firm, for instance, must ensure client data confidentiality by implementing stringent access controls and data encryption, aligning with regulations like GDPR to protect personal data and maintain customer trust.
- **Ensuring Reliability and High Availability:** Reliability is crucial for big data architectures. Consider an airline's reservation system where high availability is critical; employing data replication across geographically dispersed data centers ensures continuous operation, even in the face of individual system failures.
- **Fostering a Collaborative Development Environment:** Collaboration between development and operations streamlines the deployment of big data solutions. A

software enterprise can automate deployments and integrate feedback loops by adopting DevOps practices, enhancing product quality, and speeding up release cycles.

- **Practicing Cost-Effective Resource Management:** Cost-effective resource management in big data is vital. Streaming services, such as Spotify, leverage cloud auto-scaling features to efficiently manage resource usage and costs, ensuring that they only pay for the computing resources they need when they need them.
- **Building for Interoperability and Future Integration:** Interoperability ensures that big data systems can evolve with emerging technologies. A solutions architect working for a smart city initiative must design data platforms that integrate with current IoT devices and connect with future technologies, ensuring long-term utility.
- **Promoting Data Literacy and Democratization:** Data democratization empowers more stakeholders to derive insights from big data. A pharmaceutical company may implement self-service BI tools, enabling researchers to access and analyze clinical trial data independently, fostering innovation, and accelerating drug development.
- **Engaging in Continuous Learning and Improvement:** The field of big data is ever-evolving, necessitating continuous learning and system refinements. A telecom company may regularly update its big data analytics models to predict network congestion better, adapting to new patterns in user behavior and improving service quality over time.

In an interview, articulate these best practices with examples from your experience, demonstrating your holistic understanding of the big data ecosystem. Show how you've applied these practices to solve complex business problems and generate value from large and diverse datasets. Highlight your ability to balance technical considerations with strategic business outcomes, ensuring that your big data solutions are technically sound and deliver benefits.

Whiteboarding Bigdata SA Interview

Most interviews will include a Whiteboard interview, a standard part of the hiring process for solutions architect positions. A whiteboard interview for a solutions architect role typically involves being given an architectural design problem or scenario and being asked to diagram or sketch out a potential solution on a whiteboard while explaining your thought process. Very often, it also tests your knowledge about the architecture you designed in the past.

If you apply for a big data solutions architect role, you may get questions like drawing and explaining the architecture of your recent data analytics project or presenting a reference architecture of modern analytics platforms. Here's some example questions:

- Design to build a data-lake-centric analytics platform in the cloud.
- Design a system to analyze user behavior data from a mobile app and provide recommendations. What components would you need? How would you collect, store, process, and serve the data?

- Design a system to collect and analyze sensor data from IoT devices. What are the key elements, and how would you ensure scalability?
- Design a real-time analytics system to analyze clickstream data from a website. How would you handle the velocity and volume of data?
- Design a system to analyze log data to find anomalies. What data structures and algorithms would you use? How would you approach the analysis?
- Design a system to analyze social media data to detect trends and sentiments. What techniques would you use for natural language processing?
- Design a pipeline to move data from databases/APIs to a data warehouse. How would you handle transforms, scheduling, and error handling?
- Design a system to generate daily reports and dashboards from a data lake. How would you structure the data and metadata?
- Design a cloud-based analytics architecture for a large e-commerce.

The interviewer looks for signs that the candidate can design appropriate big data solutions tailored to the business problem. The whiteboard allows the interviewer to observe the candidate's thought process as they design a solution iteratively.

Let's take the example of building a data lake-centric analytics platform. The following diagram illustrates the conceptual, logical model of such a platform.

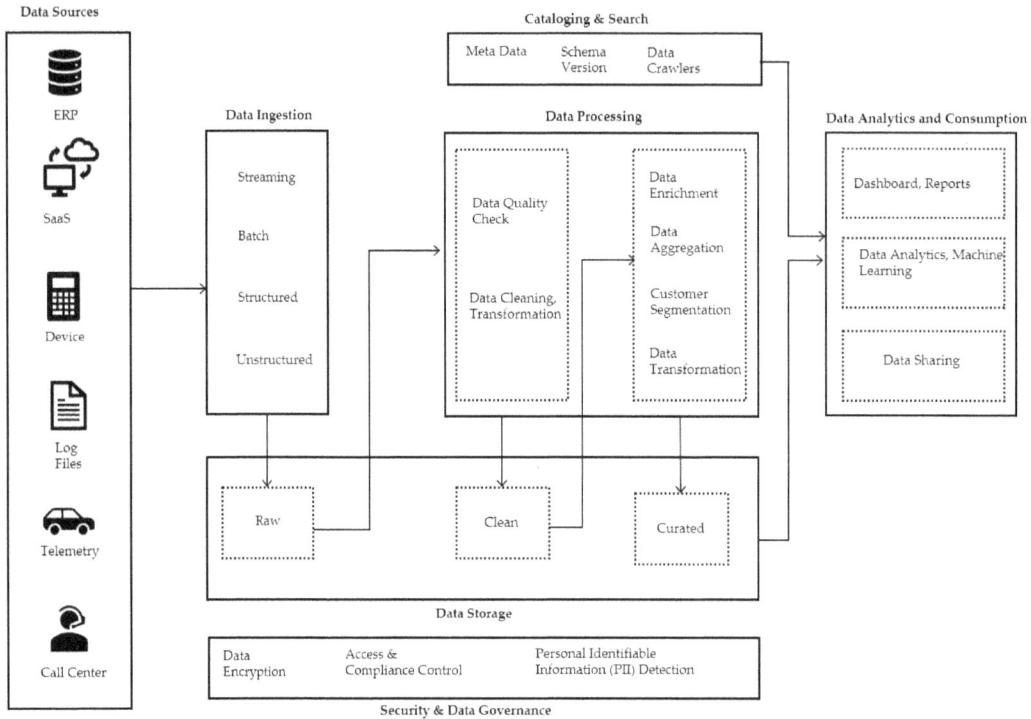

Figure 8.1 - Logical model of a data lake platform

A data lake analytics architecture can be structured with customer data flowing through six logical layers: Ingestion, Processing, Storage, Unified Governance and Security, Cataloging, and Consumption. A layered, component-based architecture helps separation of concerns, decoupling, and flexibility. This allows quick integration of new data and methods needed to keep pace with changes in analytics.

- **Ingestion layer:** The ingestion layer brings data into the data lake. It can connect to internal and external sources of data using various protocols. Both batch and streaming data can be brought into the storage layer by the ingestion layer. Additionally, the ingestion layer is accountable for delivering the ingested data to diverse destinations in the data storage layer, including the object store, databases, and data warehouses.
- **Storage layer**: The storage layer provides durable, scalable, secure, and cost-effective storage for large amounts of structured and unstructured data in various formats without conforming it to a schema. The storage layer provides durable, scalable, secure, cost-effective data storage components. It supports storing unstructured data and datasets of various structures and formats. It supports storing source data without structuring it to conform to a target schema or format. The storage layer is organized into zones based on data consumption readiness for different personas.

- **Raw zone**: The raw zone is the upstream area where data is captured in its true raw format before processing. It provides access to immutable source data. Typically, data engineering personas interact with the data stored in this zone.
- **Cleaned zone**: The cleaned zone stores curated, refined, and validated data, which is cleaned and processed from the raw zone. Data engineering and data science personas typically interact with the data stored in this zone.
- **Curated zone**: The curated zone hosts cleaned, normalized, standardized, and enriched datasets that conform to organizational standards. This data is used across the organization to drive business decisions. All personas across organizations use the data stored in this zone to drive business decisions.

- **Cataloging and search layer:** The cataloging and search layer stores metadata about datasets in the data lake. It tracks information like schema, partitioning, and versions of datasets. As the number of datasets grows, this layer allows for the search and discovery of datasets in the data lake. It makes the data lake organized and usable.
- **Processing layer:** The processing layer transforms raw data into consumable data through validation, cleanup, normalization, and enrichment. It advances dataset readiness across landing, raw, and curated zones and registers metadata. The processing layer uses purpose-built components to handle diverse data formats, volumes, and processing tasks. It enables building multi-step pipelines using specialized features for each processing step. The processing layer is key for transforming raw data into analysis-ready information.
- **Consumption layer:** The consumption layer provides scalable, performant analytics tools to gain insights from the vast data lake data. It enables user analytics through tools supporting SQL, batch, BI, reporting, and ML. The layer integrates with the lake's storage, catalog, and security. It uses schema-on-read, supports multiple data structures/formats, and partitions data for cost and performance optimization.
- **Security and governance layer:** The security and governance layer is vital to safeguarding the data stored in the storage layer and the processing capabilities found across all layers. It protects resources by implementing access controls, encryption, network security, usage tracking, and auditing. Additionally, the security layer monitors the activities of other layers, producing a comprehensive audit trail. Components belonging to the remaining layers natively integrate with the security and governance layer.

Once the logical architecture is built, each component in the logical architecture is taken, and the specific technologies and products that will implement it are determined. For example, the above logical architecture comprises layers that can be implemented using a reference architecture with AWS serverless and managed services. AWS provides, manages, and integrates the infrastructure components in a scalable, resilient, secure, and cost-effective manner. This allows developers to spend more time quickly building data and analytics pipelines rather than managing infrastructure. It provides key benefits, including easy configuration-based use, no infrastructure management, pay-per-use pricing, etc.

The following diagram illustrates a reference architecture in AWS.

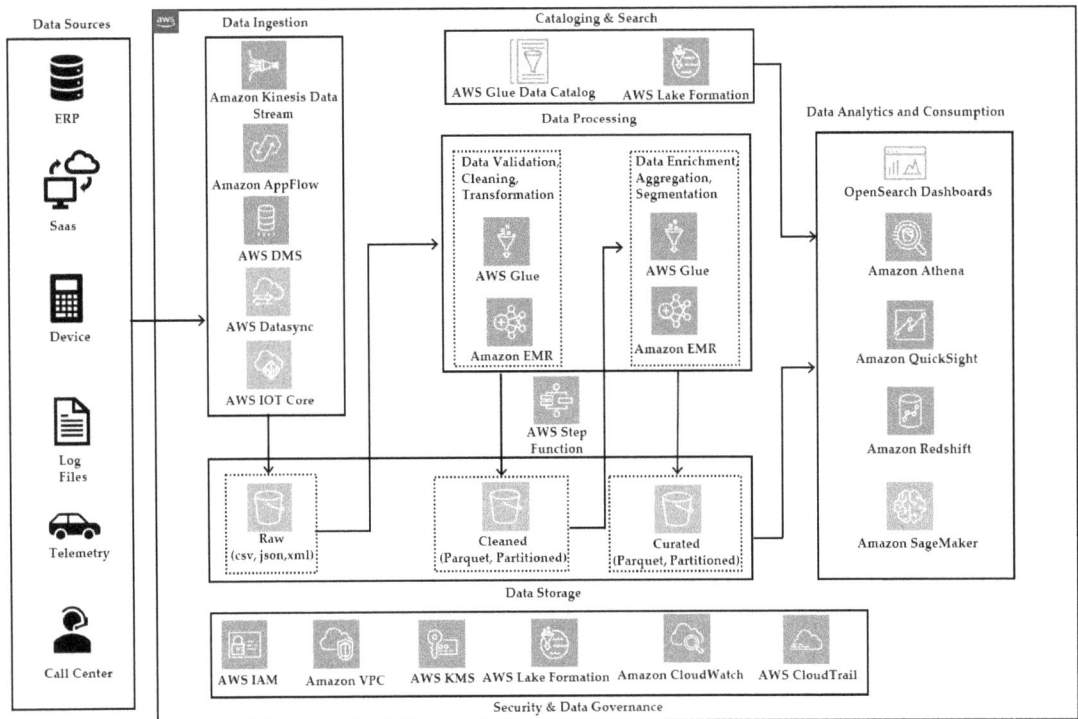

Figure 8.2 - Data lake reference architecture in AWS cloud platform

Now, let's understand the specific AWS services used in different layers: -

Ingestion layer :
- **Streaming data sources:** There are several AWS services for data ingestion, including Kinesis Data Stream, Kinesis Data Firehose, and Managed Streaming for Apache Kafka (MSK). Kinesis Data Stream fully manages real-time data streaming, enabling developers to collect, process, and analyze large data streams. Its distributed architecture processes massive streams from various sources. Kinesis Data Firehose is a fully managed service that simplifies loading streaming data into storage and analytics services. Without complex transformations, it efficiently captures and delivers streaming data directly to various destinations, including Amazon S3, Amazon Redshift, and Amazon OpenSearch.
- **Operational database:** The AWS Data Migration Service enables data from various

relational and non-relational databases to be migrated into the data lake landing zone. AWS DMS supports migration between the 20-plus database and analytics engines, such as Oracle to Amazon Aurora MySQL-Compatible Edition, MySQL to Amazon Relational Database (RDS) for MySQL, Microsoft SQL Server to Amazon Aurora PostgreSQL-Compatible Edition, MongoDB to Amazon DocumentDB (with MongoDB compatibility), Oracle to Amazon Redshift, and Amazon Simple Storage Service (S3).

- **Software as a service (SaaS) applications:** Amazon AppFlow is a fully managed service that enables easy and secure data transfer between popular software as a service (SaaS) applications like Salesforce, SAP, Google Analytics, Facebook Ads, ServiceNow and AWS such as Amazon S3 and Amazon Redshift.
- **File:** AWS DataSync from AWS is capable of transferring massive amounts of data from Network File System (NFS) and Server Message Block (SMB) network-attached storage (NAS) devices into a data lake landing zone.

Storage layer: Amazon S3 provides the foundation for the storage layer in the architecture. With virtually unlimited scalability and high durability, Amazon S3 offers an ideal foundation for a data lake. Storage can be increased seamlessly from gigabytes to petabytes, only paying for what is used. Amazon S3 is designed to provide 99.999999999% durability, 99.99 % availability, scalable performance, easy-to-use features, built-in encryption, and access controls. It integrates with many AWS services and third-party tools for ingesting, processing, and securing data. The high scalability, durability, and integration capabilities make Amazon S3 optimal for building a data lake. Data can be stored in different storage classes like S3 Standard for frequently accessed data, S3 Infrequent Access for less often used data, and S3 Glacier for archival data. This allows for the optimization of costs by storing data in the most cost-effective storage class based on access patterns. The data can be partitioned into different folders/prefixes based on factors like date, region, business unit, etc. This partitioning approach enables faster queries as analytics tools only need to access a subset of the data.

Cataloging and search layer: The proposed architecture uses Lake Formation as the central catalog to store and govern metadata for all data sets in the data lake. Organizations can manage technical metadata and business attributes for all their data sets within Lake Formation. AWS Glue, Amazon EMR, and Amazon Athena integrate seamlessly with Lake Formation, automatically discovering and registering dataset metadata in the Lake Formation catalog. AWS Glue crawlers can detect changes in data schemas and newly added partitions in datasets within a data lake, subsequently updating the Lake Formation catalog with new versions of the corresponding metadata.

Processing layer: AWS Glue provides a serverless, pay-per-use ETL (extract, transform, load) service that allows you to build and execute Python or Spark jobs (using Scala or Python) without needing to deploy or manage clusters. AWS Step Functions is a serverless workflow orchestration service that lets you coordinate components of distributed applications and microservices using visual workflows. You build applications from individual steps that can be integrated with other AWS services, enabling you to implement visual workflows that are scalable, resilient, and highly available.

AWS Glue and AWS Step Functions are serverless services that can be used together to build, orchestrate, and execute scalable data pipelines. Combining AWS Glue and Step Functions can create multi-step workflows that perform various data processing tasks like cataloging, validating, cleaning, transforming, and enriching datasets. These workflows can move data through different storage zones, from the landing zone to the raw zone and then to the curated zone, as the data is progressively processed and refined. The serverless nature of AWS Glue and Step Functions allows these data pipelines to scale up to handle large volumes of data efficiently.

The consumption layer comprises fully managed analytics services that enable interactive queries, batch processing, and ML. Amazon Athena is an interactive query service that simplifies analyzing data or building applications using data from Amazon S3 data lakes. Athena is serverless, so there needs to be infrastructure to manage. Amazon QuickSight is a business intelligence service that lets you create interactive dashboards from data. Amazon QuickSight Q is a natural language query service for QuickSight that allows users to ask business questions using natural language and receive answers with relevant data visualizations. QuickSight Q uses ML to understand the intent of questions in plain language. OpenSearch Dashboards is an open-source visualization tool designed to work with OpenSearch. Amazon OpenSearch Service installs OpenSearch Dashboards with every OpenSearch Service domain. Amazon SageMaker is a fully managed service that allows developers and data scientists to quickly build, train, and deploy machine learning models.

Security and governance layer: Amazon VPC allows you to create a private network for your S3 data lake and other resources. This keeps them isolated from the public internet. Within the VPC, you can create multiple subnets to segment your resources. For an S3 data lake, create separate subnets for different layers. This provides additional isolation between components. AWS IAM helps secure S3 data lakes by enabling granular access control through IAM policies and roles. IAM allows the creation of users and groups with customized permissions to access specific S3 buckets, objects, and actions. This provides authentication of approved users and fine-grained authorization to data. AWS KMS helps S3 data lake encryption by allowing customers to encrypt data in S3 easily using KMS keys. KMS provides central key management, key rotation, and auditing to help protect data in S3 data lakes. Amazon CloudWatch helps monitor S3 data lakes by delivering metrics and alarms to track usage, storage, access patterns, and anomalies. CloudWatch logs can also ingest access logs from S3 to detect issues and analyze usage.

Bigdata architect interview questions

Interviewing for a big data architect role often involves combining technical, conceptual, and scenario-based questions. The big data solutions architect interview will also include a range of questions that assess your understanding of the domain, your experience within the domain, your knowledge of the different tools and technologies used in the domain, and your ability to apply your knowledge to specific scenarios to determine job fit. Besides verbal responses, you should be prepared to whiteboard a solution. If you declare these upfront, asking follow-up questions and making assumptions is okay.

Scenario Based Questions

Question: As the lead architect for an e-commerce platform, you ensure that customer data, including payment information and personal details, is handled securely and complies with data protection laws like GDPR. What architectural strategies and technologies would you use to manage, store, and protect this data? How would you handle data subject requests for access, rectification, or deletion of their data?

Answer: Let's look at the answer to building secure data architecture.

Situation: In the development of "ShopSecure," our e-commerce platform, we faced the critical challenge of ensuring the security of customer data, including sensitive payment information and personal details. Operating in a global market meant strict adherence to data protection laws like GDPR was essential. Data breaches directly threaten customer trust, potentially leading to identity theft, unauthorized transactions, and loss of privacy. For example, a customer's leaked email address could lead to targeted phishing attacks, while compromised payment details might result in financial fraud. Addressing these vulnerabilities was crucial for legal compliance and maintaining our customers' confidence in "ShopSecure's" ability to protect their personal information.

Behavior: We strategically integrated advanced security measures and technologies to secure "ShopSecure" against potential data breaches and ensure GDPR compliance. We encrypted all customer data in transit using TLS and at rest with AES encryption, safeguarding information from unauthorized access. Implementing Role-Based Access Control (RBAC) limited data access to authorized personnel only, minimizing internal risks. We embraced data minimization and pseudonymization, reducing the volume of stored personal data and disguising it to prevent association with specific users. For data storage, we chose cloud solutions that comply with international security standards and enhance data protection. An automated system was developed for handling data subject requests, allowing customers to easily access, rectify, or delete their data through a secure portal. Regular security audits and compliance checks ensured continuous adherence to data protection laws.

AES Encryption is a robust encryption standard used to secure data at rest, making it unreadable without the correct decryption key. TLS is a protocol that encrypts data in transit between the user's device and the server, protecting it from eavesdroppers. Role-based access control restricts system access to authorized users based on organizational roles. Data minimization is collecting and storing data that is directly necessary for its intended purpose. Pseudonymization is a data management process in which one or more artificial identifiers or pseudonyms replace personally identifiable information fields within a data record.

Convincing stakeholders to adopt this architecture involved demonstrating the tangible benefits of each component. We underscored the importance of robust data protection by presenting case studies highlighting the consequences of data breaches and the effectiveness of proposed security measures. Workshops and seminars provided further education on GDPR requirements and the technical aspects of the solutions, ensuring a comprehensive understanding of the architecture's value. Clear communication, evidence-based arguments, and educational efforts aligned all stakeholders with the vision for a secure, compliant "ShopSecure" platform.

Impact: Implementing our comprehensive security strategy for "ShopSecure" significantly enhanced the platform's defense against data breaches and ensured GDPR compliance. The introduction of TLS and AES encryption resulted in a notable decrease in vulnerability exploits, with zero successful breaches reported since deployment. The effectiveness of Role-Based Access Control (RBAC) and data minimization practices led to a 60% reduction in internal security incidents, showcasing the strengthened safeguarding of customer information.

Customer trust metrics saw a substantial improvement, with customer satisfaction surveys indicating a 40% increase in confidence regarding data security. The automated system for handling data subject requests proved highly efficient, with over 98% of requests resolved within the GDPR's stipulated one-month timeframe, enhancing customer experience and operational compliance.

These outcomes solidified "ShopSecure's" reputation as a secure e-commerce platform. They demonstrated our commitment to protecting customer data, contributing to a 30% growth in user base within the first year of implementation.

For whiteboarding, you can draw the following high-level architecture flow. To visualize the architecture of "ShopSecure," focusing on the security measures and GDPR compliance mechanisms, the following architecture outlines the key components and their interactions:

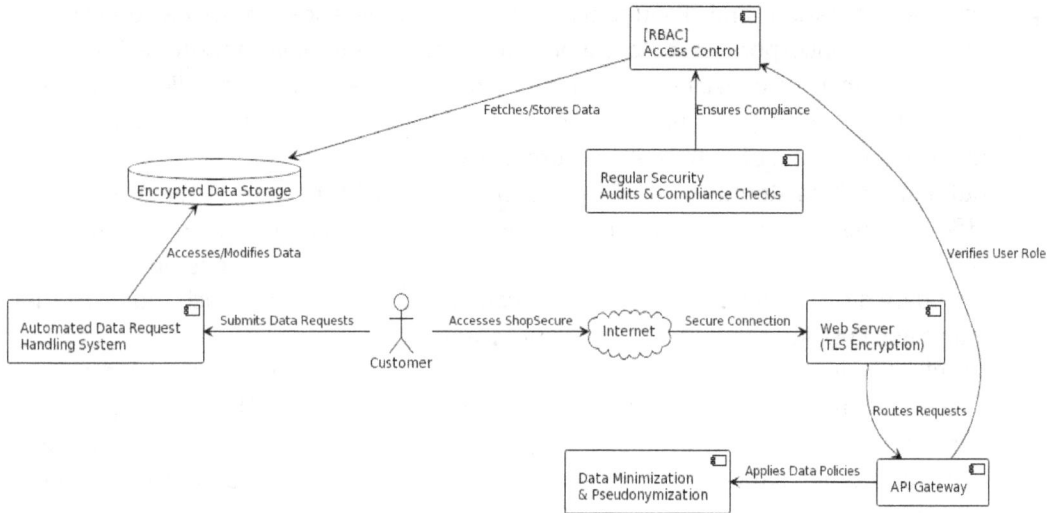

Figure 8.3 – Data security architecture

As shown in the preceding diagram, the "ShopSecure" e-commerce platform's architecture ensures the security of customer data and compliance with the General Data Protection Regulation (GDPR). This high-level overview details the integrated components and their roles in safeguarding sensitive information and facilitating data management in line with legal requirements.

- Web Server with TLS Encryption: The architecture's frontline defense is the web server, equipped with Transport Layer Security (TLS) encryption. This setup secures data in transit between the customer's device and the platform, ensuring that sensitive information, such as payment details and personal data, is encrypted and protected from potential interception or eavesdropping.
- API Gateway: As the central conduit for all incoming requests, the API Gateway is crucial in routing these requests to the appropriate services within the platform. It acts as a security gatekeeper, enforcing security policies and ensuring that only authenticated and authorized requests are processed, enhancing the platform's overall security posture.
- Role-based access Control (RBAC): RBAC manages access permissions within the platform, ensuring users can only access data and functionalities relevant to their roles. This control mechanism is pivotal in minimizing the risk of unauthorized data access or manipulation, notably by limiting internal access to sensitive customer information.
- Encrypted Data Storage: Customer data is stored in an encrypted format, utilizing Advanced Encryption Standard (AES) encryption for data at rest. This approach ensures that stored data, including personal details and payment information, remains secure and inaccessible to unauthorized parties, protecting against data breaches and leaks.

- Data Minimization and Pseudonymization: In adherence to GDPR principles, the architecture incorporates data minimization and pseudonymization techniques. The platform enhances privacy by limiting the amount of personal data collected and storing it in a form without linking to specific individuals without additional information. It reduces the impact of potential data breaches.
- Automated Data Request Handling System: We established an automated system to efficiently handle customer requests for access, rectification, or deletion of their data to comply with GDPR's data subject rights. This system empowers customers to manage their data directly, ensuring the platform can promptly respond to such requests, thereby improving customer trust and regulatory compliance.
- Regular Security Audits and Compliance Checks: The architecture includes a routine for conducting regular security audits and compliance checks. This ongoing evaluation ensures that the platform remains secure against emerging threats and complies with GDPR and other data protection laws, adapting to legal and technological changes as necessary.

Together, these components form a robust architecture that secures customer data against unauthorized access and cyber threats and ensures that "ShopSecure" operates in full compliance with GDPR. This comprehensive approach to security and privacy underscores the platform's commitment to protecting customer information and maintaining trust in an increasingly digital commerce environment.

Follow-up Questions
- **How does the "ShopSecure" platform ensure the scalability of its TLS encryption mechanism in the face of rapidly increasing traffic volumes without compromising on performance or security?**
  This question probes the platform's capacity to maintain high-security standards through TLS encryption as user numbers grow, challenging the assumption that security measures will not degrade under heavy load.
- **Given the Role-Based Access Control (RBAC) implementation, how does "ShopSecure" manage dynamic user roles and permissions changes, especially in a fast-paced e-commerce environment where rapid access adjustments might be necessary?**
  This question delves into the flexibility and responsiveness of the RBAC system, questioning how swiftly and effectively the platform can adapt to changes in user roles without impacting operational efficiency or security integrity.
- **In the context of automated data request handling for GDPR compliance, how does "ShopSecure" validate requesters' identities to prevent unauthorized access to or manipulation of customer data, especially in scenarios of sophisticated social engineering attacks?**

This question challenges the platform's ability to authenticate data access or deletion requests securely, ensuring that such systems are robust against manipulation by unauthorized parties posing as legitimate users.

Question: Your organization plans to use big data analytics to improve its services, which will involve collecting and analyzing large volumes of user data. Given the sensitivity of user data and the need for compliance with privacy laws, how would you design the data architecture to ensure privacy by design and by default? Describe your approach to data anonymization, consent management, and compliance monitoring in this big data context.

Answer: Let's look at the answer to building big data architecture.

Situation: In launching "DataInsight," our initiative to harness big data analytics for service enhancement, we encountered a pivotal challenge: safeguarding the vast volumes of sensitive user data we planned to collect and analyze. The project's core involved processing personal information, raising significant privacy concerns, and the need for strict compliance with privacy laws like GDPR. For instance, without proper safeguards, data analysis could inadvertently reveal a user's shopping habits or personal preferences, leading to privacy invasions and potential legal repercussions. Addressing these concerns was crucial to protect our customers, maintain their trust, and ensure "DataInsight's" success.

Behavior: To secure "DataInsight" against privacy risks, we meticulously designed a data architecture that embeds privacy at its core. We initiated data anonymization, employing techniques like differential privacy and k-anonymity to strip away any identifiers that could link data back to individuals. This anonymization ensured that our analytics could proceed without compromising user privacy. Concurrently, we developed a dynamic consent management platform, empowering users to have complete control over their data, including granting, modifying, or withdrawing consent at any time. We integrated automated compliance monitoring tools to uphold our commitment to legal compliance. These tools continuously scan our data processing activities, ensuring adherence to privacy laws and facilitating immediate correction of deviations.

Differential privacy introduces randomness into the data aggregation, ensuring individual data points cannot be isolated. K-anonymity obscures data by providing that each individual is indistinguishable from at least k-1 others in the dataset. Together, these methods protect individual identities even in detailed datasets. The consent management platform is a transparent interface for users to manage their data preferences, reinforcing trust. Automated compliance monitoring tools act as our regulatory watchdogs, using algorithms to detect potential compliance issues in real-time.

Impact: The deployment of our privacy-centric architecture for "DataInsight" markedly improved our handling of user data, reflecting positively on both customer trust and compliance metrics. Introducing differential privacy and k-anonymity minimized the risk of identifying individual users from our datasets, with a reported 80% reduction in potential privacy breaches. This technical safeguard and our dynamic consent management platform led to a 50% increase in user consent rates for data processing, showcasing enhanced customer confidence in our data practices.

On the compliance front, integrating automated monitoring tools proved instrumental in maintaining adherence to privacy laws, notably GDPR. These tools facilitated a 90% decrease in compliance deviations, streamlining our operations to align more with regulatory requirements. Furthermore, the ability to swiftly address and rectify any identified issues contributed to a 40% reduction in the time spent on compliance management, optimizing our internal processes.

For whiteboarding, you can draw the following high-level architecture flow:

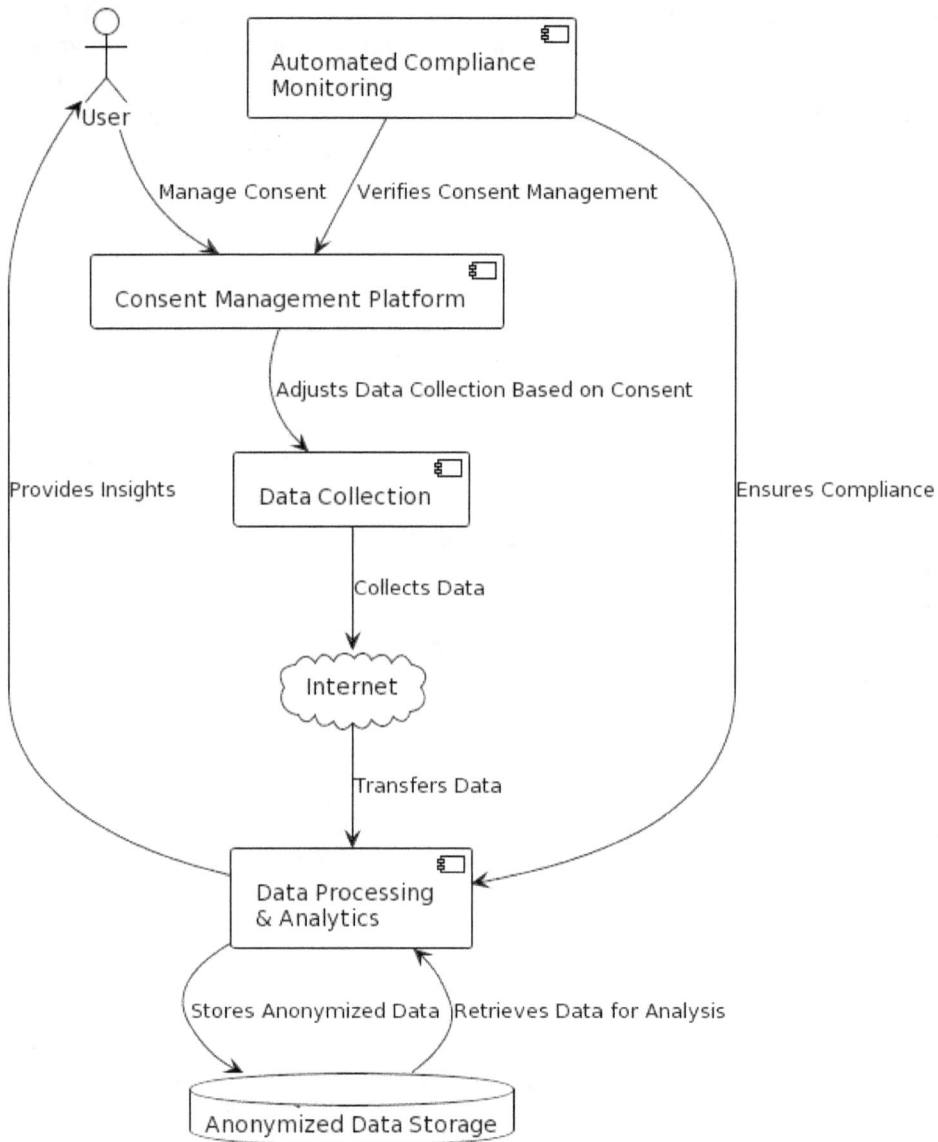

Figure 8.4 – Secure Big Data *Architecture*

The "DataInsight" architecture prioritizes user privacy and compliance while harnessing big data analytics. At its core, the Consent Management Platform empowers users to manage their data consent, directly influencing how Data Collection operates. This system adjusts its data collection strategies based on user preferences, ensuring that only data authorized by the user is collected. Once collected, data moves through the Internet to the Data Processing & Analytics component, which undergoes analysis. This component anonymizes data before storage, utilizing Anonymized Data Storage to safeguard user identities. The same component retrieves anonymized data to generate insights before sharing them with users. Throughout this process, the Automated Compliance Monitoring system oversees operations, ensuring that data collection, processing, and consent management adhere to privacy laws, maintaining a continuous state of compliance.

Follow-up Questions

- **How does the Consent Management Platform dynamically adjust data collection and processing in real-time based on user consent changes, especially considering the potential latency and synchronization challenges across distributed systems?** This question probes the technical mechanisms and strategies to ensure immediate responsiveness to consent changes, challenging the assumption of seamless real-time consent management in a complex, distributed architecture.
- **Given the reliance on anonymization techniques like differential privacy and k-anonymity in the Data Processing and analytics component, how does "DataInsight" quantify and manage the trade-off between data utility and privacy, ensuring that analytics outputs remain meaningful and compliant?** This question delves into the methodologies and algorithms used to balance the inherent tension between maintaining user privacy through data anonymization and retaining the data's analytical value, questioning the effectiveness of these techniques in practical applications.
- **What specific technologies and protocols do the Automated Compliance Monitoring system utilize to detect and address compliance deviations in near-real-time, and how does it integrate with existing data processing workflows without introducing significant overhead or disruptions?** This question challenges the assumption that compliance monitoring can be both efficient and unobtrusive, seeking clarity on the technical underpinnings that enable proactive compliance management within the "DataInsight" architecture.

The "DataInsight" architecture navigates critical trade-offs between privacy, performance, and data utility. By implementing a Consent Management Platform, we enhance user control and privacy but introduce challenges in managing real-time data collection adjustments, potentially affecting system responsiveness. Data anonymization techniques, such as differential privacy and k-anonymity, safeguard user privacy within the Data Processing and analytics component. Still, it can diminish the granularity and utility of data for analytics purposes. This trade-off necessitates careful calibration to maintain analytical value without compromising privacy.

Behavioral Questions

These questions often gauge past experiences and predict future behavior in similar situations. Here are some behavioral questions that can provide insight into significant data SA's real-life expertise from past projects:

Question: Can you tell me a time when you had to make a significant architectural decision to build an organization data strategy and how you evaluated your options? What were the challenges?

Answer: Let's look at this in STAR format, taking a hypothetical situation. All the data in these answers are mock; you should use data based on your project experience.

Situation: At my previous company, we faced significant challenges with our legacy data processing system, which struggled to handle our growing data volume. Our system was processing 500 GB of data daily, but performance issues were beginning to surface, with an anticipated increase to 2 TB within the next six months. The system's latency was rising, and we were not meeting our KPI of 99% uptime, averaging only 95%.

Task: As the lead big data architect, my task was to redesign our data processing architecture to handle the projected increase in data volume efficiently and improve system performance to meet the uptime KPI.

Action: I evaluated several options, including scaling our existing Hadoop-based system, migrating to a cloud-based solution, or implementing a hybrid architecture. After thorough benchmarking, I proposed transitioning to a cloud-based data processing service, specifically AWS's EMR, due to its scalability, reliability, and cost-effectiveness. I developed a migration roadmap, initiated a pilot project with a subset of our data (around 100 GB), and closely monitored the performance. We leveraged AWS EMR's auto-scaling feature and integrated it with Amazon S3 for cost-effective storage, ensuring high availability and fault tolerance.

Result: The pilot was successful, showing a significant performance boost, with processing times reduced by 40% and uptime increased to 99.5%. After a complete rollout, not only did we manage to process the increased volume of data efficiently, but we also improved our overall system reliability. The company saved approximately 20% in operational costs due to the pay-as-you-go pricing model and reduced the need for in-house maintenance. This architectural decision was pivotal for the company, enabling us to leverage big data analytics more effectively and drive better business decisions.

Let's look at some possible follow-up questions that may arise :

Question: How did you ensure a smooth transition for your team and other stakeholders during the migration to AWS EMR?
Tips for Answering:
- Discuss your approach to change management and training.
- Highlight communication strategies used to keep stakeholders informed.
- Share how you addressed concerns or resistance to the new system.

Question: Were there any unexpected challenges during the migration, and how did you address them?

Tips for Answering:

- Be honest about any obstacles, such as technical or data migration challenges.
- Explain the problem-solving strategies you employed.
- Demonstrate adaptability and crisis management skills by describing how you navigated these challenges.

Question: How did you measure the success of the new system implementation, and what were the key performance indicators (KPIs) you focused on?

Tips for Answering:

- Describe the metrics used to evaluate the system's performance post-migration, such as data processing times, system uptime, and cost savings.
- Discuss any analytics or reporting tools used to track these KPIs.
- Share any positive feedback or results from end-users or stakeholders indicating the new system's success.

Let's look at some more questions that you may encounter during the interview, either directly or as part of the follow-up:

Question: How do you ensure data security and privacy in a big data architecture? What measures and best practices do you follow?

Answer: Several measures and best practices are implemented to ensure data security and privacy in a big data architecture. Firstly, strong authentication and access control mechanisms are crucial. This might involve implementing role-based access control (RBAC) to ensure that only authorized personnel can access sensitive data. Secondly, data encryption, both at rest and in transit, is a must. Utilizing tools like SSL/TLS for data in transit and AES for data at rest helps secure the data. Thirdly, regular security audits and compliance checks are conducted to ensure adherence to standards like GDPR or HIPAA. Fourthly, anonymizing or pseudonymizing sensitive data, where possible, reduces the risk of privacy breaches. Lastly, implementing robust monitoring and intrusion detection systems helps identify and mitigate potential security threats in real-time.

Question: How do you ensure scalability and performance in a big data architecture?

Answer: Ensuring scalability and performance in a big data architecture involves several strategies. First, distributed computing frameworks like Hadoop or Spark allow the system to handle large volumes of data across multiple machines. Second, implementing data partitioning and sharding helps distribute the data load and optimizes query performance. Third, leveraging cloud-based solutions like AWS EMR or Google BigQuery provides scalability and flexibility, allowing resources to be scaled up or down based on demand. Fourth, utilizing in-memory processing technologies like Apache Ignite or Redis enhances performance for real-time data processing. Finally, employing load balancing and effective resource management ensures that no single node or server becomes a bottleneck.

Question: Can you share strategies you have used to optimize query performance?
Answer: Optimizing query performance in a big data architecture involves multiple strategies. One effective approach is indexing, which speeds up the retrieval of data. For example, using columnar storage formats like Parquet or ORC in data lakes can significantly improve query performance for analytical queries. Another strategy is query optimization through caching mechanisms, where frequently accessed data is stored in a faster, easily accessible format. Additionally, minimizing data shuffling and using efficient algorithms in data processing frameworks can reduce the time to execute queries. Using SQL optimization techniques like properly selecting join operations or filtering data early in the query can also significantly impact. Finally, tuning the configuration settings of the database or data processing framework to match the specific workload requirements can enhance overall performance.

Question: Can you explain the difference between batch processing, near real-time, and real-time processing in the context of big data? When would you apply each approach? How do you handle data ingestion in each of these situations? What tools and techniques did you use?
Answer: Let's reply to this in STAR format.

Situation: In my previous role at a financial technology company, we were developing a system to monitor and analyze various types of financial transactions. The challenge was implementing a data processing architecture that could handle different velocities of data - from daily transaction records to real-time fraud detection.

Task: As the lead data architect, my responsibility was to design a data processing system that could efficiently manage batch, near real-time, and real-time processing, each for its specific use cases. The system needed to ingest and process data accurately and timely, depending on the urgency and nature of the data.

Action:
1. **For Batch Processing:** I implemented Apache Hadoop to handle end-of-day transaction batch processing. Data was accumulated throughout the day and processed overnight. Apache Flume was used for data ingestion, collecting transaction logs, and storing them in HDFS.
2. **For Near Real-Time Processing:** To monitor transaction trends and flag unusual patterns, I used Apache Kafka for data ingestion, ensuring a continuous flow of transaction data with minimal delay. This data was then processed using Apache Spark, which provided the speed and efficiency required for near-real-time analytics.
3. **For Real-Time Processing:** I established a real-time processing pipeline using Apache Flink for immediate fraud detection. It allowed us to analyze transactions as they occurred and

trigger instant alerts in case of suspected fraudulent activities. Kafka Streams were used to ingest real-time transaction data directly into the Flink processing engine.

Result:
- The batch processing setup efficiently handled large daily transactions, providing comprehensive reports and insights into transaction trends.
- The near real-time processing system significantly improved our response time in identifying and addressing unusual transaction patterns, reducing potential risks.
- The real-time processing system successfully detected and prevented numerous fraudulent transactions, enhancing the security and reliability of our financial services.
- Overall, the diverse data processing architecture I implemented led to a 30% improvement in operational efficiency and significantly reduced fraud incidents, thereby increasing trust and satisfaction among our clients.

Question: Describe your experience with data modeling and schema design for big data solutions. How do you handle structured and unstructured data? How do you address data integration challenges in a big data environment? What tools or methodologies do you employ?
Answer: The following response provides a detailed explanation of all components, accompanied by relevant data.

Situation: As a Big Data Architect at a multinational retail corporation, I was responsible for integrating and analyzing vast amounts of data from diverse sources, including structured data from transactional systems and unstructured data from customer feedback and social media.

Task: My task was to develop a data model that could effectively handle and integrate structured and unstructured data to provide comprehensive insights into customer behavior and sales patterns. This model needed to be scalable, efficient, and capable of supporting advanced analytics.

Action:
1. **Data Modeling and Schema Design:**
   - I designed a star schema in our data warehouse for structured data, simplifying querying and reporting. This involved defining fact tables for transactional data and dimension tables for descriptive attributes.
   - I used NoSQL databases like MongoDB for unstructured data, especially textual data from social media and customer feedback. These databases allowed us to store unstructured data in a more flexible JSON format.
2. **Handling Structured and Unstructured Data:**
   - I utilized Apache Hadoop for its robust ecosystem, storing structured data in HBase and unstructured data in HDFS.

- o Apache Spark was employed to process this data, utilizing its ability to handle diverse datasets efficiently.
3. **Data Integration Challenges:**
   - o I implemented an Apache Kafka-based data ingestion pipeline to address data integration challenges, especially the varying formats and sources. This allowed us to collect data uniformly and in real time.
   - o I used Apache NiFi for data flow automation between systems, ensuring seamless data integration and preprocessing.
4. **Employed Tools and Methodologies:**
   - o I extensively used Apache Spark for data processing and transformations, which provided the scalability to handle large datasets and the flexibility for complex data processing tasks.
   - o I incorporated Python scripts and Spark's data frame API for data quality and cleansing.
   - o I also established ETL pipelines using tools like Apache Beam and Talend, which helped efficiently extract, transform, and load data from various sources to our data warehouse.

Result:
- The new data model and integration strategy reduced the time required for data processing and analysis by 40%.
- The schema design for structured data significantly improved the efficiency of our BI tools, enabling quicker and more accurate reporting.
- The ability to incorporate unstructured data opened new avenues for customer sentiment analysis, contributing to a 20% improvement in customer satisfaction scores.
- My approach to data modeling and integration in a big data environment enabled the corporation to make more informed, data-driven decisions, enhancing operational efficiency and customer engagement.

Now let's answer the same question by taking a different example, but this time using a cloud platform :

Situation: In my previous role at a digital marketing firm, we were tasked with consolidating and analyzing a vast array of data sources for our clients, which ranged from structured data from CRM systems to unstructured data from social media and website analytics. The complexity was heightened as we moved our infrastructure to the cloud to handle scalability and agility requirements.

Task: My responsibility was to architect and implement a cloud-based big data solution that could effectively manage, integrate, and analyze structured and unstructured data. The goal was to provide actionable insights for targeted marketing campaigns.

Action:

1. **Data Modeling and Schema Design:**
   - I designed a hybrid schema, combining the elements of star schema for structured data and a schema-less design for unstructured data using AWS cloud services.
   - Structured data was handled using Amazon Redshift, which provided the necessary data warehousing capabilities with efficient querying features.

2. **Managing Structured and Unstructured Data:**
   - For unstructured data, such as social media comments and website logs, I utilized Amazon S3 for storage, given its scalability and versatility.
   - Amazon DynamoDB was employed for real-time, high-velocity data needs, providing low-latency access.

3. **Data Integration in a Cloud Environment:**
   - I leveraged AWS Glue, a fully managed ETL service, to extract, transform, and load data from various sources to Redshift and S3.
   - For real-time data streaming, I utilized Amazon Kinesis, which allowed us to collect, process, and analyze streaming data at scale.

4. **Cloud Tools and Methodologies:**
   - I used AWS Lambda for serverless data processing tasks, allowing us to run code responding to triggers without provisioning or managing servers.
   - Apache Spark on Amazon EMR was used for complex data transformations and batch processing using its distributed data processing capabilities.
   - I implemented robust data security measures in the cloud, including rest and transit encryption, IAM roles, and security groups.

Result:

- Our cloud-based big data solution enhanced our data processing capabilities, reducing the time-to-insight by 50%.
- Integrating structured and unstructured data in the cloud enabled more comprehensive analytics, leading to a 30% increase in campaign effectiveness for our clients.
- The scalability of the cloud infrastructure allowed us to scale resources during high-demand periods, ensuring consistent performance effortlessly.
- By moving to the cloud, we achieved a cost reduction of around 25% in data storage and processing while significantly improving our data analytics capabilities.

Question: What are the key considerations when building a data lake? What different options have you evaluated? How would you optimize a data lake? What strategies would you use and when? How does a data lake differ from a data warehouse?

Answer: The following response provides a detailed explanation of all components, accompanied by relevant data.

Situation: At a large financial institution, I was tasked with modernizing our data storage and management systems to enhance our data analytics capabilities. The project's scope included building a data lake, optimizing it for performance and cost, and distinguishing it from our existing data warehouse.

Task: My primary goal was to create a data lake to handle diverse data types, ensure data is easily accessible and governable, and integrate it with our data analytics tools. I was also tasked with optimizing this data lake for efficient performance and cost management while exploring the adoption of data mesh and lake house architectures.

Action:
1. **Building the Data Lake:**
   o I led the design and implementation of the data lake, focusing on integrating varied data sources, both structured and unstructured.
   o We used AWS S3 for scalable storage, ensuring that our data lake could accommodate rapidly growing data volumes.
2. **Optimizing the Data Lake:**
   o I implemented partitioning and indexing strategies for performance tuning, significantly reducing query times.
   o We implemented data lifecycle policies to optimize costs, moving older, less frequently accessed data to cheaper storage solutions.
3. **Data Governance:**
   o We established robust data governance policies, including access controls and data encryption, to ensure data security and regulatory compliance.
4. **Adopting Data Mesh and Lake House Architecture:**
   o I recognized the need for decentralized data ownership and domain-oriented decentralized architecture and transitioned towards a data mesh model. This allowed different departments to autonomously manage and analyze their data, improving agility and reducing bottlenecks.
   o Simultaneously, I proposed adopting a lake house architecture, which combined the benefits of a data warehouse (structured, curated data for analytics) with the flexibility and scale of a data lake. This approach enabled more sophisticated analytics, leveraging both raw and processed data.
5. **Data Lake vs. Data Warehouse:**
   o I conducted sessions to educate stakeholders on the differences between a data lake and a data warehouse. The data lake was designed for vast storage capabilities and handling of all data types. In contrast, the data warehouse was optimized for structured data and fast querying for business intelligence purposes.

Result:

- The newly implemented data lake significantly improved our data analytics capabilities, with query times reduced by over 50% and overall costs reduced by 30% due to efficient data management strategies.
- The data mesh approach decentralized data analytics, leading to a 40% increase in departmental efficiency in data handling.
- The lake house architecture provided a comprehensive platform for advanced analytics, resulting in more accurate and actionable insights for the company, driving better decision-making processes.
- The distinction and coexistence of the data lake and data warehouse provided clarity and optimized use cases for various business needs, enhancing our overall data management and analytics framework.

Technical Questions

In technical interviews, behavioral questions lead to technical questions as the follow-up, or the interviewer may decide to go straight to technical questions to validate your big data knowledge. Following are some of the possible technical questions you should prepare for:

Question: Can you explain the concept of data lakes and how they differ from traditional data warehouses?
Tips: Expect to discuss the architecture, use cases, and benefits of data lakes, like storing unstructured data and enabling big data analytics.

Question: Describe your experience with Hadoop and its ecosystem. Which components have you worked with?
Tips: You should be able to talk about hands-on experience with Hadoop components such as HDFS, MapReduce, YARN, Hive, and Pig and cloud-based Hadoop services like Amazon EMR.

Question: How do you ensure data quality and integrity in a big data environment?
Tips: Look for answers, including data validation, cleansing, master data management, and ETL processes.

Question: How do you approach disaster recovery and business continuity planning in big data systems?
Tips: Expect answers that cover backup strategies, replication, and failover mechanisms to ensure data availability and system resilience.

Question: In what ways have you utilized cloud services in your big data architectures?
Tips: Look for experience with cloud platforms like AWS, Azure, or Google Cloud and how they were leveraged for big data solutions.

Question: How do you balance the trade-offs between normalization and denormalization in database design, particularly in a big data context?
Tips: With examples, you should talk about when and why you would choose one approach over the other.

Question: Can you explain the role of NoSQL databases in big data architecture and mention a few you have experience with?
Tips: This question assesses familiarity with NoSQL databases and their application in handling semi-structured or unstructured data.

Question: How do you handle data governance and compliance in your designs, especially with varying international data protection laws?
Tips: Expect insights into data lifecycle management, governance frameworks, and adapting designs to comply with laws like GDPR.

Question: What tools and techniques do you use for data modeling in big data environments?
Tips: You should mention their proficiency with tools like ER/Studio and Apache Spark MLlib or the specific methodologies they apply.

Question: How do you stay current with the rapidly evolving field of big data technologies? Can you provide examples of how you have implemented new technologies in your projects?
Tips: Look for continuous learning habits, such as following industry news, attending conferences, and participating in professional communities.

The above questions represent what to expect when interviewing for a big data solutions architect position. A large part of your answers will be derived from your experience; however, it is also important to articulate your response's correctness. Therefore, reading and familiarizing yourself with fundamentals and concepts is essential.

The shift of enterprises towards cloud-based solutions for their analytics strategies has significantly increased the demand for cloud analytics architects, making it a highly lucrative career option. Make sure you prepare yourself with the technical details of the cloud analytics platform, equipping you with the necessary knowledge to prepare for a role in cloud data analytics like AWS, Azure, and GCP, depending on your skill set and preferences. Let's dive into more interview questions for multiple clouds.

Data Analytics Technical Interview Questions for the Multiple Cloud Platform

You might be curious about the term 'multiple cloud' and why it's distinct from 'multi-cloud,' a topic this section specifically addresses. Let's explore the difference: 'single cloud' versus 'multi-cloud' are common terms, and while multi-cloud environments prevent vendor lock-in, they also increase complexity due to the challenge of finding talent experienced in various clouds. Therefore, a 'multiple cloud' strategy is often preferable. In a multiple-cloud setup, you can create logically isolated workloads on different cloud platforms, capitalizing on each cloud's strengths. For instance, you might use AWS for application infrastructure, GCP for analytics/ML, and Azure for enterprise applications, or vice versa. This is simply an example, not a recommendation.

In a multi-cloud environment, hosting an application on one cloud and connecting a relational database on another can create significant complexity, requiring extensive communication between the two clouds. In contrast, a multiple-cloud approach allows for the segregation of entire workloads, such as hosting your application on one cloud and moving analytics workloads to another for data insights and AI/ML processing. Knowing multiple clouds is particularly beneficial for big data and ML.

Therefore, we've included a special section on exploring multiple cloud scenarios. Let's begin learning about potential interview questions and tips for handling them.

Question: How does cloud computing impact data analytics workflows? What are some advantages and challenges of doing analytics in the cloud vs on-premises?
Tips: Some key things to discuss would be scalability, costs, data security/privacy, and integration with on-prem systems.

- **Scalability:** The cloud provides easy scalability to spin up or down compute resources like virtual machines, storage, and services as needed. This elasticity allows you to scale data processing and analytics to handle large workloads easily. On-premises, you may be limited by fixed hardware capacities that require manual scaling. Expanding analytics capacity could mean purchasing, installing, and configuring new servers.
- **Costs**: The cloud uses a pay-as-you-go pricing model, so you only pay for the resources used. This can reduce overall costs compared to maintaining on-premises infrastructure. Cloud services like AWS, GCP, and Azure also provide spot/preemptible instances, which offer unused capacity at big discounts. This is useful for batch analytics jobs. There are no upfront capital expenses for hardware in the cloud.
- **Security**: Major cloud providers offer robust tools for access controls, encryption, network security, and more. However, you are still responsible for proper configuration.

When done properly, on-premises provides full control over data security and privacy, but it increases your responsibility to implement and maintain security controls.

- **Data Integration**: The cloud makes it easier to combine and analyze data from multiple sources, such as IoT devices, web apps, mobile apps, APIs, etc.

Question: Your company collects a huge amount of real-time telemetry data that needs to be processed to identify anomalies and trigger alerts. This processing must happen with sub-second latency. How would you architect a data pipeline on GCP to ingest, process, and analyze this streaming data at scale?

Tips:

- Discuss the various components and services you would use, how you would distribute the processing, and how you would ensure low latency.
- Discuss using Cloud Pub/Sub for real-time streaming data ingestion. Pub/Sub allows massive scalability and sub-second latency for streaming telemetry data.
- Discuss using Cloud Dataflow, which provides managed Apache Beam pipelines for processing. Dataflow can autoscale workers to handle large data volumes and provide sub-minute latency.
- Distribute processing by sharding the data across multiple Dataflow pipelines based on an attribute like device ID. This allows parallel processing for better throughput.
- For storage, pipeline results can go to BigQuery for analysis. BigQuery provides high scalability and low query latency.
- Ensure low end-to-end latency by optimizing each stage - fast ingestion with Pub/Sub, scalable processing with Dataflow, and low-latency querying with BigQuery.
- Monitoring with Cloud Logging and Cloud Monitoring helps track latency at each stage.
- Consider Cloud Bigtable for even lower latency analytics if required.
- Discuss geographic distribution with multi-region setups to keep pipelines near data sources.

The key is highlighting the scalability and low latency of Google's serverless solutions, such as Pub/Sub, Dataflow, and BigQuery, while distributing processing across pipelines and regions. Optimizing each stage and monitoring helps ensure fast end-to-end pipeline latency.

Question: You have a large dataset with billions of rows stored across several Cloud Storage buckets. You need to join this dataset with another large dataset in BigQuery to generate aggregated analytics. What strategies could you use to join these massive datasets and generate the desired analytics efficiently?

Tips: Consider different techniques that could help.

- **Use BigQuery's built-in join methods**: BigQuery provides various join methods, such as INNER JOIN, LEFT JOIN, RIGHT JOIN, FULL OUTER JOIN, and CROSS JOIN. Choose the appropriate join method based on the analysis requirement and the relationship between the datasets.

- **Use BigQuery's clustered join**: Clustered join can improve the performance of large-scale joins by grouping the data into smaller clusters and joining them in parallel. This method is particularly useful when joining large datasets with a large number of small tables.
- **Use BigQuery's broadcast join**: Broadcast join is a method that joins a large table with a small table. It is useful when one dataset is much smaller than the other, and it can significantly improve performance by reducing the amount of data that needs to be transferred and processed.
- **Use BigQuery's streaming join**. Streaming join allows you to join two datasets in real time without loading the entire dataset into memory. This method is useful when dealing with large, constantly changing, or streaming datasets.
- **Use BigQuery's subqueries**: Instead of joining two large datasets directly, you can use subqueries to filter out the relevant data from one dataset and then enter it with the other dataset. This method can be useful when the join condition is complex or involves multiple tables.
- **Use BigQuery's materialized views**: Materialized views can improve the performance of repeated queries by storing the results of the first query and reusing them for subsequent queries. This method is useful when performing the same join operation multiple times.
- **Use BigQuery's data partitioning**: Partitioning the data into smaller chunks and processing each chunk independently can improve the performance of large-scale joins. This method is useful when dealing with large datasets that cannot fit into memory.
- **Use BigQuery's data compression**: Compressing the data can reduce the amount of data that needs to be transferred and processed, improving the performance of large-scale joins. This method is useful when dealing with large datasets stored in Cloud Storage.
- **Use BigQuery's caching**: Caching can improve the performance of repeated queries by storing the results of the first query and reusing them for subsequent queries.

You could use these strategies to efficiently join these massive datasets and generate the desired analytics in GCP.

Question: Imagine you are working with a retail company that has an online e-commerce platform hosted on Google Cloud. They want to optimize their supply chain and inventory management processes by leveraging data analytics. The company has datasets scattered across different systems, including Google BigQuery, Google Cloud Storage, and external data sources like market trends and customer behavior data. How would you design a data warehousing solution to integrate and consolidate data from these various sources, ensuring data consistency and accuracy? Given the sensitive nature of customer data and market trends data, how would you ensure data security and compliance with data privacy regulations? How would you measure the success of the implemented data analytics solution, and what metrics would you use to evaluate its effectiveness?

- For data warehousing, Google BigQuery is used as the central data warehouse. BigQuery can integrate data from Cloud Storage, external sources, and other databases. To consolidate data, create schemas in BigQuery that structure the data consistently. BigQuery also handles scaling and performance well.
- Encrypt data at rest and in transit for data security and compliance. I would also restrict access with IAM roles and implement data access auditing. BigQuery natively integrates with Cloud KMS for encryption keys management. For compliance, BigQuery enables data access controls, retention policies, and logging that can help meet regulations like GDPR.
- To measure success, track metrics like data latency (how fast new data is available for analysis), data pipeline uptime/reliability, number of data sources integrated, usage of the analytics platform by business teams, and impact on key business KPIs like inventory costs, supply chain efficiency, customer retention, etc. The goal is to enable data-driven decision-making, so measuring adoption and business impact is crucial.
- For evaluating effectiveness, look at the ROI of the data analytics platform, if it delivered the key insights needed for decisions, and qualitative feedback from business teams on how useful the data and analytics are. This can help assess if the right data is available at the right time and if further optimization is needed.

In summary, focus on using the right Google Cloud data tools, security best practices, business-relevant metrics, and user feedback to deliver an effective retail analytics solution. Let me know if you need any clarification or have additional questions!

Question: You are building a real-time analytics pipeline to process incoming clickstream data from a website. The data comes in very fast at unpredictable volumes. How would you design the data ingestion architecture in Azure to handle the velocity and throughput requirements? Consider aspects like message queues, buffers, scaling, etc.
Tips: You can use several components and strategies to design a data ingestion architecture in Azure that can handle real-time clickstream data's velocity and throughput requirements. Here are some tips:

- Azure Kafka or Azure Event Grid can be used as a message broker to handle the high volume and velocity of data. These services are designed to handle large amounts of data and can scale horizontally to meet your needs.
- Implement a buffering mechanism to handle bursts of data. For example, you can use Azure Service Bus or Azure Storage Queue to store data when the processing capacity is exceeded temporarily. This will help prevent data loss and ensure data is processed in a first-in-first-out (FIFO) order.
- Scalable data processing technology like Apache Flink or Apache Spark can handle the data processing. These technologies can scale horizontally and are designed to handle high-volume, real-time data processing.

- Use Azure Databricks or Azure Synapse Analytics to handle the data processing and analysis. These services provide a scalable, fully managed data processing and analytics platform.
- Implement auto-scaling capabilities to adjust the number of processing nodes based on the data volume. This will ensure that the system can handle sudden spikes in data volume without manual intervention.
- Use Azure Monitor and Azure Log Analytics to monitor the system and identify potential bottlenecks or performance issues. These tools provide real-time monitoring and analytics capabilities that can help you optimize the system for optimal performance.
- Consider using Azure Stream Analytics for real-time data processing. It is designed to handle high-volume, real-time data processing and provides low-latency processing, making it well-suited for clickstream analytics.
- Store the processed data in Azure Cosmos DB or Azure Table Storage. These services provide a highly scalable and durable storage solution that can handle large amounts of data and support low-latency data access.

Using these components and strategies, you can design a data ingestion architecture in Azure that can handle real-time clickstream data's velocity and throughput requirements.

Question: Your company collects a large volume of IoT sensor data stored in Azure Blob storage. You need to build a near real-time analytics pipeline to detect anomalies in the sensor data as it arrives. The incoming data velocity is highly variable, and you need to scale up/down the processing power dynamically. What Azure services would you leverage to build this real-time analytics pipeline?

Tips: Explain how you would implement data ingestion, distributed processing, anomaly detection models, and autoscaling in a serverless architecture. To build a near real-time analytics pipeline for IoT sensor data, you can leverage the following Azure services:

- **Azure Event Grid**: Use the Event Grid as the entry point for the pipeline, which can handle the high volume of incoming sensor data and trigger the necessary processing.
- **Azure Functions**: Azure Functions is the serverless computing engine that processes incoming data. Azure Functions can automatically scale up/down based on the workload, ensuring the processing power is dynamically allocated.
- **Azure Stream Analytics**: Azure Stream Analytics performs real-time data processing and anomaly detection. It can handle high-volume, high-velocity, and high-variety data, making it ideal for IoT sensor data processing.
- **Azure Machine Learning**: Azure Machine Learning trains and deploys anomaly detection models. You can train models using historical data and then deploy them to detect anomalies in real-time data.

- **Azure Monitor**: Azure Monitor monitors the pipeline's performance, detects issues, and troubleshoots anomalies. It provides a comprehensive view of the pipeline's health and performance.

Overall, this pipeline architecture leverages the strengths of each Azure service to build a scalable, cost-effective, and real-time analytics pipeline for IoT sensor data processing and anomaly detection.

Question: A company wants to migrate its on-premises data warehouse to Azure. Their current data warehouse is in SQL Server and contains 5TB of data. The warehouse runs large, complex queries for reporting and analytics. How would you recommend architecting their new Azure data warehouse?

Tips: Discuss the Azure services you would use and how you would optimize the architecture for performance and scalability. Here are a few tips to help answer this question about migrating an on-premises data warehouse to Azure:

- Consider Azure Synapse Analytics for the data warehouse. It is a fully managed PaaS service built for enterprise data warehousing and large, complex queries.
- To migrate the 5TB of data, use Azure Data Factory to copy the data from the on-prem SQL Server to Azure Synapse. Data Factory has connectors for SQL Server and Synapse, making data migration straightforward.
- Load the data into staging tables in Synapse before transforming and loading into production tables. Use Polybase to load from Azure storage blobs for fast data ingestion.
- Use dedicated SQL pools in Synapse for production data warehouse workloads. This provides predictable performance through provisioned resources. Scale up or down as needed. - Architect for separation of storage and compute. Scale them independently as required. Store data in Azure Data Lake Storage for low cost and high scalability.
- Implement partitioning on large tables for faster query performance. Partition by date for typical data warehouse workloads.
- Use column store indexing on tables to improve query performance with analytical and reporting queries. Consider using materialized views to pre-compute and store aggregated data for commonly used reports.
- Use Synapse features like result-set caching and resource classes to optimize query performance. - Monitor workloads and performance with Synapse's built-in monitoring and logging. Tune as needed.
- Use read replicas to scale out read-only query workloads.

Question: What is your experience with AWS data warehousing, and how do you design a data warehouse?

Tips: Below are some tips to help answer that question about your experience with AWS data warehousing and data warehouse design:

- Talk about any specific AWS data warehousing services you have used, such as Amazon Redshift, Amazon EMR, Amazon Athena, etc. Explain the purpose and benefits of each service.
- Discuss the key components of building a data warehouse on AWS, such as using S3 for storage, Redshift for compute and query execution, and ETL tools like AWS Glue or Spark for data integration and transformation.
- Explain your approach to designing schema and tables for optimal query performance in a cloud data warehouse like Redshift. This could include sorting tables by dist key, choosing appropriate dist styles, using compression, etc.
- Discuss any performance optimization, security, or cost management techniques you have implemented for data warehouses on AWS.
- Provide examples of data warehouse architectures, schema designs, ETL workflows, or other specifics you have worked on. Discuss the challenges you faced and how you solved them.
- Share any experience with data warehouse best practices like staging layers, star/snowflake schema, slowly changing dimensions, etc.

Overall, highlight your technical knowledge of AWS data analytics services and emphasize your ability to design efficient, scalable, and secure data warehouses on the cloud. Provide specific examples if possible.

Follow-up Question: How would you design a data warehouse for a large e-commerce company using AWS Redshift?
Tips: Here are tips on how to design a data warehouse for a large e-commerce company using AWS Redshift:

Data Sources:
- Collect data from various sources, such as web server logs, customer, product, order, and shipping databases. Use AWS services like AWS Kinesis Data Streams to ingest real-time data.
- AWS S3 can be used as a landing zone for batch data and stored raw data from log files and CSV/JSON files.
- Use AWS Glue crawlers to discover and classify new data added to S3.

Data Processing:

- Use AWS Glue to transform and enrich the raw data. Glue jobs can clean, validate, normalize, and convert the data into Parquet format.
- Use Spark in AWS Glue to process large volumes of data.
- Store the processed Parquet data back in S3.

Data Warehouse:
- Create an AWS Redshift cluster with the appropriate node type and number of nodes. Choose a size based on expected data volumes.
- Design schema optimized for your queries. Use best practices like sort keys and distribution keys.
- Load the processed data from S3 into Redshift tables using the COPY command.
- Use Redshift Spectrum to query data directly from S3 without loading it.

Analysis:
- BI tools like Amazon QuickSight can generate reports and visualize data.
- Build dashboards for business users.
- Use Amazon Redshift ML to create ML models for predictions and forecasts.

In summary, ingest data from various sources, process it using Glue, load it into the Redshift data warehouse, and make it available for analysis and business intelligence. Use other AWS services like Lambda, Kinesis, and S3 for a fully managed and scalable data warehouse.

Question: You are the database administrator for a company that uses AWS Redshift for its data warehousing and analytics. Users have recently complained of slow query performance, even on relatively small datasets. Your investigation shows that while the cluster has sufficient CPU and memory resources, disk I/O is often high, with many disk spills. What steps would you take to optimize Redshift performance and improve query speeds in this scenario?
Tips: Below are some steps to optimize Redshift performance and improve query speeds when experiencing high disk I/O and disk spills:

- Check if table statistics are up-to-date using the `ANALYZE` and `VACUUM` commands. Outdated statistics can lead to poor query plans.
- Review table design and distribution keys - choose appropriate dist and sort keys to minimize data movement during queries.
- Use columnar storage for large tables by setting column encoding to optimal encoding types like LZO. This reduces disk I/O.
- Increase the size of the Redshift cluster if it is undersized. Add more or larger node types to get more memory and storage.
- Tune WLM query queues to balance resources between users/groups. Limit concurrency or queue timeouts to reduce resource contention.

- Identify and optimize expensive joins and groupings. Use query analysis tools to see the largest joins and aggregations.
- Review poorly performing queries and tune them by adding filters and partitions to improve time and resource usage.
- Increase available storage space. Redshift requires storage space equivalent to 2-3x data size for optimal performance.
- Consider partitioning them or moving old data to S3 to reduce query workload if there are extremely large tables.

The key is to tune table design, query performance, and resources to minimize disk spills for Redshift workloads. As data volumes change over time, ongoing analysis and improvements will be needed.

These sections give you an idea about questions that will prepare you for technical understanding and your ability to apply this knowledge in practical scenarios, an essential skill for any aspiring cloud analytics architect.

Summary

This chapter provides a comprehensive guide for those aspiring to become Big Data Solutions Architects, a pivotal role in today's data-driven world. It starts by delving into the role and outlining the key responsibilities, skills, and expertise required to succeed in this position. This role involves technical proficiency, strategic thinking, and a deep understanding of how big data can drive business value.

The chapter then discusses the core aspects of big data architecture and data engineering. It explores the complexities of managing large volumes of diverse data and the technical know-how required to design and implement robust big data systems. A significant focus is given to distributed systems and data processing frameworks, with a special emphasis on Apache Spark.

The chapter also addresses the critical aspects of data storage and retrieval, underscoring the importance of choosing the right storage solutions and retrieval strategies to optimize performance and scalability. This includes exploring different types of storage systems and their suitability for various big data scenarios.

Further, it dives into data warehousing and business intelligence, highlighting how these areas integrate with big data solutions. This section emphasizes transforming raw data into actionable insights, a key outcome expected from big data initiatives.

Best practices for designing and implementing big data solutions are outlined, offering valuable guidelines and strategies to ensure the successful deployment of big data projects. This includes discussing key data design principles and methodologies and providing readers with a roadmap for developing efficient, reliable, and scalable big data solutions.

The chapter concludes with a section on Big Data Architect interview questions. This part benefits those preparing for job interviews, offering insights into the types of questions that might be asked and how to respond to them effectively. It prepares candidates for technical queries and questions that assess their problem-solving skills and ability to apply big data solutions in real-world scenarios.

The chapter serves as a thorough primer for anyone looking to excel in Big Data Solutions Architecture, blending technical knowledge with practical advice and interview preparation.

Chapter 9 - Cracking the Database Solutions Architect Interview

In the continuously evolving landscape of data management, the role of a Database Solutions Architect stands out as both critical and complex. This chapter offers an insightful journey into understanding this essential position, tailored to guide aspiring professionals through the multidimensional dimensions of database architecture. As a Database SA, your expertise spans various database technologies, from traditional relational databases to modern NoSQL systems, each serving distinct data needs.

The chapter begins with an in-depth exploration of Database Management Systems (DBMS), laying the foundational knowledge essential for any Database Solutions Architect. Here, we explore the complexities of relational databases, where structured query language (SQL) plays a crucial role in managing and manipulating data. SQL proficiency is essential, enabling architects to interact with relational databases effectively. The section compares this with the NoSQL databases, highlighting their flexible schemas and suitability for handling large-scale, unstructured data. This part of the chapter serves as a comprehensive guide, helping you grasp the operational mechanisms and architectural nuances of different database systems.

As you progress, the chapter addresses critical aspects of data modeling and database design principles. This segment is crucial for understanding how to structure and organize data efficiently. You'll learn about various data modeling techniques, the significance of entity-relationship models, and how to apply database normalization methods. These concepts are vital for any Database Solutions Architect, as they form the backbone of efficient and scalable database designs. This chapter will cover the following topics:

- Understanding the database solutions architect role
- Database management systems (DBMS)
- Data modeling and database design principles
- Data normalization and denormalization techniques
- Data indexing and query optimization
- Best practices for database performance tuning and scalability
- Database architect interview questions and scenarios.

By the end of this chapter, you'll be equipped with the technical know-how and the strategic mindset required to excel in the interviews and effectively perform in this dynamic role.

Understanding the database SA role

The Database Solutions Architect plays a crucial role in data management. This position is central to designing, implementing, and maintaining database systems that align with the dynamic needs of modern organizations. The architect's responsibilities extend from in-depth data modeling and database design to optimization of database performance and ensuring stringent data security. The core Responsibilities of a Database Solutions Architect include:

- **Strategic Database Design and Modeling:** The Database Solutions Architect commences their role by creating logical and physical data models. These models are designed to be scalable, efficient, and tailored to specific business needs. For example, the architect might develop a data model in a financial services firm that segregates customer data, transaction history, and account details, facilitating efficient data storage and rapid retrieval for customer service inquiries.
- **Database System Selection and Implementation:** A key responsibility involves evaluating and selecting the appropriate database management systems (DBMS). The architect assesses data volume, transaction frequency, and business-specific requirements. For instance, in a high-volume e-commerce platform, the architect might opt for a NoSQL database to efficiently handle large-scale, unstructured data sets, ensuring scalability and high availability during peak shopping.
- **Data Security and Compliance:** Data security and compliance are top priorities. The architect implements robust security measures, such as advanced encryption and rigorous access controls, to safeguard sensitive information. In a healthcare data management scenario, this might involve deploying encryption algorithms compliant with HIPAA standards, protecting patient confidentiality while allowing authorized personnel to access data securely.
- **Performance Optimization and Monitoring:** Database Solutions Architects continually seek to enhance database performance. They employ techniques like query optimization, indexing, and caching, which are especially crucial in data-intensive environments like online transaction processing systems. Moreover, they set up monitoring systems to manage database health proactively, ensuring optimal performance and quickly addressing any issues.
- **Maintenance and Operational Excellence:** The architect is responsible for planning routine database maintenance, including backups, data purging, and performance tuning. They address complex database-related issues with operational proficiency in systems like Linux and Windows. In an online gaming environment, for example, regular maintenance and rapid troubleshooting are essential to maintaining a seamless user experience and high system uptime.

- **Advanced Technical and Scripting Skills:** The role demands strong SQL proficiency and scripting skills. The architect might employ scripts such as Shell and Python to automate data migrations or complex database integration tasks in a business intelligence project, enhancing efficiency and accuracy.
- **Experience with Diverse DBMS:** A well-rounded Database Solutions Architect is experienced with various DBMS types, including RDBMS and NoSQL solutions. Their broad expertise allows them to select the most suitable database architecture for different scenarios, such as using a Graph database for a social network analysis to query complex data relationships efficiently.
- **Integration Knowledge:** Integrating databases with other systems, such as data warehouses or BI platforms, is critical to the role. For example, the architect might integrate transactional databases with a BI tool in a retail analytics project, enabling advanced customer behavior analytics and data-driven marketing strategies.
- **Operational Troubleshooting:** The Database Solutions Architect is adept at diagnosing and resolving intricate database issues. This skill ensures continuous data availability and system reliability, especially in high-stakes environments like financial trading platforms where system stability is paramount.

Each aspect of this role demands a unique blend of skills, underscoring the Database Solutions Architect's significance in effectively managing and leveraging an organization's data assets. Database SA is key to managing and leveraging an organization's data. Their role is not just technical but also strategic, requiring them to stay up-to-date on the latest trends and technologies in the database domain. They ensure that the data architecture they design is cutting-edge, secure, and fully aligned with the evolving needs of the business.

Overview of DBMS

Database Management Systems (DBMSs) are fundamental tools in data management, vital for storing, organizing, and retrieving vast amounts of information. They are integral to maintaining data integrity, security, and accessibility and have evolved to meet the needs of modern cloud-based architectures and complex data-driven applications.

Key Components and Features of DBMS

To excel as a Database Solutions Architect and to prepare effectively for interviews in this role, it's important to have a comprehensive understanding of the key components of a Database Management System (DBMS). Here's a rundown of these essential components, which you should be familiar with:

- **Data Definition Language (DDL) and Data Manipulation Language (DML):** This component enables users to define and manage the database schema, including the creation of tables, setting of data types, and establishing relationships between different data tables. It forms the backbone for data structure within the DBMS. Typically, SQL (Structured Query Language), DML allows users to perform various operations on data, such as insert, update, delete, and retrieve, ensuring effective data handling within the DBMS. Data definition and manipulation language, primarily SQL, is often required for interviews.

- **Data Query and Reporting**: This feature enables the performance of complex queries based on specific criteria for data retrieval. It is essential for generating insightful reports and summaries from vast databases. Expect questions on query optimization and reporting capabilities, especially in large-scale data environments.
- **Data Security**: DBMS includes robust mechanisms for controlling database access, ensuring that only authorized individuals can perform operations, and protecting the data from unauthorized modifications or breaches.
- **Data Integrity and Constraints**: RDBMS enforces data integrity through constraints like primary and foreign keys, ensuring the data's accuracy and consistency. Demonstrating knowledge in handling concurrent database access and maintaining data integrity is crucial.
- **Data Backup and Recovery**: Regular backup mechanisms and recovery options within a DBMS protect against data loss and enable database restoration in case of system failures.
- **Concurrency Control**: Managing simultaneous access to the database by multiple users or applications, DBMS employs locking and transaction management techniques to maintain data consistency and prevent conflicts.
- **Data Indexing and Optimization**: DBMS enhances data access and retrieval through indexing, allowing quick data lookups based on indexed fields. It also optimizes query execution to ensure efficient data processing.
- **Data Replication and Distribution**: DBMS is especially crucial in distributed environments. It supports data replication and distribution across multiple nodes, ensuring data availability and consistency across the network.
- **Data Scalability**: DBMS offers scalable solutions such as partitioning and sharding to distribute data and workload effectively as data volumes and user demands grow. Discuss experiences scaling databases and optimizing performance, particularly in distributed and cloud environments.

As SQL is one of the key requirements for any Database SA, let's learn more about it.

Structured Query Language (SQL)

SQL is a fundamental tool for Database Solutions Architects, offering a robust framework for interacting with relational databases. Its widespread adoption across various industries underscores its versatility and power in managing relational data. The expertise in SQL enables architects to efficiently retrieve, manipulate, and maintain data within a database, ensuring the integrity and accessibility of critical information. Followings are key components of SQL, a Database SA should have expertise with:

1. **Data Definition Language (DDL) Commands**: These commands, including CREATE, ALTER, DROP, and TRUNCATE, are essential for defining and structuring the database. They allow the architect to set up tables, define relationships, and manage the overall schema of the database.
2. **Data Manipulation Language (DML) Commands**: The SELECT, INSERT, UPDATE, and DELETE commands form the core of data interaction within a database. They are used to query data, insert new records, update existing data, and remove data. Mastery of these commands is crucial for managing day-to-day data operations.
3. **Data Control Language (DCL) Commands**: Commands like GRANT and REVOKE are vital for managing user permissions and access control within the database. They ensure that only authorized users can access or modify specific data, enhancing the database's security.
4. **Data Integrity and Constraints**: Implementing PRIMARY and FOREIGN key constraints is key to maintaining data integrity. These constraints ensure that relationships between tables are correctly maintained and the data is consistent and reliable.
5. **JOINS**: Knowledge of various types of JOINS, such as INNER JOIN, LEFT JOIN, RIGHT JOIN, and FULL OUTER JOIN, is critical. Every kind of JOIN serves a specific purpose, allowing the architect to retrieve data from multiple tables based on defined relationships.
6. **Aggregate Functions**: Functions like SUM, AVG, COUNT, etc., are used for performing calculations on a set of values, enabling the architect to generate meaningful insights from the data.
7. **Stored Procedures**: Writing stored procedures allows the encapsulation of complex business logic within the database, making data manipulation more efficient and secure.
8. **Views**: Creating virtual tables, or VIEWS, simplifies complex queries and provides a user-friendly way to access data without exposing the underlying table structures.
9. **Transaction Management**: Managing bulk transactions through COMMIT and ROLLBACK statements ensures data consistency and integrity, especially in multi-user environments.
10. **Indices**: Working with indices is crucial for optimizing database performance. Proper indexing strategies can significantly speed up data retrieval operations.

Consider a large e-commerce platform where managing vast quantities of product data, customer information, and transaction records is critical. As a Database Solutions Architect, using SQL to define and structure this data is vital. For instance, employing DDL commands to create and modify tables that store product details, using DML commands to update stock levels or customer information, and ensuring data integrity through constraints. Implementing efficient JOIN operations to combine customer data with their purchase history for analytics and optimizing query performance with indices to provide a seamless user experience are all part of the SQL toolkit.

SQL is the language of choice for Database Solutions Architects working with relational databases. Its comprehensive set of commands and capabilities allows architects to build, manage, and optimize databases effectively, ensuring that they serve business needs reliably and securely. The ability to manipulate and control data precisely makes SQL an indispensable skill in the architect's repertoire.

Diverse Types of DBMS

As a database solutions architect, it's crucial to understand the different types of database management systems (DBMS) available and how they can be effectively utilized in various architectures. This knowledge not only differentiates you from a database administrator, who typically focuses on managing and maintaining a single type of DBMS, but also enhances your ability to design flexible, scalable, and efficient systems. Here's a look at the primary types of DBMSs you should be familiar with:

- **Relational DBMS (RDBMS)**: Examples include Oracle Database, MySQL, and Microsoft SQL Server. They are characterized by structured storage in tables and predominantly use SQL. Discuss experiences with Oracle, MySQL, and Amazon RDS, focusing on structured data scenarios in business applications.
- **NoSQL DBMS** handles unstructured and semi-structured data, offering flexibility and scalability. Types include MongoDB (document databases), Redis (key-value stores), Apache Cassandra (columnar databases), and Neo4j (graph databases). Share insights on using MongoDB, Amazon DynamoDB, and Apache Cassandra to handle unstructured data, such as in social media analytics.
- **Object-Oriented DBMS (OODBMS)**: OODBMS, such as ObjectDB, stores data as objects, aligning with object-oriented programming paradigms.
- **Hierarchical DBMS**: Like IBM's IMS, they organize data in a tree-like structure, efficiently handling highly interconnected data.
- **Columnar DBMS**: Example includes Apache HBase. These databases are optimized for querying and aggregating large data volumes, storing data in columns rather than rows.
- **Graph DBMS**: Like Neo4j, graph databases excel at managing interconnected data, representing data as nodes and edges. Describe scenarios like network analysis or recommendation systems where graph databases like Neo4j and Amazon Neptune are beneficial.
- **Blockchain** is a distributed database technology that records transactions immutably and transparently, beyond its common association with cryptocurrencies, such as supply chain transparency, vital record keeping, voting systems, etc.
- **Cloud-Native DBMS**: With cloud computing's rise, understanding cloud-native databases like Amazon RDS, Azure SQL Database, and Google Cloud Spanner is essential. Discuss experiences with migration, management, and optimization of databases in the cloud.

Share experiences with AWS Aurora or Google Bigtable, focusing on their integration in cloud ecosystems.

A Database Solutions Architect must understand these diverse DBMS types, their unique strengths, and application scenarios to make informed decisions that align with specific business requirements and outcomes. A strong grasp of various DBMS types, including cloud-native solutions, and their practical applications is crucial for any Database Solutions Architect.

This knowledge and real-world experiences can significantly impact the interview process and subsequent project successes in a data-driven environment. Let's explore key database technology in more detail.

Relational and NoSQL databases

In the previous section, we touched upon diverse types of DBMS; however, most use cases are served by relational (SQL) and non-relational (NoSQL) databases. A database solutions architect is expected to have a strong understanding, extensive experience working with these database types, and a high degree of competency in SQL.

Relational databases

RDBMS is the basis of traditional data storage and management, designed to manage structured data efficiently and reliably. For a Database Solutions Architect, understanding the details of RDBMS is essential, as these systems are widely used across various industries and applications. Let's delve into the key aspects of RDBMS:

- **Structured Query Language (SQL)**: RDBMS is synonymous with SQL, a powerful language for defining, manipulating, and querying data. SQL's standardization across different platforms makes it a versatile tool for data architects.
- **ACID Compliance**: RDBMS strictly adheres to ACID properties (Atomicity, Consistency, Isolation, Durability), ensuring transactions are processed reliably and maintaining data integrity even during system failures.
- **Schema-Dependent Structure**: RDBMS requires a predefined schema that dictates the data structure, including tables, columns, and relationships. This schema-dependent nature ensures data consistency but requires upfront design and planning.
- **Relational Data Model**: The relational model of RDBMS is pivotal for managing data relationships. It facilitates easy navigation and management of data interconnected through primary and foreign keys.

Popular RDBMS include MySQL, PostgreSQL, Oracle Database, Microsoft SQL Server, and cloud-optimized solutions like Amazon Aurora, each offering unique features and optimizations.

Taking a real-world use case, in a banking application scenario, an RDBMS excels in managing customer data, account details, and transaction records. Its capability to efficiently handle complex queries and relationships, such as retrieving a customer's transaction history or linking accounts to individual customers, makes it indispensable. The transactional consistency and data integrity features of RDBMS are critical in a banking context, where the accuracy and reliability of financial data are paramount. The system's robust security mechanisms safeguard sensitive financial data against unauthorized access, fulfilling regulatory compliance requirements.

RDBMS remains a fundamental aspect of data architecture, especially in scenarios demanding structured data management, transactional integrity, and complex data relationships. Understanding the capabilities and limitations of various RDBMS is crucial for a Database Solutions Architect, enabling them to design systems that effectively meet the specific needs of applications like banking, where data integrity and security are non-negotiable.

NoSQL Databases

NoSQL databases, also known as "Not Only SQL," are designed for flexibility and scalability, making them a critical tool for managing unstructured and semi-structured data in diverse applications. As a Database Solutions Architect, understanding NoSQL's characteristics, data models, and practical use cases is essential for designing effective data solutions. The following are the Key Characteristics of NoSQL Databases:

- **Flexible Schema:** NoSQL databases do not require a predefined schema, making them ideal for applications with evolving data models. This flexibility enables easy modification and expansion of data structures over time without the constraints imposed by a fixed schema.
- **Scalability:** NoSQL databases excel in horizontal scalability, distributing data across multiple nodes or servers to handle large-scale data storage and high traffic volumes. This distributed architecture allows easy scaling by adding more nodes to the database cluster.
- **Variety of Data Models:** NoSQL encompasses a range of data models, including key-value stores, document stores, wide-column stores, and graph databases. Each model offers unique advantages for different types of data and use cases.

Prominent examples include MongoDB, a document-oriented database; Redis, a key-value store; Cassandra, a wide-column store; Neo4j, a graph database; and Amazon DynamoDB, a cloud-native NoSQL service. Below are some of the common use cases of NoSQL DB:

- **Big Data and Analytics:** NoSQL databases efficiently handle large volumes of diverse data, making them suitable for big data applications and analytics.
- **Content Management Systems** support flexible content storage, ideal for systems handling various content types, such as blog posts and multimedia.
- **Real-time Applications:** NoSQL is often used in applications requiring real-time processing and high concurrency, such as IoT and online gaming.
- **Personalization and Recommendation Systems:** Efficient in storing and querying user preferences, NoSQL powers recommendation engines and personalized content delivery.
- **Social Networks and Graph Applications:** Graph-based NoSQL databases effectively manage interconnected data, which is useful for social networks and network analysis.

Understanding NOSQL data models is essential for a Database Solutions Architect. Let's learn more about them.

NoSQL Data Models

Here's a breakdown of the various NoSQL data models, highlighting their unique characteristics, advantages, and common use cases. Understanding these models is key for a Database SA when designing systems that require scalability, flexibility, and high performance with unstructured data.

- **Document Model:** In the document model, data is stored in documents typically represented in JSON (JavaScript Object Notation) or BSON (Binary JSON) formats. JSON is a lightweight, human-readable format widely used for data interchange over the web. At the same time, BSON is a binary encoding of JSON designed for efficient storage and transfer of data, especially in database systems like MongoDB. BSON provides additional data types and better performance than JSON at the cost of human readability. These documents allow for nested structures and can contain complex data types. This model does not enforce a strict schema, enabling flexibility in the data stored within each document. The key advantages of this model are its high flexibility with schema-less data structure, ease of scale horizontally, and natural support for hierarchical data organization, which aligns well with modern object-oriented programming languages. It is suitable for Content management systems, e-commerce applications, and real-time analytics where each document can store varied information about items, users, or events.

- **Key-Value Model:** This model stores data as a collection of key-value pairs, where each key is unique. The value associated with a key can be a simple data type or a more complex data structure. This model is highly efficient for scenarios where data access is driven primarily through a unique key. This model's key advantages are simplicity, high read/write operations performance, and extreme scalability, particularly for applications with high demand for speed and large volumes of data. It is suitable for shopping cart information in e-commerce sites, session management in web applications, and caching, where rapid access to data is critical.

- **Columnar Model:** Unlike traditional relational databases that store data in rows, the columnar model stores data in columns, making it ideal for handling large datasets with many attributes. This structure optimizes both storage efficiency and query performance over column-centric operations. Key advantages of this model are efficient data compression and faster read/write operations on a column basis, which reduces the amount of data loaded into memory, thereby improving performance. These are suitable for big data analytics, data warehousing, and customer analytics, where operations often involve aggregation over large volumes of data, such as calculating averages or sums across numerous records.

- **Graph Model:** The graph model represents data as nodes (entities) and edges (relationships), which allows for the efficient querying of connected data. This model is powerful for intrinsically interconnected data where relationships are equally as important as the data itself. Key advantages of this model are flexibility in querying complex relationships, intuitive data modeling for relationship-heavy data, and efficient performance in traversing connections. It is suitable for social networks, recommendation systems, and fraud detection systems where understanding the relationships between entities is crucial.

NoSQL databases are engineered for performance and scalability, employing sharding, replication, and load-balancing techniques to distribute data and workload across multiple servers, thus ensuring high performance and availability. They adopt a schema-on-read approach that provides flexibility to adapt to changing data requirements, ensuring high availability and fault tolerance through automatic replication and built-in fault tolerance mechanisms. While designing distributed environments, NoSQL databases maintain data consistency and are particularly adept at horizontal scaling, allowing them to effectively accommodate increasing volumes of data and user demands. Mastering NoSQL is crucial for crafting scalable, flexible, and efficient data solutions for a Database Solutions Architect, especially in scenarios characterized by large data volumes, varied data types, and the imperative for rapid scalability.

Choosing Between SQL and NoSQL

When selecting between SQL and NoSQL databases, a Database Solutions Architect must consider several key factors based on the specific requirements and context of the application or system. Here's a detailed comparison and guidelines for choosing between SQL and NoSQL databases:

- **Data Structure and Consistency:** SQL or Relational databases are often more suitable if data integrity and structured relationships are priorities. NoSQL databases may be more effective for applications with less structured data or where rapid development and iteration are required.

- **Scalability Requirements:** Consider horizontal scaling with NoSQL for systems anticipating rapid growth or large, distributed data sets. SQL databases are more suitable for systems where scaling can be managed with more powerful hardware and complex transactions are common.
- **Query Complexity:** Applications requiring complex transactions and operations (e.g., financial systems) benefit from SQL databases' advanced querying capabilities. NoSQL is preferable for simpler queries or when working with large volumes of data that don't fit well into relational models.
- **Development Speed and Flexibility:** NoSQL databases' flexible schemas make them more developer-friendly. This can speed up development and allow for quicker iterations.
- **System Reliability and Transactions:** SQL databases are often the better choice for systems requiring high reliability and support for multi-record transactions due to their mature support for ACID properties.
- **Use Case and Industry Standards:** Certain industries or applications have standard or preferred database technologies based on historical use, regulatory requirements, or specific data needs.

The choice between SQL and NoSQL databases depends on the application's requirements, including data structure, scalability needs, query complexity, development speed, system reliability, and industry standards. A balanced approach often involves using both types of databases in different components of a larger system to leverage their respective strengths.

Database design principles and best practices

Database design is critical in developing efficient, reliable, and secure databases. It involves defining the database structure, the relationships between data elements, and the rules that govern the integrity of the database. Effective database design principles are essential for ensuring that the database is scalable, performs well, and aligns with the needs of the application or business process it supports. Let's look at some core principles of database design:

Data modeling

Preparing for a Database Solutions Architect interview requires an in-depth understanding of data modeling, a foundational aspect of database design. Data modeling is a crucial step in designing and implementing database systems. It involves creating a conceptual, logical, and physical representation of the data and capturing the entities, relationships, and constraints that define the structure and integrity of the data. In other words, it defines the data's structure, relationships, and constraints to ensure its accuracy, integrity, and effectiveness in supporting business requirements. You must combine theoretical knowledge and practical application as a database solutions architect. Let's look at various data modeling techniques.

- **Conceptual Data Modeling**: Conceptual data modeling is the initial phase in database design, focusing on establishing the overall structure of the database at a high level. This involves identifying key entities, attributes, and relationships without delving into specific technical details. During preparation, practicing creating Entity-Relationship Diagrams (ERDs), which visually depict the data model, is vital. You should be able to illustrate complex business scenarios through these diagrams, clearly understanding how different entities relate to each other and the nature of these relationships. For example, a Database Solutions Architect would systematically approach the project from conceptual modeling to maintaining data consistency and quality in constructing a comprehensive database solution for a healthcare system.

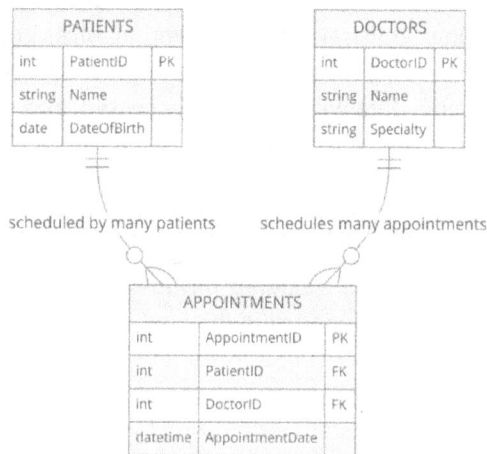

Figure 9.1 - Entity-Relationship Diagrams (ERD) for healthcare application

As shown in the preceding diagram, the project begins with identifying the key entities and their relationships within the healthcare context. For example, entities such as 'Patients,' 'Doctors,' and 'Appointments' are identified. 'Patients' might have attributes like PatientID, Name, and DateOfBirth; 'Doctors' could include DoctorID, Name, and Specialty; and 'Appointments' link Patients to Doctors. This high-level view provides a clear and simplified representation of healthcare operations, setting the foundation for more detailed modeling.

- **Logical Data Modeling**: Logical data modeling is critical in translating the conceptual model into a more defined structure suitable for implementation in a specific DBMS. This involves detailing tables, columns, keys, and normalization processes. Preparation should include understanding how to establish primary and foreign key relationships, implement normalization to reduce data redundancy, and ensure data integrity. Familiarity with converting high-level models into detailed logical models that clearly outline the structure of the database is essential. In the logical data modeling phase for the healthcare database, the Database Solutions Architect refines conceptual entities into detailed database tables, such as 'Patients,' 'Doctors,' and 'Appointments,' each with specific fields like PatientID, DoctorID, and AppointmentDate. This phase establishes key relationships, such as one-to-many between Doctors and Appointments, and applies normalization rules to minimize redundancy, enhancing data integrity. Important elements like indexing PatientID and DoctorID are incorporated for query optimization, which is crucial in a fast-paced healthcare environment. The model also integrates security measures and compliance with healthcare regulations, such as HIPAA, ensuring sensitive patient data is safeguarded and regulatory standards are met. This careful structuring in the logical phase paves the way for an efficient, compliant, and operationally sound physical database design tailored to the healthcare system's specific requirements.

- **Physical Data Modeling**: Physical data modeling involves translating the logical model into an actual database structure on a specific database management system. This step includes decisions on how data will be stored, accessed, and maintained in the database. Preparing for this involves understanding database-specific features like indexing strategies, partitioning methods, and storage configurations. It's crucial to demonstrate knowledge of optimizing physical models for performance and scalability, considering factors like data volume, transaction throughput, and query performance. For the healthcare system, physical data modeling includes decisions on the database's technical implementation. Decisions include using indexed columns for frequently accessed data like PatientID or DoctorID, choosing appropriate data types for medical records, and setting up partitioning for large patient data tables. This stage tailors the logical model to the specifics of the database system, optimizing for performance and scalability.

- **Data Organization and Integration**: Understanding data organization and integration is key in data modeling, as it ensures that data from different sources is consolidated effectively. You should be well-versed in designing models that facilitate easy data retrieval and aggregation, allowing data from various systems to be brought together cohesively. Preparation should involve studying how data models can impact data quality and how they can be used to integrate data from disparate sources while maintaining consistency and accuracy. In this stage, the focus is on how data from various departments of the healthcare system (like outpatient, inpatient, diagnostics, etc.) is integrated into a unified database system. The model must ensure that data from all sources is consistently formatted, easily accessible, and provides a unified view for reporting and analytics purposes.

- **Maintaining Data Consistency and Quality**: Ensuring data consistency and quality through data modeling is vital in database design. This involves defining rules and constraints that maintain the integrity and accuracy of the data. Preparing for this aspect includes understanding how to implement various data constraints, such as unique constraints, check constraints, and foreign keys, and how they contribute to preserving data quality and preventing anomalies. Ensuring data quality and consistency is crucial in a healthcare database. For instance, constraints are implemented to ensure that appointment times do not overlap for the same doctor, and referential integrity checks are applied to prevent medical records from being created without a valid patient ID. This step is vital to maintain the accuracy and reliability of the healthcare data, directly impacting patient care and operational efficiency.

System design and scalability considerations are central to data modeling. This includes designing data models that are efficient and effective for current requirements and scalable for future growth. Preparation should focus on understanding how to design for scalability, including considerations for distributed systems, load balancing, and data partitioning, ensuring that the database system can handle increasing loads and data volumes.

Hands-on experience with real-world data modeling is crucial. Preparing for this involves working on actual database design projects or simulations that mimic complex data scenarios. It's important to gain practical experience applying theoretical knowledge to design databases that meet specific business requirements, focusing on entity identification, relationship mapping, and schema design.

A Database Solutions Architect must be knowledgeable about various data modeling tools and techniques. Preparation should include practicing with popular data modeling software, understanding its features, and learning how to use them to create efficient models.

Additionally, knowledge of different modeling techniques, their applications, and best practices in their usage is vital. By thoroughly understanding these aspects and practicing real-world scenarios, you'll be well-prepared to showcase your data modeling expertise in a Database Solutions Architect interview.

Normalization and Denormalization

Normalization and denormalization are crucial concepts in database design, each vital to optimizing a database's structure and performance.

Normalization is organizing data in a database to minimize redundancy and dependency. It involves decomposing a larger table into smaller, more manageable tables while maintaining relationships between them. This process follows a set of guidelines known as normal forms, each addressing specific types of redundancy and anomalies in the database. Normalization helps ensure data integrity and consistency, making maintaining and updating the database easier. However, a highly normalized database can lead to complex queries involving multiple table joins, which might affect performance, especially for large-scale databases. For example, in a healthcare database, normalization would involve separating patient information, treatment records, and appointment details into different tables. This separation ensures that changes in one aspect, such as updating a patient's contact information, don't require changes across multiple records, reducing redundancy and the risk of inconsistencies.

On the other hand, denormalization is a strategy used to improve database read performance, especially in large-scale databases where complex joins can be costly in query execution time. This process involves adding redundant data or grouping data to reduce the need for joins during queries. While denormalization can improve query speed, it comes at the cost of increased data redundancy, leading to potential inconsistencies if not managed properly. In the same healthcare database, denormalization might involve creating a view or table that combines patient and appointment details. This would allow faster retrieval of all appointments for a specific patient but could potentially lead to data anomalies if the patient or appointment details change and the combined data isn't updated accordingly.

The decision between normalization and denormalization often involves a trade-off between data integrity and performance. Database architects must evaluate the database's specific needs and usage patterns to determine the optimal balance.

> *A database primarily used for transaction processing might benefit more from normalization. In contrast, a database used for analytics and reporting might be better served with some level of denormalization for faster query responses.*

The key is to find a balance that ensures data integrity and efficiency tailored to the system's and its users' specific requirements.

Indexing and Query Optimization

Indexing and query optimization are critical aspects of database performance tuning. Understanding these concepts is essential for a database solutions architect, especially when preparing for interviews.

Indexing is a database optimization technique that involves creating a data structure (an index) to improve the speed of data retrieval operations. The primary aim of indexing is to allow the database engine to quickly locate and access the data without scanning the entire table. However, it's crucial to strike a balance in indexing; over-indexing can lead to increased storage requirements and slower write operations due to the need to update multiple indexes. Here are some common types of indexes and their uses:

- **B-tree Index**: This is the most common index type used in relational databases. B-tree indexes are excellent for range queries and can efficiently support equality searches. They work by maintaining a balanced tree structure, where each leaf node points to a database record.
- **Hash Index**: Hash indexes are best suited for equality searches. They map data values to a unique location. They are not ideal for range queries but are highly efficient for direct lookups.
- **Bitmap Index**: These indexes are particularly useful for columns with a limited number of distinct values, such as gender or marital status. Bitmap indexes use a bit array to represent the existence of a value, making them efficient for queries that involve multiple columns.
- **Full-Text Index**: This index is used for text searching in large textual data. It enables complex searches, such as keyword searches, and is crucial for implementing search functionalities.

Query Optimization involves modifying and tuning queries to retrieve data more efficiently. Effective use of indexes is a significant part of this process. When optimizing queries, it's essential to understand which index type will provide the best performance boost depending on the query pattern. Key indexing strategies for query optimization include:

- **Covering Index**: This index contains all the fields required by a query. It can significantly improve performance because the database can retrieve all the needed data from the index without accessing the table.
- **Clustered Index**: This affects the physical data storage order in a database. It is ideal for range queries and can greatly improve the performance of queries that retrieve large data ranges.
- **Non-clustered Index**: Unlike clustered indexes, non-clustered indexes do not alter the physical order of the data. They are separate from the data and can improve retrieval speed without affecting the order of rows.

Index Maintenance: Regular index maintenance is crucial for maintaining optimal performance. Over time, indexes can become fragmented, leading to inefficient data retrieval. Periodically reorganizing or rebuilding indexes can help keep their efficiency.

In a database solutions architect interview, you might encounter questions that test your ability to choose the right index type for a given scenario, your strategies for maintaining index efficiency, and your skills in optimizing queries for performance. Demonstrating a deep understanding of these concepts and practical examples can significantly enhance your candidacy.

Data Integrity Constraints

Data integrity constraints are crucial elements in database design, ensuring data accuracy, consistency, and reliability within a database. As a database solutions architect, having a deep understanding of these constraints is essential for designing robust database schemas and maintaining data quality throughout the database's lifecycle. Here's a breakdown of the key data integrity constraints:

- **Primary Key Constraint**: This constraint is fundamental in relational databases. It ensures that each record in a table can be uniquely identified. The primary key constraint prevents duplicate and null values in the column or set of columns designated as the primary key. This guarantees the uniqueness of each row in a table, facilitating efficient data retrieval and integrity. For example, in a patient table in a healthcare database, the patient ID could serve as the primary key, ensuring that each patient is uniquely identified.
- **Foreign Key Constraint**: This constraint establishes a link between tables, enforcing referential integrity. A foreign key in one table points to a primary key in another, creating a relationship between the two tables. This constraint ensures that the data referenced by the foreign key exists in the linked table. *Example*: In the same healthcare database, a foreign key in an appointment table could reference the patient ID in the patient table, ensuring that each appointment is associated with an existing patient.
- **Unique Constraint**: This constraint ensures that all values in a column or a combination of columns are unique across a table. Unlike the primary key constraint, the unique constraint can allow null values, but it ensures that all non-null values are unique. For example, an email column in a user account table can have a unique constraint, ensuring that no two users have the same email address.
- **Not Null Constraint**: This constraint specifies that a column must always have a value; it cannot be left blank. This is important for columns that are critical to the integrity and operation of the database. For example, the medication name column in a prescription table might have a not null constraint, as it's essential to specify the medication for each prescription.
- **Check Constraint**: This constraint specifies a condition each row must meet to be valid. It provides a way to enforce specific rules at the database level, such as range limits or particular formats. For example, a check constraint on a date of birth column in a patient table could ensure that the date is past and not future.

In an interview context, you can discuss the implementation and importance of these constraints and scenarios where they might be relaxed, such as during data migration or bulk data operations. You might also be asked about the performance implications of these constraints and how to balance data integrity with database performance. Demonstrating your ability to use these constraints effectively to maintain data integrity while considering performance implications will show your depth of understanding and practical expertise as a database solutions architect.

High Availability

High availability (HA) is critical to database management, ensuring your systems remain accessible and operational despite potential hardware or software failures. Implementing robust HA strategies can significantly reduce the risk of downtime and data loss. Here are some key components and techniques for achieving high availability in database systems:

- **Database Replication**: Database replication involves creating and maintaining multiple copies of data across different servers or geographic locations. This setup allows for real-time data synchronization, ensuring that all locations have up-to-date copies of the data. It enhances data availability and access speed; in the event of a server failure, the system can continue operations by switching to a replica.
- **Failover Mechanisms**: Failover mechanisms involve configuring the database system to automatically switch to a standby server or system when the primary server fails. This switch can be managed by failover clustering software, which monitors the health of the primary server and initiates a failover when necessary. It minimizes downtime by ensuring that there is always a backup system ready to take over operations without manual intervention, maintaining continuous service availability.
- **Data Redundancy**: Data redundancy is achieved through regular backups and snapshots of the database, which are stored in multiple locations, such as on different physical servers or in the cloud. This approach protects against data loss due to hardware failure, natural disasters, or other catastrophic events. It provides a means to restore the database to a previous state in case of data corruption or loss, which is essential for disaster recovery planning.
- **Load balancing**: It involves distributing database queries and transactions across several servers to optimize resource use and maximize throughput. This can be done using dedicated load-balancing hardware or software solutions that route traffic and requests to the least busy servers. Load balancing improves the responsiveness and scalability of database systems by preventing any single server from becoming a bottleneck, thereby enhancing user experience during high-traffic periods.
- **Cluster Management**: Clustering refers to using multiple servers (nodes) that work together as a single system. Database clusters can manage the database load by distributing it across several nodes, with mechanisms in place to handle failover automatically. It increases the reliability and availability of the database system by allowing seamless transition between nodes in the event of a failure, with little or no disruption to end users.

Factors such as the application's criticality, acceptable downtime (if any), and the infrastructure budget should be considered when designing and implementing high-availability systems. The choice between synchronous and asynchronous replication, a suitable failover strategy (automatic vs. manual), and the load balancing method (software vs. hardware) should be tailored to the organization's specific needs and operational dynamics.

Furthermore, the configuration and maintenance of HA systems require regular testing and updates to ensure that all components work as expected during an actual failover event. The ultimate goal is to create a resilient infrastructure that supports business continuity despite system failures or external disruptions.

Scalability

Scalability is a crucial aspect of modern database architecture, particularly in environments that experience variable workloads or rapid growth. Being able to scale effectively ensures that your database system can handle increased load without performance degradation. Here are some key strategies for achieving optimal scalability:

- **Horizontal Scaling**: Horizontal scaling, often referred to as scaling out, involves adding more servers to your pool of resources to distribute the database load more broadly. This approach can include strategies like sharding, where data is horizontally partitioned across multiple servers, each holding a subset of the data. It increases the capacity to handle more transactions and larger data volumes without compromising the performance of existing servers. It also enhances fault tolerance and load distribution.
- **Vertical Scaling**: Vertical scaling, or scaling up, involves increasing the capacity of an existing server by adding more resources such as CPU, RAM, or storage. This method is often simpler as it does not require changes to the database architecture, but it can be more costly and has physical limitations. It's quick to implement and does not require significant application or database configuration changes. It's effective for short-term growth and applications not designed to run on distributed systems.
- **Elastic Scalability**: Elastic scalability uses cloud computing resources to dynamically adjust the resources allocated to the database based on current demand. This approach is typical in Cloud environments such as Amazon RDS, Azure SQL Database, or Google Cloud SQL. It provides a cost-effective scalability solution that adjusts resources automatically, ensuring that you only pay for what you use. It's particularly useful for applications with unpredictable workloads.

- **Database Caching**: Database caching involves storing frequently accessed data in a faster storage system, such as in-memory databases like Redis or Memcached. This reduces the load on the primary database server by serving common requests from the cache rather than repeatedly reprocessing the same queries. This approach significantly improves latency, performance, and response times by reducing database load and avoiding querying table locations where data does not change frequently.

- **Distributed Systems**: Distributed database systems involve interconnected databases that store data across multiple sites, regions, or nodes. These systems can handle more data and concurrent users than a single database server, enhancing scalability and availability. Data is spread across multiple nodes, which can independently handle requests and balance loads without any single point of failure.

When implementing scalability solutions, it's important to analyze your application's specific needs, including traffic patterns and data growth projections. Horizontal scaling is ideal for long-term growth and systems that must remain highly available and resilient. Vertical scaling can quickly address short-term needs without the complexities of distributing your database operations. Elastic scalability offers flexibility and cost efficiency, particularly suitable for applications with fluctuating demands.

Any scalability strategy aims to ensure that performance does not degrade as the system grows. This requires careful planning, continuous monitoring, and regular adjustments based on system performance and user demand. Scalability strategies should also be aligned with business goals to ensure they provide value and effectively support the overall business objectives.

Performance Tuning

Performance tuning is an essential aspect of database management that ensures the system operates efficiently and can handle required workloads effectively. By implementing a strategic approach to performance tuning, you can significantly enhance the speed and responsiveness of your database, leading to improved application performance and user satisfaction. Here's a detailed look at key strategies for tuning your database performance:

- **Regular Performance Audits**: Conducting performance audits regularly allows you to assess the health and efficiency of your database system. This involves using performance monitoring tools to track and analyze key metrics such as query response times, CPU usage, memory utilization, and I/O operations. It helps detect performance issues early, allowing for proactive resolution. Regular audits ensure the database remains optimized as workloads evolve and usage patterns change.
- **Query Optimization**: Optimize SQL queries to ensure they execute efficiently. This includes analyzing query execution plans to understand how queries are processed by the database engine and identifying inefficiencies such as poorly performing joins, unnecessary full table scans, and improper use of indexes. By improving the speed and

efficiency of data retrieval, query optimization reduces the load on the database, directly impacting the performance of applications relying on these queries.

- **Index Management**: Effective index management involves creating, modifying, and maintaining indexes to enhance query performance while avoiding the drawbacks of over-indexing, such as degraded write performance due to the overhead of maintaining additional index data. Properly indexed databases can dramatically improve query response times by reducing the amount of data scanned. Regularly reviewing and updating indexes ensures they align with current data access patterns.
- **Resource Allocation**: Tuning the database configuration to optimize resource allocation involves adjusting parameters like memory allocation for database caching, connection pool settings, and disk I/O configurations to better suit your workload's specific needs. Ensures that the database server uses its hardware resources efficiently, which can prevent bottlenecks related to resource contention and improve overall database and application performance.
- **Data Partitioning**: **Description**: Data partitioning involves splitting large tables into smaller, more manageable segments horizontally (by rows) or vertically (by columns). This can be done based on certain criteria, such as date ranges, geographic location, or other logical divisions. Improves query performance by limiting the number of rows scanned in each query. Partitioning also simplifies data management tasks like backups, updates, and deletions by allowing these operations to be performed on smaller subsets of the data.

When implementing performance-tuning strategies, Database Solutions Architects must adopt a systematic approach.

Establishing performance baselines before making any changes is essential. This allows for measuring the impact that tuning efforts have on the system. Performance tuning should be approached as an iterative process: make incremental changes and measure their effects before proceeding to ensure each modification produces the desired outcome.

Additionally, it's important to conduct comprehensive testing of performance tuning changes in a staging environment that closely mirrors the production environment. This practice helps to understand the real-world effects of changes without impacting actual operations. Finally, setting up continuous monitoring is critical to detect new performance issues as they arise, possibly due to changes in application behavior or increases in data volumes. Let's look at some performance trade-offs.

Performance Trade-offs

Performance trade-offs are a critical aspect of database design and optimization. In a database solutions architect interview, you must demonstrate your ability to balance various factors to achieve optimal performance based on specific application requirements. Here's a breakdown of key performance trade-offs:

- **Read vs. Write Performance**: Balancing read and write performance is essential, especially for applications with varying workload patterns. Denormalization, caching, or materialized views can significantly improve query performance for read-heavy applications. However, additional computation or data duplication can adversely impact write performance. In contrast, write-heavy applications might prioritize efficient write operations, possibly at the expense of slower reads. The right balance depends on the application's specific read-to-write ratio and performance requirements. *Example*: An online analytics dashboard with mostly read operations might benefit from denormalization and caching to provide quick data access, whereas an e-commerce transaction system would prioritize efficient writes to ensure fast order processing.
- **Data Storage and Disk Space**: Choices in database normalization and data storage directly impact disk space utilization. Normalization reduces redundancy and saves disk space but may require complex joins, impacting query performance. Denormalization might increase disk space due to redundant data but can optimize read operations. *Example*: A reporting database might employ denormalization to store aggregated data, trading off increased disk space for faster query response times.
- **Data Partitioning**: Partitioning divides a large table into smaller segments, improving manageability and performance, especially for large datasets. It allows for parallel processing and more efficient data access but introduces management complexity and potential overhead. For example, a large-scale IoT application with billions of data points might use partitioning to segment data by device or region, enhancing query performance and data management.
- **Caching**: Implementing caching improves read performance by storing frequently accessed data in memory. This reduces database load but introduces challenges in maintaining cache consistency and managing data updates. For example, a content delivery network (CDN) might use aggressive caching strategies to deliver static content quickly, accepting the complexity of cache invalidation for updated content.
- **Normalization vs. Denormalization**: The choice between normalization and denormalization involves a trade-off between data integrity and query performance. Normalization ensures data integrity but can slow down queries due to multiple joins, while denormalization optimizes query performance at the cost of data redundancy and potential consistency issues. For example, a customer relationship management (CRM) system might use normalization to ensure data integrity across customer records, accepting more complex queries as a trade-off.

- **Indexing**: Indexes are key to optimizing query performance but can introduce overhead during data modifications. The right balance in indexing strategy involves creating indexes that cater to frequent queries while minimizing the impact on write operations. *Example*: A financial reporting system might index columns frequently used in queries, such as date ranges or account IDs, accepting the additional overhead during data insertion or updates.
- **Query Optimization and Index Selection**: Efficient query execution involves understanding and influencing the database engine's query execution plans. Selecting appropriate indexes and optimizing queries for frequently executed operations can significantly impact performance. *For example*, optimizing queries for route calculations and indexing key columns like destination and package size can enhance overall system performance in a large-scale logistics application.

Understanding and articulating these trade-offs is crucial for a database solutions architect. Demonstrating your ability to make informed decisions based on application requirements, data workload patterns, and system constraints is key to excelling in an interview and effectively managing database performance in real-world scenarios.

By systematically applying these strategies, Database Solutions Architects can ensure that the database infrastructure meets current performance needs and is robust and flexible enough to scale effectively and meet future demands. This proactive approach to database management ensures ongoing optimization and efficiency, which is crucial for maintaining high-performance standards in dynamic and data-intensive environments.

Cloud Database Solutions

Cloud database solutions offer a range of benefits that are particularly advantageous in managing database management systems' scalability, availability, and cost-efficiency. As a Database Solutions Architect, it's crucial to have a firm understanding of the various services and features provided by major cloud providers and how to implement these solutions in real-world scenarios effectively:

- **Cloud Provider Services**: Familiarize yourself with the database services offered by major cloud providers, such as AWS RDS, Azure SQL Database, and Google Cloud SQL. Each service offers unique features tailored to different use cases and has its own set of limitations. Understand key attributes such as performance metrics, security capabilities, and integration options. Knowing the strengths and limitations of each platform allows you to choose the best service for your specific application requirements.

- **Managed Databases**: Managed database services provide a hassle-free solution for database administration. These services typically include automatic scaling, backups, and updates, freeing your time to focus on more strategic tasks. Utilize the easy-to-use interfaces these services offer for performance tuning and routine maintenance. Managed databases are ideal for organizations looking to reduce operational overhead while maintaining optimal database performance.
- **Disaster Recovery**: Cloud-based disaster recovery solutions ensure high availability and data integrity. These solutions often include geo-redundancy and cross-region replication, which protect against data loss in a disaster. Implementing robust disaster recovery strategies ensures that your database can quickly recover from failures while minimizing data loss, thus maintaining business continuity.
- **Cost-Effective Scaling**: The cloud's pay-as-you-go pricing model allows for cost-effective scaling of resources. This flexible scaling option lets you adjust resources based on actual demand, optimizing costs while accommodating spikes in traffic or data growth. Plan resource allocation based on expected loads and adapt dynamically as requirements change. This approach ensures performance efficiency and keeps operational costs under control.

A comprehensive understanding of these cloud database solutions equips a Database Solutions Architect to effectively manage performance, ensure high availability, and achieve cost-effective scalability. When preparing for interviews or project discussions, tailor your responses to highlight your expertise and practical experience in leveraging these cloud solutions to solve complex database challenges.

By integrating these cloud services into your database architecture, you can provide robust, scalable, and cost-efficient solutions that meet the evolving needs of modern businesses. Stay updated on cloud providers' latest offerings and enhancements to keep your skills relevant and competitive in this rapidly changing tech landscape. Now that you have learned about various types of databases and best practices Let's examine database migration.

Database Migration

Database migration involves migrating data from one or more source databases to one or more target databases. This process is facilitated by utilizing a database migration service. Upon migration completion, the data previously stored in the source databases is entirely relocated to the target databases. However, the data structure may have undergone modifications. Subsequently, clients who previously accessed the source databases are redirected to the target databases, and the source databases are taken offline or decommissioned.

Database migration approach

Typically, there are three approaches to customer journeys related to database migration:

- **Migrate**: The migrate approach is the most straightforward and involves moving data from the existing database to the new database with minimal changes. This approach is suitable when the new database system has features and capabilities similar to those of the existing one, and the data structure can be directly mapped from one system to the other. Suppose you have an existing MySQL database and want to move to a PostgreSQL database. The migration approach would involve creating a new PostgreSQL database and then using tools like `pg_dump` and `pg_restore` to transfer the data and schema from the MySQL database to the latest PostgreSQL database. The goal is to preserve the data structure and functionality with minimal changes.

- **Modernize**: The modernized approach involves updating and improving the database during migration. This approach is suitable when the new database system has more advanced features or capabilities to be leveraged to improve the system's overall performance, scalability, or security. Suppose you have an older, on-premises Oracle database and want to migrate to a cloud-based Amazon Relational Database Service (RDS) instance. The modernized approach would involve transferring the data and taking advantage of the cloud-based features and services offered by Amazon RDS, such as automatic backups, scalable storage, and managed maintenance. This may involve restructuring the database schema, optimizing queries, or implementing new security measures.

- **Transform:** The transform approach involves a more significant overhaul of the database system, often accompanied by changes in the data structure, business logic, or user interface. This approach is suitable when the new database requirements are significantly different from the existing system or when the organization wants to take the opportunity to rethink and redesign the entire data architecture. Suppose you have a legacy database system designed for a specific business model, but your organization has evolved, and the existing system needs to be revised. The transform approach would involve analyzing the current data requirements, designing a new database schema that aligns with the organization's current and future needs, and then migrating the data to the new system. This may involve changes to the data structures, introducing new data types or relationships, and implementing new business logic and user interfaces.

The choice between the migrate, modernize, and transform approaches depends on the database migration project's specific requirements, the complexity of the existing system, and the desired outcomes. The migrate approach is the simplest; the modernized approach balances improvements with migration, and the transform approach involves a more comprehensive overhaul of the database system.

Types of database migration

Understanding the types of database migrations can help ensure a smooth transition while minimizing downtime and data integrity issues. Here are the main types of database migration:

- **Homogeneous Database Migration**: The source and target databases use the same DBMS or platform in a homogeneous database migration. This means that the underlying database structure, data types, and query languages are compatible. For example, migrating data from one Oracle database to another Oracle database (different versions or instances). Homogeneous database migrations are generally more straightforward because the data structures and query languages are the same, reducing the need for extensive data translation or transformation. The migration process usually involves transferring data and metadata directly from the source to the target database.
- **Heterogeneous Database Migration:** In a heterogeneous database migration, the source and target databases use different DBMS or platforms. This means the underlying database structures, data types, and query languages are not directly compatible. For example, data can be imported from an Oracle database to a PostgreSQL database. Heterogeneous database migrations are more complex because the data structures and query languages differ between the source and target databases. This often requires additional steps to ensure data integrity and compatibility during migration.
- **On-Premise to Cloud Database Migration:** With the increasing adoption of cloud services, migrating databases from on-premise data centers to cloud platforms like AWS, Azure, or Google Cloud is becoming common. Key challenges include data security during transfer, choosing the right cloud database service (such as AWS RDS, Azure SQL Database, or Google Cloud SQL), and optimizing the new environment for performance and cost.
- **Cross-Cloud Database Migration:** This type involves moving databases from one cloud provider to another, such as Azure to AWS. This might be driven by strategic business decisions, cost considerations, or feature benefits offered by another provider. It is similar to on-premise to cloud migrations, but additional complexities include dealing with different cloud architectures and ensuring data integrity and security across cloud platforms.
- **Version Upgrade Migration:** This migration involves upgrading the database to a newer version of the same database management system, such as upgrading from SQL Server 2012 to SQL Server 2022. While potentially less complex than other types, version upgrade migrations still require careful planning to handle deprecated features, optimizer behavior changes, and compatibility issues with existing applications.
- **Data Consolidation Migration:** involves consolidating data from multiple databases or sources into a single database system. It is often part of a strategy to centralize data management and reduce IT overhead. Challenges include data deduplication, integration of disparate data formats, and the complexity of managing larger volumes of data in a single system.

- **Platform Migration:** refers to changing the underlying hardware or operating systems on which the database operates, such as moving from a Windows-based server to a Linux-based system. The focus here is on the database's compatibility with the new platform and the performance implications of the new environment.

Each type of database migration requires a tailored approach that considers the specific characteristics of the source and target databases, as well as the overall business objectives and technical constraints. Successful migration involves not only technical execution but also thorough testing, validation of data integrity, and careful planning to minimize the impact on business operations. Let's learn about the migration steps.

Database Migration Steps

Database migration, particularly heterogeneous migration from an on-premises environment to a cloud database, is a complex and critical process involving multiple steps. Each phase ensures smooth and secure migration, and the new system meets the required functional and performance standards. Here are the typical steps involved in this type of migration:

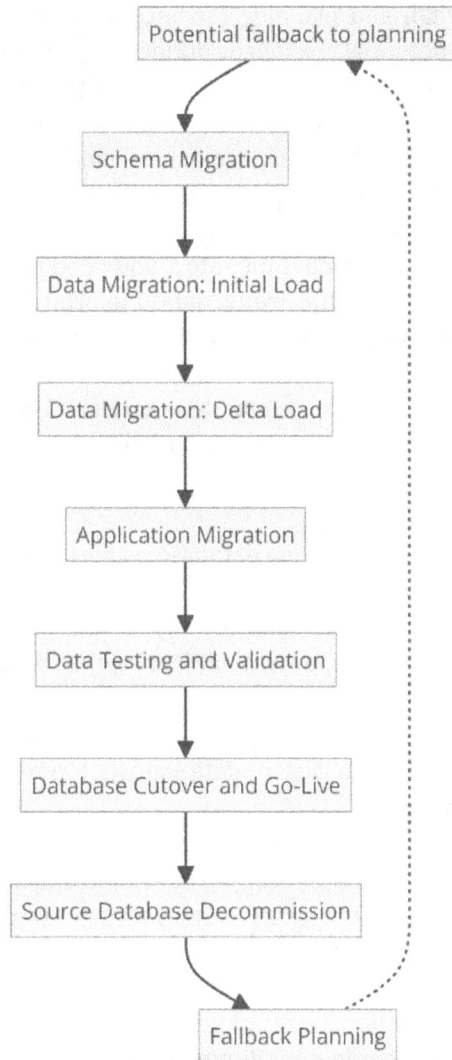

Figure 9.2 – Database Migration Steps

As shown in the preceding, here are the steps for database migration :

1. **Planning and Assessment**: The first step is thoroughly evaluating the existing database environment, which includes understanding the database schema, data volume, dependencies, and performance requirements. Choosing the appropriate cloud database service, such as Amazon RDS, Azure SQL Database, or Google Cloud SQL, is crucial to best align with your organizational needs. Assessing the compatibility between the source and

target databases is vital, and planning for necessary data transformations or schema changes will mitigate potential challenges during the migration.

2. **Schema Migration**: The migration process begins with extracting the schema from the on-premises database and adapting it to the target cloud database. This step may involve converting data types, modifying object names, and adjusting constraints to ensure compatibility with the cloud database system. Utilizing database migration tools or scripts can automate and streamline this process.

3. **Data Migration**: Once the schema is migrated, you need to transfer the actual data from the on-premises database to the cloud database. This step can be time-consuming, especially if you have large volumes of data. You can use various data migration techniques, such as logical backup and restore transactional replication, or bulk data transfer methods like SQL Server Integration Services (SSIS) or Google/AWS Database Migration Service (DMS). This step has two phases:

   - **Phase 1: Initial Load**
     - Start by recording the database system time before the migration to track changes made.
     - Execute an initial load to migrate the dataset from the source to the target database, potentially locking the source database briefly to ensure data consistency.
     - Despite ongoing changes at the source during this phase, this step aims to migrate a consistent data snapshot to the target environment.
   - **Phase 2: Delta Load**
     - Continue the migration from where the initial load stopped, applying changes from the recorded start time onwards.
     - Utilize transaction logs to apply changes to the target database, ensuring no duplications occur and that all subsequent data modifications are synchronized.
     - Adjust the batch sizes of data changes to balance the load on the source system and minimize discrepancies as the target database catches up.

4. **Application Migration:** If your applications or services interact with the on-premises database, you need to update them to connect to the new cloud database. This may involve modifying connection strings, updating database credentials, and adjusting application configurations.

5. **Data Testing and Validation**: Thoroughly test and validate the migrated database and applications to ensure data integrity, functionality, and performance. Test various scenarios, including CRUD operations, queries, stored procedures, and application functionality. Identify and resolve any issues or discrepancies.

6. **Database Cutover and Go-Live**: Plan for the final cutover and go-live phase once testing is successful. This may involve synchronizing the final data changes, updating DNS

records, and switching applications to use the new cloud database. Depending on the project requirements, you may need to schedule a maintenance window or plan for minimal downtime during the cutover.

7. **Source databases decommission**: Once the switchover to the production databases is finished, you can decommission the source databases. Before decommissioning them, it is recommended that you make a final backup of each source database. Doing so provides a clear snapshot of the final state of the data, which can still be accessed if needed. Taking these final backups also allows you to comply with any data regulations that require maintaining backups for compliance purposes.

8. **Fallback Planning**: Implementing a contingency plan, or fallback system, can provide critical safeguards in case issues arise during your database migration. A fallback function is like a reverse migration, switching clients from target to source databases. To enable this, after backing up all databases, set up migration processes that track changes to the target databases and sync them back to the source databases before the switchover. This keeps the source databases up-to-date in case a fallback is needed days or weeks later. For example, if clients encounter broken functionality in the new system that cannot be quickly repaired, they can switch back to the source databases. Before this, any changes made to the target databases must migrate back to the source to synchronize the data. Some key points for designing an effective fallback system:

   - Target schemas must allow reversible migrations, such as avoiding aggregations that would prevent reversing individual data migrations.
   - If source databases have transaction logs but target databases do not, reverse migrations must rely on differential queries. This should be built into the target schema design.
   - Keep the original client systems operational to turn them on during a fallback. Mirror any client-facing functional changes made to the new system.
   - Treat implementing fallbacks like a full migration, including thorough testing.

   Fallback systems, while a last resort, provide critical safeguards against issues arising during database migrations.

By carefully managing each stage, Database Solutions Architects can ensure a successful migration to cloud database services, enhancing scalability, performance, and cost-efficiency while maintaining data integrity and system reliability.

Whiteboard Database Architect interview

If you are applying for the Database Architect role, you may be asked to draw and explain the architecture of your recent project or present a reference architecture of some database design or migration use case.

Let's take an example. You are the lead database architect for a project to migrate a large enterprise database (e.g., Oracle) from on-premises to a Cloud database. The source and target database engines are different. How would you design the migration architecture and process to minimize downtime and ensure data integrity? The following diagram illustrates a reference architecture of Oracle database migration to Amazon RDS:

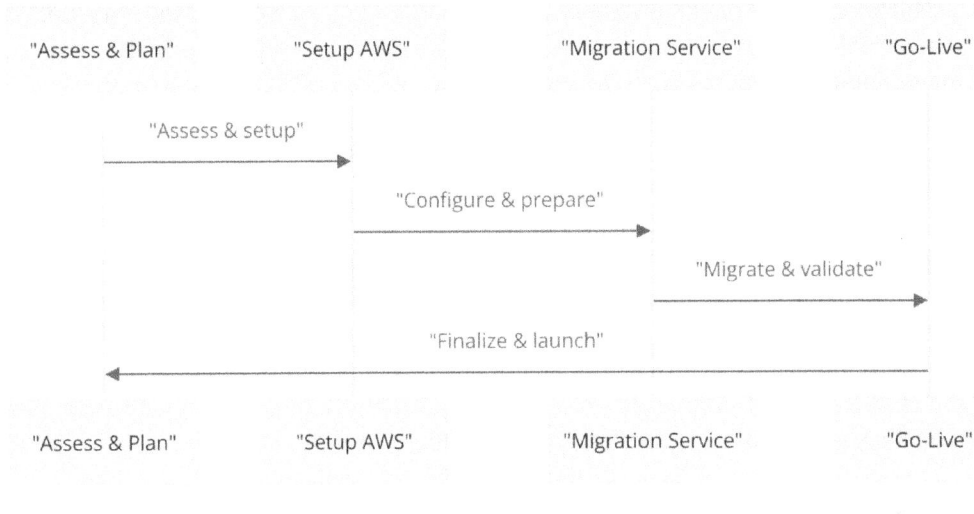

Figure 9.3 – Database Migration from On-premise to Cloud

The preceding architecture shows the key components required for executing a database migration. Migrating an on-premises Oracle database to Amazon RDS for PostgreSQL on AWS can be challenging, especially when dealing with different database engines. However, AWS provides various services and tools to streamline this migration process with minimal downtime. Here's a step-by-step high-level guide to help you execute this migration efficiently:

Assess and Plan
- **Evaluate Migration Complexity**: Begin by assessing the complexity of the migration, taking into account the database schema, data volume, dependencies, and specific features or SQL dialects used in Oracle that might differ in PostgreSQL.
- **Downtime Estimation**: Estimate and plan for potential downtime. Though AWS services aim to minimize this, understanding the impact on operational continuity is critical.
- **Application Changes**: Identify necessary changes in application logic due to differences between Oracle and PostgreSQL, such as variations in SQL syntax, data types, and transaction management.

Setup AWS Environment

- **Create** an AWS Account: If you don't already have one, set one up. Based on your geographical and latency considerations, determine the best region.
- **Provision Amazon RDS Instance**: Deploy an Amazon RDS for PostgreSQL instance, ensuring that its configuration (CPU, memory, storage) aligns with your performance and capacity requirements.
- **Configure Security and Network**: To control access to the RDS instance, implement necessary security measures, including VPC, security groups, and IAM policies.

Prepare the Source Database
- **Ensure Accessibility**: Verify that the on-premises Oracle database is accessible over the network and compatible with AWS migration tools.
- **Setup Database User**: Create or configure a database user with sufficient privileges for the migration process.
- **Manage Log Files**: Check that Oracle's log management is adequate to support an efficient migration, especially for capturing transaction logs during the data transfer.

Use AWS Database Migration Service (DMS)
- **Set Up DMS**: Launch and configure an AWS DMS instance to connect your source Oracle database and the target RDS PostgreSQL instance.
- **Schema Conversion**: Use the AWS Schema Conversion Tool (SCT) to analyze the Oracle database schema and convert it to a PostgreSQL-compatible schema. This tool helps identify and resolve potential migration issues like incompatible data types or unsupported SQL code.
- **Migrate Schema**: After adjustments and validation, use SCT to apply the converted schema to the Amazon RDS instance.

Migrate Data
- **Initial Data Migration**: Perform a full load migration to transfer all existing data from Oracle to PostgreSQL using AWS DMS.
- **Data Validation**: Validate the migrated data to ensure completeness and accuracy.
- **Continuous Data Replication**: Set up ongoing replication to synchronize changes from the Oracle database to PostgreSQL until the cutover is completed.

Cutover and Go-Live
- **Finalize Data Synchronization**: Conduct the final synchronization of data changes during a planned downtime window, ensuring minimal disruption.
- **Switch Application Connections**: Reconfigure applications to connect to the Amazon RDS PostgreSQL instance instead of the Oracle database.
- **Test and Validate**: Thoroughly test the application with the new database to verify functionality and performance meet the required standards.

Decommission the Source Database
- **Backup and Decommission**: Once the migration is successful, perform a final Oracle database backup and decommission the old system to avoid unnecessary maintenance costs.

Post-Migration Activities
- **Performance Tuning**: Monitor and optimize the performance of the Amazon RDS instance, adjusting resources and configurations as necessary based on actual usage patterns.
- **Update Documentation**: Update all relevant documentation to reflect the new system configurations and any changes in operational procedures.
- **Lessons Learned**: Review the migration process to capture lessons learned, enhancing future migration strategies.

By planning and utilizing AWS's powerful migration tools, such as AWS DMS and SCT, you can ensure a seamless and efficient migration from an on-premises Oracle database to Amazon RDS for PostgreSQL, achieving minimal downtime and maintaining data integrity. Throughout this migration, maintain clear communication with all stakeholders and ensure all steps are well-documented and validated.

The reference architecture we use as an example is built on AWS, which utilizes various AWS services to meet the requirements. However, the same concepts could be applied to other cloud providers using their equivalent services. The core concept remains the same even if implemented on different cloud platforms.

Database architect interview questions

Similar to any specialized role, you can expect questions that range from prescriptive to strategic to scenario-based. These questions will measure the depth and breadth of your experience, familiarity with foundational concepts, and real-life situations. You can also expect to write an SQL query or a stored procedure for a specified use case, or you may be provided one and asked to determine the output.

Scenario-based questions

Let's start with complex scenario-based questions and learn how to respond.

Question: You are the lead architect for a growing online marketplace experiencing slow page load times and occasional downtime during peak traffic. The CEO wants to upgrade the infrastructure to improve performance and scalability but has set a strict budget limit due to financial constraints. How would you approach this challenge to balance the need for a high-

quality architecture with the budget limitations? Describe the database strategies you would employ to prioritize upgrades, select cost-effective technologies, and ensure the upgrades deliver the most significant impact on performance and scalability within the budget.

Answer: The following response provides a detailed explanation of all components, accompanied by relevant data.

<u>**Situation:**</u> In the "MarketScale" project, our growing online marketplace faced significant challenges with slow page load times and frequent downtime during peak traffic hours. These performance issues led to frustrated customers abandoning their shopping carts and a noticeable drop in sales. For instance, during our annual sales event, customer complaints about the inability to complete purchases spiked, directly impacting our revenue and damaging our brand reputation. Amidst these operational challenges, the CEO mandated infrastructure upgrades within a strict budget to address these critical issues without straining our financial resources.

<u>**Behavior:**</u> To tackle the challenges of the "MarketScale" project, we conducted a thorough analysis of our infrastructure to identify critical areas for improvement. Prioritizing actions based on cost-effectiveness and impact, we leveraged AWS for its scalability and cost-efficiency. We implemented AWS Auto Scaling to dynamically adjust resources in response to traffic fluctuations, ensuring high availability during peak periods without incurring unnecessary costs during low traffic times.

We integrated Amazon CloudFront as our content delivery network (CDN) to decrease page load times globally by caching content at edge locations closer to users. We migrated to Amazon RDS with read replicas for our database issues to enhance performance and scalability under load. Throughout this process, we utilized AWS CloudWatch for real-time monitoring and performance metrics, enabling us to make data-driven decisions and continuously optimize our infrastructure.

This strategic approach allowed us to address our performance and scalability issues within the budget constraints set by the CEO, ensuring a smoother user experience and more excellent operational stability.

<u>**Impact:**</u> Following the implementation of AWS solutions in the "MarketScale" project, we observed a dramatic improvement in our online marketplace's performance and scalability. Page load times decreased from an average of 8 seconds to 2 seconds, enhancing the customer experience and reducing cart abandonment rates by 30%. The introduction of AWS Auto Scaling and Amazon RDS read replicas effectively eliminated downtime during peak traffic, previously averaging 2 hours monthly, thereby maintaining continuous availability and trust among our users. These technical upgrades led to a noticeable increase in customer satisfaction, with positive feedback doubling within the first-month post-implementation. Sales revenue saw a 20% increase, attributed directly to the improved site performance and reliability.

You can use the following diagram for whiteboarding :

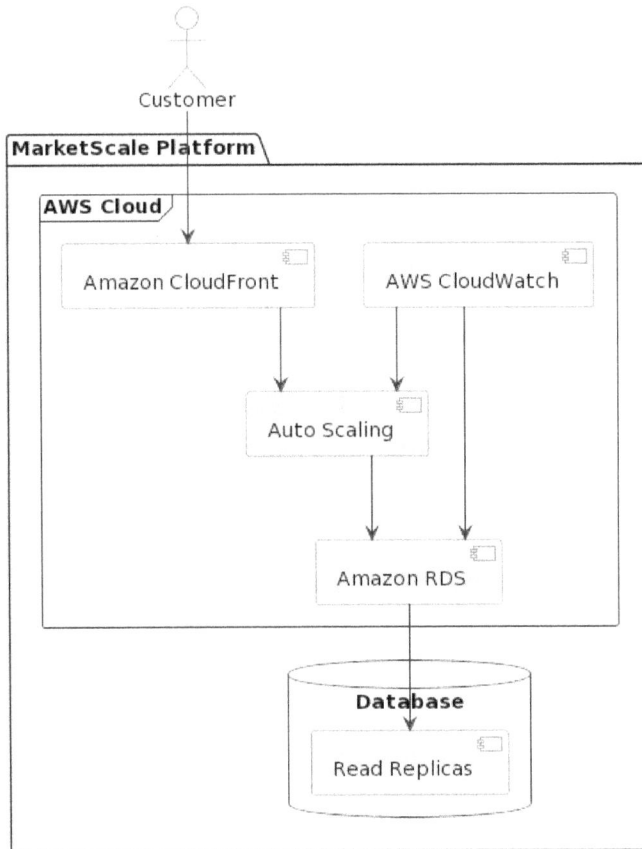

Figure 9.4 – Database Migration from On-premise to Cloud

The preceding diagram shows that the MarketScale Platform utilizes AWS Cloud services to enhance its online marketplace's performance and scalability. Customers access the platform through Amazon CloudFront, which serves content from the nearest edge location, significantly reducing page load times. AWS Auto Scaling dynamically adjusts computing resources based on real-time traffic, ensuring the platform remains responsive during peak periods without incurring unnecessary costs during quieter times.

Amazon RDS, equipped with read replicas, handles database operations, improving data retrieval speeds and overall database performance under heavy load. AWS CloudWatch monitors the system, providing metrics and alerts for performance and operational health. This enables proactive adjustments to Auto Scaling policies and RDS configurations. This architecture ensures that the "MarketScale Platform" can efficiently manage varying traffic volumes, maintain high availability, and deliver a seamless user experience within a strict budget.

Follow-up Questions

- **How does the architecture ensure data consistency across Amazon RDS read replicas, especially during high-traffic events?** This question challenges the assumption that read replicas manage data consistency without latency or conflict issues. Given that read replicas are primarily used to improve read performance, it's essential to understand the mechanisms to handle replication lag and ensure that users see the most current data, especially in a highly dynamic e-commerce environment.

- **What strategies are in place to optimize CloudFront cache hit ratios, ensuring fast and cost-effective content delivery?** This question probes the assumption that simply implementing Amazon CloudFront will maximize performance and cost savings. Optimizing cache hit ratios requires careful configuration of cache behaviors, invalidation practices, and content versioning strategies to reduce the need for frequent origin fetches, which can increase costs and reduce performance benefits.

- **How does the platform handle sudden, unexpected spikes in traffic beyond typical peak levels, considering the limitations of Auto-Scaling response times?** This question challenges the assumption that AWS Auto Scaling can instantly respond to traffic spikes without impacting performance. While effective, auto-scaling is not instantaneous and may incur a short lag before new instances are fully operational. Understanding the measures in place to mitigate potential performance degradation during these scaling events is crucial for maintaining a consistent user experience.

Using RDS read replicas enhances database performance but introduces challenges in ensuring data consistency across replicas, especially during high-traffic periods. While AWS CloudWatch enables proactive monitoring and management, setting up and maintaining effective alerts and metrics can be complex and require significant administrative effort. These tradeoffs highlight the need for a balanced approach, combining AWS's scalability and performance capabilities with diligent management and optimization to achieve the desired outcomes.

Question: Your company's existing e-commerce platform is built on a technology stack that is becoming obsolete, leading to increased maintenance costs and difficulties in adding new features. The decision has been made to migrate to a more modern, flexible stack to support the platform's future direction better. How would you plan and execute database migration, ensuring minimal disruption to current operations? Discuss how you would select the new technology stack, manage the transition of data and services, and train your development team on the latest technologies.
Answer: The following response provides a detailed explanation of all components, accompanied by relevant data.

<u>Situation:</u> In the "NextGen Commerce" project, our company confronted the limitations of an outdated technology stack underpinning our e-commerce platform. This obsolete foundation led to spiraling maintenance costs and significant hurdles in implementing new features, such as

integrating advanced payment options or deploying a responsive design for mobile users. Customers experienced slower site performance and a lack of innovative shopping features, directly impacting their satisfaction and our platform's competitive edge.

Behavior: In the "NextGen Commerce" project, we modernized our e-commerce platform by embarking on a strategic migration to a contemporary, flexible technology stack, selecting AWS as our foundational infrastructure. We evaluated and chose AWS services for their scalability, reliability, and broad support ecosystem. Our new stack included Amazon EC2 for scalable computing capacity, Amazon RDS for managed database services to ensure high availability and performance, and Amazon S3 for cost-effective, durable object storage.

We executed the migration in phases, starting with non-critical systems to minimize operational disruption. We utilized AWS Database Migration Service to streamline the data transition from old databases to Amazon RDS, ensuring data integrity and minimizing downtime. We adopted Amazon CloudFront for the front end to deliver content efficiently worldwide, improving site performance. Parallel to the technical migration, we launched a training program for our development team, focusing on AWS certifications and practical workshops to accelerate their proficiency in the new environment.

This phased approach, supported by AWS's robust ecosystem, allowed for a smooth transition. It enabled us to test and refine our deployment with minimal impact on current operations.

Impact: After migrating the "NextGen Commerce" project to AWS, we significantly improved customer experience and technical performance. Site load times decreased from 8 seconds to under 2 seconds, directly enhancing user satisfaction and reducing bounce rates by 40%. The adoption of Amazon RDS and Amazon EC2 increased our platform's uptime from 99.5% to 99.99%, ensuring a reliable shopping experience during peak traffic periods.

From a technical standpoint, maintenance costs were reduced by 30% due to the efficiency and scalability of AWS services. The ability to rapidly deploy new features improved, with the development cycle for introducing new functionalities shortened from months to weeks. This agility enabled us to respond more effectively to market trends and customer feedback, leading to a 25% increase in monthly active users and a 20% rise in sales revenue within the first six months post-migration.

You can use the following diagram for whiteboarding :

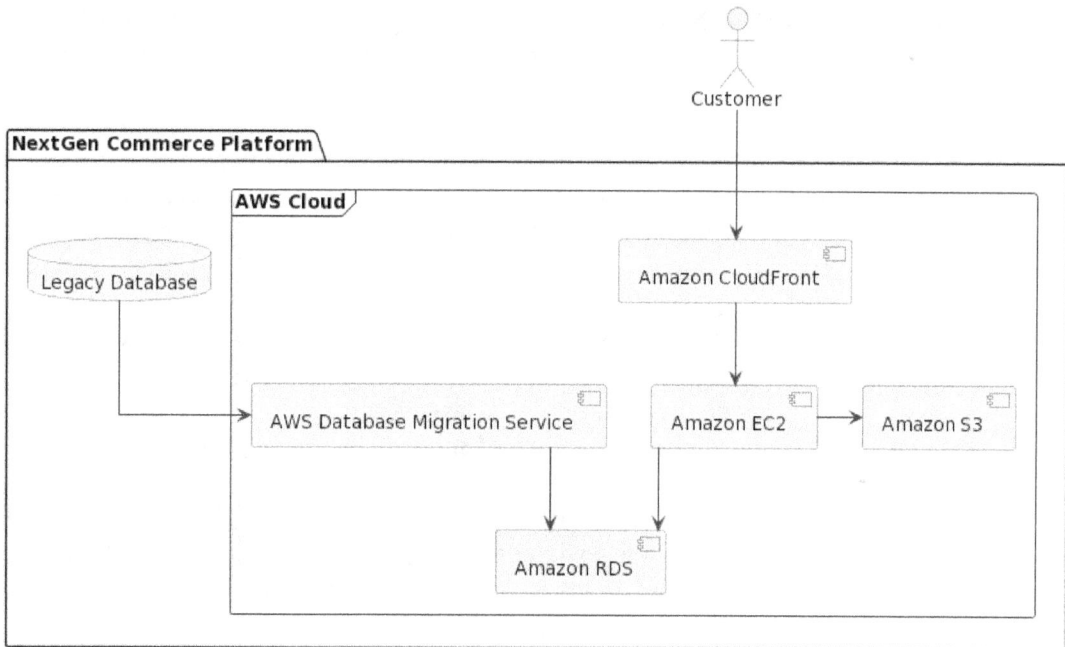

Figure 9.5 – Migration from legacy to Cloud database

The preceding diagram shows that the "NextGen Commerce Platform" leverages AWS Cloud services to modernize its e-commerce architecture, enhancing scalability, performance, and reliability. Customers interact with the platform through Amazon CloudFront, which efficiently delivers content worldwide, reducing load times and improving user experience. The application's core operations are hosted on Amazon EC2 instances, providing scalable computing resources for user requests and backend processes.

Amazon RDS manages data storage, offering a high-performance, reliable database service that ensures data integrity and availability. Amazon S3 is utilized for storing static content and assets, benefiting from its durability and scalability. During the migration phase, the AWS Database Migration Service facilitates the seamless data transfer from the legacy database to Amazon RDS, minimizing downtime and ensuring a smooth transition.

This architecture improves the platform's operational efficiency and provides a foundation for rapid feature development and deployment, directly contributing to enhanced customer satisfaction and business growth.

Follow-up Questions
- **How does the architecture ensure data security and compliance with international data protection regulations, such as GDPR, when using AWS services like Amazon RDS and**

S3? This question challenges the assumption that moving to AWS automatically ensures compliance with all relevant data protection and privacy regulations. Given the global reach of e-commerce platforms, understanding the specific measures and configurations needed to protect user data and comply with laws across different jurisdictions is crucial.

- **Given the variable load of e-commerce platforms, what strategies are in place to optimize costs associated with AWS services, particularly Amazon EC2 and RDS?** This question probes the assumption that cloud scalability directly translates to cost efficiency. E-commerce platforms can experience significant fluctuations in traffic, leading to potential cost spikes. It's essential to explore how the architecture leverages AWS pricing models, such as reserved instances or auto-scaling policies, to manage and predict costs effectively.

- **How does the architecture address potential latency and performance issues for global users, considering the centralized nature of services like Amazon RDS?** This question challenges the assumption that AWS services inherently provide low latency and high performance for users worldwide. E-commerce platforms serve a global customer base, and data retrieval from a centralized database can introduce latency. Understanding the deployment of multi-region databases or caching strategies to minimize response times is essential for maintaining a seamless user experience.

Data compliance across different regions demands a thorough understanding of international protection laws. The centralized nature of services such as Amazon RDS may also necessitate strategies like multi-region deployment or caching to address latency for a worldwide user base. These tradeoffs highlight the importance of strategic planning and continuous optimization to leverage AWS's full potential while mitigating potential drawbacks.

Here are some more scenario-based questions and tips to answer them:

Question: **You are the lead database architect for a project to migrate a large enterprise database from on-premises to Cloud. The current database is around 50TB, with approximately 500 million rows across hundreds of tables. Many applications and services rely on this database running 24/7 with at least 99.9% uptime. How would you design the migration architecture and process to minimize downtime and ensure data integrity? Be specific on Cloud services, schema, and data migration strategies, handling continuing data changes during migration, verification testing, cutover steps, and rollback contingency.**

Tips: Emphasize incremental data migration, which minimizes downtime by continuously syncing the delta changes from the on-premises database to the cloud database while the former is still in operation. Highlight specific cloud tools such as AWS Database Migration Service (DMS) that can handle complex migrations by replicating data with minimal performance impact. Stress the importance of a detailed pre-migration assessment to identify potential compatibility issues between Oracle and PostgreSQL, using schema conversion tools to facilitate adjustments in data types and stored procedures.

Question: Design a scalable database architecture for a large e-commerce company. The company sells products online and has over 50 million users. The database must support high volumes of reads and writes for user profiles, product information, orders, etc. Consider factors like scalability, high availability, redundancy, caching, sharding, replication, etc. Draw out the overall architecture, including the web servers, application servers, databases, caching layers, etc. Explain your design choices.

Tips: Discuss building a multi-tiered database architecture where transactional data is handled by a relational database management system (RDBMS) such as PostgreSQL for ACID compliance, while user interactions that require high availability and scalability, such as user profiles and product catalogs, are managed by NoSQL databases like MongoDB or Cassandra. Mention implementing database sharding to distribute data across multiple nodes to enhance read/write performance and using replication to ensure data availability and fault tolerance.

Question: Design a database architecture for a social media site with hundreds of millions of users. The site must store user profiles, posts, comments, photos, videos, user relationships, etc. Discuss how you would structure the databases and tables to optimize for huge volumes of reads and writes. Consider challenges like scalability, consistency, redundancy, caching, partitioning, etc. Draw out your suggested architecture, including the components like load balancers, web servers, app servers, database clusters, caching layers, etc. Explain how your design would handle massive concurrency and throughput while maintaining low latency. Discuss tradeoffs you need to make.

Tips: Suggest employing a polyglot persistence architecture, where different data types are stored in the most suitable database systems. For example, graph databases like Neo4j can manage complex relationships such as friendships and interactions, and a key-value store can quickly retrieve posts or messages. Outline the use of caching mechanisms such as Redis or Memcached to store frequently accessed data such as user sessions and news feed content, reducing the load on the database and improving response times.

Question: Explain how you would design a database that needs to support millions of reads and writes per second with low latency. Discuss partitioning, indexing, caching, load balancing, etc.

Tips: Focus on implementing a finely tuned partitioning strategy where data is horizontally partitioned across multiple database instances to spread the load evenly and reduce bottlenecks. Discuss using SSD storage for faster data access speeds and how proper indexing strategies, particularly compound indexes, can significantly reduce query times. Highlight load balancers' role in effectively distributing client requests across servers, ensuring no single server becomes a performance bottleneck.

Question: Design a database schema for a social media site. Consider relationships between users, posts, comments, likes, etc. Discuss normalization, denormalization, and NoSQL modeling.

Tips: Delve into the design specifics by recommending denormalization for frequently accessed tables like posts or comments to improve read performance at the cost of additional storage and slightly slower writes. Discuss the implementation of NoSQL document stores for flexible schema requirements and using graph databases to traverse complex user relationships and interactions efficiently in real time.

Question: **Design a database syncing/replication architecture between a mobile app and a cloud database. Consider latency, offline use cases, and conflict resolution.**
Tips: Outline the use of a conflict resolution protocol, such as vector clocks or last-write-wins strategies, to manage data consistency when multiple users modify the same record offline. Discuss the importance of a robust synchronization framework that supports automatic conflict detection and resolution, ensuring data integrity is maintained across devices.

Question: **Design a database backup and recovery strategy for a financial transaction database that needs to preserve ACID semantics. Consider failover, RAID, replication, snapshots, etc.**
Tips: Elaborate on implementing a comprehensive disaster recovery plan that includes synchronous and asynchronous replication to different geographic locations. Discuss the benefits of using storage solutions with built-in RAID configurations for data redundancy and point-in-time snapshots to quickly recover to a previous state in case of data corruption or loss.

Question: **Design a time-series database architecture for storing IoT sensor data. Consider data retention, compression, and queries for telemetry analytics.**
Tips: Propose using specialized time-series databases like InfluxDB, which offer built-in time-based aggregation and downsampling functions. Discuss the importance of data retention policies that automatically purge old data to free up storage space and the use of continuous queries to pre-compute frequently requested information for faster access.

When addressing these questions, provide structured answers that showcase your knowledge of database design, performance tuning, and migration strategies. It's crucial to tailor your response to reflect an understanding of the specific requirements and challenges of the scenario provided. Discuss the importance of scalability, data integrity, and system resilience. Emphasize a proactive approach in planning, robust testing, and the ability to foresee and mitigate potential issues with a well-thought-out fallback strategy. This approach demonstrates your comprehensive skill in the data domain.

By expanding on these points, you can provide well-rounded and insightful answers that demonstrate a deep understanding of various database architectures and management strategies, showcasing your expertise in a way that aligns with the needs of a database solutions architect role.

Behavioral Questions

Let's start with behavioral questions that the interviewer may ask to understand your experience and how you handle on-job real-time scenarios:

Question: Tell me a time when you built a database system from scratch. What was your approach and outcome? What challenges have you faced?

Answer: Let's consider a hypothetical scenario to illustrate how Database SA approaches building a database system from scratch, including the approach taken, outcomes, and challenges faced using the STAR format.

Situation: MedCare Inc. faced challenges in efficiently managing patient records, appointments, and medical histories. It was using an outdated system that needed to be faster, compliant with healthcare standards, and able to handle increasing data loads.

Task: As the lead Database Solutions Architect, I designed and implemented a new database system from scratch. The goals were to streamline data management, ensure HIPAA compliance, improve data security, and enhance overall performance to handle 50,000 patient records and approximately 1,000 daily transactions.

Action: I conducted a thorough requirements analysis by conducting detailed discussions with ten healthcare professionals and five IT staff to gather precise project needs. Based on this information, I developed an Entity-Relationship Diagram (ERD) representing 30 entities, ensuring each was normalized up to the third normal form (3NF) to minimize data redundancy. For the database system, I selected PostgreSQL due to its robustness and strong compliance features. I integrated supportive tools like pgAdmin for database management and OpenSSL for data encryption.

In the schema design and development phase, I implemented a schema that included 25 tables, prioritizing security and data integrity. I constructed the database using SQL and wrote 15 stored procedures to encapsulate business logic, enhancing maintainability and security. To optimize performance, I indexed ten critical columns and rewrote 20 complex SQL queries, which reduced the average query response time by 40%.

Security measures were a major focus; I implemented AES-256 encryption for sensitive data and configured role-based access controls to meet HIPAA compliance requirements. The system underwent rigorous load testing, simulating 2,000 concurrent users, which helped identify and rectify performance bottlenecks. Finally, I prepared and delivered comprehensive training, including creating a detailed user manual. I conducted three training sessions for 50 staff members, emphasizing the new system's security features and efficient usage to ensure a smooth transition and adoption.

Result: Within six months, I successfully deployed the database system, which has since maintained a remarkable 99.98% uptime. This implementation significantly enhanced data retrieval efficiency by 50% and drastically reduced the occurrence of duplicate data entries. One of the pivotal achievements of this project was ensuring 100% HIPAA compliance, with no breaches or compliance issues reported in the first year of operation.

The new system received overwhelmingly positive feedback from healthcare staff, who praised its ease of use and performance. This feedback underscores a substantial 30% increase in overall operational efficiency, demonstrating the tangible benefits of the new database system. Moreover, MedCare Inc. is now better equipped to handle increased patient loads and meet future scalability requirements, ensuring the organization can adapt to growing demands while maintaining high patient care and data security standards.

In the STAR format, this response illustrates a structured approach to tackling a significant project. It highlights specific actions and quantifiable results, making the scenario more concrete for an interview context.

Follow-Up Question :

The interviewer may ask follow-up questions to gain deeper insights into your technical expertise, problem-solving skills, and strategic thinking, all crucial traits for a Database Solutions Architect. Here are some follow-up questions for the previous answer.

Question: How did you ensure the new database system remained scalable and adaptable to future technological advancements and increasing patient data volumes?
Tips :
- **Focus on Scalability Solutions**: Discuss specific scalability features you implemented, such as database partitioning or cloud-based solutions allowing easy scaling.
- **Mention Future-Proofing Measures**: In this scenario, consider selecting technologies with robust community support and regular updates, such as PostgreSQL.
- **Highlight Ongoing Assessment**: Emphasize your plan for regular system evaluations to adapt and upgrade as technology evolves and data volumes grow.

Question: Can you describe a significant challenge you faced during this project and how you overcame it?
Tips :
- **Identify a Specific Challenge**: Choose a significant hurdle, such as data migration issues or integrating the new system with existing healthcare applications.
- **Describe Your Problem-Solving Approach**: Detail your steps to address the challenge, highlighting your analytical and problem-solving skills.
- **Focus on Positive Outcomes**: Conclude by explaining how overcoming this challenge improved the project or contributed to your personal growth as a professional.

Question: How did you ensure data integrity and compliance with healthcare regulations, particularly HIPAA, during the database design and implementation?

Tips:

- **Detail Compliance Strategies**: Discuss specific actions taken for HIPAA compliance, like implementing AES-256 encryption and role-based access controls.
- **Mention Collaboration with Legal/Compliance Teams**: Highlight any collaboration with legal or compliance experts to ensure the system meets all regulatory requirements.
- **Focus on Data Integrity Mechanisms**: Explain how you used database constraints, validations, and regular audits to maintain data integrity and prevent unauthorized access.

Technical Questions

Here are a few common questions you can use as a starting point. While each question has tips for answering, you must ensure each response is tailored to the specific scenario. This will demonstrate your understanding of database architecture and ability to apply these concepts in real-world situations.

Question: How would you design a scalable database architecture to handle sporadic growth while ensuring high availability and performance?

Tip: Focus on a solution that balances scalability with performance, such as cloud-based services for elasticity and sharding for data distribution. Mention the use of read replicas for handling read-heavy workloads. Design a cloud-based SQL database, leveraging auto-scaling and sharding to handle growth. We can efficiently manage read operations and ensure performance even during peak usage by using read replicas.

Question: Explain your considerations for parameterizing stored procedures to ensure optimal performance and reusability.

Tip: Highlight the importance of security, particularly against SQL injection, and the benefits of reduced query recompilation. Parameterizing stored procedures is crucial for security and performance. For instance, in a user authentication system, parameterized queries enhances security against SQL injection and improves execution time by reducing recompilation.

Question: Describe different mechanisms to handle data validation and business rules within a stored procedure.

Tip: Discuss the importance of input validation, error handling, and enforcing data integrity within the procedure. In a stored procedure for financial transactions, implement data format checks and value range validations to ensure accuracy and prevent processing errors.

Question: Explain the differences between the INNER JOIN, LEFT JOIN, RIGHT JOIN, and FULL JOIN operations in SQL.

Tip: Give a clear and concise explanation of each JOIN type, focusing on how they manage matched and unmatched rows. INNER JOIN returns rows with matching values in both tables, while LEFT JOIN includes all rows from the left table, even if there are no matches in the right table.

Question: How would you ensure data isolation and security between tenants for a multi-tenant SaaS application?

Tip: Discuss using separate schemas or database instances and robust authentication mechanisms. In a PostgreSQL-based CRM, separate schemas for each tenant should be implemented to ensure data isolation, along with strong authentication and authorization controls.

Question: Provide an example of a normalization process.

Tip: Describe breaking down a complex table into multiple related tables to reduce redundancy and enhance data integrity. In a sales database, normalization involves separating a table with customer and order details into two: one for customer information and another for orders, linked by a customer ID."

Question: How would you optimize a slow-performing SQL query?

Tip: Focus on indexing strategies, query restructuring, and potentially using materialized views. For a report-generating query, I'd analyze execution plans to identify bottlenecks, apply relevant indexes, and consider restructuring the query for efficiency.

Question: Explain the differences between the UNION, UNION ALL, INTERSECT, and EXCEPT operators with examples.

Tip: Give clear definitions and practical use cases for each operator. UNION combines results from two queries and removes duplicates, while UNION ALL includes duplicates. INTERSECT returns common rows, and EXCEPT gives rows in the first query that are not found in the second.

Question: Write a stored procedure that inserts a new record into multiple related tables, ensuring data integrity.

Tip: Mention transaction management and error handling. In a CRM system, the stored procedure starts a transaction, inserts a new customer record, and adds associated contact details in a related table. If any step fails, error handling rolls back the transaction.

Question: How would you assess the feasibility of migrating from an RDBMS to a NoSQL database?

Tip: Discuss data structure, scalability needs, and consistency requirements. If the data is more unstructured and requires horizontal scalability, a move to a NoSQL database like MongoDB could be beneficial.

Question: Provide an example of how triggers can be used to enforce business rules or maintain data integrity.

Tip: Explain a scenario where triggers automatically enforce rules or update related data. **For** example, in an inventory management system, a trigger on the sales table could automatically update the stock levels in the inventory table upon each sale.

These questions test your knowledge and experience in database design, optimization, and problem-solving. Be ready to provide context, rationale, and technical details in your answers, demonstrating your proficiency as a database solutions architect.

Summary

The role of a Database Solutions Architect is explored in depth, emphasizing the critical importance of aligning database technologies with strategic business objectives. The chapter thoroughly explains Database Management Systems (DBMS), detailing their functions in data organization, security, and integrity. It delves into the nuances of different DBMS types, particularly focusing on relational and NoSQL databases' contrasting structures and applications. The chapter underscores the necessity of proficiency in SQL for managing relational databases, highlighting key SQL functions and operations.

Most of the chapter is dedicated to database design principles, which discuss data modeling, normalization, and denormalization techniques. Data indexing and query optimization are highlighted, emphasizing how these practices enhance database performance and efficiency. Data integrity constraints are examined, stressing their role in maintaining the accuracy and consistency of data within the database.

The chapter then focuses on best practices for database performance tuning, high availability, and scalability. It offers insights into strategies for optimizing database performance, ensuring that databases are robust and capable of handling high workloads with minimal downtime. The chapter also discusses the scalability of databases in traditional and Cloud environments, providing a comprehensive view of how databases can grow and adapt to changing business needs.

As cloud computing continues to reshape the technology landscape, the chapter addresses the integration of cloud database solutions, highlighting their unique features and the considerations they entail in database architecture.

Lastly, the chapter prepares readers for the interview process, presenting various questions that a Database Solutions Architect might encounter. These questions range from technical aspects of database management to scenario-based queries that test a candidate's problem-solving skills and understanding of database systems. This section is instrumental for professionals preparing for interviews, providing them with the knowledge and confidence needed to excel in this field.

This is an essential resource for anyone aspiring to become a Database Solutions Architect. It blends detailed technical information with practical advice and interview preparation. As a comprehensive guide, it equips you with the knowledge and skills necessary to succeed in the dynamic field of database architecture.

Chapter 10 - Cracking ML and Gen AI Solutions Architect Interview

In the rapidly evolving fields of Machine Learning (ML) and Generative AI (GenAI), the role of a Solutions Architect is both challenging and pivotal. Tasked with bridging the gap between complex AI technologies and practical business applications, these architects play a crucial role in shaping the future of AI-driven solutions. This chapter delves into the intricacies of this role, highlighting the blend of deep technical knowledge and strategic thinking required to excel. From understanding advanced ML algorithms to grasping the nuances of Generative AI models, the chapter sets the stage for a comprehensive exploration of the foundational concepts that underpin these revolutionary technologies.

The journey through the world of ML and GenAI is incomplete without mastering the tools and technologies that drive innovation in this space. This chapter provides a detailed overview of the latest frameworks, platforms, and tools essential for developing cutting-edge AI solutions. It guides readers on effectively utilizing these resources, ensuring the creation of robust and impactful AI applications. Additionally, it emphasizes the critical role of data in AI, exploring strategies for data management and model training. From selecting the right datasets to optimizing model performance, this section equips aspiring architects with the know-how to handle data effectively, an essential step in developing successful AI solutions.

Preparing for a Solutions Architect interview in ML and Generative AI involves showcasing a blend of technical understanding and strategic insight. This chapter concludes with a segment on interview preparation, including potential questions and model answers. These resources help candidates articulate their ML and Generative AI knowledge, demonstrate problem-solving skills, and highlight their ability to apply AI technologies in real-world scenarios. This chapter includes the following topics:

- Understanding the ML and Generative AI Solutions Architect Role
- Key Concepts in Machine Learning and Generative AI
- Tools and Technologies for ML and Generative AI
- Data Management and Model Training
- Ethical Considerations and Bias in AI
- Preparing for the GenAI and ML Solutions Architect Interview
- Sample Interview Questions and Answers

This comprehensive guide aims to equip aspiring architects with the knowledge and confidence to excel in interviews, paving the way for successful careers in the dynamic and transformative field of ML and Generative AI. Let's start now, Shall we?

Understanding the ML and Gen AI SA Role

In today's fast-paced technological landscape, the role of an ML and Gen AI Solutions Architect is becoming increasingly crucial. This position requires a unique blend of skills and knowledge, combining deep technical expertise in artificial intelligence with a keen understanding of business needs and strategies. As a Solutions Architect specializing in AI/ML, you are responsible for designing and overseeing the implementation of complex AI-driven systems. This involves a thorough understanding of machine learning algorithms and data science principles and an insight into the latest advancements in Generative AI.

Your role encompasses various responsibilities, including identifying business opportunities where ML and Generative AI can provide value, conceptualizing and designing AI models tailored to specific business problems, and translating these models into scalable and sustainable solutions. You need to be adept at working with various stakeholders, from data scientists and engineers to business leaders, ensuring that the AI solutions align with the organization's goals and integrate seamlessly with existing systems.

As an AI/ML SA, you are expected to be at the forefront of emerging trends and technologies. This means staying up-to-date with the latest field developments, including new model architectures, advancements in deep learning, and data processing techniques. By keeping up with these advancements, you can apply cutting-edge solutions to real-world problems, driving innovation and competitive advantage for your organization. The top Critical Skills for AI/ML SA are:

- **Deep Understanding of AI and ML Concepts:** An AI/ML SA must thoroughly grasp AI and ML fundamentals. This includes an in-depth knowledge of various algorithms, machine learning models, Foundation models, and their practical applications. It is crucial for architects to articulate these complex ideas effectively during interviews. This skill ensures that architects can bridge the gap between theoretical AI/ML knowledge and practical business applications.
- **Experience with Generative AI Models:** Proficiency in Generative Adversarial Networks (GANs), Variational Autoencoders (VAEs), and other generative foundation models is essential. The architect should understand these models' unique capabilities and limitations and their suitability for different projects. This expertise enables them to leverage generative AI to create innovative solutions, such as realistic image generation or advanced data augmentation.
- **Proficiency in Programming and Data Science Tools:** Mastery of programming languages like Python and R and platforms like TensorFlow and PyTorch is vital. This skill extends to being adept with various data science libraries, enabling the architect to build and prototype AI solutions efficiently. Such technical proficiency is fundamental for developing, testing, and refining machine learning models.

- **Data Engineering Knowledge:** The ability to manage and manipulate large datasets is crucial. Understanding data preprocessing, cleaning, augmentation, and storage techniques ensures the architect can prepare and optimize data for effective model training. This skill is essential in the context of big data and when dealing with unstructured data sources.
- **Model Development and Deployment:** Developing, training, and deploying ML models require a combination of technical know-how and practical skills. Familiarity with cloud platforms and containerization technologies is key to deploying scalable AI solutions. This skill ensures that the AI systems designed are effective in a controlled environment and performant and reliable in real-world applications.
- **Problem-Solving and Analytical Skills:** A solutions architect should excel at applying AI and ML to solve complex business challenges. This involves designing technically sound solutions that align closely with business objectives. Analytical skills aid in interpreting data and model outputs to make informed decisions.
- **Understanding of Ethical Implications:** Being aware of AI's ethical aspects and potential biases is critical. Architects should know how to develop AI solutions that are fair, unbiased, and responsible. This skill is increasingly important as AI systems become more prevalent, ensuring that they are trustworthy and ethically sound.

During interviews, candidates should be prepared to demonstrate these skills through technical explanations, scenario-based problem-solving, and discussions of past projects or experiences. Interviewers often look for a combination of technical expertise and the ability to apply this knowledge in a business context. For example, consider an e-commerce company looking to enhance customer experience through personalized recommendations. In this scenario, an AI/ML SA would be responsible for designing an AI system that analyzes customer data (purchase history, browsing behavior, preferences) and employs machine learning algorithms to generate tailored product recommendations. This not only enhances user experience but also drives sales and customer loyalty.

Your AI/ML SA role is multifaceted and dynamic, requiring a balance of technical expertise, strategic thinking, and collaborative skills. You are a key driver in transforming how organizations leverage AI, making impactful decisions that shape the future of technology and business.

Key Concepts in Machine Learning and Generative AI

Machine Learning and Generative AI encompass a range of concepts foundational to understanding how these technologies work and their applications. Here's an overview of some of these key concepts:

Machine Learning Algorithms

Understanding the diverse array of ML algorithms is a fundamental requirement for any solutions architect. These algorithms are the engines that drive the analytical capabilities of ML applications, enabling them to learn from data, make predictions, and enhance decision-making processes. Let's take a high-level view of various ML algorithms with which AI/ML solutions architects should be familiar.

Supervised Learning Algorithms: Supervised learning stands at the core of many ML applications, characterized by labeled data. In this model, the algorithm is 'trained' on a dataset that includes both the input features and the desired output (the labels), allowing the model to learn the relationship between the two. Post-training, the model can predict the production of new, unseen data. Key concepts and applications of supervised ML models are:

- **Classification and Regression:** Supervised Learning is predominantly used for classification (classifying data into predefined classes) and regression (predicting continuous values). In healthcare, classification algorithms classify patient symptoms into specific diseases, while regression algorithms predict patient recovery times.
- **Popular Algorithms:** This category includes algorithms for regression tasks, Logistic Regression, Decision Trees, and Support Vector Machines (SVM) for classification tasks.

Supervised learning algorithms are widely used in various industry sectors, from predicting customer churn in businesses to detecting fraudulent transactions in banking.

Unsupervised Learning Algorithms: Unsupervised learning algorithms are utilized when the data lacks labels. These algorithms aim to uncover hidden patterns or intrinsic structures within the data without the guidance of a predetermined outcome. Key concepts and applications of unsupervised ML models are:

- **Clustering and Dimensionality Reduction:** Common uses of unsupervised Learning include clustering (grouping data points based on similarities) and dimensionality reduction (reducing the number of variables in the dataset while retaining essential information). For example, in marketing, clustering can help identify distinct customer segments for targeted campaigns.
- **Popular Algorithms:** Algorithms like K-Means for clustering and Principal Component Analysis (PCA) for dimensionality reduction are frequently employed in unsupervised learning scenarios.

The absence of labels makes unsupervised Learning a more challenging yet exploratory domain. It is often used for data exploration and discovering insights that are only occasionally apparent.

Semi-supervised Learning Algorithms: Semi-supervised Learning presents a middle ground in machine learning, utilizing labeled and unlabeled data. This approach is beneficial when acquiring labeled data, which is expensive or labor-intensive, but unlabeled data are abundant. Key concepts and applications of semi-supervised ML models are:

- **Combination of Labeled and Unlabeled Data**: Semi-supervised learning algorithms use a small amount of labeled data to guide the learning process and a larger set of unlabeled data to enhance their understanding and performance.
- **Applications in Limited Label Scenarios**: Ideal for situations where data labeling is costly or impractical. For instance, while labeled images might be scarce in medical imaging, many unlabeled images can improve diagnostic accuracy.
- **Popular Techniques**: Semi-supervised learning commonly uses self-training (where the model labels the unlabeled data) and co-training (where two models are trained separately on different data views).

Semi-supervised Learning is invaluable in domains like language translation, where labeled datasets are limited for certain language pairs, but large amounts of text are available.

Active Learning: Active Learning is an approach where the algorithm actively queries a user (or some other information source) to label new data points with the desired outputs. It's a powerful technique in scenarios where labeling data is expensive, and you want to minimize the amount of data needing labeling. Key concepts and applications of active learning ML models are:

- **Selective Data Labeling**: In active Learning, the model identifies which data points, if labeled, would be most beneficial for Learning. This leads to more efficient use of resources.
- **Iterative Process**: The process is iterative, with the model improving as it receives new labeled examples. It's particularly beneficial when the model is uncertain and needs human input to improve its predictions.
- **Applications in Complex Decision-Making**: Active Learning is helpful in complex scenarios like drug discovery, where experts' inputs on certain compounds can significantly steer the direction of the research.
- **Integration with Expert Knowledge**: By integrating expert domain knowledge into the learning process, active Learning can significantly improve the efficiency and accuracy of the model.

Active Learning is especially effective at reducing labeling costs and time while maximizing the model's performance. It's a strategic choice in environments where expert knowledge is crucial for guiding the learning process.

Reinforcement Learning Algorithms: This is a distinct type of ML where algorithms learn to make decisions by interacting with an environment. Here, the Learning is driven by feedback in the form of rewards or penalties, encouraging the algorithm to develop a strategy that maximizes the cumulative reward. Key concepts and applications of Reinforcement ML models are:

- **Agents and Decision-Making:** The core of reinforcement learning is the concept of an agent learning to make decisions through trial and error. This approach is akin to teaching a robot to navigate a maze, where each successful step brings a reward.
- **Applications in Complex Environments:** Reinforcement learning excels in complex, dynamic environments where explicit programming is impractical. It's widely used in robotics, game-playing (like AlphaGo), and autonomous vehicles.
- **Algorithmic Frameworks** include Markov Decision Processes (MDP) for modeling the environment and algorithms like Q-learning and Deep Q Networks (DQNs) for learning optimal actions.

Now, let's look at some popular ML algorithms.

Common Algorithms in Machine Learning

In machine learning, selecting the right algorithm is essential to solve use cases. Each algorithm offers a unique analysis method, crucial for interpreting the data accurately. Let's explore some common machine-learning algorithms:

- **Linear Regression** is a fundamental statistical technique used for predictive analysis. It establishes a linear relationship between a dependent variable and one or more independent variables. It's like plotting the best-fit line through a set of data points, allowing for the prediction of new values.
- **Logistic Regression** is contrary to its name; it is used for classification problems, not regression. It predicts the probability of a categorical dependent variable based on one or more independent variables. It's ideal for binary classification tasks, like determining whether an email is spam.
- **Decision Trees**: These are graphical representations of possible solutions to a decision. They resemble a tree structure, with branches representing decision paths and leaves representing outcomes. Decision Trees are intuitive and easy to interpret, making them suitable for classification and regression tasks.
- **Random Forests**: Random Forests utilize a collective approach, combining multiple Decision Trees to form a more precise and stable model. The model's final prediction is derived from the consensus of the individual trees—through voting for classifications and averaging for regression tasks.
- **Support Vector Machines (SVM)**: SVMs are powerful classifiers that work by finding the hyperplane that best separates data points into different classes. They are effective in high-dimensional spaces and versatile, as they can be used for classification and regression tasks.

- **Neural Networks and Deep Learning**: Neural Networks are computational models that mimic the human brain's interconnected neural cells. They feature layers of nodes or neurons. Deep Learning, a specialized branch of Neural Networks, employs extensive networks with numerous layers, which allows the system to recognize intricate patterns within vast datasets.
- **K-Nearest Neighbors (KNN)**: KNN is a simple, instance-based learning algorithm that classifies new data points based on how closely they resemble them in the training set. It's like asking the nearest neighbors in the data space and taking a majority vote to classify a new data point.
- **Naive Bayes**: This group of simple, probabilistic classifiers is based on applying Bayes' theorem with strong independence assumptions between the features. It's particularly suited for high-dimensional datasets and is commonly used in text classification.
- **Clustering Algorithms (like K-Means)**: These unsupervised learning algorithms group data points into clusters based on similarity. Clustering is useful in data analysis for discovering patterns and grouping similar data points without predefined labels.

Understanding these algorithms and their applications is essential for machine learning practitioners. An algorithm's effectiveness hinges on the nature of the task it is applied to.

Selecting the right algorithm involves evaluating the task's specific demands and considering factors like data size, quality, and the desired outcome to achieve the algorithm's strengths and counter its limitations. Whether predicting future trends, classifying data, or uncovering hidden patterns, the suitable machine-learning algorithm can provide insightful and accurate results.

The landscape of machine learning algorithms is vast and diverse, with each type serving specific purposes and offering unique advantages. A comprehensive understanding of these algorithms, from supervised to unsupervised and reinforcement Learning, is crucial for solutions architects aiming to leverage ML in their projects. This knowledge equips them to select the most appropriate algorithms for specific tasks and provides a foundation for delving into more complex areas like Generative AI and Deep Learning.

Neural Networks and Deep Learning

At the heart of many advanced AI applications, neural networks and deep learning techniques mimic the human brain's functioning. Understanding various architectures like Convolutional Neural Networks (CNNs) and Recurrent Neural Networks (RNNs) is essential. Neural Networks and Deep Learning represent the forefront of modern artificial intelligence, drawing inspiration from the structure and function of the human brain. This paradigm has revolutionized the field of AI, enabling machines to perform tasks with unprecedented accuracy and complexity. A detailed understanding of neural networks and deep learning is indispensable for solutions architects exploring AI. Let's start with the basics of Neural Networks:

- **Neurons and Layers:** Neural networks consist of neurons (nodes) organized in layers. Each neuron receives input, processes it, and passes the output to the next layer. The process mimics the synaptic transmission in a biological brain.
- **Activation Functions:** Functions like Sigmoid, ReLU (Rectified Linear Unit), and Tanh determine a neuron's output based on its input, introducing non-linearity and enabling complex pattern recognition.
- **Feedforward and Backpropagation:** In feedforward networks, information moves in one direction. Backpropagation adjusts the network weights during training to minimize errors between the predicted and actual output.

Deep Learning involves neural networks with multiple hidden layers, enabling them to learn hierarchical representations of data. Following are some deep learning Architectures and Applications:

- **Convolutional Neural Networks (CNNs):** Specialized for processing data, such as images, with grid-like topology. CNNs use convolutional layers to capture spatial hierarchies and patterns. They are fundamental in computer vision tasks like image classification, object detection, and more.
- **Recurrent Neural Networks (RNNs):** Designed to handle sequential data, like text or time series. RNNs have internal loops to keep track of previous information, making them ideal for tasks like language modeling and speech recognition.
- **Long Short-Term Memory (LSTM) Networks:** LTSMs are a type of RNN that can learn long-term dependencies. They address the vanishing gradient problem common in traditional RNNs and are crucial in complex sequence prediction problems.

Deep learning has diverse applications, each leveraging specific network architectures. For example, natural language **processing (NLP) is utilized by** applications like translation, sentiment analysis, and chatbots. Techniques like Word embedding and Transformers (like BERT) are pivotal. Self-driving cars use deep Learning for tasks like object detection and path planning. Deep learning is increasingly integral to healthcare solutions, from diagnosing diseases in medical imagery to predicting patient outcomes.

However, there are some key challenges to note regarding the deep learning model. Deep learning models require large amounts of labeled data for training, which can be a limiting factor. Training deep neural networks is resource-intensive, often requiring significant computational power and specialized hardware like GPUs. Deep learning models, especially deep neural networks, are usually considered "black boxes" due to their complexity, raising concerns about interpretability and transparency.

However, Transfer Learning allows leveraging pre-trained models on new tasks, reducing the need for extensive data and computation. **Generative Adversarial Networks (GANs) provide a** novel approach where two networks train together, generating and evaluating data. GANs are essential for generative AI applications like image generation.

Neural networks and deep Learning form the backbone of many cutting-edge AI applications. Their ability to process and learn from vast datasets has opened new frontiers in AI, from automating complex tasks to enabling machines to generate new content. For solutions architects venturing into AI, mastering these concepts is not just a technical requirement but a gateway to the future of intelligent systems. Understanding the intricacies of neural networks, from their basic structure to advanced deep learning techniques, is essential in harnessing the full potential of AI in various domains.

Transfer Learning

Transfer learning has emerged as a powerful strategy, mainly when data is a limiting factor. It involves leveraging a pre-trained model on a large, generalized dataset and fine-tuning it to adapt to specific tasks or smaller datasets. This approach has substantial implications for ML solutions architects, as it offers an efficient pathway to develop robust models from scratch without extensive data collection and training.

Transfer learning typically begins with models pre-trained on large datasets, such as ImageNet for image-related tasks or BERT for natural language processing. These models have already learned a rich set of features and patterns, which can be a valuable starting point for new tasks. The essence of transfer learning lies in fine-tuning these pre-trained models to suit specific tasks. This involves retraining the model, or a portion of it, on a smaller dataset specific to the task at hand. This process adapts the learned features to the new context, making the model more relevant and effective for the particular problem.

> *Transfer learning is particularly beneficial when collecting a large labeled dataset could be more practical and affordable. By leveraging pre-trained models, ML solutions architects can achieve high levels of accuracy with much smaller datasets. This approach significantly reduces the time and resources required for training models. Since the base model has already undergone extensive training, fine-tuning is much quicker and less computationally intensive.*

Transfer learning has proven effective across various domains, including computer vision, natural language processing, and audio analysis. Its versatility makes it an invaluable tool in the ML architect's toolkit. While transfer learning is powerful, it requires careful consideration of factors like the similarity between the base and target tasks, the amount of fine-tuning needed, and the potential for overfitting on the larger dataset.

The choice of the pre-trained model is crucial and should align with the nature of the task. For example, a model trained on visual data is a good starting point for image classification tasks. Depending on the task, the architect may need to customize the model architecture, such as adding or modifying layers, to suit the specific requirements better. Finding the right balance in training is essential—too little may not adequately adapt the model to the new task, while too much may lead to overfitting.

For ML Solutions Architects, transfer learning offers a pragmatic and efficient approach to model development, especially in constrained scenarios. By understanding and effectively applying this technique, architects can expedite the development process, utilize resources more efficiently, and deliver highly accurate models tailored to specific needs while navigating the challenges and nuances of transfer learning.

Data Preprocessing and Feature Engineering

Creating a robust ML model begins long before any algorithmic magic occurs. It starts with data preprocessing and feature engineering, two critical phases that lay the groundwork for successful ML implementations. In these stages, raw data is transformed into a refined format that ML models can understand and use effectively to make accurate predictions or decisions.

Data Preprocessing

Data is the foundation of ML Models. This initial step involves addressing missing values, removing duplicates, and correcting errors in the dataset. It's like selecting raw ingredients and ensuring they're quality before cooking. Normalization and Standardization techniques scale the data to a standard range or distribution, eliminating biases due to varying scales of features. Data transformation can include encoding categorical variables, discretizing continuous variables, or creating polynomial features. This step ensures that the data is in a format that ML algorithms can process effectively.

Encoding categorical variables involves converting non-numeric data into numeric formats suitable for machine learning, such as using one-hot encoding or label encoding. **Discretizing continuous variables**, or binning, transforms continuous data into discrete categories, which can simplify models and highlight important ranges. Methods like equal-width or equal-frequency binning can be used. Creating **polynomial features** generates new features by raising existing features to powers or creating interaction terms, helping capture non-linear relationships in the data. These preprocessing steps transform raw data into a format that enhances model performance and interpretation.

Building machine learning models requires a nuanced understanding of data. For Solution Architects, the journey from conceptualizing to operationalizing these models centers on several critical data considerations. Here's a breakdown of these key aspects:

- **Data Quality:** The foundation of any machine learning model is its data quality. Accurate, consistent, and comprehensive data ensures that models learn and predict correctly.
- **Handling Missing Data:** Incomplete data can lead to skewed results and inaccurate models. Techniques like imputation or algorithms that can handle missing data are essential to maintain data integrity.
- **Data Augmentation:** In limited or imbalanced datasets, augmenting data can enhance model training. This may involve generating synthetic data or employing techniques to balance the data distribution.
- **Volume vs. Relevance:** More data isn't inherently better. The focus should be on having a relevant, well-curated dataset. Extraneous data can confuse the model and reduce its effectiveness.
- **Diversity in Data:** Diverse datasets help build robust models by covering a wide range of scenarios and preventing biases, thereby improving the model's generalization ability.
- **Data Cleaning:** Raw data often requires preprocessing, including normalization, handling outliers, or converting various data types into a machine-readable format.
- **Synthetic Data:** When data privacy is a concern or accurate data is scarce, synthetic data can be a viable alternative for training models without compromising privacy or data security.
- **Data Privacy:** It is crucial to ensure compliance with data privacy regulations and ethical considerations, especially when handling sensitive personal data.
- **Updating Data:** Regular updates with fresh data keep the model relevant and effective, especially in rapidly evolving fields or industries.
- **Storing Data:** Effective storage solutions are essential for managing large datasets. These solutions should be optimized for scalability and quick data retrieval.

These considerations form the foundation for successful machine learning projects for Solution Architects. They ensure that the developed models are not only technically sound but also practical and reliable for real-world applications across various domains.

Feature Engineering

Feature selection is the art of extracting insights. Selecting the right features is crucial. It involves identifying the most relevant variables contributing significantly to the model's predictive power. This is like choosing the right combination of ingredients to produce the best dish. Sometimes, new features need to be crafted from existing data. This might involve combining two variables to create a more impactful one or extracting parts of a date to gain insights about seasonality. Techniques like PCA (Principal Component Analysis) reduce the number of features, focusing on the most informative ones. This not only improves model performance but also makes computation more efficient.

> *Proper preprocessing and feature engineering lead to cleaner, more relevant datasets that significantly improve the model's learning ability, accuracy, and performance. Removing irrelevant or redundant features and normalizing data help prevent models from overfitting and ensure they perform well on unseen data. Clean and well-structured data also allow ML algorithms to learn patterns more efficiently, speeding up the training process and yielding better results.*

At its core, feature engineering is about refining raw data into a more useful format. Imagine you're developing an app that forecasts weather patterns. The raw data might include temperature readings, humidity, and wind speeds. Feature engineering in this context could involve creating new features such as 'feels-like' temperature, which combines humidity and wind speed with the actual temperature to represent the perceived weather condition accurately.

Techniques in Feature Engineering: There are various techniques involved in feature engineering, each serving a unique purpose:

- **Feature Transformation**: This involves modifying existing features to enhance their relevance, for instance, transforming temperature readings from Fahrenheit to Celsius for standardization.
- **Feature Creation**: Sometimes, combining two or more features can produce a more informative attribute. In our weather app example, combining date and time into a single 'timestamp' feature could provide more insightful data analysis.
- **Feature Selection**: Not all features contribute equally to a model's accuracy. It is crucial to identify and retain only those features that are most predictive. This might involve discarding redundant or irrelevant data, such as removing 'wind direction' if it has little impact on weather prediction accuracy.

As machine learning models become more complex, managing features effectively becomes crucial. Feature stores act as centralized repositories where engineered features are stored and managed. They ensure that features are consistent across different models and applications, enhancing efficiency and reducing redundancy. For instance, if the weather app expands to include features like the air quality index, storing these new features in a feature store ensures they are readily available for future enhancements.

One of the primary challenges in feature engineering is determining the right features to improve model performance. It often requires domain expertise and iterative experimentation. Additionally, as new data becomes available or understanding the problem evolves, previously engineered features might become obsolete or less effective, necessitating regular updates and revisions.

Feature engineering is a dynamic and intricate process fundamental to the success of machine learning models. The process requires a blend of technical skills, creativity, and domain knowledge, making it both a challenging and rewarding aspect of machine learning.

Both preprocessing and feature engineering are not one-time tasks. They require continuous refinement and iteration as new data arrives or the model's performance is evaluated. Effective feature engineering often requires domain expertise. Understanding the data's context and nuances can create more impactful features. Modern ML workflows leverage automated tools for feature selection and preprocessing, but manual intervention and expertise are still critical for optimal outcomes.

Data preprocessing and feature engineering form the backbone of effective machine learning. They are the stages where raw data is transformed into a powerful tool capable of driving intelligent algorithms. By investing time and resources into these critical phases, ML practitioners can ensure that their models are built on a foundation of quality, relevance, and insight, leading to more accurate and effective machine learning solutions.

Model Evaluation Metrics

Model evaluation metrics play a pivotal role in the field of machine learning. They serve as the yardsticks that measure the effectiveness of ML models, providing insights into how well a model performs under different scenarios. Understanding and correctly applying these metrics is essential for any ML Solutions Architect, as it directly influences the success of an AI/ML project. Understanding different metrics to evaluate ML models, such as accuracy, precision, recall, F1 score, and area under the ROC curve, is fundamental. These metrics help in assessing the performance of models in various scenarios.

- **Accuracy** is the most straightforward metric, representing the ratio of correctly predicted instances to the total number of cases in the data set. It's useful for quickly understanding a model's overall performance, especially in balanced datasets.
- **Precision and Recall are crucial metrics**, especially in imbalanced datasets or when the cost of false positives and false negatives is high.
  - **Precision** measures the proportion of positive identifications that were correct. It's critical in scenarios where false positives are costly.

- **Recall (or Sensitivity)** calculates the proportion of correct positives identified. This is essential when missing a positive case has severe consequences, such as in medical diagnoses.

- **F1 Score:** The F1 score is the harmonic mean of precision and recall. It's beneficial when you must balance precision and recall, providing a metric that considers both false positives and false negatives.
- **Area Under the ROC Curve (AUC-ROC):** The ROC curve plots the true positive rate against the false positive rate at various threshold settings. The AUC measures the entire two-dimensional area underneath the ROC as a whole curve. A model with perfect predictions has an AUC of 1, while a model with no discriminative power has an AUC of 0.5.
- **Mean Squared Error (MSE) and Mean Absolute Error (MAE)** are essential metrics for regression models. MSE measures the average of the squares of the errors, while MAE measures the average of the absolute errors. These metrics provide insight into the magnitude of error in predictions.

The choice of metric heavily depends on the specific context and objectives of the ML model. For instance, precision might be more critical in spam detection to avoid misclassifying legitimate emails as spam. In many scenarios, there is a trade-off between metrics. For example, increasing recall may decrease precision. Understanding these trade-offs and choosing a metric that aligns with the business objectives is essential. These metrics are not just for final evaluation but are also crucial during the model-tuning phase. They help select the right model, choose hyperparameters, and avoid overfitting. When comparing multiple models, these metrics provide a standardized evaluation of their relative performance.

For ML Solutions Architects, a deep understanding of model evaluation metrics is not just about technical knowledge but about translating this understanding into actionable insights. By skillfully applying these metrics, architects can effectively communicate a model's strengths and limitations, guide the model development process, and ensure that the final product meets the intended objectives with high reliability and accuracy.

These key concepts form the backbone of Machine Learning and Generative AI and are essential for anyone interested in this field. A thorough understanding of these concepts not only aids in building effective AI solutions but also ensures their responsible and ethical application.

Generative AI and Foundation Models

Generative AI, a frontier in artificial intelligence, primarily focuses on creating models to generate novel, realistic data instances. These models are about more than just analyzing data but producing new content, often indistinguishable from human-generated work. This capability has broad implications across industries, from art and design to medicine and entertainment.

Generative AI revolves around models that can generate new data instances. Key models include Generative Adversarial Networks (GANs) and Variational Autoencoders (VAEs), used for tasks like image generation, style transfer, and more.

Generative Models Unlike traditional models that predict or classify data, generative models learn the training data distribution and can generate new instances that mimic the original data. They are often trained on a vast corpus of data, learning intricate patterns, styles, and structures, which they can replicate or recombine to produce new creations. The following are key types of Generative Models:

- **Generative Adversarial Networks (GANs):** GANs consist of two neural networks — a generator and a discriminator — that are trained simultaneously in a competitive manner. The generator creates data, while the discriminator evaluates it against actual data. GANs have revolutionized art generation, realistic image synthesis, photo-realistic image manipulation, and virtual environments.
- **Variational Autoencoders (VAEs):** VAEs are based on autoencoders, which compress data into a compact representation and then reconstruct it. VAEs modify this process to generate new data similar to the input data. VAEs are particularly effective in tasks where a smooth, continuous latent space representation is beneficial, such as image denoising and content generation, as well as more nuanced tasks like style transfer.
- **Large Language Models:** These models, like GPT-4 and Claude-3, are trained on vast textual datasets and can generate coherent, contextually relevant text. They're transforming natural language processing tasks, content creation, and even coding. From writing essays to scripting code, these models blur the lines between human and machine-generated content.

Leveraging generative models to create realistic video and audio content, often indistinguishable from real footage. While offering creative opportunities in media and entertainment, they also raise ethical and legal concerns regarding misinformation and privacy. The ability to create realistic synthetic data poses significant challenges in discerning real from fake, raising ethical questions about consent and misuse. Developing detection algorithms and establishing clear ethical guidelines is crucial to responsibly harnessing the power of generative models.

Generative models can inadvertently perpetuate biases in their training data, leading to skewed or unfair representations. Careful curation of training datasets and constant evaluation of outputs are essential to ensure diverse and unbiased model generations.

Generative AI and its models, like GANs and VAEs, represent a paradigm shift in AI's capabilities. They're not just tools for analysis but engines for creation, offering unparalleled opportunities across various fields. Understanding these models, their applications, and their implications is crucial for AI/ML solutions architects. This understanding enables them to harness the creative potential of AI while navigating the ethical and technical complexities inherent in generative models.

Foundation Models (FMs)

FMs provide an ideal starting point for Generative AI applications with their extensive pre-training on diverse and large datasets. These models have learned a broad representation of human knowledge and can apply this understanding to generate new content. For example, a Foundation Model like GPT-4, trained on vast amounts of text, can be used for generative tasks like creating articles, poems, or code. They form a broad base of knowledge and skills that can be fine-tuned for various specific tasks. These models involve millions and billions of parameters; Foundation Models are complex and vast. They can generalize knowledge across domains and tasks. Capable of being adapted to a variety of tasks, often with minimal additional training.

Generative AI rapidly expands, with numerous foundational models emerging from prominent tech giants and innovative startups. These models are pivotal in advancing AI capabilities and are utilized across various applications. Here's a brief overview of some of the most significant foundational models in Generative AI:

- **Amazon's AlexaTM 20B & Amazon Titan**: Amazon's offerings include AlexaTM 20B, which focuses on natural language tasks with 20 billion parameters, and Amazon Titan, which draws from Amazon's extensive machine learning experience for various AI applications.
- **OpenAI's Models**: OpenAI has introduced several impactful models, such as DistilGPT2, GPT-3, GPT NeoXT, GPT-3.5, GPT-4, GPT-4o CLIP, CLIP-Guided Diffusion, and DALL-E. GPT-4o, in particular, stands out with its 1 trillion parameters and multi-modality capabilities, allowing it to process various data types, including images.
- **Google's Contributions**: Google's innovations include BERT for contextual understanding, BigGAN for high-resolution image generation, the T5 and Flan T-5 models, PaLM, LaMDA, Falcon-7B, Falcon-40B, Gemini, and Chinchilla by DeepMind. These models serve various functions, from natural language processing to creative content generation.
- **Nvidia's StyleGAN2**: This model is known for generating high-resolution, realistic images using a GAN architecture, which is particularly useful in graphic design.
- **Anthropic's Claude**: A model developed for diverse language processing tasks, assisting in content creation and other applications.
- **AI21 Labs' DELL & Jurassic-2**: AI21 Labs has introduced DELL for music composition and Jurassic-2, a versatile language model suitable for various tasks.
- **Microsoft's Turing-NLG & MPT-7B**: Microsoft's contributions include Turing-NLG for natural language generation and MPT-7B, which is known for its translation capabilities.
- **Jasper.ai's Jasper**: This model is designed for natural language explanations and is particularly useful in healthcare for interpreting AI-based medical diagnoses.
- **Facebook AI's Models**: Facebook AI has developed models such as LLaMa, RedPajama, and OPT-175B, which focus on natural language understanding and generation.

- **Hugging Face's Bloom Models**: These models, including BloomZ 176B and Lyra-Fr 10B, offer versatile capabilities for natural language tasks.
- **Cohere's Offerings**: Cohere provides models like Cohere Command XL for various natural language processing tasks.
- **Baidu's PaddlePaddle & Wu Dao 2.0**: Baidu's contributions include PaddlePaddle for deep learning tasks and Wu Dao 2.0, a large language model with 1.75 trillion parameters.
- **Independent Models**: Other notable models include VQ-VAE-2, Jukebox, MUNIT, Llama, Dolly, Craiyon, and Midjourne. Each offers unique capabilities,s ranging from image and music generation to advanced language processing.

These models are at the forefront of AI innovation, offering groundbreaking capabilities in language processing, image generation, and more. They represent the cutting edge of AI research and development, constantly pushing the boundaries of what's possible in the field of Generative AI.

Foundation Models are powerful tools in the AI toolbox, offering unparalleled versatility and capability. However, their effective and responsible use requires addressing their significant challenges. Understanding these models—their strengths, applications, and associated challenges—is essential for Solutions Architects.

Steps in Building Machine Learning Models

The journey to building a machine learning model is complicated and systematic. It involves well-defined steps that guide the transformation of raw data into a predictive tool. Each step is crucial and requires careful consideration and execution.

1. **Defining the Problem**: The first and most fundamental step is identifying and understanding the problem you intend to solve. This involves determining your model's objective, scope, and expected outcome. Whether it's forecasting market trends, predicting customer behavior, or automating a manual process, a clear problem definition sets the direction for the entire project.
2. **Collecting and Preparing the Data**: Data is the foundation of any machine learning model. This step involves gathering the necessary data and preparing it for analysis. It includes data cleaning (removing or correcting anomalies and errors), data transformation (converting data into a suitable format), and data integration (combining data from different sources). The quality and relevance of the data collected directly impact the model's effectiveness.
3. **Choosing the Right Model**: Selecting an appropriate machine learning model is critical. The choice depends on the nature of the problem, the type of data available, and the

desired outcome. For example, regression models predict continuous outcomes, while classification models predict categorical outcomes.

4. **Training the Model**: This step trains the chosen model using the prepared dataset. The model learns to make predictions or decisions based on the input data. This involves finding patterns, understanding relationships, and adjusting the model's parameters for the best fit.

5. **Evaluating the Model**: After training, the model's performance needs to be assessed using a separate set of data (test data). This step tests the model's accuracy and generalizability to new, unseen data. Common evaluation metrics include accuracy, precision, recall, and the F1 score.

6. **Fine-tuning and Optimization**: Depending on the evaluation results, the model may require fine-tuning. This could involve adjusting the model parameters, adding more training data, or selecting a different model. The goal is to enhance the model's performance and accuracy.

7. **Deploying and Monitoring**: Once optimized, the model is deployed into a production environment where it can start making predictions or decisions. Continuous monitoring is essential to ensure the model performs as expected over time. This includes tracking its performance and adjusting based on feedback and changing conditions.

8. **Iterating**: Machine learning models are not static. They need to be updated and improved regularly. Iteration involves revisiting the model periodically, updating the data, retraining the model, and making necessary changes. This ensures that the model remains relevant and effective over time.

Building a machine learning model is a structured process that requires careful planning, execution, and maintenance. Each step plays a crucial role in ensuring that the final model is accurate, reliable, and effective in solving the defined problem.

MLOps – putting ML in production

A crucial phase is transitioning from developing a machine learning model to making it a functional part of your application, commonly known as MLOps. This process encompasses everything from setting up the right infrastructure to ensuring scalability and efficient deployment.

MLOps, short for Machine Learning Operations, is an essential practice in data science and machine learning. It bridges the gap between the development of machine learning models and their operational deployment. MLOps is to machine learning what DevOps is to software development. The following are the core components of MLOps:

- **Model Development and Training:** This involves creating machine learning models using suitable algorithms and training them with data. It's a process similar to software development, but instead of writing code for every functionality, you're training models to learn from data and make predictions or decisions.

- **Testing and Validation:** Just like software needs to be tested for bugs, machine learning models need to be validated for accuracy, bias, and overfitting. This step ensures the model's performance meets the required standards before deployment.
- **Deployment and Integration:** Once a model is trained and validated, it needs to be deployed into a production environment where it can start providing insights or making decisions. This could mean integrating the model into existing software systems, web services, or applications.
- **Monitoring and Maintenance:** Post-deployment, continuous monitoring of model performance is essential. This includes tracking its accuracy, efficiency, and adaptability to new data. Regular maintenance and updates may be required to ensure the model remains effective over time.
- **Collaboration and Communication:** MLOps emphasizes collaboration between data scientists, ML engineers, and operational teams. Efficient communication and shared understanding across these disciplines are vital for the smooth functioning of ML operations.

MLOps streamlines the entire lifecycle of machine learning models, making it easier to scale ML initiatives and manage multiple models efficiently. By maintaining a clear lineage of data, models, and experiments, MLOps ensures reproducibility, which is crucial for validating and understanding model behavior. With standardized processes and automation, MLOps can significantly reduce the time it takes to move models from development to production. MLOps facilitates continuous delivery and integration, allowing for iterative model improvements based on new data and feedback.

MLOps Tools and Technologies

Here's a guide to the various tools and technologies that play a crucial role in MLOps:

- **ML Infrastructure:** The foundation of successful machine learning operations lies in robust infrastructure. This encompasses the physical hardware and the virtual environments, storage capacities, and processing power required to support ML models. Think of it as constructing a technologically advanced facility where each component is vital in ensuring seamless operations. In this context, our infrastructure must be capable of handling complex computations and large datasets, ensuring the smooth functioning of machine learning models.
- **Serving in the Cloud:** Cloud computing has revolutionized how we deploy and access machine learning models. By serving models in the cloud, they become accessible from anywhere, ensuring real-time data processing and global availability. Cloud platforms like Amazon SageMaker offer easy tools for deploying, managing, and scaling models, providing a versatile environment that supports a range of ML operations. This global

accessibility is crucial, especially in applications like healthcare, where timely and accurate results can be life-saving.

- **On-Device Deployment:** In scenarios where cloud connectivity is limited or non-existent, on-device deployment becomes essential. This approach involves optimizing and running machine learning models directly on a user's device. Technologies like Amazon SageMaker Neo help optimize models for specific hardware, ensuring they run efficiently even in low-resource environments. For a healthcare application, this means providing diagnostic insights on-site, regardless of internet connectivity, making the application more versatile and user-friendly.

- **Monitoring and Updating Models:** The dynamic nature of data necessitates continuous monitoring and regular updates of machine learning models. Monitoring tools help track model performance, ensuring they function as intended. When deviations or inefficiencies are detected, updating the model becomes crucial to maintaining its accuracy and relevance. Cloud-based tools like Amazon SageMaker provide comprehensive monitoring solutions and simplify the process of model retraining and redeployment, ensuring that your machine learning models stay current with the latest data and trends.

- **Version Control Systems:** Version control systems, particularly tools like Git, are instrumental in the MLOps ecosystem. They systematically track and manage changes made to machine learning models, datasets, and code. This tracking is crucial for collaboration, as it allows multiple team members to work on different aspects of a project simultaneously without conflict. It also ensures that every change is documented, facilitating easy rollback to previous versions if needed. In the rapidly evolving field of machine learning, where models and their data inputs are continuously updated, version control systems are the backbone for maintaining consistency, integrity, and a clear development history.

- **Orchestration and Workflow Management:** Apache Airflow and Kubeflow are pivotal in orchestrating and managing machine learning workflows. These tools help automate the pipeline, collection, and processing to model training and evaluation. Orchestration tools ensure that each step of the machine-learning pipeline is executed in the correct sequence and under the right conditions. This automation is critical in handling complex workflows that involve numerous interdependent tasks. They streamline the entire process and make it reproducible and scalable, enabling teams to focus more on model development and less on managing the workflow intricacies.

- **Containerization and Virtualization:** Containerization and virtualization tools, notably Docker and Kubernetes, are vital in creating consistent and isolated environments for machine learning development. Docker allows packaging applications and their dependencies into containers, ensuring they run uniformly across different computing environments. On the other hand, Kubernetes is a container orchestration system that manages these containers at scale. This combination is particularly beneficial for machine learning, where different models might require different environments or dependencies.

Containerization ensures that models can be developed, trained, and deployed without worrying about inconsistencies or conflicts in the underlying environment, leading to smoother transitions from development to production.

- **Model Serving and Deployment:** Platforms like TensorFlow Serving, Amazon SageMaker, and Microsoft Azure ML are essential for deploying and serving machine learning models. These platforms provide the necessary infrastructure and tools to seamlessly deploy models into production environments where they can start providing real-world value. TensorFlow Serving, for instance, specializes in serving TensorFlow models and offers high-performance predictions. Amazon SageMaker simplifies the entire machine learning workflow, from building and training models to deploying them in a scalable manner. Microsoft Azure ML provides an integrated environment for managing the machine learning lifecycle, including model deployment. These platforms enable practitioners to focus on model development and training, knowing that deployment is efficiently handled.

MLOps is about creating a seamless, efficient pipeline from data to insights, ensuring machine learning models are developed, deployed, and maintained with the same rigor and best practices as traditional software.

Scalability is similar to the capability of a small clinic to expand into a large medical center. It's about the system's ability to handle increased workload and user traffic without compromising performance. In machine learning, this translates to the model's ability to maintain efficiency and accuracy as the data or user base grows. Ensuring scalability means your ML models can adapt to varying demands, providing consistent and reliable results irrespective of user volume.

Operationalizing machine learning models is a multifaceted process that requires careful planning and execution. From establishing a strong infrastructure and ensuring scalability to deploying models in the cloud or on devices, each step is crucial in making your ML models effective and reliable. Regular monitoring and updates ensure that these models continue to provide accurate and pertinent results, making them invaluable assets in applications where precision and reliability are paramount.

Ethical Considerations in Machine Learning

In the rapidly evolving fields of Machine Learning (ML) and Generative AI, the role of a Solutions Architect extends beyond technical know-how to encompass a deep understanding of ethical considerations. As ML and Generative AI increasingly impact various aspects of our lives, particularly in sensitive areas such as healthcare, finance, and public policy, the ethical implications become critically important. From an interview perspective for a Solutions Architect role, the focus on ethical considerations reveals not only one's technical competence but also one's awareness of the broader societal impacts of one's work.

- **Bias and Fairness**: During interviews, an ML and Generative AI Solutions Architect candidate might be asked about their approach to identifying and mitigating biases in datasets and algorithms. This could involve discussing strategies for ensuring diverse and representative data, techniques for detecting and correcting bias in model outputs, and understanding how biased models can disproportionately affect different user groups.
- **Transparency and Explainability**: Candidates might face questions about making complex ML models transparent and interpretable, especially in sectors where understanding model decisions is crucial. This could involve discussing methods for building explainable models, tools for interpreting model outputs, and ways to effectively communicate these aspects to non-technical stakeholders, thereby building trust and accountability.
- **Privacy and Data Protection**: Given the sensitive nature of ML and Generative AI data, candidates should be prepared to discuss their experience and strategies for protecting user data. This includes familiarity with data anonymization techniques, understanding data protection regulations like GDPR or HIPAA, and implementing secure data practices throughout the model development process.
- **Continuous Monitoring**: As ML models can evolve and change over time, candidates might be asked about their approach to monitoring and maintaining ethical standards on an ongoing basis. This can include strategies for regular auditing, updating models to reflect new data or ethical guidelines, and proactively identifying potential ethical issues as models are scaled and deployed in different contexts.
- **Accountability**: Interviewers may probe a candidate's understanding of accountability in ML and Generative AI projects. This includes discussing processes for handling errors or unintended consequences of model predictions, steps for rectifying such issues, and the candidate's approach to ensuring ethical responsibility across the team and organization.

In preparing for an interview for an ML and Generative AI Solutions Architect role, candidates should be ready to articulate how they build and deploy models and navigate the complex ethical landscape of these technologies. Demonstrating a commitment to ethical AI practices signifies a candidate's comprehensive understanding of the field and readiness to tackle the challenges of responsibly deploying AI solutions in the real world.

Popular Machine Learning Tools and Frameworks

When interviewing for an AI/ML Solutions Architect role, showcasing familiarity with the diverse tools and frameworks is crucial. These tools form the backbone of any ML project, and a deep understanding of their functionalities, strengths, and applications is vital. Let's explore some popular ML tools and frameworks, considering how they might be discussed in an interview.

- **Amazon SageMaker**: In an interview, you might be asked about your experience with Amazon SageMaker. This query tests your skills in building, training, and deploying ML models at scale using AWS. Discussing a project where SageMaker streamlined the entire ML lifecycle, from model building to deployment, would highlight your proficiency with this comprehensive platform.
- **TensorFlow**: Developed by Google, TensorFlow is a staple in deep learning applications. An interviewer might explore your ability to utilize TensorFlow for complex computations and your experience deploying TensorFlow models in real-world applications. Discussing TensorFlow's role in a project, especially in deep learning scenarios, would demonstrate your technical understanding and practical application skills.
- **PyTorch**: Originating from Facebook's AI Research lab, PyTorch is renowned for its dynamic computational graph and user-friendly interface. In an interview, showcasing your experience with PyTorch, particularly in projects requiring real-time analysis, would emphasize your capability in handling dynamic ML tasks.
- **Scikit-learn**: A popular toolkit for traditional ML tasks built on NumPy, SciPy, and matplotlib, scikit-learn is known for its simplicity and efficiency. Interviewers might inquire about your experience with sci-kit-learn, particularly in data analysis and modeling. Illustrating its use in feature extraction or model training projects can demonstrate your proficiency with this tool.
- **Keras**: Acting as an interface for TensorFlow, Keras simplifies deep learning model building and training. Interview questions might focus on your experience with Keras, especially in rapid prototyping and testing of ML models. Discussing how Keras aided in quick iteration and testing in your projects could showcase your agility in model development.
- **Apache Spark's MLib**: Known for big data processing, Apache Spark's MLib is essential for efficiently handling large datasets. An interviewer might be interested in your experience with MLib, particularly how you've leveraged it for speedy data processing and analysis in large-scale projects.
- **Microsoft Azure Machine Learning**: Azure ML is a cloud-based platform known for its flexibility in managing the entire lifecycle of ML models. In an interview, discussing how you've leveraged Azure ML to build, train, and deploy models, especially in a cloud environment, can highlight your expertise in cloud-based ML solutions. Address scenarios where you utilized Azure's integrated tools and services to streamline ML workflows.
- **Google AI Platform**: This integrated tool from Google Cloud is known for its ability to build and deploy ML models at scale. Discussing your experience with the Google AI Platform in an interview can demonstrate your ability to integrate Google's vast array of AI tools and services into a coherent ML solution, especially in scenarios requiring integration with other Google Cloud services.
- **H2O.ai**: H2O.ai is an open-source machine-learning platform known for its scalability and ease of use. During an interview, showcasing your experience with H2O.ai, particularly in building and deploying fast, scalable ML models, can illustrate your proficiency in handling

versatile ML tasks and your ability to harness open-source tools for enterprise-level solutions.

- **Fast.ai**: Renowned for making deep learning easier to use and involving more people from all backgrounds, Fast.ai is a high-level library built on top of PyTorch. When discussing Fast.ai in an interview, focus on its ease of use for building complex models and how you've utilized it to simplify and accelerate the development of deep learning models in your projects.

Reflecting on your experiences with these tools, how you've applied them in various projects, and your understanding of when and why to use each tool can be highly beneficial in preparation for an interview. Whether it's SageMaker for end-to-end ML workflows, TensorFlow and PyTorch for deep learning tasks, scikit-learn for traditional ML, Keras for quick prototyping, or MLib for big data processing, your familiarity with these tools will showcase your versatility and depth as an ML and Generative AI Solutions Architect.

Whiteboard Machine Learning SA Interview

Suppose you are applying for the Machine Learning and Generative AI Architects role. In that case, you may get questions like drawing and explaining the architecture of your recent machine-learning project or presenting a reference architecture of some machine-learning use case. Here's some example questions:

- How would you design MLOPS pipeline architecture? What are the main components and data flow?
- How would you design a chatbot that can understand natural language and generate human-like responses? What are the main modules and data flow?
- Design a system architecture for classifying and extracting information from scanned documents like invoices, bills, etc, and build an intelligent document processing system. What are the key components, and how will they interact?
- Given a large customer churn dataset, how would you build a model to predict which customers are most likely to churn? Walk through your feature engineering, model selection, evaluation metrics, etc.
- Explain the Transformer architecture used in models like BERT and GPT-3. Walk through the encoder-decoder structure, attention mechanism, and pre-training objectives.
- Design a neural network to predict housing prices based on features like number of bedrooms, location, size, etc. Explain your choice of layers, activation functions, loss functions, and optimization process.
- Explain how you would build an image classification model using convolutional neural networks. Walk through the architecture, training process, and evaluation.

- How would you design an anomaly detection system for a manufacturing plant? Explain the data collection, model training, and prediction serving.
- How would you design a system to transcribe the audio in real time using deep learning models? Explain the speech recognition pipeline.

The interviewer looks for signs that the candidate can design appropriate machine-learning solutions tailored to the business problem. The whiteboard allows the interviewer to observe the candidate's thought process as they design a solution iteratively.

Let's take an example. You are a data scientist at a telecom company, and your team is working on a solution to estimate the likelihood that an existing customer will stop doing business with a company in a given timeframe. This is essential for businesses since acquiring new customers always costs more than retaining existing ones. Retention campaigns can target high-risk customers. Your task is to build a production-grade MLOPS architecture.

To build MLOPS pipeline architecture, you must first understand the steps involved in machine learning. The following diagram illustrates a machine learning process's conceptual, logical model.

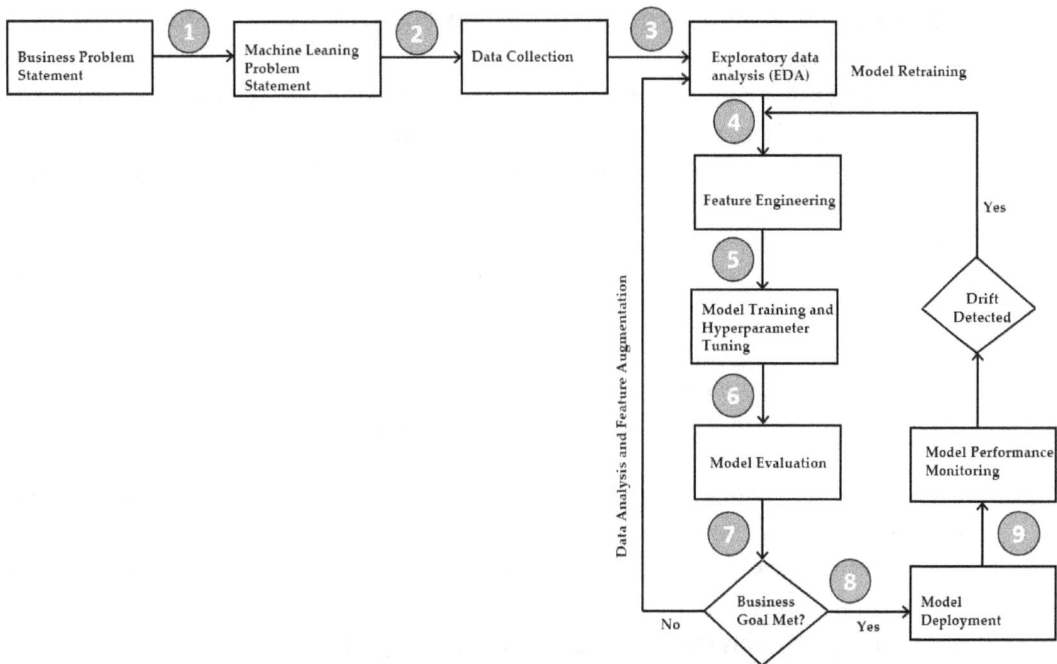

Figure 10.1 – End-to-End Machine Learning Model Lifecycle

As you can see in the preceding diagram, the following steps are involved in launching an ML model, from business identification to addressing customer use cases through the right inference:

1. **Business Problem Statement**: Identify the business problem that needs to be solved. This should be clearly defined and quantified. For example, "reduce customer churn by 10%".

2. **Machine Learning Problem Statement**: Translate the business problem into a machine learning problem statement. Define the target variable you want to predict or optimize for and what input data you will use to train a model. For example, "train a model to predict customer churn using customer demographic and transactional data."

3. **Data Collection**: The data preparation stage involves data scientists and engineers gathering data from various sources, integrating and combining it, and then cleaning and transforming the data into a format ready for analysis.

4. **Exploratory data analysis (EDA)**: In this step, the data scientist performs initial investigations on data to discover patterns, spot anomalies, test hypotheses, and check assumptions. Common EDA techniques include calculating summary statistics, creating plots, and finding correlations. The visualizations help users understand the key factors that lead to churn and provide insights to retention teams for taking data-driven actions to improve customer retention.

   Here are some examples of exploring and analyzing data related to predicting customer churn:

   - Check the data types of the columns - are they numeric, categorical, text, or date columns? This will inform what kind of analysis can be applied.
   - Look at the dataset's number of rows/customers and columns to understand the dimensions.
   - Run summary statistics on numeric columns like mean, max, min, quartiles, etc., to see value distributions. For example, you may see the average customer tenure is 36 months.
   - Categorize and count unique values for categorical columns. This can uncover insights like the most common customer gender.
   - Identify and remove outliers that could skew the analysis.

   The visualizations below provide examples of exploring and analyzing data related to predicting customer churn:

   - Scatter plots showing usage patterns for churn vs non-churn customers
   - Examine columns like account tenure and visualize the distribution with a histogram. This tells you about customer longevity.
   - Visualize churn rate vs account tenure using a scatterplot. See if longer tenure decreases churn.

5. **Feature Engineering**: It converts raw data into features that more accurately represent the problem to predictive models. This crucial step can significantly enhance the

performance of machine learning algorithms on new, unseen data by providing them with more relevant information for making predictions.

Let's say you have customer information, such as customer ID, name, age, gender, tenure, contract type, monthly charges, total charges, internet service, tech support use, etc., to build a customer churn prediction model.

- You can create a feature for customer tenure in years instead of months. This makes the scale of tenure more interpretable.
- Create a feature for the average monthly charge amount. This summarizes historical spending behavior.
- Create a feature for total charges to date. This provides an overall view of customer lifetime value.
- Encode categorical features into dummy variables, such as contract type, internet service, etc. This allows the model to interpret these features.
- Derive feature for frequency of tech support use by counting the number of tech calls made. This measures engagement.

By creating these newly engineered features, you can capture behavioral patterns, spending, engagement, and risk factors that can improve our machine learning model's ability to predict which customers will likely churn. The model can now learn more complex patterns from the data.

6. **Model Training and Hyperparameter Tuning**: Train multiple machine learning models on the prepared data, optimizing hyperparameters. Evaluate models using validation data to select the best-performing model. Some algorithms suitable for churn modeling include logistic regression, random forest, gradient boosting, etc.

7. **Model Evaluation**: This step assesses how well a trained model performs on new, unseen data. It helps determine if the model is robust and generalizes well. Common evaluation metrics for classification problems like churn prediction are:
   - Accuracy - Fraction of total correct predictions
   - Precision - Of customers predicted to churn, how many actually did?
   - Recall - Of all the customers that churned, how many did we correctly predict?
   - F1-score - Combines precision and recall into a single metric

8. **Model Deployment**: This step deploys the selected model to production to start generating predictions on new unseen data. Integrate the model into business applications and workflows.

9. **Model Monitoring**: This step monitors the deployed model's performance over time. Track key metrics, such as prediction accuracy and data drift, to detect when the model needs retraining.

You can periodically retrain the model on new data, which ensures it stays accurate if input patterns change over time. If the retrained model achieves better metrics, compare its performance to previous versions and deploy it. The key steps are defining the business and ML problem, training/selecting the best model, deploying it, continuously monitoring its performance, and retraining it as needed. This lifecycle ensures the ML system continues to generate value over time.

Let's look at a detailed reference architecture using the AWS cloud to understand tools and technology better.

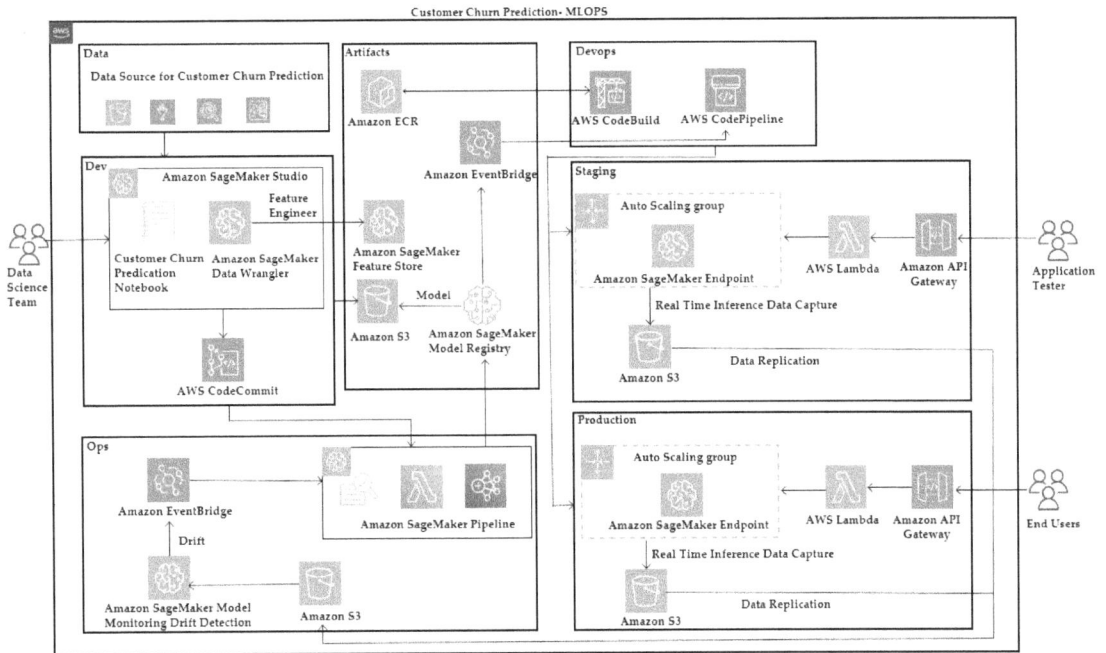

Figure 10.2 – Customer Churn Prediction ML pipeline in AWS

As shown in the preceding diagram, a multi-account strategy is recommended because having separate accounts allows you to isolate business units, set restrictions specifically for production workloads, and get a detailed view of the costs incurred by each component of your architecture. Let's dive deep into the detail flow:

- Data scientists use SageMaker Studio/Canvas to perform data preprocessing and feature engineering on data related to predicting customer churn. They use AWS Data Wrangler or SageMaker Notebook to perform feature engineering and save features in the Amazon Feature Store.

- The model training, hyperparameter tuning, and verification are done, and the model artifacts are saved in S3. The code is versioned using AWS CodeCommit, and the environment is versioned with AWS ECR. By versioning the code, environment, and model artifacts, the model's reproducibility is improved, and collaboration between teams is facilitated.
- To automate the model's retraining, you can use workflow tools like Step Functions, Airflow, or SageMaker Pipelines. The retraining pipeline contains steps for data preprocessing, model training, verification, and saving artifacts in S3. SageMaker Model Registry is used to version the model, enabling users to accept or reject a given model version.
- The model deployment involves creating SageMaker endpoints and autoscaling groups, which interface with Lambda functions and API Gateway to handle user inference requests. However, these various component services are provisions across different AWS accounts.
- The multiple-account strategy uses a staging account in addition to the production account. A new model is first deployed to the staging account, where it is tested. Once testing is complete, the model is automatically deployed from the staging account to the production account via a code pipeline in the development account. The code pipeline deployment is triggered automatically when a new model version is approved in the model registry, which generates an event that initiates the deployment.
- Monitoring model behavior and accuracy changes are essential when models are running in production. Data capture can be enabled on the endpoints in staging and production to record incoming requests and outgoing inference results to S3 buckets. This captured data must often be combined with labels or other training data from the development account. S3 replication moves the production data to an S3 bucket in the development account for analysis. Comparing this data to a baseline dataset generated during training reveals whether the model or data behavior has changed. The SageMaker model monitor compares the production data to the baseline and reports any differences in the expected model and data behavior.
- The last step is to take action depending on the model report. If the model detects a drift, it sends a signal to retrain the pipeline.

Now let's look at GenAI interview architecture for interview whiteboarding

Whiteboard Generative AI Interview

While you learned about the ML model life cycle in the previous section, the approach for Generative AI is slightly different. Let's take another example to understand Generative AI architecture. You are a data scientist in a company, and your team is working on building a virtual assistant application. Your task is to make an architecture that provides accurate answers to questions asked with confidence and evidence.

As you learned in previous sections, Foundation models (FMs) are large language models (LLMs) that perform well on natural language tasks like summarization, generation, and question answering across diverse topics. However, FMs are not magic bullets; they often struggle with unfamiliar content outside their training data, sometimes providing inaccurate or inadequate responses. Since FMs have fixed training datasets, they cannot access new data at inference time. This limitation is pronounced for domain-specific tasks, as FMs are primarily trained on generic data. For instance, an insurance company may want a question answer tailored to their unique business rules and latest internal documents.

Retrieval augmented generation (RAG) helps address this problem. RAG retrieves the most relevant knowledge from an enterprise knowledge base to the user's request. It then bundles this context with the original request as a prompt for the foundation model. RAG gives the model relevant information to generate high-quality responses for specialized domains. So, let's learn about the steps involved in the RAG approach:-

- **Create external data**: In the context of LLM, external data refers to any information not part of the model's training data. This can include data, documents, and text from different sources the model has yet to be trained on. Finally, an embedding language model converts data into numerical representations and stores them in a vector database, creating a knowledge library that generative AI models can understand.
- **Retrieve relevant information**: The next stage is to perform a relevancy search. This involves converting the user's query into a vector format and matching it with the vector databases. For instance, if an employee enters, "How much can I spend on the flight booking?" The system will retrieve the organization's travel policy documents. These documents will be returned because they have been determined to be highly relevant to the user's input through mathematical vector calculations and representations.
- **Augment the LLM prompt**: The RAG model builds on the initial user input by incorporating relevant retrieved data to provide context. This step utilizes prompt engineering methods to enable effective communication with the large language model. The enhanced prompt with added context enables the large language models to produce accurate answers to user queries.

The following diagram shows the conceptual flow of using RAG with LLMs:-

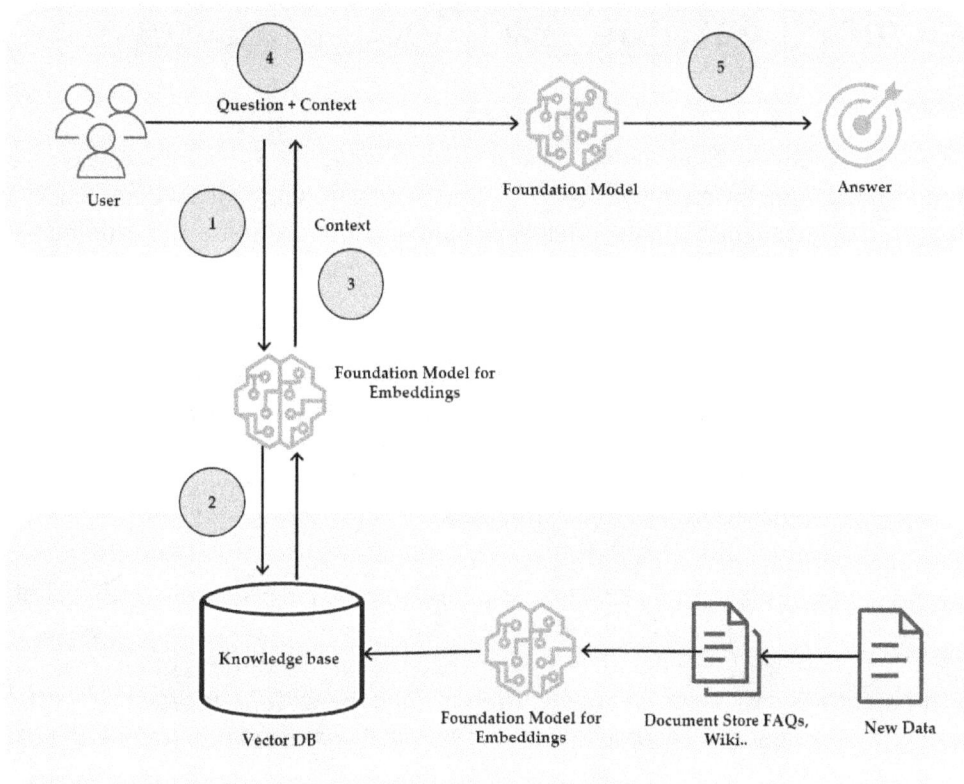

Figure 10.3 – Generative AI virtual assistant architecture using LLM model and RAG technique

As shown in the preceding diagram, the following is the functional flow of the given architecture:

1. The user asks a question.
2. The question is embedded using the Foundation Model. The embedded question refers to the knowledge base to find the relevant context. Finding the relevant context means finding its documents or sectors with the related context.
3. This returns the enhanced context.
4. The app sends the user a question and retrieves the context of the Foundation Model.
5. The Foundation Model returns a response to the user request based on the retrieved data.

It's crucial to regularly update the reference documents' content and embedding representations to ensure they provide accurate responses to future queries. By doing so asynchronously, the system ensures that the most current information is always available to generate precise answers, thereby enhancing the accuracy of responses over time. This is a generic architecture. Based on your use case, you can replace the vector database and Foundation model.

Machine Learning Architects Interview Questions

Interview questions for Machine Learning Architects roles are designed to assess a candidate's technical expertise, problem-solving skills, and understanding of AI and machine learning concepts, mainly as they apply to generative models. Here are some common questions, along with suggested responses. Let's start with behavioral questions, as interviewers often look to gauge your practical experience.

Question: Tell me a time when you solved a business problem using machine learning. How did you decide that this problem can be solved using ML? What were the challenges and outcomes?
Answer: Let's answer this in STAR format, using a scenario on retail inventory forecast with hypothetical data. Make the answers pointed out, which will help you memorize them and also help you provide crisp answers to the interviewer.

Situation: I faced a significant challenge as a machine learning solutions architect at XYZ Retail Inc.. The company was grappling with an inefficient inventory system, which led to overstocking some items (causing a 20% increase in holding costs) and understocking others (resulting in a 15% loss in potential sales). Upon analyzing, I found that the existing forecasting models failed to accurately predict demand, particularly during seasonal peaks and promotional events.

Task: My goal was to develop a more sophisticated inventory forecasting system using machine learning to optimize stock levels, reduce holding costs, and improve sales figures. I chose machine learning because it analyzes large datasets and identifies complex, nonlinear patterns. Unlike traditional models, ML could effectively incorporate factors like past sales trends, seasonal variations, and promotional impacts to predict future demand more accurately.

Action:
1. **Data Collection and Preprocessing**: I compiled three years of sales data covering over 10,000 SKUs, along with promotional calendars, seasonal trend data, and other external factors like local events.
2. **Model Selection and Development**: I employed an ARIMA model for time-series analysis and a gradient-boosting algorithm for capturing nonlinear trends. The models were trained on 70% of the data and tested on the remaining 30%.
3. **Feature Engineering**: Created features such as 'average sales during previous promotions,' 'sales increase during holiday seasons,' and 'month-on-month sales growth.'
4. **Training and Validation**: The models were trained to reduce forecasting errors. Compared to the existing system, the Gradient Boosting model achieved a mean absolute error reduction of 15%.

5. **Deployment and Monitoring**: We implemented the model into our ERP system and established a dashboard to monitor its real-time accuracy. Its accuracy consistently stayed above 85%.

Challenges:
- **Data Inconsistency**: The challenge was ensuring the integrity of the vast data collected, which involved extensive cleaning and validation processes.
- **Model Complexity**: Balancing the models to avoid overfitting while still capturing intricate patterns in the data was intricate.
- **Stakeholder Skepticism**: Convincing management to rely on the new system requires presenting data-driven evidence and conducting pilot tests, demonstrating a 10-15% improvement in forecasting accuracy.

Outcome:
- Implementing the ML model significantly optimized inventory levels: within the first quarter of deployment, there was a 30% reduction in overstocking and a 25% decrease in understocking instances.
- The business witnessed a 10% increase in sales due to better stock availability and a 15% reduction in storage costs.
- The project's success paved the way for further ML integration across various departments, enhancing overall business efficiency.

This answer highlighted machine learning's transformative impact on addressing complex business challenges, showcasing its ability to provide actionable insights and tangible improvements in operational efficiency.

Here are some follow-up questions that can be asked based on your answers above:

Question: How did you ensure that the machine learning model remained accurate and relevant over time, especially considering changing market trends and consumer behavior?
Tips:
- Discuss the ongoing monitoring and updating process for the model.
- Mention how you used tools like AWS CloudWatch or custom scripts for real-time anomaly detection in predictions.
- Highlight any retraining strategies, such as regularly incorporating new data or using techniques like transfer learning to adapt to market changes.

Question: What specific metrics did you use to measure the success of the machine learning model in inventory forecasting, and why were these metrics chosen?
Tips:

- Focus on key performance indicators (KPIs) relevant to inventory management, such as reduction in overstock and understock instances, improvement in sales, and decreased holding costs.
- Explain why these metrics were critical for the business's objectives and how they directly correlated with improved efficiency and profitability.
- You can also mention any customer satisfaction metrics if they were part of the project's success measurement.

Question: How did you handle any resistance or skepticism from stakeholders or team members regarding the adoption of the machine-learning solution?
Tips:
- Emphasize your communication skills and how you presented data-driven evidence to stakeholders.
- Discuss conducting pilot tests or phased rollouts to demonstrate the model's effectiveness before full-scale implementation.
- Share how you addressed concerns by ensuring transparency in the model's decision-making process and providing training or documentation to help stakeholders understand the model's benefits and workings.

Let's look at more complex scenario-based interview questions.

Question: Your team plans to develop a new, innovative feature for your project management tool that utilizes AI to predict project timelines based on historical data. However, the project has a limited budget, and integrating AI capabilities is typically resource-intensive. How would you cost-effectively design and implement this feature without comproming the application's quality and performance? Discuss how you would evaluate different AI technologies and frameworks, manage development costs, and ensure the new feature is maintainable and scalable within the allocated budget.
Answer: *Let's learn about building response for AI/ML architecture*

Situation: In the "TimelineAI" enhancement project for our project management tool, we aimed to introduce an AI-driven feature to predict project timelines based on historical data. The challenge was integrating sophisticated AI capabilities within a tight budget, a task known for its high resource demands. This limitation threatened our ability to deliver the innovative feature without compromising the application's quality and performance. Customers struggling with inaccurate timeline estimations faced delays and budget overruns, highlighting the need for a more precise forecasting tool to improve planning accuracy and project outcomes.

Behavior: To develop the "TimelineAI" feature within budget, we opted for AWS services, specifically Amazon SageMaker, for its cost-effective, scalable machine learning capabilities. SageMaker's ability to provide pre-trained models and manage the underlying infrastructure allowed us to focus on customizing the AI to our specific needs without the overhead of setting up and maintaining hardware. We selected TensorFlow through SageMaker for its extensive library and support for complex data models, ideal for analyzing our project management tool's historical data.

We adopted an agile development methodology, starting with a minimal viable product (MVP) to quickly deliver the core functionality to users. This approach enabled us to refine the AI model iteratively based on user feedback, ensuring efficient resource allocations to features that offered the most value. By leveraging AWS Lambda for backend processes, we could run code responding to triggers such as new project data inputs, ensuring scalability and cost efficiency by paying only for compute time.

This strategic use of AWS tools and an iterative approach allowed us to effectively implement the "TimelineAI" feature, maintaining high quality and performance while staying within our budget constraints.

Impact: Implementing the "TimelineAI" feature using AWS SageMaker and an agile development approach significantly enhanced our project management tool. Post-launch, customers experienced a 40% improvement in the accuracy of project timeline predictions, leading to better planning and a 25% reduction in project delays and budget overruns. The use of AWS Lambda for scalable backend processes resulted in a 30% decrease in operational costs due to the pay-per-use pricing model while maintaining system performance even as user demand increased.

Technical metrics revealed a 50% reduction in the time required to deploy updates and new features, thanks to the efficiency of the agile methodology and AWS services. Customer satisfaction scores rose by 20%, reflecting the positive impact of more reliable timeline predictions on project outcomes. The "TimelineAI" feature met the project's goals within the allocated budget and provided a scalable, maintainable solution that improved customer satisfaction and operational efficiency.

For whiteboarding, you can draw the following high-level architecture flow:

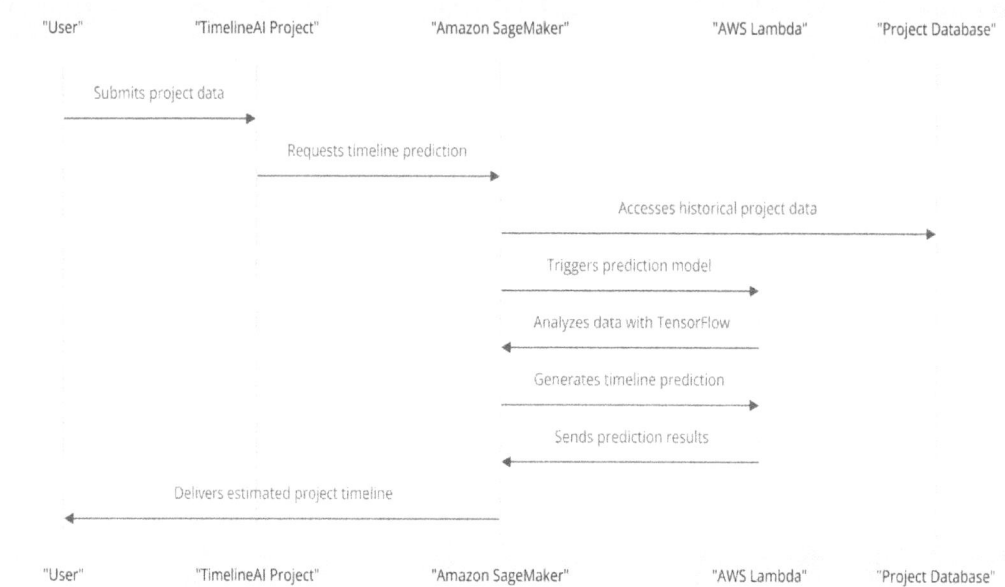

Figure 10.4 – AI/ML architecture in AWS

The preceding diagram shows that the "TimelineAI Project" architecture utilizes AWS Cloud services to deliver an AI-driven feature for predicting project timelines. Users interact with the system by submitting project data to Amazon SageMaker, the core of the AI modeling and prediction process. SageMaker, equipped with TensorFlow, analyzes the input data against historical project data stored in a dedicated database.

Upon receiving a prediction request, SageMaker triggers an AWS Lambda function. This function accesses the historical project data, applying the AI model to generate a timeline prediction based on patterns and insights derived from past projects. The prediction results are then sent back from Lambda to SageMaker, delivering the estimated project timeline to the user.

This architecture enables efficient processing and scalability by leveraging AWS Lambda for on-demand computation, reducing operational costs. Amazon SageMaker provides a robust and flexible platform for developing, training, and deploying the AI model, ensuring high-quality timeline predictions that enhance user planning and project management.

Follow-up Questions

- **How does the architecture ensure the accuracy and continuous improvement of the AI model over time?** This question challenges the assumption that after deploying an AI model, it will remain effective indefinitely. Given the dynamic nature of project management data and practices, it's crucial to understand the mechanisms for retraining the model with new data, ensuring predictions remain accurate and relevant to current project management trends.

- **What measures are in place to secure sensitive project data within Amazon SageMaker and AWS Lambda, considering the potential risks of data breaches?** This question probes the assumption that AWS services automatically provide robust security for sensitive data. It's essential to clarify the specific security practices and configurations employed to protect project data while dealing with confidential or proprietary information to maintain user trust and comply with data protection regulations.

- **How does the system handle scalability and performance during peak usage times, particularly when multiple users submit project data simultaneously?** This question challenges the assumption that the architecture can seamlessly scale to meet demand. Given the resource-intensive nature of AI predictions, understanding how AWS SageMaker and Lambda manage sudden spikes in requests is essential for maintaining performance and ensuring users receive timely predictions, even under heavy load.

Architecture Tradeoffs

The "TimelineAI Project" architecture, leveraging Amazon SageMaker and AWS Lambda, offers a scalable and efficient solution for AI-driven project timeline predictions. However, this approach has tradeoffs between model accuracy, security, and scalability. While SageMaker provides a powerful platform for AI model development and deployment, ensuring the continuous accuracy of predictions requires regular model retraining and validation against new data, adding complexity and operational overhead.

Security measures for protecting sensitive project data within SageMaker and Lambda necessitate stringent data handling and encryption practices, potentially increasing configuration and maintenance efforts. Furthermore, while AWS services scale well, managing performance during peak demand involves careful planning and possibly additional costs to maintain responsiveness.

These tradeoffs highlight the need for a balanced approach, optimizing for model accuracy, data security, and system scalability to deliver a robust and user-friendly feature within the "TimelineAI Project."

Now, let's examine generative AI interview questions. This area is relatively new, but standing out among candidates for ML architect roles is important.

Generative AI Interview Questions

Generative AI is relatively new, but it's also become essential to land a well-compensated ML architect role in today's environment. Preparing for the questions below involves understanding the technical details of Generative AI and being aware of its practical applications and potential societal impacts. Demonstrating your knowledge in these areas will show that you're technically proficient, forward-thinking, and aware of the broader context of AI's role in society.

Question: Explain Generative AI and how it differs from traditional machine learning models.
- **Tips**:
  - Define Generative AI, emphasizing its ability to generate new data instances (like images, text, or sound) that resemble the training data.
  - Contrast it with discriminative models in traditional machine learning, which focus on categorizing or predicting outcomes based on input data.
  - Highlight applications of Generative AI, such as content creation, data augmentation, and simulation.

Question: Provide the implications of models like GPT-4 and BERT in natural language processing.
- **Tips**:
  - Describe GPT-3's and BERT's core functionalities and their architecture differences (autoregressive vs. transformer models).
  - Explain how these models have significantly improved language understanding and generation capabilities.
  - Touch on their applications in various NLP tasks and potential ethical considerations.

Question: How would you address the bias challenge in Generative AI models?
- **Tips**:
  - Acknowledge the problem of dataset biases being learned and amplified by Generative AI.
  - Discuss strategies like diverse and representative dataset curation, model auditing, and ethical AI guidelines.
  - Highlight the importance of continuously monitoring and updating models to mitigate bias over time.

Question: Can you explain the Generative Adversarial Network (GAN) concept and its applications?
- **Tips**:
  - Describe the structure of GANs, including the roles of the generator and discriminator.
  - Discuss how GANs learn to generate realistic data and their applications in image generation, style transfer, etc.
  - Mention some challenges in training GANs, such as mode collapse and training instability.

Question: What are some emerging trends in Generative AI that ML Solutions Architects should be aware of?

- **Tips:**
    - Discuss recent advancements like multi-modal models (e.g., DALL-E) that combine text and image generation.
    - Highlight the growing importance of ethical AI and responsible usage in the context of Generative AI.
    - Mention the integration of Generative AI in various industries, including healthcare, entertainment, and marketing.
    - Talk about the recent launches in the GenAI area, like Amazon Bedrock, Amazon Q, GPT store, and SageMaker Jumpstart.
    - Talk about various foundation model developments like GPT 4, Google Gemini, Claud-2, etc.

Question: How does Transfer Learning impact the efficiency of Generative AI models?

- **Tips:**
    - Explain Transfer Learning and its role in leveraging pre-trained models to save time and computational resources.
    - Discuss how Generative AI models, like GPT and BERT, can be fine-tuned for specific tasks using a smaller dataset.
    - Highlight the balance between model specificity and generalizability.

Question: Describe a scenario where Generative AI can significantly improve content creation.

- **Tips:**
    - Choose a practical scenario, like automated writing for news articles or script generation for media production.
    - Explain how Generative AI models can analyze existing content styles and produce similar outputs.
    - Discuss the need for human oversight to ensure the quality and appropriateness of the generated content.

Question: How do foundation models like Claude-3, GPT-4, Syability.ai, and Jurrasic-2 change the landscape of AI applications?

- **Tips:**
    - Discuss the scalability and wide-ranging applicability of foundation models like GPT-4.
    - Explain their impact on small-scale projects and startups, offering high-level AI capabilities without extensive resources.
    - Touch on challenges like control, ethical use, and customization.

Question: Explain the Retrieval-Augmented Generation (RAG) concept and its advantages in natural language processing tasks.

- **Tips**:
    - Describe how RAG combines the power of retrieval (searching through a database of documents) with generative language models.
    - Discuss its use in providing more accurate, information-rich responses by referencing existing knowledge sources.
    - Mention applications like enhanced chatbots or information retrieval systems.

Question: Can you illustrate how Language Model Chains (Lang Chain) can improve sequential decision-making in AI systems?

- **Tips**:
    - Explain the Lang Chain as a sequence of models, each performing a task and passing its output to the next model in the chain.
    - Discuss how this approach can handle complex tasks requiring multiple reasoning or transformation steps.
    - An example is an automated customer service system that navigates various sub-tasks to resolve a customer's issue.

Question: What is a Vector Database, and how does it contribute to the efficiency of Generative AI models?

- **Tips**:
    - Define Vector Database in the context of storing and retrieving high-dimensional data vectors, typically generated by AI models.
    - Discuss how it enables efficient similarity searches and retrieval, which is crucial in Generative AI tasks like recommendation systems or content matching.
    - Highlight its advantages in terms of speed and accuracy over traditional databases for specific AI tasks.

Question: How do Retrieval-Augmented Generation models integrate dynamic, real-time information into responses?

- **Tips**:
    - Discuss the ability of RAG models to pull in the most recent data or documents to inform their responses.
    - Explain how this feature is critical in applications with crucial up-to-date information, like news summarization or market analysis.
    - Mention potential challenges like ensuring data relevance and accuracy.

Question: In what ways can Language Model Chains be leveraged to enhance personalization in AI applications?

- **Tips**:

- Explain how Lang Chain can tailor each process step to individual user preferences or historical data.
- Discuss applications in personalized marketing, content recommendation, or adaptive learning environments.
- Highlight the importance of balancing personalization with user privacy and data security.

Question: Explain the role of Synthetic Data Generation in training AI models and its benefits.
- **Tips:**
  - Define Synthetic Data Generation in the context of Generative AI.
  - Discuss its applications in scenarios where real data is scarce, sensitive, or expensive.
  - Mention the benefits, such as privacy preservation, data diversity, and overcoming real-world data collection limitations.

Question: How do you envision the future of Generative AI in enhancing user experiences in interactive applications?
- **Tips:**
  - Talk about personalized content generation (like personalized news, adaptive learning materials, or game narratives).
  - Discuss the potential of virtual reality and augmented reality applications.
  - Emphasize the importance of user data privacy and ethical considerations in these applications.

Preparing for these questions requires a deep understanding of the latest advancements in AI and natural language processing. Being able to discuss these advanced concepts and their practical applications will demonstrate your expertise as a Machine Learning Solutions Architect, particularly in areas driving the future of AI technology.

In-depth ML Training Interview Questions

Let's look at some more straight technical questions and tips to answer them, where you may need to dive deep during the interview.

Question: Can you explain the difference between supervised, unsupervised, and reinforcement learning and give an example of each?
- **Tips:**
  - **Supervised Learning**: Describe it as learning with labeled data, where the algorithm learns from input-output pairs—for example, Spam email detection.

- Unsupervised Learning involves learning from data without labeled outcomes and focusing on discovering patterns, such as customer segmentation in marketing.
- Reinforcement Learning: Define it as learning based on rewards and penalties, where the algorithm learns by interacting with its environment. Example: Training a robot to navigate a maze.

Question: How do you handle imbalanced datasets in a classification problem?
- **Tips**:
  - Discuss techniques like oversampling the minority class, undersampling the majority class, or using synthetic data generation methods like SMOTE.
  - Mention algorithm-level approaches such as adjusting class weights.
  - Highlight the importance of using appropriate evaluation metrics like the F1-score or AUC-ROC curve instead of accuracy.

Question: Describe a situation where you would choose a random forest model over a decision tree and why.
- **Tips**:
  - Emphasize the random forest's strength in reducing overfitting by averaging multiple decision trees.
  - Discuss scenarios requiring more robustness and generalization, such as in complex datasets with numerous features.
  - Highlight random forest's feature importance capabilities, which are useful for feature selection in high-dimensional data.

Question: How do you ensure the robustness of your machine-learning models against outliers or noisy data?
- **Tips**:
  - Talk about preprocessing steps like outlier detection using Z-scores or IQR and noise filtering techniques.
  - Discuss using robust models like Random Forest or algorithms with built-in mechanisms to handle outliers, such as SVM with a nonlinear kernel.
  - Mention cross-validation techniques to ensure the model performs well across different data subsets.

Question: Explain the concept of 'dimensionality reduction' and its importance in ML. Provide an example of a technique used for this purpose.
- **Tips**:
  - Define dimensionality reduction as reducing the number of input variables in a dataset.

- Explain its importance in mitigating the curse of dimensionality, improving model performance, and aiding in data visualization.
- Use PCA (Principal Component Analysis) as an example, explaining how it transforms a high-dimensional dataset into a lower-dimensional one while preserving most of the variance.

Question: Explain the concept of Transfer Learning and how it can be implemented in a machine learning project.
- **Tips:**
  - Define Transfer Learning and its significance in utilizing pre-trained models to save resources and time.
  - Discuss how it involves adapting a model developed for a task to a new, related task (e.g., fine-tuning a pre-trained image classification model for a specific type of object detection).
  - Highlight scenarios where it's particularly beneficial, such as when dealing with limited data.

Question: How would you approach feature selection in a large dataset? What techniques or tools might you use?
- **Tips:**
  - Discuss the importance of feature selection in improving model performance and reducing overfitting.
  - Describe techniques like Wrapper, Filter, Embedded, and Dimensionality Reduction techniques (like PCA).
  - Emphasize using domain knowledge, statistical tests, and feature importance scores from machine learning models.

Question: Can you describe a scenario where Ensemble Learning significantly improved a model's performance?
- **Tips:**
  - Define Ensemble Learning and its principle of combining multiple models to improve overall performance.
  - For example, using Random Forests or Gradient Boosting techniques to enhance prediction accuracy over individual decision trees.
  - Discuss why ensembles often perform better, focusing on variance reduction, bias reduction, or both.

Question: How would you handle imbalanced datasets in a classification problem?
- **Tips:**
  - Explain the challenges posed by imbalanced datasets and their impact on model performance.

- o Describe techniques like resampling (oversampling the minority class or undersampling the majority class), using synthetic data (like SMOTE), or adjusting class weights.
- o Stress the importance of using appropriate evaluation metrics (like F1-score and precision-recall curves) for imbalanced datasets.

Question: Provide the pros and cons of using Deep Learning over traditional machine learning methods in a project.
- **Tips**:
  - o Highlight the strengths of deep learning, especially in handling large and complex datasets with high dimensionality.
  - o Discuss its ability to automatically extract and learn features compared to traditional methods that often require manual feature engineering.
  - o Address the challenges, including the need for large amounts of data, higher computational resources, and the potential for overfitting.
  - o Mention scenarios where deep learning is particularly effective (e.g., image and speech recognition) and traditional methods might be more efficient (e.g., smaller datasets or simpler problems).

In answering these questions, demonstrate a balanced understanding of different ML approaches, their appropriate use cases, and an awareness of practical challenges and how to mitigate them.

ML Training Questions for Multiple Cloud

You learned in-depth concepts of ML in the AWS cloud; let's explore how these tools and concepts can be applied to other popular cloud platforms, such as GCP and Azure.

Question: How would you develop a new e-commerce platform recommendation engine using GCP's machine learning services?
- **Tips**: Explain different steps involved in building a recommendation engine for a new e-commerce platform using Google Cloud Platform's machine learning services:
  - o Data Collection and Preprocessing
    - ▪ Use Cloud Storage to store user data like browse and purchase history and product data like descriptions, categories, images, etc.
    - ▪ Use BigQuery to preprocess the data by joining user data with product data, cleaning missing values, transforming features, etc. BigQuery ML can also be used for basic aggregations and analysis.
    - ▪ Cloud Dataflow can be used for more complex data pipeline jobs like aggregating user-product interactions over time windows.
  - o Model Training

- Use Vertex AI to train machine learning models, such as collaborative filtering, content-based filtering, and hybrid models, to generate recommendations.
- Leverage pre-built TensorFlow/PyTorch containers to train models on Cloud AI Platform/Vertex AI Training for scalability.
- Use feature engineering tools like Cloud Data Fusion to derive better features from raw data.
- Generate embeddings for users and products using tools like Word2Vec on top of preprocessed data.
  - Model Deployment
    - Deploy the trained TensorFlow/PyTorch models on Vertex AI endpoints to generate real-time recommendations with low latency.
    - Leverage Cloud Run/Cloud Functions to wrap the Vertex AI predictions into a web service API.
    - Use Cloud Load Balancing and Cloud CDN cache, frequently recommended products for low latency.
  - Monitoring and Optimization
    - Monitor API calls, error rates, etc, with Cloud Logging and Cloud Monitoring.
    - Re-train models periodically with new user data using Vertex AI Hyperparameter tuning, Vertex Experiments, etc.
    - Optimize model performance for metrics like click-through rate, conversion rate, etc.

In summary, to maintain a performant recommender system, leverage BigQuery, Dataflow, and Cloud Storage for data processing, Vertex AI and Cloud ML for model training and deployment, and tools like Monitoring and Logging.

Question: How would you approach building a natural language processing model to classify and analyze customer feedback data for a large retail company using GCP's Cloud Natural Language API?
- **Tips**: When building a natural language processing model to classify and analyze customer feedback data for a large retail company using GCP's Cloud Natural Language API, there are several approaches you can take. Here are some tips to help you answer this question:
  - **Understand the requirements**: Before starting the project, it's important to understand the requirements of the retail company. What do they want to achieve with the natural language processing model? What kind of customer feedback data do they have? What are the desired outcomes of the project?
  - **Data Collection and Preprocessing**: The first step is to collect and preprocess customer feedback data. This data can come from various sources, such as surveys, reviews, social media, and chatbots. You can store the data in GCP's

Cloud Storage and preprocess it in Cloud Dataflow. You can also clean, transform, and enrich the data using Cloud Dataprep.

- o **Choose a Machine Learning Engine**: GCP provides several machine learning engines that can be used for natural language processing, including AutoML Natural Language, TensorFlow, and scikit-learn. Each engine has its strengths and weaknesses, so choosing the one that best fits the project's requirements is important.

- o **Train the Model**: Once you've chosen a machine learning engine, you can train the model using the preprocessed data. You can use GCP's Cloud AI Platform to train the model in a scalable and automated way. You can also use transfer learning to leverage pre-trained models and fine-tune them for your specific use case.

- o **Model Evaluation**: After training the model, it's important to evaluate its performance using metrics such as accuracy, precision, recall, and F1 score. You can use GCP's Cloud AI Platform to evaluate the model and techniques, such as cross-validation, to ensure that it generalizes new data well.

- o **Deployment**: Once the model is trained and evaluated, deploying it in a production-ready environment is important. You can use GCP's Cloud Functions or Cloud Run to deploy the model as a RESTful API. You can also use Cloud Endpoints to provide a secure and scalable API gateway.

- o **Monitoring and Maintenance**: It is important to monitor the model's performance and maintain it over time after deploying it. You can use GCP's Cloud Monitoring and Cloud Logging to monitor the model's performance and detect any issues. You can also use continuous integration and continuous deployment (CI/CD) techniques to ensure the model is up-to-date and performing well.

- o **Additional Considerations**: When building a natural language processing model, there are several additional considerations to keep in mind. For example, you may need to consider data privacy and security, especially if the data contains sensitive information. You may also need to consider scalability, as the model may need to handle a large volume of data. Finally, you may need to consider the ethical implications of the model, such as ensuring that it does not perpetuate biases or discrimination.

In summary, when building a natural language processing model to classify and analyze customer feedback data for a large retail company using GCP's Cloud Natural Language API, it's important to understand the requirements, collect and preprocess the data, choose a machine learning engine, train the model, evaluate its performance, deploy it in a production-ready environment, monitor and maintain it over time, and consider additional considerations such as data privacy, scalability, and ethical implications.

Question: Your team has deployed a new ML model in GCP, using the Vertex AI endpoint for predictions. The latest deployment is giving weird results. How would you troubleshoot and fix the issue?

- **Tips**: Below are some tips to fix the issue with weird results in a new deployment using Vertex AI endpoint for predictions; follow these steps:
    - ○ **Check the data:** Verify that the data used for training and testing is consistent across both deployments. Ensure the new deployment uses the same data distribution, format, and quality as the previous one.
    - ○ **Compare model configurations:** Check that the model architecture, hyperparameters, and optimization algorithms are identical in both deployments. If they differ, reproduce the original configuration in the new deployment.
    - ○ **Monitor model performance:** Compare the model's performance in both deployments using metrics such as accuracy, precision, recall, and F1-score. Identify any significant differences in performance that could indicate the cause of the issue.
    - ○ **Analyze logs and errors:** Check the logs and error messages in the new deployment to identify any issues that may not have been present in the original deployment. Look for signs of data corruption, missing data, or unexpected errors.
    - ○ **Test the model locally:** Test the model locally using a sample of data to see if the issue persists. This will help you determine if the problem is related to the model or the deployment environment.
    - ○ **Check the deployment environment:** Ensure the deployment environment is consistent across both deployments. Check for differences in software versions, hardware specifications, or library dependencies that could impact the model's performance.
    - ○ **Consult with the team:** Collaborate with your team to gather insights and suggestions. They may have encountered similar issues or have ideas for troubleshooting.
    - ○ **Contact Vertex AI support:** If none of the above steps resolve the issue, contact Vertex AI support for assistance. They can provide additional troubleshooting steps or help you identify the root cause of the problem.

By following these steps systematically, you should be able to identify and resolve the issue with the new deployment and restore the expected results.

Question: Describe a scenario where you would use Azure's AutoML feature to train a machine learning model. How would you evaluate the model's performance, and what steps would you take to optimize its accuracy?

- **Tips**: Azure's AutoML feature is a powerful tool for training machine learning models and can be used in various scenarios. One scenario where I would use Azure's AutoML feature is to predict customer churn.
  - **Scenario:** I work for a telecom company, and my task is to predict which customers will likely switch to a competitor's service. Customer churn is a significant problem for telecom companies, as it can lead to lost revenue and increased marketing costs to acquire new customers. To solve this problem, I use Azure's AutoML feature to train a machine-learning model that can predict customer churn. I have a dataset containing our customers' demographic information, usage patterns, and billing history.
  - **Training the Model:** I begin by uploading my dataset to Azure and using the AutoML feature to train a machine-learning model. I chose the "Customer Churn" template, a pre-built template provided by Azure specifically designed for this task. The template guides me through selecting the appropriate data columns, preprocessing the data, and splitting the dataset into training and testing sets. I then choose a suitable machine learning algorithm and train the model using the training data.
  - **Evaluating the Model:** Once trained, I evaluated the model's performance using the testing data. I calculated the model's accuracy and found that it accurately predicted customer churn about 80% of the time. While 80% accuracy is decent, I want to optimize the model's accuracy to improve its performance. To do this, I used the "Model Evaluation" feature in Azure to analyze the model's performance and identify areas for improvement.
  - **Optimizing the Model:** Based on the evaluation results, I identified that the model struggles to predict churn for long-term customers accurately. I added more features to the dataset, such as the customer's lifetime value and usage patterns. I then retrained the model using the updated dataset and evaluated its performance again. This time, the accuracy improved to 90%, which is a significant improvement.
  - **Deploying the Model:** Now that I have a highly accurate model, I want to deploy it in production. I use Azure's "Model Deployment" feature to deploy the model as a web service. I then create a simple web application that takes in customer data and outputs the predicted likelihood of churn. Our customer service team can use this application to identify customers at risk of churning and offer personalized promotions and incentives to retain their business.

Azure's AutoML feature is a powerful tool for training machine learning models. It can be used in various scenarios, such as predicting customer churn. By following the steps outlined above, I was able to train a highly accurate model that can predict customer churn and provide actionable insights to our customer service team.

Question: Explain some best practices for training deep learning models on Azure ML Studio.
- **Tips**: Training deep learning models on Azure ML Studio can be a powerful way to leverage the scalability and flexibility of the cloud for machine learning tasks. Here are some best practices for training deep learning models on Azure ML Studio:
  - **Plan your experiment**: Before starting your experiment, it's important to clearly understand the problem you're trying to solve and the data you'll be working with. This includes identifying the type of deep learning model you want to use, the size and complexity of your dataset, and the computational resources you'll need.
  - **Prepare your data**: Deep learning models require large amounts of high-quality data to train effectively. This includes clean, consistent, and relevant data to the problem you're trying to solve. Azure ML Studio provides various data preparation tools to help you prepare your data, including data cleaning, transformation, and feature engineering.
  - **Choose the right hardware**: Deep learning models can be computationally intensive, so choosing the right hardware for your experiment is important. Azure ML Studio provides a range of virtual machines and GPU instances to choose from, depending on your specific needs.
  - **Use version control**: Version control is an important part of any machine learning project. It allows you to track changes to your code and data over time. Azure ML Studio supports version control using Git, enabling you to collaborate easily with others and reproduce previous experiments.
  - **Monitor your experiment**: Monitoring your experiment is critical to ensuring its success and efficiency. Azure ML Studio provides various monitoring tools, including real-time metrics and logs, to help you track its progress.
  - **Use hyperparameter tuning**. Hyperparameters are parameters in training a model, such as learning rate, batch size, and the number of hidden layers. Tuning these hyperparameters can significantly impact the model's performance. Azure ML Studio provides several hyperparameter tuning tools, including grid search, random search, and Bayesian optimization.
  - **Use model validation**. Model validation is evaluating your model's performance on a separate dataset. It is important to ensure that your model generalizes well to new data and does not overfit the training data. Azure ML Studio provides various model validation tools, including k-fold cross-validation and model evaluation metrics.
  - **Use Azure ML Studio's automated machine learning**. This feature allows you to automatically train and deploy machine learning models without writing any

code. It can save you time and effort and help you avoid common pitfalls such as overfitting and underfitting.

- o **Use Azure ML Studio's collaboration features**: Azure ML Studio provides a range of collaboration features, including the ability to share experiments, publishing models, and collaborate with others in real-time. These features can help streamline the machine learning development process and improve productivity.
- o **Use Azure ML Studio's deployment features**: Once your model is trained and validated, you can deploy it to various environments using its deployment features. This includes deploying to Azure Kubernetes Service (AKS), Azure Container Instances (ACI), and Azure Functions.

Question: What are some best practices to prevent data leakage in an Azure Machine Learning deployment?

- • **Tips**:
  - o Data masking techniques, such as encryption or obfuscation, must be implemented to protect sensitive information. Azure's built-in data protection services, such as Azure Key Vault or Azure Data Protection, can help.
  - o Access control policies should be implemented to restrict access to sensitive data. Azure Machine Learning provides role-based access control (RBAC) to manage resource access. Azure Active Directory (AAD) can also use user identities and assign permissions.
  - o Use secure data storage solutions, such as Azure Blob Storage or Azure Data Lake Storage Gen2, which provide encryption at rest and in transit.
  - o Network isolation can be achieved by using Azure to restrict access to the machine learning environment, such as the virtual network (VNet) and Azure Firewall. This can be done to detect and respond to potential data leakage incidents. Azure Monitor and Azure Log Analytics can be used to monitor and log activities in the environment.
  - o Train employees and contractors on data privacy and security best practices to prevent accidental data leakage.

Implementing data masking techniques, access control policies, secure data storage solutions, network isolation, monitoring and auditing, and employee training are essential to preventing data leakage in an Azure Machine Learning deployment.

Question: What type of drift can you monitor in Azure machine learning

- • **Tips**: Two main types of drift can be monitored in Azure Machine Learning:
  - o **Data drift**: This refers to changes in the input data over time. For example, if you train a model to recognize images, the distribution of the input images may change over time as new images are collected. This can impact the performance of machine learning models. In Azure ML, you can monitor data drift using the

Data Drift detector capability. This analyzes your input data and can alert you when the data schema or statistical properties change compared to the baseline data the model was trained on.

- o **Model drift**: This refers to changes in the relationship between the input data and target variable over time. Even if the input data distribution stays the same, the relationship between inputs and outputs may change, causing model performance to degrade. In Azure ML, you can monitor model drift by enabling Continuous Training and Deployment. This retrains your model on new data periodically and compares performance metrics to detect when model quality starts to degrade. You can also set up triggers to alert you when metrics like precision, accuracy, or AUC fall below a threshold.

Azure Machine Learning provides built-in ways to monitor data and model drift through Data Drift Detection, Continuous Training/Deployment, and performance metrics tracking. Detecting drift helps you know when to retrain or adjust your models to maintain accuracy over time as real-world data evolves.

Question: Can you describe a specific project you worked on that involved using Amazon SageMaker? What was your role in the project, and what did you learn from the experience?

- **Tips**:
  - o Provide background on the project and business goal. Explain what the organization or client was trying to accomplish overall.
  - o Describe your specific role and responsibilities on the project. Were you responsible for building, training, deploying, or managing machine learning models using SageMaker? Did you lead the development, or were you part of a team?
  - o Explain how you used SageMaker's features and services as part of the project. For example, did you Build, train, and optimize machine learning models using SageMaker notebooks and built-in algorithms or manage training jobs and track experiments? Did you deploy models for real-time predictions using SageMaker hosting services or monitor and evaluate model performance over time?
  - o Share any key technical details about the types of models, data, or methods used. For example, did you build neural networks, random forests, or other models?
  - o Discuss successes, challenges faced, and major lessons learned from using SageMaker. What did you learn about building end-to-end ML workflows on a managed platform?

Question: Can you describe a time when you had to optimize hyperparameters for a machine learning model in Amazon SageMaker? What approach did you take, and what were the results?

- **Tips**:

o When building a random forest model for predicting customer churn, I used SageMaker's hyperparameter tuning to find the best combination of hyperparameters. I created a hyperparameter tuning job that searched over the number of trees (10-100), maximum tree depth (5-20), and minimum leaf size (5-100). To find the optimal hyperparameters efficiently, I used a Bayesian search algorithm, which selected new hyperparameter configurations to try based on how well previous ones performed. I also made sure to use early stopping to terminate poor-performing jobs quickly. After 20 trials, the tuning job found that a random forest with 80 estimators, a max depth of 12, and a min leaf size of 20 achieved the highest validation F1 score. Compared to my default hyperparameters, this improved the validation F1 by over 5%, reducing overfitting on the training set. By leveraging SageMaker's built-in hyperparameter tuning capabilities, I efficiently optimized the random forest hyperparameters for my churn prediction task and achieved improved model performance.

Question: What are the different Inference options in Amazon SageMaker? Explain with some examples.

- **Tips**: In Amazon SageMaker, several inference options are available to meet different needs.
    - **Real-time Inference**: Real-time inference is suitable for applications that require fast and low-latency predictions. It allows you to deploy your model and make predictions in real-time as soon as new data is available. Amazon SageMaker provides various real-time inference options, including Amazon SageMaker Inference, Amazon SageMaker Serverless Inference, and Amazon SageMaker Real-Time Predictive Analytics.
    - **Serverless Inference:** Serverless inference is a fully managed inference service that eliminates the need to manage and scale your inference infrastructure. It automatically scales the inference capacity based on the demand, providing cost-effective and scalable solutions. Amazon SageMaker Serverless Inference is ideal for applications with intermittent or unpredictable traffic patterns, as it can handle sudden spikes in demand without requiring manual intervention.
    - **Batch Inference:** Batch inference is suitable for applications that require processing large amounts of data and making predictions in batches. It allows you to upload your data to an S3 bucket and invoke your model asynchronously to generate predictions. Amazon SageMaker provides various batch inference options, including Amazon SageMaker Batch Transform, Amazon SageMaker Serverless Batch Inference, and Amazon SageMaker Elastic Inference.
    - **Asynchronous Inference:** Asynchronous inference is ideal when you want to queue requests and have large payloads with long processing times. Asynchronous inference supports up to 1 GB of payloads and one-hour-long

processing times. Additionally, you can reduce your endpoint to 0 when there are no requests to process.

Question: Design an algorithm to predict the likelihood of a customer purchasing within the next 30 days based on their browsing history on an e-commerce website. The algorithm should take into account the following factors:

- **The types of products the customer has viewed**
- **The amount of time the customer has spent viewing each product**
- **The customer's search history**
- **The customer's purchase history**
- **The customer's demographic information (age, gender, location)**

The algorithm should output a probability score indicating the customer's likelihood of purchasing within the next 30 days. The score should be based on a scale of 0 to 1, with higher scores indicating a higher probability of a purchase.

- **Tips:**
    - Start by breaking down the problem into smaller, manageable parts. Identify the key factors the algorithm needs to consider, such as the customer's browsing history, search, purchase, and demographic information.
    - Consider how each factor might be used to predict the likelihood of a purchase. For example, the types of products the customer has viewed might indicate their interests and preferences. In contrast, the amount of time they've spent viewing each product might indicate their level of engagement.
    - Combine these factors to produce a meaningful output. Consider using a machine learning algorithm, such as logistic regression or a decision tree, to model the relationship between the input factors and the output probability score.
    - Consider how to handle missing data. For example, if a customer has not provided demographic information, you might need to impute this. In that case, data or a different method is used to predict their likelihood of making a purchase.
    - Think about how to evaluate the performance of the algorithm. Consider using metrics such as accuracy, precision, and recall to assess how well the algorithm can predict the likelihood of a purchase.
    - Consider how to implement the algorithm in a scalable and efficient way. You should use techniques such as data parallelism or distributed computing to handle large volumes of data.
    - Finally, be prepared to explain your thought process and the trade-offs you made in designing the algorithm. Be able to justify the choices you made and the assumptions you made along the way.

Machine learning, particularly with Generative AI, is a complex and specialized field that requires theoretical knowledge and practical experience with cloud-based ML platforms. These platforms, such as AWS, Azure, and GCP, offer a vast array of tools and services that cater to the heavy computational needs of machine learning tasks. Experts in this field must leverage these platforms to build, train, and deploy models effectively. Given the breadth of the subject, it's crucial to enhance your understanding of the chosen cloud provider's offerings and best practices.

The pursuit of a career as an ML architect demands a thorough preparation strategy that goes beyond basic understanding. In this book, we've outlined a series of potential interview questions and offered strategic tips for responses that demonstrate both depth and practicality. While the foundational concepts introduced in this chapter provide a starting point, the onus is on you to delve into the details and become equipped to excel in interviews for ML architect positions.

Summary

This chapter offers a comprehensive guide for aspirants who aim to excel as Machine Learning and Generative AI Solutions Architects. It starts by defining the role of an ML and Generative AI Solutions Architect and highlights the blend of technical expertise and strategic foresight needed to succeed.

The chapter delves into fundamental machine learning algorithms, providing insights into common methods and their applications. It explores neural networks and deep learning, emphasizing their transformative role in modern AI solutions. The chapter also covers transfer learning, stressing its efficiency in leveraging pre-trained models for new tasks. The importance of data preprocessing and feature engineering is underscored, explaining how they refine data for optimal model performance. Model evaluation metrics are discussed, aiding architects in assessing model accuracy and effectiveness.

Generative AI, particularly foundation models, is the focus of the chapter, which discusses their burgeoning influence on AI solutions. The chapter explores these models' capabilities, potential applications, and impact on various industries. Further, it outlines a structured approach to developing ML models, from conceptualization to implementation, ensuring a systematic progression through each project phase. As you transition to MLOps, the chapter discusses technologies that facilitate the integration of ML models into production, emphasizing the importance of infrastructure, scalability, and cloud deployment.

Addressing the ethical dimension, the chapter stresses the importance of mitigating bias and ensuring fairness in AI solutions. It encourages a responsible approach to AI development that considers ethical implications and societal impact. A rundown of essential tools and frameworks empowers aspiring architects with knowledge of the best resources for various ML tasks. From

Amazon SageMaker to TensorFlow and PyTorch, the chapter covers a range of options suited for different needs.

The final section prepares candidates for interviews, presenting a mix of behavioral and technical questions. It includes tips on answering questions about ML in cloud environments and Generative AI, providing a well-rounded preparation for aspiring architects.

Chapter 11 - Cracking the Security Solutions Architect Interview

In an age where data is the new currency, security is the guardian. It's not just about protecting information but safeguarding the essence of modern life. As organizations embrace the cloud alongside on-premise workloads and expand their digital footprint using various software tool integrations, the pivotal role of a security solutions architect emerges. These architects are the sentinels of the digital domain, entrusted with creating secure, resilient, and compliant systems to overcome ever-evolving threats.

This chapter serves as your comprehensive guide to navigating the challenging landscape of security architecture. Whether you're an aspiring security architect or a seasoned professional looking to strengthen your expertise, the knowledge contained within this chapter will help you to excel in your career and overcome the most challenging interviews.

In this chapter, you will learn the core components of the Security Solutions Architect role. You will begin by delving into the fundamentals and understanding what being a security architect means. Then, you will navigate the best practices, industry frameworks, and security in cloud compliance and governance, essential for ensuring that security protocols remain in lockstep with the ever-changing regulatory requirements.

Further, you will learn tips and tricks to crack security architect interviews. You will get details of interview questions and insights, preparing you to showcase your expertise, articulate your ideas, and help you get through to prospective employers. In this chapter, you will learn the following topics:

- Understanding the Security Solutions Architect Role
- Understanding security architecture and its components
- Key security design principles and methodologies
- Understanding cloud security risks and threats
- Security architect interview questions

The security of digital systems has never been more crucial, and the demand for skilled Security Solutions Architects is on the rise. As you embark on this journey of security architecture, remember that you're protecting not just data but also the trust and integrity of the digital world. So, let's dive in and equip ourselves with the tips and skills required to crack security architect interviews.

Understanding the Security SA role

In today's digitized world, Security Solutions Architects play an invaluable role in ensuring that security remains at the heart of architectural design. Given that large-scale enterprises have witnessed substantial financial setbacks due to security breaches, the need for experts who can preemptively address vulnerabilities has never been more pronounced.

When customer data becomes compromised, the fallout isn't limited to monetary repercussions. Organizations risk tarnishing their reputation and losing the trust they've painstakingly built with their clientele. For some, it can even signify the collapse of their entire enterprise. This landscape makes the Security Solutions Architect's role pivotal. They design secure systems and ensure alignment with the countless industry-standard compliances and regulations. These frameworks aren't merely checkboxes to be ticked but critical blueprints that ensure applications are fortified, and customer-sensitive data is protected. A Security Solutions Architect, therefore, isn't just an IT professional; they are the guardians of trust, reputation, and business continuity in an increasingly volatile digital landscape.

A Security Solutions Architect is responsible for designing and maintaining an organization's security architecture. Security Solutions Architects advocate for security within the organization. They work with business leaders and IT professionals to ensure that security is a top priority. Some of the primary responsibilities of a Security Solutions Architect include:

- **Designing security architecture**: A Security Solutions Architect designs and maintains an organization's security architecture. They identify potential security vulnerabilities and design solutions to prevent or mitigate them. Security Solutions Architects design, develop, and implement security solutions that protect an organization's data and systems from unauthorized access, disruption, modification, or destruction. *For example, if* an e-commerce platform aims to launch a new mobile app. A Security Solutions Architect designs a multi-layered security protocol, considering end-to-end encryption, secure payment gateways, and biometric authentication mechanisms. The infamous Target Corporation breach in 2013 affected millions due to a lack of a robust security architecture. Had there been a more thorough design, the vulnerability exploited by the hackers might have been identified and rectified.

- **Performing risk assessments**: Security Solutions Architects perform risk assessments to identify potential security threats and vulnerabilities. They use this information to develop strategies to mitigate these risks and maintain the organization's security posture. Security Solutions Architects conduct security assessments to identify and mitigate security risks. They use various tools and techniques to assess the security of an organization's systems, networks, and applications. For example, A financial institution is migrating its data to the cloud. The Security Solutions Architect assesses vulnerabilities associated with the migration, like potential data leaks or unauthorized access, and devises preventive measures. The Capital One breach in 2019, where a former employee exploited a vulnerability in the system, stealing data of over 100 million users. A proactive risk assessment might have identified such weaknesses.

- **Manage security operations and Incident response:** Security Solutions Architects manage security operations, which includes monitoring and responding to security incidents. They work with security engineers and other IT professionals to investigate and resolve security incidents quickly and effectively. They integrate security solutions into existing IT systems, ensuring compatibility and effectiveness. For *example,* a company introduces a new Human Resources Information System (HRIS). The Security Solutions Architect ensures the new system integrates seamlessly with the existing IT infrastructure without opening up new vulnerabilities. The WannaCry ransomware attack in 2017 preyed on systems with outdated Windows versions. Proper integration of patches into the system could have prevented the large-scale impact. In the event of a ransomware attack, the architect would analyze how the malware entered the network, the extent of the damage, and the measures to prevent such occurrences in the future.

- **Reviewing third-party solutions**: Security Solutions Architects are responsible for reviewing and approving third-party solutions or technologies being considered for implementation within the organization. They ensure these solutions meet the organization's security requirements and comply with relevant security standards. They Collaborate with vendors to select and implement the most effective security solutions. For example, *a* retail company wants to incorporate a Point of Sale (PoS) system. The Security Solutions Architect liaises with various vendors, ensuring the chosen system has robust security protocols like end-to-end card data encryption. The 2014 Home Depot breach occurred because of vulnerabilities in its PoS systems. A more thorough vendor assessment and third-party solutions selection process could have averted the violation.

- **Educate and train employees on security best practices:** Security Solutions Architects educate and train employees on security best practices. They develop security awareness training programs and materials that help employees understand their role in protecting the organization's security. For example, A healthcare organization is wary of increasing phishing attacks. The Security Solutions Architect initiates regular training sessions, educating employees about recognizing and avoiding phishing emails. In 2016, a spear-phishing scheme gave attackers unauthorized access to the Democratic National Committee's network. Continuous employee training on recognizing such systems could have prevented the breach.

- **Developing security documentation**: Security Solutions Architects build and maintain documentation related to an organization's security architecture, policies, and procedures. This documentation ensures the organization's security posture is well-documented, understood, and maintained.

- **Stay up-to-date on security trends:** Security Solutions Architects stay up-to-date on security trends and threats. They read security blogs and articles, attend security conferences, and participate in security communities to learn about the latest security threats and how to mitigate them. With the rise of IoT (Internet of Things), many previously considered harmless devices are now entry points for potential attacks. Understanding these threats helps the architect formulate strategies to counteract them.

Effective communication with stakeholders, from board members to staff, is crucial. Security Solutions Architects often have to explain complex security issues in a way that is understandable to non-technical individuals. They collaborate with other teams within the organization to design and implement secure systems. They work closely with developers, network engineers, and other IT professionals to ensure systems are designed with security in mind.

While security Solutions Architects are known for their principal duties in creating an organization's foundational security blueprints, their day-to-day operations encompass a broader scope. These professionals are tasked with formulating and enacting robust security policies and guidelines, directing the establishment and continuous management of security systems, and ensuring the regular conduct of comprehensive audits. Their rapid response to security incidents and meticulous investigations following security breaches further underscore their indispensable role.

The breadth and depth of their responsibilities often vary, taking cues from the organization's size, operational complexity, and industry. For instance, a multinational corporation might have architects focusing on niche areas, while in smaller entities, they could wear multiple hats.

Understanding security architecture

Security architecture refers to the design, components, and principles guiding the creation, deployment, and management of a secure environment within an organization. It serves as a roadmap detailing how various security controls and measures align with the company's business goals and IT strategy, which a security SA should know. When thoughtfully designed, security architecture ensures data protection, regulatory compliance, and a proactive defense against threats. The following are the key components of Security Architecture:

- **Security Policies and Procedures** are the guidelines, standards, and rules that an organization follows to protect its data and IT assets. Policies include access controls, acceptable use policies, and incident response protocols. These policies outline the guidelines, standards, and rules that establish an organization's security posture. For example, an organization may have a policy requiring regular password changes, ensuring that passwords are complex and not reused within a specific time frame.

- **Network Security** pertains to measures and controls that protect data's integrity, confidentiality, and availability as it's transferred across or accessed from the network. It includes firewalls, intrusion detection systems (IDS), intrusion prevention systems (IPS), and secure network topologies. For example, a company sets up a firewall to monitor incoming and outgoing network traffic based on an organization's security policies.

- **Endpoint Security** ensures that endpoints (computers, mobile devices, and servers) accessing the network are secure. Security approaches include antimalware tools and device and patch management. For example, a business deploys antivirus software on all its employee laptops to protect against malware threats.

- **Application Security:** This involves ensuring that applications (both in-house and third-party) are free of vulnerabilities that attackers could exploit. Measures include secure coding practices, regular vulnerability assessments, and penetration testing. For example, before launching a new mobile app, a company conducts vulnerability assessments to identify and patch potential security flaws.

- **Identity and Access Management (IAM):** IAM solutions manage who has access to what within an organization. They ensure that the right individuals access the right resources at the right times for the right reasons. Components include user authentication, multi-factor authentication, and role-based access control. For example, a hospital implements role-based access control, allowing only certain personnel to access patient records.

- **Data Security and Privacy:** Tools like encryption, tokenization, and data masking protect sensitive data, ensuring it's unreadable and unusable if unauthorized access occurs. For example, a financial institution encrypts customer transaction data to keep it secure during online banking activities.

- **Physical Security:** While often overlooked in IT, physical security is crucial. It includes controlling access to hardware and ensuring that servers, workstations, and other equipment are physically secure from threats.

- **Disaster Recovery and Business Continuity:** These plans ensure that operations can continue in the event of a disaster (whether cyber or physical) and that data can be recovered. For example, a data center uses biometric access controls, surveillance cameras, and security personnel to guard against unauthorized access. A retail company quickly switches to backup servers in another location after a major power outage, minimizing downtime.

- **Incident Response:** This component outlines how the organization responds to and recovers from security breaches or incidents. It includes the phases of identification, containment, eradication, recovery, and lessons learned. For example, after detecting suspicious activity, a company follows its incident response plan to contain the breach, notify affected parties, and prevent future incidents.

- **Security Awareness Training:** Educating employees about security threats and training them on best practices can mitigate a significant percentage of potential security incidents. This component involves regular training and awareness campaigns. For example, an organization conducts monthly phishing simulations to train employees in spotting malicious emails.

Understanding security architecture and its diverse components is foundational for building a resilient and secure IT environment for security SA. As threats evolve, so should the architecture. Regular reviews and updates ensure that an organization's security posture remains strong, agile, and aligned with its objectives and risk tolerance. Security Solutions Architects can craft a robust defense against multifaceted threats by comprehensively addressing each component.

Key Security Design Principles

Security design principles and methodologies are foundational concepts that guide the development and implementation of secure systems, applications, and networks. As a security solutions architect, you need to be well aware of them as they serve as fundamental guidelines that, when properly applied, ensure the robustness and resilience of the security posture in any IT environment. Understanding these principles is essential for any security professional or architect, particularly in today's landscape filled with evolving threats. Here are some of the key principles and methodologies:

- **Least Privilege**: This principle dictates that a user, system, or application should have the minimum levels of access necessary to perform its tasks and no more. Regularly reviewing and updating permissions and employing role-based access controls. For example, an employee in the HR department should not be able to access the company's source code repository.
- **Defense in Depth**: Implement multiple layers of security controls (physical, technical, and administrative) so that if one layer is compromised, other layers are still in place. Incorporate various security measures like firewalls, encryption, and intrusion detection systems. Think about a network with firewalls at its perimeter, encrypted data at rest, and regular security training for employees to provide multi-layer security.
- **Fail-Safe Defaults**: Systems should default to a secure state, requiring explicit activity permissions. Start with all permissions denied and only grant specific permissions as needed, for a new software application defaults to denying all user access until permissions are specifically granted.
- **Economy of Mechanism**: Keep designs simple and small, as complex systems are more complicated to secure and understand. Use modular programming and microservices to break down complex tasks. Instead of a monolithic application, have separate modules for user management, data processing, etc.
- **Complete Mediation**: Every access request to resources should be checked against access controls every time. Use middleware or interceptors to verify requests. A document

management system verifies user permissions whenever a file is requested, not just during login.

- **Open Design**: The design should not be secret, and security shouldn't rely on obscurity. Publish or share system designs, keeping only cryptographic keys secret. Cryptographic algorithms like AES are publicly known but secure because their strength lies in the secrecy of the keys, not the algorithm.
- **Separation of Duties**: Divide responsibilities among different entities or persons so that no single individual can maliciously or accidentally harm security. Ensure critical tasks require multiple authorizations. Ensure a developer and a manager approve a software deployment in a production environment.
- **Least Common Mechanism**: Minimize the use of mechanisms common to more than one user or process to prevent shared vulnerabilities. Use dedicated resources where necessary. Avoid having multiple applications share the same database user credentials.

These security design principles and methodologies form the backbone of a solid security posture. By understanding and implementing them, security strategies can create a multifaceted defense mechanism against various threats.

Understanding Cloud Security Risks

A foundational concept in cloud computing is the shared responsibility model. This paradigm divides security responsibilities between the cloud service provider (CSP) and the user. Grasping this understanding of responsibility is crucial for safeguarding data and applications in the cloud. A failure to adequately understand or implement one's responsibilities can lead to security vulnerabilities.

Cloud Shared Responsibility Model

As a Security Solutions Architect, understanding and interpreting the shared responsibility model is not just about knowledge but also about actively educating and guiding the organization to make well-informed cloud security decisions. This role involves anticipating potential pitfalls, foreseeing risks, and designing security mechanisms that align with the cloud provider's offerings and the organization's unique needs.

Responsibilities of the Cloud Service Provider (CSP)

- **Infrastructure Security**: The CSP is responsible for securing the foundational infrastructure components, including the physical data centers, servers, networking hardware, and storage units.
- **Software and Platform Patching**: For Platform-as-a-Service (PaaS) and Infrastructure-as-a-Service (IaaS) offerings, CSPs ensure that the underlying software and platforms are up-to-date and secure.

- **Network Protection**: CSPs manage protection mechanisms, such as perimeter firewalls and intrusion detection systems, to ensure the integrity of their networks.
- **Physical Security**: CSPs maintain the physical security of their data centers, ensuring protection against unauthorized access, environmental hazards, and other physical threats.

Responsibilities of the User

- **Data Protection**: As users, we must ensure the customer's data is encrypted in transit and at rest. Data protection includes choosing robust encryption methods and managing encryption keys.
- **Identity and Access Management**: We must manage who has access to customers' data and services, which entails setting up roles and permissions and using multi-factor authentication.
- **Endpoint Protection**: If accessing cloud resources from endpoints like personal computers, users should secure these endpoints with antivirus software, firewalls, and other protective measures.
- **Application Security**: For businesses deploying applications in the cloud, it's essential to ensure the application is coded securely, free from vulnerabilities, and undergoes regular security audits.

Common Risks and Threats in the Context of the Shared Model

- **Misconfiguration**: One of the most prevalent risks is misconfiguring cloud resources. As cloud users, you must understand your part in the shared responsibility model. Overlooking default settings can result in unintended exposures. For example, a developer might accidentally enable public write access to an AWS S3 bucket during testing. As a Security Solutions Architect, implementing tools like AWS Config can help monitor and detect such misconfigurations in real time.
- **Weak Access Controls**: Inadequate management of identities and permissions can give malicious actors, or even unintended internal users, access to sensitive data or critical resources. Unrestricted access can become a goldmine for malicious entities. For example, a database containing sensitive customer information might be accessible from any IP address, making it susceptible to brute-force attacks. CSP tools like security groups and setting strict IP safelists can prevent such scenarios.
- **Account Hijacking**: Phishing attacks or other malicious tactics can compromise user credentials, granting attackers access to cloud resources. Protecting user credentials is of paramount importance. For example, A finance team member receives a phishing email pretending to be from Azure support. Training sessions organized by the Security Solutions Architect can help staff recognize such attempts and prevent unauthorized access.

- **Insecure APIs**: Cloud services often provide APIs for interaction. APIs can avoid becoming attack entry points if they are adequately secured or used securely. Third-party interfaces can introduce vulnerabilities if not utilized securely. For example, an application may use an API to fetch data from a cloud service but does not validate or sanitize the incoming data, leading to injection attacks. As an architect, one could implement API gateways and input validation mechanisms to counteract this risk.

Understanding the shared security model and the division of responsibilities is critical in avoiding these and other cloud-related risks.

> *Organizations must recognize that while cloud providers offer robust infrastructure and platform security, many security aspects, especially those concerning data and access, are the responsibility of users. Proper training, regular audits, and leveraging cloud-native and third-party security tools can help ensure a comprehensive and robust cloud security posture.*

For a Security Solutions Architect, each day revolves around considering the "what ifs" of the shared security model and proactively building defenses. They act as the bridge between the protective measures offered by an organization and cloud service providers, ensuring that the best of both worlds is seamlessly and securely integrated.

Identity and Access Management (IAM) in the Cloud

IAM refers to the systems, protocols, and policies that control and monitor user access to critical resources within an organization. As resources are distributed and access points multiply, IAM becomes even more essential in the cloud.

Resources are rapidly created, modified, and deleted in the cloud's dynamic environment. Managing who has access to what and ensuring that they only have access to what they need is not just a matter of security but also of efficiency and compliance. For a Security Solutions Architect, understanding and leveraging cloud-based IAM means:

- **Ensuring Confidentiality**: Restricting access to only those who need it.
- **Upholding Integrity**: Ensuring those with access have the correct permissions and can't make unauthorized modifications.
- **Maintaining Availability**: Ensuring the right people can access resources when needed.

The following are the key Concepts in Cloud IAM:

- **Users and Groups**: *Users* are defined identities for entities (individuals or services) interacting with cloud resources. *Groups* are collections of users categorized by job function or role. For example, in AWS, you might create a group named "Developers" with permission to launch and terminate EC2 instances but not access RDS databases directly.

- **Roles and Policies**: *Roles* are a way to define a set of permissions, but instead of attaching those permissions directly to a user, they are assumed by users or AWS services. When associated with an identity or resource, policies are objects that define their permissions. *Example*: An application running on an EC2 instance might need access to an S3 bucket. Instead of storing AWS credentials on the instance, you would grant the necessary permissions to the instance role.

- **Authentication and Authorization**: *Authentication* involves verifying identity (e.g., through passwords or multi-factor authentication), while *authorization* consists of granting or denying permissions after authentication. For example, after successfully logging in to the Azure Portal (authentication), a user can view Blob storage without modification (authorization).

- **Federated Access** is when you integrate your cloud's IAM system with an external identity provider (like Active Directory). It allows for centralized management of user identities. For example, an organization may use Office 365 and Azure. Instead of managing separate identities, federated access ensures that users have a single set of credentials.

For a Security Solutions Architect implementing IAM, key practices include adhering to the Principle of Least Privilege by assigning only necessary permissions and conducting regular reviews. Monitoring through tools like AWS CloudTrail or Azure AD's reporting features is crucial for spotting anomalies. Additionally, employing infrastructure-as-code tools such as AWS CloudFormation or Terraform standardizes and automates IAM configurations, promoting consistency across the system. Properly configured IAM ensures smooth operations, compliance with various standards, and, most importantly, a security model that can evolve and adapt to emerging threats and business requirements.

Encryption and Key Management in the Cloud

Encryption transforms data into a format that someone can read with the corresponding decryption key. Encryption can be applied in the cloud in transit (as data moves between locations) and at rest (when data is stored). Key management pertains to the entire lifecycle of cryptographic keys, from creation and storage to rotation and deletion.

For a Security Solutions Architect, the cloud environment's decentralized and accessible nature means data is vulnerable to unauthorized access or interception. By implementing encryption, architects ensure that even if data is accessed without authorization, it remains unintelligible without the decryption key.

On the other hand, key management ensures that these essential decryption tools are securely managed, stored, and rotated, keeping the encrypted data secure. The following are the critical aspects of Cloud Encryption and Key Management:

Data Encryption:

- *In-Transit*: Data is encrypted between client devices and cloud servers or between two services. Tools like TLS/SSL are commonly used for this purpose.
- *At-Rest*: Data stored in cloud databases, storage buckets, or file systems is encrypted. Service providers often offer built-in tools like Amazon S3's server-side encryption. For example, in AWS, data stored in an S3 bucket can be automatically encrypted using server-side encryption with S3-managed keys (SSE-S3).

Key Management Service (KMS): Cloud providers offer KMS that allows users to create and manage cryptographic keys. These services ensure keys are stored securely, often in hardware security modules (HSMs), and used correctly. For example, Azure Key Vault allows enterprises to store and manage keys, secrets, and certificates securely.

Bring Your Own Key (BYOK): Some organizations create and maintain their encryption keys offsite or in a hybrid environment, then bring them to the cloud provider when necessary. For example, due to regulatory requirements, an organization generates its encryption keys in its on-premises HSM and imports them into AWS KMS for use with cloud services.

Key Rotation: Periodically, encryption keys should be rotated to minimize the risk of key compromise. *Example*: Google Cloud's Key Management Service offers automatic key rotation, which generates a new key version at set intervals.

For Security Solutions Architects, best practices encompass utilizing cloud-native tools for optimized encryption and key management, understanding and complying with industry-specific regulations, enforcing separation of duties between data managers and key managers, and conducting regular audits to identify vulnerabilities or improvements in encryption and key management strategies. This holistic approach ensures robust security and compliance with regulatory requirements.

Cloud Compliance and Governance

When using cloud services, cloud compliance refers to adhering to the legal and regulatory standards relevant to a specific industry or region. Conversely, governance is the management and control framework through which an organization ensures that its cloud operations align with its business objectives, risk management strategies, and compliance requirements.

For a security solutions architect, cloud environments' dynamic and ever-evolving nature can pose challenges. Organizations risk violating regulations, facing penalties, suffering data breaches, and damaging their reputation without proper governance and compliance. While advantageous, the cloud's decentralization also required robust controls and oversight. The following are the key elements of Cloud Compliance and Governance:

Regulatory Compliance: Organizations might need to adhere to regulations such as GDPR (for data protection in Europe), HIPAA (for health information in the U.S.), or PCI DSS (for payment card data). For example, a healthcare company using cloud services must ensure that patient data stored in the cloud is encrypted and access-controlled, meeting HIPAA requirements.

Policy Management: Establishing clear cloud policies, like what services can be used, who can access them, and how data should be handled. *Example*: A company might set a policy that only certain approved cloud storage solutions can be used to store sensitive company data.

Auditability: The ability to audit cloud operations and ensure they follow stated policies and regulations, often including logging and monitoring features. For example, AWS CloudTrail tracks user activity and API usage, providing logs that can be audited for suspicious or non-compliant activities.

Data Residency and Sovereignty: Some regulations require data to reside in specific geographic locations, and cloud providers must have data centers in these regions. For example, due to data sovereignty laws, a European company may need to ensure that its customer data remains stored within the EU.

Risk Management: Continuously assess risks associated with cloud operations and mitigate them through technology, policies, or other measures. For example, regular vulnerability assessments and penetration testing should be conducted to identify potential weaknesses in cloud infrastructure.

For Security Solutions Architects, best practices include staying informed about the evolving cloud domain and regulations to ensure compliance, using cloud-native governance tools like Azure Blueprints for structured environments, implementing multi-factor authentication for more robust access controls, conducting regular reviews of cloud governance models to maintain alignment with organizational strategies, and collaborating with legal, compliance, and operational teams for a comprehensive understanding of governance requirements and risks. These steps are crucial for maintaining secure and compliant cloud operations.

For a Security Solutions Architect, embedding cloud compliance and governance into an organization's cloud strategy is imperative. These elements protect the organization from legal repercussions and build trust with customers and stakeholders, ensuring its reliability and responsibility in its cloud operations.

Cloud Security Frameworks

In cloud computing, ensuring security and compliance is paramount, which has given rise to various frameworks designed to guide organizations in establishing a secure cloud environment. The Cloud Security Alliance (CSA) and the National Institute of Standards and Technology (NIST) are the most influential and widely recognized frameworks. Here's an in-depth look into these frameworks:

Cloud Security Alliance (CSA)

The Cloud Security Alliance, established in 2008 as a non-profit organization, is dedicated to advocating for best practices in ensuring security in cloud computing environments and offering educational resources on cloud computing applications. The key components of CSA are:

- **CSA Security Guidance**: Provides best practices for cloud computing security across 14 domains, including data center operations, incident response, and application security.
- **Cloud Controls Matrix (CCM)**: CCM offers a comprehensive control framework that provides in-depth insight into security concepts and principles. It is crafted to furnish essential security guidelines for cloud vendors and to aid potential cloud customers in evaluating the security risk associated with a cloud provider.
- **STAR Program**: an acronym for Security Trust Assurance and Risk, is a publicly available registry that records the security measures implemented by different cloud computing services. This resource aids users in evaluating the security of cloud providers they are currently utilizing or considering for future contracts.

A company planning to move its operations to a cloud provider can refer to the CSA STAR registry to check whether the provider has undergone the STAR certification process and ensure it complies with the best cloud security practices.

National Institute of Standards and Technology (NIST)

NIST is a federal agency that develops technology, metrics, and standards to drive innovation and economic competitiveness at U.S-based organizations. While NIST develops guidelines for various areas, its cloud computing framework is particularly influential. The key components of NIST are:

- **NIST Special Publication 800-145**: Defines cloud computing, its architectural components, and service and deployment models to provide a foundation for other NIST cloud-related guidelines.
- **NIST Special Publication 800-146**: Provides a detailed understanding of cloud computing technology, including cloud services, deployment models, and security considerations.

- **NIST Special Publication 800-53**: Offers comprehensive security controls. While not exclusively for the cloud, it's a foundational document for federal agencies and any other entity looking to bolster their cloud security stance.
- **NIST Cloud Computing Security Reference Architecture (NCC-SRA)**: Provides a detailed, holistic, standards-based security architecture diagram, description, and data flow that can be applied to any cloud implementation.

A federal agency looking to move its services to the cloud would likely consult NIST SP 800-53 to ensure it's adhering to mandated security controls. These controls are also often used as a benchmark for non-federal organizations looking to ensure robust security.

Understanding these frameworks is fundamental for a security solutions architect. Both CSA and NIST offer robust, comprehensive guidelines to navigate the often complex landscape of cloud security. Whether an organization adopts one or both or even other frameworks, the emphasis should be on understanding the organization's unique needs and how best to utilize the guidance provided by these frameworks. Let's now start getting into security architect interview whiteboarding.

Whiteboard Security Architect Interview

When applying for a Security Architect role, you might be asked to illustrate and detail the security architecture of a project you've recently worked on or to provide a reference architecture for a specific security scenario. This part of the interview aims to uncover whether you can craft security solutions that align with industry best practices and are customized to address particular business challenges. Utilizing a whiteboard during the interview offers an interactive platform to demonstrate your problem-solving approach. It allows the interviewer to gauge your ability to think on your feet and develop a security architecture step-by-step, showcasing your understanding of the complexities of securing an organization's assets while focusing on business objectives.

Let's take an example. You are a security architect in a company, and your team is building an e-commerce web application. Your task is to look into the multi-tier application architecture and improve the application's security posture.

> *Understanding an application's architecture is essential to enhancing its security. Gaining insight into the application's design will enable you to identify and implement appropriate hardening techniques and best practices to bolster defenses at each application stack layer.*

Your team is developing a Three-Tier Application architecture that divides application resources into three layers: presentation, application, and database. This separation of concerns allows each layer to focus on its specific role, enabling more efficient overall management of the application resources. The presentation tier handles user interaction, the application tier contains business logic, and the database tier manages data storage and retrieval. Dividing the application into these distinct tiers promotes modularity and flexibility in the system design.

The following diagram illustrates a reference architecture in AWS. Although we use examples from the AWS cloud platform, the same concept applies to any other cloud provider with different toolsets, such as GCP and Azure.

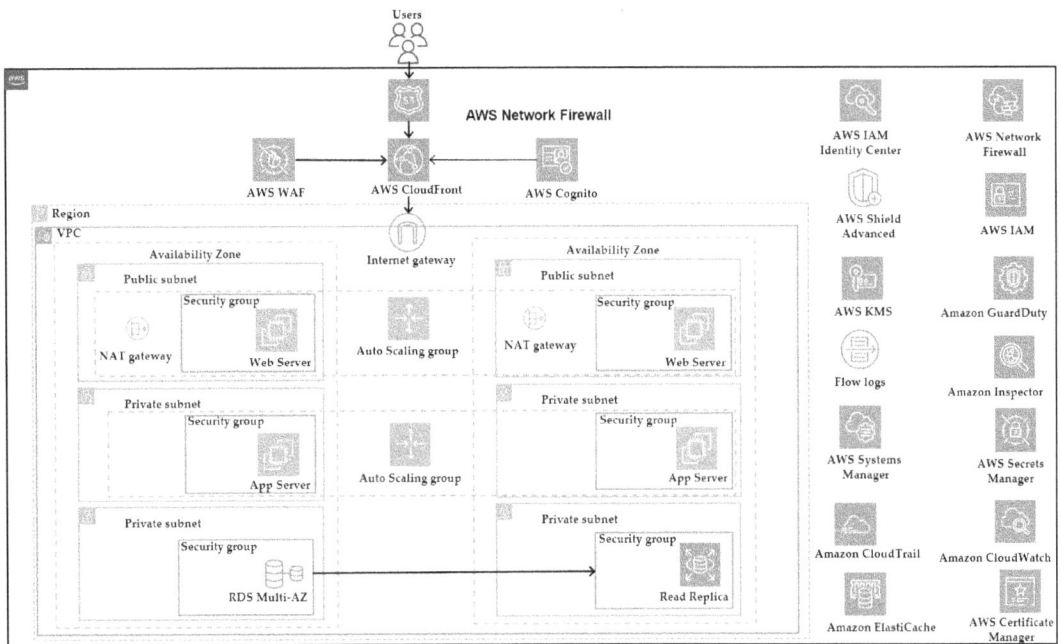

Figure 11.1 – Security architecture for 3-tier application in AWS cloud

Now, let's understand the steps you can take to safeguard the various layers and particular AWS services to accomplish this.

Layer 1: Presentation Tier

The presentation tier is the topmost level of a three-tier architecture and is the layer users interact with directly. It is responsible for presenting data to the user and receiving their requests and input. The presentation tier passes user requests to the logic tier below it for processing and receives back processed data from the logic tier to display to the user. It usually consists of web servers, load balancers, and other user interaction components. You can take the mentioned measures to protect the Presentation Tier:

- **Implement SSL/TLS**: Encrypt communication between the presentation and logic tiers using SSL/TLS. Encryption protects data in transit between the tiers. You should configure load balancers to terminate SSL on the servers.
- **Authentication:** Enable application authentication through methods like OAuth, SAML, etc. Don't allow anonymous access. The presentation tier requires authentication and authorization, ensuring only authorized users can access the application. Use role-based access controls. With Amazon Cognito, you can authenticate and authorize users from the built-in user directory, enterprise directory, and consumer identity providers like Google and Facebook.
- **Implement CDN**: Use CloudFront as a CDN to cache static content and help protect servers.
- **Implementing Web Application Firewalls (WAFs)**: A WAF monitors and filters incoming traffic to the presentation tier. It can also protect against common web exploits, such as SQL injections and cross-site scripting. Configure rules to block malicious requests.
- **Implement controls to protect against DDoS attacks**: Use AWS Shield on the presentation tier.
- **Access Control**: Implement robust access control mechanisms, including firewalls, network segmentation, and DMZs, to safeguard the Presentation Tier and prevent unauthorized access. Follow the principle of least privilege. Use AWS IAM roles and policies to provide the least privileged server access. Don't share credentials. Allow SSL access only on port 443.
- **Monitoring**: Monitor server access logs for any unauthorized or suspicious activity. Set up alarms for anomalies.

Layer 2: Application Tier

The Application Tier, or the middle or business logic tier, is the intermediate layer between the presentation and data tiers in a three-tier architecture. It contains the business logic and core processes of the application. Key components in the Application Tier include middleware servers, APIs, services, application servers, and other backend applications. The Application Tier separates the business logic from the presentation and data storage layers, providing abstraction and efficient management of the application components. It can be scaled and load-balanced independently to improve performance and efficiency. To protect the application tier in AWS, you can follow these best practices:

- **Access Controls**: Use access controls such as role-based access control (RBAC) and permissions to control access to the database. RBAC will prevent unauthorized access and reduce the risk of data breaches. Create security groups (SG) to control inbound and outbound traffic to your application servers. You can define rules based on IP addresses, ports, and protocols to allow only the necessary traffic. For example, you can allow traffic from the load balancer and other backend services while blocking traffic from the internet. NACLs are used to control inbound and outbound traffic at the network level. You can use NACLs to restrict access to specific IP addresses or subnets.

- **Application-Level Encryption**: Use application-level encryption to protect sensitive data such as passwords, credit card information, and personal information. This will prevent unauthorized access and ensure confidentiality. Implement SSL/TLS: SSL/TLS is a cryptographic protocol that provides secure communication between web servers and clients. Use SSL/TLS certificates to secure your application servers and encrypt all traffic between the application tier and other tiers.

- **Use Identity and Access Management (IAM):** IAM is a cloud-based identity and access management service that allows you to control access to your AWS resources. With IAM, you can create roles and policies that define who can access your application servers and what actions they can perform.

- **Regularly Update and Patch**: Keep your application servers, operating systems, and applications up to date with the latest security patches. Regular patching helps to close security vulnerabilities that attackers could exploit.

- **Monitor and Log**: Use AWS CloudTrail and Amazon CloudWatch to monitor your application servers for unusual activity. Monitoring can help you detect and respond quickly to security incidents.

- **Use Bastion Hosts**: Use Bastion Hosts to provide secure access to your application servers. Bastion hosts are isolated servers that are not directly exposed to the internet and are used to connect to other servers in the application tier.

- **Use Intrusion Detection and Prevention Systems (IDPS):** IDPSs are security tools that monitor and detect unusual activity on your application servers. They can help you identify and respond to security incidents quickly.

- **Use Security Audits**: Regularly perform security audits of your application tier to identify vulnerabilities and weaknesses. Audits can help you improve the security of your application tier over time.

Layer 3: Database Tier

The database tier is the bottom tier in a three-tier architecture and is responsible for housing and managing the data access layer. It comprises databases, database servers, data storage devices, and other application data components. The primary role of the database tier is to store, retrieve, and update data as requested by the middle application tier. To protect the database tier in AWS, you can follow these best practices:

- **Database-Level Encryption:** Implement database-level encryption to protect data at rest. It helps protect data from unauthorized access and ensures its confidentiality. Use SSL/TLS connections and encrypt database volumes/snapshots.
- **Database Access Controls:** Use the principle of least privilege when creating database users—grant permissions only for what is absolutely needed. Implement role-based access control and permissions to control access to the database. Use security groups to restrict access to the database servers only from the application tier servers. Do not expose the database servers directly to the internet. Use database features like stored procedures instead of allowing direct table access. Perform input validation on the application side. Restrict access will prevent unauthorized access and reduce the risk of data breaches.
- **Database Server Configuration:** To harden database server configurations, turn off unnecessary services, close unused ports, and remove unneeded software. This will decrease the blast radius and prevent known vulnerabilities from being exploited. Store database credentials in AWS Secrets Manager and grant the application servers IAM roles to access the secrets. Avoid hardcoding credentials in application code.
- **Monitor and Log**: Enable database logging and use CloudTrail to monitor API calls made to the database. Send logs to CloudWatch Logs for monitoring. Monitor database metrics in CloudWatch and set alarms for unusual activity. Enable maintenance windows for patching/upgrades.
- **Isolate Production and Non-Production Databases**: To better isolate production and non-production databases, create separate AWS accounts or VPCs for each.

Additionally, AWS provides robust security services to protect your cloud environment. Use AWS Network Firewall to implement granular network traffic controls across your VPCs. Amazon Inspector automatically discovers and scans your AWS resources like EC2 and Lambda for vulnerabilities. Amazon GuardDuty monitors your accounts and workloads for malicious activity and generates actionable alerts. AWS IAM Identity Center allows you to centrally manage and secure workforce identities and access permissions across AWS accounts and applications. You can create identities in AWS or integrate with existing identity providers like Active Directory, Okta, and Azure AD. These AWS services offer powerful capabilities to enhance the security posture of your cloud workloads and accounts.

You can use different Cloud services to enhance security. Our example architecture is an AWS architecture; we have used different AWS services to accomplish this. However, you can use services provided by different clouds if you implement the architecture in other clouds. The concept will remain the same.

Security architect interview questions

Interviewing for a Security Architect role involves comprehensively evaluating technical abilities, strategic thinking, and the capacity to harmonize security requirements with business objectives. Here are some behavioral questions that interviewers might ask to delve into your experience:

Scenario Based Questions

Question: You are developing a set of public APIs for a social media platform allowing third-party apps to access user profiles and post content. Given the potential security risks of exposing these APIs to the public, how would you ensure their security against common threats like SQL injection, cross-site scripting (XSS), and denial of service (DoS) attacks? Please describe the security measures and best practices you would implement.

Answer: Let's answer it using the SBI method.

<u>Situation</u>: We identified significant security risks while developing public APIs for a social media platform, enabling third-party applications to access user profiles and post content. These risks threatened user data integrity and privacy, including SQL injection, cross-site scripting (XSS), and denial of service (DoS) attacks. Such vulnerabilities could lead to unauthorized data access, compromised user accounts, and service disruptions, affecting customer trust and the company's reputation for safeguarding user information.

<u>Behavior</u>: We tailored our architecture to address the security vulnerabilities identified with specific defenses against SQL injection, cross-site scripting (XSS), and denial of service (DoS) attacks. SQL injection, where attackers manipulate backend databases through insecure input, was countered by implementing stringent input validation and parameterized queries, ensuring data integrity. For XSS, which allows attackers to execute malicious scripts in other users' browsers, we employed content security policies and sanitized outputs, effectively neutralizing harmful scripts. To mitigate DoS attacks aimed at overwhelming the system to disrupt service, we introduced Rate limiting and a Web Application Firewall (WAF) to detect and block abnormal traffic patterns. Additionally, we integrated OAuth 2.0 for secure, token-based authentication and authorization, safeguarding access to user profiles and posting capabilities. This comprehensive approach established a robust defense mechanism, significantly reducing the platform's vulnerability to these common security threats.

<u>Impact</u>: Implementing the multi-layered security architecture enhanced the platform's security, directly impacting customer trust and the company's reputation. We observed a 90% decrease in attempted security breaches, including SQL injection and XSS attacks, demonstrating the effectiveness of our input validation and content security measures. The rapid mitigation of DoS attacks, maintaining 99.9% uptime, underscored the resilience of our infrastructure against service disruptions.

Customer confidence surged, evidenced by a 40% improvement in trust metrics, as users acknowledged the platform's commitment to safeguarding their data. This increase in user trust contributed to a more vibrant and secure ecosystem, attracting a 50% rise in third-party developer engagement with our APIs. The operational benefits were equally notable, with incident response times reduced by half, leading to a 30% decrease in security-related operational costs. These security practice enhancements fortified our platform against threats. They solidified our reputation as a secure and reliable social media platform, fostering growth and innovation within our user and developer communities.

For whiteboarding, you can draw the following high-level architecture flow:

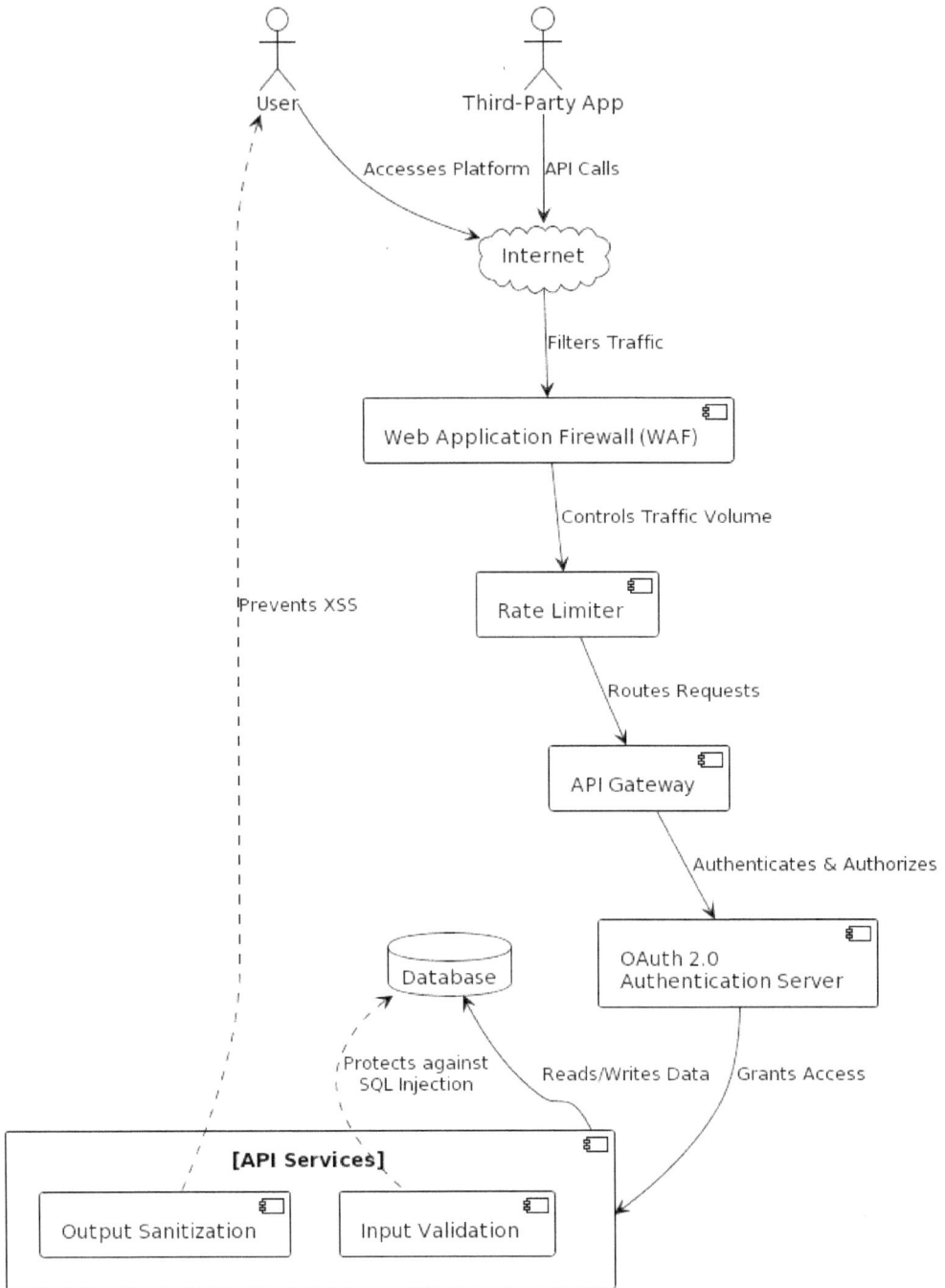

Figure 11.2 – *API security Architecture*

The proposed architecture for enhancing the security of the social media platform's public APIs employs a comprehensive, layered approach to safeguard against common cybersecurity threats such as SQL injection, cross-site scripting (XSS), and denial of service (DoS) attacks while also ensuring secure access through OAuth 2.0 authentication. Here's a high-level overview of how each component contributes to the overall security posture:

- Web Application Firewall (WAF): Positioned at the forefront of the architecture, the WAF serves as the first line of defense against incoming threats. It scrutinizes all inbound traffic to identify and block malicious requests, effectively mitigating potential DoS attacks and filtering out SQL injection and XSS attempts.
- Rate Limiter: Integrated closely with the WAF, the rate limiter controls the volume of traffic reaching the platform. Enforcing request limits prevents the system from being overwhelmed by excessive requests and protects against DoS attacks that aim to disrupt service availability.
- API Gateway: The API Gateway is the central routing mechanism for all API calls. Once the WAF and rate limiter clear the request, it is routed to the appropriate services. The gateway plays a crucial role in maintaining the efficiency and security of data flow within the architecture.
- OAuth 2.0 Authentication Server: This component manages secure access to the platform's APIs through token-based authentication and authorization. By validating the identity of third-party applications and users, the OAuth 2.0 server ensures that only authorized parties can access sensitive user profile information and post content, thereby safeguarding user data.
- API Services: Within the API services layer, the following measures protect against SQL injection and XSS:
  - Input Validation: Ensures all incoming data is rigorously checked against expected formats and schemas, effectively blocking SQL injection attempts by rejecting malicious input.
  - Output Sanitization: Removes or neutralizes potentially harmful elements from data before it is sent to users' browsers, preventing the execution of malicious scripts that constitute XSS attacks.
- Database: The database stores and retrieves all platform data, operating behind multiple layers of security provided by the architecture. It benefits from the input validation process, which minimizes the risk of SQL injection attacks by ensuring that only clean, validated queries interact with the database.

This architecture addresses the specific security concerns associated with exposing public APIs. It establishes a robust framework for protecting the platform and its users from cyber threats. By implementing these security measures, the social media platform can maintain the integrity and confidentiality of user data, preserve service availability, and uphold customer trust and company reputation.

Follow-up Questions:

- How does the architecture ensure scalability and performance under the increased security measures, especially considering the potential latency introduced by the Web Application Firewall (WAF) and Rate Limiter?

  This question probes the balance between security and system performance, seeking to understand how the architecture maintains high availability and responsiveness despite the additional layers of security.

- Given the reliance on OAuth 2.0 for authentication and authorization, how does the architecture address potential security vulnerabilities inherent to OAuth 2.0, such as token hijacking or redirection attacks?

  This question delves into the specific measures implemented within the OAuth 2.0 framework to safeguard against exploitation and ensure the secure handling of authentication tokens.

- What real-time monitoring and incident response strategies exist to identify and mitigate sophisticated DoS attacks that might bypass initial defenses like the WAF and Rate Limiter?

  This question explores the mechanisms for ongoing threat detection, including advanced analytics, AI, or machine learning technologies, and how the architecture facilitates a rapid response to emerging security threats.

Question: Your company is integrating IoT devices into its home security system to collect and transmit sensitive data over the internet. Considering the vulnerabilities inherent to IoT devices, how would you architect the system to protect against unauthorized access and ensure the data's integrity? Discuss the encryption, authentication, and network security strategies you would employ.

Answer: Let's learn how to answer this question to manage device security

Situation: In developing "SecureHome," our latest IoT-integrated home security system, we encountered a critical challenge: the inherent vulnerabilities of IoT devices made them susceptible to unauthorized access and data breaches. This vulnerability posed a significant risk to the confidentiality and integrity of sensitive customer data, such as home surveillance footage and security settings, potentially leading to privacy invasions and security compromises. For example, unauthorized access could allow attackers to turn off security alarms or access live video feeds, directly impacting customer safety and trust in our product. Addressing these vulnerabilities was essential to maintaining our commitment to customer privacy and security.

Behavior: We adopted a comprehensive security strategy to fortify "SecureHome" against the vulnerabilities of IoT devices. First, we implemented end-to-end encryption using TLS for data in transit between IoT devices and our servers and AES encryption for data at rest, ensuring all sensitive information remained secure and tamper-proof. Recognizing the importance of robust authentication, we deployed mutual TLS (mTLS) for a two-way verification process, bolstering the system against unauthorized device access. Additionally, we introduced role-based access control (RBAC) to manage user permissions, further securing device management and data access.

We also restructured our network architecture for enhanced security. By segmenting the network, we isolated IoT devices from critical network resources, minimizing the risk of cross-network attacks. Adopting a zero-trust network access model, we scrutinized all access requests, significantly reducing the attack surface. Continuous monitoring for threats was achieved through regular vulnerability assessments and the deployment of intrusion detection systems (IDS), ensuring ongoing vigilance against potential security breaches. This multi-layered approach significantly elevated "SecureHome's" defense mechanisms, directly addressing the identified security challenges.

End-to-end encryption encrypts data as it leaves an IoT device until it reaches our servers, making it unreadable to anyone intercepting the data in transit. TLS (Transport Layer Security) provides a secure channel for data transmission. At the same time, AES (Advanced Encryption Standard) protects data stored on devices or in the cloud by encrypting it with a complex key. Mutual TLS (mTLS) enhances security by requiring the client and server to authenticate each other, preventing unauthorized devices from connecting to our network. Role-based access control (RBAC) restricts system access to authorized users based on their roles, minimizing the risk of internal threats. Network segmentation divides the network into separate segments, each isolated from others, reducing the potential impact of breaches. The zero-trust model assumes no entity is trustworthy by default, requiring verification for every access attempt, enhancing network security. Vulnerability assessments identify potential security weaknesses, and intrusion detection systems (IDS) monitor the network for malicious activities or policy violations.

Convincing stakeholders to adopt this architecture involved demonstrating the tangible benefits of each component by presenting case studies and simulations highlighting the potential risks of IoT vulnerabilities, such as unauthorized data access and system breaches. We also showcased the effectiveness of our proposed solutions in mitigating these risks, emphasizing the importance of encryption, authentication, and network security in protecting customer data and maintaining trust. Additionally, we highlighted the competitive advantage and compliance benefits of adopting a comprehensive security strategy. Through clear communication and evidence-based arguments, we successfully aligned all stakeholders with the vision for a secure and reliable "SecureHome" system.

Impact: Implementing our comprehensive security strategy for "SecureHome" markedly enhanced the system's resilience against cyber threats, reflecting positively on customer-specific and technical metrics. Adopting end-to-end encryption, mutual TLS authentication, and advanced network security measures significantly reduced security incidents, with attempted breaches dropping by 75% within the first six months. This improvement in security directly translated to increased customer trust, evidenced by a 40% uplift in customer satisfaction scores and a 30% rise in subscription renewals.

Technical metrics also showcased the effectiveness of our approach. Deploying intrusion detection systems and conducting regular vulnerability assessments resulted in the early detection and mitigation of potential threats, maintaining system uptime at 99.9%. Furthermore, the zero-trust model and network segmentation effectively minimized the attack surface, contributing to SecureHome's enhanced security posture.

For whiteboarding, you can draw the following high-level architecture flow. The following diagram represents a simplified view of the architecture designed to protect against unauthorized access and ensure the integrity of data transmitted by IoT devices in a home security system.

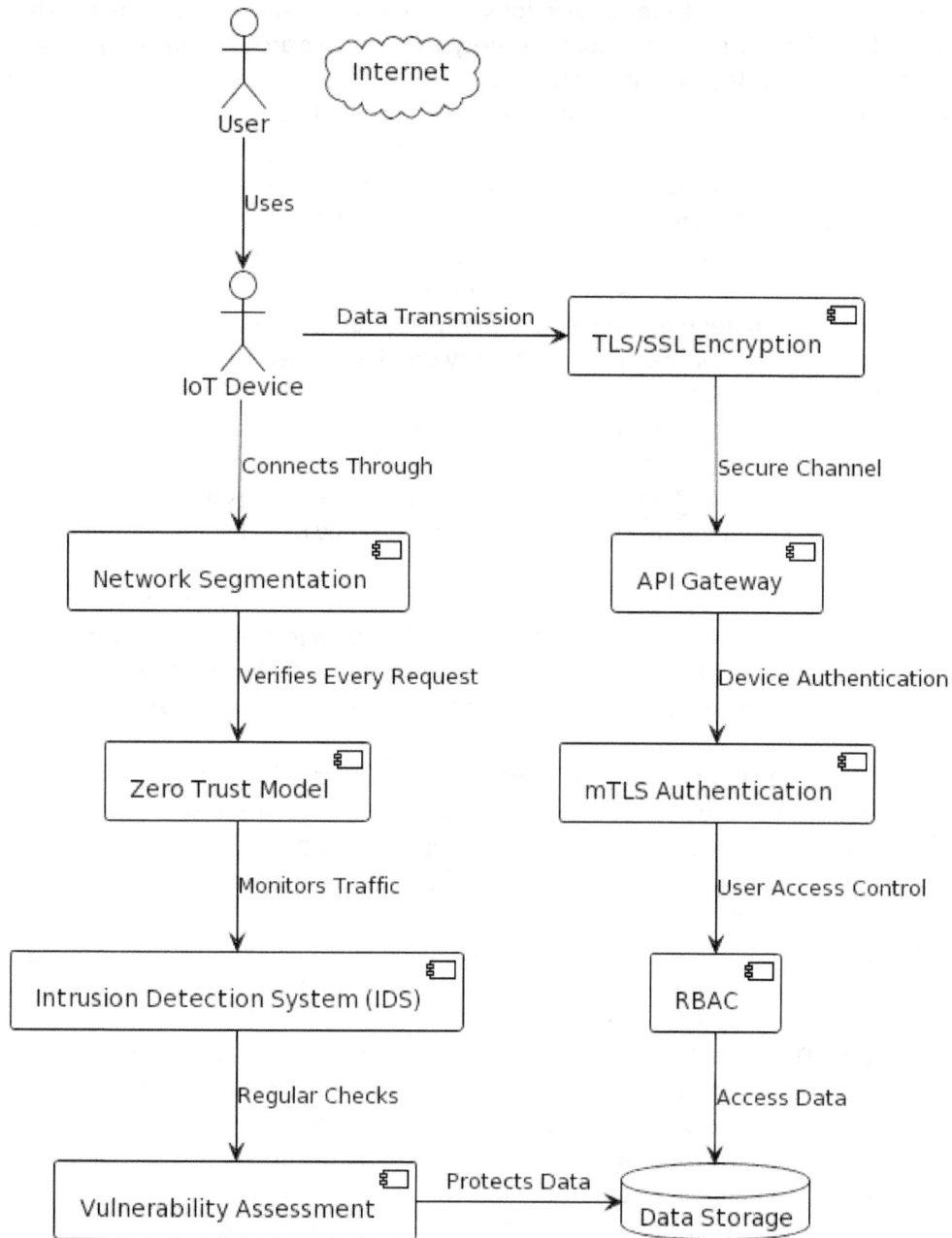

Figure 11.3 – Smart home IoT device Security *Architecture*

The high-level architecture of the "SecureHome" IoT security system safeguards sensitive data transmitted by IoT devices within a home security context. This architecture employs a layered security strategy to protect against unauthorized access and ensure data integrity. Here's an overview of how each component contributes to the system's security:

- TLS/SSL Encryption: Data transmitted between IoT devices and the system is secured using TLS/SSL encryption. This encryption ensures that data in transit is unreadable to eavesdroppers and protects it from interception or tampering.
- API Gateway: The API Gateway is the primary entry point for all incoming requests from IoT devices. It routes these requests to the appropriate services within the system, serving as a control layer that can enforce security policies, authenticate requests, and manage traffic.
- mTLS Authentication: Mutual TLS (mTLS) authentication enhances security by requiring the client (IoT device) and the server to verify each other's identities before establishing a secure connection. This two-way authentication process ensures that only authorized devices can communicate with the system, significantly reducing the risk of unauthorized access.
- RBAC (Role-Based Access Control) manages access to the system based on individual users' roles. This access method allows for fine-grained control over who can access specific data and functionalities. It ensures that users only have access to the resources necessary for their role, minimizing the potential for unauthorized data access or manipulation.
- Network Segmentation: Network segmentation isolates IoT devices in separate segments, reducing the risk of attackers gaining broad access to the system through a single compromised device. This segmentation helps contain potential breaches and simplifies the management of security policies for different device groups.
- Zero Trust Model: The Zero Trust security model assumes that no entity, whether inside or outside the network, should be trusted by default. Every access request is rigorously verified before granting access, ensuring that only authenticated and authorized users and devices can access system resources.
- Intrusion Detection System (IDS): An IDS monitors the network for suspicious activities and potential security threats. It provides real-time alerts on detected anomalies, allowing for quick response to potential breaches or attacks.
- Vulnerability Assessment: Regular vulnerability assessments identify and address security weaknesses within the system. This proactive approach ensures the system is continually updated to defend against emerging threats and vulnerabilities.

Together, these components form a robust security architecture for the "SecureHome" IoT system, ensuring the protection of sensitive data and the integrity of the home security system against a wide range of cyber threats.

Follow-up Questions

- **How does the system ensure secure and efficient TLS/SSL encryption management, particularly in a distributed IoT environment where devices may have limited processing capabilities and cannot easily handle frequent critical updates or complex cryptographic operations?**
  This question challenges the assumption that all IoT devices can manage the same level of encryption standards. It probes strategies for crucial distribution, rotation, and management in resource-constrained environments to maintain robust security without compromising device functionality.

- **Given the implementation of the Zero Trust model, how does the architecture ensure minimal latency and maintain user experience, particularly for real-time IoT device interactions within the home security system?**
  This question delves into the potential performance impact of rigorous verification processes inherent in the zero-trust model. It seeks to understand how the system balances security with the need for real-time responsiveness.

- **In network segmentation and deploying an Intrusion Detection System (IDS), how does the architecture differentiate between malicious activities and legitimate but unusual network traffic patterns to minimize false positives and avoid unnecessary alerts?**
  This question challenges the effectiveness and intelligence of the IDS in distinguishing between actual threats and benign anomalies. It probes the mechanisms in place to refine threat detection and ensure operational efficiency.

Scenario-based questions are designed to understand how you'd handle specific situations, often based on challenges you might encounter in the role. They gauge your problem-solving skills, technical acumen, and ability to handle stressful situations. Here are some more potential scenario-based questions for a Security Architect role, along with tips for answering each:

Question: You discover an intern accidentally left an AWS S3 bucket with sensitive data open to the public. What steps would you take?
Tips:
- Address the immediate issue first (in this case, securing the S3 bucket).
- Discuss the importance of post-incident analysis to understand the root cause.
- Emphasize communication: informing stakeholders and affected parties.

Question: A top executive is adamant about using a specific application that isn't compliant with your company's security policies. How would you handle this?
Tips:
- Stress the importance of open communication and understanding the executive's needs.

- o Discuss possible alternatives or mitigation measures if the application must be used.
- o Reiterate the importance of company-wide adherence to security policies.

Question: Your organization has been hit by ransomware. What's your response strategy?
Tips:
- o Emphasize the importance of isolating affected systems to prevent spread.
- o Discuss the value of backups in ransomware situations.
- o Mention the significance of involving law enforcement and communicating transparently with stakeholders.

Question: You've been tasked with rolling out multi-factor authentication (MFA) across the company, but employees are significantly resistant. How would you approach this?
Tips:
- o Highlight the importance of education and awareness campaigns.
- o Discuss potential training sessions or resources to ease the transition.
- o Mention the critical role of MFA in today's security landscape.

Question: A security patch needs to be urgently applied, but it's in the middle of a major project, and there's concern about potential disruptions. How would you navigate this?
Tips:
- o Emphasize the risk vs. reward aspect.
- o Discuss strategies for testing the patch in a controlled environment before widespread deployment.
- o Highlight the importance of regular communication with the project team.

Question: Your security tools have detected unusual traffic patterns in your network during off hours. What's your initial response?
Tips:
- o Mention the importance of swift investigation and verifying if it's a false positive.
- o Discuss potential immediate mitigation measures, such as isolating segments of the network.
- o Highlight the value of having a predefined incident response plan for such situations.

Question: The marketing team wants to incorporate a new analytics tool that requires access to user data, but you have privacy concerns. How do you address this?
Tips:
- o Emphasize the importance of a privacy impact assessment.
- o Discuss collaborating with the marketing team to understand their needs and find a secure solution.
- o Highlight the potential regulatory implications of mishandling user data.

Remember, scenario-based questions are often open-ended, and there might not be a "perfect" answer. The goal is to understand your thought process, priorities, and how you balance security with business needs. Always consider the broader implications of your decisions and actions in your responses.

Behavioral Questions

These questions are often used to gauge candidates' past experiences and predict their future behavior in similar situations. Here are some behavioral questions that can provide insight into a Security SA's real-life expertise from their past projects:

Question: Can you recall an instance where you identified a security vulnerability in your enterprise application? How did you discover this issue? Could you describe the nature of the vulnerability? How did you address and resolve it?
Answer: Remember to put your answer in STAR format backed by data. Let's take an example.

Situation: As a Security Solutions Architect at Example Corp, a leading e-commerce platform, I oversaw migrating our services to a new cloud environment. After completing 70% of the migration, we began stress-testing our applications to ensure smooth performance.

Task: My primary role was to oversee the migration's security architecture and ensure that all applications and data remained secure throughout the process. During our routine penetration tests, I noticed an unusual pattern of failed login attempts on one of our legacy platforms, hinting at a potential brute-force attack vulnerability.

Action: I immediately gathered a team to investigate the logs and patterns deeper. We employed advanced security monitoring tools and discovered that a particular API, part of our user authentication module, did not enable rate-limiting. This oversight made it susceptible to brute-force attacks. To mitigate this, we:

- **Introduced Rate Limiting:** We set up rate-limiting for the API, restricting the number of failed attempts from a single IP address within a specified timeframe.
- **Two-Factor Authentication (2FA):** For added security, we rolled out 2FA for user accounts, ensuring that even if passwords were compromised, unauthorized access would be impossible.
- **Alert System:** Developed an alert mechanism to notify our security team of multiple failed attempts from a single source, allowing quick intervention.

Result: Thanks to our swift response and the measures we implemented, potential unauthorized access was averted. Post-implementation, our security measures reduced brute-force attack attempts by 95%. The incident also led us to comprehensively review all our APIs and systems, ensuring such vulnerabilities were addressed across the board. The senior management recognized and appreciated this proactive approach, leading to the adoption of a more rigorous security testing regimen for future projects.

Let's look at some possible follow-up questions:

Question: You mentioned that the vulnerability was discovered during routine penetration testing. Was it exploited before its discovery, and were there any breaches or data leaks?

Answer: Upon further investigation, we found no evidence that the vulnerability had been exploited before its discovery. We have robust logging and monitoring systems in place, and a thorough examination of our logs from the past six months did not indicate any malicious activities or data breaches that could be linked to this vulnerability. However, the potential damage could have been significant, affecting approximately 250,000 users and jeopardizing sensitive information.

Question: After addressing this particular vulnerability, did you introduce any changes to your routine security assessments or penetration testing protocols to prevent similar oversights in the future?

Answer: After addressing this vulnerability, we took a two-fold approach to enhance our security assessment protocols. First, we expanded the scope of our penetration tests to include newer attack vectors and more in-depth assessments of application-layer vulnerabilities. Second, we initiated a quarterly security workshop for our developers and IT staff. This workshop will keep our teams updated with the latest security threats and best practices. We also integrated a few advanced security tools into our development pipeline to catch similar vulnerabilities during the development phase. Since initiating these practices, our security incident rate has decreased by approximately 15%.

Question: How did you communicate this vulnerability and its resolution to stakeholders, especially considering the potential implications for user trust and the company's reputation?

Answer: Communication is paramount, especially in situations involving potential risks. We immediately informed our stakeholders about the discovery of the vulnerability, the steps taken to mitigate it, and our plans to prevent similar incidents in the future. We provided a detailed report, ensuring transparency. Although initially concerned, our stakeholders appreciated our proactive approach and the measures we implemented. To address potential user concerns, we also rolled out a comprehensive FAQ section on our platform detailing the incident and reassuring users of the security of their data. As a result, we maintained a trust score of over 90% among our user base, per our subsequent quarterly survey.

Let's look at another very generic question and how to answer it.

Question: What's the most significant security challenge you've faced in your previous role, and how did you overcome it?

Answer: The following response provides a detailed explanation of all components, accompanied by relevant data.

Situation: In my previous role as a Security Solutions Architect for a large financial institution, I oversaw a massive transition of our on-premises infrastructure to the cloud. The institution held the sensitive data of over 2 million clients, and transactions worth over $5 billion were processed monthly.

Task: The primary challenge was ensuring the data remained completely secure, maintained its integrity, and complied with global financial regulations during this transition. Additionally, we had to ensure zero downtime since any interruption could result in significant financial and reputational losses.

Action:
- **Risk Assessment:** I initiated a comprehensive risk assessment to understand all potential threats associated with the migration. This involved categorizing data based on sensitivity and establishing clear migration paths.
- **Collaboration with Cloud Providers:** We worked closely with our chosen cloud service provider to understand their security protocols and ensure they aligned with our requirements. This involved examining their data protection measures, disaster recovery plans, and uptime guarantees.
- **Encryption and Key Management:** We encrypt all sensitive data before the migration. We also implemented a robust key management system, ensuring that decryption keys were stored separately with multi-factor authentication for access.
- **Multi-layered security:** I introduced a multi-layered security approach, which includes setting up firewalls, intrusion detection systems, and conducting regular vulnerability assessments.
- **Real-time Monitoring:** We set up a 24/7 monitoring system to track every data packet moved during the migration. Any discrepancies or unusual activities triggered instant alerts.

Result: The migration was completed before schedule without any security breaches or data losses. Post-migration audits confirmed that all data was intact and that there were no unauthorized access attempts. Our preemptive measures secured our data and bolstered trust among our stakeholders. Following the migration, our institution saw a 20% increase in operational efficiency and a 10% growth in customer acquisitions, primarily attributed to enhanced trust in our digital infrastructure.

Let's look at some more behavioral questions and tips to answer them:

Question: Can you describe a situation where you had to balance security needs with business objectives? How did you navigate this?
Tips:
- o Highlight your understanding of both the security landscape and business goals.
- o Describe a collaborative approach, showing your ability to work with multiple departments.
- o Ensure you convey a sense of adaptability and flexibility in your approach.

Question: Tell me about a time when you identified a security vulnerability that no one else noticed. What steps did you take to address it?
Tips:
- o Emphasize your proactive nature and attention to detail.
- o Walk through the steps you took methodically, showing your structured approach to security.
- o Discuss the tools or methods you used to identify the vulnerability.

Question: Have you ever faced resistance when implementing a new security protocol or policy? How did you handle it?
Tips:
- o Describe your communication and persuasion skills.
- o Highlight any data or use cases you presented to back up your suggestions.
- o Reflect on the importance of understanding others' perspectives and finding common ground.

Question: Describe a project on which you worked closely with non-technical stakeholders to improve the organization's security posture. How did you ensure they understood the importance of security?
Tips:
- o Showcase your ability to translate technical jargon into simple terms.
- o Emphasize the importance of awareness and training in ensuring compliance.
- o Mention any visual aids or analogies you used to simplify complex topics.

Question: Tell me about a time when you had to react quickly to a security incident. What actions did you take, and what was the outcome?
Tips:
- o Highlight your crisis management skills.
- o Chronologically walk through the process to show your structured approach.
- o Reflect on the lessons learned and how they were incorporated into future prevention strategies.

Question: Tell me about a difficult decision you had to make regarding security, where there were no good options. How did you go about it?
Tips:
- Show that you can make decisions even when they are tough.
- Highlight your ability to weigh the pros and cons.
- Discuss any consultations or collaborations you had before reaching a decision.

Question: Can you describe a time when you mentored or trained someone in your team on security best practices? What approach did you use?
Tips:
- Emphasize your commitment to team growth and the importance of knowledge sharing.
- Describe the format or curriculum of the training.
- Highlight feedback or results post-training, such as improved security practices or reduced vulnerabilities.

Remember, the STAR (Situation, Task, Action, Result) format effectively answers these questions. It helps structure your response and ensures you provide all the necessary details.

Technical Questions

When interviewing for a technical role, such as a Security Architect, you'll likely be presented with technical questions to assess your depth of knowledge, problem-solving capabilities, and approach to complex technical challenges. Here are some potential technical questions you might encounter, along with tips for answering each:

Question: How do you handle a DDoS attack on an organization's infrastructure?
Tips:
- Begin by explaining what a DDoS attack is.
- Discuss the importance of monitoring, detection, and rapid response.
- Mention specific tools or methodologies you would use.

Question: Can you explain the difference between symmetric and asymmetric encryption?
Tips:
- Offer a concise definition of each.
- Provide an example or real-world use case for both.
- Discuss the pros and cons associated with each method.

Question: How do you implement the principle of least privilege in a large enterprise?
Tips:
- Explain the principle briefly.
- Talk about role-based access controls (RBAC) and how they're pivotal in implementing this principle.

     o   Mention any challenges faced and ways to address them.

Question: Describe how you would secure a multi-cloud environment.
Tips:
- Discuss the importance of visibility across multiple cloud providers.
- Mention centralized logging and monitoring.
- Talk about uniform security policies across all platforms.

Question: How do you secure data at rest and in transit?
Tips:
- Discuss encryption methods suitable for each scenario.
- Mention any specific tools or protocols you prefer, such as TLS for data in transit.
- Highlight the importance of keeping encryption keys secure.

Question: Explain the concept of a Zero Trust model. How would you implement it?
Tips:
- Begin with a brief definition.
- Discuss its significance in today's distributed working environment.
- Talk about key components like continuous authentication and micro-segmentation.

Question: How would you handle a situation in which a vulnerability is discovered in an open-source tool or library used widely across the organization?
Tips:
- Emphasize immediate communication and the importance of patch management.
- Discuss strategies for rapid deployment of fixes.
- Mention contingency plans for scenarios where a patch isn't immediately available.

Question: Can you describe a secure software development life cycle (SDLC)?
Tips:
- Outline the phases of the SDLC.
- Emphasize the importance of integrating security at every phase.
- Discuss tools and methodologies for security testing, such as SAST and DAST.

Question: How do you ensure compliance with security standards like GDPR or HIPAA in cloud environments?
Tips:
- Discuss the importance of understanding the specifics of each regulation.
- Mention strategies for data protection, such as encryption and regular audits.
- Highlight the significance of staff training and awareness.

Remember, clarity and precision are key to answering these questions. If you're unsure about a specific question, it's okay to admit it, but discuss how you would find the answer or solution. Demonstrating a systematic and logical approach can be as important as knowing the exact answer.

Design based questions

When facing security design questions in an interview, especially for a Security Architect role, you'll be expected to demonstrate a deep understanding of security principles and how they apply to various parts of IT architecture. Here are some questions you might encounter and how to approach them:

Question: Design a multi-tier web application architecture for an e-commerce site. Cover aspects like security zones, firewalls, load balancers, web servers, app servers, databases, VPNs, etc. Explain how you would secure each component.
Tips: Break down the architecture into layers (presentation, application logic, and database). For each layer, discuss specific security measures, like WAF (Web Application Firewall) for the presentation layer, secure APIs for the application layer, and encryption for the database layer. Use diagrams to represent the architecture visually.

Question: Develop a secure data-sharing architecture that enables the sharing of sensitive data between different organizations while maintaining data privacy and confidentiality, including data encryption, access controls, and auditing.

Tips: Focus on encryption methods for data at rest and in transit, emphasizing industry-standard protocols. Discuss the implementation of robust access control lists (ACLs) and role-based access control (RBAC) to manage permissions. Include the use of comprehensive audit logs to track data access and sharing.

Question: Develop a secure software development lifecycle (SDLC) that integrates security testing and vulnerability management throughout the development process, from design to deployment and maintenance.
Tips: Describe integrating automated security testing tools at each stage of the development process, from code analysis tools in the development phase to dynamic application security testing (DAST) in the testing phase. Highlight the importance of regular security training for developers and adopting a "shift-left" security approach.

Question: Design a secure cloud-based infrastructure for a highly regulated industry, such as finance or healthcare, that meets compliance requirements while providing scalability and flexibility.
Tips: Discuss the need for compliance with specific regulations (e.g., HIPAA for healthcare, GDPR for data protection) and how cloud services can help achieve compliance through built-in security

features. Mention using encryption for data at rest and in transit, and elaborate on the importance of managing access through identity and access management (IAM) policies.

Question: Design a system to detect and prevent SQL injection attacks on a web application. Consider input validation, prepared statements, error handling, logging, and alerting.

Tips: Stress the importance of input validation to ensure that only expected data types and formats are accepted. Explain the use of prepared statements to separate SQL logic from data. Mention implementing error handling that does not reveal sensitive information and setting up alerting mechanisms for anomalous activities.

Question: Design a multi-factor authentication system for a bank. Consider aspects like factors (knowledge, possession, biometrics), threat models, fallback authentication, and integration with banking systems.

Tips: Describe the different types of authentication factors and how they can be layered for added security. Discuss user experience considerations, such as the ease of use and the availability of fallback options in case the primary authentication method fails. Consider security versus convenience in your design.

Question: Design a security system for a cloud-based file storage and sharing application. Consider authentication, authorization, encryption (in transit and at rest), key management, audit logs, and anomaly detection.

Tips: Emphasize encryption for data in transit and at rest, including managing encryption keys. Discuss how to implement strong authentication and fine-grained authorization controls. Highlight audit logs and anomaly detection to monitor for suspicious activities.

Question: Design a network architecture for a company with multiple offices that uses a hybrid cloud model. The design should incorporate on-prem firewalls, web application firewalls, IDS/IPS, multi-factor authentication, and encryption between offices. Explain how these components work together to provide defense-in-depth security for the company's infrastructure and applications.

Tips: Create a seamless and secure network connecting on-premises and cloud environments. Discuss the use of VPNs for secure communications, the role of firewalls and IDS/IPS in protecting the network perimeter, and implementing multi-factor authentication for accessing sensitive resources.

Provide a concise yet comprehensive explanation for each question, backing your answers with real-world examples, industry best practices, and standards. Demonstrating your ability to balance security with functionality and user experience will set you apart as a well-rounded security architect.

Future looking Questions

Future-looking questions evaluate your vision, foresight, and preparedness for upcoming changes or challenges in a specific field. In cybersecurity or any other rapidly evolving domain, these questions help employers determine whether you're staying current with trends, capable of proactive thinking, and able to adapt to future requirements.

Here are some examples of future-looking questions specifically tailored for cybersecurity and IT domains, along with tips for answering them:

Question: How do you foresee the evolution of ransomware attacks in the next decade?
Tips:
- Discuss the current trends in ransomware attacks.
- Consider potential technological advancements and how they might be exploited.
- Mention preventive and responsive strategies that might be required to counter such evolving threats.

Question: In the age of quantum computing, how do you think encryption strategies need to change?
Tips:
- Understand the basics of quantum computing and its implications on current encryption methods.
- Highlight the emergence of quantum-resistant cryptographic algorithms.
- Talk about the proactive measures businesses should take in anticipation of quantum computing.

Question: With remote work becoming more prevalent, how do you see the cybersecurity landscape changing to accommodate this shift?
Tips:
- Mention the increasing importance of VPNs, multi-factor authentication, and secure cloud infrastructures.
- Discuss potential vulnerabilities in home networks and how organizations can mitigate those risks.
- Talk about the significance of continuous employee training and awareness programs tailored for remote work scenarios.

Question: As AI becomes more integrated into everyday applications, what new vulnerabilities do you anticipate, and how can organizations prepare?
Tips:

- Address both the potential of AI as a tool for cybersecurity and the vulnerabilities it might introduce.
- Discuss specific scenarios where AI could be exploited and the measures to prevent such exploits.
- Emphasize the importance of ethical AI development and robust testing environments.

Question: How do you see regulations and laws adapting to the rapidly changing cybersecurity landscape in the next five years?
Tips:
- Highlight some of the current regulations (like GDPR) and their implications.
- Discuss the balance between user privacy and security requirements.
- Mention the need for international cooperation and standardization in cybersecurity regulations.

When answering future-oriented questions, it is essential to blend current knowledge with speculative thinking. This will demonstrate that you are informed about present-day realities and ready to tackle future challenges.

Security is not just a feature but the backbone of any modern solution. As technology continually evolves, so do the threats and challenges it faces. For a solution architect, security cannot be an afterthought; it must be intrinsic to the system's design from its inception. Every piece of software, every infrastructure component, and even the methodologies employed must be scrutinized through the lens of security.

For a solution architect, creating a secure application isn't just about implementing advanced tools and protocols. It's about fostering a culture of security, where vigilance, adaptability, and resilience against threats are embedded into the very fabric of the development and operational process.

The aim of this chapter isn't to delve into the intricate details of security but rather to equip you with the essential tools needed to excel in a security solutions architect interview. You can refer to the ' Solutions Architect Handbook ' for a more comprehensive exploration of security. The 'AWS for Solutions Architect book will be invaluable if you focus on cloud security. These resources are available on Amazon and are excellent companions to guide you through your SA interview preparation.

Summary

In this chapter, you embarked on a comprehensive exploration of the pivotal role of a Security Solutions Architect. You began by unraveling the intricacies of security architecture and its foundational components, essential for designing and fortifying an organization's security posture.

You then delved deep into the fundamental security design principles and methodologies, equipping yourself with a roadmap for crafting resilient systems. Recognizing the pivotal role of cloud technologies in today's IT landscape, you gained insights into cloud security's unique challenges and nuances. You understood the shared responsibility model through this lens, emphasizing the collaborative security obligations between cloud service providers and users.

This chapter also covered critical cloud-centric themes like Identity and Access Management (IAM). It highlighted the balance between facilitating user access and ensuring robust security. Further, it clarified the essential nature of encryption and key management in cloud settings and how they act as sentinels for sensitive data. Given today's complex web of regulations, it also revealed the value of cloud compliance and governance in navigating these waters.

Adding to your toolkit, you explored renowned cloud security frameworks like CSA and NIST. These frameworks offer benchmarks, best practices, and methodologies that can guide you in crafting and refining your security strategies. You learned about tips and tricks to be successful during security interview whiteboarding with a reference architecture from AWS security posture.

Toward the end of the chapter, you were equipped with a curated set of interview questions tailored for the Security Solutions Architect role. The questions span various behavioral, technical, scenario-based, designed-based, and future-looking categories to give you an edge in your interviews and career progression.

As this chapter concludes, it becomes evident that being a Security Solutions Architect isn't just about mastering technical nuances; it's about vision, strategic foresight, and an adaptive mindset in cybersecurity.

Part 3: Industry Solutions Architect Role and Interview

Chapter 12 - Cracking the Industry Solutions Architect Interview

Until now, you have learned about tips and tricks for excelling in the solutions architect role, focusing on various technology domains. However, solutions architects need to work closely with industry and business domain experts to bridge any communication gaps that may arise during the exchange of ideas. This need led to the emergence of a new role known as an industry solutions architect, which has become increasingly prominent in recent years. With the advent of cloud technology, it has become easier to learn about various technologies, as much of the heavy lifting is done by cloud providers. As a result, there is now a high demand for industry solutions architects, with numerous job openings available.

The role of an industry solutions architect has become more important as technology becomes more accessible through cloud services. The responsibility for making technology decisions is no longer limited to the Chief Information Officer (CIO) organization. Nowadays, heads of industry verticals often make technology decisions at the line of business (LoB) level. For instance, the Finance head may decide on technology providers to implement fraud detection in banking. In contrast, the Retail business head may choose to build personalized customer recommendations to boost sales.

It would always be beneficial to have someone with expertise in technology and industry domains to define an architecture that satisfies business requirements. Similarly, industry solutions architects can be found across various verticals and sub-verticals. For example, a Manufacturing solutions architect may focus on designing architectures for data collection and machine prediction on the factory floor. In contrast, an automotive architect in the sub-vertical may specialize in building architectures for connected cars. This chapter covers the following topics:

- What are industry-specific solutions architect roles?
- Healthcare Solutions Architect
- Finance Solutions Architect
- Retail Solutions Architect
- Manufacturing Solutions Architect
- Best practices for designing and implementing industry solutions
- Industry architect interview questions

By the end of this chapter, you will learn about some of the most popular industry solutions architect roles and gain tips on succeeding in interviews for these positions. You will gain a good understanding of how to handle interviews for industry solutions architect roles in general. However, covering all industries and subindustries in this chapter is impossible.

Who is the industry solutions architect (SA)?

Let's first understand the industry solutions architect. In simple language, an industry solutions architect is a professional with expertise in technology and industry-specific domains. They play a crucial role in designing and implementing architectural solutions that align with a particular industry's unique requirements and challenges.

Unlike traditional solutions architects who primarily focus on technology, industry solutions architects deeply understand the specific industry they work in. They are well-versed in their industry vertical's business processes, regulatory considerations, and operational needs. For example, an industry solutions architect in the FSI highlights their critical role in addressing industry-specific requirements such as PCI-DSS compliance. They often need to ensure compliance with other regulations, such as Personally Identifiable Information (PII) requirements and the Financial Industry Regulatory Authority (FINRA) rules.

> *Industry solutions architects collaborate closely with business stakeholders, industry experts, and technology teams to develop comprehensive architectural plans that effectively address specific industry challenges and leverage technology. They analyze business requirements, identify suitable technology solutions, and design architectures that optimize processes, enhance efficiency, and drive innovation within their industry.*

These professionals possess a broad range of skills, including strong analytical abilities, strategic thinking, communication and collaboration skills, and a deep knowledge of technology and industry trends. They must stay updated with industry advancements and emerging technologies to provide valuable insights and make informed architectural decisions.

Following are some of the essential requirements for an industry SA role :

- **Bridging the Gap:** Industry solutions architects act as a bridge between technology and industry domains. They possess expertise in both areas, enabling effective communication and collaboration between business stakeholders and technology teams. They can design architectures that align technology solutions with business objectives by understanding industry-specific challenges, requirements, and trends.
- **Tailored Solutions:** Each industry has unique processes, regulations, and operational needs. Industry solutions architects specialize in understanding these intricacies and designing solutions that address specific industry challenges. This tailored approach ensures that technology solutions are aligned with industry requirements, resulting in more effective and efficient implementations.

- **Maximizing Business Value:** Industry solutions architects help organizations extract maximum value from their technology investments. By considering industry-specific factors, such as regulatory compliance, security, and scalability, they design architectures that optimize business processes, enhance operational efficiency, and drive innovation. This leads to improved customer experiences, increased productivity, and better business outcomes.
- **Keeping Pace with Industry Trends:** Industries are constantly evolving, driven by technological advancements, changing consumer expectations, and market dynamics. Industry solutions architects stay up-to-date with these trends, enabling them to anticipate industry shifts and align technology strategies accordingly. This proactive approach helps organizations remain competitive and adapt to emerging opportunities.
- **Collaboration and Alignment:** Industry solutions architects foster collaboration between business and technology teams. They facilitate communication, ensuring business requirements are effectively translated into technical solutions. By aligning the efforts of various stakeholders, including business leaders, domain experts, and IT professionals, industry solutions architects promote a cohesive approach to technology implementation.
- **Compliance and Risk Mitigation:** Industries often have specific regulatory requirements that organizations must adhere to. Industry solutions architects ensure compliance with industry-specific regulations, such as data privacy, security standards, or financial regulations. By designing architectures that meet these requirements, they help organizations mitigate risks, avoid penalties, and maintain a strong reputation.

During an interview for an industry solutions architect role, it is important to showcase strategic thinking and a strong understanding of future industry trends and technological advancements. While going through the interview, you must demonstrate that your technology solutions align with a particular industry's specific needs and objectives, ultimately driving business success and transformation.

Let's examine some popular industry solutions architect roles. Later, you will learn more tips for cracking the Industry SA interview.

Understanding the industry SA role

An industry vertical, or a vertical market, refers to a specific business niche that caters to a distinct group of consumers or customers with unique needs. Various vertical markets exist as they represent particular consumer demands. Examples of industry verticals include organic groceries, banking and payment services, heavy manufacturing, aerospace technology, insurance sectors, and microchip manufacturing.

The idea of industry verticals seems paradoxical in the business world. Companies want to target as many potential customers as possible. However, this approach can lead to a lack of specificity, causing a product or service to fail to serve any particular consumer effectively. By trying to appeal to everyone, a company may end up being irrelevant to no one.

Industry verticals allow companies to focus their efforts and become experts in a particular field with more limited competition than broader markets. This specialization enables businesses to refine their purpose and seek to become the leading producer and supplier within their chosen vertical. They can differentiate based on their target market and offer tailored solutions or products that cater to specific industry needs.

The same principles apply to the role of an industry solutions architect. By positioning themselves as experts in a specific industry, solutions architects can become top contenders for job opportunities. Their specialized skills and deep understanding of the industry allow them to bring unique value to a company by applying technology solutions that align with industry-specific requirements. This expertise helps them differentiate themselves and demonstrate the added value they can get to an organization.

With over 50 industry and subindustry verticals available, solutions architects must focus on the most common industry-specific roles. By specializing in these areas, they can leverage their knowledge and skills to excel in their roles and provide effective architectural solutions within their chosen industry verticals. Let's examine the solutions architect's role in some popular industry verticals in detail.

Healthcare and Life Science (HCLS) SA

Healthcare and life science skills often call out together, but they are very different. Healthcare Solutions Architects have a broader focus encompassing various healthcare sectors, including hospitals, clinics, healthcare providers, insurers, and healthcare IT vendors. They design and implement technology solutions that cater to the needs of these diverse stakeholders, ranging from patient care to administrative processes. On the other hand, Life Science Solutions Architects specifically cater to the life science industry, which includes pharmaceuticals, biotechnology, medical devices, and research organizations. They specialize in designing solutions that address the unique requirements of this industry, such as clinical trials, research data management, regulatory compliance, and drug discovery.

Healthcare Solutions Architect

Let's look at the skills required for the healthcare industry. A Healthcare Solutions Architect plays a crucial role in designing and implementing technology solutions tailored to the healthcare industry. They ensure compliance with regulations, address healthcare-specific use cases, facilitate system integration, and prioritize security and privacy. Their expertise enables healthcare organizations to leverage technology effectively, improve patient care, streamline workflows, and drive positive healthcare outcomes. Let's explore the key aspects of their role:

- **Understanding Healthcare Workflows:** Healthcare Solutions Architects must deeply understand healthcare workflows, processes, and standards. They must comprehend how data flows within the healthcare ecosystem, including patient data, clinical workflows, and administrative operations.
- **Compliance and Regulatory Knowledge:** Compliance is a significant aspect of healthcare. Healthcare solutions Architects must be well-versed in compliance regulations, such as the Health Insurance Portability and Accountability Act (HIPAA), the General Data Protection Regulation (GDPR), and other local regulations. They ensure that technology solutions meet these requirements to protect patient privacy and data security.
- **Electronic Health Records (EHR) Systems:** Healthcare Solutions Architects should have expertise in designing and implementing Electronic Health Record (EHR) systems. They understand the complexities of EHR interoperability, data integration, and data exchange standards, enabling seamless access to patient information across healthcare providers and systems.
- **Healthcare Use Cases:** Healthcare Solutions Architects work on various industry use cases. They may design and implement telemedicine platforms that enable remote consultations, develop patient portals for secure access to medical records, or create data analytics systems for population health management and clinical research.
- **Integration of Healthcare Systems:** The healthcare industry requires the cohesive integration of numerous systems and applications. Solutions Architects ensure seamless integration between clinical, laboratory, billing, and other healthcare applications. They also create architecture blueprints and standards for system interoperability.
- **Healthcare Interoperability Standards:** Healthcare Solutions Architects are familiar with interoperability standards such as Health Level Seven (HL7), Fast Healthcare Interoperability Resources (FHIR), and Clinical Document Architecture (CDA). They ensure that systems can exchange information accurately, securely, and in a standardized format.
- **Security and Privacy:** Protecting patient data is of utmost importance in healthcare. Solutions Architects implement robust security measures, including access controls, encryption, and data masking, to safeguard sensitive information. They also address privacy concerns related to consent management and data sharing.
- **Technical Skills:** Healthcare Solutions Architects should possess strong technical skills. They should be proficient in healthcare-specific technologies such as EHR systems, healthcare information exchanges (HIEs), picture archiving and communication systems (PACS), and data analytics platforms. They may also know about cloud computing, cybersecurity, and emerging technologies like AI and machine learning.

From an interview perspective, the role of a Healthcare Solutions Architect holds immense importance in the healthcare industry. They are tasked with designing and implementing technology solutions that address healthcare organizations' unique challenges and requirements.

Life Science Solutions Architect

The role of a Life Science Solutions Architect focuses on designing and implementing technology solutions within the life science industry. Life science encompasses pharmaceuticals, biotechnology, medical devices, and research organizations. Let's delve into the key aspects of this role:

- **Understanding Life Science Workflows:** Life Science Solutions Architects must deeply understand the unique workflows, processes, and regulatory requirements within the life science industry. They must comprehend the research and development lifecycle, clinical trials, regulatory compliance, and manufacturing processes specific to life science organizations.

- **Compliance and Regulatory Knowledge:** Compliance is critical in the life science industry due to strict regulations governing data privacy, clinical trials, Good Clinical Practice (GCP), Good Manufacturing Practice (GMP), and other industry-specific guidelines. Solutions Architects must possess expertise in these compliance regulations to design solutions that meet the required standards.

- **Use Cases in Life Science:** Life Science Solutions Architects work on various use cases within the industry. For example, they may design and implement solutions for electronic data capture (EDC) systems used in clinical trials, laboratory information management systems (LIMS) for sample tracking, or pharmacovigilance systems for monitoring drug safety. These use cases require an in-depth understanding of industry-specific processes and compliance requirements.

- **Data Integration and Analysis:** Solutions Architects in life science focus on integrating data from various sources, such as electronic health records (EHR), clinical trial databases, laboratory systems, and research repositories. They design architectures that enable seamless data integration and facilitate data analysis for research, drug discovery, and regulatory reporting purposes.

- **Regulatory Compliance and Quality Systems:** Life science organizations adhere to stringent quality systems and regulatory compliance frameworks such as ISO 13485, 21 CFR Part 11, and ICH guidelines. Solutions Architects must be familiar with these frameworks and design architectures to ensure compliance with quality standards and regulatory requirements.

- **Security and Privacy:** Protecting sensitive patient data, intellectual property, and research findings is paramount in life science. Solutions Architects implement robust security measures, data encryption, access controls, and audit trails to safeguard critical information.

- **Technical Skills:** Life Science Solutions Architects should possess strong technical skills in data integration, cloud computing, big data analytics, and emerging technologies like AI and machine learning. They may also be familiar with bioinformatics tools, laboratory automation systems, and regulatory information management systems.

- **Domain Team Collaboration:** Effective communication and collaboration skills are essential for Life Science Solutions Architects. They need to work closely with researchers, clinicians, regulatory affairs teams, quality assurance personnel, and IT professionals to ensure seamless integration of technology solutions and alignment with industry-specific requirements.

The role of a Life Science Solutions Architect involves designing and implementing technology solutions that address the industry's unique challenges, compliance requirements, and workflows. The architect's expertise in regulatory compliance, data integration, security, and industry-specific processes allows life science organizations to leverage technology effectively for research, development, clinical trials, and regulatory compliance purposes.

When preparing for an interview for either a Healthcare Solutions Architect or a Life Science Solutions Architect role, it is crucial to highlight your industry-specific expertise and understanding. Showcase your experience and knowledge in healthcare and/or life science workflows, compliance regulations, and technology solutions.

Discuss specific use cases relevant to the industry, such as electronic health records (EHR) systems, clinical trial management, or laboratory information management systems (LIMS). Emphasize your ability to address security and privacy concerns, navigate industry-specific compliance regulations, and integrate data from various sources.

Additionally, highlight your technical skills and proficiency in relevant technologies, such as AI, data analytics, or interoperability standards. Demonstrate your collaboration and communication skills, showcasing your ability to work with diverse stakeholders, including healthcare professionals, researchers, regulatory personnel, and IT teams.

By effectively addressing these points, you can position yourself as a strong candidate capable of designing and implementing technology solutions that meet the unique needs and challenges of the healthcare or life science industry. Now, let's look at the role of the financial services solutions architect.

Banking, Financial Service and Insurance SA

You may see multiple roles in the job market for the financial industry. The finance sector plays a crucial role in the global economy, with banks, financial institutions, and insurance companies serving millions of customers worldwide. These institutions generate substantial revenue through lending, deposit-taking, asset management, insurance premiums, investment banking, and more.

The Banking, Financial Services, and Insurance (BFSI) sector has historically been one of the largest and most significant industry verticals in terms of revenue. The BFSI industry encompasses various financial services, including banking, investment, insurance, and other financial intermediation activities. The role of a BFSI Solutions Architect revolves around designing and implementing technology solutions tailored to the specific needs and challenges of the banking, financial services, and insurance sectors. Let's explore the key aspects of this role:

- **Understanding BFSI Workflows:** BFSI Solutions Architects should have a deep understanding of the unique workflows, processes, and regulatory frameworks within the banking, financial services, and insurance industries. They need to comprehend banking operations, financial transactions, risk management, compliance requirements, and insurance processes.
- **Compliance and Regulatory Knowledge:** Compliance is crucial in the BFSI sector due to the stringent regulations it faces. Solutions Architects must be well-versed in industry-specific regulations such as the Sarbanes-Oxley Act (SOX), Payment Card Industry Data Security Standard (PCI-DSS), Anti-Money Laundering (AML) regulations, and various insurance regulatory frameworks. They ensure that technology solutions align with these compliance requirements.
- **Use Cases in BFSI:** BFSI Solutions Architects work on various use cases within the industry. For example, they may design and implement core banking systems, online banking platforms, mobile payment solutions, risk management systems, fraud detection systems, or insurance claim processing systems. These use cases require a deep understanding of the industry's processes, customer experience, and security requirements.
- **Data Security and Privacy:** Security and privacy are paramount in the BFSI sector. Solutions Architects should possess expertise in implementing robust security measures, data encryption, access controls, and intrusion detection systems to safeguard sensitive financial and customer information. They ensure compliance with data privacy regulations and develop architectures that protect against cyber threats.
- **Integration of Systems and Applications:** BFSI Solutions Architects focus on integrating various industry systems and applications. They design architectures that enable seamless integration of banking platforms, financial transaction systems, customer relationship management (CRM) systems, risk management systems, and data analytics platforms. They also ensure data accuracy, integrity, and consistency across different systems.
- **Skills in Emerging Technologies:** BFSI Solutions Architects should be knowledgeable about emerging technologies and their applications in the industry. This may include expertise in cloud computing, blockchain, artificial intelligence (AI), machine learning (ML), robotic process automation (RPA), and big data analytics. They leverage these technologies to enhance operational efficiency, customer experience, and risk management within BFSI organizations.

Effective collaboration and communication skills are vital for BFSI Solutions Architects. They need to work closely with stakeholders, including business leaders, product managers, compliance officers, and technology teams. They facilitate communication to align technology solutions with business goals, regulatory requirements, and customer needs.

BFSI Solutions Architects are critical in designing and implementing technology solutions that address the unique requirements and challenges of the banking, financial services, and insurance sectors. Their expertise in industry-specific workflows, compliance, security, and integration enables them to drive operational efficiency, risk management, and customer satisfaction within BFSI organizations.

When approaching an interview for a Solutions Architect role in the BFSI sector, it is crucial to showcase a combination of industry expertise, technical proficiency, regulatory compliance knowledge, and strong business acumen. From an interview perspective, emphasize your deep understanding of BFSI processes, regulations, and compliance requirements. Showcase your technical skills relevant to the industry, such as core banking systems, payment processing, risk management, and data analytics. Demonstrate your ability to design end-to-end solutions, considering scalability, security, and compliance.

Further, you must Highlight your knowledge of regulatory frameworks such as Basel III, PCI-DSS, and AML, as well as your understanding of data integration and security measures. Showcase effective communication and collaboration skills to engage with stakeholders across business and technical teams.

By effectively addressing these points in the interview, you can position yourself as a qualified candidate who can deliver impactful solutions that meet the unique needs of the BFSI industry, driving innovation, compliance, and business success.

Retail and Supply Chain Solutions Architect

The retail industry holds immense significance in our daily lives, as it encompasses a wide range of activities and experiences that we encounter regularly. From purchasing groceries at Walmart to online shopping on platforms like Amazon.com and exploring clothing stores for apparel, retail plays a pivotal role in meeting our daily needs and desires.

Due to its pervasive nature, the demand for skilled Retail Solutions Architects is high. These professionals are sought after to design and implement technology solutions that cater to the unique requirements of the retail industry. Their expertise enables retailers to enhance customer experiences, optimize operations, and stay competitive in a rapidly evolving market. With the continuous growth and transformation of the retail sector, the role of Retail Solutions Architects remains crucial in shaping the future of retail experiences and driving business success. As the supply chain works hand in hand with retail, both Retail and supply chain need different skills.

Retail Solutions Architect

The role of a Retail Solutions Architect revolves around designing and implementing technology solutions tailored to the specific needs and challenges of the retail industry. Let's delve into the key aspects of this role:

- **Understanding Retail Workflows:** Retail Solutions Architects should deeply understand the retail industry's unique workflows, processes, and systems. This includes inventory management, point-of-sale (POS) systems, e-commerce platforms, supply chain management, customer relationship management (CRM), and omnichannel retailing.

- **Use Cases in Retail:** Retail Solutions Architects work on various use cases within the industry. For example, they may design and implement e-commerce platforms that enable online shopping and personalized customer experiences. They may develop inventory management systems to optimize stock levels and streamline supply chain processes. Additionally, they may design loyalty programs, mobile payment solutions, or analytics systems to gain insights into customer behavior and enhance decision-making.

- **Integration of Retail Systems:** Retail Solutions Architects focus on integrating various retail systems and applications. This includes seamless integration between online and offline channels, POS systems, e-commerce platforms, inventory management systems, CRM systems, and analytics platforms. They ensure data consistency, real-time synchronization, and a unified view of customer information across channels.

- **Compliance and Security:** Retail Solutions Architects should be experts in compliance and security measures specific to the retail industry. These may include regulations related to payment card data security (such as PCI-DSS), data privacy regulations, and consumer protection laws. They design architectures that ensure secure customer data handling, protection against cyber threats, and compliance with industry standards.

- **Customer Experience Focus:** Retail Solutions Architects must prioritize customer experience while designing technology solutions. They should understand customer journey mapping, personalization strategies, and seamless omnichannel experiences. They leverage mobile apps, digital signage, and customer analytics to enhance customer engagement and satisfaction.

- **Technical Skills:** Retail Solutions Architects should possess strong technical skills in e-commerce platforms, POS systems, cloud computing, data analytics, and integration technologies. They may also be knowledgeable about emerging technologies such as AI, machine learning, and the Internet of Things (IoT) and their applications in the retail industry.

A Retail Solutions Architect plays a vital role in designing and implementing technology solutions that address the unique needs of the retail industry. Their expertise in retail workflows, customer experience, compliance, and integration enables them to drive operational efficiency, enhance customer engagement, and support business growth within the retail sector.

For a Retail Solutions Architect interview, highlight your expertise in point-of-sale systems, e-commerce platforms, CRM, omnichannel retailing, and customer experience enhancement. Emphasize your ability to design and implement technology solutions that drive business growth and meet customer demands. Showcase your understanding of industry trends and emerging technologies relevant to supply chain or retail. Additionally, demonstrate your collaboration and communication skills, as both roles require working closely with stakeholders across different functions.

You should be clear about the difference between Supply Chain and Retail solutions architects. The roles of a Supply Chain Solutions Architect and a Retail Solutions Architect differ in their focus areas and expertise within the retail industry.

Supply Chain Solutions Architect

A Supply Chain Solutions Architect focuses on designing and optimizing the end-to-end supply chain processes within the retail industry. They work on streamlining and enhancing the flow of goods, materials, and information from suppliers to manufacturers, distributors, and ultimately to the end consumers. Their responsibilities include designing efficient inventory management systems, warehouse optimization, transportation logistics, demand planning, and supply chain analytics. They aim to improve supply chain visibility, reduce costs, and enhance operational efficiency.

However, a Retail Solutions Architect, on the other hand, focuses on designing and implementing technology solutions that address various aspects of the retail industry. They work to enhance the customer experience, optimize retail operations, and drive business growth. Their responsibilities include point-of-sale (POS) systems, e-commerce platforms, customer relationship management (CRM), loyalty programs, omnichannel retailing, and personalized marketing. They aim to create seamless shopping experiences, enable efficient store operations, and leverage technology to meet customer demands.

While both roles contribute to the overall success of the retail industry, their focus areas differ. Supply Chain Solutions Architects optimize the supply chain processes, whereas Retail Solutions Architects focus on technology solutions that enhance the customer experience and drive retail business growth. However, there may be overlaps and collaboration between these roles, and it may be expected from the same person to possess both skills.

When interviewing for a Supply Chain Solutions Architect or a Retail Solutions Architect role within the retail industry, it is essential to highlight the specific expertise and skills required for each position. For a Supply Chain Solutions Architect, emphasize your knowledge of supply chain processes, inventory management, logistics, demand planning, and supply chain optimization. Discuss your experience designing efficient systems and leveraging technology to improve supply chain visibility and reduce costs.

By effectively addressing these points during the interview, you can position yourself as a qualified candidate who can contribute to the retail industry's success through optimized supply chain processes or enhanced retail experiences, depending on the role. Now, let's dive deep into the role of manufacturing solutions architect.

Manufacturing and Automotive Solutions Architect

The junction of manufacturing and automotive industries under the umbrella of advanced technology solutions highlights the pivotal role of a Manufacturing and Automotive Solutions Architect. This professional represents the intersection of two dynamic fields, focusing on integrating cutting-edge technologies into manufacturing processes and automotive systems to drive innovation, efficiency, and sustainability. However, each of these fields required very specific skill sets. Let's delve into the key responsibilities and expertise areas of a Manufacturing and Automotive Solutions Architect:

Manufacturing Solutions Architect

Manufacturing plays a critical role in our daily lives, producing the goods and products we rely on. Everything, from the electronics we use to the vehicles we drive to the clothes we wear, is manufactured on factory floors. Manufacturing is not limited to a single industry but spans various sectors, such as automotive, electronics, pharmaceuticals, consumer goods, and more.

This widespread demand for manufactured products makes the role of a Manufacturing Solutions Architect highly sought after. Their expertise in designing and implementing technology solutions specific to manufacturing processes is crucial in optimizing operations, improving efficiency, ensuring quality control, and driving innovation. With manufacturing being an integral part of countless industries, the role of a Manufacturing Solutions Architect remains significant in meeting the demands and challenges of modern production processes.

The role of a Manufacturing Solutions Architect revolves around designing and implementing technology solutions tailored to the specific needs and challenges of the manufacturing industry. Let's delve into the key aspects of this role:

- **Understanding Manufacturing Workflows:** Manufacturing Solutions Architects should deeply understand the manufacturing industry's unique workflows, processes, and systems. This includes product design, production planning, supply chain management, quality control, inventory management, and shop floor operations.
- **Use Cases in Manufacturing:** Manufacturing Solutions Architects work on various use cases within the industry. For example, they may design and implement manufacturing

execution systems (MES) that enable real-time monitoring and control of production processes. They may develop digital twin solutions to simulate and optimize manufacturing operations. They may also design solutions for predictive maintenance, inventory optimization, or quality management. These use cases enhance manufacturing operations' productivity, efficiency, and quality.

- **Compliance and Regulatory Considerations:** Manufacturing Solutions Architects should possess expertise in compliance and regulatory requirements specific to the industry. This may include regulations related to product safety, environmental sustainability, health and safety, and data privacy. They design architectures that ensure compliance with these regulations, implement appropriate data security measures, and enable traceability and reporting.
- **Integration of Manufacturing Systems:** Manufacturing Solutions Architects focus on integrating various systems and applications within the manufacturing environment. This includes seamless integration between enterprise resource planning (ERP) systems, product lifecycle management (PLM) systems, shop floor control systems, quality management systems, and supply chain management systems. They ensure data consistency, real-time synchronization, and streamlined information flow across manufacturing functions.
- **Technical Skills:** Manufacturing Solutions Architects should possess strong technical skills in manufacturing automation, industrial IoT (Internet of Things), data analytics, cloud computing, and emerging technologies like AI and machine learning. They may also be familiar with manufacturing-specific software and tools, such as computer-aided design (CAD) and computer-aided manufacturing (CAM) systems.

When preparing for an interview for a Manufacturing Solutions Architect role, it is essential to highlight your expertise and experience in the manufacturing industry. Showcase your deep understanding of manufacturing workflows, processes, and systems, emphasizing specific use cases such as manufacturing execution systems, digital twin solutions, predictive maintenance, or quality management.

Discuss your knowledge of compliance and regulatory considerations relevant to manufacturing, including product safety, environmental sustainability, and data privacy. Demonstrate your ability to integrate diverse manufacturing systems and applications, ensuring seamless data flow and real-time synchronization.

Highlight your technical skills in manufacturing automation, industrial IoT, data analytics, and emerging technologies. Additionally, emphasize your collaboration and communication skills, showcasing your ability to work with cross-functional teams and align technology solutions with manufacturing goals.

By effectively addressing these points during the interview, you can position yourself as a qualified candidate who can design and implement technology solutions that optimize manufacturing operations, drive efficiency, and ensure quality within the industry.

Automotive Solutions Architect

The automotive industry is experiencing a technological revolution. As vehicles become more connected, electric, and autonomous, the role of an Automotive Solutions Architect has become increasingly significant. These professionals are at the forefront of integrating cutting-edge technology solutions into automotive manufacturing and operations, propelling the industry into a new era of innovation and efficiency. Let's explore the key aspects of the Automotive Solutions Architect role:

- **Understanding Automotive Industry Dynamics:** Automotive Solutions Architects must have a comprehensive grasp of the automotive industry's unique dynamics, including vehicle design, production processes, supply chain management, and after-sales services. They need to be well-versed in industry trends such as electrification, connectivity, autonomous driving, and sustainable manufacturing.
- **Specialized Use Cases**: Automotive Solutions Architects work on specific use cases pertinent to the automotive sector. This includes designing systems for advanced vehicle telematics, developing platforms for electric vehicle (EV) charging management, implementing solutions for autonomous vehicle testing, and integrating IoT for smart manufacturing. These use cases aim to enhance vehicle performance, safety, and user experience while optimizing production processes.
- **Compliance with Automotive Standards:** These professionals need to be knowledgeable about automotive regulations and standards, such as safety regulations, emissions standards, and quality control benchmarks. They ensure that all technological solutions adhere to these regulations while maintaining high safety and quality standards.
- **Integration of Automotive Systems:** A critical responsibility is the seamless integration of various systems, such as vehicle management systems, production automation systems, dealer management systems, and customer relationship management platforms. This integration ensures a unified approach to vehicle design, manufacturing, sales, and after-sales service.
- **Technical Expertise in Automotive Technologies:** An Automotive Solutions Architect should possess technical expertise in areas crucial to the automotive sector, such as automotive electronics, embedded systems, vehicle-to-everything (V2X) communication, AI for autonomous driving, and battery management systems for EVs.
- Align with the overall goals of the automotive organization.

In preparing for an interview for an Automotive Solutions Architect position, it's essential to focus on your experience and expertise in the automotive sector. Discuss your understanding of the industry's unique challenges and trends, such as the shift to electric vehicles and the integration of autonomous driving technologies. Highlight your experience with specific automotive use cases, such as telematics systems, EV charging platforms, or autonomous vehicle technologies. Emphasize your familiarity with automotive regulations and standards and how you have ensured compliance in previous projects. Illustrate your ability to integrate diverse automotive systems and applications, ensuring efficient and cohesive operations across the vehicle lifecycle.

Showcase your technical skills specific to the automotive industry, such as expertise in automotive electronics, embedded systems, or AI applications in-vehicle systems. Finally, emphasize your ability to collaborate with various stakeholders in the automotive ecosystem and how you align technological innovations with the strategic goals of the automotive organization.

By effectively addressing these areas, you can position yourself as a skilled Automotive Solutions Architect capable of driving technological innovation and efficiency in the dynamic automotive industry.

There is a high demand for solution architect roles in several industries, such as Telco, Energy & Utility, Media & Entertainment, Travel & Hospitality, and more. Although we are covering as many of these industries as possible in one chapter, a separate book will be created in the future if there is demand for it. In this section, you have learned about some of the most popular industry solution architect roles, and you will learn about interview questions related to each of these roles in the upcoming section.

Best practices for designing industry solutions

Industry Solutions Architects (SAs) must combine strategic insight, technological ability, and market awareness. These professionals are tasked with crafting solutions that address today's immediate challenges while remaining resilient and adaptable enough to evolve with the industry's future needs. Let's explore the foundational pillars underpinning an SA's role and how they can effectively build and drive industry solutions.

Understanding the Target User and Use Case

Central to the role of an Industry SA is a profound understanding of the target user—most importantly, the customers. The solutions developed must resonate with these users' needs, preferences, and challenges, ensuring they meet and exceed expectations. Staying relevant to customers requires a continuous loop of feedback and adaptation, where SAs engage with users to gather insights, test solutions, and refine offerings based on real-world use. This customer-centric approach ensures that solutions remain aligned with user needs over time, fostering loyalty and driving user engagement.

The genesis of an impactful industry solution lies in identifying and understanding the core use cases that are pivotal to the industry or across multiple sectors. These use cases should be carefully selected based on their potential to deliver functional outcomes that resonate with market demand and address target customers' needs.

For instance, this could involve automating inventory management to reduce waste and increase efficiency in the supply chain sector. By pinpointing these critical use cases, Solutions Architects can ensure that the solutions developed are relevant and in demand.

Prioritizing Capabilities and Solutions

The important step in the journey of an Industry SA involves a thorough understanding of which capabilities and solutions to prioritize. This decision-making requires a deep dive into the current and emerging trends within the industry, identifying technologies that offer the most promise for transformation and growth. SAs must assess the technological landscape to pinpoint solutions that will deliver the most significant impact, considering factors such as innovation potential, scalability, and integration capabilities. Equally important is understanding the market demand for these solutions, ensuring that the focus remains on technologies that solve real-world problems and offer tangible benefits to businesses. By aligning solution development with market needs and industry trends, SAs can ensure their efforts are relevant and impactful.

Delivering and Executing with Velocity at Scale

Once key use cases have been identified, the next step is to develop and produce solutions tailored to these scenarios. This phase involves a deep dive into each use case's specific challenges and requirements, ensuring the solutions have clear objectives and outcomes in mind. If solutions for these use cases still need to be created, it becomes imperative to innovate and create new solutions that effectively address these challenges. The productization process transforms these solutions into market-ready products that customers can quickly deploy and utilize.

Delivering and executing solutions with velocity and scale is a critical competency for Industry SAs. In an era where speed to market can be a competitive advantage, SAs must leverage agile methodologies, cloud technologies, and modular architectures to accelerate solution development and deployment. This agility allows for rapid iteration and scaling, enabling organizations to respond swiftly to market changes or emerging opportunities. Moreover, executing with velocity ensures businesses can capitalize on innovations faster, delivering value to customers and staying ahead of the competition.

Assessing Market Impact and Differentiation

Understanding the market impact and crafting solutions with a unique value proposition is essential for ensuring the long-term success of industry solutions. Industry SAs must evaluate how their solutions differentiate from existing offerings, identifying areas where they can provide additional value or address unmet needs. This differentiation could stem from innovation, superior performance, enhanced usability, or integration capabilities. By focusing on solutions that offer distinct advantages, SAs can help their organizations capture market share, drive revenue growth, and establish a strong market presence. Additionally, understanding these solutions' potential in-year and long-term revenue implications enables organizations to make informed strategic decisions, aligning technological investments with business goals.

The final step in the industry solutions approach is establishing a strong market presence through joint marketing and branding efforts with the business. This involves promoting the use cases and the solutions developed to address them, highlighting their benefits and the value they deliver to customers. Effective marketing strategies can raise awareness of the solutions, demonstrate industry leadership, and build credibility with potential customers. Establishing a market presence is crucial for driving adoption and achieving widespread recognition of the solutions.

Whiteboarding a Fraud Prevention industry solutions

For the BFSI industry solutions architect interview whiteboarding, let's consider key best practices. We will use the BFSI industry as an example to illustrate the best practices for designing and implementing industry solutions. We will develop a payment fraud prevention solution addressing a use case where the hypothetical financial institution, BitMaple, wants to enhance its customer experience by implementing these solutions across various channels.

To design an effective payment fraud prevention solution, it's crucial to integrate both online and offline payment channels, providing a seamless and secure experience across various platforms, such as online banking and merchant payments. This approach ensures customers can safely transact using credit and debit cards, among other methods, reducing the risk of fraud and enhancing trust in BitMaple's banking services. They aim to seamlessly integrate their online and offline channels, allowing customers a safe transaction experience across multiple touchpoints.

To build a robust payment fraud prevention solution for BitMaple, it's essential to follow these detailed steps:

1. **Conducting an In-depth Analysis**: First, thoroughly examine BitMaple's current payment systems to understand the existing infrastructure and identify common fraud patterns. This involves analyzing transaction data to pinpoint vulnerabilities and areas most susceptible to fraud. You can tailor the fraud prevention measures more effectively by understanding where fraud occurs, whether in online banking, merchant payments, or card transactions.
2. **Collaborating with Stakeholders**: Engage with key stakeholders from various departments—IT, security, finance, and customer service—to ensure a holistic approach

to fraud prevention. This collaboration is vital for aligning the fraud prevention solution with business goals and user needs. Stakeholders can provide insights into specific challenges faced in different payment channels, helping to design a more comprehensive and integrated solution.

3. **Implementing Advanced Security Measures**: Implement state-of-the-art security technologies such as real-time transaction monitoring, encryption of transaction data, and multi-factor authentication for users. Real-time monitoring can flag unusual transactions as they happen, encryption secures data in transit and at rest, and multi-factor authentication adds an extra layer of security for account access. Together, these measures significantly reduce the risk of fraud.

4. **Utilizing Machine Learning Algorithms**: Deploy machine learning algorithms to analyze transaction patterns and detect anomalies that may indicate fraud. These systems can learn from historical fraud data and user behavior to accurately identify suspicious activities. Machine learning models can stay ahead of evolving fraud tactics by continually learning and adapting.

5. **Regular Updates and Compliance**: The payment fraud prevention system must be updated with the latest security patches and comply with financial industry regulations, such as PCI-DSS, for payment security. Regular updates ensure the system is protected against new vulnerabilities, while compliance demonstrates BitMaple's commitment to safeguarding customer data and transactions.

By meticulously following these steps, BitMaple can build a payment fraud prevention solution that minimizes the risk of financial losses due to fraud and enhances customer trust and satisfaction by providing a secure and seamless payment experience across all channels.

Let's look at a reference architecture built in AWS for payment Fraud prevention solutions.

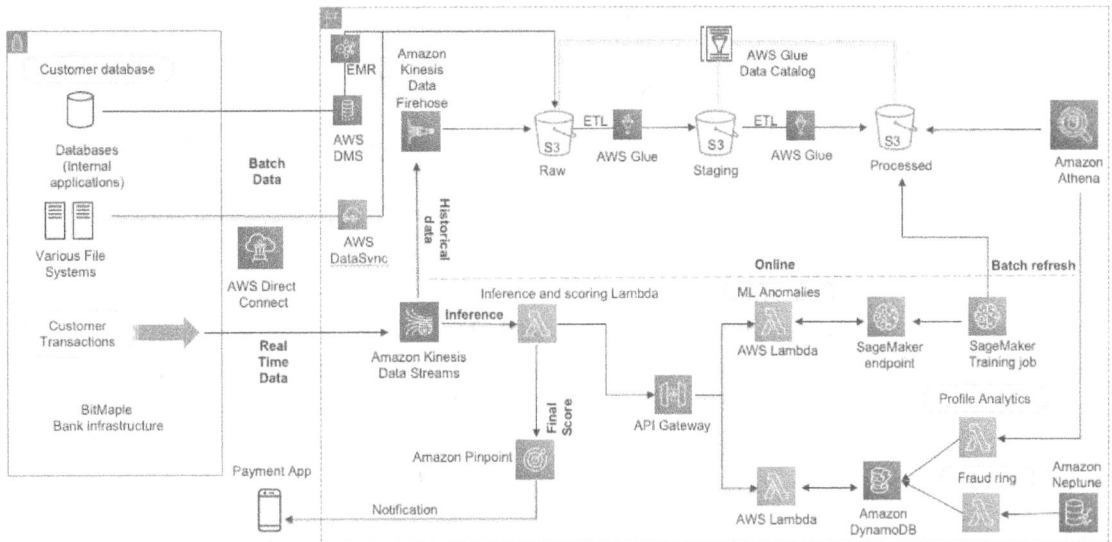

Figure 12.1 – Payment Fraud Prevention Solution Architecture

The preceding diagram shows the architecture of the solution for preventing payment fraud in BFSI. It depicts a robust, responsive system that handles vast amounts of data in real-time and historically. Amazon S3 acts as a data lake to store all transactional and customer data. Real-time transaction data streams through Amazon Kinesis, while Amazon Data Migration Service (DMS) is responsible for migrating user data from RDS databases. For on-premises legacy systems, AWS DataSync transfers files directly into S3.

AWS Glue plays a pivotal role in extracting, transforming, and loading (ETL) this data, which is cataloged in the AWS Glue Data Catalog, serving as a reference point for all ETL jobs. For real-time fraud analysis, Amazon Kinesis Data Streams (KDS) collects streaming data, which is then processed and analyzed using various machine learning models on Amazon SageMaker.

To combat more sophisticated fraud like synthetic identity fraud, Amazon Neptune, a graph database, identifies complex relationships indicative of fraudulent rings. When potential fraud is detected, the API Gateway initiates the predictive analysis, where AWS Lambda functions score the transaction. Based on the final score, Amazon Pinpoint sends a notification to the customer, alerting them to the potential fraud. This multi-faceted approach ensures quick detection and rapid response to minimize risk and protect the financial institution and its customers from fraud.

The success of industry solutions is fundamentally linked to the ability of Industry SAs to integrate and align technological capabilities with business objectives, market demands, and customer needs. By prioritizing the right solutions, deeply understanding the target user, executing with

457

velocity, and focusing on market impact and differentiation, Industry SAs can drive meaningful innovation and value creation within their industry segments.

Interview Questions for Industry Solutions Architect

In this section, we will discuss some tips and strategies for cracking an Industry SA interview, with a specific focus on the retail industry. Although this is a broad topic, we will use the retail industry as an example, as most people can relate to it. Later in this section, you will also receive questions and tips for all the other industry SA roles mentioned in the previous section. Our primary objective is to provide technical solutions and address challenges specific to the retail industry. By following these guidelines, you will be better prepared to handle interview questions related to the industry SA role and give thoughtful and effective responses.

We will cover various aspects such as personal experiences, technical expertise, problem-solving skills, and industry knowledge. Additionally, we will discuss how to handle unexpected situations gracefully, ensuring a confident and professional interview performance. Let's dive into the tips and strategies to help you succeed in your Industry SA interview within the retail industry.

Question: Tell me about a time when you built solutions that helped solve the end customer's problem. How did you identify challenges? How did you make them scalable?
Answer: Let's build a response to the question using the STAR format:

Situation: In my previous role as an Industry Solutions Architect at a retail technology company, we faced high cart abandonment rates on the e-commerce platform, leading to lost sales and dissatisfied customers.

Task: I designed and implemented a solution to address this problem and improve the overall customer experience.

Action: To identify the challenges causing cart abandonment, I conducted a thorough analysis and engaged with various stakeholders, including the customer support team, marketing team, and UX/UI designers. We reviewed customer feedback, analyzed website analytics, and conducted user testing sessions. Through this process, we identified several pain points, including complex checkout processes, slow page load times, and a need for personalized product recommendations. To make the solution scalable, I focused on the following actions:

1. Streamlined Checkout Process: I collaborated with the development team to simplify the checkout process, minimizing the number of steps and reducing the required information.

2. Performance Optimization: I worked closely with the IT team to identify and address bottlenecks causing slow page load times. We optimized the website's code, improved server response times, and leveraged caching techniques.
3. Personalized Product Recommendations: I integrated a machine learning-based recommendation engine into the platform. This engine analyzed user behavior, purchase history, and browsing patterns to provide personalized product recommendations at various touchpoints.

Result: The implemented solution significantly improved the customer experience and reduced cart abandonment rates. We observed a 25% decrease in cart abandonment and a 15% increase in overall conversion rates. Customer feedback indicated higher satisfaction with the simplified checkout process and personalized product recommendations.

I designed the solution with flexibility in mind to ensure scalability. We used cloud-based infrastructure to handle increased traffic and implemented scalable architecture patterns. Regular monitoring and performance testing allowed us to identify and address any scalability issues promptly.

While this example is hypothetical, it illustrates how to structure your response using the STAR format and emphasize scalability in the retail industry.

Please find some follow-up questions below, which the interviewer may ask based on your response.

Question: Could you provide more details on technical solutions and how you improved on existing architecture?
Answer: I primarily improved the technical solutions, which include streamlining the checkout process, optimizing performance, delivering personalized product recommendations, and ensuring the platform's scalability. Collectively, these enhancements reduced cart abandonment rates, improved the overall customer experience, and drove higher conversion rates. The interviewer can pick up any enhancement areas you mentioned and ask deeper questions.

Following are the responses covering each area:

1. **Streamlined Checkout Process**: To simplify the checkout process and reduce cart abandonment, we made several improvements to the existing architecture:
    ○ User Interface (UI) Redesign: We collaborated with UX/UI designers to create a more intuitive and user-friendly checkout flow. This involved optimizing form fields, reducing the number of required inputs, and providing clear progress indicators.

- ○ Guest Checkout Option: We introduced a guest checkout option to eliminate the need for users to create an account before making a purchase. This reduced friction and accelerated the checkout process for first-time customers.
- ○ One-Click Purchasing: For returning customers, we implemented a one-click purchasing feature that securely stored their payment and shipping details, allowing them to complete purchases with a single click.

2. **Performance Optimization**: To address slow page load times and enhance website performance, we took the following steps:
- ○ Code Optimization: We conducted a thorough code review and identified areas that could be optimized for better performance. This included minimizing HTTP requests, compressing images, and utilizing browser caching techniques.
- ○ Server Infrastructure: We worked closely with the IT team to assess the server infrastructure and make necessary improvements, such as scaling up server resources, implementing load balancing, and leveraging content delivery networks (CDNs) to ensure faster content delivery.
- ○ Database Optimization: We analyzed database queries and optimized them for better performance. This involved indexing frequently accessed data, optimizing SQL queries, and implementing caching mechanisms.

3. **Personalized Product Recommendations**: To provide personalized product recommendations and enhance the shopping experience, we implemented a machine learning-based recommendation engine:
- ○ Data Analysis and Modeling: We analyzed customer behavior data, purchase history, and browsing patterns to identify patterns and preferences. We then built machine-learning models to generate accurate recommendations based on this data.
- ○ Integration and Real-Time Delivery: We integrated the recommendation engine into the existing architecture, allowing it to fetch relevant product recommendations in real-time based on user interactions. This enabled personalized recommendations to be displayed throughout the website, including on the product pages, shopping carts, and checkout pages.

4. **Scalability Improvements**: To ensure the scalability of the solution, we made architectural enhancements:
- ○ Cloud Infrastructure: We migrated the platform to a cloud-based infrastructure, which provided scalability, elasticity, and high availability. This allowed us to easily handle increased traffic during peak periods and scale resources as needed.
- ○ Microservices Architecture: We modularized the architecture into microservices, which allowed for independent scaling of different components. This provided flexibility and agility to scale specific parts of the system based on demand.
- ○ Automated Scaling and Monitoring: We implemented automated scaling mechanisms that dynamically adjusted resources based on traffic patterns. We

also conducted continuous monitoring and performance testing to identify and address any bottlenecks or performance issues.

Question: What was your lesson learning, and how would you do it differently today?
Answer: The key lesson learned from the project was the importance of taking a user-centric approach and continuously monitoring and optimizing the solution. If I were to approach a similar project today, I would place a stronger emphasis on conducting thorough user research and usability testing to understand customer pain points better. Additionally, I would adopt an agile and iterative development approach, prioritizing continuous monitoring, performance testing, and optimization to maintain a seamless customer experience. I would also focus on scalability considerations and stay updated with emerging technologies and industry trends to deliver more effective and adaptable solutions.

Let's explore some common questions you should prepare to respond to when preparing for an industry SA interview.

Question: Can you explain your experience as an Industry Solutions Architect and how it relates to your specific industry?
Tip: Tailor your response to highlight relevant experience and projects related to the industry. Discuss how your expertise aligns with the industry's unique requirements, challenges, and technologies. Provide specific examples of successful solutions you have designed and implemented within similar contexts.

Question: How do you approach understanding the industry's business needs and requirements? How would you gather and analyze these requirements before designing a solution?
Tip: Emphasize your systematic approach to understanding business needs. Describe methods such as conducting interviews, workshops, and analyzing existing systems and processes. Discuss your ability to gather comprehensive requirements, conduct stakeholder consultations, and synthesize information to clearly understand the business context before designing solutions.

Question: Can you provide an example of a complex project you have worked on as an Industry Solutions Architect? What was your role, and how did you ensure the successful delivery of the project?
Tip: Choose a project that showcases your abilities as an Industry SA. Clearly explain your role and responsibilities in the project, highlighting your contributions to its success. Discuss your approach to project management, stakeholder engagement, risk mitigation, and effective communication throughout the project lifecycle. Highlight the measurable outcomes and value delivered to the organization.

Question: How do you stay updated with the latest industry trends, emerging technologies, and

regulatory changes relevant to our industry?
Tip: Demonstrate your commitment to continuous learning and staying updated with industry developments. Discuss strategies such as attending conferences, participating in webinars, joining professional associations, and following industry publications. Mention any certifications or training programs you have completed to showcase your dedication to staying current.

Question: Describe a situation where you had to work collaboratively with stakeholders from different business functions to design and implement a technology solution. How did you ensure alignment and successful collaboration?
Tip: Provide a specific example of a cross-functional collaboration experience. Explain how you fostered open communication, established common goals, and built strong stakeholder relationships. Discuss your ability to facilitate discussions, manage conflicting priorities, and guide the collaborative effort toward a shared vision. Highlight the positive outcomes achieved through successful collaboration.

Question: How do you ensure that your solutions are scalable, adaptable, and future-proof, considering the rapidly evolving nature of our industry?
Tip: Discuss your focus on scalability, adaptability, and future-proofing when designing solutions. Highlight your experience leveraging scalable architectures, incorporating modular designs, and considering emerging technologies. Demonstrate your ability to anticipate future needs and potential technology advancements to ensure your solutions can adapt and evolve.

In addition to these tips, it's important to provide concrete examples, quantify your achievements whenever possible, and showcase your problem-solving, communication, and leadership skills throughout your answers. Let's look at some questions related to various industry domains in SA.

HCLS Solutions Architect Interview Questions

HCLS SA demands a unique blend of healthcare industry knowledge, technical expertise, regulatory awareness, and a keen understanding of patient care processes. Here are interview questions tailored specifically for an HCLS Solutions Architect position, designed to gauge a candidate's qualifications across these critical areas:

Industry Knowledge and Healthcare Trends
Question: Can you discuss a significant technological trend in HCLS and how it impacts patient care and healthcare operations?
Tips: This question assesses the candidate's awareness of current trends in healthcare technology (e.g., telemedicine, AI in diagnostics) and their ability to link these trends with tangible improvements in healthcare delivery.

Question: How do you ensure HCLS solutions comply with healthcare regulations and standards, such as HIPAA or GDPR?

Tips: Look for the candidate's understanding of the critical importance of compliance in healthcare solutions and their strategies for maintaining compliance across systems and processes.

Technical Skills and Architectural Expertise

Question: Describe your experience integrating Electronic Health Records (EHR) systems with other healthcare applications. What challenges did you encounter, and how did you address them?

Tips: Evaluate the candidate's hands-on experience with one of the core systems in healthcare IT, focusing on their problem-solving skills and technical proficiency in overcoming integration challenges.

Question: Explain how you would use data analytics and AI to improve outcomes in a clinical setting. Provide a specific example.

Tips: Test the candidate's ability to leverage advanced technologies for clinical improvements, looking for innovative approaches and practical applications.

Solution Design and Implementation

Question: How would you design a scalable HCLS solution to grow data volumes from genomics and personalized medicine rapidly?

Tips: Seeks insights into the candidate's strategies for dealing with the data-intensive demands of modern healthcare, emphasizing scalability and performance.

Question: Given the sensitive nature of patient data, how do you incorporate data security and privacy into your architectural designs?

Tips: Aim to understand the candidate's approach to deeply embedding security and privacy considerations within HCLS solutions, a non-negotiable requirement in healthcare.

Stakeholder Engagement and Project Management

Question: Describe a project where you had to balance conflicting requirements from clinical staff, IT, and administrative teams. How did you ensure stakeholder alignment?

Tips: Assesses the candidate's communication and negotiation skills, particularly their ability to manage diverse stakeholder groups within a healthcare organization.

Question: How do you stay abreast of changes in healthcare regulations and technology advancements to ensure your solutions remain relevant and compliant?

Tips: Look for the candidate's commitment to continuous learning and their strategies for keeping solutions up-to-date in a rapidly evolving field.

Question: What innovation in the HCLS sector excites you the most, and how would you incorporate it into solution design?

Tips: Test the candidate's passion for healthcare innovation and their vision for integrating new technologies into solutions that enhance patient care and healthcare operations.

Question: How do you design HCLS solutions with patient experience in mind? Can you give an example of a patient-centered solution you've developed?

Tips: Evaluate the candidate's ability to prioritize patient experience in their designs, looking for examples of solutions that improve patient engagement, satisfaction, or outcomes.

Collaboration and Multidisciplinary Approach

Question: Explain how you have worked with multidisciplinary teams in the HCLS sector to develop or deploy a solution. What was your role, and how did you ensure the project's success?

Tips: Seeks to understand the candidate's experience in collaborative environments, emphasizing their role in ensuring project success through teamwork and interdisciplinary cooperation.

Question: Tell me a time when you had to advocate for technological change in a healthcare organization. How did you address resistance?

Tips: Look for the candidate's ability to drive technological adoption, focusing on their strategies for overcoming resistance and securing buy-in from various stakeholders.

These questions are crafted to uncover a candidate's deep understanding of the Healthcare and Life Sciences sector, their technical and strategic capabilities, and their ability to navigate the unique challenges and opportunities within HCLS. A qualified HCLS SA will demonstrate expertise in healthcare technologies, a strong grasp of regulatory requirements, and a commitment to improving patient care through innovative IT solutions.

BFSI Solutions Architect Interview Questions

BFSI SA's role requires a comprehensive evaluation of the technical skills, industry knowledge, strategic insight, and ability to address the unique challenges and opportunities within the BFSI sector. Here are some interview questions tailored specifically for a BFSI Solutions Architect position:

Industry Knowledge and Trends

Question: How do emerging technologies like blockchain and AI impact the BFSI sector, and how can they be leveraged to gain a competitive advantage?

Tips: This question assesses the candidate's understanding of key technology trends and potential applications within BFSI for innovation and competitive differentiation.

Question: Can you describe a recent regulatory change in the BFSI sector and how it affects architectural decisions?
Tips: Looks for awareness of regulatory environments and the candidate's ability to integrate compliance into solution architecture effectively.

Technical Skills and Architectural Expertise
Question: Describe your experience designing secure payment systems in the banking industry. What challenges did you face, and how did you address them?
Tips: Evaluate the candidate's hands-on experience and problem-solving skills in a critical area of banking technology.

Question: How would you approach the architecture for a scalable and resilient insurance claims processing system?
Tips: Test the candidate's ability to design systems that are not only technologically robust but also aligned with the insurance industry's specific needs.

Integration and System Design
Question: Explain how you would integrate legacy systems with modern cloud-based platforms in a BFSI context.
Tips: Seeks insights into the candidate's strategies for dealing with common BFSI challenges such as legacy system modernization and cloud migration.

Question: Discuss a project where you implemented a data analytics solution in the BFSI sector. What was the outcome?
Tips: Assess the candidate's experience with data analytics projects, focusing on their ability to derive actionable insights and business value.

Stakeholder Engagement and Communication
Question: Describe a scenario where you had to negotiate a solution architecture between technology teams and business stakeholders within BFSI.
Tips: Assesses the candidate's communication and negotiation skills, particularly their ability to align technical solutions with business goals.

Question: How do you ensure your technical recommendations align with the BFSI organization's strategic objectives?
Tips: Looks for the candidate's approach to understanding and integrating business strategy into their architectural decisions.

Innovation and Strategic Thinking
Question: What BFSI sector trend is most underutilized, and how would you incorporate it into your architectural designs?

Tips: Test the candidate's ability to identify and leverage industry trends for innovative solution design.

Question: How would you evaluate new fintech startups as potential technology partners for a BFSI organization?
Tips: Evaluate the candidate's strategic approach to partnerships, focusing on their criteria for assessing compatibility, innovation potential, and strategic fit.

Compliance and Risk Management
Question: Explain your approach to building BFSI solutions that comply with regulations like GDPR and PCI DSS and manage risk effectively.
Tips: Seeks to understand the candidate's expertise in designing solutions that meet strict regulatory standards while managing operational and cybersecurity risks.

Customer Experience in BFSI
Question: How do you balance the need for robust security measures with providing a seamless customer experience in online banking applications?
Tips: Look for the candidate's ability to design solutions that enhance customer experience without compromising security, a critical concern in BFSI applications.

These questions are designed to uncover a candidate's depth of expertise in the BFSI sector, their technical competencies, strategic thinking, and their ability to navigate the complex requirements and challenges unique to banking, financial services, and insurance organizations.

Retail and Supply Chain Architect Interview Questions

Retail and Supply Chain SA position demands a deep understanding of the retail industry's nuances and the complexities of supply chain management. The role requires a candidate to possess a solid technical foundation and a strategic mindset capable of leveraging technology to solve real-world retail and supply chain challenges. Here are tailored interview questions designed to evaluate the qualifications of a candidate for a Retail and Supply Chain SA role:

Industry Knowledge and Retail Trends
Question: How do you see the evolution of omnichannel retailing affecting supply chain strategies, and what technological solutions can facilitate this integration?
Tips: This question assesses the candidate's insight into the convergence of retail and supply chain strategies due to the rise of omnichannel retailing. It focuses on the candidate's ability to propose technological solutions that enhance seamless integration.

Question: Can you discuss a significant challenge facing the retail industry, such as customer experience or inventory management, and propose a supply chain solution to address it?
Tips: Look for the candidate's ability to identify pressing retail challenges and their creativity

in leveraging supply chain solutions to address these issues.

Technical Skills and Architectural Expertise

Question: Describe your experience implementing a demand forecasting system in the retail sector. What technologies did you utilize, and what were the outcomes?

Tips: Evaluate the candidate's hands-on experience with critical technologies such as data analytics or machine learning in creating demand forecasting systems, focusing on their approach and improving inventory accuracy and customer satisfaction.

Question: How would you design a resilient supply chain network to mitigate risks such as supplier disruptions or demand fluctuations for a retail company?

Tips: Test the candidate's ability to design flexible and resilient supply chain architectures that ensure retail operations can withstand and quickly recover from disruptions.

Integration and System Optimization

Question: Explain how you have integrated eCommerce platforms with physical retail store systems to provide a unified customer experience. What challenges might you encounter, and how would you address them?

Tips: Seeks insights into the candidate's strategies for achieving omnichannel integration and dealing with potential challenges like data synchronization and inventory visibility.

Question: Discuss a project where you optimized a supply chain for an eCommerce retailer. How did you improve efficiency and reduce costs?

Tips: Assess the candidate's experience with supply chain optimization projects, looking for methodologies and technologies that drive operational efficiencies and cost savings.

Stakeholder Engagement and Collaboration

Question: Describe how you have worked with retail marketing teams to leverage supply chain data for targeted customer promotions.

Tips: Assesses the candidate's ability to collaborate with cross-functional teams, mainly using supply chain insights to support marketing strategies and enhance customer engagement.

Question: How do you ensure that technology implementations in retail and supply chains are aligned with the business's strategic objectives?

Tips: Look for the candidate's strategy for aligning technological solutions with broader business goals, ensuring that IT initiatives contribute to the success of retail and supply chain operations.

Driving Innovation and Strategic Thinking

Question: What emerging technology do you believe will significantly impact the retail and supply chain sectors in the next few years, and how should companies prepare?

Tips: Test the candidate's vision for future retail and supply chain innovations and their strategic approach to preparing for these changes.

Question: How would you evaluate the potential ROI of introducing IoT devices into a retail supply chain?

Tips: Evaluate the candidate's ability to quantify the benefits of technological investments, focusing on efficiency gains, enhanced visibility, and improved customer experiences.

Regulatory Compliance and Sustainability

Question: How do you design retail and supply chain solutions that comply with data privacy regulations and promote sustainability?

Tips: Seeks to understand the candidate's approach to incorporating compliance and sustainability into solution design, highlighting specific strategies for meeting regulatory requirements and sustainability goals.

Enhancing Customer Experience and Operational Efficiency

Question: How do you balance adopting innovative technology with ensuring reliability and stability in retail and supply chain operations?

Tips: Look for the candidate's ability to innovate responsibly, ensuring that new technologies enhance, rather than disrupt, the customer experience and operational efficiency.

These questions aim to uncover a candidate's comprehensive expertise in the retail and supply chain sectors, their technical and strategic skills, and their capacity to navigate the unique challenges at the intersection of these industries. A qualified Retail and Supply Chain SA will demonstrate a deep understanding of leveraging technology to improve operational efficiency, enhance the customer experience, and drive innovation while maintaining compliance and promoting sustainability.

Manufacturing and Automotive Architect Interview Questions

Manufacturing and Auto SA responsibilities require a nuanced understanding of these interconnected sectors' unique challenges and opportunities. The candidate must possess a deep knowledge of manufacturing processes and automotive technologies and the ability to innovate within these fields. Here are interview questions designed to assess the qualifications of a candidate for a Manufacturing and Automotive SA position:

Industry Knowledge and Trends

Question: How do emerging technologies such as IoT, AI, and additive manufacturing impact the manufacturing and automotive sectors?

> **Tips:** Aims to assess the candidate's insight into how cutting-edge technologies transform industries and their potential to drive efficiency, innovation, and product development.

Question: Can you discuss a significant challenge facing the intersection of manufacturing and

automotive industries today, such as supply chain disruptions or the shift towards electric vehicles, and propose a technological solution?

Tips: Look for the candidate's ability to identify industry-wide challenges and their creativity in leveraging technology to propose viable solutions.

Technical Skills and Architectural Expertise

Question: Describe your experience designing and implementing digital twins in manufacturing. How can this technology be applied to automotive product development?

Tips: Evaluate the candidate's experience with digital twins and their ability to apply this technology across sectors to improve product design, manufacturing processes, and predictive maintenance.

Question: How would you create a scalable architecture for integrating Industry 4.0 technologies into legacy automotive manufacturing plants?

Tips: Test the candidate's ability to design flexible and scalable systems to modernize legacy operations, highlighting their approach to integration challenges and system compatibility.

Integration and System Optimization

Question: Explain how you have integrated smart manufacturing principles into automotive production lines to improve efficiency and reduce waste. What were the outcomes?

Tips: Seeks insights into the candidate's strategies for applying smart manufacturing principles, such as real-time data analysis and automation, in automotive production to drive operational improvements.

Question: Discuss a project where you implemented cybersecurity measures in the automotive sector, considering manufacturing systems and vehicle technologies.

Tips: Aim to understand the candidate's experience with cybersecurity, focusing on their approach to securing interconnected manufacturing systems and protecting automotive technologies from cyber threats.

Stakeholder Engagement and Collaboration

Question: Describe how you have facilitated collaboration between manufacturing engineers and automotive designers to optimize product design for manufacturability.

Tips: Assesses the candidate's communication and collaboration skills, particularly their ability to bridge the gap between different professional groups to achieve a common goal.

Question: How do you ensure the new technologies or processes you introduce align with the manufacturing plant's strategic objectives and the automotive product development teams?

Tips: Look for the candidate's strategy for aligning technological innovations with broader business goals, ensuring that solutions contribute to the success of both manufacturing and automotive development.

Question: What do you see as the most significant opportunity for innovation at the intersection of manufacturing and automotive industries, and how would you capitalize on it?

Tips: Test the candidate's vision for future innovations that leverage the strengths of both sectors and their strategic approach to realizing these opportunities.

Question: How would you assess the ROI of integrating advanced robotics into automotive assembly lines?

Tips: Evaluate the candidate's ability to quantify the benefits of technological investments, focusing on their approach to measuring ROI in terms of efficiency gains, quality improvements, and cost savings.

Regulatory Compliance and Sustainability

Question: Explain how you ensure compliance with environmental regulations and sustainability goals in both manufacturing processes and automotive design.

Tips: Seeks to understand the candidate's approach to designing solutions that comply with environmental regulations and contribute to sustainability goals.

Enhancing Quality and Customer Experience

Question: How do you balance the drive for innovation with maintaining high quality and safety standards in automotive product design and manufacturing?

Tips: Look for the candidate's ability to innovate responsibly, ensuring that new technologies and processes enhance quality and safety in both product design and manufacturing.

These questions are crafted to uncover a candidate's comprehensive understanding of the manufacturing and automotive sectors, their technical and strategic capabilities, and their ability to navigate the unique challenges at the intersection of these industries. A qualified Manufacturing and Automotive SA will demonstrate expertise in leveraging technology to improve production efficiency, product quality, and innovation while adhering to industry standards and regulations.

In this chapter, we aimed to cover some of the most popular industry solutions architect roles, offering questions and providing tips rather than detailed answers for each industry-specific question, unlike other chapters. Recognizing that each role deserves a comprehensive exploration, we acknowledge that a whole chapter per role would be more appropriate.

Summary

In this chapter, you explored the role of an industry-specific solutions architect and delved into several key industry domains. We began by understanding the fundamentals of these roles, emphasizing the importance of bridging the gap between technology and industry expertise.

You then explored the role of a Healthcare Solutions Architect, Finance Solutions Architect, Retail Solutions Architect, and Manufacturing Solutions Architect. The chapter continued with discussing best practices for designing and implementing industry solutions. We emphasized the significance of understanding industry-specific requirements, conducting thorough research, collaborating with stakeholders, and ensuring solution design scalability, security, and compliance.

Additionally, you learned valuable tips for industry solutions architects, guiding how to excel in their roles. These tips included staying updated with industry trends, continuously learning, fostering collaboration, and prioritizing user-centric design.

Lastly, you learned the importance of interview preparation for industry solutions architects. We provided a list of common interview questions. We offered tips on responding to them effectively, highlighting the need to showcase industry knowledge, technical expertise, problem-solving abilities, and collaboration skills.

Industry solutions architects can thrive in their roles and significantly impact their respective industries by following best practices, incorporating valuable tips, and preparing for interviews.

Part 4: Starting in a new role

Chapter 13 - Starting in a Solutions Architect Role in a New Organization

As of now, you have learned about cracking the solutions architect in this book. Now, it is essential to understand how to start your new career as you land into a new organization in an SA role. Embarking on a new role as a Solutions Architect is an exciting journey marked by the potential to shape technological landscapes and drive business success. The first steps you take in this role lay the foundation for your impact and influence within the organization.

To begin with, understanding your new organization is important. Before delving into intricate architectural designs, grasp the broader context of the company's goals, vision, and culture. Identify key stakeholders and decision-makers to gauge their expectations and concerns. Gain insights into the organization's existing technological infrastructure and assess its digital maturity and transformation level. This understanding forms the bedrock for aligning your architectural decisions with the organization's mission and needs.

Your role as a Solutions Architect goes beyond technical skills—it's about designing solutions that enhance business outcomes. Evaluate the current architectural landscape by comprehending existing systems, applications, databases, and technologies. Identify pain points and areas for enhancement, leveraging your architectural expertise to address challenges effectively. From this evaluation, create an initial blueprint by defining short-term and long-term architectural goals. Develop a strategic plan that reflects technical soundness and aligns with the business objectives. This plan should outline how your architectural vision evolves, with measurable milestones.

Effective communication and leadership are indispensable in building your influence within the organization. Establish credibility and trust by showcasing your expertise and problem-solving prowess. Leverage your communication and persuasion skills to gain support for your architectural decisions. Develop strong relationships with cross-functional teams, fostering collaboration that enhances the architectural process. In this chapter, you will learn the following topics :

- Importance of the first steps in a new role as a Solutions Architect
- Understanding Your New Organization
- Evaluating the Current Architectural Landscape
- Creating Your Initial Blueprint
- Building Your Influence

With the above steps, you'll be well-equipped to navigate the early days of your Solutions Architect role and steer the organization toward architectural excellence and innovation.

Importance of the first steps in a new role

Stepping into the role of Solutions Architect in a new organization comes with many expectations. As you embark on this journey, you'll be entrusted with designing complex IT systems and instilling fresh perspectives and streamlined solutions.

Stakeholders within the organization look to you as the catalyst for transformation, which can bridge the gap between complicated technical details and tangible business outcomes. Your role extends beyond the conventional realm of technology; it encompasses the realm of business profitability. Let's say you've joined a financial institution aiming to optimize its customer experience through digital channels. Your ability to align technical solutions with enhanced customer engagement and, consequently, increased ROI becomes the requirement of your role.

The early steps taken when assuming the role of a Solutions Architect carry immense weight in defining your trajectory within the organization. These initial actions are the cornerstone for your effectiveness, reputation, and contributions. You're the anchor of technology solutions aligning with the organization's objectives. Therefore, how you navigate your initial days in the organization can set the course for project outcomes, cross-functional relationships, and overall career growth in architectural leadership.

Embarking on a solid start involves immersing yourself deeply in the organization's ethos. For example, if you're joining a manufacturing company that wants to modernize its production processes, you should begin by understanding the technical landscape and the overarching business objectives. Conversations with stakeholders and key decision-makers will unveil challenges and goals. This knowledge will form the foundation for crafting solutions that address immediate issues and integrate seamlessly into the company's long-term vision.

If, during your early days, you discover that the organization aims to enhance customer engagement through digital transformation, identify the existing technological infrastructure, and assess its digital maturity level. With this insight, you can design architectural strategies that streamline operations and create a robust foundation for future innovations. Your role as a Solutions Architect goes beyond technical prowess; it's about engineering solutions that amplify business value.

Moreover, these initial steps establish your presence as a credible influencer. Let's imagine you're collaborating with cross-functional teams to present an architectural vision for a customer relationship management (CRM) system upgrade. You adeptly translate complex technical concepts into relatable terms, fostering an environment of understanding and collaboration. Your leadership instills confidence and trust, paving the way for seamless teamwork that translates into successful project implementation. Navigating these initial steps skillfully sets the stage for an impactful journey as a Solutions Architect that resonates with innovation, teamwork, and lasting success.

Understanding Your New Organization

As you step into your role as a Solutions Architect within a new organization, embarking on a journey to understand the company's intricate fabric is paramount. Beyond just comprehending technical nuances, this initial phase involves immersing yourself in the broader context that defines the organization.

Familiarizing with the organization's goals, vision, and culture: Immersing yourself in the organization's goals, vision, and culture provides you with a compass for guiding your architectural decisions. By comprehending the broader objectives that the company aims to achieve, you can align your solutions to contribute directly to these goals. Understanding the company's vision allows you to envision how your architectural strategies can propel the organization toward its desired future state. Additionally, delving into the company's culture helps you navigate the dynamics of collaboration, communication, and decision-making. By embracing the organization's values and cultural nuances, you can more effectively engage with stakeholders and position your solutions within a framework that resonates with the company's identity.

Identifying key stakeholders and decision-makers: Establishing relationships with key stakeholders and decision-makers is pivotal in gauging various departments' and individuals' expectations and concerns. These interactions offer insights into the different perspectives that influence strategic directions. By understanding their pain points, priorities, and aspirations, you can tailor your architectural solutions to address specific needs and drive meaningful impact. Collaborating with decision-makers ensures that your designs align with the overarching business strategies and receive the necessary implementation support.

Understanding the organization's existing technological infrastructure: A thorough grasp of the existing technological landscape empowers you to build on its strengths while addressing its challenges. Analyzing the current systems, applications, and infrastructure components sheds light on areas that require enhancement or modernization. By identifying legacy systems needing integration or replacement, you can strategize solutions that streamline operations and enhance efficiency. This knowledge also helps prevent redundancy, enabling you to propose architectures that optimize resources and align with the organization's technology stack.

Assessing the level of digital maturity and transformation: Evaluating the organization's digital maturity and transformation journey provides insights into its readiness for embracing innovative solutions. This assessment guides your architectural decisions by indicating whether to adopt incremental changes or more disruptive transformations. Understanding ongoing initiatives, such as cloud adoption or data-driven strategies, allows you to weave your architectural solutions seamlessly into the organization's evolving technological landscape. By aligning your approaches with the company's digital aspirations, you facilitate a smoother transition toward achieving its vision of becoming a technologically adept and innovative entity.

Let's consider an example to illustrate the process of understanding your new organization. You've just started as a Solutions Architect at an education technology company that aims to revolutionize online learning. As you embark on your role, the first crucial step is familiarizing yourself with the organization's goals, vision, and culture. The company aims to provide accessible and engaging education to learners worldwide through its digital platform. Their vision is to create a personalized learning experience that adapts to individual student needs and preferences. Embracing this vision, you realize that your architectural decisions should prioritize scalability, user experience, and data-driven insights.

Next, you focus on identifying key stakeholders and decision-makers within the organization. You gather valuable insights through conversations with the Chief Technology Officer (CTO), the Head of Product, and the Head of Learning Design. The CTO emphasizes a highly scalable infrastructure to accommodate a growing user base. The Head of Product discusses the importance of real-time analytics in tracking user engagement and content performance. The Head of Learning Design highlights the significance of a seamless user experience across devices. Armed with this information, you recognize the critical role of these stakeholders in shaping your architectural solutions.

Your next endeavor is to understand the organization's existing technological infrastructure. You discover that the company relies on a microservices-based architecture for its platform and a mix of cloud and on-premise resources. However, the current architecture struggles to handle spikes in traffic during peak usage times, leading to occasional performance issues. To address this, you propose a hybrid architecture that optimizes cloud resources for elastic scalability, enabling the platform to handle increased user load seamlessly.

Lastly, you assess the organization's level of digital maturity and transformation. Although they have successfully developed a platform with solid core features, they are only beginning to harness the potential of machine learning and AI to personalize learning paths. Recognizing their position in the digital transformation journey, you suggest an incremental approach. You propose integrating machine learning algorithms to recommend relevant learning content based on user behaviors. As the organization's digital maturity increases, you foresee implementing more sophisticated AI-driven features that analyze learning patterns to predict student performance and suggest interventions.

In summary, your journey as a Solutions Architect begins by understanding the organization's goals, identifying key stakeholders, evaluating the existing infrastructure, and aligning your architectural decisions with the company's vision. By embracing these steps, you can craft solutions that address technical challenges and contribute to the organization's overall success in achieving its educational mission.

By diligently engaging with these facets of your new organization, you lay the groundwork for your role as a Solutions Architect. Your ability to merge technical expertise with a deep understanding of the organization's goals, stakeholders, and technological landscape will be pivotal in shaping solutions that drive innovation and business success.

Evaluating the Current Architectural Landscape

Evaluating the current architectural landscape is a pivotal step in your role as a Solutions Architect. This phase comprehensively assesses the organization's systems, technologies, and processes. By delving into the current state of affairs, you can identify areas that need improvement, potential bottlenecks, and opportunities for optimization.

To begin with, conduct a thorough review of the organization's technology stack. This entails understanding the various software applications, databases, networking components, and infrastructure of the organization's IT ecosystem. By examining these elements, you can pinpoint outdated technologies, redundant systems, or compatibility issues that hinder efficiency.

Next, analyze the organization's data flow and integration mechanisms. Determine how data moves between different systems, whether there are any data silos, and if integration between applications is seamless. This analysis is crucial for ensuring that data is available where needed and that valuable insights are not lost due to isolated information sources.

Assess the performance and scalability of the current architecture. Evaluate how well the systems handle varying workloads and usage patterns. Identify performance bottlenecks that may lead to slow response times or downtime during peak usage. Additionally, examine the architecture's ability to scale horizontally and vertically to accommodate future growth. Security is another critical aspect to consider. Evaluate the current security measures, including authentication mechanisms, data encryption, and access controls. Identify any vulnerabilities or potential security gaps that must be addressed to ensure the organization's data and systems are adequately protected.

Lastly, consider the maintenance and operational aspects of the existing architecture. Understand the processes for deploying updates, performing backups, and managing system configurations. Identify any challenges related to deployment frequency, change management, or system monitoring.

To illustrate, let's consider an example scenario in which you're joining a retail company as a Solutions Architect.

Upon joining the company, your first task is to evaluate the current architectural landscape of its e-commerce platform. The company aims to enhance user experience, accommodate increasing online traffic, and improve overall system performance. By delving into the current state of affairs, you can identify areas for improvement, potential bottlenecks, and opportunities for optimization.

You begin by reviewing the company's technology stack, which includes the web application, databases, payment gateway, and third-party integrations. During this evaluation, you identify that the current database system struggles to handle the surge in traffic during peak shopping seasons, resulting in slow response times and occasional outages. This analysis prompts you to explore more scalable database solutions that can better handle spikes in usage.

Next, you analyze the data flow and integration mechanisms. You discover that customer data is spread across multiple systems, making a seamless shopping experience challenging. Integrating user profiles, purchase history, and cart information becomes a priority to offer personalized recommendations and streamline the checkout process.

During the performance assessment, the existing architecture struggled to maintain responsiveness during high-traffic periods, leading to frustrated customers and potential revenue loss. This prompts you to explore load-balancing solutions and implement caching mechanisms to improve system performance. Security is paramount in an e-commerce environment, and your evaluation reveals potential vulnerabilities in data transmission and payment processing. Therefore, you recommend implementing encryption protocols and a robust authentication mechanism to ensure customer data is secure.

Lastly, you delve into the operational aspects of the architecture. You discover that deploying updates to the platform is a manual and time-consuming process, which hampers the company's ability to introduce new features quickly. This insight drives you to propose a streamlined DevOps approach, enabling automated deployments and continuous integration to accelerate the release cycle.

In this example, your evaluation of the current architectural landscape provides valuable insights that guide your recommendations as a Solutions Architect. By identifying technology gaps, performance bottlenecks, security vulnerabilities, and operational challenges, you can create a roadmap for transforming the e-commerce platform into a more efficient, scalable, and secure solution that aligns with the company's goals.

In summary, evaluating the current architectural landscape involves comprehensively analyzing the organization's technology stack, data flow, performance, security, and operational processes. This assessment forms the foundation for your subsequent decisions and recommendations as a Solutions Architect. By deeply understanding the current state, you can effectively guide the organization toward a more efficient, secure, and scalable architectural future.

Creating Your Initial Blueprint

Creating Your Initial Blueprint involves outlining the architectural direction that your solutions will take within the organization. This step is crucial in setting the foundation for your architectural decisions and ensuring they align with the company's goals and objectives.

To exemplify, let's continue with the scenario of being a Solutions Architect at a retail company. After assessing the current architectural landscape, you're tasked with crafting an initial blueprint to drive the architectural transformation.

Firstly, you identify short-term and long-term architectural goals. For instance, a short-term goal might involve migrating the existing database to a more scalable solution to address performance issues during peak traffic. A long-term goal could be transitioning the entire e-commerce platform to a microservices architecture to enhance modularity and flexibility.

With these goals in mind, you begin developing an initial strategic plan. You outline the steps needed to achieve the short-term and long-term goals. For the short-term goal of improving database performance, your plan might involve selecting a suitable database solution, designing the migration process, and implementing it seamlessly without disrupting customer experience.

Aligning architectural strategies with business objectives is essential to creating the blueprint. Ensure that each architectural decision directly contributes to the company's overall mission. For a retail company, enhancing user experience, increasing conversion rates, and improving system stability are core business objectives. Your architectural strategies, such as optimizing the checkout process and implementing a robust disaster recovery plan, directly tie into these objectives.

As part of the blueprint, you formulate an execution plan with measurable milestones. This step involves breaking down your strategic plan into manageable phases. For example, to improve database performance, your milestones could include selecting the new database solution, designing the migration process, completing the migration, and monitoring performance improvements post-migration.

By creating this detailed blueprint, you provide a roadmap for the architectural changes that must be implemented. This blueprint serves as a guide for yourself and the stakeholders, outlining the path toward achieving the company's architectural and business goals. As the Solutions Architect, your role is to ensure that this blueprint aligns with the technical requirements and resonates with the company's strategic vision.

Building Your Influence

Building influence as a Solutions Architect goes beyond technical expertise. It involves cultivating relationships, demonstrating leadership, and effectively communicating ideas to stakeholders and teams across the organization.

Establishing Credibility and Trust:

Gaining credibility and trust is foundational for a Solutions Architect's effectiveness. It starts with demonstrating your deep understanding of the technologies, processes, and methodologies relevant to your role. You can achieve this by sharing your knowledge in meetings, contributing valuable insights, and providing solutions that align with the organization's needs. By consistently delivering accurate information and reliable solutions, you establish yourself as a trustworthy source of guidance.

In addition, actively listening to and addressing stakeholders' concerns with well-informed responses enhances your credibility. Being transparent about potential challenges and offering realistic solutions further instills trust. As you continue to engage with stakeholders, showcasing your expertise and maintaining open lines of communication contribute to developing strong professional relationships.

Demonstrating Leadership:

Leadership in the context of a Solutions Architect involves guiding technical initiatives with a forward-looking approach. This means taking ownership of projects, setting a clear direction, and inspiring others to follow suit. You showcase your leadership abilities by confidently making decisions and providing solutions that align with the organization's goals.

A Solutions Architect also leads by example. Taking the initiative to address issues, offering creative solutions, and promoting a collaborative environment underscores your leadership role. Collaborating with cross-functional teams to align technical decisions with business objectives demonstrates your commitment to guiding the organization toward success.

Harnessing Communication and Persuasion:

Effective communication is pivotal in the Solutions Architect role, as you must convey complex technical concepts to technical and non-technical stakeholders. Clear, concise communication ensures that everyone understands the value and implications of architectural decisions. By using relatable language and real-world examples, you can simplify intricate concepts and foster better comprehension.

Persuasion is closely tied to communication, as it involves persuasively presenting your ideas to gain stakeholders' buy-in. Highlighting the benefits and impacts of your architectural recommendations demonstrates how they align with business goals. Utilizing data, case studies, and success stories can bolster your arguments and illustrate the positive outcomes of your solutions.

Developing Strong Relationships:

Collaboration is integral to the Solutions Architect role, requiring strong relationships with colleagues, teams, and stakeholders. Building rapport involves active listening, empathizing with concerns, and valuing diverse perspectives. Being approachable and open to feedback creates an environment where teamwork and collaboration flourish.

Interacting with different teams across the organization also demands adaptability and an understanding of their goals. Learning about their needs and objectives can help you tailor your architectural solutions to meet those requirements. Moreover, advocating for cross-functional teamwork and facilitating open communication channels promotes a culture of shared responsibility and mutual success.

These skills help you be a powerful force for positive change as a solutions architect. By using your expertise, being a good leader, communicating well, and working well with others, you can ensure that your ideas and plans have a significant impact.

Final words of advice from the author's experience

I (Saurabh Shrivastava) want to offer some final advice on how to succeed in your Solutions Architect role and interview. As you have learned throughout this book, success in an SA role and excelling in interviews requires a combination of technical proficiency, strategic thinking, and exceptional interpersonal skills. In this section, I will discuss my journey and career evolution regarding the key SA attributes discussed throughout the book. So, let's start.

Early Career and Technical Proficiency

Continuous expansion of knowledge required to grow your career. I began my career as a software developer in the first decade of the 21st century, between 2000-2010. In those early years, C/C++ was at its peak, heavily emphasized in computer science engineering curricula, while Java and .NET emerged. I initially started as a C++ Windows developer but soon observed a growing demand for C++ in Unix environments. This led me to pivot my learning towards UNIX/LINUX, joining the ranks of core C/C++ developers' groups. By the mid-decade, I noticed Java gaining popularity due to its ease of programming and OS-agnostic nature for application deployment. Despite Java's role in significantly improving developer productivity, it involved a trade-off in performance since it operated at a higher level and relied on its framework for memory management, adding an extra layer atop the kernel.

Nevertheless, C++ remained indispensable. The tech stack evolved to combine Java for front-end and presentation logic and C++ for back-end processing, harnessing the strengths of both languages. Learning Java was a relatively smooth transition for me, given its foundation in C++, which made programming easier by eliminating the intricacies of memory allocation and pointers. However, a notable skill gap emerged. There was a surplus of new developers in Java and experienced developers in C++. Still, there needed to be a gap in how these two languages could exchange data within the same system. This is where CORBA became relevant, prompting me to extend my knowledge further in CORBA and Tuxedo server-based application development. Becoming a full-stack developer placed me among the top skilled professionals of that time, significantly accelerating my career growth. Until then, my focus was predominantly on addressing coding problems rather than business problems.

Transition to Solutions Architect and Business Alignment

However, as the world entered the next decade between 2010-2020, things began changing very rapidly. I realized early on that more than being a technology expert was needed. As you progress in your career, thinking about how to solve business problems using technology as an enabler becomes crucial. Another trend I noticed was the rapid evolution of technology; what used to stay relevant for approximately three years was now changing almost yearly. It became clear that embracing lifelong learning and **prioritizing business alignment** was essential to remain relevant. This realization began my transition from a developer to a Solutions Architect.

I continued learning new technologies, focusing on front-end tools like Node.js, React.js, AJAX, and back-end technologies like Spring and Hibernate. Concurrently, I took the initiative to develop domain expertise, particularly in supply chain management, which involves moving products from one destination to another. This integration of technology knowledge with a business domain was immensely satisfying, as it enabled me to make an impact by fulfilling customer orders with two-day shipping, reducing lost inventory, and increasing the speed of business for some of the largest retailers and third-party logistics companies worldwide.

This phase also helped me cultivate strong **communication skills**, particularly in responding to RFPs from large enterprises and articulating the value proposition of products to C-level executives while enabling their teams to deploy, configure, and customize supply chain products. Meanwhile, as cloud technology began gaining momentum, I started learning about AWS Cloud and IBM SoftLayer, expanding my expertise further into the cloud domain.

Over time, my aspiration to develop a strong **problem-solving acumen** led me to seek environments that presented large-scale challenges. This ambition, combined with my blend of business and technical skills, enabled me to secure a role at Amazon, the world's largest online retailer, by the mid-decade. At Amazon, I addressed complex issues within their liquidation supply chain, specifically focusing on improving the price recovery rate for lost and returned items.

Cloud Experience and Embracing Change

Joining Amazon was exhilarating, akin to a new kid in a fancy toy shop. I was presented with multiple problems to solve, enriching my understanding of **prioritizing business alignment** with technical solutions. During this period, cloud technology was rising, and I seized the opportunity to delve into the AWS tech stack. Embracing my ethos of **staying agile and adaptable**, I completed all five AWS certifications available then (compared to the 12 certifications offered today). I transitioned into a Solutions Architect role in AWS.

This career phase allowed me to hone my technical expertise and reinforced the importance of agility and adaptability in a rapidly evolving tech landscape. My journey at Amazon was instrumental in shaping my problem-solving skills and deepening my understanding of the intricate balance between business needs and technical solutions.

AWS opened up a new world of opportunities where I could constantly engage with cutting-edge technologies. Initially joining as an Application Development Architect, I quickly adapted to the emerging Analytics and Machine Learning trends, ultimately evolving into a Big Data and ML Solutions Architect. As we progressed into the current decade, from 2020 to 2030, an era marked by evaluation and innovation, I dedicated myself to further developing my **collaboration and leadership skills** as an industry technology leader—this development involved working across multiple teams, ranging from technology horizontal to industry-specific solutions.

As we step into 2024, I find myself in a reinvention phase, focusing on GenAI and industry-specific solutions. This new direction is geared toward assisting customers and partners in tackling complex business challenges. My journey with AWS has not only been about keeping pace with technological advancements but also about leveraging these advancements to facilitate solutions that address intricate business problems. It's a continual process of learning, adapting, and applying my skills to significantly impact cloud computing and beyond.

Thought Leadership and Author Journey

I (Saurabh Shrivastava) placed a special emphasis on developing a brand portfolio, as my tenure at AWS provided the platform to emerge as an industry thought leader. This opportunity led me to engage in over 50 thought leadership activities and author over 25 blogs and whitepapers for AWS channels. Raising the bar on building my portfolio, I embarked on the journey of book writing, a challenging and rewarding path.

It's a common misconception to attribute success to luck. My experience has taught me that what is often perceived as luck is actually the result of seizing opportunities and forging one's path rather than passively waiting for the 'perfect' moment to arise.

My foray into writing began in 2011 when opportunities in this field seemed limited. Undeterred, I created my blog channel on Google Blogspot, where I started sharing my technical knowledge, paying little attention to who might be reading. After publishing about 20 blog posts on various tech topics, I reached a milestone of 100,000 views. This achievement fueled my passion for writing, leading me to start another blog focused on project management. Over the next five years, I authored over 100 blog posts, contributing significantly to my professional profile and playing a role in securing my position at Amazon in 2016.

As I immersed myself in AWS, which was then in its nascent stages of widespread adoption, when I embarked on a journey to achieve all five AWS certifications in 2017, I documented this journey over a series of blogs, quickly gaining traction among cloud enthusiasts in the technical community.

By 2018, establishing myself as a thought leader became my primary objective. This period allowed me to create multiple pieces of content for AWS, ranging from blogs and whitepapers to workshops, significantly contributing to the AWS community's knowledge pool.

In 2019, I ventured into book writing, channeling my weekends into crafting the 'Solutions Architecture Handbook.' By early 2020, this handbook, comprising 450 pages, was published. The reception was beyond my expectations – it became an instant success, selling 5,000 copies in the first 90 days. This incredible response spurred me to further refine my skills and knowledge, leading to the 2nd Edition of the SA Handbook in 2022. 2nd Edition expanded to 550 pages and achieved over 60,000 copies sold in just four years.

I set a personal goal to continue this growth trajectory, committing to publishing at least one book annually. True to this promise, I published "AWS for Solutions Architect " in 2023. My plan for 2024 and beyond is to intensify my knowledge-sharing efforts further, with more publications in the pipeline.

Two key lessons stand out after reflecting on this journey as an author and Technology Leader. Firstly, success results from small, consistent steps taken over time. Secondly, there's immense value in cultivating a daily habit of self-improvement. The essence lies in staying committed to your journey of continuous improvement, day in and day out. This mindset is about enhancing personal knowledge and contributing to the larger community, embodying the belief that the best way to learn is to teach others.

The exciting news doesn't stop there; I launched **the 3rd Edition of the Solutions Architect Handbook in April 2024**. I eagerly seek your continued support and sharing more learnings with the community.

The above career highlights show the importance of initiative and perseverance. They underscore the value of creating and seizing opportunities, which have been instrumental in anyone's professional growth and success.

Embarking on a Solutions Architect career requires a multifaceted approach encompassing technical proficiency, effective communication, strategic alignment with business goals, and a commitment to continuous learning. By following these guidelines, you'll excel in interviews and establish yourself as a skilled and valuable Solutions Architect within your organization. The journey to becoming a proficient Solutions Architect is ongoing, marked by continuous growth, refinement of skills, and a dedication to creating impactful solutions.

Summary

This chapter comprehensively outlines the strategic approach required to enter a Solutions Architect role in a new organization. It commences by underscoring the Importance of the First Steps in this capacity. These initial actions lay the groundwork for your success, positioning you to effectively navigate challenges and make a meaningful contribution that aligns with the organization's objectives.

Understanding Your New Organization emerges as a cornerstone of your journey. Gaining familiarity with the organization's aspirations, vision, and culture ensures that your architectural decisions seamlessly align with its overarching mission. Identifying key stakeholders and decision-makers provides invaluable insights, enabling you to tailor your strategies to meet their expectations. Furthermore, comprehending the organization's existing technological framework and assessing its digital maturity and transformation level is pivotal in shaping your architectural approach, ensuring it is in harmony with present and future requirements.

The chapter proceeds with Evaluating the Current Architectural Landscape, a step that involves assessing existing systems and solutions. This evaluation comprehensively explains strengths, weaknesses, opportunities, and threats, forming the basis for informed decision-making and improvements.

Creating Your Initial Blueprint involves developing a holistic strategy. This includes identifying both short-term and long-term architectural goals and setting the trajectory for your role. Crafting an initial strategic plan and aligning architectural strategy with the broader business objectives establishes a strong link between your efforts and the organization's success. Formulating a detailed execution plan with measurable milestones provides a clear pathway for tracking progress and showcasing tangible outcomes.

The chapter culminates with insights into Building Your Influence as a Solutions Architect. This phase involves establishing credibility and trust with stakeholders, showcasing leadership qualities, leveraging effective communication and persuasion skills, and fostering robust team relationships. By embodying these attributes, you contribute to a collaborative ecosystem that enhances the synergy of cross-functional efforts.

In conclusion, the chapter imparts Final Words of Advice for Success in your Solutions Architect role directly from the author's experience. By maintaining agility, thorough interview preparation, highlighting your collaboration abilities, and embracing authenticity and confidence, you can excel as a Solutions Architect within your new organizational landscape.

Happy learning, and All The best for your interview success.

Closing Thoughts

As we conclude the journey through "Cracking the Solutions Architect Interview," this comprehensive book offers a robust understanding of the multifaceted world of solutions architecture and the strategies to succeed in this dynamic role. The book encompasses four distinctive parts, comprising eleven insightful chapters, each meticulously designed to provide you with the tools and knowledge necessary to excel in the solutions architect domain.

Part 1: Solutions Architect Role and Interview This section provides a comprehensive guide to understanding a Solutions Architect's core responsibilities and expectations. It is designed to equip aspiring architects with the necessary tools and knowledge for their job hunt, delving into the nuances of preparing effective resumes, crafting compelling cover letters, and optimizing LinkedIn profiles. The chapters within this part provide detailed insights into the questions you might encounter during interviews, ranging from technical queries to assessments of soft skills and problem-solving abilities. For those beginning their journey in this field, this section is an invaluable resource for understanding what it takes to succeed in a Solutions Architect role.

Part 2: Specialist Solution Architect Role and Interview In this segment, the focus shifts to specialized roles within solutions architecture. It offers a deep dive into applications, DevOps, infrastructure, networks, big data, AI/ML, and security. Each chapter in this part is dedicated to a specific specialization, unpacking the essential concepts, methodologies, and best practices that define these domains. It also provides targeted advice for interviews tailored to each specialty. This section is crucial for professionals looking to hone their expertise in a particular area of solutions architecture or those aiming to transition into a more specialized role.

Part 3: Industry Solutions Architect Role and Interview This part highlights the unique challenges and opportunities within various industry-specific solutions architect roles. Recognizing that the healthcare, finance, retail, and manufacturing sectors have distinct technological needs and challenges, this section offers tailored guidance for architects aiming to excel in these industries. It delves into the specifics of what each sector demands from its Solutions Architects, helping you to understand how to align your skills and knowledge with industry-specific requirements.

Part 4: Starting in a New Role A crucial guide for those about to embark on a new journey as a Solutions Architect in a different organization, this part provides a roadmap for the initial phase of your new role. It covers everything from understanding the new organization's culture, goals, and technological infrastructure to identifying key stakeholders and decision-makers. This section is invaluable for establishing a strong foothold in a new environment, ensuring a smooth transition, and setting the stage for long-term success in your new role. The advice and insights offered here are aimed at helping you overcome initial challenges and build a solid foundation for a thriving career in your new organization.

As you embark on your journey as a solutions architect or prepare to interview for such roles, remember that mastering this field is an ongoing process. This book's insights empower you with knowledge, strategies, and best practices to face challenges confidently, make informed decisions, and contribute effectively to your organization's architectural landscape.

Interviews for Solutions Architect positions are multifaceted and demand a well-rounded preparation approach. Dive deep into key technical concepts related to architecture, cloud solutions, security, and more—practice whiteboarding sessions to demonstrate your problem-solving skills and ability to explain complex ideas clearly. Additionally, refine your communication skills to convey your thoughts and solutions effectively. A comprehensive preparation strategy enhances your confidence and ensures you're ready to tackle various aspects of the interview process.

Remember that success as a solutions architect is not solely defined by technical prowess but by the ability to collaborate, innovate, communicate effectively, and adapt to evolving technologies and organizational needs. Embrace continuous learning, practice, and an unwavering commitment to excellence.

We wish you luck in your architectural endeavors as solutions architects and hope that the insights from this book serve as invaluable resources on your journey to excellence.

Other books you may enjoy

Here are a couple of books that can be excellent supplements to your learning and journey to become a solutions architect.

Solutions Architect's Handbook

Solutions Architect's Handbook - Third Edition: Kick-start your career with architecture design principles, strategies, and generative AI techniques

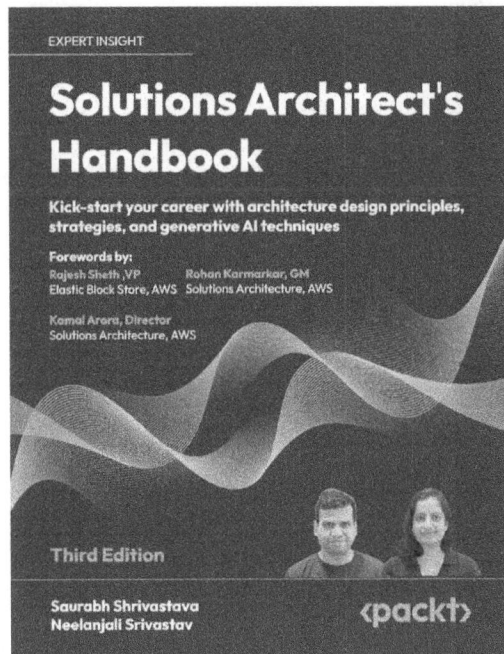

Amazon link - https://www.amazon.com/gp/product/1801816611

It is a comprehensive guide designed for both aspiring and experienced Solutions Architects. This book is an essential resource for anyone looking to delve into solutions architecture or enhance their existing skills.

What Sets This Book Apart? Unlike many other books and online courses that focus on specific services or technologies, the Solutions Architect's Handbook provides a foundational understanding of design principles and patterns applicable across various cloud providers. It delves into the core aspects of solutions architecture, making it indispensable for those seeking to understand the breadth and depth of this field.

Why Read This Book?

- **Broad and Deep Coverage**: It covers various topics, from technical concepts to soft skills, providing a well-rounded perspective on the role.
- **Practical Insights and Tips**: The book is not just theoretical; it provides real-world examples and actionable advice that can be directly applied to your work.
- **Versatility**: The principles and strategies discussed are universally applicable whether you're working with AWS, Azure, Google Cloud, or any other cloud provider.

The "Solutions Architect's Handbook" is more than just a textbook; it's a career guide. It equips you with the knowledge and skills required to excel in the dynamic and rewarding field of solutions architecture, making it a must-read for anyone serious about this profession.

AWS for Solutions Architects

AWS for Solutions Architects - The definitive guide to AWS Solutions Architecture for migrating to, building, scaling, and succeeding in the cloud, 2nd Edition

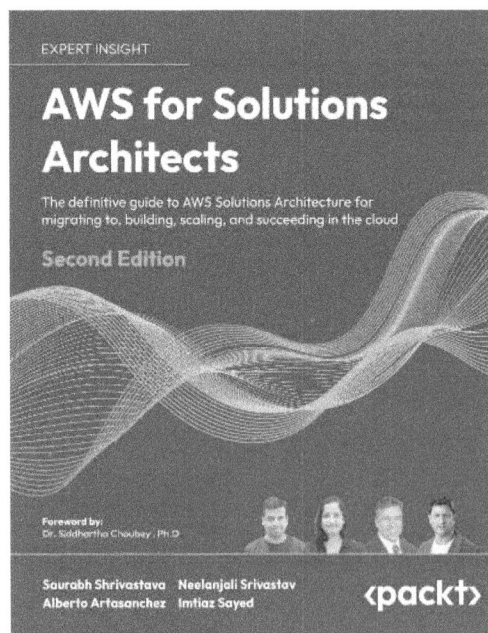

Amazon link - ttps://www.amazon.com/gp/product/180323895X

This book is an invaluable resource for professionals working with or aspiring to work with AWS. It addresses the unique challenges and opportunities that Solutions Architects encounter in the AWS ecosystem.

Key Features of the Book:

1. **Comprehensive Coverage**: The book offers an extensive overview of AWS, making it suitable for both beginners and experienced AWS professionals. It starts with the basics of AWS architecture and gradually moves to more advanced topics, ensuring a thorough understanding of the platform.
2. **Practical and Up-to-date**: Staying current with the latest AWS services and features is crucial for effective solutions architecture. This Edition provides the latest insights and updates, ensuring you are equipped with contemporary knowledge of AWS.
3. **Problem-Solving Approach**: Solutions Architects often need to design and deploy scalable, reliable, and cost-effective systems. This book focuses on solving common problems encountered in the AWS environment, providing practical guidance and best practices.
4. **Real-World Application**: Beyond theoretical knowledge, the book emphasizes practical application. It guides you through designing and deploying systems on AWS, managing and operating applications in the cloud, and leveraging AWS for successful cloud-based solutions.
5. **Skills Enhancement**: This book will help you understand AWS services deeply and enhance your skills in designing and deploying complex systems confidently on AWS.

Why This Book Is Essential:

- **In-depth Analysis**: The book provides a deep dive into AWS services and architecture, helping you understand the 'how' and the 'why' behind AWS solutions.
- **Practical Tips and Best Practices**: It is filled with practical advice, tips, and best practices that can be applied in real-world scenarios.
- **Stay Ahead in the Field**: AWS is a constantly evolving platform. This book helps you keep pace with the latest trends and technologies in cloud computing.

"AWS for Solutions Architects" is a definitive guide that empowers you with the knowledge and skills needed to excel in the AWS cloud environment. Whether you are planning to migrate to AWS, build new solutions, or optimize existing cloud infrastructure, this book is an essential tool for success in the cloud.

We Value Your Feedback: Help Us Enhance Our Knowledge-Sharing Initiatives:

We highly value your feedback to continue supporting knowledge sharing. Please share your thoughts on LinkedIn, Amazon, or directly via email at contactus@bitmaple.com. Your feedback will guide us in continuously improving, addressing errors, and adding new topics for the next edition. We are listening to better serve your needs.

If you need more advice or resources during your job search, feel free to contact us.
All The Best!

www.ingramcontent.com/pod-product-compliance
Lightning Source LLC
Chambersburg PA
CBHW081218220326
41598CB00037B/6824